PRESIDENTIAL PROFILES
THE REAGAN YEARS

Stephen F. Knott and Jeffrey L. Chidester

Checkmark Books®
An imprint of Facts On File, Inc.

Presidential Profiles: The Reagan Years

Copyright © 2005 by Stephen Knott and Jeffrey L. Chidester

Checkmark Books
An imprint of Facts On File, Inc.
132 West 31st Street
New York NY 10001

Library of Congress Cataloging-in-Publication Data

Knott, Stephen F.
  The Reagan years / Stephen Knott.
    p. cm.—(Presidential profiles)
  Includes bibliographical references and index.
  ISBN 0-8160-5343-X (hardcover : alk. paper)—ISBN 0-8160-6223-4 (pbk.)
  1. Politicians—United States—Biography. 2. United States—Politics and government—1981–1989. 3. Reagan, Ronald—Friends and associates. 4. United States—History—1969—Biography. I. Title. II. Presidential profiles (Facts On File, Inc.)
  E840.6.K58 2004
  973.9270922—dc   222004008045

Checkmark Books are available at special discounts when purchased in bulk quantities for businesses, associations, institutions, or sales promotions. Please call our Special Sales Department in New York at (212) 967-8800 or (800) 322-8755.

You can find Facts On File on the World Wide Web at http://www.factsonfile.com.

Text design by Mary Susan Ryan-Flynn
Cover design by Nora Wertz

All photographic reproductions are from the Ronald Reagan Library.

Printed in the United States of America

VB Hermitage 10 9 8 7 6 5 4 3 2 1

This book is printed on acid-free paper.

For MCD
For Rachel, Brian, Mom, and Dad

CONTENTS

❦

PREFACE

❦

The Reagan Years is a new volume in Facts On File's Presidential Profiles series that offers a comprehensive review of the presidency of Ronald Reagan. This volume begins with an introductory overview of Reagan's political career, beginning with his entry into California state politics, followed by an extensive presentation of Reagan's eight critical years in the White House. Every facet of Reagan's foreign and domestic policy is examined in detail, from his summits with Mikhail Gorbachev and the covert war in Central America, to "Reaganomics" and environmental policy. Key events from the Reagan presidency, including the assassination attempt, the air traffic controllers strike, the 1984 reelection campaign, and the Iran-contra affair, are also explored.

This extensive analysis is followed by a series of supplemental sections to help the reader gain a full perspective on the Reagan years. A lengthy time line is included which highlights the major events in the life and career of Ronald Reagan. The reader will also find over 90 biographies of key individuals in the Reagan administration, namely, cabinet officers and members of the White House staff, as well as members of Congress and world leaders, and various other friends and associates. Finally, a selection of Reagan's speeches highlights the consistency in his political thought, from the 1950s until his final statement to the American people in November 1994, disclosing his affliction with Alzheimer's disease. *The Reagan Years* also contains a lengthy bibliography designed to help readers pursue various issues in greater depth if they choose, as well as discover the most helpful general sources available on Reagan's life and career.

The Reagan years were an eventful period in the history of the United States. During his presidency, the nation witnessed a resurgence of U.S. power abroad, the highs and lows of economic recession and recovery, a revitalization of the American spirit, and the Iran-contra affair. We believe this volume captures the essence of those times and will encourage every reader to learn more about this remarkable presidency.

—Stephen F. Knott
—Jeffrey L. Chidester
Charlottesville, Va.
March 2004

INTRODUCTION

FROM "B" MOVIE ACTOR TO GOVERNOR OF CALIFORNIA

Ronald Reagan was unusual for an American politician. By all accounts, he was utterly without guile, trusted those around him, and lacked a burning ambition for power. He was, however, always interested in politics and reportedly lost his first marriage due to his somewhat obsessive focus on current events. Reagan was also unique in that, contrary to conventional wisdom, issues and ideology moved him, not public accolades or media attention. He earned more than his share of the latter during his time as a Hollywood star, and in some ways he never felt entirely comfortable with the tributes he received; his modesty and deference to others, whether in Hollywood or Washington, reinforced an impression of detachment. Opponents and even some admirers frequently misinterpreted his easygoing manner and aversion to confrontation as a lack of seriousness, but Reagan, in fact, was one of the most focused and, oddly for a conservative, one of the most radical candidates for the highest office in the nation. At some point in the 1950s Ronald Reagan concluded that he was past his peak in Hollywood and that an even bigger role awaited him on the national stage—a role that would allow him to pursue a muscular foreign policy toward the Communist world and reverse the trend toward "big government" at home.

Perhaps the most important catalyst in the transformation of Reagan from movie star to public servant came during his stint as president of the Screen Actors Guild (1947–1952) where he was embroiled in McCarthy-era controversies regarding alleged Communist infiltration of the entertainment industry. On a more personal level, he was increasingly concerned as his income eroded in the postwar era from ever-expanding state and federal taxes.

While much has been written about Reagan's aversion to taxation and "big government," it was his antipathy to communism that propelled him into a political career, a fact often slighted by many of his biographers. Reagan had a deep and abiding aversion to communism, an opinion shared by many Americans, and in particular many Californians, a large number of whom were drawn to a kind of extremist, conspiratorial view of the world found in such groups as the John Birch Society. One of Reagan's most daunting challenges as a candidate for governor was to distance himself from the radical Right, a feat he deftly performed.

Throughout much of his adult life, Reagan was a devoted supporter of the New Deal and Harry Truman's Fair Deal. He experienced

1

Ronald Reagan and *General Electric Theater,* 1954

Reagan's first real "campaign" experience (other than student politics at Eureka College, his alma mater in Illinois) came in 1954 when he signed a contract with the General Electric Corporation to serve as the "program supervisor" and host of the *General Electric Theater,* a television show that quickly established itself as one of the nation's most popular programs. Reagan's contract with GE also required that he spend much of his time off-air traveling on morale-boosting visits to GE facilities nationwide, where he spoke to managers and employees about the benefits of the free enterprise system (and electricity, of course). During the eight years he spent on the "mashed potato circuit" Reagan honed his public speaking skills and improved his knack for reading the tenor and mood of an audience. The role of GE spokesman also gave him an opportunity to reach beyond the sheltered environment of Hollywood, and gave him a strong feeling for the struggles and concerns of middle-class America.

Reagan remained a registered Democrat as late as the 1960 Kennedy-Nixon contest, but he supported his fellow Californian Richard Nixon in that election. He wrote Nixon and urged him to take the gloves off; "shouldn't someone tag Mr. Kennedy's 'bold new imaginative' program with its proper age? . . . Under the tousled boyish haircut it is still old Karl Marx—first launched a century ago. There is nothing new in the idea of a government being Big Brother to us all. Hitler called his 'State Socialism' and way before him it was 'benevolent monarchy.'"

Reagan did not formally change his party registration until 1962, by which time he had become so explicitly identified with conservative causes that General Electric released him as their spokesman. When Reagan first embraced his new ideology he veered toward the extreme, as is so often the case with converts. He was linked to a number of controver-

something of an epiphany in the early stages of the cold war when he became convinced there were organized efforts by communists to penetrate various liberal organizations in the Hollywood community. He offered his services to the FBI as an informant, and testified as a friendly witness before the House Un-American Activities Committee (HUAC). In a commencement address delivered in 1952, he delivered a blistering attack on socialism and described the ongoing struggle with communism as the "same old battle" that the United States confronted in dealing with "Kaiserism" and later "Hitlerism." Reagan told his audience "the basis of this country and our religion" is the "idea of the dignity of man, the idea that deep within the heart of each one of us is something so God-like and precious that no individual or group has a right to impose his or its will upon the people."

sial activists, many of whom believed in vast leftist conspiracies, were devotees of impeaching Earl Warren, and getting the United States out of the United Nations (and vice versa). In some instances they were neo-John Birchers and bona fide John Birchers, including Congressman John Rousselot, whom Reagan described as a "warm personal friend." One of Reagan's greatest tactical achievements as a politician was his ability to distance himself from his various extremist conservative allies and yet retain their support. This tactical achievement eluded Barry Goldwater and many other conservative candidates who were tarred by their liberal opponents as captives of the lunatic fringe of the Republican Party.

Reagan campaigned for Goldwater in his critical race in the 1964 California primary against New York governor Nelson Rockefeller, and attended the Republican National Convention in San Francisco as an alternate delegate with the California delegation. At the request of the party's nominee, Barry Goldwater, Reagan began giving speeches for the Arizona senator; one speech in particular caught the attention of the conservative faithful and helped launch Reagan's political career. "The Speech" (later frequently referred to as "A Time for Choosing") was taped on October 27, 1964, and aired later that night on the NBC (National Broadcasting Company) television network. Many Goldwater aides were concerned that Reagan's remarks would be too extreme and urged the candidate not to air the speech, but Goldwater approved the broadcast. It turned out to be a resounding success, surprising even Reagan who was delighted to learn that it generated close to $8 million for the Republican candidate.

Two California fund-raisers for Goldwater, Holmes Tuttle and Henry Salvatori, had arranged Reagan's "Time for Choosing" address, and after the 1964 electoral debacle, these two along with other wealthy Goldwater supporters, including Leonard Firestone, Ed Mills, Justin Dart, and Cy Rubel, urged Reagan to challenge incumbent California governor Edmund G. "Pat" Brown in the 1966 gubernatorial election. These men thought of Brown as a "tax and spend" liberal and believed that his higher-education appointees at the University of California had coddled student dissenters, particularly at the Berkeley campus. The first stirring of a "white backlash" against the Civil Rights movement was also in the air, partly in response to events like the Watts riots of August 1965, which left 36 people dead and more than 800 wounded. Tuttle, Salvatori, and the others were all wealthy, self-made men who believed that Reagan's cheerful demeanor, his optimism about America's future, and his genuine likability made him a far more formidable candidate than the typical scowling, pessimistic conservative who seemed to be perpetually at war with the 20th century. The hope was that Reagan could heal the wounds of a divided California Republican Party that had fractured in the heated contest between Goldwater and Rockefeller, and that his election as governor of the nation's largest state would propel him into the forefront of national politics.

Reagan was taken with the idea, a significant career change for a man in his early fifties, although he understood his best days in Hollywood were behind him. But there was much more than simple practical calculation at work in Reagan's decision to seek public office; he was a true believer in the idea that America had lost its way, that big government at home and communism abroad threatened individual liberty, and that excessive taxation and regulation threatened to prevent future generations of poor boys like himself from rising to the top. His message was fairly simple, and was frequently derided as such, but with relatively few emendations it was a message he rode all the way to the White House only 14 years after his first run for office.

Reagan first had to secure the Republican Party nomination, and his chief competition was San Francisco mayor George Christopher, a Republican moderate and champion of civil rights who portrayed Reagan as an extremist and a foe of progressive civil rights legislation. In a debate before a group of African-American Republicans in March 1966, Reagan lost his temper and stormed off the stage, in response to a series of remarks from Christopher critical of Goldwater and Reagan's opposition to the Civil Rights Act of 1964. Christopher noted that had he been a member of Congress he would have voted for the act, while Reagan had made it clear that he considered it to be a "bad piece of legislation." Reagan believed that he was being accused of bigotry and left the debate in a huff, which Christopher exploited to the hilt. Reagan dealt with the repercussions of this incident for days, and officials from Governor Brown's campaign concluded that Reagan would be an easy candidate to defeat in the general election that November. The Brown campaign actively undermined Christopher's campaign, and Reagan, despite the gaffe at the event in March, avoided attacking Christopher, adhering to the "11th commandment," that "thou shalt not speak ill of a fellow Republican." Reagan's genteel manner of campaigning, his high name recognition and his ability to tap into concerns of middle-class suburban voters, coupled with the covert attacks against Christopher in newspaper articles planted by the Brown campaign, all led to a convincing Reagan victory in the Republican primary. When the final tally was completed, Reagan defeated Christopher in a landslide, taking 77 percent of the vote. The Brown campaign now faced the opponent they wanted.

As the fall campaign began, all of the momentum was breaking in Reagan's direction, while the Brown campaign slowly disintegrated. Anxious to put the extremism charge behind him, Reagan made a point of not invit-ing Barry Goldwater to campaign for him in California. Right-wing extremists who belonged to the John Birch Society were excluded from the campaign, and Reagan spoke out against the organization. He quickly reached out to Christopher's supporters around the state to heal any wounds from the primary fight and succeeded in melding the two organizations together in a remarkably smooth transition. Brown had faced a primary challenge from Los Angeles mayor Sam Yorty, who challenged him from the Right; Yorty, a Democrat, had supported Nixon over Kennedy in 1960 and had established a reputation as a tough law-and-order mayor. Brown did not view Yorty as a serious opponent but in the end the mayor received almost a million votes in the Democratic primary, losing by only 300,000 votes. Yorty refused to endorse Brown, and many of his supporters went on to vote for Reagan in the general election, most likely including Yorty himself. Brown then tried to reach out to George Christopher, but Christopher was still nursing the bruises he had received at the hands of officials from the Brown campaign, and refused to endorse Brown. His own liberal base was in disarray; many African-American voters were upset over Brown's response to the Watts riots, which they believed fell short of addressing the root problems of the discontent, while Mexican Americans were upset that the governor had refused to meet with Cesar Chavez, the leader of the United Farm Workers union. In addition, some white liberals objected to the governor's support of the Johnson administration's war in Vietnam. On top of this, the troika that attempted to manage Brown's campaign frequently feuded with one another, while Brown refused to intervene and restore a semblance of discipline to his organization. He was weak on television as well, and had the misfortune of running against a candidate who thrived on the medium.

Governor Ronald Reagan, son Ron, Mrs. Reagan, and daughter Patti, 1967

In the end, issues matter the most in elections, and Brown appeared to be out of step with a majority of the California electorate in 1966. On civil rights, student protests, and welfare, Reagan tapped into a growing suburban revolt against the liberal position on all these issues. Many white voters concerned about rising crime rates were convinced that something

had gone wrong in the judicial system, and they pointed to lenient judges and progressive sentencing and incarceration policies. The student protests, and the "coddling" of the "free speech," or "filthy speech" movement (depending on your perspective), at Berkeley were further indicators of this social and cultural decline. "Generous" welfare programs were held responsible for undermining the traditional work ethic, it was argued, and the taxes used to pay for those programs fell disproportionately on middle-class voters. Toward the end of the campaign Brown went on the attack, arguing that Reagan was an extremist and that he lacked the compassion to be governor of a state where many depended on government assistance for their existence. The Brown campaign attempted to find some scandal in Reagan's background of the kind that had helped to derail the Christopher campaign. In the end, they resorted to belittling Reagan's career as an actor, and in one famous incident the Brown campaign ran a television documentary about the governor, which showed him chatting with two young African-American girls and telling them, "You know I'm running against an actor. Remember this, you know who shot Abraham Lincoln, don't you?" The humor was lost on many Californians, who saw the jibe as a mean and desperate remark from a candidate unsure of his own rationale for running. Reagan dismissed the comment in his usual genial way, claiming that he was sure "Pat wouldn't say anything like that." On election day, Reagan beat Brown by just under a million votes, an event that sent shock waves across the country and foreshadowed the rise of the emerging Republican majority on the national political scene.

The new governor got off to a rough start, bluntly admitting that his grasp of the details of California government was very thin at a time when the state faced a growing budget deficit. Reagan was determined not to raise taxes and instead offered an across-the-board 10 percent cut in state services, along with a freeze on hiring any new state employees. The governor proposed some additional measures that garnered media attention but did little to address the underlying fiscal problem, including a suggestion that state employees volunteer to work on Lincoln's and Washington's birthdays. In the end, Reagan's willingness to compromise prevailed over his ideological aversion to taxes, and led him, after protracted negotiations with the Speaker of the California Assembly, Democrat Jesse Unruh, to sign a $1 billion tax bill, the largest tax increase ever passed in California to that date. During Reagan's tenure as governor of California, corporate taxes almost doubled, the state sales tax increased from 3 to 4.75 percent, and the maximum state income tax increased from 7 percent to 11 percent. Despite some complaints from his conservative base, Reagan benefited politically from his willingness to compromise on taxes, in part because it revealed a pragmatic streak that many critics had believed he lacked. Over the course of his political career, Reagan was able to veer from his core beliefs if need be and emerge from such compromising positions with his reputation as a man of principle intact.

In the spring of 1967 Reagan was confronted with the first "scandal" of his administration, one involving his chief of staff, who was allegedly part of a "homosexual clique" that operated within the governor's office. The "offenders" were forced out of their positions by other members of Reagan's team, primarily Lyn Nofziger, William Clark, and Edwin Meese. The governor was forced to confront another divisive social issue when the state legislature presented him with a bill legalizing "therapeutic" abortions. Reagan agonized over this legislation more than any other bill presented to him, and despite the pleas of Francis Cardinal McIntyre of Los Angeles, he signed the act into law on June 13, 1967. The law placed California at the center of a growing movement in the United States to liberalize access to abortion; his decision to sign this bill into law was one of the few decisions, if not the only decision, that Reagan later came to regret.

Despite the fact that Reagan approved both the tax increases and the liberalization of abortion laws, he remained the darling of

American conservatives, and some of his aides began a movement to secure the 1968 Republican presidential nomination for him. The effort was led primarily by Lyn Nofziger, his director of communications, and Thomas Reed, his appointments secretary. Reagan responded lukewarmly to the idea, but never issued a flat, "Sherman-like" statement that would have removed him from the race. Nofziger and Reed enlisted the efforts of F. Clifton White, who had been one of the architects of Barry Goldwater's successful drive for the Republican nomination in 1964. Nofziger, Reed, and White, along with some members of Reagan's "kitchen cabinet," a group of wealthy California businessmen who financed his campaigns, persuaded Reagan to keep his name in contention until the convention in Miami as a "favorite son" candidate from California, whose primary election he carried in June 1968. His decision to keep his name in play until the August convention caused some ill will between Reagan and his fellow Californian Richard Nixon, whose cordial relations with Reagan concealed a certain jealousy for the latter's telegenic appeal.

In the end, Reagan lost the nomination decisively to Nixon, but he remained a viable national political figure within the Republican Party, and his name was constantly mentioned as a potential presidential candidate for the post-Nixon years. In the interim, Reagan fought to win a second term as governor in his 1970 race against the Speaker of the California State Assembly, Jesse Unruh. Unruh ran under the banner of a number of populist themes, most prominently the notion that Reagan was a "tool of the rich" and a puppet of the "half-hidden millionaires." The Speaker's campaign got off to a rough start when he decided to launch his campaign on Labor Day outside the home of one of Reagan's "kitchen cabinet" members, Henry Salvatori, whom Unruh accused of benefiting from Reagan's favoritism toward the wealthy. Salvatori, Unruh charged, was the beneficiary of a Reagan property tax relief initiative that would save him $4,000 on a home valued at $700,000. Low-income renters, Unruh claimed, would be paying $25 to the "Henry Salvatori tax relief fund." Unfortunately for the candidate, Salvatori and his wife were waiting for him when he began his press conference, and made clear their displeasure, with comments such as, "Oh, you ass, stop being so silly," or "you're a liar, Mr. Unruh." The media coverage of the event was unflattering, for it appeared that a bullying politician was harassing an elderly couple attempting to enjoy the Labor Day holiday. Unruh also stalked the governor's mansion, attempted to coax Reagan into a debate, which he had repeatedly rejected, and again the image of an apparently desperate candidate skulking outside people's homes did not appeal to most Californians. Unruh closed the gap with Reagan near the end of the race, in part due to a negative reaction in California and across the nation to a combative off-year election campaign run by President Nixon and Vice President Spiro Agnew, which was harshly critical of domestic dissent and emphasized a law-and-order theme that failed to resonate in the midst of an economic downturn. Reagan biographer Lou Cannon noted that Reagan was a much more sure-footed candidate in the 1970 election than in 1966, handling hecklers with aplomb and committing fewer gaffes. The main theme of Reagan's campaign was his promise to clean up the "welfare mess," a message that once again resonated with white middle-class voters. On election day, Reagan defeated Unruh by a margin of 52.9 percent to Unruh's 45.1 percent, with minor-party candidates dividing the remainder of the vote.

Governor Reagan spent the remainder of his tenure in office attempting to deliver on his promise of reforming the welfare system. The California Welfare Reform Act of 1971 was perhaps the most significant accomplishment of Reagan's time as governor. It came about due to the skills Reagan displayed as a negotiator, working with a new Speaker of the California Assembly, 34-year-old Bob Moretti, a protégé of Jesse Unruh. Although neither man particularly cared for the other, both came to respect the other's bargaining skills and trusted the other's word. Reagan delved into the details of policy, to the surprise of many observers of his first four years in office, and, through bargaining, horse-trading, and arm-twisting, both men reached agreement in a number of areas, which led to the Welfare Reform Act and progress toward property tax relief and enhanced school-financing schemes. The welfare reforms were hailed by observers from across the political spectrum for increasing benefits to the needy, streamlining the administration of the program, and tightening eligibility requirements. At a time when President Nixon was stymied in his attempts to overhaul the nation's welfare machinery, and in numerous other policy areas, the Reagan-Moretti reforms proved that bipartisan cooperation could be achieved if leaders put aside their suspicions and treated their opponents as men and women of good faith.

This capacity for magnanimity set Reagan apart from Richard Nixon. Reagan never viewed his Democratic opponents as disloyal or un-American, perhaps remembering his own roots in the Democratic Party, and he never wallowed in the slights that all public figures endure while pursuing elected office. Granted, Reagan's "star" quality made his rise to the top easier than Nixon's, but there was also a generosity of spirit in Reagan's character that was missing in Richard Nixon. It simply would not have occurred to Nixon to reach out to Speaker of the House Carl Albert the way that Reagan did to Speaker Tip O'Neill during his presidency. Despite their deep partisan differences on the issues, and despite O'Neill's propensity for personal attacks, Reagan came to consider O'Neill a friend, and vice versa. There were no enemies lists in the governor's "corner office" in Sacramento or in the Reagan Oval Office.

When President Nixon proceeded to self-destruct in the Watergate scandal, Reagan remained loyal to Nixon and his corrupt vice president, Spiro Agnew, long beyond the point when many Republicans had abandoned the two men. Despite this blind loyalty Reagan was not damaged by his defense of the duo; ironically, his national prospects brightened as a result of the Nixon-Agnew resignations and elevation of Gerald Ford to the presidency.

REAGAN'S 1976 CAMPAIGN FOR PRESIDENT

Reagan's tenure as governor of California ended in January 1975. He remained engaged in the public arena by recording daily five-minute radio addresses syndicated to radio stations across the nation. He also published a syndicated biweekly newspaper column, mostly ghostwritten by Peter Hannaford, Reagan's director of public affairs during his last year in Sacramento. The radio broadcasts began in January 1975, but were suspended when Reagan announced that he was challenging incumbent president Gerald Ford for the Republican nomination. Prior to Ford's assumption of the presidency, members of Reagan's inner circle, including Edwin Meese, Lyn Nofziger, and Holmes Tuttle, were convinced that Reagan was planning to run in 1976 at what was assumed would be the end of the Nixon presidency. When Gerald Ford became president in August 1974, some of Reagan's associates viewed Ford, in the words of Lou Cannon, as "a usurper." Reagan was encouraged to put aside his usual reticence about challenging a fellow Republican by an "outsider" brought into his inner circle, a Washington attorney named John Sears, who had been Richard Nixon's delegate "headhunter" during the 1968 campaign.

Whatever doubts Reagan and his entourage might have had about challenging Ford ended when the president nominated Nelson Rockefeller as his vice president. Prior to this, the Reagan camp had assumed that Rockefeller would be an opponent of Reagan's in the 1976 Republican race, and with Ford's selection of Goldwater's old nemesis from New York, Reagan believed that a signal was being sent to the conservative wing of the party that they would not have a place in the Ford White House. There had been speculation that Ford would select Reagan as his vice president, and some of the Reagan loyalists had encouraged such a step. Reagan was disappointed that he was not selected, and the conservative faithful were insulted that the very symbol of East Coast "elitist" Republicanism had won the job. Ford's amnesty for Vietnam-era draft evaders and deserters further infuriated the conservative faithful, along with the president's continued pursuit of détente in concert with Rockefeller protégé Henry Kissinger. The secretary of state was a suspect figure on the Right for a variety of reasons, including his foreign accent, his affiliation with the Trilateral Commission, (a commission founded by David Rockefeller in the 1970s that was suspected by conspiracy theorists around the globe to seek world domination), and his apparent belief that the United States was going to have to learn to live with the Soviet Union.

Ford attempted in a halting and ineffective way to persuade Reagan not to enter the presidential race, offering him various cabinet positions, including secretary of transportation and secretary of commerce, and then proposing that he serve as the U.S. ambassador to the Court of St. James (the United Kingdom), none of which appealed to Reagan, and in fact the offers verged on being insults. Some members of Ford's entourage told reporters that Reagan would not enter the race once he grasped the reality of the situation, and this talk only fueled Reagan's competitive instincts. For the most part Ford kept Reagan at a distance, and this too only heightened the latter's desire to challenge the president.

Reagan created a presidential exploratory committee on July 15, 1975, one week after Ford announced his intention to seek the Republican nomination, to gauge the depth of public support for Reagan throughout the country. Senator Paul Laxalt of Nevada was named as the head of the committee, one of the few Republican members of Congress willing to desert Ford for the Reagan camp. Reagan formally announced his candidacy for president on November 20, 1975, and spent the bulk of his first weeks as a candidate defending his proposal to transfer approximately $90 billion of federal programs to the states, in keeping with his belief in federalism and disdain for the federal government, but a concept that scared many cash-strapped states in a time of economic uncertainty. A former Reagan campaign manager, Stuart Spencer, was recruited from California by President Ford to revive his moribund effort, and Spencer knew how to exploit Reagan's weaknesses. He immediately seized on the $90 billion proposal, particularly its potential effects in New Hampshire, which depended on a significant amount of federal aid to compensate for the fact that the state had no income tax. While Reagan had promised to protect Social Security and exempted it from his $90 billion transfer proposal, the uncertainty surrounding such a radical shift in policy fed the fears of many elderly voters that Reagan was another Goldwater who would pull the safety net out from under them. As the New Hampshire and other early primaries approached, President Ford took full advantage of his incumbency and announced one federal project after another, from bridges to dams to defense expenditures, implicitly reminding voters of the benefits of federal spending and implying that Reagan would destroy this economic bonanza. The New Hampshire primary was an extremely close race, and had Reagan spent the last few days of the campaign in that state instead of in Illinois, he probably would have won the race. On election day, February 24, 1976, Ford tallied 54,824 votes to Reagan's 53,507, a margin of 1,317 votes out of more than 108,000 cast.

Reagan proceeded to lose one primary after another, including the critical Florida primary on March 9, prompting a crescendo of calls urging him to withdraw from the race for the good of the party. His campaign was essentially bankrupt by the time it staggered into the North Carolina primary, and many of his advisers were convinced that the cause was lost. Reagan refined a theme he had begun to use in the Florida primary where he charged that Secretary of State Henry Kissinger's tenure coincided "precisely with the loss of U.S. military supremacy." In North Carolina the theme was broadened to include attacks on the discussions under way to renegotiate the original treaty between the United States and Panama that would transfer control of the canal to Panama. Reagan began to repeatedly use a line that would bring his audience to their feet, "when it comes to the canal, we built it, we paid for it, it's ours and we should tell [Panamanian leader General Omar] Torrijos and company that we are going to keep it!" Reagan also criticized the president's refusal to attend a dinner honoring noted Soviet dissident Aleksandr Solzhenitsyn in the summer of 1975, in part due to Kissinger's advice that the dinner just days before a summit with Leonid Brezhnev would roil Soviet sensibilities. The secretary of state suggested a lower-profile White House meeting, which ultimately never occurred. Reagan's rhetoric about Solzhenitsyn and the Panama Canal appealed to North Carolina's conservative Republican electorate, and he ended up winning 52 percent of the vote in a dramatic victory that revived his campaign and led to a bruising battle with Ford all the way to the Republican convention in Kansas City. Reagan went on to win primary battles in Texas, Alabama, Georgia, Indiana, and his home state of California.

As the convention drew near Reagan was trailing Ford, according to most estimates, by about 100 delegates, and both men were just short of the necessary number of delegates needed to win the nomination. Ford used the power of his incumbency to pull delegates to his side, bringing them in for one-to-one meetings in the White House, using his patronage powers whenever he could, and traveling to the various remaining state conventions bringing with him all of the media attention and hoopla that accompanies a presidential visit. Reagan's campaign manager, John Sears, decided that his candidate's only remaining chance involved an unprecedented decision to name his vice presidential selection in advance of the convention, and Reagan endorsed the proposal, naming liberal Pennsylvania Republican senator Richard Schweiker as his running mate. The hope was that Schweiker would bring the large Pennsylvania delegation into the Reagan camp and thereby secure the nomination. The gambit failed, and Ford went on to win the nomination with 1,187 delegates to Reagan's 1,070, Reagan falling 70 votes shy of securing the nomination. There was some speculation that Ford might choose Reagan as his vice presidential candidate, but in the end he selected Kansas senator Robert Dole, a selection that pleased the Reagan wing of the party but at the same time kept the troublesome governor off the ticket. Reagan had one last laugh at the Kansas City convention; when Ford signaled for him to come up to the podium, Reagan delivered a brief but powerful speech that captured the hearts of the Republican faithful, and left many delegates wondering if perhaps they had nominated the wrong man.

THE 1980 CAMPAIGN

Following his defeat for the Republican nomination, Reagan returned to California and renewed his syndicated radio broadcasts, which gave him an estimated audience of some 20 million listeners. Gerald Ford lost the presidency to Jimmy Carter in 1976, and Reagan became for many the chief spokesman for the Republican opposition. He continued to criticize the policy of détente, and in fact viewed the Carter mode of détente to be a more dangerous version than that practiced by Ford and Kissinger. Reagan was convinced that America was losing ground to the Soviets and that the nation's military had fallen into disrepair and its intelligence community was shackled by restraints that prevented it from dealing with threats to American security. He avoided personal attacks on Carter, but the implication was that the president was naïve about Soviet intentions and that his criticism of allies such as South Korea and Taiwan for human rights violations played into the hands of the Kremlin. At home, Reagan contended that the federal government was growing out of control, that its regulatory policies were stifling American industry, and the growing tax burden needed to support "big government" had contributed to an odd mix of high inflation and high unemployment. A groundswell of antitax initiatives began to sweep the nation, the most important being California's "Proposition 13," a property tax–cutting initiative that passed in June 1978, and prompted voters in other states to follow suit, including in such liberal bastions as Massachusetts. As 1980 approached, Reagan seemed perfectly positioned for a run for the White House.

Reagan formally announced his candidacy on November 13, 1979. His main challengers for the 1980 nomination were Senator Howard Baker of Tennessee; former governor John Connally of Texas; former director of Central Intelligence and ambassador to the People's Republic of China, George H. W. Bush, of Texas and elsewhere; Senator Robert Dole of Kansas; and Congressmen John Anderson and Philip Crane of Illinois. Reagan's campaign team at first considered Howard Baker or John Connally to be his most formidable rivals, and they were surprised by George Bush, who ensconced himself in Iowa and New Hampshire for months on end and surprised everyone by winning the Iowa caucuses, first in the campaign, and carrying the "Big Mo" (momentum), as Bush called it, into New Hampshire. Reagan, no doubt recalling his razor-thin loss to President Ford four years earlier, redoubled his efforts in that state and in the end won the New Hampshire primary. A dramatic scene at a debate in Nashua, New Hampshire, probably tipped the election in Reagan's favor, when he rallied to the side of his other GOP opponents and insisted they be allowed to participate in a debate that Bush had hoped to limit to the two front-runners. In an event worthy of a Hollywood script, Reagan made his plea to seat the others, called them up to the stage, and promptly had to fend off requests from the moderator to shut his microphone off. "I paid for this microphone, Mr. Breen," Reagan said in anger (many reporters, particularly those who viewed Reagan as intellectually challenged, say they heard Reagan mispronounce the moderator's name as "Mr. Green." Having repeatedly viewed a tape of this event, it is impossible to determine exactly what Reagan said. Reagan claimed he said the correct name, "Breen," so this author accepts Reagan's account).

Reagan won 51 percent of the vote in New Hampshire in a seven-man field, with Bush coming in second with 22 percent, and Howard Baker third with 13 percent of the vote. That same day Reagan fired his campaign leadership team of John Sears, Charles Black, and James Lake, in part because the campaign's finances were spiraling out of control, and also due to the fact that Sears had slowly pushed Reagan's old California crowd out of the inner circle, or in some instances out of the campaign altogether. Sears first removed Lyn Nofziger, then Michael Deaver, accusing the latter of financial improprieties. Martin Anderson soon became disgruntled with the Sears operation, and left the campaign, despite pleas from Sears to reconsider. Sears's final target was apparently Edwin Meese, but this was too much for Reagan, who began to believe that Sears was making far too many decisions without consulting him, and was spending more money than the campaign could raise. The personal chemistry between Reagan and Sears was never entirely comfortable; Reagan complained on more than one occasion that John Sears was the kind of man who "looked you in the tie." William Casey was brought on board as campaign chairman and given responsibility for stabilizing the campaign's precarious finances, while Meese took over more of the day-to-day operations, and Reagan's old California gubernatorial campaign manager Stuart Spencer traveled with the candidate on his plane and made sure he stayed on message. Nofziger, Anderson, and Deaver also returned to the fold and played important roles for the remainder of the campaign.

The New Hampshire primary was a stunning victory for Reagan, and one by one his Republican opponents began to leave the race. Bush and Anderson held on the longest, with the latter eventually abandoning his party and

Ronald Reagan campaigning with Nancy Reagan in Columbia, South Carolina, 1980

running as a third-party candidate, drawing 6 percent of the vote and in so doing helping Reagan defeat Carter by siphoning liberal voters away from the president. Anderson's antipathy toward Reagan was pronounced; late in the primary season Anderson stated that he preferred Massachusetts senator Edward Kennedy, leader of the Democratic Party's liberal wing, to Ronald Reagan as president. At a Republican debate in Illinois, Reagan, acting astonished, turned to Anderson and said, "John, would you *really* find Teddy Kennedy preferable to me?" Bush fought long and hard, and won some key primaries, particularly in states where the turnout was light and the Republican Party organization supported Bush—in his two homes states of Massachusetts and Connecticut, as well as Pennsylvania and Michigan. In the end, Reagan won 60 percent of the total vote in 33 primaries.

The incumbent president faced a divisive primary challenge from Senator Kennedy. Kennedy considered Carter's refusal to embrace a more ambitious domestic agenda as a betrayal of the New Deal/New Frontier legacy, and condemned the president's fiscal conservatism along with the "tight money" policies of Federal Reserve chairman Paul Volcker. Kennedy proposed a more activist federal role in health care and blasted Carter for his unwillingness to impose wage and price controls to combat inflation and for opposing a freeze on oil prices. The Kennedy/Carter contest was a bitter battle, with the incumbent vowing to "whip his [Kennedy's] ass" and the latter stridently criticizing Carter for abandoning traditional Democratic beliefs, including his failure to endorse a comprehensive national health insurance plan. The two candidates clearly did not like each other and had little in common other than a party label; Kennedy was the wealthy heir of one of the most formidable names in American politics, with a reputation for a dissolute personal life, while Carter was

something of a self-made man who came out of nowhere to capture the White House, wore his born-again Baptist faith on his sleeve, and lusted only in his heart.

Kennedy's campaign began terribly with a nationally televised interview where he bordered on the incoherent, while Carter benefited from appearing presidential by handling foreign policy crises that in the short run redounded to his advantage. Carter easily defeated Kennedy in the Iowa caucuses, trounced the senator in his own backyard in New Hampshire, and appeared on the verge of scoring an early knockout. But Kennedy garnered surprising victories in the New York and Connecticut primaries, and later in the Pennsylvania primary and in the Michigan caucuses. These victories, along with the senator's victories in five of eight states on the final "Super Tuesday" primary in June, encouraged Kennedy to stay in the race to the bitter end. Kennedy refused repeated entreaties from the White House to concede and remained defiant through the Democratic convention in New York City, where he delivered an emotional address to the delegates and refrained from shaking Carter's hand as the flustered president chased him around the stage.

Ronald Reagan's convention in Detroit was a far less divisive affair, with the only suspense revolving around the question of who Reagan would choose as his vice presidential running mate. An unusual arrangement was proposed by some Reagan and Gerald Ford advisers where Reagan would choose the former president as his running mate and the two men would share a copresidency, with Ford managing foreign policy and Reagan overseeing domestic policy. The idea tantalized many Republicans, particularly some moderate Republicans who considered Reagan to be too extreme, and it also proved to be an alluring idea for many in the media. The extent to which Reagan seriously contemplated a Ford

vice presidency remains the subject of controversy, and like John F. Kennedy's selection of
Lyndon Johnson, there are multiple versions of
who said what to whom, depending on the
source of the story. In the end, after a face-to-
face meeting between Reagan and Ford, the
scheme collapsed and Reagan chose his toughest primary opponent, George H. W. Bush.

In his acceptance speech Reagan referred
to "three grave threats to our very existence,
any one of which could destroy us . . . a disintegrating economy, a weakened defense and an
energy policy based on the sharing of scarcity."
The main thrust of his address, and of his
entire fall campaign, was that America's best
days were still ahead. He blamed Carter for a
collapse of confidence at home and a decline in
American prestige abroad. "They say that the
United States has had its day in the sun; that
our nation has passed its zenith. They expect
you to tell your children that the American
people no longer have the will to cope with
their problems; that the future will be one of
sacrifice and few opportunities. My fellow citizens, I utterly reject that view."

Reagan left Detroit leading Carter in the
public opinion polls and having healed the
wounds with his rival candidates for the nomination. But a series of missteps, along with
Carter's claims that Reagan was outside the
mainstream of American politics and a potentially dangerous man to control the nuclear
button, began to take their toll. Reagan began
his campaign with an appearance at the
Neshoba County Fair in Mississippi, in the
same county where three civil rights workers
had been murdered in 1964, and told the
crowd that he believed in states' rights. A visit
shortly after this to the South Bronx saw the
candidate heckled by residents of one of the
most devastated inner-city neighborhoods of
the nation. In a speech to the Veterans of Foreign Wars on August 18, 1980, Reagan referred
to the Vietnam war as a "noble cause," a com-

ment which brought praise from some veterans
of the conflict but angered members of the
antiwar movement, and raised the whole divisive issue anew. This was followed by a Reagan
statement criticizing President Carter for
appearing at a rally in Alabama, at what Reagan
called the birthplace and "parent body" of the
Ku Klux Klan, a statement that was not true
and caused considerable press attention concerning Reagan's propensity for off-the-cuff
remarks that were inaccurate. Later in the
campaign Reagan's claim that trees and vege-
tation were a major source of air pollution led
a number of wits to place signs on trees at Reagan rallies reading, "Chop me down before I
kill again."

Reagan eventually got his campaign back
on track, partly because President Carter and
some members of his team underestimated
him, but primarily due to the harshness of the
attacks that Carter directed at Reagan. Carter
suggested that Reagan's election would pit
white America against black America and also
put the world at risk for war. The 69-year-old
Reagan was a master at deflecting attacks in his
homespun, genial way, and anyone who
attacked him ran the risk of appearing to abuse
America's favorite grandfather. Carter's "mean-
ness" became an issue in the race, and helped to
insulate Reagan from further attacks.

The two candidates participated in a televised debate in Cleveland on October 28, 1980.
While most observers gave Carter the edge on
debating points, Reagan was able to deflect the
president's thrusts by saying, "There you go
again," suggesting that Carter was distorting
his record and resorting to negative attacks.
Reagan also seemed to strike a nerve with a
question directed not at his opponent but at
the American people: "Are you better off now
than you were four years ago?" The gaffe of the
evening, which can often affect the media's
conclusion as to who won the debate, belonged
to Carter. The president claimed that his 13-

year old daughter had expressed concerns to him over nuclear weapons proliferation, a statement which was widely derided as manipulative if not downright comical. "Ask Amy" signs began appearing at Republican rallies. Polls taken after the debate indicated that most of the public believed Reagan won the debate, and he held a healthy lead over President Carter in the tracking polls leading up to election day.

The Reagan campaign was concerned to the very end that the Carter administration might arrange an "October Surprise" and strike a deal with Iran for the release of the 52 American hostages prior to the election. The "surprise" never occurred, although there were hints near the end of the race of a possible breakthrough. Allegations were made long after the election that some members of Reagan's team, especially William Casey and George Bush, had covertly intervened with the Iranians to block the release of the hostages prior to the election. No evidence ever emerged to support this allegation, which nonetheless persists to this day. On election day, November 4, 1980, Reagan won in an electoral vote landslide, 489 to 44; in the popular vote he received 43,901,812 votes (50.7 percent) to Carter's 35,483,820 (41 percent), with John Anderson receiving 5,719,722 (6.6 percent). As an added bonus, Reagan's lengthy coattails gave the Republican Party control of the U.S. Senate for the first time since 1954.

THE 1984 CAMPAIGN

As late as the fall of 1983, Ronald Reagan was considered by many observers to be a president whose prospects for reelection were slim. There were questions as to whether the 72-year-old president wanted to serve a second term. Reagan made it clear both publicly and privately that he missed his California ranch, even though he spent a considerable amount of time there during his presidency (almost an entire year, 345 days, of his eight years in office were spent at the ranch). One close adviser, William P. Clark, urged Reagan to think about leaving after one term. Clark, Reagan's National Security Advisor and later secretary of the interior, suggested that the president had fulfilled his 1980 campaign promises and should return to sunny California instead of seeking reelection. It is difficult to determine how seriously Reagan weighed that option, but in the end he decided to seek reelection. He formally announced his decision on January 29, 1984.

The election year began with a thaw in cold war tensions when Reagan delivered a televised address to Europe on January 16, 1984, calling for "constructive cooperation" between the United States and the Soviet Union and announcing that "1984 is a year of opportunities for peace." Reagan would never again utter the words "evil empire," unless asked to respond directly about this statement by the media. The speech muted some of the criticism from worried European allies and domestic critics who viewed Reagan as an extremist. The president followed that move by eliminating a more pressing foreign policy headache—withdrawing U.S. forces, or "redeploying" them, as Reagan preferred to call it, from Lebanon. The possibility of a quagmire in that Middle Eastern country haunted many members of his administration, and Reagan, for all his tough talk, decided to cut his losses, and remove Lebanon as a campaign issue.

In the meantime, a large field of Democratic contenders fought to win their party's nomination to challenge Reagan. The leading contender was former vice president Walter Mondale of Minnesota, who was challenged for the nomination by Senator John Glenn of Ohio, Senator Gary Hart of Colorado, Senator Alan Cranston of California, Senator Ernest Hollings of South Carolina, Governor Reuben

President Reagan and Democratic candidate Walter Mondale during the second debate in Kansas City, Missouri, 1984

Askew of Florida, former senator George McGovern of South Dakota, and the Reverend Jesse Jackson. The front-runner, Mondale, was surprised by a strong showing by Hart in the Iowa caucus, and the latter went on to defeat Mondale in the New Hampshire primary, thereby ensuring a long and at times contentious race. Mondale prevailed in the end, partly due to strong support from traditional Democratic constituencies such as organized labor. He made a dramatic move at the Democratic National Convention in San Francisco by selecting the first female vice presidential nominee of a major party, Congresswoman Geraldine Ferraro of New York. Mondale was equally bold in his acceptance speech, proclaiming, "I mean business. By the end of my first term, I will cut the deficit by two-thirds. Let's tell the truth. Mr. Reagan will raise taxes,

and so will I. He won't tell you. I just did." While Mondale's proposal may have been sensible policy in the face of a mushrooming federal deficit, it was a politically risky move. Members of Reagan's campaign team were delighted with Mondale's proposal; Stuart Spencer, Reagan's longtime political guru, noted, "I was in ecstasy . . . the political graveyard is full of tax increasers."

The Republican National Convention in Dallas was noteworthy for its unity and for its boredom. In his acceptance speech, Reagan seized on Mondale's endorsement of a tax hike, noting that "Will Rogers once said he never met a man he didn't like. Well, if I could paraphrase Will, our friends in the other party have never met a tax they didn't like or hike." Reagan claimed credit for rebuilding the nation's military, reviving the economy, and boasted that since January 20, 1981, "not one inch of soil has fallen to the Communists." America, Reagan proclaimed, was "coming back" and was "more confident than ever about the future."

In the summer of 1984, the Reagan-Bush ticket basked in the glow of the Olympic Games held in Los Angeles that summer, where the U.S. team performed especially well due to the absence of many Eastern bloc teams who were boycotting in retaliation for the U.S. boycott of the Moscow Olympics four years earlier. For Reagan it was "Morning Again in America," the theme of one of his most memorable commercials produced by San Francisco ad man Hal Riney for the fall campaign. The ad included shots of a farmhouse, a wedding ceremony, and an elderly man raising an American flag under the adoring gaze of a group of freshly scrubbed young children. The narrator proclaimed that "It's morning again in America. Today, more men and women will go to work than ever before in our country's history. With interest rates at about half the record high of 1980, nearly two thousand families today will buy new homes, more than at any time in the past four years. This afternoon, sixty-five hundred young men and women will be married, and with inflation at less than half of what it was four years ago, they can look forward with confidence. It's morning again in America. And under the leadership of President Reagan, our country is stronger, and prouder, and better. Why would we ever want to return to where we were less than four short years ago?"

Reagan held a considerable lead in the polls throughout that summer and fall, as the Mondale-Ferraro ticket lost valuable time when the latter had to deal with questions about her husband's financial dealings in the New York real estate market. Ferraro also came under heavy attack from leaders of the Catholic Church for her pro-choice position on abortion. Despite his wide lead, and his status as an incumbent, Reagan agreed to participate in two debates with his Democratic opponent, and his campaign also agreed to a debate between Vice President Bush and Congresswoman Ferraro.

The first debate in Louisville, Kentucky, on October 7, 1984, was the low point of Reagan's fall campaign. The president appeared to have aged considerably and to be unsure of himself. Reagan was aware of this as well; he turned to Stuart Spencer at the conclusion of the debate and said, "I was terrible." Suddenly, Reagan's age became an issue in the campaign, and for the first time there was cause for optimism in the Mondale camp. Public opinion polls indicated that the race was tightening, and it was clear to Reagan and his campaign team that he needed to reassure the American public that he was still physically and mentally equipped to be president for the next four years. It was no secret that America's oldest president, should he win reelection, would be just a few days shy of his 78th birthday when he left office in 1989.

The second debate was held in Kansas City on October 21, 1984, and it was apparent almost immediately that Reagan was more energetic and relaxed than he was in Louisville. Approximately 30 minutes into the debate Reagan was asked by a columnist for the *Baltimore Sun*, Henry Trewhitt, whether there was "any doubt in your mind that you would be able to function" in circumstances similar to what President Kennedy had experienced during the Cuban missile crisis. The president responded, "Not at all, Mr. Trewhitt, and I want you to know that also I will not make age an issue of this campaign. I am not going to exploit, for political purposes, my opponent's youth and inexperience." Everyone in the room laughed, including Walter Mondale, and for all practical purposes the age issue, Reagan's biggest obstacle to reelection, was negated. Reagan went on to win in a 49-state landslide, losing only Mondale's home state of Minnesota (by a narrow margin) and the District of Columbia. Reagan won 54,451,521, votes, almost 59 percent of the popular vote, to Mondale's 37,565,334, or 40 percent of the popular vote.

ASSASSINATION ATTEMPT

A little more than two months into his first term, Ronald Reagan had been the victim of an assassination attempt that seriously wounded him. Reagan became the second American president to be hit by an assassin's bullet and survive, and the only one wounded while in office who survived. (The first, Theodore Roo-

sevelt, was an ex-president when he was wounded during his Bull Moose candidacy in 1912.) By surviving, Reagan broke the so-called zero factor that captivated "psychics" and the tabloid media—every president elected in a year ending in zero since William Henry Harrison in 1840 had died in office (Harrison, Lincoln, Garfield, McKinley, Harding, Roosevelt, Kennedy). Reagan was extremely lucky, for the "Devastator" bullet, which was designed to explode on impact, had penetrated his side and lodged itself perilously close to his heart. Others in the presidential party were gravely injured, especially his press secretary, James Brady, who suffered a serious and debilitating wound to the head; Secret Service agent Tim-

President Reagan waves to the crowd outside the Washington Hilton Hotel immediately before being shot in an assassination attempt.

othy McCarthy, who may have saved Reagan's life and was shot in the chest, and Washington, D.C., police officer Thomas Delahanty, who suffered a wound near his spine.

On March 30, 1981, President Reagan delivered a somewhat lackluster speech at the Washington Hilton Hotel to an unresponsive audience, the Building Trades Council of the AFL-CIO, and left the hotel at approximately 2:25 P.M. The president was walking the short distance from the hotel's side exit to his limousine when John W. Hinckley, Jr., a mentally disturbed drifter from Colorado, fired six shots that wounded four men in a matter of seconds. Hinckley was apparently motivated by his viewing of a critically acclaimed film by direc-

tor Martin Scorsese, *Taxi Driver* (1976). In the movie the actress Jodie Foster played a young prostitute who befriends a volatile taxi driver who attempts to assassinate a presidential candidate; Hinckley took the film to heart and believed by assassinating Reagan he would impress Foster. Hinckley had been preparing for this act for some time, stalking President Carter during the final months of his presidency.

Within hours of Reagan's shooting, Reagan aide Lyn Nofziger released stories of Reagan's jocular reaction to his attack—he was quoted as saying to his attending physicians, "Please tell me you're Republicans," and to his wife, "Honey, I forgot to duck," and to members of

After the attempt, James Brady and police officer Thomas Delahanty lie wounded on the ground, March 30, 1981.

his White House troika, "Who's minding the store?" These stories reassured an anxious nation that the president was doing fine, when in fact he was not. If there was ever an instance in the short history of the Twenty-fifth Amendment when the temporary succession features should have been invoked by the vice president and the cabinet, this was it. The president had lost 3,500 cubic centimeters of blood, which amounted to considerably more than half his blood supply, and at one point he was losing blood at a rate of 300 cubic centimeters every 20 minutes. An alert Secret Service agent, Jerry Parr, noticed a tiny amount of blood on the president's lips after pushing Reagan into his limousine; if Parr had not seen this blood and didn't order the vehicle's driver to divert to George Washington University Hospital, the president may well have died. Reagan walked the 15 yards into the emergency room doorway after arriving at the hospital but collapsed immediately after passing the threshold. At first Reagan believed Parr had broken one of the president's ribs when he fell on Reagan after forcing him into the vehicle. "Jerry, get off, I think you've broken one of my ribs," was the way the two men remembered it later, along with Parr's command to the Secret Service driver, "Haul ass! Let's get out of here!"

The operation was a delicate one, for the surgeons had to remove a "Devastator" bullet that was lodged less than an inch from the president's heart. Reagan was on the operating table for close to two hours, and a considerable amount of time was spent searching for the bullet and then gingerly extricating it from his lungs. The president was well enough the next day to sign a routine piece of legislation, and joked with aides that "I should have known I wasn't going to avoid a staff meeting." Reagan recovered quickly, but developed a serious fever four days later that stubbornly resisted multiple doses of antibiotics but ultimately broke. On April 11, 1981, the president

President Reagan with Mrs. Reagan inside George Washington Hospital four days after the shooting

returned to the White House, noting in his diary "I know it's going to be a long recovery . . . whatever happens now I owe my life to God and will try to serve Him every way I can."

John Hinckley was ultimately found not guilty by reason of insanity, and his repeated requests for unescorted visits to his family prompted objections from the Reagan family and members of the other victims' families. In December 2003, a federal judge approved Hinckley's request for a limited amount of unsupervised travel in the Washington, D.C., area.

Some Reagan intimates were convinced that the president's determination to undermine the Soviet Union deepened after his brush with death; that he believed he had been spared for this purpose. One immediate result of the shooting was that Nancy Reagan became more involved in the president's scheduling decisions and began routinely consulting an astrologer for suggestions on planning the president's travel. Former White House chief of staff Donald Regan revealed this news to a startled nation in 1988 in a bitter memoir that recounted his difficulties with the first lady. Additionally, security around the president was tightened drastically after the March 1981 attempt on Reagan's life, and he began to wear protective body armor for almost every major public event.

The image of control and coolness that the White House staff labored to create in the first hours and days after the assassination attempt was generally successful. There was, however, one glaring exception, and that was the performance of Secretary of State Alexander Haig during a nationally televised statement from the White House briefing room. Shortly after the news broke on March 30, Haig watched Deputy Press Secretary Larry Speakes refuse to answer a question about who was in charge at the White House, and Haig decided to offer more reassurance that the situation was under control. Haig went to the briefing room and responded to a question about who was in control while Reagan was undergoing surgery. He noted, "Constitutionally, gentlemen, you have the president, the vice president, and the secretary of state, in that order, and should the president decide he wants to transfer the helm, he will do so. He has not done that. As of now, I am in control here, in the White House pending return of the vice president, and in close touch with him. If something comes up, I would check with him, of course." Haig incorrectly cited the order of presidential succession but worst of all, appeared somewhat out of breath and perspiring. Many viewers did not find Haig's performance particularly reassuring.

Reagan's ability to make light of the circumstances surrounding the attempt on his life resonated with the American public, and was perhaps the foremost event of his first term in office. It crystallized a perception that had already taken hold among many Americans that Reagan was a "stand-up guy," a genial but tough man who spoke from his heart, and while he may occasionally misspeak, he meant well and could be trusted. His apparent rapid recovery (impressive for a 70-year-old man) also reinforced the image that Reagan was a lucky man.

On April 18, 1981, one week after leaving George Washington University Hospital, President Reagan spoke to a joint session of Congress and urged passage of his tax and budget cut proposals. It was the beginning of a campaign that led to the adoption of much of his economic agenda, and set the stage for the implementation of Reaganomics. Once again Reagan appealed directly to the American people, reinforcing his reputation as a "great communicator." The president thanked the American people for their prayers and support, and read a letter from a young admirer who urged him to get well so that he would not have to deliver a speech in his pajamas. Reagan rolled over his congressional opponents that summer, in no small measure due to the emotional reaction to the assassination attempt.

JUDICIAL APPOINTMENTS

President Reagan and his domestic affairs team considered the appointment of federal judges to be a top priority of his administration. According to Attorney General Edwin Meese, the goal was to "institutionalize the Reagan revolution so it can't be set aside no matter what happens in future presidential elections." These judicial appointees, according to Reagan's White House counsel Fred Fielding, were "Ronald Reagan's best legacy." The administration achieved its goal, appointing nearly half of all lower-court judges, and also three nominees to the Supreme Court, one of whom, Antonin Scalia, became the leader of a small but sometimes influential conservative bloc on the high court. If Reagan had succeeded in appointing Robert Bork to the Supreme Court, that body may well have reversed the controversial abortion decision of *Roe v. Wade*, a dream of conservative activists since the decision was handed down in 1973.

Edwin Meese was the point man for the administration's judicial strategy, and he and his staff methodically and efficiently identified and recruited young, talented conservatives for the bench. They placed great emphasis on youth, hoping to find appointees who could serve 30- or 40-plus years and thereby undo what Meese and others perceived to be decades of judicial activism dating back to the New Deal. While there was not a "litmus test," the Reagan administration searched for judges who were "strict constructionists," in other words, justices who interpreted the Constitution by discerning, as best they could, the intent of the architects of that document. These judges tended to be more likely to defer to the decisions of the elected branches of government, defer to states' rights at the expense of the federal government (in some instances even narrowing the scope of the commerce clause, which for 200 years was the main instrument the federal government used to enhance its authority at the expense of the states), narrowly construe the Fourth Amendment protections extended to criminal defendants (particularly the so-called Miranda rights, which had been a target of conservative critics since 1966), and were skeptical of the reproductive rights the courts had expanded through the *Griswold v. Connecticut* (1965) and *Roe v. Wade* decisions, which introduced the concept of a right to privacy. In keeping with their strict construction-

ism, Reagan's judicial appointees also tended to reject expansive notions of what constituted free speech and "expression," opposed affirmative-action programs as a remedy for institutions that had engaged in discriminatory practices, and generally permitted the executive branch wide discretionary authority when dealing with cases involving executive power and national security.

President Reagan appointed almost half of the federal judiciary during his two terms in office, including 83 appellate court judges, 292 district court judges, and three members of the Supreme Court. Meese, at first working in concert with Attorney General William French Smith, and later as attorney general himself, was proud of the "exhaustive" process of interviewing and background checking that the administration created. They altered the traditional process of allowing members of Congress to suggest one nominee by requiring that three names be submitted, and if those names were unacceptable to the White House then more names were requested. In some instances the administration went outside the list of names provided by Republican senators and congressmen, and turned to candidates recommended by other sources. The ultimate control over judicial selection was moved from the Department of Justice into the White House itself. As legal scholar David O'Brien observed, "a White House Judicial Selection Committee was created to decide whom the President should nominate. It met weekly in the White House and included the Attorney General; the Deputy Attorney General; the counselor to the President [in the early years of the Reagan administration, Edwin Meese]; the assistant attorneys general for the Office of Legal Policy . . . as well as other White House advisors, including the chief of staff. This reorganization concentrated power, [and] institutionalized the role of the White House." President Reagan was not directly involved in this process, but his interest in these matters could be seen in the fact that every Reagan judicial nominee was personally contacted by the president by telephone offering the nomination to the candidate. In this arena, as David O'Brien has observed, Reagan remained "devoted to the principles of his presidency and a master of the 'personal touch.'"

Reagan's three Supreme Court nominees, Sandra Day O'Connor, Antonin Scalia, and Anthony Kennedy fulfilled the administration's hopes in terms of longevity in office, but two of the three disappointed their benefactors by emerging as "moderates" on the Court. Reagan promised during his campaign in 1980 that "one of the first Supreme Court vacancies in my administration" would be filled by a woman. When Justice Potter Stewart announced in 1981 that he would step down from the Court, Reagan nominated Sandra Day O'Connor to fill the seat. O'Connor was an Arizona Republican who had served in the state legislature and was a judge on the Arizona Court of Appeals. On September 25, 1981, she became the first woman to take a seat on the Supreme Court, and in her decades on the bench she proved to be a major crafter of decisions that upheld elements of abortion rights and affirmative action, to the dismay of Reaganites.

Antonin Scalia's name was at the top of the list for potential Supreme Court nominees throughout the Reagan years, and when Chief Justice Warren Burger announced his retirement, President Reagan, on the advice of Attorney General Meese, decided to elevate Justice William Rehnquist to the position of chief justice, and fill the open slot with Scalia. A number of factors helped Scalia easily win confirmation—he was the first Italian-American nominated to the Court, a former law professor at the University of Virginia and the University of Chicago, and at 50 he was young and assured of a lengthy tenure. He was con-

firmed by a vote of 98-0 after a five-minute debate. After the debilitating defeat of Robert Bork, many conservatives questioned the wisdom of the administration's strategy of nominating Scalia while the Republicans controlled the Senate. These critics argued that by waiting to nominate Robert Bork until after the Republicans lost the Senate, the administration miscalculated; the more controversial Bork should have gone first, the argument went, while the Senate was in Republican hands. Scalia emerged as the ultimate Reagan judicial appointee, spending his years on the Court crafting lively and often acerbic decisions lambasting judicial activism. He reached particular heights of passion when dissenting from decisions in the privacy arena dealing with abortion, gay rights, and pornography.

Rehnquist's nomination encountered stiff resistance led by Senator Edward Kennedy of Massachusetts, who managed to convince 33 of his colleagues to vote against the nomination, the second-highest tally against any confirmed justice in the 20th century (Clarence Thomas won that dubious honor). Kennedy's effort to block Rehnquist's elevation presaged his campaign against Robert Bork's nomination. The Massachusetts senator claimed that Rehnquist was "too extreme on race, too extreme on women's rights, too extreme on freedom of speech, too extreme on separation of church and state, and too extreme to be chief justice." Rehnquist's position on segregation during the 1950s and his prior residence in a community with a restrictive covenant (prohibiting the sale of property to minority buyers) were examined at great length, but in the end the Senate voted to confirm the nomination, with Rehnquist winning the support of all but two Republican senators and of most southern Democrats.

The administration's practice of appointing judges who practiced strict-constructionism and spurned judicial activism was vigorously challenged after the Democrats took control

Supreme Court justices with President Reagan in the Supreme Court Conference Room. From left to right: Justice Harry Blackmun, Justice Thurgood Marshall, Justice William Brennan, Chief Justice Warren Burger, President Reagan, Justice Sandra Day O'Connor, Justice Byron White, Justice Lewis F. Powell, Jr., Justice William Rehnquist, and Justice John Paul Stevens, September 1981

of the Senate in January 1987. Judge Bork was nominated on July 1, 1987, to fill a vacancy on the Supreme Court created by the retirement of Justice Lewis Powell. Reagan's selection of Bork was the breaking point for most Democrats. Bork had created a lengthy paper trail during his many years as a Yale law professor and a judge on the U.S. Court of Appeals, and had criticized a number of Warren Court decisions, including privacy decisions such as *Roe v. Wade*. He was the nation's foremost proponent of the doctrine of original intent, and for a nation grown accustomed to having the courts settle almost every major political and legal dispute, his position struck many as antiquated. But perhaps the foremost reason that the Bork nomination failed was due

to the concerted public relations campaign waged against him by Senator Edward Kennedy and organizations such as People for the American Way. The White House, still reeling form the Iran-contra affair, was slow to react to the opposition, and failed to appreciate how deep and visceral it was.

Senator Kennedy set the tone for the opposition when he spoke on the Senate floor just hours after Bork was nominated and charged that "Robert Bork's America is a land in which women would be forced into back-alley abortions, blacks would sit at segregated lunch counters, rogue police could break down citizens' doors in midnight raids, schoolchildren could not be taught about evolution, writers and artists could be censored at the whim of government, and the doors of the federal courts would be shut on the fingers of millions of citizens for whom the judiciary is—and is often the only—protector of the individual rights that are the heart of democracy." Techniques formally reserved for political campaigns were brought to bear on the Bork nomination, including newspaper and television advertisements, and direct mail campaigns. People for the American Way sponsored a series of television advertisements in which the actor Gregory Peck (who played Atticus Finch in *To Kill a Mockingbird*) urged voters to contact their senators to oppose Bork, because "if Robert Bork wins a seat on the Supreme Court, it will be for life—his life and yours."

Bork did not help his cause with his intellectually impressive but somewhat brittle testimony before the Senate Judiciary Committee. In a media era where image counted as much as judicial experience, Bork faced many obstacles, which he and the White House ultimately could not overcome. Apparently following instructions from the White House, Bork tried to portray himself as a moderate, which caused many senators to wonder if Bork was experiencing a "confirmation conversion" that would be discarded once he was on the bench. Additionally, President Reagan's efforts on behalf of the nominee were somewhat tepid, and in the end Bork was defeated in a lopsided vote of 58 to 42. The Bork nomination was the opening salvo in an increasingly partisan struggle over judicial nominations, and the legacy of that battle persists to this day.

After Bork's defeat, the administration nominated Judge Douglas Ginsburg, a former Harvard law professor whose name was quickly withdrawn after it was revealed that he had smoked marijuana. Reagan then selected Judge Anthony M. Kennedy of the U.S. Court of Appeals, 9th Circuit, a Ford appointee who, unlike Bork, truly was something of a moder-

ate. Kennedy was easily confirmed, and proved to be a disappointment to conservatives, serving as something of a "swing vote" on the Court and frequently differing with the opinions of Chief Justice Rehnquist and Scalia.

In the end, through the sheer number and quality of his federal judicial appointees, Reagan succeeded in shifting the federal judiciary to the Right. Law enforcement agencies were given greater latitude in terms of "good faith exceptions" to the exclusionary rule, and states saw a restoration of some of their authority in a handful of controversial commerce clause cases. However, many of the administration's most cherished objectives, such as the reversal of abortion rights and affirmative-action programs, were not realized.

CIVIL RIGHTS AND AFFIRMATIVE ACTION

No criticism offended Ronald Reagan more than the charge that he was insensitive to the plight of minorities, yet this accusation was frequently directed at him during his eight years as president. Reagan was raised in an era when segregation and racism were the norm, and yet his parents seem to have instilled in him the idea that all human beings deserved to be treated with respect, regardless of color. He recounted in his memoir how he told Supreme Court justice Thurgood Marshall that "Jack and Nelle had raised me from the time I was a child to believe racial and religious discrimination was the worst sin in the world, how I'd experience some of it as the son of an Irish Catholic in a Protestant town; how as a sports announcer I'd been among the first in the country to campaign for integration of professional baseball."

Despite his professed belief in racial equality, Reagan opposed every major civil rights act of the 1960s, and this made him a target of criticism in both California and around the nation. Reagan's opposition was based on his belief that these acts enhanced the power of the federal government at the expense of the states; for instance, he opposed the Voting Rights Act of 1965 because he believed voting procedures should be the responsibility of local officials. During the 1980 campaign he affirmed his commitment to civil rights, claiming "I am heart and soul in favor of the things that have been done in the name of civil rights and desegregation and so forth." Yet he chose to open his 1980 campaign at the Neshoba County Fair in Mississippi, near the site of the murder of three civil rights workers in 1964, and proclaimed his fidelity to the cause of states' rights.

According to Roger Wilkins, during Reagan's presidency long-term unemployment among whites increased 1.5 percent from 1980 to 1984, while for African Americans, it increased 72 percent. By May of 1986 the unemployment rate for African Americans was 15 percent, more than double the white rate, and more than double what the rate had been for African Americans, in 1970—6.7 percent. Slightly more than a third of all African Americans (more than 9 million) were classified as poor, which represented an increase of 2 million from 1978. Black family income fell by 3.7 percent during Reagan's first term.

Reagan made few efforts to reach out to civil rights organizations, believing that he would not receive a fair hearing. He did address the National Association for the Advancement of Colored People in Denver in 1981, his only such appearance before that organization, and received a chilly reception. In his speech the president claimed that federal policies had created a "new kind of bondage" for blacks, which only served to increase the chill. One policy in particular drew Reagan's wrath—affirmative action. During the 1980 election Reagan claimed that affirmative action was "becoming

a kind of quota system . . . a kind of reverse discrimination." His inaugural transition team on the Equal Employment Opportunity Commission charged that the commission, by pursuing affirmative-action policies, had created a "new racism in America," while his attorney general, Edwin Meese, said that "a new version of the separate-but-equal doctrine is being pushed upon us." Some members of the Reagan administration wanted the president to rescind President Lyndon Johnson's Executive Order 11246, requiring government contractors to "take affirmative action to ensure that applicants are employed . . . without regard to their race, creed, color, or national origin," but the president never accepted this advice. His first secretary of labor, William Brock, supported certain types of affirmative action, but most members of the Reagan administration, from the president on down, were steadfastly opposed to "reverse discrimination," as they called it. The most prominent opponents of affirmative action during the Reagan years were Edwin Meese, White House counsel and later attorney general, and the assistant attorney general for civil rights, William Bradford Reynolds.

Meese, Reynolds, and others were allied in their aversion to "group remedies." This was the fundamental principle of the administration's civil rights agenda and served more than any other factor to tarnish Reagan's image among civil rights advocates. In one prominent instance, the administration argued before the Supreme Court for a narrow interpretation of instances where courts could provide relief in discrimination cases. This interpretation was called "victim specific" and allowed that only specific victims of proven discrimination by a particular employer must be given relief or compensation, but the Supreme Court rejected this interpretation.

But there were other events that contributed to the contentious relationship between the administration and civil rights activists. In 1982, Reagan opposed a bill that would have extended provisions of the 1965 Voting Rights Act. The bill passed with overwhelming majorities in both the House and the Senate, and became law. In 1988 Reagan vetoed the Civil Rights Restoration Act, which he said would "vastly and unjustifiably expand the power of the federal government over the decisions and affairs of private organizations," but the act became law over his veto with 21 Republicans in the Senate and 52 in the House supporting it. Even more galling to civil rights leaders was the fact that the president sided with Bob Jones University in early 1982 in a controversy involving tax-exempt status for schools that practiced segregation. The Inter-

nal Revenue Service had followed the practice of denying exemptions for segregated schools, and Bob Jones University filed a lawsuit attempting to reverse the IRS policy. Bob Jones admitted a small number of black students each year but banned interracial dating and marriage, and Reagan and many conservative Christians viewed these cases as an issue of religious freedom. Reagan later said, "All I wanted was that these tax collectors stop threatening schools that were obeying the law." No one in his administration told him that he was repealing the civil rights policy of Nixon, Ford, and Carter, and when the news reached the media there were cries of outrage. He proposed a compromise on the issue that would give the

President Reagan at the signing ceremony for Martin Luther King holiday legislation in the Rose Garden of the White House, November 2, 1983

IRS the right to deny tax exemptions, but in the end he ended up pleasing no one, neither his conservative allies who thought he abandoned his principles nor civil rights advocates who were looking for a clear statement of support for the IRS action. The compromise proposal went nowhere, and the Supreme Court ultimately upheld the IRS action. The whole Bob Jones affair revealed the disarray in the president's domestic policy staff, and strained his relations with African Americans.

Reagan further angered African Americans with his comments about Martin Luther King, Jr., and he had opposed making the civil rights leader's birthday a national holiday. At a press conference on October 19, 1983, Reagan said he understood Senator Jesse Helms's request to have King's FBI files opened before approving the holiday. Helms had suggested that King may have been a communist sympathizer, and Reagan appeared to endorse Helms's view that before mandating the King holiday "we should know everything there is to know about an individual." He compounded the damage when he was asked to respond directly to Helms's suggestion that King had communist sympathies, "We'll know in about 35 years, won't we," a reference to the opening of sealed FBI evidence. Nonetheless, Reagan spoke admiringly of Martin Luther King in 1987, telling students to "accept nothing less than making yours a generation free of bigotry, intolerance, and discrimination." Reagan ultimately agreed to sign the King holiday bill, but the damage had been done.

Throughout his tenure in office Reagan tried to reach out to some African Americans through a series of symbolic gestures. Although he had an aversion to meeting with organized civil rights groups, tales of individual hardship moved him, and often prompted a response. After reading news reports about the harassment of a black family in suburban Washington, D.C., Reagan met with the family, and he also visited the same black high school in Chicago twice to commend the students for their academic achievements. He delivered the commencement address at Tuskegee University in 1987 and spoke of the important contributions of African Americans in building American society. But in the end these symbolic gestures did little to bolster his standing, and he consistently received some of his lowest approval ratings from African Americans. One indicator of Reagan's troubled legacy in this area could be seen in the rhetoric of his hand-picked successor, George H. W. Bush. Bush tried to distance himself from Reagan's civil rights record, promising during the 1988 campaign to usher in a "new day" for African Americans if he was elected president.

DEFICITS

Ronald Reagan pledged during his 1980 campaign for president to balance the federal budget but never once submitted a balanced budget in his eight years in office. He was critical of the budget deficits of the Carter years, which in fiscal year 1981, the last budget year of President Carter's administration, stood at $79 billion; in 1986, at the peak of the deficit spending of the Reagan years, the budget deficit stood at $221 billion. In 1981 the federal debt was $994 billion; by 1989, the year Reagan left office, the national debt had almost tripled, approaching $3 trillion. This was a remarkable development coming from the same man who in 1979 argued that we "need both a limit on spending and a ban on unbalanced budgets. . . . Let's hear it for fiscal responsibility."

Many economists blame the hemorrhaging red ink on Reagan's adherence to what became known as "Reaganomics" or supply-side economics, coupled with his commitment to large increases in the nation's defense budget. Supply-side economists, particularly economist Arthur Laffer, had been arguing that cuts in the nation's tax rates would spur economic growth and that the nation's treasury would not lose, as one of Reagan's economic policy advisers Martin Anderson put it, "as much revenue as one might expect. People would work harder, and their incomes would rise over time to offset a substantial part of the revenue loss due to the tax rate cut." Much of this did come to pass, but in the short term, a deep recession and dramatic increases in defense spending and in spending for entitlement programs led to the explosion of the nation's deficit, especially during Reagan's first term.

Reagan was firmly committed to his tax cuts and spent considerable political capital during his first year in office winning congressional support for the (Jack) Kemp–(William) Roth tax cut legislation, a proposed 25 percent cut in personal income taxes phased in over three years at 10 percent in 1981, an additional 10 percent in 1982, and then a final 5 percent cut in 1983. (Reagan and Kemp-Roth had initially proposed a 30 percent cut, but had to settle for the smaller 25 percent cut to win congressional approval). Reagan was also firmly committed to increasing defense spending, and resisted pressure from his Office of Management and Budget (OMB) director David Stockman and some congressional Republicans to push for smaller increases in the Pentagon's budget. If forced to choose, between cutting defense or tolerating deficits, Reagan would choose the latter. There were numerous confrontations between Stockman and Defense Secretary Caspar Weinberger over the size of the Department of Defense (DOD) budget, and Stockman privately began to harbor doubts about Reagan's economic prowess as he repeatedly rejected OMB's arguments for belt tightening. According to Stockman, Reagan, along with his secretary of the treasury and some members of the White House staff, were "almost entirely innocent and uninformed." Reagan held on to the hope that some of the deficit problem could be cured by cutting "waste, fraud, and abuse" out of the budget, a position Stockman and others considered hopelessly naive. Yet Stockman himself contributed to a misleading public relations campaign in the early days of the administration, when he predicted that strong economic growth and "phantom tax revenues" would generate a balanced budget by 1984.

Stockman fell out of favor with his administration colleagues when he gave a series of interviews in 1981 to the *Atlantic Monthly* describing the behind-the-scenes machinations involved in Reagan's tax and spending proposals. When "The Education of David Stockman" was published in November 1981, the White House was forced to defend itself against charges of incompetence and deception. Regarding the budget, Stockman claimed that "none of us really understands what's going on with all these numbers." He referred to supply-side economics, in particular the Kemp-Roth bill, as a Trojan horse for the old notion of trickle-down economics; the idea that help for those at the top eventually "trickled down" to those at the bottom of American society. "It's kind of hard to sell 'trickle-down,' so the supply-side formula was the only way to get a tax policy that was really 'trickle-down,'" Stockman noted. The 35-year-old OMB director was supposed to have been "taken to the woodshed" by Reagan in a concocted effort to make it appear that the president was disciplining him for his indiscretions. Edwin Meese, Michael Deaver, and Nancy Reagan all urged the president to fire Stockman, but the president decided not to remove him, partly out of an innate sense of compassion but also due to his belief that Stockman was a victim of sabotage by the press. Stockman also had some powerful patrons, including White House chief

President Reagan addresses the nation from the Oval Office on tax reduction legislation, July 27, 1981.

of staff James Baker, who urged the president to retain his young OMB director. Stockman did not repay Reagan's kindness; in 1986 he published a bitter memoir highly critical of Reagan, Weinberger, Meese, Deaver, and others. Stockman's revelations provided ammunition to those who believed that Reagan's economic and fiscal proposals were based on false premises.

It should be noted that there were economists outside the administration who adopted the same rosy economic projections as Reagan's team. In fact, the Carter administration predicted robust economic growth through 1984 and forecast a balanced budget for that year. The Congressional Budget Office in 1981 also anticipated strong economic growth, even with Reagan's tax and spending initiatives. All of these faulty projections foresaw strong economic growth and a gradual decrease in the inflation rate. None of these projections anticipated the sharp recession that took hold in 1981–82, along with the rise in real interest rates, nominal income growth, and an unexpectedly rapid fall in the inflation rate. The deficit exploded as a result, surging to $128 billion in 1982 (4.1 percent of the nation's gross national product) and $208 billion (6.3 percent of the nation's GNP, the highest level it reached during the Reagan years) in 1983.

Defenders of the Reagan record, including the president himself, blamed excessive congressional spending as the chief culprit for the deficit problem. Reagan later wrote in his memoir that "in the first six years after tax rates started coming down late in 1981 . . . Congress increased spending by $450 billion. So, we lost our chance to slash the deficit. Deficits, as I've often said, aren't caused by too little taxing, they are cause by too much spending. President's don't create deficits, Congress does." This analysis does not appear to be accurate; most budget experts argue that if Congress had not altered Reagan's budgets but accepted them as proposed, the resulting deficits would still have been as large as the actual deficits. According to Reagan biographer Lou Cannon, Congress contributed $90 billion to the deficit during the Reagan years, or $15 billion per year. Additionally, the Republican Party controlled the Senate for six years of Reagan's presidency, and the president held considerable sway over that body for much of his first six years in office.

The United States was $1.8 trillion deeper in debt by January 20, 1989, the day Ronald Reagan left the White House, than it had been on January 20, 1981. The debt amounted to one-fourth of the nation's GNP, or $15,000 per family. However, the annual deficits had begun to shrink after peaking in fiscal year 1983, when the deficit had represented 6.3 percent of the nation's GNP; by 1988 it was 3.2 percent. Nevertheless, Reagan left office believing that his inability to contain government spending was his greatest failure, and he repeatedly called for an amendment to the Constitution mandating annual balanced budgets, a provision found in many state constitutions. At the conclusion of his presidency, a poll of American public opinion found that nearly one-fifth of all Americans cited budget deficits as the issue that most disturbed them about Reagan's presidency, only slightly behind the Iran-contra affair.

It is accepted by most economists and political scientists that the Reagan administration deserves the bulk of the responsibility for the large deficits that marked his years in office. The larger question of just how serious Reagan's deficits were to the long-term health of the country remains unanswered. The accusation that Reagan was "mortgaging" the nation's children's and grandchildren's futures by accumulating mountains of debt had not come to pass by the turn of the century, although many argue that the tax hikes of his successors, achieved at great political cost to both President George H. W. Bush and to President Bill Clinton, prevented the dire consequences from occurring.

AGRICULTURE POLICY

The Reagan years witnessed the greatest expansion of federal aid to farmers since the creation of the Department of Agriculture. The federal government devoted $8.8 billion in its fiscal year 1980 budget to agriculture; that figure rose to $31.5 billion in 1986, although it sharply declined to $17.2 billion by 1988. Nonetheless, while President Reagan often spoke of the need to apply the principles of the free market to farming, the importance of the farm vote to Reagan's coalition, and to many Republican members of Congress, led his administration to expand the federal role in the nation's agricultural economy. According to an analysis by political scientist Larry Schwab, the Reagan administration "end[ed] up supporting a huge expansion of most of the existing farm programs, [and] his administration even added new ones."

The nation's farmers were saddled with debt when Reagan became president in 1981, their total debt having increased from $70 billion in the early 1970s to more than $210 billion in the early 1980s. Robert Thompson, a longtime observer of the American agricultural scene, notes that in 1981 Congress passed, and Reagan signed into law, a farm bill establishing minimum price supports up to four years in advance, without regard to exchange rates or domestic and global supply and demand balances. As a result, farm exports fell from $44 billion in 1981 to $26 billion in 1986. In the long run, the 1981 bill transformed the United States, in the words of one commentator, "into the Saudi Arabia of the international grain cartel.... We ended up making all the production cutbacks necessary to support the world price of grain at our loan rates." In 1983, the United States government paid American farmers to remove 80 million acres from production, under a program called Payment-in-Kind (PIK), the largest acreage reduction program ever sponsored by the federal government. The PIK program took more land out of production than all of the land planted by farmers in Western Europe.

In 1985, President Reagan threatened to veto a farm bill that he considered an example of excessive spending—the price tag for the bill was $168 billion, of which $82 billion would go to price and income support programs. Electoral considerations appear to have moved him to support the bill in the end, although the administration influenced some elements of the package, including a 25 percent reduction in price supports in the first year of the bill's implementation, followed by a 5 percent reduction each year until the supports reached 75 percent of the market price. The administration was forced to accept a freeze on target prices, and this had the effect of increasing agricultural spending from $19 billion to $26 billion in 1986. The acreage reduction programs, which required farmers to retire 25, 27.5, or 35 percent of their land to qualify for government payments, remained in place, as did daily price supports. However, the 1985 farm bill did restore some level of competitiveness to the export market by reducing domestic price supports.

Ronald Reagan frequently invoked free-market principles when addressing agricultural issues, arguing that the government needed to reduce its entanglement with the farm economy, and he often attacked the price and income support programs as a violation of those principles. He consistently held that "if we believe in a free market, shouldn't our farmers be allowed to sell their produce anywhere in the world for the best price they can get? To not allow this is to subsidize and make available to our own consumers low priced food at the expense of our own farmers." However, in the final analysis, electoral pressures led Reagan and many of his conservative supporters to abandon their principles and avoid any significant alterations of farm programs during his presidency.

1981 AIR TRAFFIC CONTROLLERS STRIKE

One of the most noteworthy actions of Ronald Reagan's first term in office was his handling of the strike by air traffic controllers in August 1981. The Professional Air Traffic Controllers Organization (PATCO) went on strike on August 3, demanding more compensation and a reduction in the number of overtime hours they were required to work. In a dramatic Rose Garden announcement the president gave the striking controllers 48 hours to return to work. Most did not return to work, and Reagan dismissed more than 12,000 controllers for engaging in an illegal strike against the government. "I'm sorry, and I'm sorry for them," the president said as he fired the strikers, "I certainly take no joy out of this." Legislation had been in place for some time prohibiting strikes by government employees; all Federal Aviation Administration (FAA) employees, including all air traffic controllers, were required to sign an affidavit agreeing not to strike. In addition to firing the striking workers, Reagan refused to grant amnesty to those controllers who reversed their position after walking off the job.

Reagan's action sent shock waves through the American labor movement and around the world. Gerald Ford's White House chief of staff, Donald Rumsfeld, no fan of Reagan's, commented "it struck me as singular . . . you had a president who was new to the office and not taken seriously by a lot of people. It showed a decisiveness and an ease with his instincts." In Great Britain, Margaret Thatcher's press secretary, Bernard Ingham, recalled that "Reagan rapidly became a folk hero because he fired the striking air traffic controllers. There were a very large number of people in this country who had put up with an extremely large number of strikes, who thought that it was about time that somebody did something like that here. . . . so people here began to sit up and take notice of this man."

Ironically, PATCO was one of the few unions that endorsed Reagan in his 1980 campaign against President Carter. Reagan was proud of his lifetime membership in the American Federation of Labor—Congress of Industrial Organizations (AFL-CIO) and his six terms of service as president of the Screen Actors Guild, leading that organization in its first strike. But Reagan was consistently opposed to the idea that public employees could strike. In 1977 Reagan made the following observation on the difference between public and private employees and their right to strike: "when are public servants not public servants? When they go on strike. . . . No amount of rhetoric or reciting clichés . . . can change the fact that there is a fundamental difference between private and pub[lic] employment." He admired the position of his favorite president, Calvin Coolidge, who observed that "there is no right to strike against the public safety by anybody, anywhere, at any time." According to Reagan, "this was the first real emergency I faced as president. . . . I don't like firing any-

body. But I realized that if they made the decision not to return to work in the full knowledge of what I'd said, then I wasn't firing them, they were giving up their jobs based on their individual decisions." He later observed that "I suppose the strike was an important juncture for our new administration. I think it convinced people who might have thought otherwise that I meant what I said."

Many union supporters predicted that the replacement controllers (military air traffic controllers, along with some supervisory personnel, and PATCO members who defied the strike organizers) were unqualified and would cause a "safety incident," but this never materialized. The reaction among American labor leaders to the PATCO firings was furious, and a massive protest by organized labor, "Solidarity Day," took place on September 19 in Washington, D.C. The protest was one of the largest in the history of the capital, with some 250,000 union members and sympathizers in attendance.

But Reagan's decision to fire the air traffic controllers won the support of a majority of the American public, and coming on the heels of his surviving an assassination attempt, and in the midst of his tax cut victories, the PATCO firings contributed to his image as a decisive leader. The failed strike was a watershed event in the Reagan presidency, and may well have contributed to the successful effort to contain inflation in the early 1980s, as labor reverted to a somewhat more defensive posture regarding its demands from management.

HEALTH CARE

Ronald Reagan showed little interest in health care policy during his tenure in office. Despite being the nation's oldest president and a Social Security recipient, his bond with elderly voters concerned about health costs and Social Security benefits was always tenuous. Reagan held to a consistent ideological position regarding all domestic health and welfare programs—that market alternatives and competition were preferable to government regulations and transfer payment programs.

This was true in the health care policy arena, where he hoped the forces of competition would make the American health care industry more efficient in terms of costs and delivery of services. The so-called competition strategy was based on the idea that consumers should be able to choose between competing health care plans, that employers or the government would contribute a fixed sum toward a health care plan, and that all available plans would follow identical rules and that health care providers would be organized in such a way as to encourage competitiveness. However, Reagan never took the lead in pushing for a shift in government health care policy toward a competition strategy; during the first two years of his administration, his most active domestic policy years, health policy was run by the White House Office of Domestic Policy, in particular Reagan aide Jack Svahn; by Secretary of Health and Human Services Richard Schweiker; and by Office of Management and Budget director David Stockman. Following Schweiker's departure in 1983, OMB took the bulk of responsibility for health care, after Schweiker's successor, Margaret Heckler, proved to be an ineffective cabinet secretary. OMB's primary concern was the budget deficit, the immediate bottom line. Health care innovations relying on a competition strategy would have led to short-term cost increases, and were thus ruled out by the cost-averse OMB. As one observer of health care policy during the Reagan years noted, the early "health policy triangle" became "unbalanced" by 1984–85, with HHS "no longer exerting leadership that could offset the budget cutters

at OMB. This was precisely the time when strong leadership might have spelled the difference between success and failure for the competition strategy."

There were a few significant changes in health care policy during the Reagan years, some of which were proposed by the administration in a February 1983 health care policy initiative submitted to Congress, although many of the initiatives died on Capitol Hill. The administration succeeded in winning a temporary freeze on Medicare fees at 1983 levels beginning in June 1984. The administration contended, and Congress apparently agreed, that Medicare payment rates to hospitals in 1983 were 6.1 percent higher than necessary that year. One successful initiative stood in stark contrast to Reagan's normal aversion to expanding government programs, and that was a catastrophic-illness proposal designed to protect the elderly from, as Reagan put it, "the worst fear of old age," by assisting in the payment of all hospital and doctor bills that exceeded the first $2,000 in out-of-pocket expenses. Reagan appears to have been influenced by a somewhat emotional appeal from his HHS secretary, Otis Bowen, a physician and former governor of Indiana, who reduced a complicated issue to a very personal level that appealed to Reagan. In a contentious cabinet meeting, Bowen stood his ground against the pressure from OMB budget cutters and in a rare instance won the president's approval to enlarge a government program. A compromise catastrophic health care bill was passed by Congress in May 1988, and President Reagan signed it into law the following July, creating the largest expansion in Medicare's 23-year history. (This legislation was eventually rescinded in 1989 under the Bush administration due to pressure from senior citizens upset over a surtax provision).

More in keeping with his small-government philosophy and his free market principles, Reagan eliminated the Federal Health Planning Program, enacted in 1974 to oversee hospitals' building and expansion plans, along with the purchase of capital equipment. The administration believed the FHPP contributed to higher hospital costs. The program was completely phased out by October 6, 1986, and the power to oversee hospital expansion was effectively turned over to the states. Additionally, Reagan reduced or eliminated some federal health manpower programs. For instance, the National Health Service Corps of the U.S. Public Health Service was drastically curtailed during the Reagan years. The NHSC awarded scholarships to medical and dental students who promised in return for scholarship money to work in rural or inner-city areas following their graduation. More than 10 percent of the students defaulted, and large numbers of graduates, from a third to a half, did not remain in the areas to which they were assigned. Reagan viewed the corps as an example of government waste and abuse of taxpayers' money, and reduced the number of scholarships from well over 2,000 per year in the 1970s to 35 in 1986.

Overall, while the administration's goal was to make health care more competitive and market-oriented, many of the health-related proposals that became law during the 1980s relied on price controls, not market forces. Conservative critics, in particular, were upset over the administration's acquiescence in, if not support for, a prospective-payment system for Medicare that relied on a price-control system, as well as a provision in the Tax Equity and Fiscal Responsibility Act of 1982 (TEFRA) permitting prepaid health care plans to enroll Medicare beneficiaries, which was also based ultimately on price controls.

Spending on health care skyrocketed during the 1980s; from 1979 to 1988 federal spending on health programs increased from $48 billion to $128 billion, a 167 percent increase. As a percentage of the nation's gross national product, it expanded from 1.9 percent to 2.7 percent of GNP; health care programs grew at a much faster rate than the economy, and faster than the rate of all federal spending. The Medicare program alone grew from $24 billion in 1980 to $85.6 billion in 1989, while Medicaid spending ballooned from $13.2 billion in 1980 to $29 billion in 1988.

However, a compelling case can be made that the relative fiscal conservatism of the Reagan administration in the health care field prevented spending in this area from increasing at an even faster rate. Paul Pierson, professor of government at Harvard and a longtime observer of American health and welfare policy, notes that cuts from Reagan's first term reduced Medicare spending over time by 6.8 percent and Medicaid by 2.8 percent. It was estimated that by 1993, these cuts and others made in later years under both the Reagan and Bush administrations kept Medicare expenditures 27 percent lower than they would have been without these changes. These reductions in spending were ultimately passed on to consumers, as many of Reagan's critics were quick to point out. One study estimated that between 1980 and 1988, expenses for health care for the elderly rose from 12.8 percent of total income to over 18.2 percent. Many of these critics referred to Reagan's cuts as draconian, including the president of the American Medical Association, Dr. James H. Sammons, who labeled the administration's cuts as a rationing of health care and said, "this administration has an absolute commitment to only one thing and that's money," while many of the president's defenders claimed that his actions succeeded in containing health care costs in the 1980s. Regardless of the outcome of that debate, there was no disputing the fact that health care remained a hot-button issue in American politics. While an ambitious effort during the Clinton years to nationalize the American medical system died in Congress in 1994, issues of health care equity and efficiency continued to roil the body politic in the new millennium.

WELFARE

Ronald Reagan believed that American social welfare programs, particularly programs created under Lyndon Johnson's Great Society program, were failing both recipients and taxpayers. One special target of Reagan's ire was Aid to Families with Dependent Children (AFDC), which he believed to be morally corrupting to many recipients and excessively expensive to maintain. Reagan was not opposed to the concept of providing government assistance to the truly needy—the aged and the infirm, the very young and the disabled, and in fact often cited his support for FDR's New Deal, and the assistance it had provided his father at a critical point during the Great Depression when he was hired to work for the Works Progress Administration (WPA). But Reagan believed programs like AFDC encouraged promiscuity and contributed to the breakdown of the American family, which Reagan proclaimed in 1986 had reached "crisis" proportions. This type of welfare, Reagan argued, was a "tax-financed incentive for immorality that was destroying the family" and "was responsible for an endless and malignant cycle of despair in which generation after generation went on the dole and never had any incentive to leave it." Welfare's "spider's web of dependency" had made some Americans vassals of the state, and to Reagan, a staunch believer in individual liberty, this was an abomination. To make matters worse, Reagan believed that government programs, or more precisely the bureaucrats who administered them, sought to expand their client lists; "they go out and actually recruit people to be on welfare."

As with most domestic issues, Reagan viewed welfare through the lens of federalism, believing that government governed best when it was administered closest to the people. In one of his prepresidential radio addresses, Reagan urged "for the sake of the people we are trying to help & for the taxpayers, welfare should be administered at the state & local level without the benevolent hand of Wash[ington] laying a finger on it." His goals for welfare reform during his presidency were succinctly described by his domestic policy adviser, Martin Anderson: (1) the establishment of fair and sensible eligibility levels; (2) the elimination of fraud, waste, and extravagance; (3) returning control of welfare programs back to the states and localities, along with adequate tax resources to pay for the programs; (4) the avoidance of any guaranteed income proposal along the lines of the Family Assistance Plan (FAP), one of the most progressive pieces of legislation ever proposed by an American president, but one that, ironically, a Democratic-controlled Congress killed due to a suspicion of Richard Nixon's motives, among other factors. Nixon's FAP proposal would have set an income floor below which no American would be allowed to fall, and Reagan, generally a Nixon admirer and supporter, strongly disagreed with Nixon on this issue.

During his second term as governor of California, Reagan's dispute with the Nixon administration over welfare policy became heated at times, with the administration pressuring the state to increase its cost-of-living payments to recipients, while Reagan was seeking ways to reduce the state's welfare rolls and trying to put welfare recipients to work. In 1971 Reagan reached a compromise with Nixon's Department of Health, Education, and Welfare, headed by Elliot Richardson, whom he came to dislike. Nonetheless, Reagan was always able to strike a deal, if a deal was possible, and he agreed to bring California into compliance with federal regulations in return for a promise from HEW that it would not block a pilot program requiring able-bodied recipients to work as a condition for receiving public assistance. It took Nixon's direct intervention to win HEW's approval of the "workfare" experiment, but Reagan was satisfied with the compromise. Although the program had mixed results, it established Reagan as the leading proponent of "workfare," and further enhanced his reputation among conservatives nationwide. Reagan believed the California Welfare Reform Act of 1971, which came about partly through face-to-face negotiations between Assembly Speaker Bob Moretti and Reagan, was "probably the most comprehensive" welfare reform in American history. Reagan's ability to go around the Assembly and appeal directly to Californians to support his welfare initiative contributed in part to the passage of the act. Speaker Moretti, in a story Reagan loved to tell, supposedly came into the governor's office one day "holding his hands in the air as if I had a gun on him, and said, 'Stop those cards and letters!'" The act inspired many other American states to follow suit with similar reforms. Reagan's biographers are almost unanimous in calling the act "Reagan's proudest achievement in the eight years of his governorship."

In the early years of Reagan's presidency, during the deep recession of 1981–82, the number of Americans who fell below the poverty line increased, and by 1984 approximately 13 million children, many in the inner cities, were living in poverty. This was more than had lived in poverty in 1965 when Lyndon Johnson launched his "Great Society" programs and vowed to wage war on poverty. But while Reagan was clearly hostile to the welfare state, his elevation to the presidency produced no major reform of the welfare system. There was an effort in the early days of his administration to cut programs, such as AFDC, school lunch programs, and subsidized housing, that were targeted at poor Americans. Programs

designed to benefit households with incomes under $10,000 per year declined by 8 percent, while federal subsidies that benefited the middle class for the most part remained untouched. His OMB director, David Stockman, disputed the claim that the administration was attempting to balance the budget on "the backs of the poor," arguing instead that they were "interested in curtailing weak claims rather than weak clients." Nonetheless, the perception that Reagan was indifferent to the plight of the poor took hold at this time, despite the president's repeated attempts to convince voters that he was a child of poverty and hoped to create opportunities for all Americans to advance up the socioeconomic ladder. He wrote to one supporter in 1983, "I've been frustrated and angered by the attempts to paint me . . . as lacking in compassion for the poor. . . . we [Reagan's family] were poor in an era when there were no government programs to turn to," and to another correspondent he wrote in defense of his record, "I was raised in poverty."

Yet while some welfare programs were initially curtailed during the Reagan years, including job training, unemployment insurance benefits, and AFDC, all major welfare programs survived the 1980s and even grew by billions of dollars. Charles Hobbs, a member of Reagan's Office of Policy Development, notes that the rate of growth of welfare programs decreased during the 1980s years, but there was no real decline in any major program—in fact, welfare spending actually rose faster during the Reagan years than did the cost of living. Following the 1981 cuts, Congress went on to restore some of the benefits, increasing spending on food stamps and expanding eligibility requirements for AFDC. In fact, the criticism Reagan received from the Left for "balancing the budget on the backs of the poor" was matched by critics on the Right who accused him of tinkering with these programs only to make them more efficient. Their hope was that

Reagan would dismantle Lyndon Johnson's Great Society program, but no effort of that sort ever materialized. Some conservative supporters of the president argue that the large deficits of the Reagan years acted as a restraint on federal spending, including spending for welfare programs, but generally there was disappointment that no wholesale effort was made to overthrow the Great Society. One conservative critic, and former member of Reagan's White House staff, Kevin Hopkins, observed that "the president explicitly wanted to preserve the Great Society pretty much as it was— he just hoped to make it work better . . . there never was even an incipient Reagan revolution in welfare policy, only a proposed changing of the guards." Without question some of Reagan's advisers, and perhaps even Reagan himself, secretly harbored the idea of repealing the Great Society, but political realities intervened to render it impossible. There was a caution and a moderation in Reagan that critics on both ends of the political spectrum repeatedly failed to discern; he treasured his political capital, nurtured it, and used it sparingly.

The most important change in welfare policy during the Reagan years was the Family Support Act, which the president signed in October 1988. The chief architect of the legislation was Senator Daniel Patrick Moynihan of New York, a Democrat who had once worked for President Nixon and was the architect of the Family Assistance Plan that Reagan had opposed. Moynihan and the administration were able to reach an agreement on the first major overhaul of welfare since its inception, and ushered in the most sweeping overhaul of AFDC in its brief history. The bill required the states to offer job training and support to poor parents if they attempted to get off welfare, and offered matching federal funds to assist in the effort. It also required that by 1994 one parent in each welfare household must look for work and if they failed in that pursuit, then they would be required to work a 16-hour week on a state-sponsored project. Reagan balked at signing the bill without a "workfare" provision, but once it was included, he signed the legislation and referred to it as "a message of hope" to those seemingly locked in a cycle of poverty and dependence.

It was not until 1996 that a Democratic president, Bill Clinton, facing a Republican-controlled Congress eager to "end welfare as we know it," reached agreement on sweeping welfare reforms incorporating many of the workfare themes that Reagan once championed. What had once been an argument confined to the conservative side of the American political spectrum, that welfare bred a "culture of dependency" and had potentially negative effects on the character of the recipients, was by the mid-1990s accepted by many on both sides of the ideological divide. Some Republicans, including Speaker of the House Newt Gingrich of Georgia, credited Reagan and the ideological movement he spearheaded for laying the foundation for the reforms adopted in 1996 under the Personal Responsibility and Work Opportunity Reconciliation Act, which, among other things, eliminated the AFDC program.

THE 1981 BUDGET AND TAX CUT BATTLES

President Reagan gave top priority to winning passage of his economic program in his first term. This was the topic of his first televised speech to the nation on February 5, 1981, when he told the American people, "I regret to say that we're in the worst economic mess since the Great Depression . . . it's time to try something different." On February 18 Reagan followed with an address to a Joint Session of Congress where he announced his "Program for Economic Recovery," which proposed a 30 percent, three-year tax rate cut, increased defense spending, cutting $41 billion from Jimmy Carter's projected budget for fiscal year 1982, including cuts in some 83 programs, all of which, Reagan contended, would balance the budget within three years. Reagan believed that "if we cut tax rates and reduced the proportion of our national wealth that was taken by Washington, the economy would receive a stimulus that would bring down inflation, unemployment, and interest rates, and there would be such an expansion of economic activity that in the end there would be a net increase in the amount of revenue to finance important functions of government."

Reagan's rhetorical pitch succeeded with the public, as opinion polls taken in the aftermath of the speech to the joint session showed that public support for his proposals was better than 2 to 1. But many congressional Democrats, particularly in the House, were adamantly opposed to the proposals, and Speaker Thomas P. "Tip" O'Neill vowed to defeat the package. According to Reagan, "Tip was an old-fashioned pol: he could be sincere and friendly when he wanted to be; but when it came to the things he believed in, he could turn off his charm and friendship like a light switch and become as bloodthirsty as a piranha. He was a politician and a Democrat to his roots. Until six o'clock, I was the enemy and he never let me forget it."

Speaker O'Neill was not the only skeptic regarding Reagan's proposed economic package; in fact, his own vice president, George H. W. Bush, had referred to supply-side economics as "voodoo economics" during their 1980 primary fight, and some traditional Republican fiscal conservatives were wary of the proposals as well. Senate Majority Leader Howard Baker referred to the Reagan package as a "riverboat gamble," a clear reflection that at the very top of the party there were doubts about Reagan's supply-side approach to closing the deficit, while some Republicans and many

Democrats suggested that Reagan's ambitious military expansion, coupled with tax cuts, would only deepen the deficit. O'Neill and the Democrats responded to Reagan with an alternative proposal that included deep cuts in the defense budget.

The president engaged in a concerted personal lobbying campaign to win the support of members of Congress for his economic and budget package, and was aided by a highly skilled congressional liaison office headed by Max Friedersdorf, a veteran of the Nixon and Ford White House congressional liaison operation. Throughout the spring and summer of 1981, Reagan "worked the phones" and held face-to-face meetings with legislators, including 69 meetings with 467 members in his first 100 days in office. At a critical point in the process, on April 28, 1981, just weeks after being seriously wounded in an assassination attempt, Reagan spoke again to a joint session of Congress, and urged passage of his proposals. "Our government is too big and it spends too much . . . high taxes and excess spending growth created our present economic mess. . . . Isn't it time that we tried something new?" Reagan was pleased with the response, observing later, "At one point, forty or so Democrats stood up and applauded and I felt a shiver go down my spine. I thought to myself: 'Boy, that took guts; maybe our economic package has a chance.' Later, I joked to someone, 'that reception was almost worth getting shot for.'" The package cleared a major hurdle on May 7, 1981, when the Democratic-controlled House of Representatives passed a proposal mandating $35.2 billion in budget cuts by a vote of 253-176. Sixty-three "boll weevils" (conservative Democrats, mostly from the South) joined every Republican member and supported the president.

Reagan then moved to secure the passage of his tax cut package of 30 percent spread over three years. Democrats rejected this proposal and offered an alternative of a 15 percent cut stretched over two years, with most of the cuts aimed at those in low-income brackets. Reagan reluctantly agreed to alter his plan somewhat; agreeing to a 25 percent tax reduction over three years, phased in at 5 percent, 10 percent, and 10 percent annually. This was done to win some wavering Democrats in the House, whose support was essential to securing passage there. The final package also reduced the top tax rate on income from 70 to 50 percent, a proposal which Reagan believed was essential to reinvigorate the economy, but one that he feared exposed him to the charge of pandering to the wealthy. The final vote on the bill was uncertain, and Reagan was prepared to issue a statement condemning Congress for its inaction. In the end, the Democratic alternatives were defeated in both houses, and the Economic Recovery Act of 1981 passed on July 29, 1981, by a vote of 89-11 in the Senate and 238-195 in the House, where 40 Democrats crossed the aisle and supported the president's package, and only one Republican, James Jeffords of Vermont, defected from his party's ranks. The largest income tax cut in American history, estimated at $750 billion over five years, was now enacted, and from this point on, the "economy," for better or worse, was

President Reagan celebrates the passage of federal tax legislation with his staff in the Oval Office; (from left to right) Richard Williamson, Elizabeth Dole, Dennis Thomas, Don Regan, Ann McLaughlin, Ed Meese, Vice President George Bush, Karna Small, David Gergen, and President Reagan, July 29, 1981.

now Reagan's. As his legislative liaison, Max Friedersdorf, remarked at the time, Reagan would "be blamed if anything goes wrong . . . snow, bubonic plague." In the short run, "Reaganomics" became a term of derision, but as the decade progressed Reagan was more than happy to embrace this label.

By the end of 1981, Reagan's success at generating public support and maneuvering his economic package through the Congress impressed a normally skeptical press corps, and even some of his Democratic adversaries. The journal *Congressional Quarterly* concluded that "Reagan dominated Congress like no President since Lyndon B. Johnson, perhaps even Franklin Roosevelt . . . Reagan succeeded where the Carter administration had failed—in pushing Congress into a coherent effort to pass major and policy changing economic programs." In 1981 Reagan scored an 82.4 percent in a *CQ* presidential support voting study, which measured how frequently congressional votes followed the president's positions. *CQ* noted, "not since [Lyndon] Johnson (who scored 93 percent in 1965) had the CQ study recorded such harmony between a President and Congress." Hedrick Smith wrote in the *New York Times* that "to the electorate, he [Ronald Reagan] has come across as Mr. Nice Guy with the Eisenhower grin and the infectious optimism of the boy next door. But on Capitol Hill, they have discovered his political grit and competitive streak." *Washington Post* columnist David Broder described Reagan's 1981 legislative victories as "one of the most remarkable demonstrations of presidential leadership in modern times." Representative Leon Panetta, a Democrat from California, noted the difference between the Carter and Reagan legislative liaison operations, stating that Reagan was quick to send him a pen he had used to sign a bill Panetta moved through the House, while "I ha[d] yet to get a pen" from the

Carter administration for a piece of legislation Panetta crafted in 1980.

Reagan's first-year legislative successes curtailed an organized effort, led by Carter's White House counsel, Lloyd Cutler, former Treasury secretary Douglas Dillon, and scholar James MacGregor Burns, which sought to fundamentally revise the American system of separation of powers by adopting certain aspects of a parliamentary system. Cutler and others contended that the presidency was no longer functioning effectively in facing the demands of 20th-century America. This effort to break the "gridlock" in Washington quietly faded and was replaced by accusations from some Democrats in Congress that Reagan's "imperial presidency" once again threatened congressional prerogatives. Majority Leader Jim Wright of Texas observed, "there has never been an administration that has demanded to dictate so completely to the Congress, certainly not Lyndon Johnson in his heyday or Franklin Roosevelt in his. I don't know what it will take to satisfy them, I guess for the Congress to resign and give them our voting proxy cards." It was a successful first year for a president whose opponents once again underestimated him.

IMMIGRATION POLICY

Despite being governor of a state noted for dealing with a large legal and illegal immigrant population, Ronald Reagan virtually ignored immigration policy both as governor and as president. A review of Reagan's memoirs, radio addresses, and private letters finds scant references to the issue. When the issue was raised during his eight years as governor, Reagan would often demur, describing it as a responsibility of the federal government. Reagan's first major comments on the issue came during the presidential campaign of 1980, when he proposed a "North American

Accord," comparable to what would become the North American Free Trade Agreement (NAFTA), in which people and commerce could freely move throughout the North American continent. This vision eventually came to pass, and it revealed Reagan's preference for open borders and a willingness to pursue a moderate immigration policy.

The 1980 Republican Party platform contained the standard "Statue of Liberty" rhetoric about the need for inclusion of all those who immigrate to America's shores, but it advocated no particular policy goals. In his acceptance speech Reagan observed, "Can we doubt that only a Divine Providence placed this land, this island of freedom, here as a refuge for all those people in the world who yearn to breathe free—Jews and Christians enduring persecution behind the Iron Curtain, the boat people of Southeast Asia, of Cuba and Haiti, the victims of drought and famine in Africa, the Freedom Fighters in Afghanistan?" But Reagan offered no specific policy preferences regarding legal or illegal immigration to America.

By the time of his inauguration in 1981 there was considerable discussion in Congress and the media about the need for immigration reform, and calls for change grew louder as the economic recession of 1981–82 deepened. Public opinion polls showed that most Americans were concerned about the effect of legal and illegal immigrants on the nation's sagging economy, a reaction quite common in any society whenever jobs become scarce. The issue was further highlighted by the release of a report two months into the Reagan presidency, from the Select Commission on Immigration and Refugee Policy, chaired by Theodore Hesburgh, the president of Notre Dame University. The report was highly critical of the deficiencies in U.S. immigration policy, and prompted the White House to announce the formation of a cabinet-level task force on

immigration and refugee policy, headed by Attorney General William French Smith. Despite the creation of the task force, evidence indicates that Reagan's advisers saw immigration as a waste of the president's political capital. Reagan received a memo on June 3, 1981, from Chief of Staff James Baker and White House counsel Edwin Meese telling him "immigration is a no-win" issue.

The White House saw immigration as primarily a political problem and hoped to find some middle ground between the supporters of open borders and those who wanted to seal the borders and crack down on illegal immigrants. On July 30, 1981, the Smith task force proposed a series of moderate changes including (1) penalizing employers who hired illegal immigrants, (2) creating an "experimental" guest worker program that would allow up to 50,000 Mexican farmhands to work nine to 12 months in instances when American labor was unavailable, (3) a declaration of amnesty for immigrants who came to the United States prior to January 1, 1980, (4) stronger border protection to stop the flow of illegal immigrants. The Smith proposals were softer than the Hesburgh proposals regarding illegal immigration, and to the dismay of some commentators, did not include any recommendations for a national identity card. The latter proposal was removed after the strenuous objections of Reagan's domestic policy adviser, Martin Anderson, who viewed it as an infringement of American civil liberties, an argument that Reagan found persuasive.

Little came of the Smith task force's recommendations, and the administration lost interest in the issue, effectively conceding the agenda to Congress. Congress took the lead on immigration policy, and on March 17, 1982, Republican senator Alan Simpson of Wyoming and Congressman Romano Mazzoli, a Democrat from Kentucky, introduced the Immigration Reform and Control Act, a proposal for comprehensive immigration reform regarding both legal and illegal immigration. Simpson-Mazzoli set a ceiling on overall immigration levels, eliminated the preference for those with brothers and sisters already residing in the United States, called for the creation of a national identification card, mandated penalties for people who hired illegal aliens, and placed greater focus on a potential immigrant's working skills over family reunification. In a private letter written in October 1983 to Governor Meldrim Thomson of New Hampshire, Reagan expressed his support for Simpson-Mazzoli and noted that "we have lost control of our borders" but also observed that "it is a very complex issue with our agriculture dependent on migrants, several million people as residents undetected and a dozen other facets."

Simpson-Mazzoli unleashed strong emotions on both sides of the issue; labor unions supported the measure as a way of protecting jobs and keeping wages high, while some civil rights groups and proponents of open borders deemed it a racist piece of legislation. Reagan felt the sting of this accusation and felt compelled on a number of occasions to publicly state that he welcomed new immigrants to the United States. The bill easily passed the Senate, but bogged down in the House, which adjourned before it reached a vote.

Simpson-Mazzoli was reintroduced in 1983 and once again easily passed in the Senate, but Speaker O'Neill initially refused to let the bill go to the floor of the House for a vote. This prompted an outcry in Congress from both Democrats and Republicans, and Speaker O'Neill eventually relented. The bill was hotly debated, and passed by a thin margin of 216-211 on June 20, 1984. The White House issued a statement contending that the bill was "unacceptable" due to the costs involved with the amnesty provision, and once again the bill expired as Congress adjourned.

A milder version of Simpson-Mazzoli passed the House in October 1986 by a much wider margin, as Democrats rallied to the bill, while Republicans defected in large numbers due to the weakening of border control provisions. The Senate passed its version shortly after, and a conference bill was agreed upon by both houses, with President Reagan signing it into law on November 6, 1986. Under the provisions of the Immigration Reform and Control Act (IRCA), employers who hired illegal immigrants faced fines ranging from $250 to $10,000, and employers who demonstrated a pattern of hiring such "undocumented workers" faced up to six months in prison. Illegal aliens who had lived in the United States prior to January 1, 1982, were granted amnesty and allowed to gain status as U.S. citizens. In addition, IRCA created a "guestworker program" that gave permanent resident alien status for 350,000 farmworkers.

More than 7 million legal immigrants came to America during Reagan's tenure; another 1 million were granted amnesty and legal status. In his farewell address, Reagan again reiterated his belief in America as a "city with free ports" and doors "open to anyone with the will and the heart to get there." In retrospect, many critics believe the Immigration Reform and Control Act of 1986 did not adequately address the problems of immigration. As far as controlling the flow of both legal and illegal immigrants into America, IRCA was, in the words of Otis L. Graham, Jr., a "dismal and costly policy failure." The act did not produce a reliable way of determining workers' legal status, and it simply ignored the whole question of the appropriate levels of legal immigration. The attacks of September 11, 2001, elevated the issue of border security to new heights, and cast IRCA in an even harsher light.

SOCIAL ISSUES: ABORTION, SCHOOL PRAYER, AIDS, PORNOGRAPHY

Ronald Reagan was unequivocal in his support for school prayer and adamant in his opposition to abortion, pornography, and safe-sex education. He was quite comfortable with mixing elements of church and state and frequently expressed his frustration and "shock" at those who "used" the First Amendment to the Constitution "as a reason to keep traditional moral values away from policymaking." Yet Reagan made it clear from the start that the economy and foreign and defense policy would be his primary focus, not a conservative social agenda. With relatively few exceptions, Reagan, though offering unwavering rhetorical support for conservative positions, relegated the social issues to the second or third tier of his priorities.

Abortion

Reagan's record on abortion was somewhat mixed throughout his political career. As governor of California, he signed into law one of the most liberal abortion laws in the country—the Therapeutic Abortion Act of 1967, which permitted abortions in cases where the physician believed there was a risk to the mental health of the mother. The mental health standard was loosely interpreted by many physicians and essentially allowed for abortion on demand. Commenting on this in 1975, Reagan noted that "when I became governor I found myself involved almost immediately in a controversy over abortion. It was a subject I'd never given much thought to and one upon which I didn't really have an opinion. . . . Suddenly I had to have a position on abortion." Reagan later claimed that he signed the law in the interests of women's health and that he was appalled by the way it had opened the door to more abortions, but this was followed a few years later by his signing another bill as governor that funded about one-third of California abortions with state dollars. By the time Reagan left office in Sacramento, the abortion rate in California had increased considerably, due in some measure to the permissive laws he signed as governor.

Many pro-choice advocates were disheartened when Reagan was elected president in 1980, and believed that he was determined, through his judicial appointment powers, or possibly through the adoption of a constitutional amendment, to repeal the landmark *Roe v. Wade* decision of January 1973, which struck down state restrictions on abortion. Reagan often used the presidential "bully pulpit" to proclaim his opposition to abortion, and in fact used one of his most memorable speeches on the Soviet Union, the "evil empire" speech, to give a passionate and often forgotten plea to end abortion. "Human life legislation ending this tragedy will someday pass the Congress, and you and I must never rest until it does. Unless and until it can be proven that the unborn child is not a living entity, then its right to life, liberty, and the pursuit of happiness must be protected." Ending abortion, Reagan said, was the centerpiece of a "great spiritual awakening in America, a renewal of the traditional values that have been the bedrock of America's goodness and greatness."

Shortly after this speech Reagan wrote an essay for the spring 1983 edition of *Human Life Review* entitled "Abortion and the Conscience of the Nation." He did so against the advice of many of his image-conscious advisers, including Deputy Chief of Staff Michael Deaver, and possibly Nancy Reagan as well. The essay was written in response to the 10th anniversary of the Supreme Court's *Roe v. Wade* decision, and Reagan argued that the "culture" of abortion in America was leading to "infanticide" and he called for Americans to unite in prayer to end abortion. Public statements in opposition to abortion were common throughout the remainder of his presidency. In July 1984 Reagan said America would give money to population control efforts only if the funds were not used for funding abortions. In January 1985 Reagan told a pro-life rally of his dedication to "ending the terrible tragedy of abortion." He promised in July 1987 to halt federal funding to any health organization that offered abortion counseling to poor women. And in his final month in office, Reagan was still urging Americans to unite to fight for the rights of the unborn so that "the voice of life" could be heard "over all the others."

The Reagan administration argued a number of cases before the Supreme Court in support of efforts designed to curtail the *Roe* decision. One such effort involved a dispute over an Ohio law that placed a litany of restrictions on abortions—for example, requiring that women seeking abortions be told that a fetus is a "human life," and that second-trimester abortions be performed in hospitals only. The pro-life movement suffered a defeat when the U.S. Supreme Court invalidated this law in *Akron Center for Reproductive Health v. City of Akron* (1983), holding that the restrictions were excessive. In another case, *Thornburgh v. American College of Obstetricians and Gynecologists of Pennsylvania* (1986), challenges were raised to restrictions similar to those in the *Akron* case, and Reagan's Justice Department, under Attorney General Edwin Meese, submitted a supplementary brief arguing on the side of the restrictions mandated by the state of Pennsylvania. However, this law was also ruled unconstitutional by the Supreme Court, which held that it was an overt attempt to discourage a legal medical procedure. In fact, the majority's decision in the *Thornburgh* case was the most forceful assertion to date of a woman's right to an abortion.

Throughout his presidency Ronald Reagan supported legislation sponsored by pro-life members of Congress. After he won passage of his economic and defense programs, Reagan told members of Congress in the summer of 1982 that "the national tragedy of abortion" was an "assault on the sacredness of life" and that his administration was behind legislative efforts to restrict or eliminate abortions in

America. He lent his support to North Carolina senator Jesse Helms's Human Life bill, which recognized the unborn as human beings and protected them as persons under the Constitution, and the Respect Human Life bill, introduced by Congressman Henry Hyde of Illinois and Senator Roger Jepsen of Iowa, which prohibited the federal government from performing abortions or assisting those who do so, except to save the life of the mother. Reagan also called for congressional adoption of the so-called Kemp amendment, which prohibited the use of American foreign aid for birth-control efforts that included abortions forced on unwilling women.

The most important piece of pro-life legislation introduced during the Reagan years was the Human Life Amendment, a proposed constitutional amendment that sought to invalidate *Roe v. Wade*. This amendment was a major event in the abortion debate as pro-lifers moved from a strategy of curtailing specific features of *Roe* to a direct attack on the entire ruling. Reagan was resolute in support of the amendment, saying "I pledge to you that I will not rest until a human-life amendment becomes a part of our Constitution." Reagan believed, as he bluntly stated in one of his pre-presidential radio commentaries, that he could find "no evidence whatsoever that a fetus is not a living human being with human rights." The Human Life Amendment fell far short of garnering the necessary two-thirds majority in the Senate required to submit it to the states for ratification, winning only 50 votes.

The failure of the Human Life Amendment was indicative of the tremendous opposition Reagan faced in changing American attitudes toward abortion. According to some surveys dating from the 1980s, nearly two-thirds of the public supported abortion under all circumstances, and 62 percent opposed the Human Life Amendment. It was an uphill struggle for the pro-life movement even with the backing of the "Great Communicator," for the issue was a divisive and "hot" one, which many members of the Washington political community hoped to avoid; it was divisive even within Reagan's camp, where close advisers such as Michael Deaver and Lyn Nofziger were pro-choice, and perhaps Nancy Reagan as well. In the end, Reagan's support of the pro-life position was genuine—he endorsed several unpopular antiabortion proposals and coupled that with forceful denunciations of abortion in various speeches and writings. But the issue never rose to the importance of the economy and foreign policy, and after Reagan's two terms pro-life supporters were left with few gains from his presidency. It is possible, perhaps likely, that had the president succeeded in placing Robert Bork on the Supreme Court, as he attempted to do, a five-person majority may have eventually overturned *Roe v. Wade*, but Bork's replacement, Justice Anthony Kennedy, tended to side with the "middle" of the Court and voted to sustain the *Roe* legacy.

School Prayer

Ronald Reagan made it clear early during his presidency that he abhorred the 1962 Supreme Court decision, *Engel v. Vitale*, which struck down organized prayer in public schools, a decision he labeled "affirmative action for atheists." In 1977 Reagan commented on *Engel v. Vitale*, claiming that "a few years ago, egged on by an avowed Atheist, voluntary prayer was banned in our schools. Have we let some among us make Atheism a religion and impose that religion on those of us who believe in our Judeo-Christian traditions?" Reagan believed that some element of moral education was essential in the classroom and that the ban on prayer was another example of "overreaching" on the part of the federal government. "I don't believe," he once observed, "[that] we should have ever expelled God from the classroom. And who knows, if we get the federal govern-

ment out of the classroom, maybe we'll get God back in."

In March 1984 he took a step in that direction when his administration proposed a constitutional amendment on school prayer. The amendment would have essentially restored the pre-1962 understanding of the separation of church and state; the amendment's language read as follows, "Nothing in this Constitution shall be construed to prohibit individual or group prayer in public schools or other public institutions. No person shall be required by the United States or by any state to participate in prayer. Neither the United States nor any state shall compose the words of any prayer to be said in the public schools." In addition to proposing and supporting this amendment, the president made it clear that he believed the theory of evolution was flawed and he supported the teaching of biblical creationism alongside evolution in public schools.

Reagan told the National Religious Broadcasters in January 1984, "I think Americans are getting angry. I think they have a message and Congress better listen. We are a government of, by, and for the people. And people want a constitutional amendment making it unequivocally clear our children can hold voluntary prayer in every school across the land. And if we could get God and discipline back in our schools, maybe we could get drugs and violence out." He also personally lobbied members of the Senate to pass the amendment in a private meeting in March 1984. Yet for all of his public support for the amendment, Reagan was unwilling to spend any real political capital to get it passed. The proposed amendment fell shy of the necessary two-thirds majority in the Senate by 12 votes, 56-44. In response, the president vowed to continue fighting to repeal the 1962 decision—"we have suffered a setback, but we have not been defeated. Our struggle will go on"—but the school prayer debate did not receive serious attention for the remainder of his administration.

AIDS Policy

The outbreak of the Acquired Immune Deficiency Syndrome (AIDS) virus in the United States occurred under Reagan's watch, and he approached dealing with the new disease with apprehension. Sexual transmission was the leading cause for the spread of the disease, and some of Reagan's supporters viewed this "gay plague" as an act of divine retribution. It is possible that Reagan felt this way as well. As a result his administration's response was widely condemned as late and ineffective at best, and genocidal at worst.

Reagan was certainly not the only person to misinterpret the severity of the disease or the most effective means to contain its spread. Yet even as scientific knowledge increased, he remained slow to join the fight against AIDS and his administration's policies never surpassed half-hearted measures. As a result, many critics have accused his administration of ignoring research breakthroughs and perpetuating a disease that has now reached epidemic proportions. When Reagan entered the White House in 1981 there were only 199 reported AIDS cases in the United States. In fact, the disease was so anomalous at the time that it was seen by many as an epidemic of Kaposi's sarcoma, a rare type of tumor AIDS patients frequently contracted. In 1982 Congressman Henry Waxman convened the first congressional hearings on this mysterious new disease. As knowledge of the virus grew and cases increased sharply, the federal government lagged behind in committing large resources to research, health care, and prevention. Some of this tardiness was doubtless attributable to the fact that AIDS was seen by some as a problem confined to Haitians or a "gay plague" that could be solved by alterations in homosexual behavior.

Reagan was among those who failed to take AIDS seriously when the disease first appeared. At one point, according to his physician John Hutton, Reagan thought that AIDS was like "measles and it would go away." Only when Reagan's friend and fellow Hollywood star Rock Hudson died of AIDS in October 1985 did Reagan begin to change his opinion on the virus. Reagan spoke to Dr. Hutton and asked questions about the causes and effects of AIDS and engaged in his first substantial discourse on the reality of the disease. He told Hutton, "I always thought the world would end in a flash, but this sounds like it's worse."

Even after the shock of Hudson's death, Reagan was slow to act. Responding to the actor's death, the House of Representatives voted 417-8 to give Surgeon General C. Everett Koop the authority to close down bathhouses and massage parlors as a means of fighting AIDS, but Reagan continued to avoid the subject. In February 1986 Reagan spoke at the Department of Human Services and said that "one of our highest public-health priorities is going to continue to be finding a cure for AIDS . . . we're going to focus on prevention." But on this same day his administration proposed a budget that would cut funding for AIDS research. This met with strong criticism from the National Academy of Sciences, which criticized the administration's response and called for greater spending; Congress eventually appropriated it.

The issue divided members of Reagan's administration, particularly when Surgeon General Koop released a report on AIDS on October 22, 1986. Koop reported that AIDS could not be prevented or controlled without altering people's personal behavior and educating them on the importance of safe sex "at the lower possible [school] grade." Koop suggested that the public follow these preventive steps, "one, abstinence; two, monogamy; three, condoms." Reagan's conservative supporters could agree on the first point, and most on the second as well. But educating young students about safe sex and the use of condoms met with fierce opposition from Education Secretary William Bennett; from Gary Bauer, Reagan's domestic policy adviser; and from White House Communications Director Patrick Buchanan, who had once written a column in 1983 observing, "the poor homosexuals. They have declared war on nature and now nature is exacting an awful retribution."

Koop shared the belief of Reagan's hard-core conservative cadre that abstinence was the most important lesson to teach young people, but he also believed that the reality of sexual behavior in America suggested that effective prevention could only come through educating the public on safe sex. Secretary Bennett proceeded to distribute 300,000 pamphlets to public schools that stressed abstinence as the key to AIDS prevention, and dismissed the use of condoms as unreliable. In March 1987 a frustrated surgeon general went to the president and asked him to take a leadership role in fighting AIDS. A public opinion poll taken during this period revealed that two-thirds of the public thought that AIDS was the greatest health menace facing America. Feeling the pressure, Reagan announced on April 1, 1987, that AIDS was "public health enemy Number One." However, even with such a declaration, Reagan refused to call for the use of condoms and support safe-sex education.

First Lady Nancy Reagan urged her husband to take a more proactive stand on the issue and asked the president to speak at a fund-raising dinner for the American Foundation for AIDS Research in May 1987. According to Reagan biographer Lou Cannon, Nancy Reagan arranged for Landon Parvin, a former Reagan speechwriter, to write the AIDS address. Parvin had left the White House in 1983, but he remained a favorite of the first lady. Despite recruiting Parvin to craft the address, Mrs. Reagan feared that the more conservative members of the White House staff would tone down the address, which is precisely what happened. For AIDS activists the speech confirmed to them that Reagan was not serious about the AIDS epidemic. The address broke little new ground and failed to endorse the surgeon general's recommendations. The president was also booed during the speech when he called for testing for certain individuals, such as immigrants, federal prisoners, and anyone seeking a marriage license. The address to the American Foundation for AIDS Research indicated that Reagan rejected many of the proposals coming from public health advisers and the scientific community.

In July 1987 Reagan created a presidential commission to examine the HIV epidemic filled with opponents of AIDS education and including no physicians who had treated AIDS patients nor scientists involved in AIDS research. Admiral James Watkins chaired the commission. Despite the initial concerns of AIDS activists, in 1988 the Watkins Commission issued a report critical of the government response to this health crisis and offered nearly 600 recommendations for change. But for many, the effort was too little, too late. The White House ordered that the report be further studied by the attorney general, a move that fueled criticism that the administration was not serious about confronting AIDS.

The presidential commission was emblematic of the eight-year struggle within the administration over how to confront the AIDS epidemic. The supporters of Surgeon General Koop were pitted against the supporters of Gary Bauer and William Bennett, who genuinely believed that AIDS was a behavioral disease and safe-sex education sent precisely the wrong message to America's youth. It was in this situation that Reagan could have intervened to end the internecine conflict in the administration, but he chose not to. His biographer,

Lou Cannon, wrote that "on an issue on which he might have demonstrated great leadership, Reagan was content to play the role of an exceptionally passive president." It was far more likely, however, that Reagan agreed with the position enunciated by Bauer and Bennett, and acted accordingly. By 1989, the number of reported AIDS cases had increased from 199 in 1981 to 82,762, and the death toll had risen to 46,344. The former president hinted in a 1990 interview that his administration's response might have been ineffective. "It wasn't easy," Reagan said. "Here suddenly was a brand-new disease and you didn't have the facts or figures." Unfortunately, these figures were available well before the end of his presidency, and Reagan's response to the AIDS epidemic will likely be remembered as halting and ineffectual.

Pornography

One element of Reagan's social agenda that received the president's unequivocal support was the fight against pornography. As a man who grew up decades before the sexual revolution, Reagan detested pornography and saw it as the culprit in the decline of America's moral values. He worried that the advances in mass communication were quickly turning the industry into a virus that was almost out of control. In 1986 Reagan noted that the "distributors of obscenity and child pornography have expanded into new areas. They are employing new technologies and reaching new audiences. This is how any business grows and develops, except that this business is illegal. This administration is putting the purveyors of illegal obscenity and child pornography on notice: your industry's days are numbered." Reagan called for an assault to "break the back" of the porn industry. The administration emphasized that the fight against pornography would focus on child pornography, an effort that enjoyed widespread support amongst the American public. Yet while the administration made great

strides in reducing child pornography, their larger agenda was to restrict and ultimately eliminate any kind of pornography. The most important step taken was the formation of the Attorney General's Commission on Pornography, chaired by Attorney General Edwin Meese, to examine the scope and nature of pornography in America. Meese was a strong advocate of antipornography legislation to curb what he referred to as the "obscenity epidemic."

The Meese Commission held public hearings in six cities and reviewed thousands of books, magazines, and films. On July 9, 1986, the 11-member commission released its 1,960-page final report, which recommended 92 changes in federal law dealing with pornography. Among the many changes were proposals to prohibit the distribution of obscenity through computers, cable television, and telephone lines; prohibitions on the sale of children by parents or guardians for the production of child pornography; and requirements that producers of pornography keep accurate and complete records of the ages and names of persons in films. The Meese Commission concluded that sexually explicit materials caused "anti-social acts of sexual violence," including sex crimes. By linking pornography to criminal violence, the commission sought to marginalize those who claimed that pornography was an art protected by freedom of expression and that the commission was promoting censorship. The attorney general put it bluntly: "We are not in favor of censorship . . . we are talking of something that is not protected by the Constitution."

Free-speech advocates and civil libertarians were opposed to the commission's recommendations and viewed the attorney general and his commission as a threat to the First Amendment. Many of these critics believed that the administration was simply pandering to the religious Right and that its commission had reached its conclusions even before launching the inquiry. These critics contended that the Reagan administration was determined to challenge the conclusions of a 1970 commission created during the Nixon years that argued pornography had no adverse effect on sexual behavior. The founding father of *Playboy* magazine called the commission's final report "a circus show of misinformation" and a "seek and destroy mission" against the publishers and producers of "adult entertainment."

Despite some opposition, the administration succeeded in upgrading the federal government's role in prosecuting those involved in the pornography industry. To crack down on the illegal distribution of pornography, a National Obscenity Enforcement Unit was created, along with a Center for Obscenity Prosecution at the Justice Department, staffed with lawyers trained specifically to deal with pornography cases. Attorney General Meese required all of the 93 U.S. Attorneys' offices to have one lawyer dealing specifically with obscenity cases.

Perhaps the most significant action was the passage of legislation in 1988 called the Child Protection and Obscenity Enforcement Act. The bill was cleverly packaged, because it dealt with all facets of pornography, not just child pornography. The legislation was designed to update federal law to take into account the new technological explosion that made pornography more accessible. In addition it strengthened existing laws by removing loopholes and mandating stronger enforcement. Reagan urged passage of the bill, arguing that "if this nation can send men to the moon, then we can certainly do some cleaning up here at home, and give our sons and daughters the simplicity and beauty that an American childhood should entail." The bill passed unanimously in both houses of Congress and was signed in November 1988, the president proclaiming that it was part of a "spiritual reawakening" in America. It

was one of the few significant victories for the administration's social agenda, but the legislation did little to curtail the multibillion-dollar American pornography industry, and the seemingly insatiable consumer demand for its products. If there was any tempering of the sexual revolution in the United States during the 1980s, it came about because of the fear of AIDS, not because of any change in the nation's moral climate. As the century drew to a close, America's sexual and cultural revolution continued unabated, with pornography becoming somewhat standard fare in American television, music, and movies.

EDUCATION

Ronald Reagan's commitment to limiting the role of the federal government was particularly evident in his views on education policy. Reagan believed in local control of education and in broader choice for parents and was committed to his party's 1980 platform, which called for the abolition of the Department of Education, created during the Carter administration. Reagan had opposed the new department when it was first proposed—"when will we learn the wisdom of the old saying—'if it ain't broke, don't fix it.'" He believed that the decline in the quality of the nation's schools "began when Fed[eral] aid to ed[ucation] became Fed[eral] interference in ed[ucation]." In his memoirs, Reagan claimed that the Department of Education's bureaucracy gave parents little recourse to improve failing schools; "if parents didn't like the way their schools were being run, they could throw out the Board of Education at the next election; but what could they do about the elite bureaucrats in the U.S. Department of Education who sent ultimatums into their children's classrooms regarding curriculum and textbooks?" The Department of Education, for Reagan, was emblematic of a federal government that had overreached its authority and lacked an effective means of accountability. The department also symbolized for him the excessive clout the National Education Association wielded within the Democratic Party and with bureaucrats in Washington, D.C. He wrote in 1977, "It would be wonderful if we could give the National planners, those social engineers who tinker with our social structure a years sabbatical."

Reagan also hoped to reduce the federal government's control over local school districts. He wanted to get school districts out from under a litany of regulations and also return federal funds to the states to spend on education as they saw fit. Additionally, he was an early advocate of "school choice"—giving parents tax credits or vouchers to select the schools their children would attend. Although it was not mentioned in the Republican platform for 1980, Reagan strongly supported teaching "traditional values" in the classroom, a goal promoted by his second education secretary, William J. Bennett, and resisted by teachers' unions and many civil libertarians.

The administration's first major initiative in education policy came early in Reagan's first term when Education Secretary Terrel H. Bell (who was selected for the task of dismantling his department) was ordered to produce a study on the quality of education in America's public school system. On August 26, 1981, Bell created the National Commission on Excellence in Education, and in April 1983, he released the commission's conclusions in a report entitled, "A Nation at Risk: The Imperative for Educational Reform." While most commission reports are consigned to the ash heap of history, this report captured the attention of the news media, prominent members of government and the business community, along with the public at large. The report made education a national issue, and received cover stories in popular publications such as

Time and *Newsweek*. The report was highly critical of the state of education in America, arguing that "the educational foundations of our society are presently being eroded by a rising tide of mediocrity that threatens our very future as a Nation and a People." It recommended changes in a variety of areas, including greater focus on the basics of education, increasing standards and expectations in colleges and universities, lengthening the amount of time children would attend school, and increasing the salary and education levels of teachers.

While the Reagan administration can be credited with elevating the issue of the quality of the nation's schools, the president was stymied in his goal of abolishing the Department of Education. This proposal never received serious consideration in Washington, primarily because Reagan never made the issue a top priority. It was strenuously opposed by Democratic members of Congress, and by the nation's oldest and largest teachers union, the National Education Association. Secretary Bell proposed to replace the DOE with an agency called the "Foundation for Education Assistance" which would have operated in a fashion similar to the National Science Foundation, but this had little appeal, probably even to the president himself, since it would have retained virtually the same level of federal control as the DOE. Nevertheless, the proposal was ignored by Congress, which for all practical purposes ended talk of abolishing the DOE. "A Nation at Risk" had raised education close to the top of the nation's domestic agenda, and the president's Democratic opponents were able to attack him for claiming to be concerned about education while seeking to abolish the cabinet agency created to improve the nation's schools. Politically, abolition became an albatross, and the White House announced that the idea was "moot" in June 1983. It was officially abandoned during the confirmation hearings of

Bell's successor, William Bennett, in the winter of 1984–85.

Ronald Reagan was a longtime supporter of school choice, and he instructed the Department of Education to construct a school voucher policy, but the administration made little progress with its voucher proposals. In 1985 Secretary Bennett unveiled the TEACH proposal (The Equity and Choice Act), which was designed to give a voucher to children eligible for Federal Assistance under the "Chapter 1" program to pay part of the cost of attending a private school. These vouchers, averaging about $600 per student, would have been available to close to 5 million children, but the proposal was defeated after many of the nation's teachers unions and public school advocates mobilized against them.

Despite these setbacks, the Reagan administration made the issue of school vouchers a credible alternative in the national debate on education. But while Reagan clearly influenced this debate, shifting it to the Right, in raw practical terms there were no major changes in education policy during the Reagan years. His top priorities of abolishing the Department of Education and creating a school voucher program were unsuccessful, and he also failed to substantially reduce the federal government's control of local education policy. He was successful in getting some minor cuts in what he saw as the wasteful areas of the education budget, but some of his proposed cuts, such as in the college loan program, brought a severe backlash from the public, especially among the middle class. In fact no federal education programs were eliminated during Reagan's tenure, and some new education and training programs were added.

Ironically for a president who campaigned to eliminate the Department of Education, his second education secretary, William Bennett, gave the department its most visible role in its short history. Bennett was adept at using his position to lobby for reform and altered many conservatives' perceptions of the usefulness of his department. As an outspoken advocate of "character education" and school vouchers, Bennett became a lightning rod for criticism in the media but simultaneously pushed education policy into the headlines. Bennett never hesitated to speak his mind and often alienated teachers' unions, academic administrators, and occasionally even students. In February 1985 he defended the administration's proposed cuts in loans for college students, holding that "tightening the belt can have the function of concentrating the mind." He added that the government did not have the responsibility to "assure that every student can go to the school of his or her choice." Bennett then commented on what he saw as self-indulgent, affluent college students receiving federal aid, noting that loan cuts could lead to "divestiture of certain sorts—stereo divestiture, automobile divestiture, three-weeks-at-the-beach divestiture." These remarks were made at the height of a student movement designed to force trustees at the nation's colleges to divest funds from firms doing business with South Africa.

Reagan's policy initiatives introduced ideas into the political discourse that remain key issues today—the state of America's public schools revealed in "A Nation at Risk" and the proposal for school vouchers are both topics that dominate the education debate in the new millennium. In the end, Reagan left his successors with a stronger Department of Education, a greater number of federal programs devoted to education, and a heightened awareness of the status and future of education in America.

CAPITAL PUNISHMENT AND GUN CONTROL

As governor of California, Reagan was twice confronted with requests for clemency during his stewardship. The first case involved Aaron Mitchell, who was convicted of murdering a Sacramento police officer. Reagan spent the night of April 11, 1967, listening to opponents of capital punishment chanting in protest against his refusal to grant clemency to Mitchell. Reagan let the execution proceed, and Mitchell was put to death at 10:00 the next morning in San Quentin's gas chamber. Reagan later commented that it was the worst decision he had had to face. Reagan granted a clemency request in the only other capital case that came to him, due to the fact that the condemned prisoner was severely brain damaged.

Reagan supported the death penalty throughout his public career, and it angered him deeply when his appointee as chief justice of the California Supreme Court wrote the majority decision overturning the state's capital punishment law. During his presidency, Reagan pushed for the extension of the death penalty for certain crimes, such as dealing drugs. In November 1988, Reagan won the passage of a drug bill that permitted the death penalty for drug traffickers involved in killings of law enforcement officers.

On the issue of gun control, Reagan had a somewhat mixed record, and, befitting a life-long member of the National Rifle Association, he interpreted the Second Amendment as prohibiting the government from regulating personal ownership of firearms. In 1967, while serving as California's governor, Reagan signed the Mulford Act, which prohibited "the carrying of firearms on one's person or in a vehicle, in any public place or on any public street." The law was aimed at curtailing the Black Panthers, an Oakland-based radical group that viewed American society as inherently racist and called for the overthrow of the government. In June 1981 President Reagan commented that in general he was opposed to gun control legislation as "virtually unenforceable" and that Congress should focus its attention on stiffening existing laws for carrying weapons. Referring to his own encounter with handgun violence, the president noted, "there are more than 20,000 gun control laws in effect, federal, state, and local, in the United States . . . They didn't seem to prevent a fellow a few weeks ago from carrying one down by the Hilton Hotel. In other words, they are unenforceable." He signed a law in May 1986 that relaxed the nation's gun laws, reversing a trend toward stricter gun control that began with the violence and assassinations of 1968.

However, shortly after he left the White House, he shifted his position and became a proponent of one of the most far-reaching federal gun control laws, the Brady Bill, named after his former White House press secretary, James Brady. "It's just plain common sense that there be a waiting period to allow local law enforcement officials to conduct background checks on those who wish to buy a handgun. I support the Brady Bill, and I urge Congress to enact it without further delay."

DRUG ABUSE

The Reagan administration conducted an aggressive assault on drug use in America, particularly regarding the importation, or "supply" side, of the problem, while the "demand" side, according to the administration's critics, was downplayed. President Reagan believed that drugs were endangering American society and threatening the security of the nation, that in fact drugs were "as dangerous to our national security as any terrorist or foreign dictatorship." The administration's "war" on drugs was symbolized by Nancy Reagan's "Just Say No" campaign, but its efforts were much broader in scope encompassing law enforcement, interdiction efforts, and, despite the allegations of their critics, attempts to bolster treatment and rehabilitation programs. Reagan's efforts yielded

First Lady Nancy Reagan, speaking at a "Just Say No" rally in Los Angeles, California, May 13, 1987

During his first term, Reagan focused largely on "interdiction," or law enforcement efforts designed to curb the flow of illegal drugs into America. In 1982 he established the Organized Crime Drug Enforcement Task Force (OCDEF), officially declaring war against drug traffickers. The OCDEF was an agency composed of members from the U.S. Attorney's Office, the Drug Enforcement Administration, the Internal Revenue Service, the U.S. Marshals Service, and the Coast Guard, among others, all given a mission to coordinate and execute a comprehensive strategy against the influx of drugs. In March 1983 Reagan placed Vice President George Bush in charge of the newly created National Narcotics Border Interdiction System. The NNBIS was charged with coordinating enforcement efforts among federal agencies to stop the flow of drugs across America's borders, particularly along the 2,000-mile border with Mexico. With the establishment of the OCDEF and NNBIS, Reagan clearly delineated his frontline of the drug war: interdiction.

The emphasis on interdiction that characterized the administration's drug control policy during the first term appeared to come at the expense of prevention and treatment programs. Reagan was roundly criticized for cutting the federal budget in these areas by nearly 50 percent during his first years in office. The administration's policy was criticized by one of its original architects, Jeffrey Harris, a former Justice Department official. Harris later argued that the focus on stopping the flow of cocaine and heroin into the United States was a lost cause, as both substances continued to flow freely into the country. The administration, Harris contended in 1984, was losing the war on drugs.

For many observers the notion that such a war could be won was ludicrous. Arnold Trebach of the *Wall Street Journal* said that it shouldn't come as a surprise that the drug war

some legislative successes, particularly the 1986 and 1988 drug bills. He also succeeded in substantially increasing the percentage of the budget devoted to the drug problem and boosting the number of federal employees focused on the "drug war." Yet this comprehensive effort, which was another focus of the administration's desire to repeal the 1960s, ultimately failed. In fairness it should be noted that the Clinton administration downgraded the war on drugs, leading many defenders of Reagan's policy, such as former "drug czar" William Bennett, to argue that "victory" could have been achieved if the war had been sustained across administrations.

was a lost cause, since every attempt in the "70-year American crusade against these chemicals had also failed." Even staunch allies of the president questioned the wisdom of the administration's approach, including Senator Alphonse D'Amato of New York, who claimed that "the administration has been totally inept and unwilling to admit the seriousness of the situation. The administration says, 'we're winning the drug war.' We're not winning the drug war. We are shoveling against the tide. When are we going to wake up? It's an absolute scandal." A growing tide of discontent forced Reagan to reevaluate his efforts, leading to a more comprehensive strategy during his second term in office.

The new strategy was announced in August 1986, when Reagan gave a speech outlining a six-point strategy to fight drugs, one that combined tougher penalties and stronger border enforcement with expanded drug prevention and rehabilitation programs. Reagan claimed that this new approach had never been tried before, and vowed "not to announce another short-term government offensive but to call instead for a national crusade against drugs, a sustained, relentless effort to rid America of this scourge." This was a fight Reagan was deeply committed to for the duration of his presidency—the goal was a "drug-free America, period."

Reagan launched a campaign to eliminate drug use in schools and in the workplace, and suggested that mandatory drug tests begin for federal workers and those in highly sensitive jobs. He encouraged voluntary testing in all other places of business and offered to take a drug test himself, committing his cabinet officers to do the same. This campaign ended abruptly, however, when a federal judge ruled in September 1986 that such tests were unconstitutional.

The president took action in the international arena, announcing "Operation Alliance," a program designed to fight drug trafficking on the Mexican border. Seven months earlier,

on his way to visit Mexican president Miguel de la Madrid, Reagan labeled drug trafficking, along with terrorism, as "the most insidious and dangerous threat" to the Western Hemisphere. The administration had long argued that international cooperation was essential in closing America's borders to illicit drugs. Vice President Bush and Attorney General Edwin Meese assured the American people that the Mexican government had promised its full cooperation, a pledge that was called into question in the years to come.

On September 14, 1986, Reagan took the drug issue directly to the American people, only this time the Great Communicator had a little help. The president invited the first lady, the most visible spokesperson for the war on drugs, to deliver a joint televised address on the issue. The Reagans called on Americans to "mobilize for a national crusade against drugs . . . menacing our society . . . threatening our values and undercutting our institutions . . . there is no middle ground. Indifference is not an option." The next day, Reagan sent to Congress his antidrug proposal, the Drug Free America Act of 1986. The legislation moved rapidly through Congress, becoming law in little more than a month, having passed the House by a vote of 378-16 and passing by a voice vote in the Senate. Reagan hailed the passage of the legislation as a "major victory" in the drug war, yet he was quick to note that this was only the first step toward a "drug-free generation." The legislation doubled the federal antidrug budget to $1.7 billion, and sought to combine stricter laws and tougher enforcement with funds for drug treatment and rehabilitation, though close to 75 percent of the budget was still devoted to enforcement.

In his last year in office, Reagan was confronted with questions from Congress about the sincerity of Mexico's efforts in the battle against drug trafficking. Fighting trafficking introduced a foreign policy element into the antidrug strategy, and the administration struggled to satisfy the demands of its congressional overseers and the concerns of the Mexican government over sovereignty issues and other matters. Reagan came under fire from Congress for not being tough enough in dealing with Mexico when laspses were revealed in their effort to stop the flow of drugs. When the president declared in April 1988 that Mexico was "fully cooperating" with the war on drugs, the Senate rebuked the administration and voted 63-27 to reject his finding. Congressional criticism intensified the following month when it became known that the administration had made an offer to drop drug charges against Panamanian dictator Manuel Noriega if he agreed to resign and leave Panama.

Reagan signed one other major piece of antidrug legislation into law on November 18, 1988, after the 100th Congress, responding to public opinion polls labeling drugs as the public's foremost concern, passed an act that went further than the 1986 legislation in toughening penalties for drug-related crimes, and substantially increasing drug education and rehabilitation programs. Proponents of capital punishment won a victory because the bill included the death penalty for drug trafficking and drug-related murders of law enforcement officers. The bill also created a cabinet-level "drug czar" responsible for the entire federal antidrug campaign. At the bill-signing ceremony, Reagan said, "now in the 11th hour of this presidency, we give a new sword and shield to those whose daily business it is to eliminate from America's streets and towns the scourge of illicit drugs."

While it is clear that the Reagan administration was successful in securing passage of antidrug legislation and making drug policy a prominent issue in the national debate, the evidence is mixed for the effect of their policy in reducing drug use. The president frequently pointed to a list of positive statistics to demonstrate the effectiveness of the administration's policies, including evidence that marijuana use had declined for seven straight years, and that 1987 had marked the first reduction in cocaine use by high school seniors in 13 years. One 1988 study claimed that the number of high school seniors using illicit drugs dropped from 53 percent in 1980 to 39 percent during Reagan's final year in the White House. Reagan also presided over a record number of drug seizures and convictions.

Critics contended that these were carefully selected statistics that concealed the fact that the drug problem was as bad, if not worse, than before he took office. The statistics simply do not show that the Reagan administration was on its way to "winning" the war on drugs. However, this does not mean that Reagan's drug policy was a failure. Ronald and Nancy Reagan's primary achievement was to elevate the problem of illicit drug use to a preeminent position in the national debate; since their departure from the White House the issue has never received the same level of attention. Additionally, Reagan's administration created a more coherent and efficient organization to wage the drug war, and also, belatedly, increased funding for rehabilitation programs to those Americans suffering from drug addiction. He also brought both parties together on an issue where agreement on broad objectives led to further cooperation and success in the drug war. This new consensus and commitment, although dismantled somewhat during the Clinton years, nonetheless remains one of the more impressive domestic accomplishments of the Reagan years.

ENVIRONMENT

Ronald Reagan's position on environmental matters was well documented as he entered the White House, after he embroiled himself in several high-profile controversies with the Sierra Club and other environmental interest groups. He was reputed to have little regard for environmental protection, although recent scholarship regarding his gubernatorial years has challenged that notion. He appointed several pro-environment advisers to his staff in Sacramento and lobbied for passage of several proposals, most notably the California Environmental Quality Act, which was supported by some environmental groups. But Reagan was labeled, somewhat accurately, as having a cursory understanding of many environmental issues, and comments such as the one he made during his 1966 campaign for governor haunted him throughout his public career: "You know, a tree is a tree—how many more do you need to look at." Trees tripped him up again during the 1980 campaign when he remarked that they were major sources of air pollution; this comment prompted Reagan's opponents at his rallies to place signs on trees warning, "Chop me down before I kill again."

The most important force shaping Reagan's environmental position was his strong belief in the right of individuals to own private property, and he was deeply concerned about the tendency of the federal government to "take" lands for public use. He referred frequently to the fact that the federal government owned one-third of the land in the United States, a development that Reagan called "the greatest threat in 200 years to our traditional right to own property." Beyond the threat to individual freedom, Reagan believed that the federal government's environmental policies had impaired economic growth and contributed to the stagnation of the 1970s, and for this reason much of his deregulatory agenda was directed at environmental regulations.

President Reagan hoped to restore what he viewed as the proper balance between environmental protection and economic growth. Polls taken in 1981 revealed that Reagan faced

an uphill battle in garnering support for his agenda, even with his election mandate, as a vast majority of Americans favored environmental protection over the interests of business and industry. One poll showed two-thirds of the public wanted to maintain the status quo, while only 21 percent of Americans wanted to relax environmental laws for the sake of economic growth. As a result, what Reagan saw as establishing an equilibrium between competing interests was regarded by most Americans as an aggressive, pro-business agenda.

Reagan tried to change environmental policy by avoiding confrontations in Congress and instead pursued an "administrative strategy," by focusing on his appointment power, use of executive orders, and other means to influence the various environmental regulatory agencies to alter their policies. Changing the policymaking process and agenda requires strong leadership at the cabinet and agency level; unfortunately for Reagan, his nominees to run the Environmental Protection Agency and the Department of the Interior were the most controversial appointments of his two terms in office. The administrator of the Environmental Protection Agency, Anne Gorsuch Burford, immediately became a target of attack when she proposed massive cuts in the EPA's budget—for instance, her fiscal year 1983 budget proposal called for a 28 percent cut from 1981 levels. Burford became embroiled in a bitter dispute with Congress after she refused to hand over subpoenaed documents dealing with the mandatory cleanup of hazardous waste dumps. In December 1982 she was cited for contempt by a vote of 259-105 in Congress, demonstrating that the disapproval of her conduct as EPA administrator crossed party lines. Less than three months later, Burford was forced to resign her position, along with other EPA employees, in the midst of a scandal involving the cleanup of the toxic waste dumps.

Reagan's choice to head the Department of the Interior fared little better, for James Watt received bad press from the day it was announced that he was Reagan's nominee. Watt had spent much of his professional life jousting with environmental groups, most recently during his stint as president of the Mountain States Legal Foundation. Once in office he fired a number of Carter administration holdovers, some of whom had close ties to various environmental groups, and he seemed to take a certain delight in challenging organizations such as the National Wildlife Federation and the Audubon Society. Remarkably blunt, he horrified environmentalists with claims such as "We will mine more, drill more, cut more timber." Watt quickly became a lightning rod for anyone opposed to the administration's policies. One observer of Watt's rocky tenure in office observed, "as a personality, he proved easy to ridicule, dislike, even despise, and he came to symbolize what was widely perceived to be the administration's environmental insensitivity." Insensitivity of another stripe surfaced on September 21, 1983, when Watt addressed the U.S. Chamber of Commerce and referred to an Interior Department commission as having "every kind of mix you can have. I have a black, I have a woman, two Jews and a cripple. And we have talent." Watt was quickly sent packing to his beloved West.

By the time of Burford and Watt's departure from the administration, Reagan's environmental policy was facing serious opposition, and threatened to become a major issue in the 1984 presidential campaign. An overwhelming majority of the public was opposed to Reagan's agenda, and significant numbers of congressional Republicans were voting with their Democratic colleagues to block or reverse Reagan's environmental proposals. Reagan sought to defuse the issue as the 1984 election approached, in part by replacing Burford with William Ruckelshaus, who had been the first administrator of EPA under President Nixon and had a good reputation with many environmental interest groups. Reagan turned to an old California hand, William Clark, to replace Watt at Interior, and due to the latter's checkered reputation Clark was a welcomed replacement, despite his lack of experience in environmental or land management issues. Clark left his post as National Security Advisor to take the Interior post; his departure from that office was welcomed by Chief of Staff James Baker and Deputy Chief of Staff Michael Deaver (and possibly by Nancy Reagan as well). They saw Clark as too ideological and too anti-Soviet, because they wanted to moderate the president's cold war views as the 1984 election approached. Despite his alleged hardline views, Clark was known as something of a conciliator, and at Interior he succeeded in snuffing out the fires ignited by Watt by making some concessions to Congress, including placing federal wildlife refuges off limits to future oil or gas drilling.

Nonetheless, this new approach by the Reagan administration did little to dispel the notion that Reagan was an enemy of environmental protection. During his 1984 reelection campaign Reagan claimed that his administration had renovated the nation's national parks, bolstered the protection of endangered species, and had taken a "common sense" and "balanced" approach to environmental policy. Reagan's opponent, Walter Mondale, pounded away at the issue, charging that Reagan "would rather take a polluter to lunch than take him to court." Nonetheless, the environment remained a minor issue in the 1984 election; a *Los Angeles Times* poll taken after the election showed that only 4 percent of American voters believed the environment was an important issue when they cast their vote. Of those voters, 75 percent cast their ballots for Mondale, but Reagan's sweep of 49 states indicated that environmental policy played a marginal role in the 1984 election.

Reagan ignored environmental issues for the remainder of his tenure despite the pleas of EPA administrator Ruckelshaus that action was needed to curb acid rain. Reagan and many of his advisers viewed the proposed solutions as too costly and detrimental to midwestern industries, prompting the president to delay any action and call for more research. Ruckelshaus knew after the president's November 1984 victory that the environment would be a minor issue for Reagan, and he quietly resigned his post at EPA three weeks after the election. His low standing in the administration was exemplified by Reagan's tendency to refer to him as "Don" (confusing him with Donald Rumsfeld) in various White House meetings.

Congress dictated environmental policy during Reagan's second term, forcing him to accept policies that he half-heartedly opposed. Many of his conservative supporters hoped that the president would build on his reelection landslide and fight to lift various environmental restrictions, but instead Reagan was forced to accept expanded regulations from an assertive Congress. The first step in this direction involved an increase of the Superfund in 1986. Congress had passed the Comprehensive Environmental Response, Compensation, and Liability Act of 1980 (CERCLA), in response to highly public incidents involving the improper disposal of toxic wastes, including at Love Canal, New York. The original legislation allocated $1.8 billion over five years to the Superfund to clean abandoned chemical waste sites. The fund had to be renewed in 1986, and Reagan's own EPA administrator, Lee Thomas, and Republican leaders in Congress all strongly supported the renewal measure. Reagan was concerned about the fund's cost, but after votes of 386-27 in the House and 88-8 in the Senate, the president reluctantly signed the bill on October 17, 1986,

increasing Superfund's budget nearly fivefold to $8.5 billion.

The most overt setback for the president's environmental agenda occurred when Reagan challenged Congress over the issue of clean water standards in 1986. Late in 1986 Congress passed the $18 billion Water Quality Act, which Reagan pocket-vetoed. The 100th Congress, now totally under Democratic control, revisited the issue in January 1987, and passed an even costlier $20 billion clean water bill by a large majority. Reagan immediately vetoed the bill, claiming that it was "loaded with waste and larded with pork." Reagan believed the water bill was yet another example of the federal government encroaching on the prerogatives of the states and localities—he believed it was inappropriate for the federal government to spend $100 million to clean Boston Harbor or spend $50 million for sewage treatment in Des Moines, Iowa. Reagan offered his own version of a water quality act that would have reduced the bill's price tag to $6 billion, but his proposal received virtually no congressional support. In early February 1987 the House overrode Reagan's veto by a vote of 401-26, and the Senate by a vote of 86–14. The passage of the Water Quality Act of 1987 was not only an impressive victory for environmentalists, it also was a further indicator that Reagan had been damaged by the Iran-contra revelations that were dominating the nation's headlines at the time.

President Reagan never recovered from the negative coverage his environmental team received during his first few years in office. Even after Watt's and Burford's departures, his "balanced" environmental agenda was viewed with suspicion by Congress, environmental interest groups, and by many American citizens. In April 1986 Reagan's former EPA chief, William Ruckelshaus, observed that the public's distrust of the president's environmental policies "was worse today than it's been at any time in the past." Reagan never expressed regret over the direction he pursued in the early years of his presidency, telling his biographer Lou Cannon in 1990 that James Watt "was darn good" as secretary of the interior. Ironically, Reagan's support for environmental budget cuts and his attempt to restrain the EPA contributed to a rejuvenated environmental movement, supported by large majorities in Congress and among the public. Opinion on this issue was so overwhelming that Reagan's vice president, George H. W. Bush, ran in the 1988 presidential election pledging to become the nation's "environmental president."

DEREGULATION

Ronald Reagan believed that government regulations strangled the American economy by stifling the ingenuity and creativity of the American people. Government was best when it governed least, and the best thing it could do was get out of the way of the American people. His philosophy toward regulation was summarized in the famous line from his first inaugural address, that "government is not the solution to our problem, government is the problem." The economic distress of the 1970s—high inflation, declining productivity, stubborn unemployment—coincided, Reagan contended, with the "intervention and intrusion in our lives" from "unnecessary and excessive growth of government." Reagan's deregulatory plans were designed to increase individual liberty and reduce the power of the federal government.

There had been a fairly rapid expansion of federal regulatory power in the 1970s under both Republican and Democratic administrations. As Lou Cannon has noted, the decade began with 12 federal regulatory agencies and ended with 18, and the budgets of these agencies increased from $1.4 billion to $7.5 billion.

One measure of their increasing reach could be found in the *Code of Federal Regulations*, whose pages of rules almost doubled from 54,000 to nearly 100,000 pages. One of Reagan's economic advisers, Murray Weidenbaum, suggested that federal regulations were costing American businesses nearly $100 billion each year. These regulations, Reagan proclaimed, were part of "the tentacles of excessive government . . . which are strangling our economy."

During the Carter administration the federal government had taken steps to deregulate the airline, trucking, and railroad industries, among others. There was something of a bipartisan consensus on this issue—traditional liberals such as Senator Edward Kennedy joined a number of congressional conservatives in pushing a deregulatory agenda. Reagan hoped to build on this momentum, applying a standard by which government "regulates only where necessary and as efficiently and fairly as possible." The incoming president wasted little time in moving toward his goals—just weeks into his first term he signed two executive orders shifting more power to the executive branch for drafting and enforcing regulations. This was a significant departure from the practice of the Carter administration, which had worked largely through the Congress. Reagan's first order gave the OMB's Office of Information and Regulatory Affairs (OIRA) greater control over proposed regulations and required each agency to prove to the OIRA that the benefits of each new regulation outweighed the costs imposed on business and the public. The second executive order established a task force, headed by Vice President Bush, to review "regulations with an eye towards getting rid of as many as possible." This "Presidential Task Force on Regulatory Relief" recommended that hundreds of federal regulations be either changed or eliminated altogether.

The administration's deregulatory agenda prompted critics to accuse it of maintaining a cozy relationship with "big business" and informally delegating decision-making authority to groups such as the U.S. Chamber of Commerce. The Commerce Department forwarded a list to the president of what the chamber labeled the "terrible 20"—a list of the most offensive regulations in the eyes of American business. Reagan also appointed businessmen to regulatory positions, all of whom were strong advocates of deregulation. John Shad, a former vice president of E. F. Hutton, was appointed director of the Securities and Exchange Commission, and Thorne Auchter, an executive of a construction firm that had been cited numerous times for Occupational Safety and Health Administration (OSHA) violations in the 1970s, was appointed director of that agency. These appointments and others guaranteed that significant deregulation would be one of the hallmarks of the Reagan years.

Reagan was predisposed to accept any recommendations from his advisers reducing federal regulations—his belief in deregulation was so deeply felt that he had a tin ear when it came to appreciating the political repercussions of some of his deregulatory decisions. It is also quite possible that he did understand these repercussions and yet believed he was doing the right thing, regardless of the political consequences. Some have argued that Reagan did not appreciate the distinction between economic regulations designed to control prices and entry into certain markets, and social regulations designed to clean the environment or create a safer workplace. The former were somewhat unpopular and open to challenge on the grounds of stifling economic growth, while the latter enjoyed widespread public support. But Reagan chose to wage war against all forms of regulation, including many popular social regulations such as standards for classifying hazardous waste, lowering air pollution levels, licensing nuclear power plants, and classifying and restricting the use of carcinogens. Since

Reagan was quickly immersed in the controversies surrounding EPA administrator Anne Gorsuch Burford and Interior Secretary James Watt, his attempt to weaken or eliminate many social regulations reinforced the impression that his administration put the interests of business above public health and safety. All of this produced a tremendous backlash from consumer groups, Congress, and the courts, which stopped, and in some cases reversed, many of the administration's deregulation efforts.

As public opinion grew increasingly hostile to the administration's policies, pragmatists within the White House began to see little value in pushing the agenda; the Bush deregulatory task force submitted its final report in August 1983 and dispersed. Proposals for regulatory reform languished in Congress, and some members of the business community urged the administration to move with caution to avoid creating even further public backlash. As with most presidencies, Reagan achieved his most significant objectives in his first two years in office, including his deregulatory agenda.

Although the issue was relegated to a lower priority during Reagan's second term, it was hardly ignored. On December 15, 1986, Reagan reestablished the Bush task force, which quickly moved to dismantle more rules. The task force had learned from its earlier mistakes and this time focused largely on economic deregulation. Just one week after the task force was brought back into business, Bush and his colleagues proposed abolishing U.S. fuel economy standards, claiming they were hurting the automotive industry. The task force also recommended eliminating the Interstate Commerce Commission, the major regulatory agency of the trucking and rail industries, and proposed making changes in banking regulation. In July 1987 the administration proposed deregulating the American Telephone and Telegraph Company and opening the telecommunications markets to local phone companies.

Most of Reagan's second-term deregulatory initiatives did not come to pass, but overall, his presidency succeeded in building on the momentum of the Carter years in dismantling many economic regulations, most notably in banking, securities, trucking, airline, and the interstate bus industries. More modest success was achieved in telecommunications, where regulations on television advertising and cable rates were removed. Oil-price controls were also eliminated during the Reagan years—although these controls were already set to expire, Reagan hastened their demise, and this move contributed to the impressive economic growth of the 1980s. The price of crude oil decreased from $35 per barrel in 1981 to $14.50 in 1989, and the price of gasoline at the pump dropped from $1.35 per gallon to $1.00 during the period. The administration attempted to deregulate in several other areas—natural gas, for example—but this was resisted by Congress, consumer groups, the courts, and elements of the bureaucracy.

Perhaps the most significant regulatory change of the Reagan years was in the manner by which regulations were reviewed and implemented. The executive branch, specifically OMB's Office of Information and Regulatory Affairs, was given enhanced authority to review existing and proposed regulations, each of which had to undergo a rigorous cost-benefit analysis. The effect of this was to slow the rate of regulatory expansion and reduce the annual production of new federal rules by 25 percent from the rate of the Carter administration. Spending by regulatory agencies dropped from 4.5 percent during Carter's term to 1.4 percent in Reagan's first term. In his final year in office, President Reagan claimed that his legacy of deregulation was "one of our administration's proudest achievements."

The president's critics vehemently disagreed, citing among other problems the savings and loans crisis of the late 1980s and early 1990s, which was left to the Bush administration to clean up. By the summer of 1990, 600 savings and loan institutions had defaulted, and almost twice that number were on the edge of insolvency. During the Reagan years legislation was passed (in part due to the unscrupulous actions of some members of Congress, both Democrat and Republican recipients of lucrative campaign contributions from S&Ls) allowing the thrifts to expand their investments beyond home loans. Many of these institutions went on spending sprees encouraged by the fact that their deposits were ensured by the "full faith and credit" of the federal government. Reagan's thrift industry watchdogs were asleep at the wheel, partly because they had authorized accounting changes that made it easier for the thrifts to hide their growing insolvency. All of this began to unravel after the stock market crash of October 1987; only a massive federal bailout averted an even greater disaster. The bailout costs reached $161 billion by 1999, the bulk of which was paid by the American taxpayer. It was the worst deregulatory fiasco of the Reagan years.

Ironically, Reagan's predecessor, Jimmy Carter, was more successful in advancing a deregulatory agenda than the stalwart Republican opponent of "red tape" and "big government." During the Carter years four major deregulatory initiatives were passed; during the Reagan years only one such reform, the Bus Regulatory Reform Act of 1982, became law. Reagan also failed to change any of the major pieces of social regulation, even though several of them, including the Clean Air and Clean Water Acts and the Superfund came up for renewal during his administration. In fact, the real costs of regulation for the three major health, safety, and environmental programs—the EPA, OSHA, and the National Highway Traffic Safety Administration—increased from 5.3 percent to 9.9 percent during Reagan's first term.

Many Americans shared Reagan's belief that government was too intrusive and endorsed the notion of "getting the government off their backs." Yet public support appeared to be somewhat disingenuous on this matter; Reagan's attempts to roll back social regulations involving health, safety, and protection were roundly condemned in opinion polls. There was no Reagan Revolution in the field of deregulation—ironically, Reagan may have contributed to this result, having increased the level of confidence that Americans had in the presidency and ultimately in the government itself.

SOCIAL SECURITY

Social Security was one of the most troublesome issues for Ronald Reagan, both as a presidential candidate and as president. A veteran of Barry Goldwater's 1964 campaign for president, Reagan was aware that Social Security was a sensitive topic, one that Republicans could not raise without the risk of committing electoral suicide—it was the "third rail" of American politics. Yet Reagan often violated this rule and spoke out on the issue, much to his political detriment. As Lou Cannon has observed, Reagan was captivated by the idea of making Social Security voluntary and giving people the choice to make their own retirement investments. This position cost him dearly in his 1976 race against President Ford, especially in states with a large population of retirees, such as Florida, where Ford captured more than 60 percent of the vote of those older than 65. He said that year that the government should make "a provision for those who could do better on their own" and that if people proved they could pay for their retirement, they should be able to opt out of the program. He reiterated this position in a November 1977 radio address, claiming that most Americans could "buy in the open insurance market a retirement policy with life protection paying far more than present social security benefits." He tried to stay clear of the issue in 1980 and was surrounded by advisers who did their best to convince him to avoid the subject.

Nevertheless, Reagan still hoped to reorganize Social Security when he became president. He tried to ride the momentum from his economic victories in the summer of 1981 and restructure what he saw as an ailing and costly program, but he was met with a firestorm of criticism. He did succeed in getting some minor cuts passed through Congress, such as the elimination of the minimum benefit, but he abandoned the idea of any major overhaul of Social Security. The outcry was so great that he was forced to reassure an anxious public that Social Security and other middle-class entitlement programs would not be dismantled during his presidency.

Despite the political hazards of dealing with the issue, the Social Security system remained on the road to insolvency. A report issued in 1979 by the trustees of the Social Security Trust Fund said that the fund for old-age and survivors' insurance would be depleted by the end of 1981 or in early 1982. Senators Pete Domenici (R-N.M.) and Fritz Hollings (D-S.C.) drafted a bipartisan proposal on Social Security to freeze or reduce cost-of-living allowances, an idea that Reagan was attracted to, but many of his advisers opposed the move, in part because the president had promised in his campaign not to cut Social Security. Reagan remained faithful to his campaign pledge, thereby missing a rare opportunity to forge a bipartisan consensus on Social Security in the Congress.

Following the collapse of the Domenici-Hollings proposal, Reagan's OMB director, David Stockman, crafted his own proposal that called for a $4 billion cut in basic benefits, a three-month delay in cost-of-living allowances

(COLAs), and an increase in the penalty for retiring at age 62 from 20 percent to 55 percent. The Stockman proposal was backed by Reagan's domestic policy adviser, Martin Anderson, and Health and Human Services Secretary Richard Schweiker, and Reagan approved it with relatively little debate. Within hours the Democrats in the House denounced Stockman's plan, with Speaker of the House Thomas P. O'Neill saying, "It is a rotten thing to do. It is a despicable thing." O'Neill was pleased that Reagan had finally given the Democrats an issue on which they could win, and his party seized the moment. Members of Reagan's own party were also furious at the White House for dropping this plan in their laps unannounced. They joined their fellow Democrats in denouncing it on May 20, 1986, when the Senate voted 96-0 to oppose any "unfair" or "precipitous" cuts in Social Security. The message was clear—any proposed cuts to Social Security would be subject to great scrutiny, if not outright rejection.

Presidents who are confronted with issues that are deeply divisive and charged with partisanship often turn to bipartisan commissions as a way to break the deadlock, and Reagan was no exception. In December 1981 Reagan named a 15-member commission, the National Commission on Social Security Reform, chaired by Alan Greenspan, to examine the growing Social Security crisis and offer recommendations. The Greenspan Commission recommended increasing payroll taxes in two stages, and gradually boosting the retirement age from 65 to 67 by the year 2027, as well as taxing the benefits of high-income recipients, and delaying COLA payments by six months. On April 20, 1983, these recommendations were enacted into law, and they resulted in a savings of about $165 billion. Speaker O'Neill, in response to the passage of the commission's proposals, said, "This is a happy day for America." In the political climate of the day, this was perhaps the most politically viable option available, although it failed to find a long-term solution to Social Security, simply salvaging the program until the end of the 20th century.

The political fallout from this bill was substantial, for Reagan was signing into law one of the largest tax increases in U.S. history. It probably would have been better for Reagan to have approved the earlier Domenici-Hollings initiative, but as was often the case with Reagan, the damage that might have been expected, particularly among his base, did not occur. Ronald Reagan could maneuver on issues like this with greater ease than most politicians, particularly his immediate successor. His conservative credentials were so unassailable that he could abandon the faith on occasion and not be deemed a heretic. However, Reagan was still vulnerable from the Left of the political spectrum for David Stockman's 1981 proposal, and his party paid dearly in the off-year elections of 1982. His Democratic opponent in 1984, Walter Mondale, accused Reagan of having a "secret plan" for cutting Social Security. This accusation was very effective in unnerving senior citizens, and forced Reagan and his advisers to repeatedly pledge that the Social Security program was essentially off limits.

Reagan was content to relegate the issue to the bottom of his domestic agenda during his second term, wishing to avoid being burned, once again, by an issue that constantly seemed to threaten his party. In 1985 Republicans in Congress tried to cut Social Security, in part from a fear that ballooning deficits would hurt their party in the 1986 midterm elections. The effort, led by Senate Majority Leader Robert Dole (R-Kans.), called for a one-year COLA freeze, the proceeds going to deficit reduction. The president hinted that he was in favor of the bill, but he soon abandoned his congressional allies when he was told that the House was going to reject the bill. Instead, he cut a deal with Speaker Tip O'Neill to preserve COLA levels in exchange for higher defense spending. This infuriated the president's allies in the Senate, including Charles Grassley of Iowa, who commented, "if the president can't support us he ought to keep his mouth shut. It would be better if the president sticks behind us rather than Tip O'Neill."

Reagan remained opposed to any cuts in Social Security even as the pressure grew throughout his second term to control the deficit. After the stock market crash of October 1987, he conducted a "budget summit" with 12 members of Congress and three members of his economic team, in which he specifically excluded cuts in Social Security. He told the summit team that he was "putting everything on the table with the exception of Social Security, with no other preconditions." It seemed that Reagan had been burned too often in his first term to go near the issue again.

This refusal to meddle with Social Security, based on political calculations, was antithetical to Reagan's principles and to the agenda that carried him into the White House in 1981. When Reagan left office, Social Security had become bigger and a more permanent part of American life, with the combined payroll tax rising from 12.26 percent in 1980 to 15.02 percent in 1988. In the short run, Reagan deserves some credit for sponsoring and endorsing the Greenspan Commission proposals, which left the system solvent until the end of the 20th century. But the commission, and the president and Congress, left it to future generations to deal with many of the structural problems facing the system. In the 2000 presidential election, Republican candidate George W. Bush offered proposals that were somewhat similar to those offered by Reagan in the 1970s, including one that would allow the government to invest a small portion of the system's revenue in the stock market, but the proposal faded away in light of the poor market performance during the recession of 2000–2002.

THE "REAGAN DOCTRINE"

The "Reagan Doctrine" was the president's alleged strategy to hasten the demise of the Soviet Union through economic pressure, rhetorical assaults, and overt and covert military action against its allies and the Soviet Union itself. It should be noted that many observers, including some former members of the Reagan administration, assert that this "doctrine" was acknowledged as doctrine only after the fall of the Soviet Union. The influence of this doctrine, and whether it actually existed, is a major point of contention between those who credit Reagan with the collapse of the Eastern bloc and those who view it as an inevitable result of internal contradictions within the Soviet system.

As with many of Reagan's policies, the so-called Reagan Doctrine was not the result of careful analysis and planning, although it did represent something of a congealing of ideas that had been percolating in Reagan's mind for some time. According to his National Security Advisor, Robert McFarlane, "not one nanosecond" went into crafting the Reagan Doctrine. The term itself was actually coined by columnist Charles Krauthammer in a *Time* magazine essay and was never officially adopted by the Reagan administration. Yet despite the slapdash evolution of the Reagan Doctrine, Reagan's clearly stated antipathy toward communism and his belief in its inevitable failure provided some semblance of intellectual cohesion and guidance to Reagan's foreign policy and national security team. Krauthammer arrived at the Reagan Doctrine by extrapolating from a passage in Reagan's 1985 State of the Union address, which argued that "we must not break faith with those who are risking their lives—on every continent, from Afghanistan to Nicaragua—to defy Soviet-supported aggression and secure rights which have been ours from birth." In practice, not breaking faith was to come to mean launching an offensive that, unlike previous policies, "supports not the status quo but revolution."

Reagan, along with the more conservative members of his foreign policy team, among them Director of Central Intelligence (DCI) William Casey, Defense Secretary Caspar Weinberger, UN Ambassador Jeane Kirkpatrick, and National Security Advisors Richard Allen and William Clark, all favored a policy of pressuring the Kremlin, particularly by bleeding the Soviets and their proxy forces in Poland, Afghanistan, Angola, and Nicaragua. They were convinced that the Soviet economic system was teetering on the brink of collapse, and believed that economic sanctions and a costly arms race would force the Kremlin into bankruptcy. Additionally, they shared the view that it was time to talk bluntly about the Soviet Union, and that in Ronald Reagan the West had an effective communicator to speak the truth about the "evil empire," as Reagan labeled it in 1983. In his first press conference as president, Reagan claimed that the Soviet leadership reserved the right to commit "any crime, to lie, to cheat" to advance its interests. In a May 1981 commencement address at Notre Dame University he proclaimed that the West would not contain communism, it would "transcend" it. Communism was a "sad, bizarre chapter in human history whose last pages are even now being written." The most vital anti-Soviet movement in Eastern Europe, Poland's "Solidarity," led by shipyard worker Lech Walesa, was encouraged by the words and actions of Reagan and the Polish-born pope, John Paul II. Reagan's CIA director and officials in the Vatican cooperated, if not outright coordinated their efforts, to undermine

the pro-Soviet Polish government of General Wojciech Jaruzelski.

DCI Casey served as the point man for Reagan's covert war against the Soviets. Casey was a veteran of the World War II Office of Strategic Services (OSS), which had served as a hatchery for many CIA operatives, and Casey admired the founder of the OSS, William Donovan. He was impressed by Donovan's boldness, by his willingness to approve operations in the face of daunting odds. Casey brought this same spirit to a somewhat moribund CIA, which had lost much of its autonomy and penchant for risk-taking after the exposure of its misdeeds in the mid-1970s. Casey believed that a more assertive congressional oversight regime operating since that time had crippled the CIA's ability to conduct covert operations, and he was determined to reinvigorate his agency.

It remains an open question how much Reagan's policies contributed to the collapse of the Soviet Union. The evidence is mixed, with many high-ranking former Soviet officials denying that American policy played any role, while some contend that Reagan's commitment to the Strategic Defense Initiative (SDI) and his rhetorical and material support to Solidarity and other anti-Soviet movements helped to hasten the collapse of the Warsaw Pact and ultimately the Soviet regime itself.

LIBYA

A favorite target of President Reagan during his eight years in office was Colonel Muammar al-Gadhafi of Libya. Gadhafi seemed to especially irritate Reagan, and the latter enjoyed tweaking him whenever possible. According to Reagan, Gadhafi was "a madman . . . an unpredictable fanatic [who] believed any act, no matter how vicious or cold-blooded, was justified to further his goals." Reagan's secretary of defense shared the commander in chief's contempt for the Libyan leader, calling him "one of the strangest heads of state in the world . . . a theatrically posturing, fake mystic, with a considerable dollop of madness thrown in. Rumors have long circulated in intelligence circles that he suffers from an incurable venereal disease. . . ." A series of minor air and naval engagements between the United States and Libya occurred throughout Reagan's presidency. The first occurred in August 1981, in the midst of American naval maneuvers in the Gulf of Sidra inside Gadhafi's "zone of death," an arbitrary boundary that jutted far into the Mediterranean. Two American F-14s were confronted by two Soviet SU-22s of the Libyan Air Force, and the latter were destroyed by heat-seeking missiles in an engagement that lasted less than a minute. The incident caused a stir beyond the usual repercussions that occur with any use of force, in that White House counsel Edwin Meese decided not to wake the sleeping president to inform him of the engagement, since the event had ended so abruptly. This incident contributed to the perception of Ronald Reagan as a detached chief executive excessively reliant on, if not controlled by, his staff.

In general, the public reaction to this minor skirmish was positive, and it bolstered Reagan's standing among the American people as someone who "stood tall" and was determined to rebuild America's military strength. When it was later revealed that Reagan instructed a navy admiral that his forces could engage in the "hot pursuit" of enemy aircraft inside Libyan territory "all the way into the hangar," the story became part of the Reagan lore.

The most serious confrontation with Libya occurred in March–April 1986. Once again it was American naval exercises in the Mediterranean that prompted Gadhafi to strike at the Sixth Fleet. On March 24, 1986, the Libyans used SAM missiles, aircraft, and small naval

vessels to attack the American forces, at a substantial cost to the Libyans. Four days later, Gadhafi issued a statement encouraging "all Arab people" to attack American interests. On April 5, a bomb exploded in a West Berlin discotheque, killing an American serviceman and one civilian, and injuring 230 people, including 50 American servicemen. The National Security Agency intercepted Libyan communications that indicated the bomb had been planted by Libyan agents. In response President Reagan ordered air strikes against military and "terrorist" targets inside Libya, including the "command and control" center, Gadhafi's compound in Tripoli. Air Force F-111s were dispatched from the United Kingdom, but the French government refused to allow the American aircraft to fly over its airspace. Nonetheless, five separate targets were hit, and one F-111 was lost in the attack. Gadhafi later claimed that an adopted child of his had been killed, while many Americans seemed particularly pleased that the French embassy had suffered minor damage in the raid. While the administration denied they were attempting to kill Gadhafi in the attack, they made it clear that whoever was killed in a strike on a terrorist headquarters was fair game. The American attack appeared to put Gadhafi on the defensive, at least for a time, as he began to restrain his rhetoric and curtailed his public appearances. In the final days of Reagan's presidency, in January 1989, two Libyan MiG-24s were shot down by pilots from the USS *John F. Kennedy*, the final salvo of Reagan's showdown with "this unpredictable clown."

GRENADA

The island of Grenada seemed an unlikely spot for the largest American military action since the end of the Vietnam War. The roots of the conflict went back to 1979 when Maurice

Bishop and his "New Jewel Movement" over-threw the government of Eric Gairy, a some-what eccentric and heavy-handed prime minister. Bishop's coup was hailed by many Grenadans, for he promised free elections and to protect the human rights of the island's 100,000 residents. These promises were quickly broken, as Bishop suspended the nation's constitution, refused to hold early elec-tions, and turned increasingly to Fidel Castro as his role model and benefactor, while enhanc-ing his nation's ties to the Soviet Union. Con-struction of an airport that was largely undertaken by Cuban soldiers raised suspicions in Washington that the island would become a supply depot for Soviet aid to the Sandinista regime in Nicaragua and to rebels in El Sal-vador. There was some saber-rattling in Wash-ington directed at the Bishop government from the administration's earliest days in office, but when Bishop was overthrown by a more hard-line faction within the New Jewel Movement in October 1983, and the island's neighboring countries requested that the United States intervene, the administration eagerly con-sented to the request.

Belittled at the time as something of a "phony war," the operation, or "invasion" as its critics called it, or the "rescue mission" as the administration called it, was hastily con-ceived and occurred during the worst foreign policy fiasco of the administration's first term, the terrorist bombing of the barracks in Lebanon that killed 241 U.S. Marines. In a pat-tern that would repeat itself throughout much of the Reagan years, Secretary of State Shultz was one of the more hawkish advisers urging the president to intervene in Grenada, while Secretary of Defense Weinberger tended to be more cautious about the use of force, and often engaged in delaying tactics in the face of Shultz's demands for action. Shultz believed that Weinberger's request for "far greater preparation and a much larger force before an

operation could begin" was "the counsel of no action at all."

The assault began on October 25, 1983, and was marred by a series of operational problems. Fighting in some locations was fierce: 19 U.S. servicemen were killed and 115 wounded, while 59 Cubans in a force of 800 soldiers and laborers were killed, and another 25 wounded. The remaining Cubans surren-dered, while 45 Grenadans were killed and 337 wounded. The worldwide reaction to "Opera-tion Urgent Fury" was generally negative, including from such stalwart allies as Margaret Thatcher, who was angry that Reagan had not consulted with her before authorizing force against a British Commonwealth nation. The UN General Assembly denounced the assault in a 108 to 9 vote, while at home, seven mem-bers of the House of Representatives moved to impeach Reagan. The *New York Times* argued that the attack on Grenada was "a reverberating demonstration to the world that America has no more respect for laws and bor-ders, for the codes of civilization, than the Soviet Union." There was skepticism in the media and among some members of the Democratic Party that the attack had been launched to divert attention from the debacle in Lebanon. But the American public sup-ported Reagan's decision in large numbers, and the images of American medical students returning from Grenada and kissing the tar-mac upon their arrival in the United States solidified that support. The invasion of Grenada reinforced the perception that Rea-gan was far more inclined to resort to force than President Carter, delighting those on the Right and dismaying those on the Left.

LEBANON

While Grenada may have been seen as evi-dence that the United States had exorcised the ghost of Vietnam, the American experience in Lebanon ran the risk of becoming Ronald Reagan's "quagmire." Reagan sent American marines into Lebanon in August 1982 as part of a multinational force that included troops from Italy and France, and it was hoped that this force would stabilize the situation and keep Israeli, Syrian, Palestinian, and various Lebanese militias from further reducing Beirut to rubble. The chain of events leading to the deployment of American forces began when Israel invaded Lebanon in June 1982 to destroy the Palestine Liberation Organization (PLO) and other groups that had launched attacks into northern Israel from sanctuaries in southern Lebanon. While the Israelis had scored impressive military victories during their invasion, the prospect of an Israeli attack on an Arab capital, Beirut, in the company of their Christian allies, raised the prospect of many casualties and an outcry in the Arab world. Reagan persuaded Israeli prime minister Menachem Begin to halt the Israeli advance at the outskirts of Beirut, and eventually an agreement was reached allowing for the withdrawal of PLO forces and the insertion of the peacekeeping contingent. For a brief time there was relative calm in Beirut, as the PLO and Syrian forces withdrew from the city. The Christian Phalangist leader Bashir Gemayel was elected president in late August, and shortly after this the U.S. Marines were evacuated to ships offshore. On September 14 President Gemayel was assassinated, and in response Israeli troops moved into Beirut, thereby violating the agreement under which PLO forces had been removed. At the same time Christian militias entered the Palestinian refugee camps at Sabra and Shatila and killed over 700 people. This prompted Reagan to send the marines back into Beirut, in the hope of creating a stable environment that would allow the Lebanese government to restore order.

On Sunday, October 23, 1983, at 6:22 A.M. a yellow Mercedes truck worked its way over and around a series of obstacles at the Beirut airport, into the lobby of the four-story building that served as the headquarters of the First Battalion, Eighth Marine Regiment, and detonated approximately 12,000 pounds of TNT, the largest nonnuclear blast on record. The rubble of the building buried 346 marines, and 241 would die from their wounds. When Reagan was informed of the attack by his National Security Advisor, Robert McFarlane, he asked a series of questions, "How could this happen? How bad is it? Who did it?" and when news of the high casualty count arrived he reacted with "a look of deep grief" and "a long, thoughtful staring at the carpet." Reagan later wrote that he was "in a state of grief, made almost speechless by the magnitude of the loss" and that the bombing of the marine barracks, in contrast to Grenada, which produced "one of the highest of the high points" of his presidency, had produced "the lowest of the low." It was one of the few instances in Reagan's presidency where his sunny optimism was overwhelmed by tragedy.

The disaster in Lebanon only exacerbated tensions between Caspar Weinberger and George Shultz, for Weinberger had opposed the peacekeeping mission to Lebanon, while Shultz and Robert McFarlane had championed the deployment. Weinberger was bitterly opposed to the idea of "presence" missions, the notion that the presence of American forces could stabilize a hostile situation and add an element of leverage to any ongoing diplomatic efforts. In the case of Lebanon, Weinberger believed that the presence of the U.S. Marines at the Beirut airport was particularly futile, in part because of the tactical disadvantage for the marines of the airport location, which offered, in Weinberger's words, a "'bull's-eye' of a large target." Under a State Department–negotiated agreement, the marines were prevented from taking routine military steps to protect themselves, and thus

The Reagans honor the victims of the bombing of the U.S. embassy in Beirut, Lebanon, at Andrews Air Force Base, Maryland, April 23, 1983.

became the targets of repeated sniping and artillery fire. Of course, as secretary of defense, Weinberger felt a particular obligation to look out for the welfare of the troops under his command. After the bombing of the barracks with its horrible death toll, a rueful Weinberger told Colin Powell, "I wished I had been more persuasive with the president."

Shultz's and Weinberger's paths had crossed many times over the years, and a number of longtime Reagan observers are unsure about the origins of the bad blood between the two men. They had served together in the Nixon administration in the Office of Management and Budget, with Shultz as director and Weinberger as his deputy, and later both men joined the multi-

national construction firm Bechtel, with Shultz serving as the president of the corporation, and Weinberger as the general counsel. In frequent debates inside Reagan's National Security Council, Shultz believed that Weinberger was excessively cautious regarding the use of force, and that he was inflexible and prone to talk an issue to death. In his memoirs Shultz wrote that Weinberger "exhibited a technique he used on many issues before and after: take a position and never change. He seemed to feel that the outcome, even if different from his position, would likely move further in his direction when he was difficult and intransigent."

Lebanon was one of many examples of these two stubborn, proud men differing over the use of force. The conventional interpretation holds that Reagan did not like this intra-cabinet squabbling, but his detached and lethargic governing style allowed the situation to fester. But it is equally possible that Reagan welcomed this kind of balancing act in his cabinet, and shaped his foreign policy by splitting the difference between these two headstrong cabinet members.

EL SALVADOR AND NICARAGUA

President Reagan's policies in Central America generated more controversy than any other foreign policy initiative, in particular his decision to launch a covert war against the Sandinista government of Nicaragua, and to support Center-Right political parties in El Salvador. Critics of the administration's policies were convinced that Reagan was running against the tide of history in the region, and that his policies continued the decades-old tendency of the United States to act as an imperial power in Latin America. The ghost of Vietnam also loomed large over this debate, with many of the administration's opponents convinced that the United States was on the verge of entangling itself in a Central American quagmire. Reagan viewed the struggle in Central America as another venue for the cold war, and the "contra" forces fighting the pro-Cuban, Soviet-leaning Sandinistas were the moral equivalent of the Founding Fathers.

The United States provided military, economic, and covert assistance to the government of El Salvador to help it defeat a leftist insurgency known as the FMLN (the Farabundo Martí National Liberation Front). Ten days before Reagan's first inauguration, the FMLN launched a "final offensive" against the American-backed government and did so with the support of the Sandinistas. The incoming president moved cautiously in Cen-tral America during the first months of his administration, not wanting to divert the focus from his foremost issue, his proposals to reinvigorate the American economy through tax and spending cuts. His secretary of state talked tough, arguing at one point that the United States should be "going to the source" of the trouble in Central America, Cuba, and suggested a blockade would be the appropriate response. Defense Secretary Weinberger and the Joint Chiefs of Staff opposed the blockade plan, and Reagan never seems to have seriously considered such a proposal. It was the first of many setbacks for Secretary Haig, who remained outside the loop for much of his tenure in the Reagan administration.

Reagan opted instead for a policy of providing assistance to the centrist government of José Napoleón Duarte and guardedly increased the American military presence in El Salvador, raising the number of advisers to 55. Reagan's policies produced a mixed result; leftist forces in El Salvador were held at bay throughout the 1980s, but their hit-and-run attacks continued to harm an already devastated economy. The El Salvadoran military engaged in human rights abuses, the most notorious being the massacre of anywhere from 700 to 1,200 peasants in the village of El Mozote. At the same time, right-wing death squads targeted anyone suspected of leftist inclinations; their victims included countless Salvadorans, a Catholic bishop, six Jesuit priests, along with journalists and aid workers.

Nicaraguan support for the FMLN was cited in the early months of Reagan's presidency to justify his covert war against the Sandinistas. Reagan had campaigned in 1980 promising to curtail all aid to the Nicaraguan government, and the 1980 Republican platform sharply criticized the "Marxist Sandinista takeover of Nicaragua." In the first weeks of his presidency the administration threatened to cancel all assistance to the Sandinistas unless they ceased aiding the rebels in El Salvador. By the end of 1981, the president had adopted the recommendations of William Casey, a somewhat reluctant Alexander Haig (who preferred more overt means), Jeane Kirkpatrick, and William Clark, for an ambitious operation designed to assist anti-Sandinista forces in Honduras. On November 17 he approved a $20 million program to organize these forces, and on December 1 he signed a "finding" authorizing the CIA to organize a 500-man "interdiction force."

Reagan later wrote in his memoirs that the Sandinistas had merely replaced "one dictatorship with another," and had allied themselves "with Castro, Moscow, and the Eastern bloc . . . Bill Casey and others at the CIA drafted a plan . . . [that] would provide for the support of anti-Sandinista Nicaraguans who would try to halt the flow of Soviet-made arms from Cuba to Nicaragua to El Salvador. These men, just a few in the beginning, were the nucleus of Nicaragua's Contra freedom fighters."

Reagan's "covert" war became an open secret and a source of bitter controversy at home and abroad when the *Washington Post* reported the approval of the aid package to the contras in February 1982. In March the *Post* ran a story noting that Reagan had personally approved the plan. Congress, particularly members of the House, were uncomfortable with the Nicaraguan operation from the start. They were skeptical of the interdiction argument, concerned about the prospect of the United States being drawn into another Vietnam, and convinced that America's support for the repressive, corrupt regime of Anastasio Somoza had led to the rise of the Sandinistas. Reagan attempted to keep the nation's focus on his domestic economic priorities, but slowly the covert war moved to the front pages as the size of the "interdiction force" grew from 500 men into the thousands, and the contras' campaign of economic sabotage and attacks against

regime officials escalated. In response to this heightened violence and protests from Nicaragua and other nations, the House Intelligence Committee, chaired by Representative Edward Boland of Massachusetts, included language in the Intelligence Authorization Act of 1983 prohibiting the use of CIA funds to overthrow the Nicaraguan government. This was the first in a series of shots fired across the administration's bow, and would ultimately culminate in the worst crisis of the Reagan presidency, the Iran-contra affair.

For much of Reagan's first term the Republican-controlled Senate tended to support the president's policy, but this support began to dissipate near the end of the term when it was revealed that the CIA had mined harbors in Nicaragua. The CIA had included mining as an option in their initial "interdiction force" proposal to Congress in 1981, and Reagan gave his approval to that option in December 1983. DCI Casey briefed the House Intelligence Committee on January 31, 1984, about three weeks after the operation began. It appears that some senators and their staff members were told about the mining at this time; the full Senate Intelligence Committee was informed on March 8 and March 13, 1984. When the story broke in the media on April 6, 1984, many members claimed they were hearing about it for the first time and demanded that it stop.

To this day there is confusion as to who knew what and when. Director Casey is generally cited as the guilty party in this episode; his propensity to mumble and his reluctance to share information with Congress undoubtedly contributed to the confusion. Members of Congress were not alone in having difficulty understanding William Casey; President Reagan once remarked, "He'd give you problems . . . because of his mumbling." Reagan frequently attempted to read Casey's lips but failed at times. National Security Advisor

William Clark joked that Casey was the only director of the CIA who didn't need a telephone scrambler. But it also appears that some members of Congress knew about the operation and either endorsed it or remained silent until it became public. Later in 1984, support for the contra war declined even further when it was revealed that the CIA had produced a guerrilla warfare manual that included references to "neutralizing" members of the Sandinista government.

Reagan's covert war in Nicaragua collapsed in his second term after the Iran-contra revelations generated vigorous congressional and foreign opposition to his policy. Costa Rican president Oscar Arias emerged as an eloquent spokesman for peace in the region and organized leaders of the Central American nations to push for a change in U.S. policy. The fate of the contras was sealed when Representative Jim Wright of Texas became the Speaker of the House in 1987. Wright launched his own effort to secure the peace in Nicaragua, and while his proposals were viewed with suspicion by the Reagan administration, the incoming Bush administration declared a cease-fire with Congress and endorsed Wright's proposal to cut off aid to the contras and to allow all of the parties to participate in elections in 1990. In those elections the Sandinista government of Daniel Ortega was defeated by Violeta Chamorro, a disgruntled former Sandinista who was one of the leading voices of opposition to that regime.

The verdict on Reagan's Nicaraguan policy is as contentious as that on his policy toward the Soviet Union: admirers see the covert war as so costly to the Sandinistas that they ultimately agreed to the free and fair elections that led to their demise. Supporters of Reagan's policies contend that, absent this pressure, the Sandinistas would never have held open elections. Detractors see the policy as one that ravaged the Nicaraguan economy, caused countless deaths and assorted violations of human rights by the contras, and led to a scandal in the United States that rocked Reagan's presidency and for a time generated serious discussion of impeachment.

THE IRAN-CONTRA AFFAIR

The Iran-contra affair was the most serious crisis of Ronald Reagan's presidency. Two factors contributed to Reagan's decision to proceed down a path that could well have led to his impeachment: his concern for the American hostages held by Shi'ite militiamen in Lebanon, and his desire to keep the Nicaraguan contras alive.

In 1985 Congress had tacked onto an appropriations bill the Boland Amendment, which prohibited the CIA or "any other agency or entity of the United States involved in intelligence activities" from spending funds in support of the contras. Reagan was confronted with a difficult decision: had he vetoed the appropriations bill the government would have been shut down; but signing it could mark the end of the contras. He chose to sign the bill, but refused to accept this as the death knell for the contras. While no evidence had ever been produced linking the president to the diversion of funds to the contras, it is clear that a general edict had been issued to keep Reagan's "freedom fighters" intact.

After the passage of the 1985 amendment, Reagan's National Security Council staff began to explore alternative methods of sustaining the contras. Foreign governments and wealthy conservative Americans were asked to assist in the cause, and many did, including the sultan of Brunei and American beer magnate Joseph Coors. While these actions may have violated the spirit of the Boland Amendment, they were probably legal. Other elements of the NSC's plan were clearly illegal. The National Security

Council, first under Robert McFarlane and later John Poindexter, with Lt. Col. Oliver North as the "point man" for the operation, hatched a scheme whereby arms (desperately needed HAWK antiaircraft missile parts) would be sold to Iran, which was locked in a bitter war with Iraq, and the funds from those arms sales would be placed in a secret bank account in Switzerland accessible to the contras. While McFarlane's role in the diversion of funds is unclear, he was a driving force behind the opening to Iran, at one point traveling there himself on a secret mission. McFarlane, and Director of Central Intelligence William Casey, believed that there were moderate elements within the Iranian government with whom the United States could deal, and who would eventually hold key positions of power inside Iran. But it was also hoped, as a gesture of goodwill, that these Iranians would use their influence to free the American captives in Lebanon. It was believed that Iran was the major benefactor of the terrorist groups behind the kidnappings, and they could exert their influence over these groups. Despite the president's repeated claims that he would never negotiate with terrorists, his administration did negotiate with the benefactors of terrorism. Reagan could never bring himself to admit this was the case, with one notable exception, which was an address to the nation on March 4, 1987, in which he observed, "a few months ago I told the American people I did not trade arms for hostages. My heart and my best intentions still tell me that's true, but the facts and the evidence tell me it is not." Yet despite this admission, which helped put the scandal behind him, Reagan would later claim that the Iranian initiative was an attempt to make an opening to so-called moderate elements.

The NSC's scheme began to unravel in the fall of 1986, after Nicaraguan forces shot down a plane carrying supplies to the contras, and captured an American member of the crew,

Eugene Hasenfus. Less than a month later, on November 3, 1986, a Lebanese newspaper, *Al-Shirra*, ran a story claiming that the United States was selling arms to Iran. Three days later, President Reagan claimed that the United States had not sold any arms to Iran. However, on November 13, 1986, Reagan held a news conference and admitted that arms were sold to Iran but claimed that they were not intended to secure the release of the hostages. This was followed by the biggest bombshell of the entire story, the revelation by Reagan and Attorney General Edwin Meese on November 25, 1986, that funds from the arms sales had been diverted to bank accounts designated for the contras.

It was this revelation that led to widespread calls in the media and in Congress for the appointment of an independent counsel and for congressional investigations into the affair. President Reagan tried to preempt these actions by announcing the appointment of the Tower Commission on December 1, 1986; the commission, headed by former senator John Tower, also included former National Security Advisor Brent Scowcroft and former secretary of state Edmund Muskie. The Tower Commission issued a report on February 26, 1987, that was critical of the president's detached management style, and that recommended reforms for the NSC, but it in no way deterred the independent counsel or the congressional committees from proceeding with their investigations.

Lawrence Walsh was appointed independent counsel on December 19, 1986, and he and his staff began a lengthy and costly probe that would stretch well into the 1990s. Walsh's investigation led to a number of convictions, although two of the prime targets of the investigation, Oliver North and John Poindexter, had their convictions overturned due in part to the use of immunized testimony. A number of CIA operatives were indicted and convicted, but an attempt to try former defense secretary Caspar Weinberger on felony charges of perjury and obstruction of justice was short-circuited when he was pardoned, along with five other figures (including Robert McFarlane) by President George H. W. Bush on Christmas Eve, 1992.

A joint House-Senate committee began its public hearings on May 5, 1987, and the highlight of the hearings came in July when Oliver North testified (wearing his U.S. Marine Corps uniform) and appeared to win the public relations battle with the committee members. He contended that he had followed the president's orders in implementing the arms sales and the diversion of funds, and he appealed to the patriotism of the American people and their animosity toward Congress in making his case. Many Reagan loyalists were not impressed, and they remain convinced to this day that North embellished his story and had engaged in a rogue operation that the president would not have approved.

Perhaps the critical moment in the entire saga occurred during July 15–17, and July 20–21, 1987, when John Poindexter testified that he had not told the president about the diversion of funds. Poindexter's testimony may well have prevented Reagan's impeachment. Poindexter claimed that he wanted to protect Reagan and therefore kept him uninformed, but he believed at the same time that he was

President Reagan and Senator Edmund Muskie listen as Senator John Tower (left) reports on his commission's investigation into the Iran-contra affair.

doing what the president wanted him to do. Some committee members remained skeptical, and to this day the extent of President Reagan's knowledge remains a subject of controversy. It may be the case that Poindexter was simply relying on the old but discredited doctrine of plausible deniability, whereby the president makes known his general wishes about a controversial covert operation but leaves no paper trail to link him to the dirty details. The few instances where Reagan was questioned about the details proved to be an exercise in futility for the investigators. For instance, in a videotaped deposition presented during John Poindexter's trial on February 16–17, 1990, Reagan had great difficulty remembering names, places, and events from his time in the White House.

President Reagan eventually recovered from the fallout of the Iran-contra affair, leaving office a popular figure in January 1989. But some of the damage was irretrievable; for instance, his reputation for tough talk against terrorism seemed to be hollow boasting in light of the arms deal, and jokes about his detached management style became routine. Those who knew Reagan best never saw him more deflated than he was during late 1986 and early 1987 when the revelations of mismanagement and illegal activities dominated the headlines. Family members have attested to this, as have some of his closest advisers. It was a sharp fall from grace for a man who formerly seemed to glide through life.

In retrospect, it would appear that the Iran-contra affair was a continuation of a struggle that began in the mid-1970s between Congress and the president over the control of the covert instruments of American foreign policy. Reagan, and his DCI William Casey, wanted to restore presidential discretionary authority in this area. Members of Congress, both Democrats and Republicans, wanted the legislature to play a more assertive role, if not become outright partners, in the management of the American intelligence community. In attempting to play by the old rules, Reagan, Casey, McFarlane, Poindexter, and North almost cost Reagan his presidency.

AFGHANISTAN

Nowhere was the "Reagan Doctrine" more effectively applied than in the covert war in Afghanistan, which bled the Soviet Union of desperately needed treasure and killed thousands of its soldiers. Afghanistan became the Soviet Union's "Vietnam," although the comparison is understated in that Afghanistan contributed to the collapse of the Soviet regime. In a classic case of underestimating the tenacity of their foes, the Soviets invaded Afghanistan in December 1979 to prop up a faltering Marxist government. The Western world roundly condemned the invasion, and the Carter administration retaliated by shelving SALT II (the Strategic Arms Limitation Treaty), implementing a grain embargo against the Soviets, and canceling American participation in the 1980 Summer Olympic games in Moscow.

In the 1980 election, Republicans characterized the Soviet invasion of Afghanistan, along with the seizure of the American embassy in Iran, as evidence of the sagging fortunes of the United States. Candidate Reagan talked in bold but vague terms of restoring American strength and prestige around the globe, while President Carter's push for increased defense spending and his tougher talk vis-à-vis the Soviet Union came too late to reverse an image of drift and decline. Unlike the divisive covert war in Central America, there was near bipartisan unanimity on the need to support the "freedom fighters," or Mujahideen, in Afghanistan. No Democrat disagreed with Reagan's assessment that in Afghanistan the Soviets "were attempting to subdue winds of freedom with a ruthlessness bordering on barbarity."

Covert assistance to the Mujahideen began during the Carter years, and involved cooperative efforts with the governments of Egypt, Saudi Arabia, and, most important, Pakistan. But the turning point of the war came in 1985 when President Reagan signed National Security Decision Directive 166, which sought the defeat and complete removal of the approximately 90,000 Soviet troops in Afghanistan. The American assistance provided to the Mujahideen in Afghanistan was the largest covert operation the CIA had conducted to date. About $2 billion worth of aid was provided to the "freedom fighters," including satellite data on Soviet targets, intercepts of Soviet communications, the establishment of clandestine communications networks for the Mujahideen, long-range sniper rifles, wire-guided antitank missiles, and a targeting device for mortars that was linked to a U.S. Navy satellite.

But the key item in the American aid package was the Stinger antiaircraft missile, the arrival of which tilted the war in favor of the Mujahideen. Reagan had been under pressure for some time to provide the Stinger, and much of that pressure came from members of Congress, particularly Democratic congressman Charles Wilson of Texas. DCI Casey championed the Stinger as well, and he found an ally in Secretary of State George Shultz, a powerful partnership, since the two were often at odds with one another. There was intense bureaucratic opposition to the Stinger transfer, with many officials in the Department of Defense concerned that the weapon would fall into the wrong hands, particularly terrorist hands. Shultz believed that it was important to "hurt the Soviets in Afghanistan" and that ultimately the Stingers made "a huge, perhaps even decisive, difference." The Stingers denied the Soviets the control of the air they had

enjoyed for most of the war, forcing their *Hind* helicopters out of action, and causing their bombers to fly at high, ineffective altitudes. Seven weeks after the Stingers made their first kill in September 1986, Mikhail Gorbachev held a politburo meeting in which he made clear his impatience with the war, and in December of that year it was announced that the Soviets would withdraw from Afghanistan no later than December 1988.

In the wake of the Soviet withdrawal from Afghanistan, that devastated nation reverted to a state of nature as the Mujahideen allies and various clans turned against one another. The attention of the United States drifted elsewhere, and that nation became a breeding ground for a virulent form of Islamic fundamentalism. The verdict of history on Reagan's covert war in Afghanistan, which at first glance appeared to be a stunning cold war success, lost some of its luster when, as the years wore on, the Taliban regime in Afghanistan provided shelter for Osama bin Laden and his al-Qaeda terrorist organization.

POLAND

"Solidarity" was founded in the shipyards of Gdansk, Poland, by Lech Walesa and other activists and had become a powerful force within Poland; for a time the union cowed the Polish government of the prime minister, General Wojciech Jaruzelski. Under pressure from the Soviet Union to curtail anti-Soviet activities, Jaruzelski imposed martial law on December 13, 1981, and his secret police began arresting 5,000 activists in an attempt to crush the first independent trade union in a Communist nation. Jaruzelski justified his actions on the grounds that if he had failed to act, the Soviets would have invaded Poland in an attempt to restore order, which was likely the case. Nonetheless, Western intelligence agencies were convinced that, as Reagan later put it, "the entire exercise had been orchestrated by Moscow." Soviet leader Leonid Brezhnev had engaged in considerable saber-rattling throughout 1981 as Jaruzelski's government made grudging concessions to Solidarity, and at one point in the spring of that year Soviet forces engaged in troop maneuvers along the Polish border. Jaruzelski's imposition of martial law and his arrest of the Solidarity leadership caused an uproar in the Western world, although in many ways Reagan's response was quite tempered. He imposed sanctions on the Soviet Union and Poland, suspended negotiations on a long-term grain sale, banned the Soviet airline Aeroflot from flying into the United States, stopped a number of exchange programs, and, in his most controversial step, he embargoed shipments of pipeline equipment that was to be used in the construction of a natural gas pipeline from Siberia to Western Europe. This last step caused a fissure between the United States and some Western European government who continued to support the pipeline project. It was this moderate response that prompted Reagan ally and conservative columnist George Will to remark in disappointment that the Reagan administration "loved commerce more than it loathed communism."

But behind the scenes Reagan opted once again for a covert response to a foreign policy problem. In May 1982 the president signed National Security Decision Directive 32 to destabilize the Polish government. The destabilization was to be accomplished by keeping Solidarity alive with help from the Catholic Church and from the Polish-born pope, John Paul II. Reagan's first National Security Advisor, Richard Allen, later described this effort as "one of the great secret alliances of all time." The CIA, along with Western trade unions, the Vatican (operating through its secret bank accounts), and the newly created National Endowment for Democracy, funneled tons of communications equipment into Poland. This equipment permitted numerous underground newsletters to flourish (more than 400 such newsletters by 1985) and, more boldly, allowed Solidarity to routinely break into government radio broadcasts with messages like "Solidarity Lives!" or "Resist!" Overt pressure on the part of the pope also hastened the demise of the Soviet-backed government; the pope traveled to Poland and was hailed as a hero by the people. On one such trip, the pope publicly scolded General Jaruzelski while the latter stood on an airport tarmac literally shaking in his boots. By 1987 the pressures exerted by Solidarity and the Catholic Church forced the Jaruzelski government to begin discussions with the church that ultimately led to the election of Lech Walesa as president of Poland. Walesa later claimed that Reagan's anticommunist rhetoric and his policies "gave strength and sustenance" to the people of Poland, and "helped defeat the Communists."

PERSIAN GULF REFLAGGING

In September 1980 Saddam Hussein ordered the Iraqi military to invade Iran, igniting a war that led to the slaughter of hundreds of thousands, perhaps more than 1 million, Iraqi and Iranian soldiers and civilians. The war initially went well for Iraq, but by 1982 Iranian forces had regrouped and counterattacked, causing Iraq to withdraw from its occupied positions in Iran. The Iranian leader, Ayatollah Ruhollah Khomeini, vowed to continue the war until Saddam's regime was destroyed. For the next six years some of the worst fighting of the 20th century occurred, including a return to trench warfare and, for the first time since World War I, the use of chemical weapons. In an example of realpolitik in its starkest form, the Reagan administration tilted its policy back and forth, throwing its support behind whichever side appeared to be losing ground. Unofficially it seemed that the United States was content to let both regimes bleed themselves to death.

Iran gained a clear advantage in the conflict in early 1987, advancing north of Baghdad and south of Basra in a movement that threatened to topple Hussein's government. Around this time the Iranians began to lay mines in the Persian Gulf and threatened the oil tankers plying that body of water with land-based anti-ship Silkworm missiles. Oil-rich Kuwait began to seek assistance, first from the Soviet Union, and later from the United States, in the hope that one, or both, of the superpowers would protect its fleet of tankers, preferably by letting them fly the flag of the United States or the USSR. While there was some concern in the administration about Soviet involvement in the operation, Secretary George Shultz reluctantly accepted the idea of a Russian role, and, in one of their rare instances of agreement in the Reagan era, so did Secretary of Defense Caspar Weinberger, at least according to Shultz. As Shultz later noted in his memoir, "For once, on an issue involving the use of our military force, Cap Weinberger and I were on the same side. . . ." Weinberger disagreed in his memoir, observing that at a meeting of members of Reagan's cabinet, an "extensive but sterile and fruitless" debate over reflagging ensued "with the other [cabinet] members . . . particularly with George Shultz, who did not share my enthusiasm for this mission. . . ." The president ultimately approved the reflagging mission, announcing it two days after the USS *Stark* was struck by Exocet missiles fired from a French-built Iraqi F-1 fighter. The attack appeared to be an accident; the Iraqi pilot apparently thought he was firing at an oil tanker. Thirty-seven American sailors were killed in the attack; Iraq eventually apologized and paid the United States $27 million in compensation.

Congress reacted negatively to President Reagan's initiative, with the Senate voting 91–5

that the president must report on the security situation in the gulf prior to launching the reflagging effort. At one point 110 members of Congress brought suit against the president to force him to initiate the procedures under the War Powers Act. The specter of a quagmire was raised again, with the editorial position of the *Miami Herald* representative of much of the sentiment of the day: "Congress must do whatever is necessary to stop presidential ego and pugnacity from leading this nation into disaster once again." A frustrated George Shultz later proclaimed, "Once again, the signal was being sent to the world that if the United States took on this responsibility, Congress, the press, and the public would probably seek to compel us to pull back at the first sign of danger to our forces. Under those circumstances, other countries did not want to be associated with our effort."

The reflagging effort began inauspiciously—on July 22, 1987, a reflagged tanker, the *Bridgeton*, hit an Iranian mine while being escorted by three U.S. Navy ships. A series of minor skirmishes followed between American and Iranian forces, one of which involved a publicity coup for the United States when it disabled and captured an Iranian vessel that had been laying mines in the Persian Gulf. On October 8, 1987, three Iranian gunboats were sunk by U.S. helicopters, and a week later an Iranian oil rig that served as a base for these gunboats was destroyed. In April 1988 the USS *Roberts* struck a mine and in response the United States attacked oil rig sites and engaged in combat with Iranian vessels; the U.S. Navy destroyed a number of patrol gunboats and small craft; in one day, half the Iranian navy was destroyed. On July 3, 1988, in the final incident prior to the end of hostilities in the region, the USS *Vincennes*, in the midst of an engagement with Iranian speedboats, shot down an Iranian civilian airliner it mistook for a warplane, killing 290 persons on board. In the following days, mediation efforts at the United Nations made progress toward bringing the Iran-Iraq War to a close. Some credit the increasing isolation of Iran, brought about in part by the U.S.-Soviet effort to protect Persian Gulf shipping, coupled with Iraqi success on the battlefield in the spring and summer of that year, in forcing a more flexible negotiating position from Iran. On August 8, 1988, Iran and Iraq accepted a UN-mandated cease-fire.

ANGOLA

In 1975 Portugal granted Angola, the last European colony in Africa, its independence. The newly independent government was controlled by one of the guerrilla factions that fought against Portuguese colonial rule, the Marxist MPLA (Popular Movement for the Liberation of Angola). Two other guerrilla factions, the FNLA (National Front for the Liberation of Angola) and UNITA (National Union for the Total Independence of Angola) formed a coalition government and controlled another region of the country, but by early 1976 UNITA and the FNLA were defeated by MPLA forces with Cuban and Soviet aid. In the mid-1970s the CIA provided covert assistance to the non-Marxist forces in Angola, but Congress, reacting to the Vietnam War and revelations of CIA misdeeds at home and abroad, passed the Clark Amendment in 1976 prohibiting covert aid to Angola.

When the Reagan administration came to power, one of DCI William Casey's top priorities was to overturn the Clark Amendment. Casey allied himself with many members of Congress and pushed for a lifting of the ban, which was seen by some as an example of congressional "micromanagement" of foreign policy and an excessive reaction to the misdeeds of the "imperial presidency." The large Cuban military presence in Angola was a major factor

in this reversal of congressional sentiment. On August 8, 1985, President Reagan signed a foreign aid authorization bill which included a provision repealing the Clark Amendment. At a National Security Planning Group meeting later that month Reagan proclaimed, "we want [Jonas] Savimbi [leader of UNITA] to know the cavalry is coming," and signed a finding that provided $13 million of covert military assistance.

Covert operations in the Reagan years seldom remained covert, and news of the Angola operation soon appeared in the media. President Reagan chose to confirm this operation during a meeting with journalists and television anchormen in November 22, 1985: "we all believe that a covert operation would be more useful to us and have a better chance of success right now than the overt proposal." Reagan was referring to an effort in Congress to provide overt aid to Savimbi's forces, a proposal vehemently opposed by Secretary of State George Shultz, who thereby earned the wrath, or perhaps more accurately, the greater wrath, of conservative true-believers. Shultz later observed, "conservatives in Congress, always suspicious of me and the State Department, went on a virtual rampage. Congressman Jack Kemp called for my resignation because I opposed open assistance to Savimbi. He did not want to listen to realities; the conservatives wanted an open vote as a matter of thumping their collective chests." However, the administration openly invited Savimbi to visit Washington, and he did so in January 1986.

In October 1987 UNITA forces scored an impressive victory in the largest battle of the 12-year Angolan civil war; this victory came in the wake of an increase in covert lethal aid from the United States from $18 million to $40 million. In the last years of the Reagan presidency, Shultz elevated the issue to near the top of his agenda, giving Assistant Secretary of State for African Affairs Chester

Crocker wide latitude to pursue a negotiated settlement to end the civil war. The policy of covert support for UNITA, coupled with attempts at a diplomatic solution, prevailed despite heated opposition from some conservatives in the administration who opposed the negotiating track. Angola was one beneficiary of the cold war thaw between Reagan and Gorbachev in that the United States and the Soviet Union cooperated to achieve a settlement of the contentious civil war; a settlement in which the United Nations also played a key role. The Soviet Union had tired of the Angola conflict as well, and Shultz urged Moscow to pressure the Cubans to be more flexible. In 1988, Cuba agreed to withdraw its troops from Angola, and the withdrawal was completed in 1989. At the same time agreement was reached to remove South African forces from Namibia and allow that nation its independence and freedom from apartheid.

Shultz believed this diplomatic success was attributable to the Reagan Doctrine, which was, as the secretary put it, "replacing the now-retreating Brezhnev Doctrine." As for Angola itself, the progress of the late 1980s vanished during the 1990s, primarily due to Jonas Savimbi's unwillingness to participate in a coalition government. A cease-fire between UNITA and the MPLA was achieved in 1991, when the MPLA agreed to allow UNITA to share power, but Savimbi later rejected the election results after raising accusations of fraud. A series of ineffectual agreements were brokered throughout the 1990s; Savimbi, for all practical purposes defeated and isolated, nonetheless continued to wreak havoc.

TERRORISM IN THE REAGAN YEARS

American interests in the Middle East were repeatedly subject to terrorist attacks during the Reagan years. For an administration viewed as "hawkish" both at home and abroad, the United States, with few exceptions, either did not respond to these attacks, or did so in a restrained manner. Reagan's 1980 campaign had implicitly capitalized on the image of a shackled superpower epitomized by the seizure of American hostages in Iran—the suggestion was that Ronald Reagan would be far more aggressive in dealing with acts of terror against the United States. Like his predecessor, Ronald Reagan found it difficult to deal with an increasingly virulent form of Islamic fundamentalism and its terrorist appendages.

The first major act of terror during the Reagan years occurred on April 18, 1983, when a pick-up truck packed with explosives destroyed the American embassy in Beirut, killing 63 people, including 17 Americans, among them Robert Ames, the CIA's station chief for Beirut, the deputy station chief, and six other CIA officers. (William Buckley, Ames's replacement in Beirut, was kidnapped on March 16, 1984, by Islamic Jihad, who repeatedly tortured him; he died sometime in 1985). In October 1983 Shi'ite suicide bombers destroyed the U.S. Marine barracks in Beirut, killing 241 Marines and 58 French paratroopers in a separate attack on the French military headquarters. In December of that year, car bombs were detonated in front of the U.S. and French embassies in Kuwait City, killing five and injuring 86.

The new year brought no respite from terror; on January 18, 1984, Malcolm Kerr, the president of the American University of Beirut and an expert on Arab politics, was murdered in the stairwell leading to his university office. On September 20, 1984, another car bomb exploded in front of the U.S. embassy annex in East Beirut, killing 16 and injuring the American ambassador. Reagan came under heavy criticism when he was asked how the United States would respond; he commented that it

President Reagan holds a National Security Council meeting on the TWA hijacking in the White House Situation Room, June 16, 1985.

would be a simple matter of repairing the building, comparable to remodeling the family kitchen. On June 14, 1985, Hezbollah gunmen hijacked TWA Flight 847 en route from Athens to Rome and demanded the release of 700 Arabs held by the Israelis. A U.S. Navy diver, Robert Stetham, 23 years old, was killed by the hijackers and his body dumped on the tarmac in the midst of the 17-day hijacking. The passengers' ordeal ended after a successful Syrian mediation effort. On October 8, 1985, the Italian passenger liner *Achille Lauro* was hijacked by four PLO terrorists, and a wheelchair-bound American passenger, 69-year-old Leon Klinghoffer, was killed and dumped at sea (his body was later returned to the United States after being found on a beach in Syria). The four hijackers eventually released the passengers, and attempted to fly from Egypt to Algiers, but the United States intercepted the Egyptair jet and forced it to land in Sicily. An armed standoff ensued between U.S. and Italian authorities, with the Italians refusing to hand the hijackers over to the United States. Italy eventually tried the four hijackers, but allowed the mastermind of the hijacking, Abu Abbas, to go free, refusing to extradite him to the United States. He later reemerged as a member of Yasser Arafat's PLO leadership cadre.

In April 1986 a bomb was planted in a Berlin disco that killed one U.S. serviceman and one civilian and wounded 230 others. The administration had electronic intercepts indicating that the Libyans were behind the attack, and President Reagan responded by ordering an attack by U.S. Air Force and Navy aircraft. The final major act of terror directed against the United States during the Reagan years occurred on December 21, 1988, when a Pan American Boeing 747 traveling from London to New York exploded over Lockerbie, Scotland, killing 259 passengers and 11 people on the ground. On January 31, 2001, a former Libyan intelligence agent, Basset Ali al-Megrahi, was sentenced to 20 years to life for placing the bomb on the flight. Some observers contended the Pan Am bombing was an act of retaliation for Reagan's April 1986 bombing of Libya, while others argued that the bombing was orchestrated by the Iranians. But in August 2003 Libya formally accepted responsibility for the bombing in a bid to end its international isolation.

During the mid to late 1980s a number of Westerners, including many Americans, were kidnapped by the Iranian-backed Hezbollah terrorist group in Lebanon, and the fate of these hostages haunted President Reagan. He later observed in his memoir, "long before I ever entered the Oval Office, I had adopted a very simple philosophy regarding the question of what we as a nation should do if an American was held captive abroad . . . it was up to the rest of us to do everything we could to restore those rights, wherever it took us, anywhere in the world that person was. It was a policy I followed for eight years as President." He was determined to secure their release, and made it a priority to stay in contact with the families of the hostages. It was his deep personal concern for the hostages in Lebanon that led Reagan

into the morass of the Iran-contra affair, and caused the greatest damage to his presidency. The revelation that Reagan traded arms for hostages (although he never believed he had) was devastating, for this was the same tough-talking president who once vowed that terrorists "can run but they can't hide" and that "America will never make concessions to terrorists—to do so would only invite more terrorism."

Overall, the Reagan administration found it as difficult as any other administration in the last quarter of the 20th century to deal with sporadic but deadly incidents of terrorism rooted in the Middle East. To his credit, Secretary of State George Shultz made a concerted effort to elevate the issue of terrorism to the top of the nation's agenda, advocating the use of military force to strike at terrorist havens. In a speech delivered in October 1984, Shultz argued that "we cannot allow ourselves to become the Hamlet of nations, worrying endlessly over whether and how to respond . . . we must reach a consensus in this country that our responses should go beyond passive defense to consider means of active prevention, preemption, and retaliation . . . the public must understand before the fact that occasions will come when their government must act before each and every fact is known—and the decisions cannot be tied to the opinion polls." But Secretary of Defense Weinberger disagreed; his Weinberger "doctrine" listed certain conditions that had to be met before the United States could employ the "last resort," the use of force. Weinberger argued that there must be a "reasonable assurance" that the action would have the support of the American people before forces could be sent into harm's way. In Shultz's view, "in the face of terrorism, or any other . . . unclear, gray-area dangers facing us in the contemporary world . . . his was a counsel of inaction bordering on paralysis." The lack of accord between the two key cabinet members muddled the administration's stance on terrorism; it finally lost all credibility with the Iran-contra revelations. It took the September 2001 attacks on the World Trade Center and the Pentagon for the United States to formulate a coherent and concerted response to terrorism.

THE REAGAN DEFENSE BUILDUP AND "STAR WARS"

Ronald Reagan made the condition of the nation's armed forces one of the principal themes of his 1980 campaign for the presidency. He claimed that the Carter administration had allowed the nation's defenses to deteriorate, that the armed forces had become a "hollow" military. Reagan's supporters cited as an example the failure of the Iranian hostage rescue mission in April 1980. The dead bodies and the wreckage of American aircraft at the "Desert One" landing site in Iran convinced many Americans that the nation's military had not recovered from the debacle of Vietnam. The "Desert One" tragedy came on the heels of the Soviet invasion of Afghanistan; both issues fed the image, fair or not, that President Carter was a weak executive presiding over an ineffectual military. Reagan claimed that "militarily, our nation was seriously in danger of falling behind the Soviet Union at a time a former naval officer was holding the watch as Commander in Chief . . . on any given day, I was told that as many as half the ships in our navy couldn't leave port because of a lack of spare parts or crew and half our military aircraft couldn't fly for lack of spare parts; the overwhelming majority of our military enlisted personnel were high school dropouts."

Reagan selected as his secretary of defense a man with a reputation as a cost cutter, fellow Californian Caspar Weinberger. As OMB director during the Nixon years, Weinberger was tagged with the nickname "Cap the Knife," due to his propensity for penny-pinching. Yet Weinberger would go on to preside over the largest peacetime buildup of military force in the nation's history, or for that matter, in the history of the world. "My brief," Weinberger noted, "was to regain our military and defensive strength. The President had said many times—on the stump and many times to me personally—that if it ever came down to a question of a balanced budget or a strong military, he would always choose a strong military." During the campaign, candidate Reagan had called for a 5 percent increase in real growth per year for the Defense Department, but once in office he proposed what amounted to a real growth rate of 10 percent per year, according to OMB director David Stockman. One of the first steps taken in that direction was to add $32 billion to the Carter administration's defense requests for fiscal years 1981 and 1982. The defense budget increased in real terms by 13.3 percent in fiscal year 1981; 11.5 percent in fiscal year 1982; 7.9 percent in fiscal year 1983; 4.7 percent in fiscal year 1984; 7.6 percent in fiscal year 1985, but then decreased in real terms for the remainder of Reagan's presidency.

These increased defense appropriations were used to purchase some big-ticket items for the services. Weinberger and navy secretary John Lehman were concerned over a growing Soviet fleet with improved war fighting capabilities, and they set a goal of building a 600-ship U.S. Navy, including 15 aircraft carrier task forces. The administration inherited a 455-ship navy with 12 carrier task forces, and many of those 455 ships were in need of repair. The army had been eager to acquire a new tank as part of its conventional arsenal, and Weinberger succeeded in deploying the M-1 "Abrams" tank, after, as he put it, "years of design, redesign, and indecision." Additionally, Reagan revived the air force's B-1 program, which had been cancelled by President Carter, and eventually built 100 of the swing-wing bombers. Secretary Weinberger saw the B-1 as a replacement for the aging B-52 fleet, which was a part of the triad of strategic weapons arrayed against the Soviet Union, including sea-launched nuclear missiles housed on submarines, and land-based intercontinental ballistic missiles (ICBMs).

In the strategic weapons arena, the administration pushed for the development of the MX missile to replace the Minuteman missile, which was deployed in the 1960s. President Reagan rejected the Carter administration's "race track" proposal to house the MX in multiple shelters in which 200 missiles would be constantly moved among 4,600 shelters to be built in the western United States. Instead the administration proposed housing the MX in hardened Minuteman sites, a position which prevailed after Reagan's lobbying produced some narrow legislative victories from a reluctant Congress.

But by far the most controversial defense program of the Reagan years was the Strategic Defense Initiative (SDI), which was quickly labeled by its critics as "Star Wars." Reagan's visit to the North American Aerospace Defense Command at Cheyenne Mountain in Colorado Springs, Colorado, on July 31, 1979, reaffirmed his belief that the doctrine of Mutual Assured Destruction (MAD) was immoral; that the U.S. government owed its people more than agreeing to an unwritten pact whereby both sides would exercise restraint because of a shared capacity to incinerate each other. Reagan was accompanied on his visit to Cheyenne Mountain by Martin Anderson, his domestic policy adviser, and according to Anderson, Reagan was "deeply concerned about what he learned. He couldn't believe the United States had no defense against Soviet missiles. . . . 'The only options he [the President] would have,' Reagan said, 'would be to press the button or

do nothing. They're both bad. We should have some way of defending ourselves against nuclear missiles.'" Reagan described his reaction to the MAD doctrine in his memoir: "Somehow this didn't seem to me to be something that would send you to bed feeling safe. It was like having two westerners standing in a saloon aiming their guns at each other's head— permanently. There had to be a better way."

The Republican Party, which nominated him in 1980, seemed to agree—the platform for that year, thanks to the efforts of its two key drafters, Martin Anderson and Richard Allen, included the following passage, "We reject the mutual assured destruction (MAD) strategy of the Carter Administration which limits the President during crisis to a Hobson's choice between mass mutual suicide and surrender" and committed the party to the development of an "effective anti-ballistic missile system."

Early in his first term, Reagan asked the Joint Chiefs of Staff to begin exploring the feasibility of a defensive system that could intercept ballistic missiles. Reagan received encouragement for his project from an ad hoc group of advisers both official and unofficial, including one of the fathers of the hydrogen bomb, Edward Teller; from air force general Daniel Graham, former head of the Defense Intelligence Agency; and from his own science adviser, George Keyworth, a Teller protégé, and Republican senator Malcolm Wallop of Wyoming.

Reagan publicly unveiled his SDI proposal in an address to the nation on March 23, 1983. The president defended his buildup of conventional and nuclear forces to counter the Soviet Union, and went on to deal with the problem of Soviet and Cuban influence in Central America, particularly in Grenada. To the surprise of many, Reagan concluded his remarks with an appeal to change America's strategic doctrine from offense to defense to insure that the nightmare scenario of nuclear war was rendered obsolete. The "specter of retaliation," of "mutual threat," was a "sad commentary on the human condition," the president noted, "Wouldn't it be better to save lives than to avenge them? Are we not capable of demonstrating our peaceful intentions by applying all our abilities and our ingenuity to achieving a truly lasting stability? I think we are. Indeed, we must." Reagan's "vision" of a more hopeful future rested on his belief that America's technological creativity could lead to the development of systems that could "intercept and destroy strategic ballistic missiles before they reached our own soil or that of our allies."

The Strategic Defense Initiative was greeted with skepticism by members of the scientific community, many of whom contended that this system would require such sophisticated technology as to be unaffordable, not to mention unworkable. Traditional allies were uneasy with SDI as well, fearing that the system would allow the United States to disengage from NATO and its other alliances, and retreat into a fortress America. Many prominent Republicans and Democrats from the Kennedy, Johnson, and Nixon administrations, who considered MAD to be a morally questionable doctrine, nonetheless argued that it kept the peace for decades. SDI would be destabilizing, these critics argued, and would likely fuel an arms race to build weapons that could evade SDI, such as "suitcase" nuclear weapons, or additional submarine-launched missiles capable of being fired at close range and underneath the "high frontier" SDI systems. Some argued that SDI ran the risk of fueling an arms race to create weapons capable of destroying elements of the defensive systems themselves as they orbited the earth. Many fiscal conservatives and congressional Democrats viewed SDI as a Reagan-Weinberger boondoggle guaranteed to push the DOD budget, and more important, the federal deficit, fur-

ther out of control. Reagan's defense spending, coupled with his tax cuts, were seen as coming at the expense of social programs designed to assist the poor.

SDI was never funded to the extent that Reagan desired, but it was proceeding fast enough by 1986 that it became the major point of contention between Gorbachev and Reagan at the Reykjavik summit of October 1986. By that time the project had met with some success, and funding had more than doubled since fiscal year 1985 to approximately $3.3 billion in fiscal year 1987. Gorbachev was determined to stop SDI, and Reagan was just as determined to preserve it. The latter refused to yield on SDI, and both men left the summit disappointed and convinced that the other had missed a historic opportunity to dramatically reduce, if not outright eliminate, the two countries' nuclear weapons stockpiles. In the following months, however, the two sides reached an agreement on intermediate nuclear forces.

It was, and remains, a major point of contention whether Reagan's SDI program contributed to the collapse of the Soviet Union, or whether such a system is even feasible. To this day SDI remains a controversial and divisive issue. It was claimed by some critics, including the authors Frances Fitzgerald and Garry Wills, that SDI was a Hollywood fantasy of Reagan's, inspired by the movies *Torn Curtain* and *Murder in the Air*. In the latter film the future president played the role of Brass Bancroft, who was assigned to protect a secret wonder weapon, the "inertia projector," that shot down enemy aircraft by disabling their electrical systems.

Defenders of the Strategic Defense Initiative contend that the Soviets feared American technological prowess, and that in a head-to-head competition in such an advanced high-tech undertaking, the Kremlin understood it would lose. The Soviet economy had been staggering for some time and Mikhail Gorbachev had staked his future and the future of the Communist regime on the success of "glasnost" (openness) and "perestroika" (reform and restructuring). Underlying much of Gorbachev's campaign to change the Soviet system was the desire to transfer resources away from defense to boost the standard of living for Soviet citizens. The pressure to counter SDI, either through building a Soviet version of an antiballistic missile defense or countering with new offensive innovations was a disturbing prospect for the Kremlin, so the admirers of SDI contend. After the fall of the Soviet Union, some former Soviet officials endorsed this view, including former foreign minister Alexander Bessmertnykh, who observed that Reagan's policies, particularly SDI, "accelerated the decline of the Soviet Union." Former George H.W. Bush secretary of state James Baker claims that he knew "from talking to Gorbachev, that the SDI thing scared the Soviet Union to death; they couldn't compete." But publicly, most former Soviet officials, including Mikhail Gorbachev, denied that this was the case.

Funding for SDI all but evaporated in the early 1990s, but Speaker of the House Newt Gingrich's "Contract with America" committed congressional Republicans to SDI, and with the Republican takeover of Congress in 1994 the project was resurrected. The George W. Bush administration elevated missile defense to the top of its agenda, but justified the program on the grounds of protecting the United States from a missile attack from a "rogue" state such as North Korea.

THE "EVIL EMPIRE" AND FLIGHT KAL 007

The most controversial speech Ronald Reagan delivered during his eight years in office was his address in Orlando, Florida, to the National

Association of Evangelicals on March 8, 1983. The speech focused on issues important to religious conservatives, including prayer in school, abortion, and parental consent requirements for teenagers using contraceptives. The president also shared with his audience his belief that "there is sin and evil in the world" and that "our nation . . . has a legacy of evil with which it must deal," a reference to slavery and the struggle of African Americans for equal rights. But the passages that ignited a firestorm in the American media and overseas appeared in the closing paragraphs, when Reagan claimed that the Soviet Union was preaching the "supremacy of the state" and declaring its "omnipotence over individual man" and seeking to dominate "all of the peoples on the Earth." They were, therefore, "the focus of evil in the modern world." Reagan urged his listeners to heed the lessons of "history," which taught that "simple minded appeasement or wishful thinking about our adversaries is folly." Referring to the nuclear freeze movement, Reagan called on the evangelicals to resist the argument that the superpowers were "equally at fault," for to do so one would have to "ignore the facts of history and the aggressive impulses of an evil empire." He also urged his audience to fight the temptation to "call the arms race a giant misunderstanding" and "remove yourself from the struggle between right and wrong and good and evil."

Reagan later reflected on the "evil empire" speech, noting that for "too long our leaders were unable to describe the Soviet Union as it actually was. The keepers of our foreign-policy knowledge—in other words, most liberal foreign-affairs scholars, the State Department, and various columnists—found it illiberal and provocative to be so honest. I've always believed, however, that it's important to define differences, because there are choices and decisions to be made in life and history." The reaction among the "keepers" of American foreign policy was harshly critical, including from some fellow Republicans. Media reaction was highly critical, with Strobe Talbott of *Time* arguing that Reagan's use of the bully pulpit to "bait" the Soviet bear "made a bad situation worse," for when "a chief of state talks that way, he roils Soviet insecurities." Columnist Anthony Lewis of the *New York Times* described the speech as "simplistic" and "terribly dangerous" and finally, "primitive . . . the only word for it." Historian Henry Steele Commager called it "the worst presidential speech in American history," because it was a "gross appeal to religious prejudice." Reaction in the USSR and in Eastern Europe differed between the man on the street and those in leadership positions; Soviet leader Yuri Andropov accused Reagan of deliberate provocation and claimed he was obsessed by a "bellicose, lunatic anti-communism," while years later many Soviet and Eastern European dissidents talked about the euphoria they felt when Reagan bluntly endorsed their view of the illegitimacy of the Soviet government.

The original draft of the speech was crafted by a cigar-chomping White House speechwriter by the name of Tony Dolan, a graduate of Yale more comfortable with his Boston Irish roots. Dolan had been a Pulitzer Prize–winning reporter and was a frequent contributor to William F. Buckley's *National Review*. Like Reagan and Buckley, Dolan considered Whittaker Chambers to be a hero, and the "evil empire" speech was clearly influenced by Chambers's *Witness*. In fact, the speech included a reference to Chambers and a passage from *Witness*, which was the bible for cold war American conservatives. Dolan was considered an extremist by the pragmatists in the White House, among them communications director David Gergen, who was upset with "the outrageous statements" in an earlier draft of the "evil empire" speech and worked with Deputy National Security Advisor Robert McFarlane to moderate the final draft. But as Reagan biographer Lou Cannon has observed, the "evil empire" speech was seminal Reagan, and reflected his deep disdain for communism as an immoral ideology destined for the ash heap of history.

Reagan had a bond with his speechwriters, for they shared his love of ideas, and his writers always believed they held a special place in his administration. As Dolan noted, "Ronald Reagan knows how important his speeches are. Not only do they provide a statement of purpose for the government; it is through his speeches that [government] managers understand where they're going." Reagan was well known for not paying attention to the details of governing, but he paid attention to his speeches, and frequently offered suggestions or corrections to his speechwriter's drafts. This was true of the "evil empire" speech, where the president actually toughened the language about the Soviet Union. Dolan had written "surely historians will see they are the focus of evil in the modern world," and Reagan changed it to "they are the focus of evil in the modern world."

Reagan's assessment of the Soviet government seemed to be vindicated six months later when a Korean Air Lines 747 drifted into Soviet airspace and was shot down with 269 passengers on board, including Congressman Lawrence McDonald of Georgia and 60 other Americans. Reagan was notified of the attack while vacationing at his California ranch (Rancho del Cielo), when he was notified by his National Security Advisor, William Clark, that a Korean airliner was "forced down or shot down by the Soviets." Reagan responded, "Bill, let's pray that it's not true." The Soviets had tracked the commercial airliner for two and a half hours, and refused for days to admit they had shot the plane down, insisting that it had "crashed," and yet at the same time the Kremlin claimed the plane was on an intelligence mission, a theory that persists to this day. Soviet marshall Nikolai Ogarkov said that KAL 007 was on a "deliberate, thoroughly planned intelligence operation." The Soviets, although they denied it at the time, discovered the black boxes carried by civilian aircraft; in fact, the orders to shoot the aircraft down came from a four-star general, obeying an Andropov-era decree allowing no leeway for any type of "intruder planes."

President Reagan initially referred to the incident as a "barbarous act" and many in his administration lobbied for, as Secretary Shultz put it, "drastic responses," but while Reagan's rhetoric was tough his response was muted. In a public address to the nation on September 5 he observed that "what can only be called the Korean Air Line massacre" was not a surprise, for "such inhuman brutality" conjured up memories of "Czechoslovakia, Hungary, Poland, the gassing of villages in Afghanistan." In the end Reagan accepted George Shultz's counsel that a restrained response would be best, and he refused suggestions that he tighten American economic sanctions, break off arms talks in Geneva and Vienna, or order a wholesale expulsion of KGB agents in the United States. Reagan and Shultz believed that the beating the Soviets were taking in the world media would have a lasting impact on the Kremlin's standing in international public opinion. Despite the restrained American response, the downing of KAL 007 was part of a chain of events in the fall of 1983, some violent, others less so, that elevated superpower tensions to levels not witnessed since the Cuban missile crisis.

THE INF TREATY (INTERMEDIATE NUCLEAR FORCES)

During the Carter years certain NATO countries, West Germany in particular, had raised concerns over the Soviet deployment of the SS-20 medium-range missiles throughout Eastern Europe and portions of Asia. President Carter decided to meet this challenge in 1979 by deploying 572 U.S. missiles, Pershing IIs and ground-launched cruise missiles (GLCMs), while at the same time proceeding with negotiations to achieve parity in medium-range forces between the Warsaw Pact and NATO. This "two-track" approach was ultimately endorsed by the Reagan administration, and the so-called zero option was the name given to Reagan's negotiating stance, since he called for the complete removal of all Soviet SS-20s in Europe and Asia, in return for the United States canceling deployment of the Pershing IIs and the GLCMs. At the time the proposal was made in 1981, it was assumed by many that it was non-negotiable, that the Soviets would never agree to an arrangement requiring them to eliminate an entire weapons system before the United States had deployed a single missile. There is some evidence that Defense Secretary Weinberger and Assistant Secretary of Defense Richard Perle, the architect of the "zero option," believed this as well. Nonetheless, the proposal appealed to Reagan's dream of eliminating nuclear weapons from both countries' arsenals, and it was formally presented to the Soviets, who promptly rejected the proposal.

Reagan's decision to continue with the deployment of the Pershing IIs and GLCMs generated deep opposition from the budding nuclear freeze movement. When the deployment decision was coupled with Reagan's hardline rhetoric toward the Soviet Union, many observers were convinced that the superpowers were drifting toward conflict. Senator Edward Kennedy (D-Mass.) remarked in 1982 that "the arms race rushes ahead toward nuclear confrontation that could well mean the annihilation of the human race." Former secretary of state Cyrus Vance found the administration's stance toward the Soviet Union to be "needlessly provocative . . . bear-baiting," and added that "the clock is ticking." The nuclear freeze movement reached its peak in the months leading to the deployment of the Pershing IIs and the cruise missiles on November 23, 1983, the first day of deployment in West Germany. Dr. Helen Caldicott, one of the leaders of the American freeze effort, called for a universal order free from "artificial distinctions" imposed by male politicians, "We're thinking of our babies; there are no Communist babies; there are no capitalist babies. A baby is a baby is a baby." Discussions of the effect of "nuclear winter" were held on television newscasts, in university classrooms, and on the nation's editorial pages. More than 2 million protesters turned out in Europe on October 22 and 23, and the American Broadcasting Company ran a drama called "The Day After," three days before the West Germany deployment; the drama depicted the impact of a nuclear strike on Kansas.

Perhaps most worrisome to the Reagan administration was the fact that the National Conference of Catholic Bishops supported the freeze. Catholic voters represented a substantial bloc within the Reagan electoral coalition, and as the 1984 election neared, the prospect of a public confrontation with the bishops worried the administration. Their most vocal opponent was Chicago archbishop Joseph Bernardin, whose Committee on War and Peace issued a statement labeling elements of U.S. nuclear strategy "immoral." Reagan and his advisers tried to convince the bishops that their stance would weaken the American arms control position, but to no avail. Reagan, bolstered by the support of British prime minister Margaret Thatcher, German chancellor Helmut Kohl, and French president François Mitterrand, held firm, and proceeded with the deployment throughout the fall of 1983. On November 23, 1983, the day the first Pershing IIs arrived in West Germany, the Soviets promptly walked out of the INF negotiations in Geneva, vowing never to return until the Pershing IIs and the GLCMs were removed.

They also refused to set a time to resume the START talks (Strategic Arms Reduction Talks), as well as refused to set a time for negotiations on conventional forces (Mutual Balance Force Reductions) being held in Vienna. They would eventually reverse these position, but as the winter of 1983 began, the cold war rarely seemed chillier.

Almost a year would elapse before there was any significant movement on the arms control front. In the aftermath of Ronald Reagan's landslide victory in November 1984, Secretary of State Shultz called on the Soviet Union for "concrete deeds" that could lead toward improved relations between the United States and the Soviet Union. The Kremlin responded by indicating a willingness to participate in arms control talks between Shultz and Soviet foreign minister Andrei Gromyko, and hinted at a possible resumption of the suspended negotiations. In January 1985 Shultz met with Gromyko in Geneva for talks that were described as "procedural and philosophical," but at the conclusion of the talks Shultz announced, "there are many tough and complicated issues still to be resolved, but we have here in Geneva agreed on the objectives for new negotiations on nuclear and space arms."

The most important breakthrough came with the elevation of Mikhail Gorbachev as the leader of the Soviet Union. Reagan dealt with four Soviet leaders in his eight years in office—Leonid Brezhnev, Yuri Andropov, Konstantin Chernenko, and Gorbachev. This frequency of turnover prompted the president to remark that the Soviet leaders "kept dying on me." In fact the septuagenarian American president seemed a positively spry and robust leader in comparison to his sclerotic Communist counterparts—Gorbachev excepted. On Monday, March 11, 1985, Gorbachev was named Chernenko's successor after the latter died the preceding weekend (as was the custom, the Kremlin provided almost no information on the circumstances or time of Chernenko's death). The initial reaction in the West to Gorbachev's rise to power bordered on the euphoric; many in the West shared the view of British prime minister Margaret Thatcher, who stated, "I like the man. We can do business together." (Some in the West remained skeptical about Gorbachev; they recalled in the early days of the ascension of Yuri Andropov there were similar glowing accounts in the media of the former KGB chief as a renaissance man who loved to listen to American jazz).

The day after Gorbachev assumed power, the Soviet Union and the United States resumed arms negotiations in Geneva, and in July 1985 Shultz met with Soviet foreign minister Eduard Shevardnadze (who had replaced Andrei Gromyko as foreign minister earlier that month) in Helsinki to begin planning for a Reagan-Gorbachev summit in November (*see* Reagan and Gorbachev Summits on page 92). Shevardnadze was a fresh face, a Georgian who seemed intent on breaking with the past and offering, for the first time on the Soviet side, proposals to reduce nuclear arsenals. The November summit in Geneva was a success; Reagan and Gorbachev developed a rapport and each vowed to accelerate arms control talks, including the INF negotiations, and hold additional summits in 1986 and 1987. The "spirit of Geneva" was captured in a widely circulated photograph of the two smiling leaders seated in front of a roaring fire.

President Reagan and Soviet general secretary Gorbachev at the first summit in Geneva, Switzerland, November 19, 1985

In April 1987 Secretary Shultz visited Moscow and was presented with a proposal from the Kremlin of "equality at zero in short-range INF missiles." This was followed in July by another breakthrough, when Gorbachev announced that he would agree to eliminate long-range INF missiles; the zero option now became known as the "double-zero" option. Additional obstacles regarding the disposition of British and French nuclear weapons and the status of German-owned Pershing missiles that were equipped with nuclear weapons owned and operated by the United States were overcome in the following weeks. As word of an agreement neared, serious opposition to the treaty began to emerge among Reagan's fellow Republicans, in particular from former president Nixon, Henry Kissinger, Brent Scowcroft, and Republican senators Jesse Helms, Dan Quayle, and Malcolm Wallop. Many NATO allies had qualms about the agreement as well, fearing that it would "decouple" the United States from Europe. Doubts were raised about Reagan's ability to withstand Gorbachev's charm, and some former conservative allies on Capitol Hill and in the media began to wonder if a politically wounded President Reagan, still reeling from the Iran-contra affair, was abandoning his anticommunist principles and embracing a flawed arms control agreement in order to bolster his standing in the history books.

Reagan was undeterred, and at one point referred to his critics as having accepted the inevitability of war and suggested they were uninformed. Reagan proceeded ahead, and the INF treaty was signed in the East Room of the White House on December 8, 1987; for the first time the superpowers had committed themselves to eliminate an entire class of nuclear weapons, and had agreed to an intrusive inspection regime allowing inspectors to visit each one another's facilities on very short notice. It also lopsidedly favored the United States by requiring the destruction of approxi-

mately 1,500 deployed Soviet warheads as opposed to 350 American missiles. As Secretary Shultz observed, the treaty's terms were "almost exactly what Ronald Reagan, to the scoffing of arms control experts, had proposed back in 1981 . . . all of those were 'Reagan proposals' that had been dismissed by the people 'who knew everything' as impossible to attain!" During the signing ceremony Reagan repeated, to the distress of Gorbachev, one of his favorite lines in dealing with the Kremlin, "Doveryai, no proverayyai—trust but verify." Gorbachev laughed and said in response "you repeat that at every meeting," to which Reagan responded, "I like it."

Reagan's success in the INF negotiations derived in part from his persistence and stubbornness, a quality that aides and associates had observed for some time. Once he settled on a course of action he was often unmovable. This trait was a source of strength and of weakness, for Reagan would often hold a position even in the face of overwhelming factual evidence to the contrary (for instance, his contention during the Iran-contra affair that he never traded arms for hostages). But in the case of the "zero option," Reagan's determination to deploy the Pershing IIs and GLCMs in the face of international protest, followed by his resolve to eliminate this class of nuclear weapons, led to the most significant foreign policy triumph of his second term in office.

THE REAGAN AND GORBACHEV SUMMITS

The first summit between Ronald Reagan and Mikhail Gorbachev took place in Geneva November 19–21, 1985. This highly anticipated meeting generated extensive news coverage, since it was the first personal contact between an American president and a general secretary of the Communist Party of the Soviet

Union since Jimmy Carter and Leonid Brezhnev met in Vienna in June 1979. The fact that as recently as 1983 the president had deemed the Soviet Union an illegitimate regime served to fuel interest in the summit—many tuned in to news coverage simply to see how Ronald Reagan would deal with the Number One Communist of the "evil empire."

The presummit expectations were that the younger Gorbachev, with his mastery of detail and his vigor, would overwhelm the older American president. Gorbachev did outmaneuver Reagan in the weeks leading up to the summit by proposing a 50 percent cut in strategic weapons, and this, coupled with Reagan's oft-stated devotion to SDI, appeared to put the Americans on the defensive. Those presummit speculators who gave Gorbachev the advantage underestimated Reagan's ability to hold his own in negotiations when he had done his homework, and in this instance, as his long-time biographer Lou Cannon has noted, Reagan had done it. According to Cannon, "Reagan probably prepared with greater care for the Geneva summit than for any other event of his presidency." Those who bet on Gorbachev also ignored the fact that the White House "spin" operation led by Michael Deaver (who was brought out of retirement to assist in the planning for the Geneva summit) was far more adept at image making than its Soviet counterparts.

On that chilly November day when the two men first met, much was made of the fact that the elder Reagan appeared coatless, while the youthful Gorbachev was bundled against the cold wearing an overcoat, scarf, and hat. An image-conscious White House staff was delighted to see that the opening salvo in the media war went to Reagan. The two leaders immediately met one on one (not counting interpreters) in what was supposed to have been a 10-minute exchange. As the clock ticked away well past the 10-minute deadline, President Reagan's personal assistant, James Kuhn, asked Secretary Shultz whether he should enter the room and give the president an opportunity to stop the meeting, to which the often prickly Shultz replied, "if you're dumb enough to do that, you shouldn't be in your job." Instead, Reagan and Gorbachev spent an hour and 15 minutes with each other and emerged smiling. The ice was broken. In part, Reagan was charmed by Gorbachev, as he later admitted, "there was this warmth in his face and his style, not the coldness bordering on hatred I'd seen in most senior Soviet officials I'd met until then."

The warmth of the initial morning session did not extend into the afternoon, when the conversation turned to Afghanistan, and then on to arms control issues, and in particular the subject of SDI. After Gorbachev talked about the withdrawal of Soviet troops from Afghanistan in the context of a "general political settlement between us," the subject quickly turned to arms control and SDI, and Reagan vigorously defended SDI and expressed his revulsion at the doctrine of mutual assured destruction. Gorbachev claimed that SDI would expand the arms race and was skeptical of Reagan's pledge to share the technology with the Soviets. When things got heated the two men left the room for a walk in the bitter cold, and spent time alone again in the villa's pool house. They agreed on reciprocal summits, first in Washington and then in Moscow, but while this was a sign that the personal rapport between Gorbachev and Reagan continued to improve, there was little progress on the substantive issues. A dinner that evening at the Soviet mission was also filled with warmth, but again no real progress on the major points of contention between the United States and the Soviet Union was achieved by day's end.

Day two's discussions were held at the Soviet embassy in Geneva and began with another private exchange between the two leaders, with the focus on human rights and regional conflicts in Nicaragua and Afghanistan. Gorbachev responded to Reagan's criticism of the USSR's human rights record by criticizing the unemployment rate in the United States and argued that the American record regarding its treatment of African Americans and women was a violation of human rights, to which Reagan replied that Gorbachev's information was out of date; "things have changed," the president countered. At a later plenary session the exchanges became more heated with Gorbachev making his strongest criticism of SDI, and Reagan "exploded," according to Secretary Shultz. The president "spoke passionately" about missile defense and "expressed his abhorrence at having to rely on the ability to 'wipe each other out' as the means of keeping the peace." Once again, the evening festivities belied the fact that there were considerable differences between the two sides, for each man warmly toasted the other. The problem was that an agreed statement between the two leaders was due to be issued the next morning, and there was no agreement in either delegation as to the language that statement should contain. A marathon, all-night negotiating session ensued between the American and Soviet delegations and by 4:45 A.M. an agreed statement had been crafted. The statement committed both sides to a 50 percent reduction in nuclear weapons and called for "early progress" on an interim INF agreement. A renewed commitment was made to talks on conventional and chemical weapons, and lesser agreements were reached on air safety in the northern Pacific, resuming talks on airline flights between the two nations, and opening consulates in Kiev and New York. At the closing ceremony Reagan and Gorbachev again appeared at ease with one another; Reagan, in fact, later told Lou Cannon, that he "shared 'a kind of chemistry' with Gorbachev."

This "chemistry" was not in evidence at the summit in Reykjavik, Iceland, on October 11 and 12, 1986. The exchanges between Reagan and Gorbachev in "Hofdi House," which Icelanders believed was a haunted house, were as chilly as the wind blowing off Faxafloi Bay. Gorbachev arrived at the summit determined to achieve substantial cuts in nuclear stockpiles and block the development of Reagan's Strategic Defense Initiative, but on this point the American president was equally determined not to yield. Gorbachev announced that he was prepared to accept much of what President Reagan had proposed regarding the "zero option" on intermediate nuclear forces in Europe, although he excluded the Soviet INF systems in Asia from his proposal. Both leaders expressed their desire, much to the consternation of many of their advisers (Caspar Weinberger on the American side), and foreign allies (Margaret Thatcher, for instance), to eliminate all nuclear weapons through a process of phased reductions. The prospect of such a radical agreement between the world's superpowers was hard for many to grasp, and yet it came close to becoming reality. Prime Minister Thatcher later wrote that "my own reaction when I heard how far the Americans had been prepared to go was as if there had been an earthquake underneath my feet." Before, during, and after the Iceland summit doubts were again raised about the president's ability to go "head to head" with his younger, more technically knowledgeable counterpart.

Gorbachev pressed the issue of compliance with the 1972 Anti-Ballistic Missile (ABM) Treaty, of which Article Five of the treaty stated, "Each party undertakes not to develop, test, or deploy ABM systems or components which are sea-based, air-based, space-based, or mobile land-based." Gorbachev was aware that there was a deep division within the Reagan administration, primarily between the State Department and the Pentagon, whether to interpret the treaty narrowly or broadly in terms of allowing development of SDI. He also understood that there was widespread opposition to SDI in the United States Senate, and that many senators were urging the administration to strictly abide by the ABM treaty as well as the unratified SALT II treaty negotiated by Jimmy Carter and Leonid Brezhnev. Weinberger and Richard Perle, his assistant secretary of defense for international security policy, were strong advocates for a broad interpretation of the ABM treaty. Much to their delight Weinberger and Perle's position was supported from an unlikely quarter, that of the State Department's legal adviser Abraham Sofaer. But for Weinberger "this arcane legal argument" was neither "relevant [n]or very useful" because the president was determined to develop SDI and "it was clear that we could not deploy the system without changing the ABM treaty." One of Weinberger's most vocal opponents within the administration was veteran arms control negotiator Paul Nitze who apparently viewed Reagan's devotion to SDI as an impediment to negotiating an arms control treaty. Nitze played an active role at the Iceland summit, and while Weinberger did not attend, he dispatched his deputy Richard Perle to ensure the Pentagon's position was heard at the negotiating table.

Rapid progress was made on that first day of the summit, when both sides, but particularly the Soviets, made one dramatic proposal after another for substantial reductions in all types of strategic, and perhaps even conventional, weapons. Reagan and Gorbachev appeared to be on the verge of a historic arms control agreement that would change the face of the world for decades to come, but as Secretary of State Shultz observed, Gorbachev's strategy was to "concede and press," and press he did, telling Reagan at one point, "this all depends, of course, on you giving up SDI." For Gorbachev, the ABM treaty had prevented a

nuclear war, while Reagan considered the treaty to be a vestige of a dying strategic doctrine that held both nations' populations as hostages to terror. In defense of SDI Reagan pointedly told Gorbachev "I'm older than you are. . . . When I was a boy, women and children could not be killed indiscriminately from the air. Wouldn't it be great if we could make the world as safe today as it was then?" Reagan again offered to make SDI available to the Soviets, but Gorbachev was skeptical of this offer, noting that the United States was unwilling to share "oil-drilling equipment or even milk-processing factories." Gorbachev argued that SDI would "take the arms race into space" and make it more likely that the United States would be tempted to launch a first strike from the heavens. Gorbachev insisted that SDI research be confined to the laboratories in what he believed would be adherence to the ABM treaty, which Reagan thought would be the death knell for SDI. The final meeting grew heated as both men traded barbs with one another; in one instance when Gorbachev insisted on strict observance of the ABM treaty, Reagan responded, "If you feel so strongly about the ABM treaty, why don't you dismantle the radar you are building at Krasnoyarsk in violation of the treaty." (Krasnoyarsk was a "phased array radar station" that violated provisions of the ABM treaty signed by Richard Nixon and Leonid Brezhnev. The Soviets admitted in November 1989 that the Krasnoyarsk installation violated the ABM treaty.) Back and forth it went, with Gorbachev arguing that he had made great concessions to the United States on issues like the zero option, and that he had to return to the Soviet Union with some evidence of a concession on the American side; that concession should be Reagan's agreement to limit SDI research and testing to the laboratory; in the intervening 10 years both sides would move toward the elimination of all nuclear weapons. Late on that marathon Sunday, Gorbachev looked at Reagan and said, "It's 'laboratory' or good-bye." In the ensuing silence the president passed a note to Shultz: "Am I wrong?" Shultz whispered back, "No, you are right." With that Reagan said, "The meeting is over," and then he stood and said, "let's go George, we're leaving."

The grim-looking delegations departed Hofdi House in the full glare of the media, with Reagan and Gorbachev sharing some final barbs; the president accusing Gorbachev of planning "from the start to come here and put me in this situation," and Gorbachev insisting that the American president had missed "the unique chance of going down in history as a great president who paved the way for nuclear disarmament." Reagan responded, "That applies to both of us," to which Gorbachev pleaded that he didn't know what else he could have done. Reagan snapped "you could have said yes." When he reached the seclusion of his limousine, the president turned to Don Regan, his chief of staff, and said, "Goddammit, we were *that* close to an agreement."

As Reagan returned to the United States he was greeted by news reports and statements from members of Congress that the summit was a failure and that the U.S.–Soviet relationship had taken a dramatic turn for the worse. A woeful Secretary Shultz contributed to this impression at a post-summit conference in which he appeared to have been a survivor of a death march, which to some extent he was. In the following weeks conflicting accounts emerged from the administration about what had transpired in Reykjavik, while prominent Republicans such as Henry Kissinger and James Schlesinger argued that Reagan had been duped by a cunning Gorbachev. Former president Richard Nixon echoed this charge, observing that "No summit since Yalta has threatened Western interests so much as the two days at Reykjavik. . . . No deeper blow has ever been dealt to allied confidence in the

United States than by the incorporation of the nuclear-free fantasy into the American negotiating position at Reykjavik." But in hindsight it now appears that the haunted house on Faxafloi Bay was the site of the beginning of the end of the cold war.

The dire predictions of a breakdown in superpower relations did not come to pass, and a third summit was held in Washington, D.C., on December 7–10, 1987. The Washington summit came at the end of a year when Gorbachev's reform initiatives captured the imagination of many in the West, while Ronald Reagan spent much of the year dealing with the fallout from the Iran-contra affair. Reagan escaped from the scandal news in Washington by traveling to Europe in June 1987, where he attended an economic summit in Venice and then delivered one of the most notable addresses of his presidency in West Berlin at the Brandenburg Gate. The president questioned whether the reforms in the Soviet Union and the Eastern bloc were genuine changes or "token gestures," and challenged Gorbachev to take a step that would provide "unmistakable" evidence of a Soviet commitment to openness: "General Secretary Gorbachev, if you seek peace, if you seek prosperity for the Soviet Union and Eastern Europe, if you seek liberalization: Come here to this gate! Mr. Gorbachev, open this gate! Mr. Gorbachev, tear down this wall!"

But by the time of the Washington summit Gorbachev once again dominated the headlines with dramatic proposals for change in Soviet foreign and domestic policy. This summit was a publicity bonanza for the Soviet leader, for the nation's capital was in the midst of "Gorby fever," as *Washington Post* columnist Tom Shales dubbed it. Gorbachev's motorcade was repeatedly cheered by Americans who lined the streets of the capital, and in one instance he ordered his entourage to stop on Connecticut Avenue so he could shake hands

President Reagan speaks in front of the Brandenburg Gate at the Berlin Wall, Federal Republic of Germany, June 12, 1987.

with his American admirers. The savvy Russian leader was the clear winner in the photo-op competition. The highlight of the summit was the signing of the Intermediate Nuclear Forces (INF), Treaty in the East Room of the White House (*see* INF treaty on page 89). After the glittering White House ceremony the two leaders met for a discussion in the Cabinet Room, where Reagan infuriated Gorbachev by telling him one of his favorite anecdotes about the Soviet Union, a practice Reagan frequently engaged in, much to Gorbachev's irritation, but one he usually tolerated. Gorbachev was not so tolerant on this occasion, and according to George Shultz and Chief of Staff Howard Baker, the meeting did not go well for a seemingly ill-prepared and distracted Reagan. The president admitted that he had performed

poorly, and his National Security Advisor, Colin Powell, later described Reagan's telling of the old anecdote as "offensive." The president's performance improved markedly in later meetings, but no significant breakthroughs were achieved for the remainder of the summit. The two men were wedded to their conflicting positions on SDI, and that blocked any progress in the negotiations on strategic weapons. Inconclusive discussions were also held on Nicaragua and on conventional weapons, but the real story from the Washington summit was the rapport that had developed between Reagan and Gorbachev (the awkward meeting in the Cabinet Room excepted) and also between Secretary Shultz and Soviet foreign minister Eduard Shevardnadze. When it was announced that a summit would be held in

Moscow in 1988, it was further evidence of just how far and how fast the U.S.-Soviet relationship had evolved. The same president who four years earlier had referred to the Soviet Union as an evil empire would soon be exchanging toasts with Gorbachev inside the Kremlin.

The Moscow Summit was held from May 29–June 1, 1988, with the president arriving in Moscow two days after the Senate had ratified the INF treaty on a 93-5 vote (four Republicans voted against the treaty negotiated by their president). While Gorbachev had taken Washington by storm the previous December, Reagan now stole the headlines with a series of assertive remarks and gestures focusing on human rights and the plight of Soviet dissidents. Reagan was greeted warmly by large crowds that lined the streets, and in particular by a crowd of Muscovites at the Arbat, a pedestrian mall that the Reagans visited, to the dismay of his KGB escorts, who promptly pummeled their fellow citizens. The two leaders strolled through Red Square in a carefully staged photo opportunity and even stooped to kissing babies. The president visited a monastery in Moscow and talked of a "new age of religious freedom in the Soviet Union," addressed a gathering of dissidents at the U.S. ambassador's house, and quietly arranged with the Soviets to allow many of them to emigrate in the following months. The event that captured the most attention at home and in the Soviet Union was Reagan's speech in front of an enormous bust of Lenin to students at Moscow State University. The president extolled "the riot of experiment that is the free market" and again spoke of "one sad reminder of a divided world: the Berlin Wall. It's time to remove the barriers that keep people apart." Many of Reagan's remarks had been drafted by Tony Dolan, the primary author of the "evil empire" speech, who now accompanied the president to Moscow and who was mischievously reported by Secretary Shultz as hav-

ing been seen "worshiping at Lenin's Tomb." The Gorbachev-Reagan relationship was so chummy that the press, anxious to report on some conflict that might generate public interest, opted to focus on the somewhat chilly relationship between Nancy Reagan and Raisa Gorbachev. The summit ended on a high note with a joint press conference of the two leaders, the first ever held in the Soviet Union by a Soviet leader.

The unusual Reagan-Gorbachev "friendship," which it became over time, was arguably the most significant relationship of the cold war. Ten months after Ronald Reagan left office the Berlin Wall fell; the Soviet Union itself ceased to exist in December 1991. The issue of who deserved the credit for ending the cold war is a contentious one, and most scholars tend to give the honor to Gorbachev, or contend that the collapse was inevitable, that internal contradictions within the Soviet system were destined to destroy the regime. While Gorbachev's reforms were intended to save the Communist system, they may have in the end helped destroy it. What is indisputable is that Reagan claimed as early as June 1981 that in the Soviet Union "we are seeing the first beginning cracks: the beginning of the end." These remarks roiled foreign leaders, not to mention the Soviet leadership and Soviet experts in the United States, including Richard Nixon, Henry Kissinger, and Strobe Talbott. Testimony from various dissidents revealed that Reagan's rhetorical assaults, such as the "evil empire" speech, encouraged dissent within the Soviet Union and the Eastern bloc, and that his "Reagan Doctrine," particularly as applied to Afghanistan, helped bleed a tottering Soviet regime. Yet at the same time Reagan was deft enough to alter his position in response to the rise of Gorbachev. Reagan did this despite the resistance of his own secretary of defense and sharp criticism from long-time conservative supporters such as William F. Buckley and columnist George Will, who wrote after the Moscow summit that Reagan had engaged in "moral disarmament." Reagan was repeatedly accused by leaders of conservative interest groups of having lost his anticommunist edge, if not his mind. One such leader, Paul Weyrich, claimed shortly before the Washington summit that "Reagan is a weakened president, weakened in spirit as well as clout, and not in a position to make judgments about Gorbachev at this time." Reagan brushed off this criticism as he had brushed off earlier criticism from the Left about the installation of the INF, and by "staying the course" in both instances he paved the way for a radical transformation of U.S.–Soviet relations, leaving his successors a far more peaceful superpower relationship than either he or any president since Harry Truman had enjoyed.

The Reagan Legacy

At the dawn of the 21st century Ronald Reagan's standing with the American public remained high, and his reputation also improved in the rankings conducted by historians and political scientists of "presidential greatness," where he hovered near or occasionally broke into the "top 10." Much of Reagan's high standing with the public was attributable to his geniality and his good nature, qualities that stood in stark relief in the Bill Clinton–George W. Bush era of deep partisan division and rancor. Ronald Reagan epitomized the notion that political figures could adhere to their principles and also view their opponents as loyal Americans. He never took political criticism personally and avoided strident language when discussing his adversaries. Having been a Democrat for much of his adult life, Reagan understood that members of the Democratic Party were also capable of acting on principle.

Perhaps Reagan's greatest accomplishment as president was one also attributed to the Democratic hero of Reagan's youth, President Franklin Roosevelt. Roosevelt is often credited with restoring the confidence of the American people during the Great Depression, even if many of his economic programs were ineffective in ending the depression. By almost any measure, Reagan restored the confidence of the American public during the 1980s, including, ironically, their confidence in the same federal government that Reagan viewed as part of what ailed America. When Reagan took the oath of office on January 20, 1981, the nation had witnessed five of his immediate predecessors leave office under duress; Kennedy by assassination, Johnson forced into retirement by the Vietnam War, Nixon forced to resign, Ford defeated in a close reelection campaign, and Carter defeated by Reagan. The upheavals of the 1960s still reverberated throughout the nation: racial tension, exploding crime rates, employment insecurity and runaway inflation, defeat in Vietnam coupled with renewed Soviet assertiveness in the developing world, and a sense that the nation's political institutions were no longer functioning. It is not surprising that many commentators at the time suggested that the nation's best days were behind it, that the United States was in decline.

Reagan's immediate predecessor, Jimmy Carter, appeared at times to be overwhelmed by the presidency, and despite his renowned attention to detail never seemed to master the job. There was also a kind of cramped style to the Carter presidency, a kind of uninspired casualness that perhaps suited the nation's mood in the immediate aftermath of Watergate and Vietnam, but did not wear well over time. Reagan restored many of the "imperial" trappings to the Oval Office and seemed to revel in presidential pomp and circumstance. On the proverbial tug-of-war that presidents seem to walk between Jeffersonian simplicity and high-toned Hamiltonianism, Reagan clearly leaned toward the latter in his proclivity for White House pageantry.

In the policy arena, his rebuilding of the demoralized American military had the collateral benefit of repairing the pride of a public whose confidence had been seared by Vietnam, Afghanistan, and the fiasco of "Desert One," the failed rescue mission of the American hostages in Iran. Reagan was able to restore American confidence by the time of his reelection in 1984 through a combination of assertive rhetoric, jocular defiance in the face of an assassination attempt, military skirmishes in Grenada and with Libya, the deployment of the Euro-missiles, the PATCO firings, and a focus on breaking the back of inflation by avoiding domestic "pump priming" programs and endorsing a tight-money policy from the Federal Reserve. Setbacks, including serious ones like the debacle in Lebanon that led to the deaths of hundreds of U.S. Marines, did not seem to hurt Reagan. He became, much to the dismay of his opponents, the "Teflon president," to whom no bad news would stick. It was only well into his presidency, near the end of his sixth year in office, that bad news finally stuck to Ronald Reagan (the Iran-contra revelations) and for a time his buoyant optimism seemed to elude him.

Reagan succeeded in lifting a demoralized nation and restoring the reputation of the battered office of the presidency. Radical surgery of the kind floated by Jimmy Carter's White House counsel Lloyd Cutler (incorporating elements of a parliamentary system) was quietly forgotten in the early 1980s after Reagan scored a number of legislative successes. But Reagan's legacy regarding the restoration of presidential power is less impressive when one looks for evidence that he challenged Congress's inclination to micromanage the executive branch. Terry Eastland, a former deputy of Attorney General Edwin Meese and

an advocate of a strong presidency, has observed that Reagan paled in comparison to George H. W. Bush in terms of using the formal powers of his office, including the veto power, to protect presidential prerogatives. Eastland was also unimpressed with Reagan's reluctance to spend political capital to withstand congressional and judicial incursions into territory once considered the province of the executive, including the appointment of independent counsels and in the war power and intelligence arenas.

By husbanding his formidable resources, Eastland believed, Reagan squandered an opportunity to restore the balance that was lost in the 1970s after Congress asserted itself during the Vietnam and Watergate eras. Reagan left the office weaker than he found it in intelligence: one of Reagan's 1980 campaign goals was to restore the Central Intelligence Agency, and in particular to restore the autonomy the president once possessed over the intelligence community. By the time Reagan left office the CIA was subject to further restrictions and heightened congressional oversight due to the Iran-contra affair. Reagan's reluctance to challenge some of the underlying assumptions and prescriptions for change offered by the congressional Iran-contra committees and his acquiescence to the demands of independent counsel Lawrence Walsh disappointed Eastland and other advocates of executive power.

Throughout Reagan's presidency, he often appeared to be pulled in conflicting directions, between his wife's inclination (along with Michael Deaver's) to tack according to the shifting winds of public opinion, and the instinct of those "purists" around him, such as Edwin Meese and William Clark, who believed that Reagan was at his best when he sailed against the wind. Of course all successful politicians and statesmen in a republic have to both sail with, and at times against, the wind, but Reagan was particularly adept at doing so, and could merge conflicting currents into a seemingly coherent direction. He had an ability to make concessions while at the same time convincing himself and his fellow countrymen that he had not altered his position. In this regard he once again resembled his hero Franklin Roosevelt. One of Reagan's strengths throughout his time in office was the perception that he was ideologically consistent, although a close examination reveals a politician who knew when to cut his losses; the two most glaring examples of this were his decision to withdraw the marines from Lebanon in early 1984 and his endorsement of a Social Security revenue "enhancement," that is, a tax increase, despite his often repeated opposition to new taxes.

One of the strongest criticisms leveled against President Reagan when he left office in 1989 was that the national debt had tripled during his watch, from $914 billion in fiscal year 1980, to $2.7 trillion in fiscal year 1989, and that large annual budget deficits were accepted as the norm. This occurred despite the fact that Reagan had promised in 1980 to balance the federal budget in four years. The Republican Party in recent times had been a party of balanced budgets, but by the end of the Reagan presidency many Republicans were sounding more Keynesian than Keynes himself.

Many observers predicted that Reagan's red ink would ruin the American economy, and that his fiscal policies had simply provided a short-term but superficial fix for the economy; that the deficits and debt "as far as the eye can see" would undermine the nation in the long run. The doomsayers appeared to be wrong, for the American economy did not collapse. Depending on which economist you choose to believe, this was due either to courageous tax increases supported by Reagan's two immediate successors, or, according to unrepentant supply-siders, to the Reagan boom, after a recession in the early 1990s, returning with a vengeance in the mid to late

1990s. What is indisputable is that the federal government began running budget surpluses in the late 1990s under President Clinton, and even began to reduce the national debt. The surpluses did not last long, however, as the recession of the early 2000s, coupled with tax cuts advocated by President George W. Bush and the costs of the War on Terror, put the federal budget back in the red in the new millennium.

Reagan's legacy within the Republican Party cannot be overestimated. Twenty years after his first election to the White House, he remained a revered figure among the GOP's rank and file. Some of his conservative admirers succeeded in naming Washington's National Airport after him; many wanted to put him on Mount Rushmore; others sought to put him on the $10 bill, replacing Alexander Hamilton; while some wanted him on the dime, replacing his idol, Franklin Delano Roosevelt. Reagan transformed the Republican Party into a homogeneous conservative party, and his legions of followers found a second home in an unofficial "party" of sorts, over the nation's talk-radio airwaves on programs such as the Rush Limbaugh Show, and on the Fox Television Network. The Republicans who led the effort to win the House of Representatives in 1994, primarily Representative Newt Gingrich of Georgia and Richard Armey and Tom DeLay of Texas, were devout Reaganites, determined to radically reform welfare, which they succeeded in doing, shrink the size of government, and cut taxes. They generally followed Reagan's hawkish views on foreign and defense policy, and in particular remained committed to the development of a missile defense system similar to Reagan's Strategic Defense Initiative. President George W. Bush, only the second president who was the son of a president, looked less to his father for inspiration, molding himself instead into a sort of mini-Gipper, invoking language similar to the "evil empire" speech to mobilize the nation for the War on Terror, and sticking to a tax-cutting agenda that made Reagan's cuts seem timid by comparison. More than any president since FDR, Reagan shaped his party in his own image.

Reagan had an impact on his opponents as well, pulling the Democratic Party to the center and forcing it to abandon its more liberal policy positions, particularly on welfare and some foreign policy issues. A number of southern Democrats defected to the Republican Party throughout the 1980s and 1990s; one of the most prominent defectors was Representative Phil Gramm, a Democratic "boll weevil" who backed Reagan's tax and spending cuts,

and went on to become a Republican senator from Texas. Beyond the defectors, evidence that Reagan altered the political landscape could be seen in the creation of the Democratic Leadership Council (DLC) in 1985, in the wake of Reagan's landslide reelection win over Walter Mondale. The DLC was formed by a group of moderate Democrats concerned about the party's "soft" image on foreign and defense policy, and determined to restore notions of "responsibility" to domestic programs designed to assist the poor. After being soundly defeated in three presidential races in a row with candidates Carter, Mondale, and Dukakis, labeled, fairly or not, as liberals, the party nominated two DLC members, Bill Clin-

President Reagan's last day saluting, as he boards *Marine 1* at the U.S. Capitol, Washington, D.C., January 20, 1989.

ton and Al Gore, to head the party's ticket for its next three races. President Clinton's support for a radical welfare reform proposal was further evidence that Reagan shifted the nation's center of gravity to the Right. The proposal contained workfare elements first proposed by Governor Reagan in the 1960s, and limited the amount of time a beneficiary could receive assistance. Clinton's welfare reforms were strongly opposed by many members of his own party; nonetheless, these reforms and many other Clinton domestic policy initiatives were markedly moderate in tone and content.

Ronald Reagan's communicative skills set a high standard for his successors to follow, for he elevated the presidential "bully pulpit" to a level of excellence not witnessed since the days of John F. Kennedy. His memorable "evil empire" speech and his "tear down this wall" plea to Mikhail Gorbachev, along with his pledge to leave Marxism and Leninism on the "ash heap of history," may well have contributed to the end of the Soviet Union by inspiring dissidents behind the Iron Curtain. His rhetoric during periods of national mourning lifted the nation time and again: during the Challenger disaster of 1986 or during the memorial service for the American soldiers killed in an airplane crash in Newfoundland (soldiers from the 101st Airborne were on their way home for Christmas) in 1985. His comments on Anne Frank at the Bergen-Belsen concentration camp, or his remarks at the 40th anniversary of D day at Pointe du Hoc, France, or his remarks at the 1984 dedication of the Tomb of the Unknown Soldier from the Vietnam Conflict were some of the most moving rhetoric about war and heroism in the history of the presidency. In the end, Reagan's words, like those of Thomas Jefferson, Abraham Lincoln, Franklin Roosevelt, and John F. Kennedy, may prove to be his most durable legacy.

BIOGRAPHICAL
DICTIONARY A–Z

Allen, Richard V.
(1936–) *National Security Advisor*

A transplanted Californian, Richard Allen was part of the inner circle that guided Ronald Reagan's successful quest for the White House in 1980. Allen was an ardent opponent of communism, and his hawkish views on U.S.–Soviet relations shaped the administration's foreign policy during its critical first year in office.

Allen received his B.A. from the University of Notre Dame in 1957, then continued there to earn an M.A. in political science the following year. He also did graduate work at the Universities of Freiburg and Munich in West Germany. Following his studies, Allen moved to the University of Maryland to become a lecturer in the Overseas Division. He taught at Maryland for three years before taking a job as assistant professor of social sciences at the Georgia Institute of Technology. In 1962, Allen accepted a position at Georgetown University's Center for Strategic and International Studies as research principal and chairman of the study program on communism, where he stayed until 1966. After this, he became a senior staff member for two years at Stanford University's Hoover Institution.

In 1968 Allen entered politics as a senior foreign policy adviser to the Nixon-Agnew presidential campaign. Following Nixon's victory, Allen was appointed to a senior staff position in the National Security Council, but it was reported at the time that he had an uneasy relationship with Henry Kissinger, Nixon's National Security Advisor. He went on to serve as a consultant on National Security Affairs in 1970 and 1971 and a member of the presidential Commission on International Trade and Economic Policy from 1970 to 1972. He earned several key appointments in the Nixon administration, including deputy executive director on the Council on International Economic Policy and deputy assistant to the president on international economic affairs.

Allen served as Reagan's chief foreign policy adviser from 1977 to 1980, advocating increased defense spending and a firm stance toward the Soviet Union, both of which became prominent components of the Reagan foreign policy agenda. In 1981, he was appointed Reagan's National Security Advisor. He was a strong supporter of the Strategic Defense Initiative, or "Star Wars," and laid the groundwork for Reagan's March 1983 SDI proposal. Early in his tenure Allen was accused of taking a $1,000 check from NANCY REAGAN and was forced to resign his post on January 4,

National Security Advisor Richard V. Allen meets with President Reagan in the Oval Office, January 21, 1981.

1982. The money, given as a gift to the first lady after an interview with a Japanese magazine, was simply placed in the White House safe at Allen's request and forgotten, but by the time his innocence was proven he had already submitted his resignation.

Following his departure from the White House, Allen remained involved in national politics. He served as an adviser for the 1996 presidential campaign of Republican challenger PAT BUCHANAN. He is currently president of the Richard V. Allen Company, a consulting firm specializing in U.S.–East Asia business. He also serves on the Defense Policy Board and is a fellow at several think tanks, including the Heritage Foundation, the Hoover Institution, and the Center for Strategic and International Studies.

Anderson, Martin
(1936–   ) *assistant to the president for policy development*

Martin Anderson was a key member of Ronald Reagan's conservative brain trust and a staunch supporter of supply-side economics. He was part of Reagan's inner circle during the 1976 and 1980 campaigns for president and later became one of the foremost domestic policy advisers to Reagan during the first years of the new administration.

Anderson graduated summa cum laude from Dartmouth College, and later completed his master's degree from Dartmouth, then moved to the Massachusetts Institute of Technology and earned his Ph.D. in 1962. Immediately after completing his doctorate, Anderson joined the faculty at Columbia University's Graduate School of Business Administration as an assistant professor of finance. In 1965, he became an associate professor of business, a position he held until 1968.

Anderson became the director of research for the 1968 presidential campaign of Richard Nixon. Following Nixon's election victory, he joined the administration as a special assistant and consultant to the president. After nearly three years in the White House, Anderson returned to an academic setting with an appointment at Stanford University's Hoover Institution. Over the next 10 years, he served on a number of different boards and committees in both business and politics while maintaining his status as a senior fellow at the Hoover Institution.

In 1976, Anderson became part of a network of neoconservative intellectuals who were beginning to exert their influence in Republican circles. He served as a key economic adviser for Ronald Reagan in the 1976 GOP presidential primary race, and a year later joined the Committee on the Present Danger, the group responsible for developing many of the ideas later championed by the Reagan administration. He enlisted in the Reagan campaign again as an economic adviser in 1980, and after the election became assistant to the president for policy development, where his views on free-market economics and federal welfare policy were very influential to the president in his first two years in office. He was also a member of the Economic Policy Advisory Board and the Foreign Intelligence Advisory Board, underscoring his role as a major player in the White House. He left his post in the administration in 1982 and returned to the Hoover Institution.

Anderson has written a number of books on politics and economics. In *Welfare: The Political Economy of Welfare Reform in the United States*, he examined the government's failed attempts at achieving a successful welfare system. In *Impostors in the Temple: A Blueprint for Improving Higher Education in America*, he addressed the problems with America's colleges and universities. He also wrote a memoir of his time in the Reagan White House, *Revolution*, in which he defended the job of the administration and argued that it advanced the cause of capitalism and democracy across the globe. Yet Anderson's greatest success has been a series of recent works on Reagan. In 2001, along with his wife, Annelise Anderson, and Kiron Skinner, he released a collection of Reagan's radio broadcasts from the late 1970s entitled *Reagan, in His Own Hand*. Two years later, they completed a volume of Reagan letters called *Reagan: A Life in Letters*. These books helped more than any other works to decipher the mystery of Ronald Reagan. Anderson remains a senior fellow at the Hoover Institution.

Andropov, Yuri
(1914–1984) *general secretary, Communist Party of the Soviet Union*

After the death of LEONID BREZHNEV in November 1982, Yuri Andropov, chief of the KGB for the previous 15 years, edged out Brezhnev's chosen successor, KONSTANTIN CHERNENKO, to become leader of the Soviet Union. He initiated a series of reforms to deal with the Soviet Union's economic and social

malaise, but his efforts were cut short when he died after just 15 months in office.

Andropov first became involved in Communist politics at the age of 22 when he served as an organizer of shipyard workers in the Communist Youth League (Komsomol). He rose to first secretary of the Komsomol organization in Yaroslavl after just two years, then joined the Communist Party of the Soviet Union (CPSU) in 1939. A year later, Andropov earned his first appointment in the CPSU as head of the Komsomol branch in the Karelo-Finnish republic, the former Finnish region then under Soviet control after the Soviet-Finnish war of 1939–40. He remained in the region throughout World War II organizing guerrilla operations by Komsomol members against the German military. He was highly regarded by Otto Kuusinen, head of the Finnish Communist Party, who used his influence to make Andropov a party secretary in Karelia after the war.

After working briefly for the Central Committee in Moscow, Andropov entered the Soviet diplomatic service in 1953 and earned a position in the Ministry of Foreign Affairs. Later that year, he was appointed to a post in the Soviet embassy in Budapest, Hungary, then in 1954 he was promoted to ambassador. Andropov served in Hungary during the leadership of reformist Imre Nagy, whose push for democracy posed the first major challenge to Soviet power in postwar Eastern Europe. Andropov repeatedly assured the Nagy government that the Soviet Union had no intention of intervening in Hungary's internal affairs, yet behind the scenes he was maneuvering to eliminate Nagy and replace him with Communist leader János Kádár. Shortly after the Red Army entered Hungary in October 1956, Andropov had Nagy arrested and executed, and the Communists restored to power. His ability to maintain party unity was lauded by the Soviet leadership, who called Andropov to Moscow in 1957 to head the new Department of Relations with Communist Parties in Power. This position, held by Andropov for the next 10 years, required him to work closely with the governments in Eastern Europe, Asia and Cuba, giving him valuable experience in foreign affairs. In 1967 LEONID BREZHNEV appointed Andropov head of the Soviet secret police force, the Committee for State Security (KGB). Over the next 15 years, he restored prestige to an agency in serious decline after revelations of vast abuses of power during the Stalin years. He was also successful in suppressing the growing human rights movement of the 1970s popularized by the writings of "dissenters" such as Andrei Sakharov and Alexander Solzhenitsyn.

Andropov's 15-year tenure with the KGB launched him to the top of the party apparatus. In 1973, he earned full membership to the Politburo. In May 1982, when Brezhnev's health was in serious decline, he resigned his post as head of the KGB and positioned himself to become the next general secretary. When Brezhnev died six months later, Andropov, backed by Foreign Minister ANDREI GROMYKO and Defense Minister Dmitri Ustinov, took over as general secretary of the CPSU. Andropov went to work immediately to confront the social and economic malaise plaguing the Soviet Union in the last years of the Brezhnev regime. He initiated a series of reforms to increase productivity and efficiency in the workplace, including giving workers rewards for higher productivity. He also made changes in the party organization by removing corrupt officials and bringing younger, reformist politicians, such as MIKHAIL GORBACHEV, into the party leadership. These changes were somewhat successful in increasing industrial productivity and reducing absen-

teeism, but opposition from party conservatives was so strong that Andropov was never able to fully implement his reforms.

In foreign affairs, relations with the United States declined to their lowest state in years, although initially Andropov was optimistic about rekindling a détente between the two nations. In his first major speech to the Central Committee on November 22, 1982, he rejected the platform of the party conservatives who advocated taking a harder line with Washington and instead spoke of his plans for arms reductions and increased cooperation. Then, on March 8, 1983, President Reagan gave a speech to the National Association of Evangelicals where he described the Soviet Union as an "evil empire"; two weeks later, he outlined his plan to build a national missile defense system called the Strategic Defense Initiative (SDI). These two speeches served to dampen any hopes of a renewed détente. In September 1983 a Soviet jet shot down a Korean Airlines passenger airplane, killing all on board and bringing a sharp rebuke from Reagan. A long chill in relations between the United States and the Soviet Union followed the Korean Airlines incident, including an end to Intermediate Nuclear Forces and Strategic Arms Reduction negotiations, which prohibited any real progress from being made during Andropov's brief time in office.

Andropov died of kidney failure on February 9, 1984, and was replaced by longtime Brezhnev aide, Konstantin Chernenko, who worked to dismantle the reforms made by Andropov and reverted to a more conservative posture. When Mikhail Gorbachev took power in March 1985 the reforms begun by Andropov came to fruition, dramatically changing the landscape of Soviet society and the nature of the cold war.

B

Baker, Howard, Jr.
(1925–) *chief of staff*

A one-time opponent of Ronald Reagan who became a valued ally and indispensable chief of staff, Howard Baker was born into politics. His father, Howard, Sr., was a Republican congressman from Tennessee from 1951 to 1964, and his stepmother took over the seat following his father's death. He studied at both the University of the South and Tulane University before entering the United States Naval Reserve. After serving in World War II and reaching the rank of lieutenant, junior grade, he entered the University of Tennessee for studies in law, receiving his LL.B. in 1949. Baker went on to practice law in his grandfather's Knoxville, Tennessee, firm, Baker, Worthington, Barnett and Crossley. He also became involved in several lucrative financial deals during this time that made him very wealthy.

In 1964, Baker made his first entry into national politics, running for a seat in the U.S. Senate once held by Estes Kefauver. His ardent conservatism was unpopular in Tennessee at this time and he lost the race to a moderate Democrat. The seat came up for election again two years later, and a more moderate Baker won the seat, becoming the state's first Republican senator since the Civil War and the first popularly elected Republican senator in the history of Tennessee. He stayed in the U.S. Senate for the next 18 years. He was seen by many as a moderate, favoring the usual conservative planks of smaller government and high military spending, while also supporting traditionally liberal policies such as environmental protection and civil rights. His thoughtful approach to each separate issue earned him the respect of his peers and a reputation as an admirable public servant.

Baker ran for Senate minority leader in 1969 and 1971, but failed both times. His star rose, however, in 1973 when he served as vice chairman of the Senate Select Committee on Presidential Activities, the committee charged with investigating President Nixon's role in the Watergate scandal. Although he had been one of Nixon's strongest allies on the Senate floor, Baker remained objective throughout the investigation and was steadfast in his search for the facts. His question, "what did the President know, and when did he know it," became something of a battle cry for the Watergate committee investigators. His impartial attitude, though offensive to some conservatives, won him the respect of both Democrats and Republicans. In 1977 Baker edged out Michigan senator Robert

Griffin by a vote of 19 to 18 to become minority leader.

In 1980, Baker sought the Republican nomination for president. He failed in his attempt, losing the nomination to Ronald Reagan, but with the Republican victory in the general election, Baker became majority leader in the Senate. In this role, Baker served as one of Reagan's key allies in Congress, supporting the president on several controversial defense and budget issues. In 1983, amid speculation that he was eyeing the 1984 GOP nomination, Baker announced he would retire from the Senate at the end of his term. He abandoned his plan to seek the nomination when Reagan announced he would seek reelection, and following his retirement he went back into law practice as a senior partner at Vinson and Elkins in Washington, D.C. He stayed connected to national politics with a seat on the president's Foreign Intelligence Board from 1985 to 1987.

In the years after he left the Senate, Baker began to lay the groundwork for a presidential campaign in 1988. After the resignation of DONALD REGAN, however, Baker once again abandoned his presidential aspirations to join the Reagan administration as the chief of staff. The appointment was widely praised by Democrats and Republicans, and Baker's professionalism and conciliatory attitude during the Iran-contra investigations boosted the morale of the White House staff and dampened Democratic calls for Reagan's impeachment.

Following his departure from the White House in 1989, Baker returned to a quiet life with his wife and his favorite hobby, photography. He published his second pictorial book, *Big South Fork Country*, in 1993. His wife, Joy, died of cancer in the same year, and in 1996 Baker married former Kansas senator Nancy Kassebaum. In June 2001 President George W. Bush named Baker to the coveted post of U.S. ambassador to Japan, where he still serves today.

Baker, James A., III
(1930–) *chief of staff, secretary of the Treasury*

As Ronald Reagan's chief of staff during the president's first term, James Baker earned a reputation as a savvy political infighter and a skilled administrator. A pragmatic deal maker in an ideological White House, Baker's loyalty was often questioned by Reagan's more conservative advisers, but he retained the confidence of the president and Mrs. Reagan during his nearly eight years of service in the administration.

Baker received his B.A. from Princeton University in 1952, and later joined the U.S. Marine Corps, where he served until 1954. Upon his return from the service, he entered law school at the University of Texas and received his LL.B. in 1957. Baker accepted a job at the Houston law firm Andrews, Kurth, Campbell, and Jones, where he practiced law full time for almost 25 years.

Baker's first involvement in politics came in 1970 when he ran the unsuccessful Senate campaign of his friend, GEORGE H. W. BUSH. In 1975 he entered government service as Commerce Department under secretary in the GERALD FORD administration. He stayed in the Ford camp during the 1976 election, serving as chairman of President Ford's campaign committee. Baker returned to his firm in Houston following Ford's defeat, but came back to politics for the 1980 presidential election as the campaign chairman for Bush. The Reagan campaign was impressed by Baker's skill in managing Bush's race for the Republican nomination, and after Reagan became the Republican nominee Baker joined his campaign as a senior adviser.

Following Reagan's victory, it was clear that Baker would play a senior role in the new administration. To the surprise of many in Washington who believed Reagan would select EDWIN MEESE or MICHAEL DEAVER as his chief of staff, Baker was chosen for the position and remained until the second term. Meese and Deaver also held senior positions within the White House, and the three men became known as the "troika" of Reagan's closest advisers. Baker displayed strong political acumen during his tenure as chief of staff, managing the White House staff with skill and playing a key role in formulating and implementing Reagan's agenda.

He remained chief of staff through the first term, then at the beginning of the second term, in an unusual personnel move, Reagan allowed Baker and Treasury Secretary DONALD REGAN to switch posts. Many saw this as a poor decision by Reagan, particularly when the Iran-contra scandal broke and Regan failed to shield the president from the political firestorm that resulted. Baker left the Treasury Department in 1988 to concentrate on the presidential campaign of George Bush. He served as campaign chairman for Bush and was widely praised for managing a strong campaign that ended in a comfortable victory over Michael Dukakis.

Baker served as secretary of state during the Bush administration and presided over one of the most dynamic and successful periods in U.S. foreign policy. He played a key role in shaping policy toward the Soviet Union and Eastern Europe, in the reunification of Germany, and in the Gulf War. However, toward the end of the term he left his post in the State Department to become Bush's chief of staff, primarily so he could concentrate on the reelection campaign. Following Bush's 1992 defeat to Bill Clinton, Baker returned to practicing law, and was the guiding hand behind George W. Bush's legal challenge to secure the contested vote in the 2000 presidential election in Florida.

Baldrige, Malcolm
(1922–1987) *secretary of commerce*

Malcolm Baldrige left a successful business career in 1981 to become commerce secretary in the Reagan administration. He became a close ally of President Reagan and a supporter of his agenda to cut expenditures, reduce business regulations, open up new trade markets, and increase America's exporting power around the world. He also became a friend of Ronald Reagan, joining him on horseback riding expeditions at Camp David and elsewhere in the Washington, D.C., area.

"Mac" Baldrige earned his B.A. in English from Yale University in 1944, then joined the U.S. Army to fight in the remaining years of World War II. He served in the 27th Infantry Division in the Pacific Theater, fighting in the Battle of Okinawa and taking part in the occupation in Honshu, Japan. Following the war, he joined the Eastern Malleable Iron Company in Naugatuck, Connecticut, as a foundry foreman. He was promoted to managing director of the Frazer and Jones division in 1951, then became company vice president in 1957. In 1960, after 15 years with the company, Baldrige was named president. He left Eastern Malleable two years later to take an executive vice president position at Scovill Manufacturing Company. He rose through the ranks at Scovill as well, becoming president and chief executive officer, then chairman of the board of directors. Scovill was losing money when Baldrige joined the company, but by the time he left nearly 20 years later it was earning about $1 billion in annual revenues.

Baldrige had close ties to the Republican Party his entire life; his father, H. Malcolm Baldrige was a U.S. congressman from 1931 to 1933. He served as a delegate to the 1968, 1972, and 1976 Republican National Conventions, and as cochairman of the United Citizens for Nixon-Agnew in Connecticut. He also served on a number of prestigious panels, including the Council on Foreign Relations, the International Chamber of Commerce, and the Business Council. During the 1980 GOP primaries, he was campaign chairman for fellow Yale graduate GEORGE H. W. BUSH.

When Reagan entered office in 1981, he took the advice of his vice president and appointed Baldrige as secretary of commerce. Baldrige became known for his simple, straightforward style, an approach that earned the respect of both friends and adversaries around the world. He was faced with a trade deficit of nearly $170 billion when he entered office, thus his main focus became the increase in productivity and exports. To make up part of the trade deficit, he supported protectionist measures against countries with unfair import restrictions against the United States, particularly Japan. He was a driving force behind the high tariffs the administration placed on Japanese imports. He was, however, an advocate of free trade, and his efforts in opening up trade routes with China, India, and the Soviet Union were key accomplishments of his tenure. He also worked to reduce regulations adversely affecting American businesses.

On July 25, 1987, Baldrige, a professional steer roper, died after suffering massive injuries to his heart and pancreas from a fall during a rodeo practice. After serving six and half years as commerce secretary, he was seen by many as the most successful department leader since Herbert Hoover under presidents Harding and Coolidge. His death was a great blow to the administration. In August 1987, the Malcolm Baldrige National Quality Award was established to encourage greater efficiency and competitiveness of American businesses abroad. He was succeeded as commerce secretary by C. WILLIAM VERITY, JR.

Bell, Terrel H.
(1921–1996) *secretary of education*

Ronald Reagan's first secretary of education, Terrel Bell was originally charged with shutting

down his own department, but ultimately moved the issue of education to the top of the nation's domestic agenda and spared his department from extinction.

Bell stayed in his home state of Idaho following high school to attend Southern Idaho College of Education. He left school to join the U.S. Marine Corps, serving from 1942 until 1946 in the Pacific theater, and reaching the rank of first sergeant. He returned to southern Idaho after the war, earning his B.A. in 1946. Immediately following graduation, he took a job as a science teacher at Eden Rural High School in Eden, Idaho. After only two years at Eden, at just 26 years of age, Bell was hired as the superintendent of Rockland Valley Schools in Rockland, Idaho. He stayed at this job until 1954 before taking another superintendent's position at Star Valley Schools in Afton, Wyoming. Also in 1954, Bell received his M.Sc. from the University of Idaho. He served as superintendent of Weber County School District in Ogden, Utah, from 1957 to 1962, earning his doctorate in education from the University of Utah.

In 1962, Bell moved into college education, taking a job as professor of school administration and chairman of the department of educational administration at Utah State University. After just one year at Utah State, he took a job in state government as Utah's superintendent of public instruction. Throughout the next three decades, Bell would alternate between education and government service. He left his job in the state government in 1970 to join the U.S. Office of Education in Washington, D.C., as deputy commissioner for school systems. He also joined the Department of Health, Education, and Welfare as the acting U.S. commissioner of education. He came back to Utah a year later to become superintendent of Granite School District in Salt Lake City, but returned to Washington in 1974 to serve as U.S. commissioner of education. Following Gerald Ford's defeat in the 1976 election, Bell once again moved back to Salt Lake City and became the commissioner and chief executive officer of the Utah System of Higher Education.

In 1980, Ronald Reagan campaigned to abolish the newly created Department of Education, arguing that it was the responsibility of each state to set its own education policy. When Bell took the post as Reagan's education secretary, he was in the awkward position of trying to dissolve his own department. However, once Reagan took office the idea was essentially abandoned and Bell set out to execute a new agenda. With the 1983 release of a departmental study on America's public school system entitled *A Nation at Risk*, he succeeded in increasing national awareness of the problems facing public education.

Following his resignation from the Reagan administration, Bell returned to the University of Utah as a professor. In 1988, he completed *The Thirteenth Man: A Reagan Cabinet Memoir* about his days as education secretary and his battles with conservative elements in the administration. Bell died of pulmonary fibrosis in Salt Lake City on June 22, 1996.

Bennett, William J.
(1943–) *secretary of education*

William Bennett served as the secretary of education under President Reagan, advocating such controversial measures as character education, cuts in student aid, and school vouchers. His outspoken personality often made him a lightning rod for criticism, but by the end of the Reagan administration he had become the most visible education secretary in the department's history and had elevated education policy to the forefront of the national debate.

Bennett received his B.A. in philosophy from Williams College in 1965, then moved to the University of Texas for his doctoral work, where he received his Ph.D. in political philosophy in 1970. Bennett then went to Boston and completed his J.D. at Harvard University Law School in 1971. Between 1967 and 1973, he taught courses on both law and philosophy at the University of Southern Mississippi, the University of Texas, Harvard University, Boston University, and the University of Wisconsin. In 1972, Bennett was promoted to the position of assistant professor of philosophy at Boston University, where he remained until 1976.

Beginning in 1976, Bennett alternated between academia and government service. He was appointed executive director of the National Humanities Center from 1976 to 1979, then president and director of the National Humanities Center until 1981. Between 1977 and 1981, Bennett was also associate professor of philosophy at North Carolina State University. In 1981, he left the National Humanities Center to take the post of chairman of the National Endowment for the Humanities. During his tenure at NEH, Bennett was a harsh critic of multiculturalism and affirmative action.

His work at NEH caught the attention of senior Reagan administration officials, and in 1985, after the resignation of TERRELL H. BELL, Bennett was selected to head the Department of Education. He became one of Reagan's most controversial cabinet members, often upsetting the Left with his advocacy of character education and his drive for a school voucher plan. These positions and others earned him the lasting enmity of the National Education Association (NEA), the nation's largest teacher's union. Although he faced perhaps the most criticism of any cabinet member, Bennett had Reagan's strong support. By the time he left his post, Bennett had elevated education to the forefront of domestic policy.

In 1989, Bennett joined the Bush administration as the director of the Office of National Drug Control Policy (the "drug czar"), presiding over the war on drugs. Once again, he became a magnet for criticism as he focused largely on law enforcement and interdiction and less on education and rehabilitation programs. He left the Bush administration in 1990, but remained deeply involved in politics. He published two books, *The Book of Virtues* and *The Index of Leading Cultural Indicators*, in 1993 and 1994, both of which charged liberalism with the decline in American culture. Bennett later became cofounder of Empower America, a conservative policy group.

Block, John R.
(1935–) *secretary of agriculture*

When John Block was named secretary of agriculture in 1981, he supported President Reagan's plan to cut farm subsidies and foster a greater reliance on free-market mechanisms. However, a deep recession in the agricultural sector during the first Reagan term forced Block to largely abandon those ideas and initiate one of the largest budget expansions in the department's history.

Block grew up on a family-owned farm in Galesburg, Illinois. Following high school, he entered the United States Military Academy at West Point, New York, graduating in 1957. He served as an infantry officer in the U.S. Army for the next three years, then moved back to Galesburg and started Block Farms with his father. Over the next 20 years, Block Farms grew from 300 to 3,000 acres, and Block earned himself the reputation of a gifted businessman. He was also awarded the Outstanding Young Farmer of the Year honor in 1969 by the American Jaycees. In 1977, Block was named Illinois director of agriculture by Republican governor James Thompson; he pushed for major revisions in Illinois's conservation laws, including a financial incentives program that rewarded farmers who protected their land from erosion. He also proposed the creation of various overseas trade offices to promote Illinois farm products abroad.

In 1981 Block joined the Reagan administration as secretary of agriculture. Like Reagan, Block supported a major reduction in government subsidies to farmers, but the agricultural sector, a major source of political support for the Republican Party, suffered a recession in Reagan's first term in office, forcing the administration to rethink its agenda. Instead, the agriculture department expanded during the Reagan years and subsidies were actually increased. Block played a key role in the construction of both the 1981 and 1985 farm bills, and the 1983 Payment-in-Kind Program, all of which combined to increase the department's budget from $8.8 billion in 1980 to $31.5 billion in 1986. He was committed to opening global markets for American agricultural products and he negotiated several important farm agreements with other nations. His department also joined the fight against starvation in Africa by initiating the Food for Peace Program.

In 1986, facing strong criticism from farmers and consumer groups over the declining number of family farms, Block resigned his position and was replaced by RICHARD LYNG. He became president and chief executive officer at Food Distributors International and the International Foodservice Distributors Association, then in December 2002, executive vice president of the Food Marketing Institute and president of its wholesaler division, a position he still holds. Block also delivers a syndicated weekly radio broadcast and serves on the board of several governmental and agricultural organization.

Boland, Edward P.
(1911–2001) *congressman; chairman, House Permanent Select Committee on Intelligence*

Edward Boland devoted most of his life to public service, spending the last 36 years of his career representing his western Massachusetts district in the U.S. House of Representatives. As chairman of the House Intelligence Committee, he pushed for limits on aid to the Nicaraguan contras, known as the Boland Amendments, which led some members of the administration to pursue illegal means and jeopardize Reagan's presidency.

Boland spent his entire career in the political arena. After college, he entered Boston College Law School, but dropped out and took a job as the playground director in his hometown of Springfield, Massachusetts. He won his first political office in 1934 when he joined the Massachusetts state legislature. He stayed there until 1940, when he was elected county recorder of deeds. In 1952, Boland decided to run for a seat in the U.S. Congress. He defeated his opponent with a bare majority of the vote, but over the next 36 years he would successfully win reelection 17 times with no less than 60 percent of the vote in any election. Boland was known as a liberal in the House and a close ally of fellow Massachusetts representative, Speaker of the House TIP O'NEILL.

In 1977, he was named chairman of the House Permanent Select Committee on Intelligence, the committee charged with overseeing the nation's intelligence community. The appointment was particularly important in 1977 due to the recent restructuring in congressional authority over covert operations. The Intelligence Authorization Act of 1975 gave the House and Senate intelligence committees the power to oversee actions of the Central Intelligence Agency. In 1981 President Reagan appointed WILLIAM CASEY as the new head of the CIA, replacing Carter appointee Stansfield Turner. Casey, a veteran of the Office of Strategic Services, the forerunner to the CIA, was contemptuous of congressional oversight, making Boland, in the Democratic-controlled House, his chief adversary during his six years as DCI.

The most noted conflict between Casey and the congressional panels concerned covert aid to the Nicaraguan rebels, known as the contras, who opposed the Marxist Sandinista government. Early in the operation, Boland proposed an amendment to the Intelligence Authorization Act cutting lethal aid to the contras. The proposal, known as the Boland Amendment, was passed by Congress in 1982. Shortly after, Boland proposed a second amendment that cut off any type of aid to the contras, this one passing in 1983. The amendment expired two years later and was not renewed by Congress. Congress passed a substantial aid package to the contras the following year. This new wave of contra support in Congress was not expected by the administration, and in 1985, anticipating continued congressional restrictions on contra aid, a group of National Security Council officials began a clandestine operation, selling arms to Iran and diverting the funds to the contras. This illegal operation, known later as the Iran-contra affair, led to a massive investigation and the near downfall of the Reagan administration. Administration officials have made the case that the arms sale would never have occurred without the passage of the Boland Amendments.

A man who disliked the limelight, Boland was nonetheless proud of the amendments that bore his name, believing they upheld congressional prerogatives and enforced the system of checks and balances created by the founding fathers. Boland left the House of Representatives in 1988 after 18 terms in Washington. He returned to his home in Springfield and died on November 4, 2001, at age 90.

Bork, Robert H.
(1927–   ) *federal judge, Supreme Court nominee*

A controversial Reagan nominee for the Supreme Court, Robert Bork grew up in Pittsburgh during the Great Depression as a New Deal liberal and loyal Roosevelt Democrat. Following graduation from high school, he joined the marine corps reserves and served in China in 1945 and 1946. He then entered the University of Chicago where he abandoned his New Deal liberalism and became a free-market conservative. After receiving his B.A. from Chicago in 1948, he went back to the marines to serve in the Korean War. He served until 1952, then returned to the University of Chicago to study law, earning a J.D. in 1953.

He passed the Illinois bar exam that same year, but instead of entering practice right away, Bork stayed at the University of Chicago as a research associate for free-market economist Aaron Director.

Bork's work on business regulations and antitrust laws proved beneficial when he joined Kirkland, Ellis, Hodson, Chaffetz, and Masters, a well-known Chicago corporate law firm, in 1955. He worked for this firm in both Chicago and New York City until 1962, specializing in antitrust litigation. In 1962, he left the firm to take a teaching position at Yale University Law School. Bork continued to devote his energy to the area of antitrust law, yet as a university professor he had more time for independent research and writing. In 1978 he published *The Antitrust Paradox: A Policy at War with Itself,*

President Reagan talks with his Supreme Court nominee, Judge Robert H. Bork, July 1, 1987.

which criticized past antitrust rulings and advocated the elimination of many antitrust laws on the books.

Bork also became known for his work in the field of constitutional law during his tenure at Yale. He advocated judicial restraint and a strict interpretation of the Constitution. He also believed strongly in the right of the majority to make law and would only uphold challenges to these laws if they explicitly violated a person's constitutional rights. He wrote frequently on the latest Supreme Court rulings and often criticized the high court for its judicial activism. He opposed many of the seminal legal victories in the Civil Rights movement, as well as numerous other issues regarding free speech, religion, and privacy rights, earning him high marks in conservative circles. By 1973, he had gained the attention of the Nixon administration and was selected as solicitor general. Just months into his term, Bork rose to the unenviable position of acting attorney general after the infamous "Saturday Night Massacre." After Attorney General Elliot Richardson and Deputy Attorney General William Ruckelshaus were dismissed for disobeying Nixon's order to fire Watergate special prosecutor Archibald Cox, Bork rose to the head of the department and followed Nixon's order. Although his decision was widely unpopular, he was able to keep his position as acting attorney general until 1974, then returned to his post as solicitor general until the end of the Ford administration.

After government service Bork returned to Yale as a professor of law, a position he kept until 1981. He also became associated with the American Enterprise Institute for Public Policy Research (AEI), a Washington-based think tank, during this time, serving as a resident scholar in 1977, then an adjunct scholar until 1982. Following his exit from Yale in 1981, Bork became a partner at the Washington law firm Kirkland and Ellis. In 1982, another con-

servative, President Ronald Reagan, selected Bork to join the U.S. Court of Appeals for the District of Columbia Circuit. When Supreme Court Justice Lewis Powell retired in 1987, Reagan tapped the conservative Bork to be his replacement on the bench. Almost immediately, a firestorm of opposition embroiled the nomination as numerous political organizations challenged his positions on a variety of social issues. Senator Edward Kennedy argued that if Bork were placed on the Supreme Court, "women would be forced into back-alley abortions, blacks would sit at segregated lunch counters, rogue police would break down citizens' doors in midnight raids, school children would not be taught about evolution, writers and authors could be censored at the whim of government and the doors of the federal courts would be shut on the fingers of millions of citizens." President Reagan, already weakened by the Iran-contra scandal, belatedly entered the fray on Bork's behalf, but his lobbying effort came too late to sway any votes. Bork tried to paint himself as a moderate and sought to assure the Senate that his political beliefs would not affect his ability to fairly judge the law, but in October 1987, his nomination was defeated, 58 to 42.

Bork returned to his seat on the Circuit Court for a few more months but retired in February 1988 to write and work with the American Enterprise Institute. In 1989, he released *The Tempting of America: The Political Seduction of the Law*, a widely read work that criticized the judicial activism of many judges in America and called for a return to a strict interpretation of the Constitution. Years later, Bork published *Slouching toward Gomorrah: Modern Liberalism and American Decline*, where he warned that the absence of a shared morality was leading to the decline of American culture. Bork currently serves as John M. Olin Scholar in Legal Studies at the AEI in Washington, D.C.

Bowen, Otis R.

(1918–   ) *secretary of health and human services*

Dr. Otis Bowen joined the Reagan administration as secretary of health and human services (HHS) in December 1985 and served the remainder of Reagan's second term, becoming the longest-serving secretary in HHS history. Before his entry into national politics, he served 14 years in the Indiana General Assembly and two terms as one of the most popular governors in Indiana's history. A gentle man with the demeanor of a country doctor, many observers thought Bowen would be overwhelmed by the ways of Washington, but he proved to be an able administrator and an effective advocate for his agency.

Bowen was born in Richland Center, Indiana, and remained in his home state following high school to attend Indiana University in Bloomington. He earned his A.B. in chemistry in 1939, then continued at the Indiana University School of Medicine for his medical degree, which he received three years later. He began his internship at Memorial Hospital in South Bend, Indiana, before joining the U.S. Army Medical Corps during World War II. Bowen served with the medical corps in the Pacific theater until 1946. He took part in the first wave of attacks by American troops in the famous battle for Okinawa.

Following the war, Bowen started his own private practice in Bremen, Indiana. In 1953, he made his first foray into politics when he won election as the coroner for Marshall County, Indiana, where he served for the next four years. In 1957, he won a seat in the Indiana General Assembly. He was elected again the next year, then after a brief time away from politics served 12 consecutive years in the state legislature from 1961 to 1972. In 1965, Bowen was named House Minority Leader, and two years later he became Speaker of the House, a position he

held until 1972. He also served on the Indiana General Assembly Legislative Council as vice chairman in 1970 and as chairman in 1972. Bowen lost the 1968 gubernatorial election to Democrat Edgar Whitcomb, but four years later he succeeded Whitcomb as governor of Indiana. That same year, Indiana passed a constitutional amendment allowing governors to serve two consecutive terms in office. In 1976, Bowen won reelection and became the only Indiana governor to serve back-to-back terms.

Bowen moved from the governor's office into academia in 1982, becoming the Lester D. Bibler Professor of Family Medicine and the director of Undergraduate Family Practice Education at the Indiana University School of Medicine. He continued his involvement in government during this time, serving on a number of boards and presidential commissions, including the Presidential Advisory Committee on Federalism and the Advisory Council on Social Security, where he served as chairman. In December 1985 President Reagan nominated Bowen as HHS secretary to replace MARGARET HECKLER. He joined the administration the following month and remained until the end of the Reagan presidency, making Bowen's tenure the longest of any secretary in the history of the department.

Following his service in the Reagan administration, Bowen and his wife, Carol, returned to Bremen, Indiana, for retirement. In 2001, he released his autobiography, *Doc: Memories from a Life in Public Service*, which offers an intimate portrait of his career in public life. Bowen continues to write and speak frequently on health, welfare, and education issues.

Brady, Nicholas F.

(1930–   ) *secretary of the Treasury*

As treasury secretary for the Reagan and Bush administrations, Nicholas Brady successfully dealt with the Latin American debt crisis and the near collapse of the savings and loan industry. Nonetheless, his support for a tax increase, which caused Bush to renege on a campaign promise and ultimately led to his electoral defeat in 1992, made Brady the target of criticism from within his own party.

Brady grew up in Far Hills, New Jersey, a suburb of New York City, and attended Yale University for undergraduate work, earning a B.A. in 1954. He received his M.B.A. from Harvard University two years later. He joined the prestigious Manhattan investment banking firm Dillon, Reed, and Company, immediately after graduating from business school. Brady moved up the ladder quickly at Dillon Reed, becoming president and CEO in 1971, and chairman of the board three years later. In 1971, he was named chairman of the Fortune 500 company Purolator, where he remained until 1987.

In 1980, Brady entered the political arena as cochairman of former CIA director George Bush's campaign for the Republican presidential nomination. After the Bush defeat, Brady went back to his job as chairman of Purolator, but in 1982 he returned to politics with a surprise appointment to the U.S. Senate. New Jersey senator Harrison Williams had recently resigned after being convicted in the anticorruption Abscam operation. Upon his resignation, Governor Thomas Kean selected Brady to serve the final eight months of Williams's term. During this short stint, he advocated cuts in Social Security and criticized the Reagan administration's economic forecasts.

Brady remained in government service after he left the Senate. In 1983, he was named to the President's Commission on Strategic Forces, the National Bipartisan Commission on Central America, and the Commission on Security and Economic Assistance. A year later, he became chairman of the President's Commission on Executive, Legislative, and Judicial

Salaries. In 1985, he joined the Blue Ribbon Commission on Defense Management. And in 1987, following the stock market collapse in October of that year, President Reagan named Brady chairman of the Presidential Task Force on Market Mechanisms, the commission charged with investigating the causes of the collapse and recommend ways to prevent another such crash. Known as the Brady Commission, the panel recommended many stock market reform measures that were later approved by Congress.

In the summer of 1988, Treasury Secretary JAMES BAKER III left the Reagan administration to work again for Vice President GEORGE BUSH's presidential campaign. Reagan then tapped Brady to replace Baker at Treasury, and Brady took over the post on September 15, 1988. He quietly served the final four months of the Reagan presidency. Brady was reappointed as secretary of the Treasury by President Bush in January 1989 and served the entire term. This was a difficult time to serve at Treasury as the nation plunged into recession. Brady also drew sharp criticism from his party for supporting Bush's tax increase, leading many Republicans to call for his resignation. Bush, known for his loyalty, kept Brady for the remainder of his term, and Brady was able to achieve some successes in other areas. He played a major role in bailout of the savings and loan industry by creating the Resolution Trust Corporation. He also initiated what is known as the Brady Plan to solve the debt crisis in Latin America. Following Bush's defeat by Bill Clinton in 1992, Brady returned to the business world.

Brady remains active in both politics and business, serving as the chairman and CEO of Darby Overseas Investments and as a member of the Council on Foreign Relations. He is also on the board of several other companies, including Amerada Hess Corporation, H.J. Heinz Company, and Templeton Funds.

Brezhnev, Leonid

(1906–1982) *general secretary, Communist Party of the Soviet Union*

During his 18-year tenure, Leonid Brezhnev greatly enhanced the stature of the Soviet Union abroad, reaching strategic parity with the United States, solidifying Moscow's control over Eastern Europe, and expanding the communist revolution to the developing world. However, in his last few years in power, the Soviet Union was plagued by economic stagnation and social malaise, while at the same time Moscow entered a new period of conflict with the United States during the Reagan years.

Brezhnev grew up in a pro-communist, working-class family in the Ukraine and was 11 years old when the Bolsheviks took power in the 1917 October Revolution. He was immediately attracted to the new system, joining the Komsomol, the Communist Party's youth organization, in 1923 and working as a land surveyor for the party in Byelorussia. A few years later, he moved to the Ural Mountain region to administer Stalin's massive land redistribution program. In 1931, he formally joined the Communist Party of the Soviet Union (CPSU). He studied agronomy at the Timiryazeff Academy briefly before entering the Kamenskoe Metallurgical Institute, completing his degree in metallurgical engineering in 1935. For two years after graduation he served as the institute's technical college director.

In 1938 Brezhnev turned his attention full time to the party, working in propaganda, agriculture, and defense policy at the Dnepropetrovsk Regional Communist Party Committee. He met future general secretary Nikita Khrushchev, who was sent to purge the Ukrainian Communist Party leadership, during his time in Dnepropetrovsk. From 1939 to 1945, he served in the Red Army in World War II, under Khrushchev for a short time, as head of party propaganda, where he rose to the rank

of major general by the end of the war. Following the war, Brezhnev was named first secretary of a regional Communist Party committee in the Ukraine, where he managed the postwar reconstruction. In 1950 he was promoted to first secretary of the Central Committee of Moldovia, and charged with socializing the former Romanian territory into the Soviet sphere. Two years later he moved to Moscow after being elected to the Central Committee and appointed one of 10 members of the Secretariat.

Following the death of Joseph Stalin in 1953, Brezhnev was temporarily demoted from the party structure and appointed second secretary of the Central Committee in Kazakhstan. While in Kazakhstan the new Soviet leader, Khrushchev, commissioned Brezhnev to administer his "Virgin Lands" program, a 90 million–acre agricultural development project in western Siberia and Kazakhstan. Over the next two years, Brezhnev ran the program so successfully that he was reappointed to the Secretariat in 1956, and in 1960 was named chairman of the Presidium of the Supreme Soviet, the formal head of state in the Soviet Union. This largely ceremonial role gave Brezhnev the opportunity to travel extensively and become well versed in international affairs. In October 1964, following the removal of Nikita Khrushchev by a party coup, Brezhnev became first secretary of the Communist Party. Although this was the most powerful position within the Soviet Union, an informal agreement made after Khrushchev's ouster gave Prime Minister Aleksei Kosygin and Presidium chairman N.V. Podgorny equal power with Brezhnev. He did not emerge as the sole leader until the 23rd Party Congress in March 1966, when he was given the title of general secretary.

Brezhnev led perhaps the most successful foreign policy in the history of the Soviet Union. In 1965, he began a massive arms buildup to put the Soviet arsenal on an equal footing with that of the United States. By the end of the decade, the Soviets had achieved parity in a number of key weapons systems and had passed the United States in the amount of intercontinental and submarine-launched ballistic missiles (ICBMs and SLBMs). The expansion of the Soviet arsenal, coupled with the American public's disillusionment with the Vietnam War, led President Richard Nixon to seek a rapprochement with Brezhnev. Between 1972 and 1974, Nixon and Brezhnev reached a number of economic, scientific, and cultural agreements, marking a significant easing of tensions between the two superpowers. The most important agreement of this period was the Strategic Arms Limitation Treaty (SALT I), signed in 1972, which placed a five-year freeze on strategic launchers and prohibited the development of an antiballistic missile (ABM) system.

Brezhnev also increased the power of the Soviet Union around the globe. The Warsaw Pact nations of Eastern Europe remained firmly in the Soviet sphere, in large part due to the credibility of the "Brezhnev Doctrine," which gave Moscow the right to intervene militarily in any nation where communist rule was under attack. He put this doctrine into action early in his tenure when Soviet forces invaded Czechoslovakia and crushed an uprising led by reformer Alexander Dubcek. He actively supported communist revolutions in the developing world, gaining Soviet satellites in countries like Angola, Somalia, Yemen, and Afghanistan, among others, during the 1970s. Finally, with the signing of the Final Act of the Conference on Security and Cooperation in Europe in August 1975, Moscow's hegemony over the Eastern bloc was formally recognized by the Western powers.

Brezhnev and his foreign minister, ANDREI GROMYKO, continued to work with the Ford and Carter administrations to improve relations, but by the mid-1970s the American public began to repudiate détente. When the Red Army invaded Afghanistan in December 1979, the Carter administration withdrew the SALT II agreement from the Senate and canceled a number of agreements with Moscow, formally ending the rapprochement. The confrontational posture taken by Carter in his last year in office was augmented in 1981 by incoming president Ronald Reagan. Reagan, part of the neoconservative movement of the 1970s, which fought for an end to détente, initiated the largest arms buildup in American history shortly after entering office. With neither side making a concerted effort at reviving détente, relations between Reagan and Brezhnev remained chilly until Brezhnev's death.

Domestically, the final years of the Brezhnev regime were equally bleak, with the economic and social situation causing widespread malaise throughout the country. The Soviet economy, growing at a 3 percent annual rate in the early 1970s, was now sputtering at less than 2 percent a year. Rigid bureaucratic control of industry had led to inefficiency, low productivity, and a declining standard of living. In addition, widespread patronage and corruption within the party organization caused cynicism and disillusionment among the Soviet public. Because Brezhnev and the conservative wing of the party never made any serious effort to redress these problems, the economic and social conditions remained this way until the end of his tenure.

On November 10, 1982, Brezhnev died from heart and vascular disease in Moscow. Two days later, former KGB chief YURI ANDROPOV beat out Brezhnev's hand-picked successor, KONSTANTIN CHERNENKO, to become general secretary of the CPSU.

Brock, William E., III
(1930–   ) *U.S. trade representative, secretary of labor*

William Brock served as U.S. trade representative during the first term of the Reagan administration, then replaced RAYMOND DONOVAN as secretary of labor, a position he held until 1987. Prior to joining the administration, he served four terms in the U.S. House and one term in the Senate, and was chairman of the Republican National Committee from 1976 to 1980.

Brock graduated from Washington and Lee University with a degree in commerce in 1953, then joined the U.S. Navy where he served for the next three years and reached the rank of lieutenant, junior grade. He returned to his home town of Chattanooga, Tennessee, in 1956 and began working in the family candy business as an assistant in production and control. In just five years, he rose through the ranks to become director of the company and vice president in charge of marketing.

In 1962, Brock won his first bid for public office when he took Tennessee's Third District seat in the U.S. House of Representatives, becoming the first Republican to win the seat in more than 40 years. He served the next eight years in the House, then in 1970 he defeated three-term Democratic senator Albert Gore. After Brock lost his seat to Democrat James R. Sasser in 1976, he ran for the chairmanship of the Republican National Committee (RNC), winning the post as a compromise candidate over Richard Richards and JAMES BAKER III. He was credited by many in the party for his role in rebuilding a fractured GOP in the wake of the 1976 presidential election, where President GERALD FORD, after a difficult primary challenge from Ronald Reagan, was easily defeated by JIMMY CARTER in the general election. He was also head of the RNC when Reagan took 44 states and 489 electoral votes, and the Republican Party took control of the Senate in the 1980 elections. Nonetheless, Brock's failure to use his position as RNC chairman to oppose Carter's policies, particularly the ratification of the 1978 Panama Canal treaties, caused resentment among the conservative wing of the party.

In 1981, Brock joined the Reagan administration as U.S. trade representative, a position that was given cabinet-level status by Carter. He served at this post until the end of Reagan's first term in office, then in 1985 he replaced RAYMOND DONOVAN as secretary of labor. He resigned from the Labor Department in 1987 to join the presidential campaign of Kansas senator ROBERT DOLE as chairman of the Dole for President Committee. After Dole failed to defeat Vice President GEORGE H. W. BUSH in the GOP primary, Brock remained in Washington, D.C., as a political consultant. In 1994, he made another run for the Senate, this time from Maryland, but lost to Democrat Paul Sarbanes.

Brown, Edmund G.
(Pat)
(1905–1996) *governor of California*

Ronald Reagan's first opponent in a race for public office, Edmund Brown was a pillar of the Democratic Party who had defeated Richard Nixon in the 1962 race for governor of California. Four years later, Brown was soundly defeated by Reagan, a development that sent shock waves throughout the nation and launched Reagan on the path to the White House.

Following graduation from high school, Brown entered the San Francisco College of Law, receiving his LL.B. in 1927. He passed the California bar exam the same year and began to practice law in San Francisco. Brown entered politics early in his career, and in 1928, at the age of 23, he ran for the California State Assembly. Running as a Republican, Brown lost the race and returned to his law practice where he would remain until 1943. He ran several more unsuccessful campaigns for public office during his time in private law practice. During the Great Depression, he became an admirer of Franklin D. Roosevelt, and in 1943 he made another run for public office, this time as a Democrat. He won the election as district attorney of San Francisco and stayed at this post for seven years. In 1951, Brown was elected attorney general of the state of California.

In 1958, Brown challenged Republican senator William Knowland for the state's highest office, defeating the well-known senator by over 1 million votes. He won reelection four years later over another powerful California politician, former vice president Richard Nixon. Brown governed as an unabashed liberal who believed in the power of the government to make people's lives better. For most of his tenure as governor, California enjoyed tremendous growth and prosperity, allowing Brown to greatly increase the state budget. He added 11 new state college campuses, over 1,000 miles of highway, and one of the largest state public works programs in American history. He worked hard to implement his liberal social policies, including laws to end racial discrimination, health care for the poor, and increased benefits for the unemployed, the handicapped, and senior citizens.

Toward the end of his second term, the days of unprecedented growth came to an end and Brown was forced to confront many of the problems facing the nation at the dawn of a period of discord at home during the Vietnam War. In the 1966 election, he was challenged by the former actor, Ronald Reagan, who ran as a Goldwater conservative, but a genial conservative. Brown dismissed Reagan as just an actor, but Reagan was successful in tapping into the anxiety many average Californians were feeling about taxes, race relations, and the increasing power of the student movement, and he easily defeated Brown in the election.

Following his exit from the governor's office, Brown became a partner at the Los Angeles firm of Ball, Hunt, Hart, Brown, and Baerwitz. In 1970, he wrote a book about California under Reagan entitled *Reagan and Reality: The Two Californias*. He also coauthored a book, *Public Justice, Private Mercy: A Governor's Education on Death Row* (1989), on the subject of capital punishment, which Brown passionately opposed. He retired from his law practice in the early 1990s. Brown died of a heart attack in his Beverly Hills home on February 16, 1996.

Buchanan, Patrick J.
(1938–   ) *director of communications*

In 1992, 1996, and 2000, Pat Buchanan ran for president on a platform of populist conservative beliefs such as cutting illegal immigration, protecting American industries, and maintaining traditional American values. Starting as a young aide to Richard Nixon, Buchanan emerged over the years to become one of the most recognizable faces on cable television news and public affairs programming. His lengthy career in politics and journalism made him one of the nation's foremost conservative spokesmen.

Following high school, Buchanan remained in his hometown of Washington, D.C., where he was born and raised, to attend Georgetown University for studies in English. During his senior year, he assaulted a police officer after being cited for a traffic violation and was arrested and fined, and suspended from school for a year. The year away from school had a profound effect on Buchanan's career path: he made the decision to pursue a career in journalism. The next year, he returned to Georgetown and earned his B.A., with honors. He moved to New York immediately after to study journalism at Columbia University and received his Master of Science degree in 1962.

Buchanan joined the conservative *St. Louis Globe-Democrat* as a reporter the following year and was quickly promoted to editorial writer,

President Reagan and Director of Communications Patrick J. Buchanan looking at a television monitor, Blue Room, White House, March 22, 1985, moments before Reagan gives a press conference

becoming the youngest editorial writer of any major U.S. newspaper at that time. After just two years at the job, he was promoted to assistant editorial editor, but a year later he left the newspaper to pursue a career in Washington. In 1966, Buchanan met with former vice president Richard Nixon, who was working as a lawyer in New York City at the time. Nixon was taken by Buchanan's conservative philosophy and hired him as an assistant, where Buchanan served as a speechwriter until Nixon's victory in the 1968 presidential election. Buchanan was fortunate to join with Nixon at such an early stage and following the victory he was named a special assistant to the president.

Buchanan was pleased with his new career and enjoyed working in the White House. He stayed in the administration until Nixon's resignation in August 1974, primarily writing speeches for Nixon and Vice President Spiro Agnew, and serving as a strategist for the 1972 reelection campaign. In 1973, he became a consultant to Nixon for the growing Watergate scandal. He went on to serve as an adviser for President GERALD FORD in the first few months of his administration, but left shortly after to lecture and write a syndicated column. He also wrote *Conservative Voices, Liberal Victories: Why the Right Has Failed*, which was released in 1975. In 1978, he joined NBC Radio as a commentator and also became a cohost of the "Buchanan-Braden Show." In 1982, he became a cohost on CNN's adversarial political talk show, *Crossfire*, and a panelist on the PBS program, *The McLaughlin Group*. Buchanan's visibility on these programs earned him a reputation as a leading figure in the conservative wing of the Republican Party.

Buchanan moved back into politics in 1985 when he joined the Reagan administration as director of communications, but he stayed in the White House for only two years before returning to journalism. He rejoined the casts of *Crossfire* and *The McLaughlin Group*, and in 1988 he joined the panel of CNN's *Capital Gang*. He also became editor-in-chief of the newsletter *PJB: From the Right* in 1990. In 1992, he challenged incumbent President GEORGE H. W. BUSH for the Republican presidential nomination. Bush had angered much of the party faithful who believed he had sacrificed his conservative principles in favor of a more centrist ideology. Buchanan capitalized on this sentiment and ran on quintessential conservative values— what he termed "street corner" conservatism— such as lowering taxes, fighting illegal immigration, and eliminating a woman's right to an abortion. The message resonated with many in the party and Buchanan stunned the incumbent by winning the New Hampshire primary with 37 percent of the vote. His campaign stalled after New Hampshire and Buchanan returned again to journalism after the election.

In the years following the 1992 election, Buchanan prepared to run once again for the Republican presidential nomination. He used his large audience on *Crossfire* and as host of *Pat Buchanan and Company* to lay out what would become the major themes of his 1996 campaign. His major opponent was longtime Kansas senator ROBERT DOLE, the sentimental favorite for many in the party. Buchanan started off strong, winning the New Hampshire primary for the second time, but eventually lost the nomination to Dole. In 1999, he prepared for his third run

for the GOP nomination, but after an Iowa straw poll showed his support within the party waning he left the Republican Party and became the nominee for the Reform Party. His candidacy was ineffectual in the general election as he took only 1 percent of the popular vote.

Since the 2000 election, Buchanan has remained one of the most visible ambassadors of the conservative wing in America. He continues to write a syndicated column and is currently a political analyst for MSNBC.

Burford, Anne McGill
(1942–) *director, Environmental Protection Agency*

President Reagan's controversial choice to head the Environmental Protection Agency, Anne McGill Burford was a target of Democrats in Congress for her alleged insensitivity to the environment. She resigned her office under a cloud, and along with her colleague JAMES WATT, fostered the impression that the Reagan administration favored business interests over environmental protection.

Burford received her B.A. from the University of Colorado in 1961. She went immediately into law school at Regis College in Denver, earning her LL.B. in 1964. Burford was awarded a Fulbright scholarship in 1964 to study in Taipur, India. Following her studies in India, she returned to Denver and took a job at First National Bank as an assistant trust administrator. In 1968, she became assistant district attorney in Jefferson County, Colorado. She was appointed deputy district attorney in Denver in 1971 and remained at this position until 1973 when she became a Colorado State hearing officer. In 1975, Burford joined the Mountain Bell Corporation as an attorney. While at Mountain Bell, she entered into politics for the first time, winning a seat in the Colorado House of Representatives in 1976 and serving until 1980.

In 1981 Burford was selected by President Reagan to serve as administrator of the Environmental Protection Agency. She was criticized almost immediately for the massive cuts she proposed in the EPA's budget. Much of Burford's notoriety, however, came when the EPA was investigated by Congress in October 1982 over the use of money allocated for the cleanup of hazardous waste. When Congressman John Dingell (D-Mich.) demanded that Burford supply Congress with the relevant information, she invoked executive privilege and refused to hand over the documents, a move that led Congress to charge her with contempt. President Reagan publicly supported his EPA chief, but in early 1983, in response to serious pressures from both parties, Burford resigned her post at the agency.

Following her departure from the EPA, Burford unleashed a scathing critique of environmentalists, Congress, and administration officials in a book she coauthored with John Greenya, *Are You Tough Enough? An Insider's View of Washington Power Politics* (1985).

Burnley, James H., IV
(1948–) *secretary of transportation*

James H. Burnley, IV, served in the Transportation Department under President Reagan from 1983 to 1989, beginning as general counsel and eventually leading the department in December 1987. His agenda included greater focus on safety and efforts to increase cooperation between the Transportation Department and private business and industry, both of which were largely achieved during his tenure as transportation secretary.

Burnley attended Yale University after high school and earned his B.A., magna cum laude, in 1970. He moved on to rival Harvard University for studies in law and completed his J.D. in 1973. Immediately after law school,

Burnley moved back to his hometown of Greensboro, North Carolina, and joined the law firm of Brooks, Pierce, McLendon, Humphrey, and Leonard as an associate. He stayed there for two years before becoming a partner at Turner, Enochs, Foster, Sparrow, and Burnley, another Greensboro firm. In 1981 and 1982, he served as director of the VISTA program.

Burnley joined the Reagan administration in 1982 when he was named associate deputy attorney general for the Justice Department. The next year he moved to the Department of Transportation and became general counsel. He was only at this post for a short time before becoming deputy secretary of transportation. As deputy secretary, Burnley played a key role in maintaining an air traffic control workforce, an industry that was still seeing the effects of the ill-advised August 1981 PATCO strike. He also assisted in the negotiations of the sale of Conrail, spearheaded the efforts to privatize Amtrak, and helped establish the department's aviation safety and security policies. Burnley took over as head of the Transportation Department in December 1987 after Secretary ELIZABETH DOLE left to assist her husband, Senator ROBERT DOLE, in his 1988 presidential campaign. During his 13 months in office, Burnley implemented an agenda focused on greater safety and a higher degree of private-sector partnership with the Transportation Department. He remained at his post until the end of the Reagan administration in January 1989.

Burnley is currently a partner at Venable LLP, a Washington law firm.

Bush, George H. W.
(1924–) *vice president*

The 41st president of the United States was a lifelong public servant who was tapped by

Ronald Reagan (his 1980 Republican primary opponent) to serve as the nation's vice president during the Reagan years. A loyal vice president, Bush was the first president since Martin Van Buren to inherit the office from his running mate.

George H. W. Bush had a long and distinguished career in business and public service, spanning more than 25 years in politics and culminating in his election as America's 41st president in 1988. Although he was soundly defeated in his bid for reelection in 1992, Bush has been increasingly praised by historians and political scientists as a successful president.

Bush grew up in a privileged household in the town of Greenwich, Connecticut. As the son of a Wall Street businessman and U.S. senator, Bush was able to attend prestigious private schools like Greenwich Country Day School and Phillips Academy. Immediately following high school, Bush volunteered in the U.S. Navy Reserve to fight in World War II. During the war, Bush served in the Pacific as a navy pilot and was shot down in action, earning a Purple Heart for his bravery. Following the war, Bush entered Yale University to study economics, and he graduated after just three years. He moved to Midland, Texas, and entered the oil business with a job as an oilfield supply salesman for Dresser Industries. By 1953, Bush had a firm grasp of the oil business and opened his own gas and oil drilling company, Zapata Incorporated. By the end of the decade, he had become a millionaire.

Bush became involved in Texas Republican politics during this time, serving as GOP chairman of Houston County. In 1964, he tried to follow in his father's footsteps and win a seat in the U.S. Senate. He lost the race to incumbent Democrat Ralph Yarborough, but returned two years later to win a seat in the House of Representatives. He served in Congress for two terms, then made another run for the Senate in

President-elect George H. W. Bush and President Reagan shake hands in the Oval Office, January 19, 1989.

1970, losing this time to moderate Texas Democrat Lloyd Bentsen. During his second term in Congress, Bush became one of President Nixon's strongest allies in the House, and after Bush's failed attempt at the Senate, Nixon made him ambassador to the United Nations. Although new to international affairs, Bush exhibited prudence and skill in this forum, honing a diplomatic style that would later serve him well in the White House.

Bush left the United States at the end of 1972 to become chairman of the Republican National Committee. This proved to be one of the most difficult times in the history of the party as the Watergate scandal was erupting. Bush remained steadfast in his support of Nixon, but as new evidence came to light, he began to shift his agenda to salvaging the reputation of the Republican Party. One month after Nixon's resignation, Bush left the RNC to run the U.S. Liaison Office in China, the highest diplomatic post to the People's Republic of

China, where formal diplomatic relations had not yet been established. He remained at this position for just over a year before taking over as GERALD FORD's director of Central Intelligence in January 1976. He worked hard to restore the efficacy of the CIA after a series of damaging revelations generated by congressional investigations in the mid-1970s.

Bush left his position at the CIA after the election of JIMMY CARTER and returned to Texas to become chairman of the First National Bank of Houston. He immediately began to eye the 1980 GOP nomination, starting the Fund for Limited Government to finance his campaign efforts. In May 1979 Bush formally announced his candidacy for the presidency. He went up against a formidable opponent in Ronald Reagan, who successfully captured a large part of the conservative wing of the party, to the detriment of the Bush campaign. Bush also lacked the simple, broad vision for America that Reagan offered in his campaign, a problem that followed Bush into his own presidency. He stayed in the race until the convention, but he quickly ended his run when Reagan selected him as his running mate the day before the formal balloting.

Although he had run a tough and often biting nomination campaign against Reagan, after the election Bush became a faithful ally to the president. He was instrumental in the execution of several of Reagan's policy initiatives; chairing the National Narcotics Border Interdiction System, for example. Also, through a regular weekly lunch with the president, Bush developed a warm friendship with Reagan. In 1988, Reagan gave Bush his endorsement for the GOP nomination.

Even with the damage of the Iran-contra scandal, Reagan left the White House with an approval rating nearing 60 percent, and Bush was able to ride much of that popularity to a victory over Massachusetts governor Michael Dukakis. During his tenure in the White House, Bush led with prudence and pragmatism, which served him well in most cases but led many to decry his lack of vision. In this sense, he was the antithesis of Reagan. Yet by governing in his own style, Bush was still able to achieve significant victories, particularly in foreign policy. His finest moment was in organizing an international coalition to defeat Iraqi dictator Saddam Hussein in the Gulf War. He also presided over the reunification of Germany, the capture and conviction of Manuel Noriega, and the collapse of the Soviet Union.

Bush's domestic policy, however, became a major liability in his campaign for reelection. His approval rating had surpassed 90 percent in the wake of the Gulf War, the highest rating ever by a president, but soon the country slipped into recession and Bush was admonished for failing to propose a domestic agenda and restore an ailing economy. To make matters worse, Bush broke his 1988 campaign promise and raised taxes, essentially insuring his defeat in the 1992 election. By the end of 1992, the economy was recovering strongly, but it was too late for Bush to gain politically.

His loss to Arkansas governor Bill Clinton marked the end of Bush's career in national politics. Since that time, he has focused largely on writing, spending time with his family, and supporting the electoral efforts of his two sons, President George W. Bush and Florida governor Jeb Bush. He finished his first memoir, *A World Transformed* (1998), coauthored with Brent Scowcroft; a book that, not surprisingly, focused on his administration's foreign policy. A more personal memoir, *All the Best, George Bush*, was published the following year. He is also actively involved in the work of the George H. W. Bush Presidential Library and Museum, which opened in College Station, Texas, in 1997.

C

Carlucci, Frank C., III
(1930–) *National Security Advisor, secretary of defense*

During the depths of the Iran-contra scandal, Frank Carlucci played a critical role in restoring the credibility of the National Security Council in the turbulent months following the departure of JOHN POINDEXTER and OLIVER NORTH. Carlucci also served as Reagan's second secretary of defense, and earned a reputation as an able administrator and a team player.

Carlucci didn't travel far from his hometown of Scranton, Pennsylvania, to attend Princeton University, where he earned a B.A. in 1952. He joined the U.S. Navy after graduation and stayed in the service for two years before entering Harvard Business School for his M.B.A.

Carlucci entered government service early when he joined the foreign service in 1956. He became vice consul and economic affairs officer in Johannesburg, South Africa, in 1957, serving at this post until 1959. He stayed in Africa until 1962 after taking a position as second secretary and political officer in Kinshasa, Congo. With six years of experience in Africa, Carlucci moved to Washington, D.C., in 1962 and resumed his career in the State Department as

the officer responsible for Congolese political affairs. After two years, he was promoted to consul general for Zanzibar. In 1965 Carlucci took his expertise to South America and accepted a position as counselor for political affairs for the American embassy in Rio de Janeiro, Brazil.

In 1969, Carlucci returned to Washington, D.C., and shifted his attention to U.S. domestic policy. He became assistant director of operations for the White House Office of Economic Opportunity (OEO) during the Nixon administration. One year later, he was promoted to OEO director. In 1971, Carlucci took a position as associate director in the Office of Management and Budget (OMB), moving to deputy director in 1972. Later that year, he moved over to the Department of Health, Education and Welfare (HEW) to become an under secretary. Coincidentally, CASPAR WEINBERGER served as the director of OMB and secretary of HEW during Carlucci's tenure at both offices, and the two became close associates during that time. After six years in the domestic arena, Carlucci returned to work in foreign affairs in 1975 when President Ford named him ambassador to Portugal. He remained at this position even after Ford's defeat in the 1976 general election, winning reappointment by President JIMMY CARTER, which would later make him suspect in the eyes of some conservatives. He left his post in Lisbon when Carter appointed him deputy director of the Central Intelligence Agency in 1978.

Carlucci rejoined Caspar Weinberger in 1981 when he became deputy secretary of defense for the Reagan administration. After 25 years in government service, he entered the private sector in 1982 for Sears World Trade, first as president, then as chairman and CEO. In 1986, he returned to the Reagan administration to take over as National Security Advisor, replacing the embattled John Poindexter, who had been forced to resign because of the Iran-contra affair. He became secretary of defense in 1987 after Weinberger left the administration.

Carlucci agreed with much of Weinberger's agenda. He was a firm supporter of SDI and consistently fought against any attempts to trade research and development on the program for arms cuts by the Soviet Union. He also strongly supported the Intermediate Nuclear Forces Treaty, signed with the Soviet Union in December 1987. Unlike his predecessor, however, Carlucci forged good relations with both Congress and Secretary of State GEORGE SHULTZ. He presided over a difficult time at the Pentagon as Congress was demanding deep cuts in the defense budget. Yet Carlucci, by cutting waste and eliminating a series of unneeded military bases, was able to bridge the gap between Congress and the White House while preserving much of the president's agenda.

Carlucci left the Pentagon in January 1989 and took a position as vice president and managing director with the Carlyle Group, a Washington-based investment firm. He later became chairman of Carlyle. Carlucci has also written and lectured extensively on national defense policy.

Carter, Jimmy
(1924–) *former U.S. president*

The 39th president of the United States was soundly defeated by Ronald Reagan in the 1980 presidential election. A decent man with a powerful intellect, Carter was one of only three presidents awarded the Nobel Peace Prize (along with Theodore Roosevelt and Woodrow Wilson) and established a reputation as a master of detail and a dogged worker. His campaign for the presidency in 1976 was first dismissed as a joke, but he surprised the nation and the world with his successful capture of the Democratic Party's nomination, and his defeat of incumbent President GERALD FORD.

Jimmy Carter attended Georgia Southwestern College and the Georgia Institute of Technology until 1943, when he was accepted into the U.S. Naval Academy in Annapolis, Maryland. He planned on a career in the navy, but his father's death in 1952 brought him back to Georgia to run the family farm and peanut warehouses. Carter became interested in politics in his hometown of Plains, Georgia, and was actively involved in community affairs, earning a reputation as a liberal, particularly on issues regarding race. In 1962, he won his first bid for political office, running for a seat in the Georgia Senate. He was a meticulous and disciplined legislator, promising his constituents that he would examine every piece of legislation that came across his desk. In 1964, Carter won a second term in the Senate.

After just four years in state politics, Carter made a run for the Democratic gubernatorial nomination. His loss to Lester Maddox in the primary marked a major turning point in his life. Following the defeat, he was born again, both spiritually and politically, and over the next three years Carter traveled around Georgia campaigning for his vision for the state. His tireless efforts earned him notoriety throughout the state and in 1970 he became governor of Georgia. Carter fought hard for social justice during his tenure in Atlanta. He was a staunch supporter of civil rights for African Americans; as a consequence the number of minorities holding state government posts rose by large numbers during his administration. Carter was also a champion of the poor, advocating equal education funding for rich and poor school districts and equal employment opportunity for all citizens.

Carter assumed leadership roles in the Democratic Party during this time, running the Democratic Governors Campaign Committee in 1972 and the Democratic National Campaign Committee two years later. At the end of his term as governor, Carter announced his plans to seek the Democratic presidential nomination in 1976. He rose from relative obscurity, even within his party, to the top of the 11-man field, winning more than half the party primaries and earning the nomination on the first ballot at the 1976 Democratic National Convention. Carter ran as an honest, moral leader and a Washington outsider with no ties to special interests groups, an image which had large appeal to voters in the wake of the Watergate scandal. The general election was a close contest, but in the end Carter won 297 electoral votes to Ford's 240.

President Carter focused largely on the energy crisis and the high unemployment rate, two issues GERALD FORD was unsuccessful in solving during his two and a half years in office. Like his predecessor, Carter found it difficult to deal with the ailing American economy. Although the economy briefly improved in the beginning of his term, by 1978 unemployment and inflation were both in double-digits and the economy was faltering once again.

Carter's foreign policy yielded similar results. Although he scored a major victory in September 1978 with the signing of the Camp David accords, establishing normal relations for the first time between Israel and Egypt, his foreign policy often gave the impression of weakness and inconsistency. His negotiation of a treaty to relinquish U.S. control of the Panama Canal in 1977 was seen by conservatives as a sign of American retreat. Carter's pursuit of détente while the Soviets were actively expanding their influence in the developing world contributed to a perception of naiveté. The most damaging event of Carter's presidency, however, came in November 1979 when militant Iranian students stormed the U.S. embassy in Tehran and took 52 Americans hostage. Five months later, a failed rescue attempt by the administration crystallized the perception of American weakness and loss of world status. During his final year in office, Carter took a tougher stance on foreign policy, particularly after the December 1980 Soviet invasion of Afghanistan, but it was much too late to overcome the image of weakness. In the 1980 election, Republican candidate Ronald Reagan capitalized on this feeling and easily defeated Carter on a platform of stronger defense and restoration of American pride.

Since his exit from the White House, Carter has worked assiduously as a promoter of democratic values and humanitarian ideals across the globe. He founded the Carter Center in 1981 to promote human rights, mediate conflicts, and fight disease in the Third World. In 1986, he became president of the Carter-Menhil Human Rights Foundation, another organization devoted to human rights in the Third World. He has also resumed his role as a major player in international politics. In an effort to resolve potentially explosive situations around the globe, Carter has met with various world leaders, including Nicaragua's DANIEL ORTEGA, Somalia's Mohammed Farrah Aidid, North Korea's Kim Il Sung, and Haiti's Lt. Gen. Raoul Cedras.

Carter spends his private time fishing, hunting, and writing. He has written several

CIA director William Casey meeting with President Reagan, January 23, 1983

books, including *Living Faith* (1997), *The Virtues of Aging* (1998), *Christmas in Plains* (2001), and *Hornet's Nest* (2004). He has also been an active participant in the Habitat for Humanity program. In 1999, President Clinton presented Carter with the Presidential Medal of Freedom.

Casey, William J.
(1913–1987) *director, Central Intelligence Agency*

William J. Casey was one of the more controversial and colorful figures of the Reagan era. As director of Central Intelligence, Casey was the point-man for Reagan's campaign to undermine the Soviet Union and its allies, the

"enforcer" of the so-called Reagan Doctrine. According to some testimony, he may have been involved in the Iran-contra affair, which had all of the hallmarks of Casey's penchant for off-the-shelf, ad hoc clandestine initiatives. His most ardent defenders reject this accusation, seeing the effort undertaken by OLIVER NORTH and JOHN POINDEXTER as lacking in Casey's sophisticated touch. Regardless of his role in that scandal, Casey was one of the most colorful figures to head the CIA since its founding; he resembled, in many ways, his mentor, William Donovan, the director of the Office of Strategic Services during World War II.

After attending both public and private schools as a youth, William Casey entered

Fordham University with plans to pursue a career in social work. He graduated from Fordham in 1934, then after a brief stint at Catholic University in Washington, D.C., moved on to St. John's University Law School in the Bronx, where he received his J.D. in 1937. The following year, Casey entered the workforce when he took a job at Leo Cherne's Research Institute of America. In December 1941, following the Japanese bombing of Pearl Harbor, Casey joined government service with jobs at the Bureau of Economic Warfare and, after receiving a commission as a navy lieutenant, in the navy's Office of Procurement. Casey eventually settled into the Office of Strategic Services, foreshadowing his later work as director of the CIA. He began work in the OSS's London office, and was quickly put in charge of Allied spies in occupied Europe and Nazi Germany as head of the OSS Secretariat for the European Theater of Operations.

Casey entered the business world after the war, starting the Institute for Business Planning, where he became a successful venture capitalist and part owner of several lucrative corporations. He also lectured frequently on tax law at New York University and became known as one of the leading tax experts in America. In 1957, Casey left IBP to practice law in New York City as a partner in Hall, Casey, Dickler, and Howley, where he remained for the next 14 years. It was during these years that Casey became an active participant in Republican Party politics, campaigning for Thomas Dewey in 1948. In 1966, he threw his own hat in the ring for a Long Island congressional seat, but was unsuccessful in his bid.

Casey worked for the 1968 Nixon campaign, and was rewarded three years later with an appointment as chairman of the Securities and Exchange Commission. In December 1972 he left the SEC to become undersecretary of state for economic affairs. He moved again in 1974 to the post of president of the Export-Import Bank, where he earned a reputation for mastering the intricacies of economic policy. He returned to practice corporate law for a brief period, but came back into government service in 1976 when Gerald Ford selected him to join the Foreign Intelligence Advisory Board.

Casey first came to know Ronald Reagan during the 1980 presidential campaign. During the Republican primaries he was appointed campaign director for Reagan, and received widespread praise for helping Reagan successfully gain the nomination. Casey was rewarded with the post of director of Central Intelligence following Reagan's victory and immediately set out to rebuild the agency. According to the *Los Angeles Times*'s Don Irwin, "Casey vowed to build the world's best intelligence operation." This was a major element of Reagan's agenda, for the president believed in the importance of an assertive intelligence community.

Because of the increased emphasis placed on intelligence during these years, Casey played a significant role in implementing Reagan's foreign policy. He was a key force behind what was later known as the Reagan Doctrine, which provided covert support to anticommunist forces throughout the world. Elaborate covert operations were conducted in Eastern Europe, Central America, Africa, and especially Central Asia, where American weapons given to Afghan rebels played a crucial role in the eventual defeat of the Soviet Union.

The CIA's operations ran into considerable opposition, however, in Central America where both Congress and the public feared American involvement in "nationalist" struggles. This opposition crystallized with the passage of the Boland Amendment in December 1983, which prohibited money for overthrowing the Sandinista government in Nicaragua. Casey, however, continued to support the contras, and the CIA came under fire in April 1984 when it was discovered that the agency had mined three harbors in Nicaragua without properly informing the members of the Senate Select Committee on Intelligence. After strong protest, Casey apologized and signed a pledge that required him to notify the committee of future covert operations.

Opposition to Casey and the CIA subsequently hardened and on October 12, 1984, a second Boland Amendment was passed, this one prohibiting any support to the contras. Certain members of the National Security Council staff were determined to evade the Boland Amendment restrictions, and sold arms to Iran and diverted the proceeds to the contras. In December 1986, a day before Casey was scheduled to testify before Congress about the scandal, he suffered a seizure and was treated for a malignant brain tumor. He resigned his post in January 1987, and died from pneumonia four months later in Long Island, New York.

The Tower Commission blamed him for failing to keep Reagan informed of the deal as it progressed. Others have been more critical of his involvement, saying that he played an active role in all facets of the operation. Yet, due to his illness, Casey never testified to his knowledge or involvement in Iran-contra.

Cavazos, Lauro F.
(1927–) *secretary of education*

Lauro Cavazos spent his entire career in education, beginning as a university professor and rising to several prestigious administrative positions including university president and later secretary of the U.S. Department of Education. During his two and a half years in the Reagan and Bush cabinets, he was a strong advocate of bilingual teaching, higher minority college enrollment, and greater parental involvement in education. He kept a lower profile at the Education Department than either his predecessor, WILLIAM BENNETT, or his successor, Lamar Alexander, and this prompted some criticism of his performance.

Cavazos grew up on the Spanish-speaking King Ranch, a small cattle ranch for Mexican workers in southern Texas. After high school, he joined an infantry unit in the U.S. Army near the end of World War II. He wanted to work as a commercial fisherman following the war, but on the advice of his father, who placed a priority on receiving a good education, he entered college. He began his studies at Texas A&I, then transferred and earned a zoology degree from Texas Technological College. He continued his education at Texas Tech, receiving his M.A. in zoological cytology in 1951, then moved east to earn his Ph.D. in physiology from Iowa State University in 1954.

Cavazos went directly into academia out of Iowa State, landing a job as an instructor at the Medical College of Virginia. He stayed in Virginia until 1964, eventually being promoted to assistant professor, then associate professor of anatomy, and serving on the editorial board of the *Medical College of Virginia Quarterly*. He then joined the anatomy department at the Tufts University School of Medicine in 1964. He began as professor and department chair, then in 1975 he became dean of the medical school. In 1980, he returned to his alma mater, Texas Tech, to become the new president of the university and its Health Science Center, the first Hispanic president in the university's history. During his tenure at Texas Tech, Cavazos focused on increasing the number of minority students at the university. By the time he left, the number of Hispanic students had doubled and the number of black students had increased by more than 30 percent. He also attacked the university's tenure policy, which resulted in a substantial backlash from professors. However, it earned him praise from the

Reagan administration who gave him the Outstanding Leadership Award in 1984.

When William Bennett resigned his post as secretary of education, President Reagan called on Cavazos to take over the department. He became education secretary and the first Hispanic member of the administration on September 20, 1988, and served the remaining six months of the Reagan presidency. Cavazos's agenda and personal style ran in stark contrast to Bennett, who was known for his aggressive demeanor and draconian cuts in federal education programs. Upon entering office, Cavazos said that "education is perhaps our most serious deficit." He advocated bilingual education and greater minority college enrollment, two new issues for the administration. He did agree with his predecessors in encouraging parental involvement and in finding local, not federal, solutions to problems in education.

In 1989, President GEORGE H. W. BUSH reappointed Cavazos as education secretary. During his tenure in the Bush administration, he continued to focus on higher standards, greater accountability, and reductions in the high school dropout rate. His views on bilingual education came under attack when he argued that children who cannot speak English are not ready for public education. He also challenged the notion that increased federal funding leads to better performance, choosing instead to encourage greater parental and community involvement. Cavazos was forced to resign his post in December 1990. He then took a position as adjunct professor at Tufts University Medical School.

Chernenko, Konstantin
(1911–1985) *general secretary, Communist Party of the Soviet Union*

Konstantin Chernenko spent more than five decades as an apparatchik in the Communist Party of the Soviet Union, rising quickly through the leadership ranks and eventually succeeding YURI ANDROPOV as general secretary in February 1984. His tenure as general secretary lasted just 13 months due to illness and marked one of the shortest and least eventful tenures in Soviet history.

Chernenko was born into a peasant family in Siberia and had little formal education as a youth, instead spending the majority of his time working on a farm, or kulak. He joined the Communist Youth League (Komsomol) in Novoselovo at the age of 18 and shortly after was named head of his district's propaganda and agitation department. After two years in the Komsomol, he joined the Red Army and spent the next three years in Kazakhstan near the Chinese border. One year into his military service, he became a full member of the Communist Party of the Soviet Union (CPSU). He returned to Siberia in 1933 and began serving as a party propagandist, steadily rising through the party structure over the next decade. In 1941, he was named party secretary in the Krasnoyarsk region of Siberia.

Chernenko's work as a propagandist was noticed by his superiors within the party, and in 1943 he was selected to study at Moscow's Higher School for Party Organizers. After graduation in 1945, he worked for three years as secretary of the CPSU's Penza Region Committee, then took over as head of the Moldavian Community Party Central Committee's Propaganda and Agitation Division in 1948. Two years into his tenure, LEONID BREZHNEV, who would later serve as general secretary of the CPSU, became head of the Moldavian party, and Chernenko quickly became one of his closest aides. In 1956, Brezhnev, now a member of the Presidium, got Chernenko a position in the Central Committee's Department of Agitation and Propaganda in Moscow. Four years later, Chernenko became Brezhnev's chief of staff when Brezhnev was named chairman of the

Presidium of the Supreme Soviet. He remained in this position when Brezhnev was named general secretary of the CPSU in 1964, taking over for Nikita Khrushchev.

Chernenko's quick rise to the top of the party organization began when he joined Brezhnev in Moscow; in 1966, he joined the Central Committee as a candidate member, and was given full membership in 1971; in 1976, he was appointed to the Secretariat; and in 1977, he was offered alternate membership to the Politburo, eventually gaining full membership the following year. At just 67 years of age, he was the youngest party official to be a member of both the Secretariat and the Politburo. Although he was among the elite in the CPSU, Chernenko still had little experience running any major government or party organization and was hesitant to outline his own positions, choosing instead to remain in the shadow of Brezhnev. When Brezhnev died in November 1982 Chernenko was passed over as his replacement in favor of former KGB chief YURI ANDROPOV. During Andropov's brief tenure, Chernenko took over as the chief ideologist for the party, a powerful position that allowed him to concentrate largely on foreign policy. He wrote many articles on foreign policy in the party journal, *Kommunist,* many of which dealt with U.S.–Soviet relations. In a major speech to the Central Committee in June, 1983, Chernenko called on the party to fight President Reagan's anticommunist "crusade" by increasing the propaganda war, foreshadowing the state of relations when he became general secretary.

Chernenko assumed many of the duties of the general secretary when Andropov's health began to decline in mid-1983, and when Andropov died in February 1984, Chernenko was selected to head the CPSU. In domestic affairs, Chernenko vowed to continue the social and economic reforms introduced during Andropov's tenure, but in reality he delayed the progress that was made in the previous 15 months. His for-

eign policy was shaped largely by the counsel of Foreign Minister ANDREI GROMYKO and Defense Minister Dmitri Ustinov, who wanted to take a harder line toward the Reagan administration. Nonetheless, a breakthrough in U.S.–Soviet relations occurred in January 1985, when U.S. secretary of state GEORGE SHULTZ held a meeting with Gromyko in Moscow and agreed to begin a new series of arms control talks in March. His regime also eased tensions with the Soviet Union's other major adversary, China, when the two nations signed a trade agreement in December 1984. Chernenko became gravely ill after less than a year in office, allowing young reformer MIKHAIL GORBACHEV the chance to take control of many of the general secretary's duties, much as Chernenko had done for Andropov the previous year. On March 10, 1985, Chernenko died of heart failure in Moscow.

Clark, William P.
(1931–   ) *National Security Advisor, secretary of the interior*

Perhaps no man was closer to Ronald Reagan than William P. Clark, a longtime California-born adviser and horseback riding partner of the president. The two men were remarkably similar, and despite a significant difference in age, might well have been brothers.

Clark studied at Stanford University for two years before joining the U.S. Army in 1951. He served in the army Counter Intelligence Corps for two years, then he entered Loyola University Law School in Los Angeles. He never received a degree from Loyola, but after being able to pass both the California and federal bars in 1958, he joined the Oxnard firm of Clark, Cole, and Fairfield, as a senior partner. While working at this firm, Clark also started a business doing what he truly loved: ranching. He served as president of Clark Land and Cattle Company from 1963 to 1973.

In 1966, Clark received his first government position as the chief of staff for California governor Ronald Reagan, where he stayed until 1969. He became part of Reagan's first troika of close advisers, along with EDWIN MEESE and MICHAEL DEAVER. After his service in Sacramento, he returned to the law, though this time on the other side of the bench. Clark became a judge in the Superior Court of San Luis Obispo County, California. He rose quickly within the California judicial system, becoming an associate justice of the California Court of Appeals, then in 1973 an associate justice of the California Supreme Court.

Clark had become an established and highly respected member of the California legal system by this time, but following the victory of Ronald Reagan in the 1980 presidential election, he left his seat on the Supreme Court and returned to government service. He was appointed deputy secretary of state under ALEXANDER HAIG in 1981, after a rocky confirmation hearing in which he confessed to a lack of knowledge about foreign nations and their leaders. In early 1982, following the resignation of RICHARD V. ALLEN, Clark was appointed as Reagan's second National Security Advisor. Allied with WILLIAM CASEY and JEANE KIRKPATRICK, he was at the center of many controversial actions taken by the president during his first term, including his proposal for a Strategic Defense Initiative and his address labeling the

President Reagan and National Security Advisor William P. Clark, December 7, 1982

Soviet Union an "evil empire." His conservative views brought him into conflict with the more moderate members of Reagan's staff, particularly Michael Deaver and JAMES BAKER, and possibly with NANCY REAGAN as well. He was asked in 1983 to move to the Department of the Interior to restore confidence in the office previously held by the unpopular JAMES WATT. Clark was successful in dampening criticism of the Interior Department and removing this as an issue in the 1984 campaign. In 1985 Clark left Washington to resume his legal career. He remained a loyal confidant of Ronald Reagan until the two ceased to have contact after Reagan's 1994 declaration that he was afflicted with Alzheimer's disease.

D

Darman, Richard G.
(1943–   ) *assistant to the president, deputy secretary of the Treasury*

Richard Darman served under four different U.S. presidents in six cabinet departments. As an adviser and deputy secretary of the Treasury for President Reagan and OMB director for President GEORGE H. W. BUSH, Darman played a key role in the economic policy of the 1980s and early 1990s. Known for his abrasive manner and keen intellect, Darman was a deficit hawk in an administration that had difficulty coming to grips with that issue. He used his tenure as President Bush's OMB director to rectify the deficit situation created during the Reagan years, urging Bush to abandon his 1988 "no new taxes" pledge.

Darman graduated with honors from Harvard University in 1964, then stayed at Harvard and earned his M.B.A. three years later. He went directly into public service after graduation with an appointment to President Richard Nixon's Department of Health, Education and Welfare (HEW). He became a close associate of HEW secretary Elliot Richardson during this time, and would later follow Richardson as he moved to the Departments of Defense, Justice, and Commerce in

the Richard Nixon and GERALD FORD administrations. He made another important friendship during his time in the Commerce Department when he met Undersecretary JAMES BAKER III. Following the election of JIMMY CARTER in 1977, Darman returned to his alma mater as a professor at the John F. Kennedy School of Government, where he remained until 1981. He also served as principal and director of ICF Consulting from 1977 to 1981.

When his old friend James Baker joined the Reagan administration as chief of staff in 1981, Darman again joined the government as an adviser to President Reagan. He worked on a variety of subjects regarding domestic policy and speechwriting, yet his major focus was economic policy, where he helped with budget policy and tax reform legislation. In 1985, he followed Baker to the Treasury Department when he was named deputy secretary. He continued to fight for changes in the tax laws, and when the sweeping Tax Reform Act of 1986 was passed he was awarded the department's highest award, the Alexander Hamilton Medal. He also played a key role in the Plaza Accord and the Louvre Accord, two major international economic policy reform agreements. In 1987, he left the Reagan administration and entered the private sector as a managing director at Shearson Lehman Brothers.

Darman returned to politics a year later as a key economic adviser for Vice President Bush in his 1988 presidential campaign. Following the election, Bush appointed Darman as director of the Office of Management and Budget. Due to the onset of recession, he was faced with difficult budget decisions during his time at OMB. He advised Bush to go back on his campaign promise and agree to a tax increase, advice that caused resentment from many in his own party who demanded he be replaced. Darman advocated budget cuts as well and played a major role in the inclusion of a federal spending cap in the 1990 budget agreement. He remained the head of OMB until the end of the Bush administration.

In February 1993, Darman joined the Carlyle Group as a senior adviser and managing director. He has written several articles for the top newspapers, magazines, and journals in the country, including the *New York Times*, *U.S. News & World Report*, and *Foreign Affairs*. He also wrote a book about the dangers of gridlock in the democratic process, called *Who's in Control? Polar Politics and the Sensible Center*, released in 1996. In 1998, Darman returned to the faculty at Harvard's Kennedy School of Government as a professor of public service.

Deaver, Michael K.
(1938–) *deputy chief of staff*

Michael Deaver was a member of Ronald Reagan's inner circle for much of the president's public life. Deaver forged an unusually close relationship with NANCY REAGAN as well, serving as her eyes and ears in the West Wing of the White House. A mastermind at creating visuals for his president, Deaver set the standard by

which many future White House communications operatives have been judged. Whether it was on the cliffs at Pointe du Hoc, Normandy, or at a campaign rally in Toledo, Deaver had a knack for finding the setting that would convey the White House's message of the day.

Michael Deaver graduated from San Jose State University in 1960 with a B.S. in political science. Unable to put his degree to use immediately after college, he joined IBM in 1960 as a management trainee. He remained at IBM until 1962 when he began working with the Republican Central Committee of Santa Clara County. In 1966, following the gubernatorial victory of Ronald Reagan, Deaver joined the staff of the new administration. After just one year, he became one of Reagan's closest advisers as assistant to the governor and director of administration, remaining at this post until the end of Reagan's tenure in 1974.

Following his years in Sacramento, Deaver opened up a public relations firm with Reagan aide PETER HANNAFORD. His primary focus during this time, however, was continuing the political ascendancy of Ronald Reagan. He was a close adviser to Reagan during his 1976 presidential bid, serving as the chief of staff to the Reagan Presidential Campaign Committee. He returned to the private sector after Reagan failed to win the GOP nomination, but joined Reagan again in 1980 and played a key role in his successful campaign.

Deaver was offered the position of deputy chief of staff and became, along with Chief of Staff JAMES BAKER and counsel EDWIN MEESE, one of Reagan's closest advisers. He had a particularly good relationship with Nancy Reagan, something that undoubtedly kept him in good favor with the president. Deaver's expertise in media communications became an important asset for the administration, and in 1984 he was instrumental in the success of Reagan's reelection campaign.

The Reagans attend a farewell ceremony for Michael K. Deaver (right), May 20, 1985.

He left the administration in 1985 to start his own lobbying firm, Michael K. Deaver Incorporated, in Washington, D.C. He ran into some legal trouble shortly after his departure regarding improper lobbying practices, and was eventually indicted for breaking federal ethics laws and convicted of lying to Congress. He has written several books on his days with the Reagans, including *A Different Drummer: My Thirty Years with Ronald Reagan; Behind the Scenes;* and *Nancy: A Portrait of My Years with Nancy Reagan.* Deaver currently lives in Washington and serves as vice chairman international of Edelman Public Relations Worldwide.

Dolan, Anthony R.
(1948–) *chief speechwriter*

Anthony Dolan served as chief speechwriter for President Reagan from November 1981 until the end of his presidency in January 1989. During this time, he was responsible for constructing some of Reagan's memorable speeches, including his address to the British parliament, the "evil empire" speech, and the 1989 farewell address. Dolan was known as a hard-liner inside the Reagan White House, and he was viewed with suspicion by moderate elements in the State Department, many of whom suspected him of covertly inserting inflammatory anti-Soviet passages into Reagan's speeches. Reagan, however, was very engaged in the speechwriting process, and shared his young speechwriter's disdain for the Soviet Union and his admiration for anticommunists such as Whittaker Chambers. The two men saw eye to eye on most issues, and the speeches Dolan produced and Reagan delivered were the result of a collaborative effort.

Dolan's first experience as a writer came during his undergraduate studies at Yale University, where he worked as a columnist for the *Yale Daily News.* After earning his degree in 1970, he became the deputy press secretary for James Buckley's Senate campaign in New York. Following the election, he took a job with F. Clifton White Associates as a political campaign consultant, and stayed at this firm until 1974 when William F. Buckley advised him to begin a career in journalism. Between 1974 and 1980, Dolan worked as a reporter for *The Advocate* in his home state of Connecticut and was awarded the Pulitzer Prize for Special Local Reporting in 1978 for an article dealing with municipal corruption in Stamford, Connecticut.

In May 1980 Dolan joined the Reagan campaign as a speechwriter and special research director, where one of his tasks was to find information that made President JIMMY CARTER seem "unpresidential." He continued working in the Office of the President-elect following the election and in March 1981 was named special assistant to the president and speechwriter. In November 1981 Dolan was promoted to chief speechwriter. Over the next seven years, he crafted some of the most memorable foreign policy speeches of the Reagan presidency, consistently focusing on the evils of communism and the necessity for the West to defend freedom around the world. In May 1981, in the commencement address at the University of Notre Dame, Reagan said the West would "transcend Communism" and "dismiss it as a sad, bizarre chapter in human history whose last pages are even now being written." Speaking to the British parliament in June 1982, Reagan called for a "crusade for freedom" so that liberty could "triumph over evil." Nine months later, Reagan sharply described the Soviet Union as the "evil empire." In each of these speeches, Dolan tried to stress the inevitable victory of freedom over communism, a belief of utmost importance to Reagan. Dolan also played a role in writing all of Reagan's State of the Union speeches, both inaugural speeches, and his farewell address in January 1989.

Dole, Elizabeth Hanford
(1936–   ) *secretary of transportation*

Elizabeth Hanford Dole became the nation's first female secretary of transportation when she was named to the post in 1983 by President Reagan. With service under six different U.S. presidents, nine years as head of the American Red Cross, and her election to the U.S. Senate, Dole earned her spot as the better half of Washington's most famous power couple.

Dole grew up in North Carolina and after high school followed her brother to Duke University. She earned a degree in political science, graduated Phi Beta Kappa, and served as president of her class. Dole then moved to Massachusetts and earned a master's degree in education from Harvard University in 1960. She got her first close look into Washington politics during this time, working as a secretary for Democratic senator B. Everett Jordan of North Carolina in the summer of 1960. The following two summers, Dole worked at the United Nations Public Information Section. She then returned to Cambridge and completed her J.D. from Harvard Law School in 1965, graduating as one of only 24 female graduates out of 550 students.

Following graduation, Dole took a job in Washington as a staff assistant to the assistant secretary for education in the Department of Health, Education and Welfare. She then worked briefly as a public defender in Washington before being appointed by President Johnson to the Committee for Consumer Interests. When the committee was renamed the White House Office of Consumer Affairs a few years later by President Nixon, Dole stayed on as executive director. In 1971, Nixon named Dole, still a registered Democrat, deputy assistant to the president for consumer affairs. Two years later, Nixon placed Dole on the five-member Federal Trade Commission.

She resigned from the FTC in 1976 when her husband, Senator ROBERT DOLE, whom she had married the previous year, was selected for the number two spot on the GOP ticket with President GERALD FORD. After her husband's defeat, Dole returned to her job at the FTC, only to resign again in 1979 when her husband made another run for the GOP nomination. When Senator Dole lost the nomination again, Elizabeth joined the Ronald Reagan campaign.

Dole helped the incoming Reagan administration with its transition and was rewarded with the job of director of the White House Office of Public Liaison. In 1983, following the resignation of DREW LEWIS, Dole became the first woman in U.S. history to be appointed secretary of transportation. She also became the first woman to head a branch of the armed services, because the transportation secretary served concurrently as director of the U.S. Coast Guard. Dole was known to many as the safety secretary for the high priority she placed on the passage of safety legislation, such as requirements for air bags and a third brake light on cars, increasing the legal drinking age to 21, and increasing the number of Federal Aviation Administration inspectors. She also allocated $70 million to renovate Washington's Union Station.

Dole left her job in 1987 to help her husband campaign once again for the Republican presidential nomination. After he lost again, Elizabeth campaigned for the nominee, Vice President GEORGE H. W. BUSH, who rewarded her with an appointment as labor secretary. She worked to raise the minimum wage and also made efforts to break the so-called glass ceiling that hindered women and minorities from earning high-level executive positions. After nearly two years at the Labor Department, Dole resigned and was named president of the American Red Cross, where she focused on world relief efforts and protecting the U.S. blood supply against the AIDS virus. She took a one-year leave in 1996 to help her husband run one more time for the GOP nomination. Senator Dole won the nomination, and though Elizabeth proved to be a substantial asset on the campaign trail, he lost the general election to incumbent president Bill Clinton. She returned to the Red Cross in 1997 and stayed on with the organization until 1999. In March 1999, she followed in her husband's footsteps and made a bid for the Republican presidential nomination, but a lack of money forced her to abandon her campaign before the first primary. In 2002, Dole won the U.S. Senate seat from North Carolina vacated by Jesse Helms.

Dole, Robert J.
(1923–   ) *U.S. senator*

Robert Dole was a dominant figure in Republican Party politics for more than 30 years, serving as a member of the House, chairman of the Republican National Committee, a candidate for vice president, the majority leader of the Senate, and finally as a candidate for president of the United States. A highly decorated veteran of World War II, Dole could be vindictively partisan on occasion, but at other times he was deeply respectful of his opponents and profoundly inspiring when discussing his love of country.

Dole grew up in the small farming town of Russell, Kansas. He entered the University of Kansas in 1941 where he studied premed and became a star on the school's track team. However, a year after the United States entered World War II, Dole joined the U.S. Army Enlisted Reserve Corps. Over the next year, he traveled around the United States training in several different military bases before becoming an infantry second lieutenant at the Officer Candidate School in Fort Benning, Georgia. He joined the fighting in Italy as a platoon leader for the 10th Mountain Division in early 1945, then, in April, he received a serious wound that left him temporarily paralyzed from the neck down. He spent the next four years in the hospital and in physical therapy, eventually gaining use of his entire body, with the exception of his right arm, which became permanently disabled. For his service, Dole earned two Purple Hearts and a Bronze Star with Cluster.

When Dole returned from the war, he entered Washburn University in Topeka, Kansas, where he completed his bachelor's degree in history, then continued to earn his law degree. Becoming a physician was no longer a goal for Dole, who had become enamored with politics during his time at Washburn. While he was still in law school, he ran for a seat in the Kansas state legislature and won, becoming the youngest legislator from his county to serve in the statehouse at age 27. After one term in the House, Dole was elected as the prosecutor for Russell County, where he stayed for the next eight years.

In 1960, Dole won his first national election, taking the seat of retiring Kansas congressman Wint Smith. He faced a difficult challenge in 1962 when, following the reapportionment of Kansas' congressional seats, he was forced to face incumbent Democrat J. Floyd Breeding in the midterm elections, winning by just 21,000 votes. During his eight years in the House, he became associated with the conservative wing of the GOP, opposing much of President Johnson's Great Society legislation and fighting hard for America's farmers, a large part of his constituency in Russell, Kansas. He broke with many members of his party on the issue of civil rights, voting for both the 1964 Civil Rights Act and the 1965 Voting Rights Act.

Dole ran for the U.S. Senate in 1968 following the retirement of longtime Kansas senator Frank Carlson, taking more than 60 percent of the vote in his victory over Democrat William Robinson. He continued to be a strong conservative on both economic and social policy, and an advocate for agricultural interests. From 1971 to 1973, he served as chairman of the Republican National Committee, where he said, he was fortunately "cut out of the action" of Nixon's inner circle, emerging from the Watergate scandal unscathed. In 1975, Dole met and married his second wife, Elizabeth Hanford, a powerful activist lawyer who later became secretary of transportation for President Reagan. Together, they made up one of Washington's most powerful couples.

In 1976, Dole was asked by incumbent president GERALD FORD to join him on the presidential ticket following the retirement of Vice President Nelson Rockefeller. The selection of Dole was a strategic move to gain the support of the conservative wing of the party, most of whom backed Ford's major challenger, Ronald Reagan, and to attract voters in states with large farming interests. Dole ran a tough campaign against Democrats JIMMY CARTER and WALTER MONDALE, earning the label of Ford's hatchet man, after making vitriolic comments on the campaign trail. Following the defeat in the general election, he returned to his seat in the Senate. He made a brief run for the GOP presidential nomination in the next election, but the conservative wing of the Republican Party quickly threw their support behind Ronald Reagan. Nonetheless, the Republicans gained a surprise majority in the Senate in the 1980 election, giving Dole the chairmanship of the powerful Finance Committee where he allied himself with President Reagan's economic agenda. Late in 1984, Dole took over as Senate majority leader, but held this post for only two years before the Democratic Party took over the Senate in 1986.

Dole ran for the Republican presidential nomination again in 1988 against Vice President GEORGE H. W. BUSH, but he was unable to overcome the support behind Reagan's chosen successor. His wife, Elizabeth, joined the Bush administration as secretary of labor, and Dole served as a loyal ally to the new president in the Senate. Dole's best role, however, was as the fighting underdog in the Senate, and in 1994, following the huge Republican victory in the midterm elections, he returned to his position as majority leader, this time opposing Democratic president Bill Clinton's agenda. For the next two years, Dole served as Clinton's lead adversary in the Senate, opposing many of the president's policies and earning the respect of the party faithful.

In 1996, he made his third run for the GOP presidential nomination, this time with the full backing of the party establishment. The beginning of the nomination campaign was a difficult period for Dole as he lost two early races to outsiders Steve Forbes and PATRICK BUCHANAN. These insurgency campaigns, however, could not overcome Dole's lock on the party organization, and in March Dole wrapped up the presidential nomination. He tried to keep his post as Senate majority leader during the campaign, but in June he was forced to leave his seat, ending a 35-year run in the Senate. In the general election, Clinton received 49 percent of the popular vote and 31 states to Dole's 41 percent.

Following the election, Dole joined Verner, Liipfert, Bernhard, McPherson, and Hand, a Washington, D.C., law firm that represented many of America's largest corporations. Elizabeth Dole also left politics to become president of the American Red Cross, enhancing their reputation as one of Washington's preeminent "power couples." Dole remained involved in politics after his retirement from the Senate. In 1999, for example, President Clinton commissioned him to take part in the negotiations for a NATO peace accord with Serbia. Dole and his wife currently live in Washington where his wife serves as the junior senator from North Carolina.

Donovan, Raymond J.
(1930–) *secretary of labor*

Raymond J. Donovan's four years as labor secretary during the Reagan administration were shrouded in controversy after allegations surfaced about his relationship with organized crime figures during his tenure at a New Jersey construction company. Two separate federal investigations and a criminal trial in state court led to his acquittal on all charges, but his reputation was permanently damaged by the controversy.

Donovan grew up in Bayonne, New Jersey, a small, industrial town in the northern part of the state where he learned early about labor and industry. He attended Notre Dame Seminary in New Orleans and earned his B.A. in philosophy in 1952, then returned to New Jersey to take a job with the American Insurance Company. In 1959, Donovan joined Schiavone Construction Company in Secaucus, New Jersey, working with construction workers' unions on contract negotiations. He was named executive vice president in 1971. Donovan developed a reputation as a tough, but fair, negotiator while at Schiavone. In

1976, he became actively involved in national politics, campaigning for Ronald Reagan for the GOP presidential nomination against President GERALD FORD. He supported Reagan again in the 1980 election, this time as chairman of the Reagan-Bush campaign in New Jersey.

In 1981, President Reagan chose Donovan to serve as his labor secretary. He underwent a grueling nomination process after allegations surfaced that he was linked to organized crime and labor racketeering, and the FBI and the Senate Labor and Human Resources Committee conducted investigations into Donovan and the Schiavone Construction Company. On February 3, 1981, by a vote of 80-17, Donovan became the last member of Reagan's cabinet confirmed by the Senate. The 17 votes against his nomination, all made by Senate Democrats, marked the largest opposition to any of Reagan's cabinet nominees.

As soon as he entered office, Donovan went to work on the Reagan agenda, eliminating or easing a number of federal regulations affecting American business and cutting the staff and budget of the Labor Department. He remained in the headlines, however, not for his work as labor secretary but as a public figure mired in controversy. Shortly after his confirmation, the FBI alleged that Donovan and his construction company had ties to the mob and that Donovan had conspired with William "Billy the Butcher" Masselli, a notorious organized-crime figure in New Jersey. The Masselli connection initiated a federal investigation by Independent Counsel Leon Silverman that would last the remainder of Donovan's tenure at the Labor Department. In 1987, Silverman ended the investigation without any charges. Donovan was charged with 10 criminal counts in a separate New York trial, but was acquitted on all charges by a Bronx jury in 1987. At the conclusion of both investigations, Donovan, exhausted from years of defending himself against criminal charges, asked, "Where do I go to get my reputation back?"

Donovan left the Reagan administration at the end of the first term and was succeeded by WILLIAM BROCK.

Duarte, José Napoleón
(1926–1990) *president of El Salvador*

President José Napoleón Duarte was one of the Reagan administration's closest allies in Central America, and one of the largest recipients of U.S. aid in the fight against leftist guerrillas. Facing pressures from both the Left and Right, he was never able to achieve his political and economic reforms, and was voted out of power after less than five years in office.

Duarte was born to a seamstress and a tailor in El Salvador's capital city of San Salvador. After his father won the national lottery in 1944, Duarte was able to move to the United States to study civil engineering at Notre Dame University, where he earned his degree in 1948. He returned to El Salvador after graduation to work for his father-in-law's construction company and teach college part time, while also volunteering for community service organizations, such as the Red Cross and the Boy Scouts.

In 1960, following the overthrow of the Lemus government by leftist rebels, Duarte showed his first interest in national politics, joining a group of middle-class, Roman Catholic citizens to form the Christian Democratic Party (PDC), a "third way" political organization between capitalism and communism. For the next four years, Duarte served as general secretary of the PDC. In 1964, he was elected mayor of San Salvador. By focusing largely on improving the lives of the middle and lower classes, Duarte became a popular figure, winning reelection two more times. His most noted achievements during his tenure as mayor were the installation of the city's first modern street light system, and forcing the wealthy to pay years of back taxes to fund the city's budget.

In 1972, after being named president of the PDC, Duarte made a bid for the presidency of El Salvador. Joining with the National Revolutionary Movement (MNR) and the Nationalist Democratic Union (UDN), he ran on the National Opposition Union (UNO) alliance ticket against Colonel Arturo Armando Molina of the National Conciliation Party (PCN). Duarte looked to be on the way to a strong victory before the government stopped coverage of the election and declared Molina the winner the following day. In response, Duarte's supporters launched a failed coup attempt on March 25, 1972, where hundreds lost their lives and Duarte fled to the Venezuelan embassy to seek asylum. Government officials soon stormed the embassy and arrested and tortured Duarte. After appeals from the Venezuelan government, the Vatican, and Notre Dame University, Duarte escaped a death sentence and was allowed to live in exile in Venezuela, where he lived and worked as an engineer until 1979.

In October 1979, a group of reformers succeeded in overthrowing the authoritarian government of Colonel Carlos Humberto Romero, opening the way for Duarte to return to his country the following year. When the new ruling junta was dissolved in December 1980, Duarte, still very popular with the people, was appointed provisional president of El Salvador. Balancing pressures from both the Left and the Right, he initiated a series of reforms on key industries such as banking and agriculture. In March 1982, Duarte's PDC won a plurality in the Constituent Assembly elections, but lost power when a right-wing coalition, led by Robert D'Aubuisson's Nationalist Republican Alliance (ARENA), took control of the government and named businessman Alvaro Magana as provisional president.

Two years later, Duarte returned to power after he defeated D'Aubuisson in a runoff election, becoming the nation's first elected president in 53 years. One of his campaign promises was to foster negotiations with the leftist FDR/FMLN coalition that had been waging a guerrilla campaign against the government for more than five years. Progress seemed likely when the Christian Democrats won a majority of seats in the March 1985 legislative elections, strengthening Duarte's position to negotiate, but in 1985, one of Duarte's daughters was kidnapped, forcing the president to releasing 100 leftist guerrillas from prison and greatly weakening his ability to continue the efforts toward reconciliation. The economic situation in El Salvador was also on the decline as inflation neared 40 percent and nearly half the population was unemployed. In addition, a severe drought and a massive earthquake struck the nation in 1986, bringing $1 billion in damages and putting more strain on El Salvador's feeble economy. After a precipitous decline in popular support, the Christian Democratic Party split into two separate factions, leaving Duarte virtually powerless by the end of his term. On March 19, 1989, ARENA's Alfredo Cristiani took 54 percent in the general election and succeeded Duarte as president of El Salvador.

With the departure of Duarte, the United States lost a key ally in Central America. Duarte had been closely aligned with the Reagan administration during most of his presidency, securing over $3 billion in financial assistance from Washington during his tenure to help in the fight against leftist guerrillas. Although the Reagan administration had doubts about his abilities, they played a central role in his rise to the presidency in both 1980 and 1984. Both Reagan and Bush praised Duarte's drive toward democratic reforms and his efforts to bring warring parties to the negotiating table for a peaceful solution.

Late in his term, Duarte was diagnosed with stomach and liver cancer, and on February 23, 1990, he died in San Salvador.

Duberstein, Kenneth M.
(1944–) *chief of staff*

Kenneth Duberstein served Ronald Reagan in different capacities, first in his legislative liaison operation, and finally as the fourth and final White House chief of staff. Duberstein understood that maintaining a good relationship with the first lady was one of the key ingredients for succeeding as Reagan's chief of staff. During Reagan's final months in office, Duberstein presided over a smooth transition of power to the Bush administration, which was potentially more difficult than it appeared from the outside.

Duberstein earned his A.B. from Franklin and Marshall College in Lancaster, Pennsylvania, in 1965. A year later, he completed his master's degree at American University. While he was studying for his M.A. in Washington, D.C., Duberstein worked as an intern for Republican senator Jacob Javits of New York. He began studying law at New York University Law School after he completed his M.A. but left after only one year to take a position as a research assistant to Senator Javits. In 1967, he returned to Franklin and Marshall and became the administrative assistant to the president. From 1972 to 1976, he served in the U.S. General Services Administration as director of congressional and intergovernmental affairs. He also served as deputy undersecretary of labor for President GERALD FORD. In 1977 he was named vice president and director of business-

government relations of the Committee for Economic Development.

Duberstein joined the Reagan administration in January 1981 as a deputy assistant for legislative affairs. After a year at this post, he was promoted to assistant for legislative affairs. He left the administration in December 1983 and worked in the private sector as vice president of Timmons and Company, a government relations firm in Washington. He returned to the White House in March 1987 to serve as deputy chief of staff under HOWARD BAKER, who had recently replaced the embattled DONALD REGAN. When Baker left his post in July 1988, Duberstein took over as White House chief of staff. Several high-level posts were vacated in the last year of the Reagan administration as many key figures left to help Vice President GEORGE H. W. BUSH in his presidential campaign. Duberstein, a political pragmatist, was instrumental in getting many moderates, such as Attorney General RICHARD THORNBURGH, into the administration to assist the Bush campaign. Duberstein remained with the Reagan administration until the end of his term. In January 1989 President Reagan awarded him the President's Citizens Medal.

Duberstein is currently chairman and chief executive officer of the Duberstein Group, a Washington-based planning and consulting firm. He serves on the board of directors for a number of prestigious companies, including the Boeing Company and the American Stock Exchange, and several educational and volunteer organizations, such as Ford's Theater and Harvard University's John F. Kennedy School of Government. He is also a member of the Council on Foreign Relations.

Edwards, James B.
(1927–) secretary of energy

James B. Edwards worked as an oral surgeon for 15 years before entering state politics as a senator and, later, as governor of South Carolina. He served for two years in the Reagan administration as secretary of energy before returning to South Carolina as the president of the College of Charleston's medical school.

Edwards joined the U.S. Maritime Service in 1944, at the age of 18, and served until 1947 as a deck officer. After his military service, he entered the College of Charleston and earned his B.S. in 1950. For two years after his undergraduate studies, he worked as a deck officer for the Alcoc Steamship Company. In the fall of 1951, he went back to school at the University of Louisville School of Dentistry, completing his D.M.D. in 1955. From 1955 to 1957, Edwards served in the U.S. Navy as a dental officer. For the next 10 years, he would continue to serve in the naval reserve as a lieutenant commander. In 1957, he entered the University of Pennsylvania Medical School for one year of postgraduate studies, then moved to Michigan to begin a two-year oral surgery residency at Detroit's Henry Ford Hospital. Following his residency, he moved back to Charleston, South

Carolina, and worked as an oral surgeon for the next 15 years.

Edwards became actively involved in the South Carolina Republican Party during these years, serving as chairman of the Charleston County Republican Party from 1964 to 1969, and chairman of the First Congressional District Republican Committee from 1970 to 1971. In 1968, he joined the state executive branch as a member of the South Carolina Governor's Statewide Committee for Comprehensive Health Care Planning, serving on this board for four years. In 1971, he lost a bid for the U.S. Congress, but the following year he won his first elected public office in the South Carolina Senate. After serving one term, he successfully ran for governor of South Carolina, becoming the first Republican governor of this state since the end of Reconstruction. During his one term as governor, Edwards's most notable achievements were the signing of legislation reinstating the death penalty and the passage of the Education Finance Act, which increased education funding to poor districts.

Edwards backed Reagan in the 1976 GOP primary against President GERALD FORD, but in 1980 he endorsed former Texas governor John B. Connally. After Connally's exit from the campaign, Edwards supported Reagan again and played a key role in Reagan's victory in South Carolina in the general election. In 1981 Reagan selected Edwards as secretary of energy, one of several cabinet-level departments Reagan wished to dismantle during his tenure. Edwards supported Reagan's position on eliminating the department, saying shortly before his nomination, "I'd like to go to Washington and close the Energy Department down and work myself out of a job." However, during his confirmation hearings he backed away from this position and did not make any serious attempts to dissolve the department while in office. Edwards's nomination was strongly opposed by various environmental groups because of his support of nuclear power; as governor of South Carolina, he was an outspoken proponent of nuclear energy and continually sought ways to expand nuclear power in his state. Some members of Congress were also wary of the nomination due to Edwards's lack of experience in energy policy. The only indication he gave of the direction he would take as secretary was to pursue the administration's broad agenda of deregulation and lower taxes. Despite various misgivings, he was confirmed by the Senate, 93 to 3, on January 22, 1981.

As energy secretary, Edwards fought for deregulation of the oil and natural gas industries, hoping to rely more heavily on market forces to determine the price of energy. He left the Reagan administration in November 1982, after less than two years in office, to become president of the Medical University of South Carolina in Charleston. Since his exit from government service, Edwards has continued to serve in various governmental organizations, but spends the majority of his time working in the medical field.

Ferraro, Geraldine
(1935–   ) *U.S. congresswoman,*
vice presidential candidate

During her six-year tenure in the U.S. House of Representatives, Geraldine Ferraro did much to advance the cause of women in America. In 1984, she became the first woman ever chosen by a major party for a national ticket when Democrat WALTER MONDALE selected her as his running mate for the presidential campaign.

Ferraro moved to the South Bronx, in New York City, with her mother and sister at the age of eight, after her father died of a heart attack. After graduating from high school at just 16 years of age, she decided to stay close to home and attended Marymount Manhattan College. She also took classes on teaching at nearby Hunter College during this time. After earning her B.A. from Marymount in 1956, she took a job as a schoolteacher while studying law in the evenings at Fordham University. She completed her law degree in 1960 and passed the New York State bar exam in 1961, but decided to practice law only part time so that she could raise her children.

In 1974, Ferraro was named assistant district attorney for New York's Queens County where she focused largely on cases dealing with women, children, and senior citizens. She also joined the Advisory Council for the Housing Court of the City of New York and was named president of the Queens County Women's Bar Association. After gaining notoriety in this position, she made a run for the U.S. House of Representatives from her district in Queens. She ran as a candidate tough on law and order, and was able to garner 54 percent of the vote in her victory. As one of only 17 women in Congress in 1979, Ferraro gave a voice to the growing women's movement and publicized several women's issues such as salary discrimination and the problems facing single-parent mothers. Serving on the Congressional Caucus for Women's Issues, she helped secure the passage of the Economic Equity Act and fought hard for the unsuccessful Equal Rights Amendment.

Ferraro easily won reelection to the House in 1980 and 1982. In 1980, she was elected to serve as secretary of the House Democratic Caucus. She also served in numerous positions in the party organization, most notably as chairwoman of the Democratic Party Platform Committee for the 1984 convention. In July 1984, Democratic candidate Mondale selected Ferraro as his running mate for the presidential election, marking the first time a woman had been chosen for the position by a major party in U.S. history. The announcement was made on the 64th anniversary of the day when women were given the right to vote. Ferraro was not only valuable as a woman; she was very popular among working-class Americans, whom she represented in Queens, and she was from New York, the state with the second-highest electoral vote in the country. It remained an uphill battle nonetheless, with President Reagan enjoying a booming economy and high approval ratings. The Mondale-Ferraro ticket lost with just 41 percent of the popular vote and 13 electoral votes, one of the more lopsided defeats in American history.

After the election, Ferraro completed the remainder of her term in Congress and returned to private life. She wrote a memoir of the presidential election a year later entitled *Ferraro, My Story*. She stayed out of the public eye until 1992 when she launched a political comeback and ran for the Democratic nomination in the New York Senate race. After a tough primary battle, Ferraro lost the nomination by less than 1 percent. Following the defeat, she became managing partner at Keck, Mahin, Cate, and Koether in New York. She also released a collection of speeches and essays called *Changing History: Women, Power and Politics* in 1993.

Ferraro continued to serve in a variety of prestigious political appointments including representative to the United Nations Commission on Human Rights and vice chair of the U.S. delegation at the Fourth World Conference on Women in Beijing. In 1996, she became a cohost on CNN's *Crossfire*. With the help of publicity from the show, she hinted at another comeback in 1997 by weighing a run for mayor of New York City. She abandoned the idea, but considered running for senator or governor of New York the following year. After losing the Democratic nomination for the Senate for the second time, Ferraro officially retired from political life. In 1999, she took a

position running the Women's Leadership Group at the Washington-based public relations firm, Weber McGinn.

Ford, Gerald R., Jr.
(1913–) *former U.S. president*

The 38th president of the United States and Ronald Reagan's opponent in the 1976 race for the Republican presidential nomination, Gerald Ford restored credibility to the White House following the "long national nightmare" of Watergate. The nation's first and only appointed president was, admittedly, "a Ford, not a Lincoln," but his fundamental decency and his courageous decision to pardon Richard Nixon helped extricate the nation from the Watergate morass, at the expense of his own election prospects.

After graduating from high school, Gerald Ford did not journey far from his hometown of Grand Rapids when he entered the University of Michigan to pursue a degree in economics. He had earned a full athletic scholarship to play football, and while at Michigan he excelled as a center, winning a spot in the Shrine College All-Star game. Following graduation, Ford took a position as an assistant coach for Yale University's football team. He stayed with the team for two years before entering Yale Law School, graduating in the top 25 percent of his class in 1941. He returned to Grand Rapids that year to start his own law firm, but after the Japanese attack on Pearl Harbor in December, Ford joined the U.S. Navy. He served in the navy for the remainder of World War II and left in February 1946 with the rank of lieutenant commander.

Ford returned to practice law following the war, although it was clear that he had his eyes on a career in politics. In 1948, he ran for a seat in the U.S. Congress, defeating Republican Bartel Jonkman in the primary with 62 percent of the vote, then taking the general election by a similar margin. Ford cast himself in the mold of another Michigan Republican, Senator Arthur Vandenberg, who was conservative on domestic issues but favored an increased role for the United States in the international community. Ford's stock rose when another such Republican, Dwight D. Eisenhower, entered the White House in 1953, giving the internationalist wing of the GOP a preponderance of power in Washington. Ford earned a reputation as a loyal party man and moved quickly up the ranks of the House of Representatives. He became chairman of the House Republican Conference in 1963, then two years later, following the Democratic rout of 1964, he was elected minority leader.

Ford was a strong opponent of President Lyndon Johnson on both foreign and domestic policy. He rejected the premise of the Great Society and the expansive role of the federal government, and instead pushed for returning power to the states. He also broke early with President Johnson's strategy in Vietnam, questioning the gradual escalation approach, and calling for a strong show of American military might. Ford became a key ally of Richard Nixon after his victory in the 1968 election. Although he disagreed with Nixon on many policy issues, he served as a loyal friend in the House, supporting the president even at the height of the Watergate scandal when many of his GOP colleagues had already abandoned Nixon.

Realizing that it was unlikely he would ever become Speaker of the House, Ford planned to leave politics in 1976. But following the resignation of vice president Spiro T. Agnew in October 1973, Ford was asked to become Nixon's vice president. Nixon considered offering Democrat John Connally the post, but Ford's good reputation made him an ideal choice; he was confirmed 92-3 in the Senate and 387-35 in the House. Although he was not Nixon's first choice, he served the president

well during his tenure, faithfully defending Nixon throughout Watergate. When Nixon resigned the presidency on August 9, 1974, Ford became the first unelected president in American history. He stumbled in his first few months in the White House—his popularity plummeted due to his pardon of Richard Nixon and his declaration of amnesty for Vietnam draft evaders. Both actions weakened his ability to govern, but were seen by many as statesmanlike acts in retrospect. Over time he regained his footing and learned the intricacies of the office and helped restore respect to a severely damaged presidency.

It was a recalcitrant Congress, however, that proved to be Ford's most difficult obstacle as president. With the downfall of Nixon, the imperial presidency had given way to the imperiled presidency, and Congress, with a weak executive and large Democratic majorities following the 1974 midterm elections, was ready to reassert its authority. Because of this, Ford was often at the mercy of the legislature. He frequently vetoed legislation only to be overridden by Congress. There were a host of other problems confronting the Ford administration, including high inflation, high unemployment, and the energy crisis. He advocated lower federal spending, lower taxes, greater state and local power, and deregulation of domestic oil and natural gas, an agenda that made him much more conservative than his predecessor. However, Ford was able to get only a small tax cut and limited deregulation through Congress. By the time of the 1976 election, inflation had been reduced slightly, but unemployment and the energy crisis remained major problems.

There was also the issue of the gradual decline in America's world standing and the rising power of the Soviet Union. Public support for détente had slipped by the time Ford took office, but he remained committed to the policy, supporting two key agreements with the

Soviets during his tenure. The November 1974 Vladivostok Accords limited the number of missile launchers allowed for each country, and the Helsinki Agreement at the Conference on Security and Cooperation in Europe bound the Soviets to human rights standards in Europe in exchange for recognition of their Eastern European borders. However, the fall of both Vietnam and Angola to communist movements crystallized in the minds of most Americans the idea that détente was not working. Congressional limitations prohibited Ford from supporting the South Vietnamese government, but two weeks after its fall he asserted American power with the rescue of the *Mayaguez* freighter in the Gulf of Siam. Although 41 lives were lost to save 39 hostages, Ford's decisive action was popular in America, underscoring the prevailing opinion toward détente.

Even with the success of the *Mayaguez* incident, Ford faced fierce opposition for the 1976 GOP presidential nomination. Former California governor Ronald Reagan had tapped into the growing conservative movement in America, calling for an end to détente and a reassertion of American power abroad. Détente had become so unpopular by the 1976 election, especially among conservatives, that Ford stopped using the word in his campaign. Reagan succeeded in battling Ford all the way to the Republican National Convention, although Ford was able to narrowly win the nomination in the end. Nevertheless, he entered the general election against JIMMY CARTER as a weakened candidate. His campaign came on strong at the end, but it was not enough; Carter defeated Ford with 297 electoral votes to 240.

During his retirement from politics, Ford enjoyed great success in the business world. He served on the boards of several major corporations and his personal investments, according to *Business Week*, have earned him nearly $300 million over the last two decades. He has also spoken out periodically on issues in national politics, and authored a memoir, *A Time to Heal: The Autobiography of Gerald R. Ford*, published in 1979. In August 1999 Ford was awarded the Presidential Medal of Freedom by President Clinton.

Gadhafi, Muammar al-
(Mu'ammar Qadhafi)
(1942–) *president of Libya*

Muammar al-Gadhafi's regime was the target of a series of American military actions during the Reagan years. Gadhafi seemed to particularly irk the American president, who frequently referred to the mercurial leader as "a madman." In light of this assessment, Reagan seemed to take a certain delight in tweaking Gadhafi with military probes that prompted a predictable suicidal response on the part of the Libyan armed forces. The two men engaged in a blood feud throughout Reagan's time in the White House, and at one point it was reported in the American media that Gadhafi had dispatched hit squads to the United States to assassinate the president. Reagan also seemed determined to dispatch Gadhafi, authorizing an air attack in April 1986 that struck Gadhafi's compound in Tripoli and apparently killed a member of his family.

Gadhafi came to power in Libya after a successful coup in September 1969, quickly installing a socialist government blended with Muslim law, a system he called Islamic socialism. His association with international terrorism and the consequences that have resulted, most notably economic sanctions and military confrontation with the United States, have forced him to take a more pragmatic approach in recent years and seek reentry into the world community.

Gadhafi took a strong interest in politics in his youth. Heavily influenced by the rise of General Gamal Abdel Nasser in neighboring Egypt and his calls for Arab unity, Gadhafi quickly became involved in Libyan youth politics. He organized a secret revolutionary group called the Command Committee, and as a result in 1961 he was expelled from school. His family then moved and Gadhafi was able to complete his high school education in 1963, but he refused to give up his political ambitions and he continued to involve himself in the revolutionary movement.

Following high school, Gadhafi entered the Military Academy of Benghazi. Several of his best friends and fellow revolutionaries joined him at the academy and started the Free Unionist Officers Movement, a group committed to overthrowing Libya's king Idris and the Sanusi monarchy. He took courses in history during this time at the nearby University of Benghazi, although he did not complete his degree. In 1966, he moved to Britain to enter a six-month signals course at Beaconsfield Military Academy. Upon his return from Britain, Gadhafi, now a lieutenant, joined the Libyan

Army's Signal Corps and served near Benghazi. Even as he was serving in the king's army, he continued to cultivate his political ambitions and increase the membership of his revolutionary organization. By 1969, his group had gained enough power to change the government, and on September 1, 1969, the Free Unionist Officers Movement overthrew the Libyan monarchy in a bloodless coup and declared the Libyan Arab Republic.

Less than two weeks after the coup, Gadhafi was named president of the leading political body, the Revolutionary Command Council. Some of the elder members of the movement resented the rise of Gadhafi, only 27 years old at the time, but by the beginning of 1970 he had eliminated his opposition and was firmly in control. He immediately launched a series of dramatic reforms, many of which mirrored those of his hero, General Nasser. It took him only four months to expel the American and British military bases from Libya, and this was followed by the exit of the Italians in October 1970. He also nationalized major portions of the Libyan economy, including the banking and oil industries. In addition, Gadhafi made changes in the social structure, declaring Islamic law and strictly forbidding many things, such as dancing and alcohol consumption, prohibited by the Koran. With the death of General Nasser in 1970, Gadhafi also moved to become the new leader of a unified Arab world. In 1972, he came close to convincing Egypt and Syria to join Libya in the Federation of Arab Republics, though disagreements on the terms of the alliance prevented it from coming to fruition. He also tried to achieve union with neighboring Tunisia, but this, too, failed to develop.

Frustrated by the lack of progress with his Arab neighbors, Gadhafi concentrated on completing the revolution at home. In May 1973, he released his "Third International Theory," which sought to unite the principles of social-

ism with Islamic law, a system he called a third way to "capitalist materialism and Communist atheism." In 1976, he published *The Solution to the Problem of Democracy*, the first part of his political manifesto *Green Book*. The second and third parts, focusing on economics and social issues, were released in 1977 and 1979. Throughout the remainder of the decade, Gadhafi worked to achieve the changes outlined in these writings. With the money gained from nationalization, he initiated housing, farming, and health care programs for the public. Gadhafi also made moves to extend political power to Libyan citizens, creating "elected people's committees" to deal with local issues and the General People's Congress to replace the Revolutionary Command Council. On March 2, 1977, the government changed its name from the Libyan Arab Republic to Socialist People's Libyan Arab Jamahiriyya ("government by the masses") to further show its commitment to pure democracy, and Gadhafi was named president and head of the people's revolution. Two years later, he symbolically left this post and became the "leader, theoretician, and symbol" of the Libyan revolution. In general, his efforts in building a "democracy" were largely cosmetic, for Gadhafi remained firmly in command of a repressive police state.

In the international sphere, Gadhafi was increasingly becoming a nuisance to many Western nations. When he aligned with the Soviet Union and showed a penchant for wars, including conflicts with Chad, Egypt, and Tunisia in the 1970s, many Western leaders viewed him as a serious threat to the region. Yet it was his involvement in international terrorism that brought him into direct confrontation with President Ronald Reagan. Early in his first term Reagan increased political and economic sanctions against Libya in an attempt to remove Gadhafi from power. There were also several military incidents between Libya and the United States in the 1980s. In 1981, American pilots shot down two Libyan fighters over the Gulf of Sidra, which Gadhafi had claimed was Libyan airspace. In 1986, responding to terrorist bombings in airports in Rome and Vienna, and the firing of a Libyan missile at an American aircraft over the Gulf of Sidra, the United States bombed military sites off the Libyan coast. A month later, in response to a terrorist attack on a Berlin nightclub where one U.S. soldier was killed, Reagan ordered military strikes on government sites, killing 37 Libyans, allegedly including one of Gadhafi's daughters. One final incident occurred in January 1981, when two Libyan pilots flew directly at American planes and were shot down by U.S. forces.

There were also serious internal problems facing Gadhafi at this time. By the late 1980s, the Libyan economy was suffering from economic sanctions and the drop in the price of oil, and many of Gadhafi's social programs were either frozen or eliminated altogether. This led to a vast erosion of his political support, which threatened the stability of his government. After surviving several coup attempts, Gadhafi heeded the advice of pragmatists in his government and instituted a series of reforms aimed as easing the economic burden on his nation.

Gadhafi also sought a new relationship with his African neighbors toward the end of the 1990s. In 1998, he helped create the Community of the Sahel-Saharan States with Burkina Faso, Chad, Mali, Niger, and Sudan, to foster economic and cultural ties. Later that year, he changed the name of Libya's national radio station from "Voice of the Greater Arab Homeland" to "Voice of Africa." He also participated in the mediation of several conflicts on the continent, such as sending in Libyan forces to quell a coup attempt in the Central African Republic, and he became involved in the African Union.

Gadhafi has mended some fences with the international community in recent years. After years of sanctions by the United Nations, he agreed to extradite two Libyan intelligence officers suspected in the bombing of Pan Am Flight 103 over Lockerbie, Scotland, which killed nearly 300 people in 1988. Most recently, in December 2003, Gadhafi acquiesced to American and British demands and agreed to dismantle his weapons programs under UN supervision, indicating a willingness to shed his terrorist reputation and reenter the world community. Nonetheless, his comments on issues such as terrorism and the Israeli-Palestinian conflict raise doubts about his intentions, and many governments continue to view the Libyan leader with skepticism.

Gergen, David R.
(1942–   ) *assistant to the president for communications*

David Gergen served as director of communications during the first two years of the Reagan administration and played a key role in the development of Reagan's public image. Serving under four different U.S. presidents, Gergen became known for his mastery of media relations, developing many techniques that are widely used today.

Gergen grew up in Durham, North Carolina, where his father was head of Duke University's mathematics department. Following high school, he traveled to Connecticut to study journalism at Yale University. He became managing editor of the *Yale Daily News* and earned his B.A. in 1963. He returned home to work for North Carolina's governor, Terry Sanford. He was only at this position for a brief period, however, before entering Harvard Law School, where he completed his J.D. in 1967. Gergen then began a three-and-a-half year stretch in the U.S. Navy, serving as a damage control officer in Japan

In 1971, Gergen met with Ray Price, a fellow Yale alumnus and the chief speechwriter for President Nixon, who recommended Gergen for the speechwriting team. Gergen became the head of the White House writing and research team and stayed until the end of the Nixon administration in August 1974. He took part in several key events while in this job, including the coordination of the 1972 Republican National Convention, and writing and researching public statements given by Nixon's lawyers in the midst of the Watergate scandal. Gergen's career was unharmed by Nixon's resignation, and after working briefly for Treasury Secretary William Simon, he joined GERALD FORD's White House as director of communications. He worked for Ford until the end of his term, then joined a conservative think tank, the American Enterprise Institute (AEI), as a resident fellow. He also served as managing editor of AEI's journal, *Public Opinion.*

Gergen left AEI to work as an adviser for former CIA director GEORGE H. W. BUSH in his bid for the 1980 Republican presidential nomination. When Reagan won the nomination, Gergen joined his campaign, then was appointed assistant to the president for communications. He became famous for his work as communications director as he revolutionized the way the White House presented its message to the public. Many in the administration, however, were wary of Gergen's moderate positions, particularly those on the speechwriting team who repeatedly had their speeches softened by Gergen himself. In 1983, realizing that he would not be appointed to his choice position as director of the U.S. Information Agency, Gergen left the administration and was named a resident Fellow at the Institute of Politics at Harvard University's John F. Kennedy School of Government.

Gergen stayed at Harvard until 1985 when he was offered a job as managing editor of *U.S. News & World Report.* After just a year at the magazine, he was promoted to editor and editor-at-large and stayed until 1993. Also during this time, Gergen worked as a commentator for PBS on the *MacNeil/Lehrer News Hour.* In both his magazine columns and his television commentary, Gergen displayed a moderate, pragmatic approach to the nation's most pressing problems and was widely respected for his objectivity. In 1993, Gergen joined the Clinton administration as a counselor to the president. This was the fourth president he served, and the first from the Democratic Party. He was brought on to improve the image of President Clinton after a difficult first few months in office and to restore his commitment to moderate, centrist policies. In June 1994, he moved to the foreign policy field as special adviser to the president and the secretary of state.

Gergen left the Clinton administration in December 1994 and returned the next year to *U.S. News & World Report* as editor-at-large. In 1999, he rejoined Harvard University as Public Service Professor of Public Leadership, and director of the Center for Public Leadership at the John F. Kennedy School of Government. The following year, he completed his memoir, *Eyewitness to Power: The Essence of Leadership, Nixon to Clinton.* Gergen is currently on the staff at Harvard University and is a frequent political commentator on PBS, CNN, MSNBC, and the Fox News Channel.

Gorbachev, Mikhail
(1931–) *general secretary, Communist Party of the Soviet Union*

Mikhail Sergeyevich Gorbachev became general secretary of the Soviet Union at the most turbulent time in its 74-year history. In an attempt to reform a failing system, he introduced a series of

Soviet general secretary Gorbachev meets with President Reagan and Vice President Bush on Governor's Island, New York City, December 7, 1988.

radical economic, political, and military reforms, only to see the collapse of the Soviet empire and the eventual dissolution of the Soviet Union in December 1991.

Gorbachev grew up near the city of Stavropol in the southern part of Russia, a major center for Soviet agriculture, where he learned the fundamentals of collective farming and the deficiencies of the Soviet agricultural system. Growing up during the reign of Stalin, he appreciated the power of the KGB and the iron fist of the Soviet leadership. Like most other ambitious

Russians, he joined the Communist Party (CPSU) and in 1952 entered Moscow State University to study law. While at Moscow State, Gorbachev joined the Youth Communist League—Komsomol—and became deeply involved in CPSU politics. He became the leader of the Komsomol chapter in 1954. Following the death of Stalin in 1953, he was excited at the changes being made in the party and chose to begin a career in government service.

Gorbachev took his first government position as an organizer with the local Komsomol chapter in Stavropol. He immediately distinguished himself as a capable party leader, and in 1962 he was appointed as the party organizer for collective and state farms in Stavropol. Just four years later, General Secretary LEONID BREZHNEV promoted him to first secretary of the Stavropol Communist Party. By the late 1960s, he had established himself as a rising young leader in the party, particularly in the agricultural sphere. He was also gaining influential friends within the CPSU such as KGB head and future general secretary Yuri Andropov, who was from Stavropol.

Gorbachev went back to school at the Stavropol Agricultural Institute for an advanced program in agrarian economics, and with this added credential he took the job of first secretary of the Stavropol Territorial Party Committee in 1970, a job similar to a U.S. governor. That same year, he was also appointed as a representative to the Supreme Soviet and a year later he was named to the elite Central Committee. Gorbachev was quickly becoming a leading figure in Soviet national politics. In 1978, he gained a key promotion into the upper echelon of the party when he was named agriculture secretary. Despite the fact that Soviet agriculture went through a difficult period in the late 1970s as a result of a series of poor harvests, Gorbachev earned a reputation as an active and intelligent administrator. In 1979, he joined the Politburo as a nonvoting member, then after just one year he was given full membership, a rare accomplishment for a person his age.

With Brezhnev's death in 1982, Gorbachev was able to enact some of the reforms he believed the Soviet Union desperately needed. His political ally, YURI ANDROPOV, succeeded Brezhnev, and Gorbachev immediately became his chief assistant. Together they worked for a broad reform agenda to improve accountability in the party structure and efficiency in the Soviet economy. After just 14

months in office, Andropov fell ill and died, putting the reform agenda on hold with the appointment of KONSTANTIN CHERNENKO as the next general secretary.

Chernenko was gravely ill from the beginning of his tenure, and Gorbachev quickly emerged as the next in line of succession. He had secured the support of key party leaders in Moscow, and after the death of Chernenko in March 1985, Gorbachev was named general secretary of the CPSU. He proceeded immediately with a radical reform agenda to dramatically reorganize key elements of Soviet society, particularly the economy and the party structure. His economic program, called *perestroika* or economic restructuring, was intended to increase productivity and quality through decentralization and greater private ownership of industry. His political reforms centered around *glasnost*, or openness, which sought to reform the party structure and give the Soviet people greater involvement in the political debate.

He also earned a reputation as a different kind of Soviet leader in the eyes of the West, or, according to British prime minister MARGARET THATCHER, as someone they could "do business" with. As he entered office, Gorbachev considered the level of military commitments abroad to be a drain on the Soviet economy and attempted to drastically reduce the Soviet presence in Afghanistan and Eastern Europe. He also made great strides in reducing the arms race with the United States. He met four times with President Reagan, once in Geneva, and then in Reykjavik, Washington, and Moscow, to negotiate reductions in nuclear weapons. The two men developed a mutual respect for one another, and before long, much to the consternation of Reagan's conservative allies, they were referring to each other as friends. Reagan's tendency to tell the same stale anticommunist jokes tested this friendship on occasion, but in the end their shared desire to put the cold war behind them, and in particular their desire to reduce, if not eliminate, their nuclear arsenals, overrode all other considerations. In December 1987, Gorbachev and Reagan signed the Intermediate Nuclear Forces Treaty, the first treaty ever to reduce the nuclear stockpiles of the United States and the Soviet Union. One year later, Gorbachev stunned the world with the announcement that the Soviet Union intended to pull 50,000 troops from Eastern Europe and reduce its military force by half a million men.

After two short years in office, Gorbachev's popularity abroad was at an all-time high. He was viewed by many as a champion of peace and freedom, particularly in the West where "Gorby-mania" became the new phenomenon. However, at home his popularity rapidly plummeted. *Perestroika* was slow in bringing results, leading to a decline in the quality of life and bringing the Soviet economy to the verge of collapse. More important, *glasnost*, though still in its nascent stages, was giving the Soviet public a channel to form opposition to the government.

Gorbachev's ultimate goal was to restructure the Communist Party, not to destroy it, yet in pushing for greater political freedom he sowed the seeds of his own destruction. In 1989, he agreed to allow nonparty members to challenge party officials in free elections. Later that year, he formally ended the CPSU's monopoly on political power. This was supposed to rid the party of the extreme elements and bring more reform-minded politicians to Moscow, but instead it gave political power to nationalist groups and democrats who wished to end the Soviet system. Nationalism became a particularly difficult problem for Gorbachev as tensions in places like Armenia, Azerbaijan, and Lithuania highlighted the growing impotence of the party in the republics.

The collapse of communism in Eastern Europe in late 1989 further accelerated the drive for democracy in the Soviet Union. Many of the republics declared independence in 1990 and a popular movement began to grow in Russia under the leadership of Boris Yeltsin. During this time of great turmoil, Gorbachev was awarded the Nobel Peace Prize in 1990 for his efforts to ease international tensions. In a last-ditch effort to save the Soviet Union, hard-liners staged a coup against Gorbachev on August 18, 1991. The coup ended, however, within days, and Gorbachev returned to Moscow virtually powerless. In the months that followed, he slowly disassembled the remaining power of the CPSU and on Christmas 1991, the Soviet Union was officially dissolved.

Greenspan, Alan
(1926–) *Federal Reserve chairman*

Alan Greenspan spent nearly 20 years running a successful Wall Street economic consulting firm before entering public service in 1974. During his 17 years as chairman of the Federal Reserve Board, he skillfully managed the U.S. economy through expansion and recession, earning him high marks from both the business world and the general public.

Although he is known primarily as an economist, Greenspan's first career choice was music. Following high school, he entered New York City's world-famous Juilliard School of Music to play saxophone and clarinet but dropped out after just a year to join a swing band. In 1944, he joined New York University to study economics, earning a B.A. with highest honors in 1948, then a master's degree in economics two years later. He then went to nearby Columbia University to work on a doctorate, where he studied under famed economist and future Federal Reserve chairman Arthur Burns but left before he completed his dissertation.

Greenspan's first job out of graduate school was researching issues relating to heavy industry for the National Industrial Conference Board. After just one year at this position, he joined William Townsend in creating Townsend-Greenspan and Company, a Wall Street economic consulting firm. Greenspan and Townsend quickly established themselves as a major corporation, and they soon held a client list that included U.S. Steel, J.P. Morgan and Company, and Aluminum Company of America.

Greenspan became involved in politics in 1968 when he joined Richard Nixon's presidential campaign as a domestic policy adviser. When Nixon won the presidency, he asked Greenspan to join the administration, but Greenspan chose instead to stay in business; he did, however, serve on a number of presidential commissions, such as the Task Force on Economic Growth and the Commission for an All-Volunteer Armed Forces. In 1974 he took the advice of Arthur Burns and accepted the position as chairman of the Council of Economic Advisers (CEA). He joined the CEA at a precarious time; Nixon had resigned shortly before Greenspan's confirmation as chairman, and the U.S. economy was battling rising inflation. Greenspan succeeded in bringing the inflation rate down from 11 percent to 6.5 percent during his short time at the CEA. He left his post at the end of the Ford administration and returned to his firm in New York City. In 1977, Greenspan officially completed his Ph.D. when

Alan Greenspan shakes hands with President Reagan, June 2, 1987.

his alma mater, New York University, awarded him his doctoral degree without a formal dissertation due to his contribution to the field of economics.

In 1980, Greenspan joined the presidential campaign of Ronald Reagan as an economic adviser. He continued in that role following the election but not in any official capacity. In 1981 Social Security became a major issue in the national debate, prompting Reagan to create the National Commission on Social Security Reform to recommend ways to keep the program solvent into the distant future. He named Greenspan chairman of the commission, and two years later they recommended changes that were largely adopted in the 1983 Social Security Amendments.

Greenspan returned to private business for four years before Reagan selected him to replace Paul Volcker as chairman of the Federal Reserve Board on June 2, 1987. He was approved by the Senate 91-2 and joined the Federal Reserve on August 11. Just two months into his term he faced the gravest threat to the U.S. stock market since the Great Depression, when the Dow Jones Industrial Average fell a record 508 points in one day. Greenspan reacted quickly to the collapse by flooding the economy with money so that banks would be able to accommodate those who feared their money would be lost. His actions allowed the economy to recover more quickly than many expected.

In 1991 Greenspan was reappointed to a second four-year term by President GEORGE H. W. BUSH, and later to a third and fourth term by President Clinton. He became a popular chairman among both businessmen and the public for his policies and his candid appraisal of the American economy. A 1996 poll gave him a 96 percent approval rating among America's top 1,000 executives; that number rose to 97 percent in a similar poll two years later. Although this support was tested

with the recent recession of the Bush administration, Greenspan remains the trusted vicar of the American economy. He was reappointed to a fifth term in June 2004.

Gromyko, Andrei
(1909–1989)   *foreign minister of the Soviet Union*

Andrei Gromyko spent 28 years as foreign minister of the Soviet Union, serving under each general secretary from Nikita Khrushchev to MIKHAIL GORBACHEV. His influence in foreign affairs reached a pinnacle under LEONID BREZHNEV, but in 1985, Gorbachev brought his "new thinking" to the foreign ministry and replaced Gromyko with the more reform-minded EDUARD SHEVARDNADZE.

Gromyko was just eight years old when the October Revolution swept the Communist Party into power in Russia. As the son of a peasant farmer, he was impressed by the new system and became an early believer in the party, formally joining in 1931. He graduated from an agricultural technical school in Byelorussia in 1936, then moved to Moscow to become a senior researcher at the Institute of Economics in the Soviet Academy of Sciences, concentrating on the American economy. Two years later, he was promoted to academic secretary at the Institute of Economics.

Gromyko's rise in the party organization began in 1939 when he joined the Soviet diplomatic service. Stalin purged a large number of senior party officials in the late 1930s, leaving a power vacuum in the diplomatic corps, which Gromyko used to his advantage. After six months at the American department in the Commisseriat for Foreign Affairs, he was promoted to counselor to the Soviet embassy in Washington, D.C., the second position below the ambassador. Gromyko's command of the English language and his deep understanding of the U.S. economy earned him promotion to ambassador to the United States in 1943, at the youthful age of 34. He was involved in all of the major conferences between the Soviet Union and the United States at the end of World War II and in the early stages of the cold war, including the Tehran, Yalta, and Potsdam conferences. He headed the Soviet delegation to the Dumbarton Oaks talks from August to October 1944, which laid the foundation for the creation of the United Nations. During the talks, he proposed giving each permanent member of the UN Security Council veto power, a proposal later approved when the UN Charter was signed at the San Francisco Conference in April 1945. The following year, he was chosen as the Soviet Union's first permanent representative to the Security Council.

Over the next several years, Gromyko displayed a rigid view of the Soviet national interest, becoming known for his repeated use of the word *nyet* in Security Council proceedings—he used the veto 26 times in his two years at the UN. He returned to Moscow in 1949 to become deputy foreign minister, serving during the first major conflicts of the cold war—the Berlin blockade, the creation of NATO, the Korean War, and others. In 1952 he fell out of favor with Stalin and was moved from the Foreign Ministry to London, as ambassador to Great Britain. When Stalin died in March 1953, Gromyko returned to his position as deputy foreign minister and worked for the next four years under longtime foreign minister Vyacheslav Molotov. His standing rose in the party in 1956 when he was offered membership in the Central Committee. Molotov was fired from his post in February 1957 after taking part in a failed coup attempt against General Secretary Nikita Khrushchev, giving Gromyko, who was not part of the coup, the job of foreign minister. Khrushchev had little faith in his new foreign minister, seeing him as nothing more

than a loyal party official; thus, Gromyko had little effect on the foreign policy of the Khrushchev era.

In October 1964 Khrushchev was peacefully removed from power by a party coup and replaced by Brezhnev, who kept Gromyko as his foreign minister. During the 18 years of the Brezhnev regime, Gromyko gradually gained power and influence in Soviet foreign affairs. In 1968 he urged Brezhnev to send military forces into Czechoslovakia to suppress the democratic uprising in Prague and restore Soviet power. He also directed the détente with Western Europe in the late 1960s and early 1970s that led to the 1970 treaty between West Germany and the Soviet Union, and the 1975 Final Act of the Conference on Security and Cooperation in Europe, which formally recognized the postwar borders in Eastern Europe for the first time.

Gromyko's central focus throughout the 1970s was détente with the United States. He worked closely with President Richard Nixon and his secretary of state, Henry Kissinger, both of whom he greatly respected as skillful politicians, to reach the Strategic Arms Limitation Talks (SALT) Treaty in May 1972, as well as several other substantial agreements. Less than a year after the signing of the treaty, Gromyko was given full membership in the Politburo. He worked with the Ford and Carter administrations to continue cooperation, reaching arms control agreements in Vladivostok in 1974 and Vienna in 1979, but détente ultimately collapsed after the Soviet invasion of Afghanistan in December 1979. As Brezhnev's health began to decline in the early 1980s, Gromyko assumed greater control over Soviet foreign policy, representing the conservative wing of the party, which advocated a tougher approach to the United States under President Ronald Reagan. His influence was seen in the final three years of the Brezhnev regime and the tenures of YURI ANDROPOV and KONSTANTIN CHERNENKO, as relations with the United States deteriorated to their worst state in decades.

When Chernenko died in March 1985, Gromyko backed the Soviet secretary for military-industrial affairs, Grigori Romanov, as the new secretary general, but the party leadership chose Gorbachev instead. Gorbachev sought a new direction in foreign policy, different from the conservative platforms of Brezhnev and Chernenko that Gromyko had ardently supported, so in July 1985 he named the pragmatic Shevardnadze the new Soviet foreign minister. Gromyko was given the largely symbolic title of chairman of the Presidium of the Supreme Soviet, a position he held until he was removed from office in April 1989 as part of Gorbachev's effort to rid the party of more conservative members and replace them with younger, reform-minded politicians. Three months later, two weeks before his 80th birthday, Gromyko suffered a stroke and died in Moscow.

Haig, Alexander M., Jr.
(AI)
(1924–) *secretary of state*

Alexander Haig built an impressive career of government and military service, serving four U.S. presidents and attaining the rank of four-star general. He reached the position of secretary of state in the Reagan administration, but after less than two years on the job, his desire to be the vicar of U.S. foreign policy caused his star to fade, and his resignation in June 1982 effectively ended his career in national politics.

Haig began his undergraduate work at the University of Notre Dame, but after just two years of study he transferred to the United States Military Academy at West Point. He graduated in the bottom half of his class in 1947 before joining active service as a second lieutenant. Haig was impressive in his service as administrative assistant to the chief of staff of the Far East Command and as an aide to the X Corps commander in Korea. He took part in major action during the Korean War, most notably in the famous landings at Inchon.

After the war, Haig returned to academic life, joining the faculty at West Point and working on his graduate studies in business administration at Columbia University. He was promoted to the rank of major in 1957,

then worked two years as an army staff officer in Europe. Haig returned to academia with a one-year position at the Naval War College, and in 1961, he completed his master's degree in international relations at Georgetown University. A year later, Haig was promoted to lieutenant colonel and was then appointed as the deputy chief of staff for military operations. In 1964, Cyrus Vance, who had recently accepted the position as deputy secretary of defense in the Johnson administration, asked Haig to join his staff as his deputy special assistant.

After two years at this job, Haig was appointed as a brigade commander in Vietnam. He served in Vietnam until 1967, earning widespread respect as a leader and receiving a host of awards for distinguished service, including the Distinguished Service Cross and the Bronze Star. After his tour of duty in Vietnam, and his subsequent promotion to the rank of colonel, he returned to West Point as regimental commander and deputy commander of the U.S. Military Academy.

With the election of Richard Nixon, Haig came back to Washington to serve as military assistant to National Security Advisor Henry Kissinger. In this role, he immediately earned a reputation for a sharp mind and was given access to the Oval Office to speak directly with

President Reagan meets with Secretary of State Al Haig, April 20, 1982.

President Nixon in Kissinger's absence. He also played a role in many facets of the Nixon-Kissinger foreign policy, advocating bombing campaigns in Cambodia and Vietnam, assisting in negotiations in the 1972 cease-fire, and taking part in preparations for Nixon's landmark visit to China. Haig was promoted rapidly during his time under Kissinger, rising to brigadier general, then major general, and finally four-star general and vice chief of staff of the U.S. Army in 1973.

His service as vice chief of staff, however, lasted less than a year. With the onset of the Watergate scandal in 1973, and the subsequent resignation of many senior officials in the executive branch, Haig decided to return to the administration as Nixon's chief of staff. He played an integral role in keeping order in the executive during the waning months of the

Nixon presidency and in the transition to the Ford administration. Many observers in the media contended that Haig was in virtual control of the White House during the final days of the Nixon administration, as the president adopted a bunker mentality and appeared detached and depressed. Haig was an integral player in GERALD FORD's decision to pardon President Nixon, and left the White House shortly after Ford became president. He was selected by Ford in 1974 to become NATO supreme allied commander and commander in chief of U.S. European Command. He served as head of NATO until 1979 when, after more than 30 years of service, he retired from the army and joined United Technologies Corporation as president and chief operating officer.

Haig was not out of the public arena for very long. His stellar record in military and government service and his reputation as a fervent anticommunist drew the admiration of President-elect Ronald Reagan, and shortly after the election Haig was chosen to become secretary of state. He caused a stir early in the administration with talk of "going to the source" of the problem in Central America, that is, Cuba, and raising the possibility of some type of blockade. Haig was largely an adherent of the Reagan foreign policy agenda, particularly its firm stance on the Soviet Union and its clients among developing countries. Yet Haig thought of himself, not Reagan, as the vicar of American foreign policy and his stint at Foggy Bottom was marked by turf wars and infighting with other senior members of the Reagan administration, leading to his early resignation in June 1982, just 18 months into his tenure. His resignation came on the heels of a failed but well-intentioned effort to mediate a dispute between Great Britain and Argentina over the status of the Falkland (Malvinas) Islands. Engaging in 8,000-mile shuttle diplomacy, Haig tried in vain to convince the military junta in Buenos Aires to withdraw its forces from the islands, where they had landed (or invaded, depending on your perspective) in April 1982. The Argentineans rebuffed Haig's request for a diplomatic solution to the problem, leading Prime Minister MARGARET THATCHER to dispatch a British military expedition to remove their forces from the islands. The British soundly defeated the Argentineans just days before Haig's resignation.

Haig returned to private life and wrote his memoir, *Caveat: Realism, Reagan, and Foreign Policy*, which was published late in Reagan's first term. In this work, he portrayed Reagan's senior advisers in an unflattering light, and charged them with making foreign policy decisions based on political calculations. He also blamed Reagan's advisers for his early exit from the administration. He tried to return to national politics in 1988, running for the

Republican presidential nomination, but his campaign never got off the ground, and Haig made an early exit from the race. Since this failed run, he has focused largely on business ventures, serving on the boards of several major corporations and becoming president of Worldwide Associates, an international consulting firm.

Hannaford, Peter
(1932–) *presidential adviser*

A longtime friend and associate of Ronald Reagan, Peter Hannaford grew up in Glendale, California, and attended the University of California at Berkeley. After receiving his A.B. in 1954, he joined the U.S. Army's Signal Corps, serving the next two years and reaching the rank of first lieutenant. In 1956, Hannaford joined the Helen A. Kennedy Advertising firm as an account executive, but he stayed at this position for just one year before joining with Kennedy and forming Kennedy-Hannaford in San Francisco. He served as partner and vice president until 1962, then as president between 1962 and 1965. Hannaford also became a part-time instructor at Merritt College, teaching advertising until 1967. He moved across the bay to Oakland in 1965 to start Kennedy, Hannaford and Dolman, working as a partner and president until 1967. He soon started another firm and was president of Pettler and Hannaford until 1969. In 1969 Hannaford became vice president of Wilton, Coombs, and Colnett, and by 1973 he decided to start his own company, Hannaford and Associates.

Hannaford became involved in California state politics in the late 1960s, shortly after Governor Ronald Reagan took office. He joined the Alameda County Republican Central Committee and Republican State Central Committee of California in 1968 and sat on both committees for the next seven years. He also served as president of the East Bay Division of Republican Alliance in 1968 and 1969. In 1972 Hannaford made a bid for a seat in the U.S. Congress, but was unsuccessful. After the defeat, Governor Reagan appointed him vice chairman of the governor's Consumer Fraud Task Force. In 1975 Hannaford was named director of public affairs for Governor Reagan. He was in this position only for a year before returning to advertising as chairman of the board at Deaver and Hannaford, and at Hannaford Company, both Los Angeles–based advertising firms.

Hannaford continued his relationship with Reagan after Reagan won the presidency in 1980, serving as a speechwriter and adviser to the president, and a member of the Public Relations Advisory Commission of the U.S. Information Agency. He also wrote and edited a number of books on Reagan, including *The Reagans: A Political Portrait* (1983), *Recollections of Reagan: A Portrait of Ronald Reagan* (editor, 1997), and *The Quotable Ronald Reagan* (editor, 1998).

Heckler, Margaret
(1931–   ) *secretary of health and human services, ambassador to Ireland*

Margaret Heckler set out to battle the most visible health dangers in America during her two years as secretary of health and human services (HHS) in the Reagan administration, but a shrinking departmental budget virtually guaranteed her inability to achieve real results. In 1985 Heckler resigned her post and was named ambassador to the Republic of Ireland where she remained until the end of Reagan's presidency.

Heckler grew up in Flushing, New York, and attended Albertus Magnus College. She became involved in politics while in college, majoring in political science and participating in student government organizations. After graduating in 1953, she entered Boston College Law School, becoming editor of the law review and earning her J.D. in 1956. Heckler and her family stayed in Massachusetts, and in 1962 she became the first woman elected to the governor's council in state history. Four years later, she won a seat in the U.S. House of Representatives from Massachusetts's 10th District.

Heckler was technically a Republican, although she frequently broke from her party, especially on women's issues. She was a strong advocate of equal credit laws, child care for working mothers, and the Equal Rights Amendment. She lobbied for the creation of the Congresswomen's Caucus in 1977 to further encourage pro-woman legislation. One issue, however, where Heckler remained firmly in the Republican camp was abortion, where she repeatedly opposed the pro-choice position. She won reelection to Congress seven times before losing her seat in 1982 to Democrat Barney Frank.

A year later, Heckler was selected by President Reagan to succeed RICHARD SCHWEIKER as secretary of health and human services. She was criticized frequently for poor leadership qualities and, by many on the Right, for her support for liberal policies and for her refusal to endorse the conservative position on welfare. She concentrated most of her energy on AIDS, Alzheimer's disease, and breast cancer research during her tenure at HHS.

In October 1985 Reagan asked Heckler to leave the department and take a position as ambassador to the Republic of Ireland. She stayed in Dublin until August 1989, then retired from public life.

Herrington, John S.
(1939–   ) *secretary of energy*

John Herrington left his private law practice in California to serve for eight years at various posts in the Reagan administration. As secretary of energy for Reagan's second term, he continued the drive for deregulation and encouraged greater use of coal and nuclear energy to ensure America's energy independence and stability.

Herrington left his home in Los Angeles to attend Stanford University where he earned his A.B. in 1961. He stayed in northern California and earned his L.L.B. and J.D. from the University of California at San Francisco Law School in 1964. From 1965 to 1967, he served as deputy district attorney in Ventura County, California. In 1967, Herrington started his own private practice, Herrington and Herrington, where he served as partner and general manager until 1981.

Herrington was a strong supporter of California governor Ronald Reagan throughout his terms in office, and when Reagan ran for president in 1980, he volunteered full time for the campaign, serving as western regional director for advance. When Reagan was elected president, he appointed Herrington deputy assistant to the president for personnel. Late in 1981, he moved from the White House to the Pentagon as the assistant secretary for manpower and reserve affairs in the Department of the Navy. He returned to the West Wing in 1983 when he served again in the personnel office as well as special assistant to chief of staff James Baker III.

At the beginning of Reagan's second term, Herrington was appointed secretary of energy to replace DONALD HODEL, who had accepted the post of secretary of the interior. He continued Hodel's drive for more deregulation, particularly in the natural gas industry where he urged Congress to lift all controls on the price of natural gas in April 1986. He also focused on increasing the stability of America's energy resources by encouraging greater use of coal and nuclear power as alternative energy sources to oil. His push for increased use of nuclear power was unfortunately followed by the melt-

down of the Soviet Union's Chernobyl nuclear power plant, which raised doubts among the America public about the safety of nuclear energy. In response, Herrington commissioned an independent safety study of all U.S. nuclear reactors by the National Academy of Sciences and the National Academy of Engineering in May 1986. Environmental groups were also concerned about his drive for greater coal technology, which they contended would result in an increase in acid-rain pollution. Herrington worked closely with the Canadian government and with environmental groups to address these concerns and find ways to limit pollution.

Herrington stayed at the Department of Energy until the end of the Reagan administration, then returned to California to serve as chairman of the state Republican Party.

Hodel, Donald P.

(1935–) *secretary of energy, secretary of the interior*

Donald Hodel held two cabinet posts for President Reagan, remaining an active spokesman for conservative issues related to resource development, nuclear energy, and exploration of the potential oil reserves in the Artic National Wildlife Refuge in Alaska.

Hodel was born in Oregon and attended Harvard University, where he received his B.A. in government in 1957. He moved back to Oregon that same year to study law at the University of Oregon, where he served as the editor of the law review and completed his J.D. in 1960. His first job out of law school was as an associate at the law firm of Rockwood, Davies, Biggs, Strayer, and Stoel. In 1963, he left this private firm to become general counsel for Georgia-Pacific Corporation. He left Georgia-Pacific in 1969 to become deputy administrator for the Interior Department's Bonneville Power Administration, a federal agency that manages

President Reagan listens to a report from Secretary of the Interior Donald P. Hodel, August 1, 1988.

dam-generated electricity. He was promoted to administrator three years later and remained at this position until 1977. During his tenure at Bonneville, Hodel was a strong proponent of nuclear energy and a critic of the environmental lobby, two positions that later attracted him to the Reagan administration. He left Bonneville in 1977 to work as an energy consultant.

Hodel joined the Reagan administration in 1981 when he was named undersecretary of interior, where he served under the controversial secretary, JAMES WATT. Although he supported, and in many cases proposed, most of Watt's initiatives, his likable demeanor allowed him to avoid much of the criticism levied against his boss. In 1983, Hodel left Interior and replaced JAMES EDWARDS as secretary of

energy. Reagan selected Hodel thinking that he would dismantle the newly created department, but Hodel made no efforts in this direction. Nonetheless, he did implement much of the Reagan agenda regarding the easing of environmental regulations and the development of nuclear power. In February 1985, Hodel returned to the Interior Department to replace WILLIAM CLARK as secretary. He continued the Watt-Clark agenda of selling publicly owned lands to business and industry for commercial use, and the drive for further deregulation. Hodel remained at the Interior Department until the end of the administration.

Hodel was awarded the President's Citizens Medal in January 1989. He is currently the managing director of the Summit Energy Group.

Jaruzelski, Wojciech
(1923–) general secretary, Polish Communist Party

In August 1989, under the leadership of Wojciech Jaruzelski, Poland became the first Eastern European nation to undergo a peaceful transfer of power from communism to democracy. Poland's rejection of communism sparked similar uprisings throughout the region, leading to a complete collapse of Soviet power in Eastern Europe and hastening the fall of the Soviet Union two years later.

Jaruzelski was born into a privileged family in interwar Poland and attended an elite Catholic boarding school near Warsaw as a youth. At the age of 16, following the Soviet invasion of Poland in September 1939, he and his family were taken by the Red Army to the Soviet Union. He was separated from his family, all of whom died during this period, and forced to work in the Karaganda coal mines in Kazakhstan until 1943, when he entered a Soviet military school in Ryazan. He then joined the First Polish Army, moving west with the Soviet army until the liberation of Berlin. From 1945 to 1947, he took part in defeating an underground anticommunist resistance movement in Poland called the Home Army.

Jaruzelski moved quickly up the military hierarchy in the years that followed. In 1947, he entered the one-year Senior Infantry School, then went on to Warsaw's General Staff Academy the year after, graduating from the latter in 1951. He was promoted to brigadier general in 1956, becoming the youngest person at that rank in the entire Polish army. He was promoted to division general in 1960, heading the army's Main Political Administration, then to deputy minister of defense in 1962 and chief of the army's general staff in 1965. In March 1968 Jaruzelski was named general of arms for the army, and appointed as Poland's minister of defense.

Jaruzelski's rise through Poland's Communist Party organization was equally impressive. He formally joined the Polish Union Workers' Party (PUWP) in 1948, and by 1964 he was already a member of the Central Committee. He was selected as a candidate member for the Politburo in 1970 and earned full membership a year later. With his ascension to the Politburo, Jaruzelski was considered both a leading military and a political figure in Poland. When the Solidarity trade union was established in August 1980, it presented the most serious threat yet to the PUWP, and many looked to Jaruzelski to lead the party in confronting this challenge. In addition to serving as defense minister, he became Poland's premier in February 1981, then first secretary of the PUWP in October. In November 1983 he was appointed supreme commander of the Polish military and head of the National Defense Committee, solidifying his position as the head of government, party, and military in Poland.

On December 13, 1981, in response to the rising popularity of the Solidarity movement, martial law was declared, and many of the union's top leaders were imprisoned. Ten months later, Solidarity was officially outlawed in Poland, completing the state's repression of the movement for democratization. The United States responded by placing limited sanctions on the Polish government, and, with the help of the Vatican, began giving covert aid to Solidarity through the National Endowment for Democracy and the AFL-CIO. Many of the leaders of Solidarity would later say that this assistance was key to the survival of the movement and its return to power later in the decade. Although martial law was lifted in July 1983, the PUWP continued to repress Solidarity.

In the mid-1980s, Poland's economic and political situation grew steadily worse as the popularity of the PUWP was in decline, and the country fell deeper into financial crisis. Jaruzelski resigned as premier in 1985, but continued as head of the PUWP and the military. After a series of workers' strikes, coordinated largely by Solidarity, broke out in the spring and summer of 1988, and the Soviet Union under Mikhail Gorbachev refused to intervene in Poland, Jaruzelski realized that he would have to either open talks with the opposition or run the risk of his nation falling into chaos. Preliminary talks with the leaders of Solidarity began in late 1988, followed by the relegalization of Solidarity in January 1989, and the beginning of the historic Round Table talks a month later. In April, both sides agreed to hold semi-free elections in June where noncommunist candidates were guaranteed a third of the seats in the legislature. In the elections held for open seats, the Communists received virtually no popular support, highlighting their rapid decline in popularity and the concurrent rise of the pro-democracy movement. When the PUWP was unable to form a coalition government following the election, a Solidarity-led governing alliance formed a new government in August. In an effort to ensure some semblance of political stability, Jaruzelski was elected president by the Polish parliament with the intention of his serving a five-year term until the transition to democracy was complete. The general public, however, did not want to wait five years for free elections and LECH WALESA, the most prominent figure in the Solidarity union, urged Jaruzelski to call for a presidential election, which he did in November and December 1990.

When the popular Walesa announced his candidacy for the presidency, Jaruzelski resigned from office and pledged to usher in a peaceful transition of power for the incoming president. As he left office, Jaruzelski publicly apologized to the nation for his role in suppressing the drive for freedom and democracy in Poland in the 1980s.

Kemp, Jack
(1935–) *U.S. congressman*

After 11 seasons in professional football and
two AFL championships, Jack French Kemp,
Jr., entered national politics and became a leading voice for supply-side economics. During
his nearly 30 years in politics, Kemp held the
positions of U.S. congressman, secretary of
housing and urban development, and 1996
Republican candidate for vice president. Kemp
was a font of ideas for the Republican Party,
and in many ways he personified the spirit of
the Reagan years. He persistently urged the
Republican Party to reach out to the African-
American community, and was the leading
advocate of "urban enterprise zones," a policy
of encouraging tax breaks and other government incentives designed to attract businesses
to the inner city. As HUD secretary, he supported programs permitting residents of public
housing to purchase their units, and promoted
an aggressive campaign of enforcement against
suspected drug dealers, including expulsion
from federally subsidized housing.

Kemp's lifelong goal was to become a professional football player. Following high school,
he entered Occidental College in Los Angeles
and studied physical education. His primary
focus, however, was football, where he became

the starting quarterback and captain of the
team. He graduated from Occidental in 1957,
then began graduate studies at Long Beach
State University and California Western University while seeking a career in professional
football. He was drafted by the Detroit Lions of
the National Football League in 1957, but was
released soon after. He joined the Pittsburgh
Steelers for the rest of the season, but he did not
see any action the entire year. In 1958, Kemp
moved north to play in the Canadian Football
League. After two years in the CFL, Kemp was
drafted by the Los Angeles (later San Diego)
Chargers of the newly formed American Football League. He served as the starting quarterback and captain of the Chargers for two years,
but during the 1962 season, Kemp, battered
from injuries, was sold to the Buffalo Bills for
$100. He sat out much of the 1962 season, but
the next year he joined the Bills and helped lead
the franchise to their first-ever winning season.
The next two years, the Bills won the AFL
championship, and in 1965, Kemp was named
both AFL Player of the Year and championship
Most Valuable Player.

It was during this time that Kemp began to
develop an interest in politics. He cofounded
the American League Players Association in
1965 and served as president for five terms. He
then came to the attention of the new governor

of his home state of California, Ronald Reagan, and served as a special assistant to the governor in 1967. Two years later, Kemp was named a special assistant to the chairman of the Republican National Committee. In 1970, he ended his 11-year career in professional football and moved into politics.

He made a bid that year for an open seat in the U.S. Congress from a district in the Buffalo, New York, area. Kemp was such a high-profile candidate that President Nixon and vice president Agnew both came to Erie County to campaign for him, and he won 52 percent of the vote. He served in Congress for the next 18 years, easily winning reelection nine times. Kemp was seen as moderate to liberal on many social issues, but a staunch conservative on economic policy, becoming one of the strongest proponents of supply-side economics. When another supply-sider, Ronald Reagan, came to office in 1981, Kemp became one of his leading allies in fiscal policy, helping to push through Reagan's economic program. From 1981 to 1987, he served as chairman of the House Republican Conference.

By 1988, Kemp had developed such a strong national reputation that he decided to make a run for the GOP presidential nomination. However, his campaign sought to continue the conservative politics of the Reagan administration at a time when the public was seeking a more moderate leader, and by March he was out of the race. Following the victory of Republican GEORGE H. W. BUSH, Kemp was selected as secretary of housing and urban development. He set out immediately to restore the reputation of the department after eight years of scandal and fraud, demanding the resignation of nearly all the department's appointees and suspending a series of programs enacted during the Reagan administration. His efforts to increase the HUD budget and initiate bold new programs were widely praised by both Democrats and Republicans. Kemp became a leading advocate of helping the poor by creating opportunity and incentives for economic development.

Following President Clinton's victory in 1992, Kemp cofounded Empower America, a policy organization aimed at fostering opportunity while preserving individual freedom and economic liberty. He also received fellowships at the Heritage Foundation and the Hoover Institute. In 1996, he became the Republican vice presidential candidate for ROBERT DOLE, but lost the election to Bill Clinton and Al Gore. Kemp is currently affiliated with both Empower America and Habitat for Humanity.

Khachigian, Kenneth L.
(1944–) *chief speechwriter*

Kenneth Khachigian served on and off in the Reagan administration as a consultant to the president and a speechwriter, crafting some of Reagan's most important speeches, including his 1981 inaugural address and his 1985 speech at the Bergen-Belsen concentration camp in West Germany. In more than 30 years as a political consultant, he has been involved in a number of major Republican national campaigns, including the presidential runs of Reagan, GEORGE H. W. BUSH, ROBERT DOLE, and John McCain.

Khachigian grew up in the town of Visalia in central California and attended the University of California at Santa Barbara, completing his B.A. in 1966. He moved across country following graduation to study law at Columbia University. After earning his J.D. in 1969, Khachigian returned to California and was admitted into the state bar the following year.

In 1970, at the age of 25, Khachigian was appointed deputy special assistant to President Richard Nixon. He remained with the administration until Nixon's retirement, then returned to private law practice back in California. In the summer of 1980, Khachigian was sought out by STUART SPENCER to join the Reagan presidential campaign as a speechwriter. Over the remaining months of the campaign, he drafted a number of key stump speeches that effectively laid out the Reagan message, earning him appointment as chief speechwriter and special consultant to the president after the election. He wrote a series of important speeches during Reagan's first year in the White House, including his inaugural address and the speech on the Economic Recovery Program. In September 1981 he left the administration and returned to private life as a public affairs consultant in San Clemente, California.

Over the next seven years, Khachigian alternated between private consulting work and service in the Reagan administration. In May 1982 he was appointed by Reagan to the advisory board of the National Institute of Justice, serving on that board until 1985. He also served on the boards of directors of several private organizations, including the California Chamber of Commerce, the University of California at Santa Barbara Foundation, and the Hoover Institution. He returned to speechwriting in the fall of 1984 to draft some campaign speeches and to help the president prepare for a series of debates with Democratic challenger Walter Mondale. In May 1985 he was again commissioned to write a speech Reagan was to deliver during his controversial visit to the Bergen-Belsen concentration camp in West Germany. For the remainder of Reagan's tenure, Khachigian was periodically called back to Washington to collaborate on major speeches, including the 1987 State of the Union address and Reagan's 1988 speech to the Republican National Convention.

In 1988, Khachigian was named communications director for the Bush campaign, and crafted numerous speeches for both Bush and his vice presidential nominee, Dan Quayle. Following Bush's victory over Michael Dukakis

in the general election, Khachigian returned to California to work in private law practice. He remained involved in a number of state and national elections during this time, most notably serving as national senior adviser for Senator Dole's 1996 presidential campaign and Senator John McCain's bid against George W. Bush in 2000.

Khachigian is currently a partner at the law firm of Smiland and Khachigian in Los Angeles. He is also director of the Richard Nixon Library and Birthplace Foundation, and the California Council for Environmental and Economic Balance.

Kirkpatrick, Jeane J.
(1926–   ) *United Nations representative*

A former Democrat and supporter of Hubert Humphrey, Jeane Kirkpatrick was an instrumental member of Ronald Reagan's conservative foreign policy brain trust. As the American ambassador to the United Nations, Kirkpatrick earned a reputation for blunt talk, including vowing to hold developing nations accountable for their support of the Soviet

President Reagan meets with UN Ambassador Jeane J. Kirkpatrick, December 11, 1984.

Union in the General Assembly. Her frank manner endeared her to American conservatives, many of whom had little regard for the United Nations, and, in an administration dominated by men, gave her a high profile in the media.

Kirkpatrick graduated from Missouri's Stephens College with an A.A. in 1946, then completed her B.A. two years later at Barnard College in New York City. She went immediately into graduate work after Barnard and received her M.A. from Columbia University in 1950. After the completion of her master's degree, Kirkpatrick entered government service for the State Department, working in Washington, D.C., for the next two years as a research analyst. She returned to her studies in 1952, starting graduate work at the Institut de Science Politique at the University of Paris, where she remained for two years.

Upon her return from Paris in 1953, Kirkpatrick moved to Washington, D.C., where she would live for the next 27 years. In 1962, she took the position of assistant professor of political science at Trinity College in Washington, and in 1967, Kirkpatrick completed her Ph.D. from Columbia University. She then became associate professor of government at Georgetown University and went on to become a full professor at Georgetown in 1973. In 1978 she was appointed as the Government Department's Leavey Professor in Foundations of Freedom.

Kirkpatrick began her career in public service shortly after she moved to Washington, D.C. In 1955 she married a State Department foreign service officer named Evron Kirkpatrick, who was a good friend of Hubert Humphrey and a strong supporter of the Democratic Party. Kirkpatrick quickly became involved in Democratic Party politics, serving for a time as an aide to Senator Humphrey. In 1972, she became vice chairman of the Democratic National Commission on Vice-Presidential Selection, then in 1976 she served

as a member of the Credentials Committee at the 1976 Democratic National Convention. During the Carter administration, Kirkpatrick became disillusioned with the direction of the Democratic Party, particularly on foreign policy issues, and began associating herself with Democrats like Senator Henry Jackson, who supported a strong defense policy and was a critic of détente with the Soviet Union. She was an active participant in the neoconservative movement, joining such groups as the Coalition for a Democratic Majority, and the Committee on the Present Danger, the latter closely associated with the Reagan presidential campaign.

Kirkpatrick attacked Carter's policies in Iran and Nicaragua in an article in the November 1979 issue of *Commentary* entitled "Dictatorships and Double Standards." She contended that President Carter's human rights policy had the effect of undermining pro-U.S. governments, which, while they were authoritarian, were preferable to the alternative. She was referring to Iran under the shah, Chile under General Pinochet, the Somoza government in Nicaragua, and the military regime in South Korea. These governments were threatened from within and without, and, unlike many totalitarian regimes, they were capable of change and tolerated a degree of freedom. Kirkpatrick argued that Carter's human rights policy was effective only against pro-American governments, which were then replaced by leftist, anti-American regimes with little regard for human rights.

The article caught the attention of RICHARD ALLEN and through him, candidate Reagan, who invited Kirkpatrick to join the campaign as a foreign policy analyst. After Reagan's victory, she was appointed the U.S. permanent representative to the United Nations, a post she held for the next four years. During her tenure at the United Nations, Kirkpatrick was best known for implementing a distinction between autocracies that she thought America could support, and totalitarian regimes, whose revolutionary and expansionist aims she strongly opposed. She shared her president's disdain for the Soviet Union, and was particularly vocal in condemning the crackdown against the Solidarity Movement in Poland; the destruction of Korean Airlines Flight 007 in September 1983; and Soviet (and Cuban) intervention in Central America. Kirkpatrick returned to her job as professor at Georgetown University after she left the Reagan administration. She cofounded the public policy group Empower America in 1993, thus solidifying her credentials as a leading advocate of neoconservatism in America.

Kohl, Helmut
(1930–   ) *chancellor of the Federal Republic of Germany*

A faithful ally of Ronald Reagan and MARGARET THATCHER, Helmut Kohl shared many of their views on economic policy and on relations with the Soviet Union. He also entangled Ronald Reagan in one of the most awkward episodes of his presidency by inviting him to a visit to Germany in 1985 that included a stop at a military cemetery in Bitburg containing the remains of members of Adolf Hitler's SS units.

Kohl grew up in Germany during the rise of Adolf Hitler and the Nazi Party. His parents were not Nazis, but their loyalty to the government, even during World War II, kept them secure. Kohl was only a youth during the war (15 years old when it ended), but he took a keen interest in politics at an early age. He took part in organizing the Christian Democratic Union's (CDU) youth wing, the "Young Union," in 1947. He formally studied politics, history, and law at the Universities of Frankfurt and Heidelberg, and finished his doctorate in 1958.

Kohl began working in government even before he was out of college. After holding local government posts for a few years, he won his first election to the parliament of the Rhineland-Pfalz province in 1959, at just 29 years of age. In 1964, Kohl was selected to serve on the CDU's national board. He rose to the position of minister president of Rhineland-Pfalz in 1969, serving until 1976. It was during his days as the governor of this province that Kohl gained notoriety in the national political arena, and by 1973 he was chairman of the CDU and, following the 1969 victory of the Social Democratic Party (SPD), leader of the opposition.

Kohl made his first bid for chancellor in 1976 as the candidate for the CDU/Christian Social Party (CSU) alliance, but lost to incumbent SPD leader Helmut Schmidt. Following the election, Franz Josef Strauss, leader of the more conservative CSU, blamed Kohl for the loss, leading to the dissolution of the 27-year-long alliance of the two parties at the CSU party conference a month after the election. The party reunited in time for the 1980 election, and Strauss ran as the CDU/CSU candidate in that election, but his defeat proved that a right-wing party could never form a government in West Germany, thus boosting the standing of Kohl in the CDU/CSU alliance. He took over as leader again and moved the alliance back to a more moderate position.

In 1982, Kohl was successful in getting the Free Democratic Party (FDP) to split from its governing alliance with the SPD and cast a vote of "no confidence" in the Schmidt government. Elections followed in March 1983, and Kohl was able to form a three-party government with members of the CDU, CSU and FDP. As leader of this loose coalition, Kohl took over as chancellor. The no-confidence vote and the ascendancy of Kohl marked a shift in German politics—a "turning point," according to Kohl—as the Christian Democrats gained 38.2 percent of the vote, their highest share in more than 25 years.

Kohl ruled in the mold of Reagan and Thatcher, preaching tax relief and economic recovery; he also favored a strong defense and championed the Western alliance. His economic policies were only mildly successful, however. In response to West Germany's financial woes, he promised to obtain a no-interest loan from the wealthy, but this was later found unconstitutional by the highest court, leaving the government in desperate need of additional revenues. Unemployment also continued at a high rate. Nonetheless, Kohl did succeed in bringing the first real economic growth since 1980 when the GDP rose 1.3 percent in 1983.

Kohl met with much greater success in foreign policy. He worked closely with President Reagan to increase West German security, supporting Reagan's proposal to place Pershing II missiles on German soil in 1983. Although this was an unpopular decision, particularly in Western Europe where the nuclear-freeze movement was at its zenith, it demonstrated Kohl's commitment to a strong defense and the alliance with the United States. Another major aspect of Kohl's foreign policy was the symbolic reconciliation with other Western European nations who fought against Germany in World War II. Visits to military graveyards at Verdun with President FRANÇOIS MITTERRAND and Bitburg with President Reagan showed a willingness on the part of the German leader to heal the wounds of World War II. But the latter visit caused a firestorm in the United States when it was revealed that the Bitburg graveyard included soldiers from various Waffen SS units. American Jewish leaders pleaded with Reagan to cancel his visit to the cemetery, but Kohl implored Reagan to fulfill his commitment and keep Bitburg on his itinerary. Reagan agreed to do so, and used the occasion to call for reconciliation among old foes. He also added a visit to the Bergen-Belsen concentration camp, and

gave a moving tribute to the victims of the Holocaust, including Anne Frank.

By far Kohl's most important, and far-reaching, foreign policy accomplishment was the reunification of Germany in 1990. He consistently championed the idea of reunification throughout his tenure, although to many this seemed like wishful thinking that was likely never to materialize. But in a stunning succession of events in the fall of 1989, the Communist East German government lost its grip on power and the Berlin Wall, the most prominent symbol of the East-West struggle, fell on November 9, 1989. Kohl immediately called for reunification of East and West Germany, but this was met by strong resistance from the Soviet Union as well as France and Great Britain, both of whom feared the power of a unified Germany in the middle of Europe. In a brilliant tactical move, President GEORGE H. W. BUSH threw his support behind Kohl's initiative, giving the United States a prominent position in the execution of reunification. In September 1990, the United States won a significant victory when a united Germany agreed to remain in the Western alliance. Economic and political reunification was completed on October 3, 1990.

Kohl served as chancellor for 15 years, winning reelection in 1987, 1990, and 1994. The economic and political difficulties associated with a task as complex as reunification occupied a majority of his time during the 1990s. Kohl lost his bid for a fifth term in 1998, and in 2000 he left politics altogether after a party funding scandal forced his resignation. He later admitted his involvement in the scandal, and in March 2000 Kohl rejoined the Reichstag.

Koop, C. Everett
(1916–   ) *surgeon general*

As surgeon general for the Reagan administration, Dr. C. Everett Koop challenged the tobacco industry and lobbied for "safe sex" practices to inhibit the AIDS virus, both positions that generated criticism from the conservative wing of his party. Despite this opposition, his pragmatic solutions to these public health dangers brought him widespread respect from a majority of Americans.

Koop wanted to become involved in medicine at a very early age, and took courses at Dartmouth College when he was just 16 years old, earning a B.A. in 1937 at the age of 20. After Dartmouth, he moved back to his home state of New York and attended Cornell Medical College for a degree with a focus on pediatric surgery. He trained at Boston Children's Hospital and Pennsylvania Hospital, then completed his Sc.D. degree in medicine from the University of Pennsylvania. He remained in Pennsylvania following graduation to take a position as surgeon-in-chief at the Children's Hospital in Philadelphia.

Koop devoted his early career to the advancement of pediatric surgery. Surgical procedures for babies and children had not yet been fully developed and the child mortality rates were still substantially high. In fact, there were less than 10 pediatric surgeons in the country at that time. Through his tireless dedication over the next 33 years, he became responsible for a number of major breakthroughs that improved knowledge of pediatric surgery and contributed to a declining child

Surgeon General C. Everett Koop shakes hands with President Reagan in the Cabinet Room, White House, January 22, 1986.

mortality rate. In addition to his work at the Children's Hospital, Koop was also a member of the University of Pennsylvania School of Medicine faculty. He joined the school as an assistant professor in 1949 and rose quickly through the ranks, becoming full professor of pediatric surgery in 1959, then professor of pediatrics in 1971.

In 1981 Koop accepted his first political appointment when he was named U.S. surgeon general by President Reagan. His nomination generated controversy, because many Democrats were concerned with Koop's reputation as an ardent conservative and particularly with his strong feelings on abortion and homosexuality. Koop also was over the maximum age allowed for a surgeon general. After a difficult nine-month nomination process, and a change in the age requirement law, Koop was confirmed by the Senate in a close vote in November 1981.

Koop's number one priority while in office was to improve the public health of Americans. He tried to bring about greater public awareness of dieting and exercise. He also advocated a ban on the advertising of alcoholic products. Koop's greatest fight, however, was against the tobacco industry, which he claimed was responsible for the greatest threat to public health. He argued that nicotine was an addictive drug in much the same way as cocaine and heroin. He also pushed to eliminate smoking from the workplace and ultimately to create a "smokeless society by the year 2000." This battle was extremely unpopular within conserva-

tive circles, particularly with North Carolina senator Jesse Helms, who represented a state with a thriving tobacco industry. Nonetheless, it dispelled the myth that Koop was controlled by the right wing of the Republican Party.

Another issue unpopular among conservatives was Koop's views on the AIDS virus. AIDS had been ignored by the Reagan administration until 1984 when Koop was asked to prepare a report on the subject. In October 1986 he released a report that said the most effective means to control the spread of the virus, beyond abstinence, was early sex education and condom use. This position was vociferously attacked by conservatives who advocated an "abstinence-only" approach to sex education in schools. Koop adhered to his position, earning widespread respect from the public for his compassionate and objective response to the disease.

After nearly eight years as surgeon general, Koop found his support among conservatives foundering. In October 1989 he decided to leave office and return to Dartmouth as a professor of surgery. He helped establish the C. Everett Koop Institute at Dartmouth in 1992. President Clinton awarded Koop with the highest civilian honor, the Presidential Medal of Freedom, in 1995 for his dedication to public health issues. Koop has also written several books and articles, and has continued to advocate health awareness through public lectures and initiatives such as drkoop.com and Shape Up, America! He currently runs the C. Everett Koop Institute and serves as a senior scholar.

L

Laxalt, Paul
(1922–) *U.S. senator*

Paul Laxalt was a rarity among members of Congress—he was a friend of the Reagans prior to their arrival in Washington and was a stalwart supporter of Ronald Reagan's effort to unseat GERALD FORD in 1976. During the Reagan presidency, Laxalt kept his finger on the pulse of Capitol Hill, providing valuable intelligence to the White House about the mood of his Republican and Democratic colleagues.

Laxalt entered Santa Clara University in 1944 but left school to serve in the army during World War II. Upon his return, he enrolled in Denver University, earning his B.A. and LL.B. in 1949 and passing the Nevada state bar exam the same year. He began his law career as the district attorney of Ormsby County, Nevada, staying in public service until 1954. Following his days as district attorney, he went into private practice as a partner in the firm Laxalt, Ross, and Laxalt, where he worked until 1962.

Laxalt left private practice in 1962 to enter politics, winning the office of lieutenant governor of Nevada. He served one term in this role, then in 1966 was elected governor of Nevada. As governor, Laxalt established a community college system, battled organized crime in Las Vegas, and left office with a surplus in the state's budget. After one term in office, he returned to private practice in Carson City, Nevada, as a senior partner at Laxalt, Berry, and Allison. His hiatus from politics, however, was short-lived as he ran and won a seat in the U.S. Senate in 1974. In 1976, Laxalt broke with many members of his party and supported the candidacy of Ronald Reagan against President Ford, forming the campaign group "Citizens for Reagan" and nominating Reagan for president at the GOP convention in Kansas City. He remained a loyal supporter of Reagan and served as chairman of his Campaign Committee again in 1980 and 1984.

Laxalt was one of Reagan's closest allies in the Senate. He was an ardent conservative who agreed with the bulk of the Reagan agenda, particularly on defense issues and the size of government. Laxalt was also heavily involved in intraparty politics, serving as general chairman of the Republican National Committee from 1983 to 1987. He toyed with the idea of running for president in 1988 but quickly abandoned the effort.

Laxalt served two terms in the Senate before returning to private law practice once again, although this time he remained in Washington, taking an associate's position at Finley, Kumble, Wagner, Heine, Underberg, Manley, Myerson, and Casey. After less than two years at this job, he joined another Washington-based firm, Laxalt, Washington, Perito, and Dubuc, as an associate. In 1990, Laxalt founded his own business, the Paul Laxalt Group, in Washington, D.C.

Lewis, Andrew L., Jr.
(1931–   ) *secretary of transportation*

Ronald Reagan's secretary of transportation was at the center of a storm that helped define the Reagan presidency in its first months in office: the strike of the nation's air traffic controllers. Reagan's decision to fire the controllers, with Drew Lewis at his side, confirmed for some Americans that Reagan was a resolute leader of deep conviction.

Born and raised in Philadelphia, Lewis attended nearby Haverford College and received his B.S. in economics in 1953. After college, he went to the Harvard Graduate School of Business and earned his M.B.A. two years later. His first job out of Harvard was as a foreman for Henkels and McCoy, Incorporated. He remained with this company for the next six years, quickly earning promotions to production manager, then director. In 1960, he left Henkels and McCoy and became vice president for sales at the American Olean Tile Company. Lewis also became involved in politics in 1960 as the organizational chairman for the Richard Schweiker for Congress Committee. Eight years later, he served as the chairman of the Schweiker for Senator Committee. In 1969 Lewis was promoted to vice president and assistant to the chairman of National Gypsum Company, the parent company of American Olean Tile. A year later, he became president and chief executive officer of Simplex Wire and Cable Company, and of Snelling and Snelling. In 1974 he created Lewis and Associates, a consulting firm that focused on advising struggling businesses.

Lewis remained closely involved in politics during these years, serving as county commit-

President Reagan receives a briefing from Secretary of Transportation Andrew L. Lewis, Jr., January 8, 1986.

tee member and chairman of the Pennsylvania Republican Party's finance committee. In 1974, he also made a bid for the Pennsylvania governor's seat, but was unsuccessful in his campaign. He was chairman of the Pennsylvania delegation to the 1976 Republican National Convention as well as deputy chairman of the Republican National Committee, and his support of President GERALD FORD for the GOP nomination, even after a personal plea from friend and fellow Pennsylvanian RICHARD SCHWEIKER, played a key role in Reagan not receiving the nomination. While only in his mid-40s, Lewis was quickly becoming a major force in the Republican Party.

Lewis was one of the first in the party leadership to support Reagan in his 1980 bid for the presidential nomination. He managed the Reagan campaign in Pennsylvania and secured a majority of the state's delegates even after Reagan failed to win the popular vote. Following Reagan's victory over President JIMMY CARTER in the general election, he joined the transition team as the deputy director of the office of the president-elect and a member of the transportation task force. On January 23, 1981, after a vote of 98 to 0 in the

Senate, he was sworn in as the nation's seventh secretary of transportation. During his confirmation hearings, Lewis said, "We don't plan to back off deregulation in any way," and during his two years in office he worked to scale back or eliminate a variety of regulations adversely affecting the transportation industry. The biggest issue he faced during his tenure was the strike by the Professional Air Traffic Controllers Organization in August 1981. Lewis worked closely with the Federal Aviation Administration to maintain safe air travel while the strike was proceeding. He also succeeded in modernizing America's airspace system and gaining passage of the Surface Transportation Assistance Act of 1982. Lewis left the administration in February 1983 for a job in the private sector. He was succeeded by ELIZABETH DOLE.

Lyng, Richard E.
(1918–2003) *secretary of agriculture*

Richard Lyng spent his entire career in the agricultural sector, moving up from his father's bean and seed company to become secretary of agriculture in the Reagan administration. Lyng played a key role in shaping Reagan's farm policy, which saw one of the largest budget increases in the department's history.

Lyng attended the University of Notre Dame for undergraduate studies and earned his degree, summa cum laude, in 1940. He returned to his home state of California following graduation and began working for his father as a field representative for his bean and seed company. Shortly after, Lyng joined the U.S. Army to fight in World War II and served in the South Pacific until the end of the war. When the war ended in 1945, he came back to California and resumed work for his father. In 1949, Lyng became president of the bean and seed company and remained at this position

for the next 18 years, doubling the company's earnings in that time.

In the 1960s, Lyng began to take a part in California Republican politics. He made a bid for the California state senate in 1966, but was defeated by the incumbent Democrat. A year later, he was appointed associate director of the California Department of Agriculture under Governor Ronald Reagan. He served the Reagan administration until 1969, when he was named assistant secretary of agriculture by President Richard Nixon. He stayed in the Nixon administration for the duration of his first term, then in 1973 he moved to the other side of the negotiating table and became a lobbyist for the American Meat Institute. He stayed at the AMI as president until 1979.

Lyng left his lobbying position in 1979 after he heard his former boss, Ronald Reagan, was making a second run for the White House. He joined the campaign and helped to win votes in America's farm regions, a major constituency for Reagan throughout his two terms in office. When Reagan took office in 1981, he named Lyng deputy secretary of agriculture. There was speculation that Lyng was going to be tapped to become secretary, but the post was given to JOHN BLOCK on the advice of Senator ROBERT DOLE, who argued that a midwestern farmer be given the position. Heart surgery forced Lyng to leave the department in 1985, but the following year he returned after being nominated as secretary of agriculture. He served in this position for the remainder of Reagan's second term. During his eight years in Reagan's Agriculture Department, Lyng presided over a massive increase in the department's budget, as policies such as the 1981 and 1985 farm bills and the 1983 Payment-in-Kind program substantially increased the federal government's role in the agricultural sector.

Lyng returned to California after leaving the administration and died on February 1, 2003.

M

McFarlane, Robert C.
(Bud)
(1937–) *National Security Advisor*

Robert McFarlane was one of six National Security Advisors to President Reagan, and his tenure was marked by controversy. He became embroiled in the Iran-contra affair, and was generally considered to be one of the key players in the administration's failed attempt to establish a relationship with moderate elements in Iran.

Like many of his colleagues on Reagan's National Security Council staff, McFarlane had a strong military background. He entered the U.S. Naval Academy in 1955 for studies in electrical engineering, and later that year joined the U.S. Marine Corps for active duty as a second lieutenant. McFarlane graduated from the naval academy in 1959, then six years later entered the Institute of International Studies in Geneva, Switzerland, for graduate work. He became Oldsted scholar and received his M.S. in strategic studies, magna cum laude, in 1967. He retired from the military in 1979 as a lieutenant colonel after a distinguished career that included service in Vietnam, Korea, and Japan.

McFarlane entered public service in 1971 when he took a job as White House Fellow in the Nixon administration. In 1973, he became military assistant to President Nixon's National Security Advisor, Henry Kissinger. He remained at this position until 1975, serving also under President Ford's National Security Advisor, Brent Scowcroft. In 1976, McFarlane became special assistant to the president for national security affairs under President JIMMY CARTER. He left the Carter administration in 1977 to take the position of senior research fellow at the National Defense University. He stayed at NDU for two years before joining the staff of the Senate Committee on Armed Services, where he stayed until the beginning of the Reagan administration.

McFarlane joined the Reagan administration in 1981 as an undersecretary in the State Department. After a year at State, he moved back to the NSC with a job as deputy National Security Advisor. He stayed at this job until July 1983, when he took the post of special presidential envoy to the Middle East.

Just three months into this appointment, McFarlane was asked to become Reagan's third National Security Advisor, which he accepted in October 1983. A major issue confronting McFarlane was how to provide support for the Nicaraguan contras in the face of congressional restrictions on such assistance.

President Reagan was determined to keep the contras active, and the extent of his knowledge of what became known as the "diversion" of funds remains a subject of controversy, although no evidence has been produced indicating that the president knew of the diversion. Reagan did, however, approve of the opening to Iran, and hoped that one benefit from this initiative would be the release of the American hostages held in Lebanon by groups supported by Iran. McFarlane, along with other members of the NSC staff and members of other government agencies, constructed a plan to sell weapons to Iran, then to reroute the profits from the arms sales to aid the contras, an illegal action under the provisions of the Boland Amendments, which prohibited U.S. aid to the Nicaraguan rebels. As the deal progressed, McFarlane's opening to Iran seemed to become almost exclusively focused on freeing the American hostages in Lebanon, despite President Reagan's repeated assurances that he would never deal with terrorists. McFarlane resigned his position as National Security Advisor on

National Security Advisor Robert C. "Bud" McFarlane talks to President Reagan and George Schultz at the Augusta golf course, October 23, 1983.

November 30, 1985, but he continued to assist the effort in a private capacity. He even traveled to Tehran in May 1986, attempting to work out a deal that would free the hostages, but this ultimately failed.

Soon after the Iran-contra scandal became public, McFarlane attempted suicide by overdosing on tranquilizer pills. He said the impetus behind this was his feeling that he had misled Congress and the American public, and thus "failed the country." The investigation conducted by Independent Counsel LAWRENCE WALSH charged McFarlane with involvement in the arms deal and he pleaded guilty to four of the misdemeanor charges. He was given two years' probation, 200 hours of community service, and a fine of $20,000 for his role in the scandal. In 1992, President GEORGE H. W. BUSH pardoned McFarlane and others for their involvement in the Iran-contra affair.

McLaughlin, Ann Dore
(1941–) *secretary of labor*

Ann Dore McLaughlin served in the Departments of Treasury, Interior, and Labor for the Reagan administration. As secretary of labor for the final 13 months of the administration, she focused on finding private sector solutions to key labor issues. Ann McLaughlin was the wife of a prominent Washington media figure and former Nixon aide, John McLaughlin, and the two of them were one of the more prominent "power couples" of the Reagan years.

McLaughlin earned her B.A. from New York's Marymount College in 1963. Her first job out of college was working for the American Broadcasting Company in New York as a supervisor of network commercial scheduling. She left ABC after just three years and returned to Marymount College as the director of alumni relations. In 1970, she became an account executive for Myers-Infoplan International and a consultant and literary agent for Perla Meyers' International Kitchen.

In 1971, McLaughlin took her first job in politics when she was named director of communications for the Presidential Election Commission. Following President Nixon's victory in the general election, she worked as the press secretary and assistant to the chairman of the Presidential Inaugural Committee. In 1973 she joined the Nixon administration as director of the Environmental Protection Agency's Office of Public Information. She returned to the business world after Nixon's resignation with a job at Union Carbide Corporation. After four years at Union Carbide, she started her own business, McLaughlin and Company, and also served as Washington manager of Braun and Company, staying at both positions until 1981.

McLaughlin joined the Reagan administration's Treasury Department in 1981 as assistant secretary for public affairs, working under Secretary DONALD REGAN. In 1984, she became undersecretary of the Interior, but left this post in 1987 to manage Kansas senator ROBERT DOLE's presidential campaign. Following Dole's defeat, McLaughlin worked briefly at the Center for Strategic and International Studies in Washington, D.C., and the University of Pennsylvania's Wharton School of Business, then returned to the Reagan administration as secretary of labor, replacing WILLIAM BROCK, who had also left the administration to work for the Dole campaign. During her 13 months in the Labor Department, McLaughlin encouraged private economic growth and increased private sector initiatives to improve the lives of American workers. She focused specifically on drug use in the workplace, day care services for workers with children, unemployment insurance, and job training programs. She served the remainder of the second term as labor secretary.

Meese, Edwin, III
(1931–) *counselor to the president, attorney general*

Edwin Meese was a longtime, loyal adviser to Ronald Reagan and was a critical member of Reagan's inner circle in Sacramento and in Washington. Reagan rewarded Meese by nominating him for attorney general, but his tenure at the Department of Justice was controversial, in part because he was determined to implement the president's conservative legal agenda.

After a childhood spent in the Oakland area, Meese entered Yale University on academic scholarship and received his B.A. in 1953. He then moved west to attend the University of California at Berkeley Law School, where he earned a J.D. After serving in the U.S. Army for two years, Meese became the deputy district attorney of Alameda County, California. He stayed in this position from 1958 to 1967, gaining notoriety for his tough stance against student protesters and the Black Panther Party. In 1964, Meese supervised the arrest of several hundred students of the Berkeley Free Speech Movement.

During his time as deputy district attorney, Meese became involved in the political career of Ronald Reagan, campaigning in his successful 1966 bid for the governor's office. In 1967, he joined Reagan's administration in Sacramento as the secretary for legal affairs and became one of Reagan's most trusted legal aides. After two years, Meese became an executive assistant to the governor, then one year later was appointed as Reagan's chief of staff. He worked closely with the governor on the rising social unrest in California over the conflict in Vietnam. He became so close to Reagan and so influential in the governor's office that he was even called the deputy governor by some.

After Reagan left the governor's office in 1975, Meese went briefly into the business world, joining Rohr Industries as vice presi-

President Reagan and Edwin Meese III on *Marine 1,* March 24, 1982

dent for administration. After a short tenure at this job, he accepted a position teaching law at the University of California, San Diego. He also became director for the Center of Criminal Justice Policy and Management at UC, San Diego.

Meese, however, remained close to Reagan during his hiatus from government service, and in 1980 he joined the Reagan campaign as an adviser. After only a short time, he replaced campaign manager John Sears and became chief of staff and senior issues adviser, and following the election victory Meese was appointed as director of the transition. He was certain to have a major post in the new administration, but several Reagan aides opposed making Meese chief of staff. Nonetheless, Reagan wanted him as a senior adviser and he was eventually appointed to the new cabinet-rank

position of counselor to the president. Along with JAMES BAKER and MICHAEL DEAVER, Meese was part of the troika of Reagan's closest advisers. As counselor to the president, he advised Reagan on nearly every policy area, from covert operations and personnel moves to tax cuts and judicial nominations, and became known as a loyal adherent to the Reagan agenda, earning him respect among the GOP's conservative wing.

In early 1984 Meese was selected to replace Attorney General WILLIAM FRENCH SMITH, but questions about Meese's financial dealings and ethical behavior caused his nomination to take more than a year before clearing the Senate on February 23, 1985. Once confirmed, Meese worked hard to advance two key pieces of Reagan's social agenda, the "war on drugs" and the battle against child pornography. Meese was also credited with recruiting a wide array of talented, young conservative lawyers who brought an intellectual vitality into the Justice Department.

Nonetheless, new questions about unde-clared capital gains, bribery, and insider deals arose throughout his term, tainting his reputa-tion and prompting some prominent officials, including Republicans, to call for his resigna-tion. Throughout all of Meese's legal troubles, Reagan remained loyal. The most publicized scandal Meese became involved in was the Iran-contra affair. At first he claimed he was never consulted about the arms sale and the transfer of funds to the Nicaraguan contras, but subsequent investigations asserted that at the very least Meese greatly mishandled the investigation and provided the president with questionable legal advice.

Although Meese was able to avoid legal culpability in every scandal he was implicated in during his time in Washington, the number of legal probes and the appearance of impro-priety raised the specter of a "sleaze factor" in the Reagan administration. Many Republicans wanted to remove Meese before the 1988 elec-tions, and in July 1988 Meese resigned his post at the Justice Department. His memoir, *With Reagan: The Inside Story*, showed a continuing, unyielding loyalty to Reagan and pride in what the administration was able to accomplish in eight years.

Mitterrand, François
(1916–1996) *president of France*

As the first Socialist president of the Fifth Republic, François Mitterrand embarked on a series of dramatic economic and social reforms in his first year before a recession forced him to take a more centrist approach for the remainder of his tenure. An unlikely ally of Ronald Rea-gan, he proved to be a strong supporter of the NATO alliance and a loyal friend to the United States in its struggle with the Soviet Union.

Mitterrand grew up in the small village of Jarnac in southwestern France, and at age 18 moved north to the capital to study political science and law at the University of Paris. Dur-ing his time at the university, he became involved in the rising pro-fascist movement, joining the League of National Volunteers and regularly attending far-right rallies. In 1938, he completed his degrees in law and political science, then began his required service in the French army. Mitterrand was wounded and taken prisoner in May 1940 in the Battle of Verdun, and was held as a prisoner of war for 18 months before escaping and returning to France. He took a job in Marshall Petain's Vichy government, but after two years on the job he joined the French resistance, earning a Rosette de la Resistance for his work.

At the end of World War II, Mitterrand joined the postwar government of Charles de Gaulle as the secretary-general of the Organi-zation of Prisoners of War, War Victims, and Refugees. In 1946, he was elected to the National Assembly, where he would remain for the next 12 years. During this time, he also served in a variety of ministerial positions, including the minister of war veterans, minis-ter for information, minister for overseas terri-tories, minister of state, minister for the Council of Europe, minister of the interior, and minister of justice. Even as a member of de Gaulle's government, Mitterrand remained independent from the Right, and in 1958, fol-lowing the establishment of the Fifth Republic, he joined the ranks of the opponents of de Gaulle's government. His political career nearly ended that year when, in an attempt to show his opposition to de Gaulle's policy toward Algeria, he staged an assassination attempt on his own life, which was discovered and ridiculed in the press. However, he quickly recovered from the incident and won both the mayorship of Chateau-Chinon and a seat in the French senate.

In 1965, Mitterrand joined with the Federation of the Democratic and Socialist Left (FDGS), an alliance of anticommunist leftist parties, to face de Gaulle in the presidential election. He lost the contest after a close battle with de Gaulle, taking 44.8 percent in the final round of voting. Over the next few years, Mitterrand continued to build his leftist alliance to take on de Gaulle in the next election, but in 1968, the Events of May, a massive student-worker revolt, nearly destroyed the French Left. In legislative elections called for the following month, the Left was routed and a disillusioned Mitterrand left his post as head of the FGDS. The next several years, as leader of the Convention of Republican Institutions, he worked to restore the viability of the French Left, primarily through an alliance with the Communist Party (PCF) in France. In 1971 he became the leader of the new Socialist Party (PS), made up from the remnants of the former socialist party, the SFIO. The following year, he helped to establish the Common Program, an alliance of the PS, the Communists, and the radical leftist party, MRG.

This relationship between the Socialists and Communists proved to be tenuous at best. In the 1973 legislative elections, the PCF gained more votes (21.4 percent to 18.9 percent) than the PS. Mitterrand made his second bid for the presidency the following year, taking 49.2 percent of the popular vote in the final round, but losing to Valéry Giscard d'Estaing. By 1976, the PS had become the preeminent leftist party in France, taking 30.8 percent of the vote in the 1976 cantonal elections to just 17.3 percent for the PCF, and leading to the collapse of the Common Program two years later.

In the 1981 presidential election, the PS and the PCF each ran their own candidates, Mitterrand for the Socialists and Georges Marchais for the Communists. After Marchais gar-

nered only a small percentage of the vote in the first round, the PCF threw their support behind Mitterrand, helping him gain 52 percent in his victory over Giscard d'Estaing to become the first leftist president of the Fifth Republic. One month later, the PS took a majority of seats in the National Assembly, giving the Left control over both the executive and the legislature for the first time since 1789.

Mitterrand quickly initiated a bold reform agenda that greatly increased the size of the public sector and moved France toward a more socialist government. His most significant change was in social policy where the government reduced the workweek to 39 hours, increased the minimum wage, lowered the retirement age to 60 years old, and extended the vacation period to five weeks, just to name a few. He also brought a number of changes to the economic sector, including nationalization of nine French industries, a series of wage and price reforms, and higher taxes for the rich. The reforms, though popular, proved to be too expensive for a French economy already in recession, leading to higher inflation and large budget deficits. In June 1982 conservatives in the legislature forced Mitterrand to accept an austerity program that included a devaluation of the franc, a wage and price freeze, and a cap on public expenditures. Another austerity program nine months later, along with rising unemployment, led to a dramatic decline in Mitterrand's popularity. This dissatisfaction came to a head on June 24, 1984, when more than 1 million demonstrators gathered at the Bastille to protest the Mitterrand government, forcing the president to take a more centrist approach to domestic policy for the remainder of his tenure.

Mitterrand's popularity was actually rising during this time in the NATO countries as his government proved to be a strong ally in the cold war. He supported President Reagan's effort to place Pershing II and Cruise missiles in West Germany in 1983, rejecting the pleas of the growing nuclear freeze movement in France. Although he continued the Gaullist tradition of French independence in the international community, he was a believer in the importance of the NATO alliance for the security of France and Western Europe. He also tried to cultivate a close relationship with the West German government under Helmut Schmidt and his successor, Helmut Kohl, which ultimately facilitated cooperation in the European Union.

In 1986 the PS lost its majority in the National Assembly to the new Gaullist party, the Rally for the Republic (RPR), forcing Mitterrand to select conservative Jacques Chirac as the new prime minister. With the French economy flourishing in the second half of the decade, Mitterrand turned his focus to European issues. He continued to encourage increased economic cooperation of the European nations and was a strong advocate of the Maastricht Treaty, the agreement which provided the foundation of the European Union.

Mitterrand was diagnosed with prostate cancer in 1992. He served the remainder of his second term in office, then retired from political life. He died on January 8, 1996.

Mondale, Walter F.
(1928–) *U.S. senator, presidential candidate*

Reagan's Democratic opponent in the 1984 presidential election was a protégé of former vice president Hubert Humphrey and a devoted believer in New Deal and Great Society liberalism. In the 1984 election, Mondale carried only his home state of Minnesota (by a scant 3,000 votes) and the District of Columbia, enduring one of the most lopsided defeats in the nation's history. Mondale left a more positive mark in the history books by choosing GERALDINE FERRARO as the first major-party female candidate for vice president.

The son of a Methodist minister, Mondale grew up in a deeply religious household. He excelled in both athletics and academics in his early years, becoming president of his high school class, before he moved on to Macalester College in 1946. His father, Theodore, died three years into his studies at Macalester, forcing Walter to leave school so that he could work and earn enough money to complete his degree. He returned to school the following year at the University of Minnesota, where he graduated cum laude in 1951.

It was during his days at Macalester College that Mondale first became interested in politics. Mondale became involved in the early political career of Hubert Humphrey, volunteering for his mayoral and senatorial campaigns. He also organized a Macalester College chapter of the anticommunist Students for Democratic Action. Because of his work with SDA, Mondale was offered a position as SDA executive director in Washington, D.C., where he remained until 1950.

Following his graduation from the University of Minnesota, Mondale spent two years serving in the U.S. Army in Fort Knox, Kentucky. In 1953, he entered law school at the University of Minnesota, where he graduated in the top quarter of his class in 1956. He also met Joan Adams during his time in law school, and the two were married on December 27, 1955. Mondale joined the law firm of Larson, Loevinger, Lindquist, Freeman, and Fraser upon graduation and remained at the firm until 1960.

However, politics was gradually becoming the centerpiece of Mondale's life, and he was heavily involved in campaigns for the Democratic–Farmer–Labor Party in Minnesota, working as Orville Freeman's campaign manager in his gubernatorial bid. Mondale's work on Freeman's campaigns earned him the reputation as a gifted party strategist. In 1958, he was given his first post as special assistant to the Minnesota attorney general, Miles Lord.

Two years later, Mondale was elected attorney general of Minnesota. He was reelected to the office by a very wide margin, and proved that he was quickly becoming a major force in Minnesota politics. Attorney General Mondale exhibited a strong commitment to progressive politics. He often fought on behalf of average people against big businesses or the government, and was particularly vigorous in enforcing civil rights. His most notable work was writing a brief in the seminal *Gideon v. Wainwright* Supreme Court case, which won the rights of criminal defendants to legal counsel.

In 1964 Minnesota's governor selected Mondale, at the age of 36, to complete the term of Hubert Humphrey after the latter left the Senate to become vice president. Mondale quickly became a leading proponent of Johnson's Great Society programs and a key Johnson ally in the U.S. Senate. He won his own senatorial election in 1966 with 54 percent of the vote. Mondale spent the next 10 years in the Senate, fighting for liberal causes and becoming a leading spokesman for the Democratic Party. But by 1968 he had become an outspoken critic of Johnson and the Vietnam War, and saw his party tear itself apart over the issue in 1968, when his friend Hubert Humphrey was nominated at the Democratic National Convention in the midst of riots in the streets.

Mondale refused to join George McGovern as the vice presidential candidate in the 1972 election, choosing instead to run for reelection, which he easily won with 57 percent of the vote. He considered running for president in 1976, and organized a brief exploratory effort, yet he soon abandoned the idea. The eventual winner, JIMMY CARTER, then selected Mondale as his running mate, which he readily accepted. During his years in the Carter White House, Mondale took on a more active role than past vice presidents, becoming a key adviser to the president and lobbying hard for Carter's agenda in Congress.

After losing their bid for reelection in 1980, Mondale returned to practicing law with the Washington, D.C., firm Winston and Strawn. His time in the private sector would be short-lived, however, as Mondale eyed the 1984 Democratic presidential nomination. After a tough battle with Senator Gary Hart (D-Colo.), Mondale won the nomination and ran with the first female vice presidential candidate in American history, New York Representative Ferraro. Mondale was defeated in a landslide by the popular incumbent Ronald Reagan, gaining only 13 electoral votes.

Following his defeat, Mondale alternated once again between private law practice and politics, speaking out frequently against the policies of the Reagan administration. In 1993 President Clinton appointed him U.S. ambassador to Japan, where he remained until 1997. Mondale's most recent attempt to return to national politics ended in defeat as he lost the 2002 Minnesota senatorial election to replace Paul Wellstone.

Mulroney, Brian
(1939–) *prime minister of Canada*

In 1988, Brian Mulroney became Canada's first Conservative Party leader to win consecutive elections in nearly 100 years. During his 10 years as prime minister, he established close ties with the Reagan and Bush administrations, signing two major free trade agreements and serving as a key ally in the cold war. This did not endear him to many Canadians who believed Mulroney sacrificed Canadian sovereignty and pride to the interests of the United States. Mulroney had an affection for Reagan that was returned by the president—

each enjoyed the other's capacity for story-telling and an ability to crack a joke, especially jokes dealing with their ancestral homeland of Ireland.

Mulroney became involved in politics at an early age, joining Canada's Conservative Party at age 16 while studying political science at St. Francis Xavier University. He became active in the campaign of prominent conservative Robert Stanfield, who later became party leader, in 1956. After earning his B.A., with honors, from St. Francis, Mulroney went to Dalhousie University for graduate studies. After just one year, he decided he was more interested in law and transferred to Laval University. He continued his active involvement in Canadian politics during this time, serving as a party organizer in Quebec and as an unofficial adviser to Conservative prime minister John Diefenbaker. He earned his law degree from Laval, then went to work in Montreal's biggest law firm.

Mulroney remained at this firm until 1976, eventually becoming a partner. He specialized in labor law while at the firm, and through his work he made contacts with many leading business and political figures, many of whom would help him later in his political career. He rose to prominence in 1974 when he served as cochairman of the Cliche Royal Commission on union violence and corruption in the construction industry. Mulroney then tried to turn his popularity into political fortune by running for the Conservative Party leadership, but his third-place finish led him back to the private sector, this time as vice president of the American-owned Iron Ore Company of Canada. This high-powered business position allowed Mulroney to remain a major figure in Conservative Party politics.

In 1983, Mulroney made another bid for the party leadership, defeating Joe Clark, and became the first party leader never to have previously run for public office. Because he was required to hold a seat in Parliament, he won an open seat in an off-year election in traditionally conservative Nova Scotia in 1983, then captured a seat in his home district in the 1984 general election. Mulroney quickly came out against Prime Minister Pierre Elliott Trudeau, whose 16 years in the prime minister's office were beginning to wear on the Canadian public. Trudeau retired from office in 1984 and his successor, John Turner, called for a general election after just nine days in office. Mulroney then led his party to the biggest victory in the history of Canadian politics, taking 211 out of 282 seats in the House of Commons and ending the rule of the Liberal Party who had governed for 42 of the previous 50 years. He was sworn in as prime minister on September 4, 1984.

Yet even after receiving a mandate from the Canadian public, Mulroney had a difficult first year in office. Scandals forced six of his ministers to resign from office, all of which reflected badly on Mulroney's judgment. Then, in a move to reduce the rising federal deficit, he proposed a partial deindexing of Canada's social security benefits and family allowances, resulting in a severe backlash that forced Mulroney to retreat. These early mistakes led the public to question the ability of the new prime minister; after just his first year in office 60 percent of Canadians felt he could not be trusted, and by 1985, the same percentage said they wanted a new prime minister.

Mulroney's political situation began to stabilize in 1985 as the Canadian economy, beset by high unemployment and slow economic growth, took part in the worldwide economic boom. Although the budget deficit remained high, both inflation and unemployment dropped dramatically and the economy grew at an impressive rate. In May 1987 Mulroney brokered the Meech Lake Accord, where Quebec, after being fully recognized by the other Canadian provinces as a francophone society, became a partner in the 1982 Canadian constitution.

In foreign affairs, Mulroney was unequivocally pro-American. Shortly after he took office in September 1984, he was in Washington, D.C., pledging to change his predecessor's policies on issues of energy and investment. Although many of his political opponents charged the prime minister with being Reagan's lackey, the majority of Canadians approved of closer ties with the United States. Mulroney became one of Reagan's strongest allies in the cold war, agreeing to cooperate on missile defense systems, strengthening air defenses, and increasing Canada's military force. The most important bilateral agreement of Mulroney's tenure came on January 2, 1988, when the United States and Canada signed the Free Trade Agreement. There were issues of disagreement between the two nations, most notably regarding America's response to the problems of acid rain, but on the whole, the Mulroney era marked one of the closest periods in U.S.–Canadian history.

In November 1988, after years of low personal and political approval ratings, Mulroney won reelection as prime minister. Once again, his popularity dropped sharply following the election as the Meech Lake Accord collapsed, a new tax on goods and services was introduced, and the government became more closely aligned with the United States than most Canadian citizens desired. In December 1992 Mulroney, along with America's president Bush and Mexico's president Salinas, signed the North American Free Trade Agreement (NAFTA). Estimates showed that Canada lost well over 100,000 jobs as a result of the agreement, and with unemployment again at high levels, Mulroney's approval rating was less than 20 percent. Facing insurmountable opposition, on February 24, 1993, Mulroney resigned as prime minister and was replaced by Canada's first female leader, Kim Campbell.

Following his departure from Ottawa, Mulroney became chairman of the Sun Media Corporation in Montreal. Shortly after, writer Stevie Cameron released a book titled *On The Take*, levying numerous serious charges against the prime minister, including misappropriation of budgets, political favors for corporate supporters, and manipulating government contracts. A more serious charge came when Canadian police and Swiss authorities accused Mulroney of accepting $5 million in kickbacks and taking part in a tax fraud conspiracy during the government's 1988 purchase of 34 Airbus jets. In response, he filed a $50 million libel suit against his accusers, eventually winning an out-of-court settlement and a formal apology from the government.

N

Noonan, Peggy
(1950–) *speechwriter*

As a speechwriter for Ronald Reagan and GEORGE H. W. BUSH, Peggy Noonan wrote some of the most memorable and emotional phrases in presidential speechmaking. She crafted Reagan's *Challenger*-disaster speech and Bush's 1988 GOP convention address where he infamously pledged, "no new taxes." Noonan had an uncompromising, passionate writing style that made her a favorite of conservative true believers.

Noonan cared little for school as a teenager in Long Island, New York. Following graduation from high school, she skirted the idea of college and instead worked as a clerk at Aetna Insurance Company in Newark, New Jersey. In 1970, she began taking classes at Fairleigh Dickinson University part time, and after two years, she was accepted as a full-time student. Noonan shed her Democratic roots and became a Republican during this time, after becoming disillusioned by the anti-war protests and extreme liberalism on college campuses, and being introduced to the conservative magazine, *National Review.* She became the first from her family to earn a college degree when she received her B.A. in 1974. She then moved to Boston and took a job as a news and editorial writer for WEEI radio. Three years later, she became broadcast writer and producer of CBS News Radio in New York City, writing commentary for Dan Rather. She stayed at CBS for the next eight years.

In 1984, Noonan caught the eye of the head of Reagan's speechwriting department, Ben Elliott, and she went on to spend the next two years in the administration. She wrote some of the most famous speeches of the Reagan years, including the address on the 40th anniversary of the D day invasion, the speech to the nation on the *Challenger* space shuttle disaster, and the remarks following the U.S.-Soviet summit in Geneva, Switzerland. Noonan wrote with a deep and palpable emotion, and constructed phrases that matched Reagan's deepest convictions, often to the chagrin of pragmatists within the administration. She also became one of the first presidential speechwriters to publicly take credit for her work, a practice rare for speechwriters who usually revel in their anonymity. In 1986 Noonan, frustrated by her lack of direct contact with Reagan and by the number of changes made to her speeches by administration moderates, left the White House and began working as a freelance writer.

Noonan returned to politics in 1988, helping Reagan with his farewell address and

Bush with his Republican National Convention speech and his inaugural address. She is credited with constructing some of Bush's most famous phrases as well, including "a thousand points of light," and a "kinder, gentler America." She left the Bush administration after his inauguration and returned once again to writing. She moved to New York City and wrote *Life, Liberty, and the Pursuit of Happiness,* a work describing life as a single mother in national politics. She has written two successful books on her years in the Reagan administration, *What I Saw at the Revolution: A Political Life in the Reagan Era and When Character Was King. Revolution* was so well-received that it spent six months on the *New York Times* best-seller list. Noonan also released *The Case against Hillary Clinton,* a scathing critique of the first lady and her years in the East Wing of the White House.

North, Oliver
(1943–) *National Security Council member*

Probably the most famous lieutenant colonel in the history of the U.S. Marine Corps, Oliver North achieved his notoriety in his role as the coordinator of both the arms sales to Iran and the diversion of funds to the Nicaraguan contras. After spending his early years in San Antonio, Texas, North moved to New York, where he remained after high school to attend the State University of New York at Brockport. In 1962, North left Brockport to attend the U.S. Naval Academy in Annapolis, Maryland, where

President Reagan meeting with his staff concerning Nicaragua, April 4, 1985. Lt. Col. Oliver North is seen standing on the far left of the picture.

he became middleweight boxing champion. A serious car accident in February 1964 slowed his progress at the academy, but he recovered and was able to graduate in 1968. North immediately joined the marine corps as a second lieutenant, fully aware that he would soon enter the war in Vietnam.

North spent a brief period in basic officers' school in Quantico, Virginia, before receiving his orders to join the war. Following his honeymoon, he embarked on an 11-month tour of duty in Vietnam where he served as platoon patrol commander. After receiving a Silver Star, a Bronze Star with a V for valor, two Purple Hearts, and a host of other prestigious commendations, he returned to Quantico to teach a tactics course at basic officers' school. He remained at Quantico until 1973 when he was moved to Okinawa, Japan, to supervise jungle training exercises. North left this assignment mentally exhausted, so much that he checked himself into Bethesda Naval Hospital after his return. Although he was cleared for active duty after his release, he opted to take a staff position at marine corps headquarters in Washington, D.C. He stayed in this position for four years before deciding in 1980 to enter the Naval War College in Newport, Rhode Island.

North's work at the war college earned him a position in the National Security Council's Defense Policy Staff (DPS) in August 1981. Although he preferred to stay with the marines and away from politics, North was drawn to the anticommunist rhetoric of President Reagan and willingly accepted the chance to serve in his administration. During his five and a half years on the DPS, he became known for his action-oriented style and unmatched work ethic, usually working 16-hour days. He was involved in planning a variety of covert operations, most notably against Lebanese and Libyan terrorists. He was best known, however, for his involvement in what became the most damaging scandal of the Reagan years, the Iran-contra affair.

In 1983 and 1985, after Congress voted in the Boland Amendments to end funding for covert aid to the Nicaraguan contras, North pursued various alternatives to ensure that the contras remained funded. North coordinated a clandestine sale of arms to Iran in exchange for the release of American hostages, funneling the profits from the arms sales to the contras. When the scandal came to light in November 1986, North was immediately accused of playing a central role in the operation and was fired by Reagan. In a series of nationally televised hearings before Congress, North, dressed in full uniform, spoke of his unfailing loyalty to the president and the cause of democracy in Central America: "I am proud of what we accomplished. I am proud of the efforts that we made, and I am proud of the fight that we fought. I am proud of serving in the administration of a great president." His performance led to an outpouring of support from many Americans, so much so that *Time* magazine declared that "Olliemania" had swept the nation. Many Reagan loyalists, including NANCY REAGAN, believed that North embellished his account with stories of meetings with President Reagan that they claim never occurred.

Late in 1986, North took a staff position at Marine Corps Headquarters in Washington and began lecturing across the country. He was indicted by a federal grand jury and found guilty of three felonies, but this conviction was later overturned when a federal appeals court ruled that his immunized testimony could not be used against him. He made a bid for a Senate seat in Virginia in 1994, but lost to Democratic incumbent Charles Robb. He has also written three bestselling books, *Under Fire, One More Mission,* and *Mission Compromised.* North currently writes a syndicated column, hosts the weekly show *War Stories* on the Fox News Channel, and hosts his own daily radio talk show, *Common Sense Radio.*

O'Connor, Sandra Day
(1930–) *associate justice, U.S. Supreme Court*

The first woman appointed to the U.S. Supreme Court, Sandra Day O'Connor emerged as a crucial "swing" vote on the Court, disappointing many conservatives, including members of the administration that nominated her, for her moderate stance on a wide variety of cases.

A native of the American Southwest, O'Connor completed high school at the age of 16, then entered Stanford University to study economics. She received her B.A. in 1950 and stayed at Stanford to complete a law degree. She compiled an impressive record in law school, graduating third in her class in 1952. The valedictorian of her class was William H. Rehnquist, who would later become a colleague of O'Connor's as chief justice of the U.S. Supreme Court.

O'Connor was appointed deputy county attorney of San Mateo County (California) from 1952 to 1953. The following year, she took a position as a civilian lawyer for the Army's Quartermaster Market Center in Frankfurt, West Germany. She stayed in West Germany until 1957 when she and her family moved to Maryvale, Arizona, and she began to practice law. From 1965 to 1969,

O'Connor was an assistant attorney general in Arizona.

In 1969, O'Connor moved from the judicial to the legislative branch, winning a seat in the Arizona state Senate and serving three two-year terms in Phoenix. She also became the first woman in history to hold the position of majority leader. After her service in the state legislature, O'Connor was elected as judge of the Maricopa County Superior Court, where she remained for the next four years. In 1979, she received an appointment to the bench of the Arizona Court of Appeals.

After the resignation of Potter Stewart from the Supreme Court in July 1981, O'Connor's name was widely circulated around Washington as a possible replacement. Reagan had hinted several times about his desire to appoint a woman to the highest court and O'Connor was acceptable to most Republicans. Reagan nominated her as an associate justice and on September 25, 1981, O'Connor became the first woman to sit on the Supreme Court. The selection was received well by most Americans, although some on the far Right were disappointed Reagan had not chosen a more conservative justice. Her nomination was endorsed by members of both parties, including conservative senator Barry Goldwater and liberal senator Edward Kennedy. O'Connor has been a moderate justice on the

President Reagan and his Supreme Court Justice nominee Sandra Day O'Connor at the White House, July 15, 1981

Supreme Court, holding conservative positions on several issues, particularly federalism cases, but consistently voting to uphold abortion rights for women as well as affirmative action programs for minorities.

O'Neill, Thomas P.
(Tip)
(1912–1994) *Speaker, U.S. House of Representatives*

The Speaker of the House was a fierce opponent of "Reaganomics" and of Reagan's policies in Central America during the president's first six years in the White House. Nonetheless, the two partisan rivals became friends "after six o'clock," as President Reagan liked to put it. Both men shared a love of Ireland and off-color jokes, and they developed an unlikely mutual respect for one another.

Thomas (Tip) O'Neill dedicated more than 50 years of his life to public service in Massachusetts and Washington, D.C. His first involvement in politics came during his senior year at Boston College when he lost an election for Cambridge City Council—this would be the only defeat of O'Neill's political career. He received his degree from Boston College in 1936, then went immediately back into politics, winning a seat in the Massachusetts state House of Representatives the same year. During his early service in the Massachusetts House, O'Neill worked a second job in the Cambridge city treasurer's office, learning more about government and cultivating important political allies in the process. He moved quickly up the ladder in the Massachusetts Democratic Party, becoming minority leader in 1947 and then in 1948 becoming the youngest Speaker of the Massachusetts legislature since the Civil War.

After 16 years of service at the state level, O'Neill moved to national politics, winning an election in 1952 for the seat previously held by John F. Kennedy, who had been elected to the U.S. Senate. O'Neill became friendly with key members of the House, including Majority Leader John McCormack and Speaker Sam Rayburn, and was quickly seen as a loyal party man. He was a staunch supporter of the New Frontier and Great Society domestic programs, but his loyalty to President Johnson ended in 1967 over the war in Vietnam. O'Neill was the first "establishment" Democrat to challenge Johnson's Vietnam policy.

In 1971, O'Neill, by then a major player in the Democratic Party, was elected majority whip in the House. He became majority leader less than two years later. After four years as majority leader, O'Neill was elected the Speaker of the House, where he remained until his retirement in 1987—the longest consecutive tenure in the history of the office. O'Neill's reputation as a shrewd and competent politician was particularly evident during his years of leadership in the House. Although he disagreed with President Carter on several policy areas, he was a loyal adherent to the president and was an integral part of getting much of his legislation through Congress. A quintessential party man, O'Neill even stayed neutral in the 1980 nomination battle between Carter and fellow Massachusetts politician Edward Kennedy.

With the 1980 election victory of Ronald Reagan and the Republican takeover of the Senate, O'Neill became the ranking Democrat in Congress. He became the heart and soul of the Democratic opposition to Reagan's agenda. Because of Reagan's popularity, O'Neill lost some early legislative battles, particularly on tax cuts and the budget. He was infuriated by the defection of many southern Democrats, the so-called boll weevils, but was helpless to stem the tide. But after Reagan's "honeymoon" with

Congress ended in 1982, O'Neill reasserted his influence over the House of Representatives during the next four years. He accused the administration of callousness toward the poor, and was particularly effective at convincing many Americans that Reagan was intent on cutting Social Security benefits. O'Neill was a passionate opponent of the administration's policies in Central America, and claimed that Reagan was engaging in a jingoistic pursuit of American hegemony. It was reported that one of O'Neill's sisters was a Catholic nun, and that she had influenced her brother's position on this issue with reports from members of her order regarding atrocities committed by the contras and right-wing paramilitary forces in

President Reagan and House Speaker Tip O'Neill discussing the budget in the Oval Office, January 31, 1983

El Salvador. O'Neill's closest friend in the House of Representatives, Congressman EDWARD BOLAND of Massachusetts, was a thorn in the administration's side over its covert support of the contras in Nicaragua. It was JOHN POINDEXTER and OLIVER NORTH's decision to violate the Boland Amendments that led to the gravest crisis of Reagan's presidency, the Iran-contra scandal.

O'Neill retired from politics in early 1987 after more than 30 years in the U.S. House and 50 years in public service. He died in January 1994 in Boston.

Ortega, Daniel
(1945–) *president of Nicaragua*

In the eyes of Ronald Reagan Daniel Ortega was a villain, a Marxist who betrayed a popular movement and installed a Soviet-style dictatorship in Nicaragua. Reagan directed some of his harshest rhetoric toward the Nicaraguan regime and considered Ortega's opponents, the contras, to be the "moral equivalent of the Founding Fathers." Some members of the Reagan administration put his presidency at risk with their effort to remove Ortega's government. While it is the subject of deep historical controversy, Reagan's defenders argue that the pressure applied throughout the 1980s on Ortega's Sandinistas by the contra forces ultimately led to the calling of genuine elections and the downfall of that regime.

Daniel Ortega was born in a mining and ranching town named La Libertad in Chontales, Nicaragua, but after his father lost his job as an accountant for a local mining company the Ortegas moved to Juigalpa, near the capital of Managua. He attended both private and Catholic schools and was so devoted to his faith at one point that many felt he would study for the priesthood. After his parents could no

longer pay the tuition for his schooling, Ortega was forced to leave school and received much of his education at home. During his teenage years, his parents tried to keep him away from the revolutionary student movements, but because of his family's poverty and his hatred of the Somoza regime, these movements had a great appeal to Ortega. He was also a great admirer of Augusto César Sandino—whose followers later became known as the Sandinistas—after hearing stories of his guerrilla campaign against the U.S. Marines in the 1920s.

Ortega joined and participated in several demonstrations with the country's youth movement, the Nicaraguan Patriotic Youth (JPN), against the Somoza regime. He was detained and tortured during one such protest in 1960. That same year, Ortega formed his own youth movement, the Nicaraguan Revolutionary Youth (JRN), with members of Nicaragua's communist revolutionary organization, the Sandinista National Liberation Front (FSLN). He went back into formal schooling in 1961 to study law at Central American University, but left after just one year to return to the revolution.

In 1963, Ortega joined the FSLN and committed his life to armed resistance against the Somoza government. He held other Latin American revolutionaries such as Che Guevara and Fidel Castro in the highest esteem and used their tactics as a template for the Sandinistas. He took part in the creation of the FSLN's youth wing, the Federation of Secondary Students (FES). He was captured and tortured several times over the next two years by the Somoza government. In 1965, Ortega, undeterred by the government's brutality, continued with the revolution and cofounded the official newspaper of the Revolutionary Student Front, *El Estudiante*. That same year, he was selected to join the FSLN's top policy council, the National Directorate, solidifying his place in the highest levels of the Nicaraguan revolutionary movement.

He took over control of the urban insurgency movement, the Internal Front, in 1966, leading the FSLN in a new phase of resistance. He organized a new wave of violence in Managua that included several armed robberies and the FSLN's first political assassination, the killing of Gonzalo Lacayo of the National Guard in 1967. Ortega and several of his comrades were arrested for the murder and sent to prison for lengthy terms. Ortega served seven years in harsh conditions, suffering torture, beatings, and near starvation. After the FSLN kidnapped several of Somoza's top officials in December 1974, Ortega and many other Sandinista prisoners were set free in exchange for the hostages and sent to live in exile in Cuba.

Ortega's revolutionary fervor increased in exile, for he was inspired by the success of the Castro regime in resisting the United States. In 1975, he quietly came back to Nicaragua and assumed his post in the National Directorate. He returned, however, to great changes in Nicaragua and in the FSLN. President Anastasio Somoza Debayle had declared martial law in 1974 and was cracking down on opponents of the government. Also, the FSLN was experiencing internal strife and breaking off into many different factions based on differences in ideology.

Regardless of these differences, Ortega continued on, joining his brother Humberto to guide the Tercerista (Third Force) faction of the FSLN. The Sandinistas gained a major victory in 1978 when the assassination of *La Prensa* journalist Pedro Joaquin Chamorro exhibited the brutality of the Somoza government and united much of the public against the regime. The revolution spread quickly across Nicaragua and by the middle of 1979 the Somoza government was on the brink of collapse. The FSLN reunited and launched a major offensive in June 1979, leading to the collapse of the Somoza government on July 19, 1979.

In 1981 Ortega emerged as the key leader of the ruling junta, and became the recognized face of the new Nicaraguan government. He immediately consolidated his ties with other communist and revolutionary governments such as Cuba and the Soviet Union, making him a prime target for the staunch anticommunist American president, Ronald Reagan. His administration worked assiduously for years to provide aid to opponents of the Sandinista government, the contras, but this cause never garnered large support from either Congress or the public. After a series of congressional restrictions to contra aid, the administration illegally funded the contras through what became known as the Iran-contra affair, a scandal that effectively ended America's attempt to topple the Sandinista government.

Ortega was selected by the National Directorate as the FSLN nominee for the November 1984, presidential election and he easily won with 67 percent of the popular vote. His government faced many severe challenges, particularly from the U.S. economic embargo, which began in May 1985; this action, coupled with aid to the contras, put severe strains on the Nicaraguan economy. In March 1988 the FSLN agreed to a cease-fire with the contras. Ortega also agreed to open elections in February 1990, when the FSLN suffered a major defeat against the center-right Union of National Opposition. Ortega lost the presidency to Violeta Barrios de Chamorro, the widow of journalist Pedro Chamorro, and left office in April 1990. He continued as a major player in national politics, winning reelection as the leader of the Sandinistas in May 1994. He reemerged in the October 1996 elections, but lost to Arnoldo Aleman by 51 to 38 percent. Ortega made his last run for the presidency in 2001, losing this time to Enrique Bolanos, 56 to 42 percent.

P

Perle, Richard
(1941–   ) *assistant secretary of defense*

Richard Perle was one of the leading nuclear strategists in the neoconservative movement, opposing every major arms control agreement between the United States and the Soviet Union and claiming such agreements were dangerous to America's national security. Working for Senator Henry "Scoop" Jackson (D-Wash.) and President Ronald Reagan, Perle played a major role in shaping the arms control debate throughout the 1970s and 1980s.

When Perle was a student at Hollywood High School, he became friends with the daughter of a well-known logician and strategist from the RAND Corporation named Albert J. Wohlstetter, who went on to become Perle's mentor in a number of subjects. He entered the University of Southern California and earned a B.A. in philosophy. During his undergraduate years, he also studied nuclear strategy and arms control for one year abroad at the London School of Economics. He attended Princeton University for graduate work after USC, but left before finishing his doctoral dissertation.

In 1969, Perle moved across country to Washington, D.C., where Albert Wohlstetter got him a job with the Committee to Maintain

a Prudent Defense Policy. The committee was established by Paul Nitze and Dean Acheson to gain support for President Nixon's antiballistic missile (ABM) program, which passed narrowly through the Senate in the summer of 1969. Perle's work on the committee was noticed by Senator Jackson, who soon asked him to join his staff. He quickly became the leading voice in Jackson's office on defense and foreign policy issues. His influence was seen clearly in Jackson's position on the SALT I Treaty, which Perle argued allowed the Soviets to hold a monopoly in "heavy" intercontinental ballistic missiles (ICBMs). Jackson's amendment to the treaty, requiring that future arms control agreements be based on numerical equality of weapons, was written by Perle. He was also a strong proponent of linking trade with the Soviet Union to the emigration of Soviet Jews, an idea later proposed as the Jackson-Vanik amendment. This proposal became a major source of contention between Washington and Moscow and almost led to the downfall of détente on several occasions, something which Perle, an ardent anticommunist, was eager to achieve.

Perle joined the Reagan administration in 1981 as assistant secretary of defense for international security policy. He continued to work against arms control agreements during this time, arguing, with great success during Reagan's first term, that such agreements were not in the best interests of American national security. He succeeded in persuading Reagan to adopt the "zero option" in 1981 over the advice of powerful figures in the administration, including Secretary of State Alexander Haig. This proposal required the Soviet Union to remove its intermediate-range nuclear missiles in Europe and Asia in exchange for the United States agreeing not to deploy its own nuclear missiles in Europe. Perle knew the zero option would be unacceptable to the Soviets and would prohibit an arms control agreement between the two powers. In 1983, he persuaded Reagan not to accept the "walk in the woods" proposal, a proposal constructed by chief U.S. negotiator Paul Nitze that would have limited the number of intermediate-range weapons in Europe to 75 each for the United States and Soviet Union. Perle even attempted to dismantle the SALT I Treaty through support of Reagan's Strategic Defense Initiative, which was apparently in violation of the ABM Treaty.

Perle resigned from the Pentagon in March 1987, just nine months before Reagan and MIKHAIL GORBACHEV would sign the most sweeping arms control agreement in history, the Intermediate Nuclear Forces Treaty. He then joined the conservative American Enterprise Institute in Washington, where he still serves as a Senior Fellow. Perle has also written numerous books and articles on defense policy.

Pierce, Samuel R., Jr.
(1922–) *secretary of housing and urban development*

The longest-serving cabinet member of the Reagan administration and its only African-American member, Samuel Pierce's tenure at the Department of Housing and Urban Development was marred by a late-breaking scandal. His reserved demeanor at cabinet meetings and

elsewhere led some to dub him Silent Sam, an unfair label that belied the fact that he was a man of great accomplishment in both the public and the private sector. He was so reserved, in fact, that President Reagan once greeted him at a White House reception as "Mr. Mayor," although that faux pas is perhaps more attributable to Reagan's difficulty in remembering names than to Pierce's detachment.

Samuel Pierce grew up in a Republican home, and his father, a small-business owner in Long Island, emphasized to his three sons the virtues of success and self-determination. He was a standout both athletically and academically in high school and following graduation he earned an academic scholarship to Cornell University. He left the university before graduating to join the U.S. Army in World War II, breaking ground for many black Americans in the armed forces. He was the only black agent in the army's Criminal Investigation Division in the Mediterranean, and he was one of only a few black soldiers to enter officer's training. After serving in North Africa and Italy, Pierce left the army in 1946 with the rank of first lieutenant. He returned immediately to Cornell University and graduated with honors in 1947. Pierce stayed at Cornell and continued on to the law school following graduation, earning his J.D. in two years and serving as president of the Cornell Law School Association.

After he received his law degree, Pierce went to work as an assistant for Manhattan district attorney Frank Hogan. During this time, he was also taking courses at New York University's School of Law, earning an LL.M. in taxation in 1952. In 1953, he left Hogan's office and took a post as an assistant U.S. attorney for the Southern District of New York. He entered the political arena in 1955 when he became the first black assistant to the under secretary of labor in the Eisenhower administration. Pierce left the Labor Department the following year to take the post of associate counsel to the

President Reagan meets with HUD secretary Samuel R. Pierce, Jr. in the Oval Office, December 14, 1981.

Antitrust Subcommittee in the House Judiciary Committee, and was promoted to counsel after just one year. In 1957, he took a job as adjunct professor at New York University's law school where he remained until 1970.

During his time at NYU, Pierce quickly gained notoriety not only in academia but also in law, business, and politics. He raised the bar of success for black Americans in each of these fields, becoming the first black board member of a Fortune 500 company, and the first black partner in a major Manhattan law firm, and helping to found the first black-owned bank in New York, Freedom National Bank. He fought for civil rights by joining the legal team that defended major black leaders, including Martin Luther King, Jr. He was also an active partici-

pant in Republican Party politics, working on the side of prominent New York Republicans Nelson Rockefeller and Kenneth Keating.

After playing an instrumental role in the 1968 presidential campaign with the Committee of Black Americans for Nixon-Agnew, Pierce, after turning down the post of Civil Service Commission chairman, returned to government service as general counsel to the Treasury Department. He played a key role in several of the department's major policies, such as the wage-price freeze, and was rewarded in 1973 with the Alexander Hamilton award, the highest honor bestowed by the Treasury Department. He left the Nixon administration in 1973 and returned to his law practice at Battle, Fowler, Stokes, and Kheel in New York City.

Pierce continued to serve in a number of high-level commissions and boards during his hiatus from government, and in 1980 President-elect Ronald Reagan tapped him for the job of secretary of Housing and Urban Development. He declined the post at first, hoping for the position of attorney general or labor secretary, but joined after a personal plea from Reagan. Pierce's primary goal at HUD was to bring efficiency to what he believed was a wasteful department. He supported cuts in HUD staff and budget, bringing a savings of billions to the federal government, while at the same time initiating several new programs to increase home ownership among the poor and reduce the rising costs of federal housing. His last few years in office were clouded by accusations of fraud and bribery in his department, and Pierce, although never formally charged, left office in 1989 with his integrity in doubt. Nonetheless, Pierce remained a respected public servant and received a host of awards upon his resignation, including the Martin Luther King, Jr., Salute to Greatness award and the Presidential Citizens Medal. Following his days at HUD, he took a position as a consultant with the Turner Corporation.

Poindexter, John M.
(1936–) *National Security Advisor*

John Poindexter approved and supervised the Iran-contra operation that almost toppled the Reagan presidency. An odd choice for the position of National Security Advisor, Poindexter was a far cry from the strategic thinkers who had previously occupied the NSC post, such as Henry Kissinger, Zbigniew Brzezinski, and McGeorge Bundy. All of Reagan's NSC advisors seemed to rapidly burn out, and this frequent turnover contributed to a considerable amount of instability and incoherence in Reagan's foreign

policy making. Perhaps the most significant moment of Poindexter's time with Reagan was his testimony under oath that he kept the details of the Iran-contra affair from the president to protect the presidency. This spared Ronald Reagan from the prospect of impeachment.

As with ROBERT MCFARLANE, COLIN POWELL, and many Reagan-era NSC staffers, John Poindexter was a career military officer. He graduated first in his class at the U.S. Naval Academy in 1958 and continued his education at the California Institute of Technology, receiving his doctorate in nuclear physics in 1964. Poindexter was appointed as military assistant to Reagan's first National Security Advisor, RICHARD ALLEN, in 1981. After working under both Allen and his successor, WILLIAM CLARK, Poindexter was promoted to deputy National Security Advisor to Bud McFarlane. He served in this role until December 4, 1985, when he was appointed as Reagan's fourth National Security Advisor.

When Poindexter became head of the NSC, he inherited an ongoing secret operation that later became known as the Iran-contra affair. He continued to approve the sale of weapons to Iran and the transfer of monies to

President Reagan talks with National Security Advisor John M. Poindexter (right), April 14, 1986.

the Nicaraguan contras, and when the details began to emerge in November 1986, Poindexter became one of the prime targets of investigation. At a critical moment in the Iran-contra hearings before a joint congressional investigative committee in the summer of 1987, Poindexter testified that he had not informed President Reagan about the diversion of funds to the Nicaraguan contras. He claimed he had done this to protect the president; this testimony probably spared Ronald Reagan from impeachment. In 1988, he was indicted by a grand jury for obstruction of justice, diversion of public funds, stealing public funds for private ends, and lying to Congress and other government officials. However, with many key documents either unreleased or destroyed by the administration, special prosecutor LAWRENCE WALSH could charge Poindexter only with providing false information and lying to Congress. During his trial, it was proven that Poindexter lied to Congress and destroyed thousands of documents relating to the operation, leading a jury to convict him on both charges. Poindexter's conviction was overturned in 1991 on a technicality after it was found that his testimony before Congress was unfairly used in his conviction. During the administration of George W. Bush, Poindexter served in the Defense Advanced Research Projects Agency and on the Total Information Awareness Project, generating ideas for the war on terrorism, many of which produced controversy, including a proposal for a "futures market" that would help predict the likelihood of terrorist attacks.

Pope John Paul II
(Karol Wojtyla)
(1920–) *religious leader, statesman*

On October 6, 1978, Karol Wojtyla became the first Polish pope in the history of the papacy and the first non-Italian pope in 455 years. With more than 25 years of service at the Vatican, Pope John Paul II became one of the most important spiritual, political, and social forces of the 20th century. The early years of his papacy coincided with the Reagan presidency, and the two men's passionate anticommunism rhetoric provided encouragement to dissidents in the Eastern bloc, particularly among Poland's Solidarity movement.

Karol Josef Wojtyla was born in Wadowice, Poland, in 1920. He grew up with tremendous personal suffering; his sister died before he was born, his mother when he was just nine years old, his brother four years later, and his father, who fought for Poland in World War II, died in 1942, when Wojtyla was 22. Wojtyla focused early on studying the arts, entering Krakow's Jagiellonian University in 1938 to study literature, poetry, and drama. When Germany invaded Poland the following year, the university was closed down, and Wojtyla was forced to study underground. He became interested in the priesthood at this time and secretly entered the seminary while working for the Nazi army as a manual laborer. The combination of personal tragedy, religious study, and political oppression helped to form Wojtyla's perspective on the importance of God in society, which later had a great effect on his views toward communism.

Wojtyla became an ordained priest in November 1946, then went on to earn a doctorate in divinity from Pontifical University of the Angelicum in Rome in 1948. He moved back to Poland after graduation to serve as a parish priest in the Roman Catholic Church and also to work as a professor of ethics at the Catholic University of Lublin, the only independent school in the Eastern bloc. Wojtyla was an accomplished scholar during his time at the university, publishing several articles and books, and becoming intimately involved in the struggle for religious freedom in communist Poland, a struggle which would occupy him

President Reagan meeting with Pope John Paul II in Miami, Florida, September 10, 1987

over the next four decades. In 1958, he was named auxiliary bishop of Krakow under Archbishop Eugeniusz Baziak, and when Baziak died in 1962, Wojtyla became vicar capitular of the See and head of the archdiocese of Krakow. Two years later, he was officially consecrated Archbishop of Krakow, and in 1967, Pope Paul VI made Wojtyla a cardinal.

Pope Paul VI died in August 1978, and his successor, Pope John Paul I, died after just one month in the papacy. In October 1978, the College of Cardinals named Cardinal Wojtyla the 263rd successor to St. Peter, and Wojtyla took the name John Paul II. In an expression of humility, he chose a simple mass in St. Peter's Square over a coronation ceremony. In stark contrast to his successors, John Paul II was an active, energetic pope, traveling to Latin America, North America, Africa, Europe, and the Far East in his first few years. He became a strong advocate of human rights and an outspoken supporter of traditional Catholic social values, opposing birth control, divorce, premarital sex, and abortion. In June 1979, John Paul II made perhaps his most important trip, visiting his home country of Poland, where his masses and rallies attracted millions and fostered the growth of opposition movements against the Polish communist government that had stifled religious freedom. Many have credited his visit for the rise of the Solidarity movement, which became the most powerful movement for change in Eastern Europe in the 1980s.

In May 1981, John Paul II was shot in an assassination attempt by Turkish national Mehmet Ali Agca. Agca's connection to a group of Bulgarian nationals led to allegations that the Soviet KGB was involved in the attempt in response to the pope's support of Solidarity. Soon after the attempt, President Reagan, himself recovering from a March 1981 assassination attempt, met with the pope and discussed ways to disrupt the communist system in Poland. Reagan and John Paul II shared a sense of religious obligation in bringing freedom to the communist bloc. The Vatican later cooperated with the White House, the AFL-CIO, and the National Endowment for Democracy in supporting Solidarity. In 1983, John Paul II visited Poland again and renewed the country's desire for religious and political freedom. When the Polish communist government fell from power in the fall of 1989, John Paul II played a key role in mediating between the government and the leaders of Solidarity.

In addition to his spiritual role as the leader of the Catholic Church, John Paul II serves as the formal head of Vatican City. His foreign policy has been marked by the push for greater international cooperation to solve the problems of human rights violations and hunger in developing nations. Relations between the Vatican and the former Soviet Union and Eastern Europe have improved dramatically since the collapse of communism in the early 1990s. Pope John Paul II also became the first pope in more than 100 years to speak to the Italian parliament in an attempt to reconcile a longstanding breach between the state and the Catholic Church in Italy. Most recently, he has called for an independent Palestinian state and opposed the U.S.-led war against Iraq.

Pope John Paul II has written extensively on the Catholic faith. In addition to several religious treatises, poems, and plays, he has written numerous books including *Crossing the Threshold of Hope* and *Every Child a Light*. He also released an album of religious hymns in 1999. In 2001, one of John Paul II's doctors confirmed that the pope was suffering from Parkinson's disease. His health has been in visible decline since; he usually reads only a portion of his mass before being replaced by one of his cardinals. Nonetheless, Pope John Paul II remains one of the most influential spiritual and social forces in the world today.

Powell, Colin L.
(1937–) *National Security Advisor*

One of the most impressive figures to emerge during the Reagan years, Colin Powell served as President Reagan's last National Security Advisor and went on to become chairman of the Joint Chiefs of Staff and George W. Bush's secretary of state.

Colin Powell was born in Harlem, New York, but spent a large part of his childhood in the Hunts Point area of the South Bronx, a rough, multiethnic neighborhood outside Manhattan. His family was very close, and although Powell was considered to be a slow learner his family instilled in him the value of hard work and a good education. His dedication to his studies earned him acceptance into the City College of New York, where he graduated with a B.S. in geology in 1958. His primary focus in college was the Reserve Officers' Training Corps (ROTC) program, where Powell exhibited great leadership skills and received straight A's. He completed the program with Distinguished Military Graduate honors and the highest rank possible upon graduation, cadet colonel.

Powell began his military service as a second lieutenant in Fort Benning, Georgia, and then went overseas to West Germany where he served in the Third Armored Division. He was promoted to first lieutenant after one year,

President Reagan holds a National Security Council meeting on the Persian Gulf with National Security Advisor Colin Powell in the Oval Office, April 18, 1988.

and after two years in West Germany he was transferred to the First Battle Group, Fourth Infantry, Second Infantry Brigade at Fort Devens, Massachusetts. Powell completed his three-year requirement in the military in 1961, but by this time he was committed to a career in the U.S. Army.

Powell's first tour of duty came in late 1962 when he served as an adviser to an infantry division in Vietnam. He was wounded in the foot near the Laos border and received a Purple Heart for his service. Powell came back to the United States in 1963 and quickly added several successes to his résumé. He graduated first in his class at a Pathfinder paratrooper course in Fort Benning, Georgia, and first again at the Infantry Officers Advanced Course, leading to his promotion to the rank of major. In 1967, Powell moved to Fort Leavenworth, Kansas, to begin work at the Command and General Staff College, where he graduated second out of more than 1,200 officers. He returned to Vietnam in July 1968, for his second tour of service with the 23rd Infantry Division. He was awarded the Soldier's Medal this time for his bravery in rescuing several men from a burning helicopter.

Following his second tour of duty, Powell returned to school at George Washington University for graduate studies in business administration, receiving his M.B.A. in 1971. He returned to the army with an assignment at the Pentagon in July 1971, but shortly thereafter he was awarded a White House fellowship to work in the Office of Management and Budget. Powell considered this his "dream job," and while at OMB he worked under Director CASPAR WEINBERGER and Deputy Director FRANK CARLUCCI, both of whom figured prominently in the Reagan administration.

After his fellowship in Washington, Powell returned to the army with an assignment at Camp Casey in South Korea. He returned to the Pentagon in September 1974 for a one-year stint, then in August 1975 entered the National War College, where he graduated with distinction a year later. He also received a promotion to full colonel during this time. Powell was then assigned as brigade commander of the 101st Airborne Division, Second Brigade, in Fort Campbell, Kentucky.

During the Carter administration, Powell took his first in what would eventually become a long list of government posts, serving as a senior military assistant to the deputy defense secretary. He also served in President Carter's Energy Department for a brief period in 1979 as Secretary Charles Duncan's executive assistant. Powell also earned promotion to brigadier general in June 1979.

The failed attempt to rescue American hostages in Iran led Powell to support Republican presidential candidate Ronald Reagan in the 1980 election. He was offered positions within Reagan's Defense Department, but declined them to return to the army. He served as assistant division commander for the Fourth Infantry Division in Fort Carson, Colorado, until 1983. He then moved back to Fort Leavenworth to lead the Combined Arms Combat Development Activity, in the process receiving a promotion to major general.

Late in 1983 Powell joined the Reagan administration as the senior military assistant to his former boss, Defense Secretary Caspar Weinberger. The most notable event of his time in the Pentagon regarded the illegal sale of arms to Iran, what later became the Iran-contra scandal. Powell was aware of the transfer of arms, and in a written memo he told National Security Advisor JOHN POINDEXTER and OLIVER NORTH of their obligation to notify Congress of the transaction, thus removing him from any implications of wrongdoing and enhancing his reputation as a man of integrity. In March 1986 he took command of the Fifth Corps in Frankfurt, West Germany, but stayed at this position only a short time before returning to Washington as Deputy National Security Advisor under Frank Carlucci.

Powell and Carlucci were charged with the difficult task of rebuilding the NSC's credibility in the wake of the Iran-contra scandal. Powell was successful in reorganizing the staff at NSC and headed its policy review group, and in November 1987, following Carlucci's move to the Pentagon as defense secretary, he became Reagan's sixth National Security Advisor. During his time as NSA, he was influential in shaping the administration's foreign policy, particularly regarding Nicaragua and the Soviet Union. After his service in the Reagan administration, Powell returned to military service at Fort McPherson, Georgia, as the head of U.S. Forces Command.

Shortly into the term of President GEORGE H. W. BUSH, Powell was promoted over scores of more senior officers as chairman of the Joint Chiefs of Staff. He became the first black officer and the youngest man to rise to this top position in the history of the U.S. military. He demonstrated great leadership during the invasion of Panama in December 1989 and, more notably, against Iraq in the Gulf War of 1991, earning respect from the vast majority of the American public. He was awarded the Congressional Gold Medal for his successful execution of Operations Desert Shield and Desert Storm.

In September 1993, after an illustrious career, Powell retired from the military and received the highest civilian award from President Clinton, the Presidential Medal of Freedom with Distinction. His star rose quickly in private life as he lectured across the country on community service, education, and issues in politics and business. By the mid-1990s, Powell was considered one of the most trusted and respected figures in America, and many were disappointed both in 1996 and 2000 when he decided not to run for president. Instead, he continued to work with education and community programs, serving as chairman of the 1997 President's Summit for America's Future.

In 2000, Powell returned to government service as secretary of state in the cabinet of President George W. Bush. He was a leading advocate of the diplomatic approach to foreign affairs and the importance of maintaining good relations with the rest of the international community. Powell resigned as George W. Bush's secretary of state on November 15, 2004. His resignation came as no surprise to most Washington observers, since his concerns about the American intervention in Iraq and his multilateralist tendencies placed him at odds with the more "hawkish" members of the Bush administration.

R

Reagan, Nancy
(1923–) *first lady*

President Reagan's "best friend" and the love of his life was also his most trusted confidante. Throughout his career as a public servant, Nancy Reagan worked tirelessly to ensure that Ronald Reagan's aides put her husband's interests first, and she did not hesitate to remove those she distrusted. In their postpresidential years, the Reagans faced one of their greatest tests of all when the ex-president was diagnosed with Alzheimer's disease, and Mrs. Reagan was called upon to play the role of an around-the-clock caregiver as the president slowly succumbed to that crippling disease. By all accounts, Mrs. Reagan's caregiving bordered on the heroic.

Born Anne Frances Robbins, she was adopted by Dr. Loyal Davis in 1937 and had her name legally changed to Nancy Davis. She spent most of her childhood in Chicago before entering Smith College, where she graduated with a degree in drama in 1943. Following graduation, Davis immediately began her acting career, appearing first in local plays, but eventually moving to New York City and working on the stage in Broadway and Off-Broadway productions. Her first big break in the film industry came in 1949 when she caught the attention of executives at MGM who signed her to a seven-year movie contract. Between 1950 and 1956, she was cast in 11 films. Davis married fellow actor Ronald Reagan in March 1952, and thereafter her film career slowed down considerably. She appeared with her husband one time in the 1956 film, *Hellcats of the Navy*, but the majority of her time was spent away from the studio and with her family.

In 1967, Nancy Reagan was thrust into political life as the first lady of California following her husband's election as governor. She became involved in a variety of civic activities and participated in several projects dealing with wounded and missing soldiers from Vietnam, eventually writing a regular newspaper column on this issue called "Questions for Nancy." She also became deeply involved in the Foster Grandparent program, which joined needy children with senior citizens, and she continued working with this organization throughout her time in Washington.

In November 1980 Nancy Reagan became first lady of the nation after her husband defeated incumbent president JIMMY CARTER. She continued her active involvement in many community programs during her time in the White House, although she was most remembered for her work in fighting drug and alcohol abuse. Serving as the spokeswoman for the "Just Say No" Foundation, she lectured on this issue all across America. She even delivered an unprecedented, televised speech with her husband on the issue. Her campaign brought nationwide attention to the problem of drug abuse among American teenagers, and she was widely praised for her work both at home and abroad.

Although she was consistently among the most admired women in America every year, she still had her detractors. Many within the administration felt she was too protective of the president, and occasionally she was criticized for being too heavy-handed in dealing with personnel decisions. She also received public criticism for her expensive decoration of the White House during an economic downturn and for

Official portrait of Mrs. Reagan in the Red Room, February 7, 1981

her involvement with astrologer Joan Quigley after her husband's near assassination. However, the criticism seemed to have minimal effect, for she remained a popular figure during and after her days as first lady.

She left the White House in 1989 and returned to private life with her husband, who was then in the early stages of Alzheimer's disease. She continued her campaign against drug abuse with the Nancy Reagan Foundation, but since 1993 the majority of her time has been spent caring for her ailing husband. Since her departure from Washington, she has written two memoirs, *Nancy* and *My Turn*, and a book on the Foster Grandparent program entitled *To Love a Child*. She has also released a collection of letters from her husband called *I Love You, Ronnie: The Letters of Ronald Reagan to Nancy Reagan*, which has given America a much deeper and more personal understanding of Ronald Reagan.

Reagan, Ronald
(1911–2004) *president*

Ronald Reagan's presidency was arguably the most significant presidency of the latter half of the 20th century. During his eight years in office Reagan shifted the tone of political discourse to the right, pursued an aggressive policy toward the Soviet Union that may have contributed to its decline, directed the largest peacetime expansion of the American military in the nation's history, and accumulated mountains of debt. The battered office of the presidency, which witnessed a succession of presidencies cut short by death, resignation, or electoral defeat, regained its luster for most of the Reagan years. In January 1989 the nation's oldest president transferred power to his handpicked successor (the first time this occurred since 1837) and returned to California an immensely popular figure. While Reagan's accomplishments where significant, he was a detached chief executive who delegated considerable authority to staff, neglected personnel issues throughout his tenure, and often misspoke at press conferences. But there was something quintessentially American about Reagan that his countrymen responded to, and unlike Richard Nixon or Bill Clinton, Reagan's opponents liked him—it seemed as if everyone wanted to win the affections of the "Gipper."

Reagan was born on February 6, 1911, in Tampico, Illinois, the second son of John and Nelle Reagan. Nelle seems to have had the greatest influence on her son, imparting a strong religious faith and a love of reading, among other qualities, while his relationship with his alcoholic father was more complicated and distant. The family moved to Dixon, Illinois, when Reagan was nine years old, and it was here that he spent his summers serving as a lifeguard on the Rock River, rescuing some 77 swimmers over the course of his tenure. Reagan graduated from Eureka College in 1932, where he majored in economics and was actively involved in student government, sports, and in the college's drama society. Reagan then began a career as a broadcaster for radio stations in Davenport and Des Moines, Iowa, where he did the "play by play" for various sports including Chicago Cubs baseball games. It was on a trip to the Chicago Cubs spring training camp on Catalina Island, California, that Reagan detoured to Hollywood, took a screen test for the Warner Brothers studio, and went on to become one of America's favorite B-movie actors. Reagan was married twice; first to the actress Jane Wyman in 1940, and then, following a divorce in 1948, he married another actress, Nancy Davis, in 1952. Reagan had a daughter, Maureen, and an adopted son, Michael, with Jane Wyman, and two children, Patti and Ron, with NANCY REAGAN.

Ironically, this conservative president lived much of his adult life as a devoted New Deal

Ronald Reagan in Dixon, Illinois, 1920

Democrat. Reagan's ideological transformation began in the 1950s when he started to question the "tax and spend" policies of the New Deal and Fair Deal; in later years he would recall losing over 90 percent of his actor's paycheck to some form of taxation. Reagan's tenure as president of the Screen Actors Guild (1947–52) also contributed to his ideological transformation, for he was disturbed by what he viewed as a concerted effort on the part of American Communists to infiltrate the entertainment industry, and he went on to testify before the House Un-American Activities Committee. Reagan did not officially change his party registration until 1962, but by the time of the 1960 presidential election, Reagan observed in his memoir, "I had completed the process of self-conversion."

Ronald Reagan as a WHO radio announcer in Des Moines, Iowa, 1937

Reagan's first significant political activity was in 1964 when he spoke on behalf of Arizona senator Barry Goldwater in his race against President Lyndon Johnson. On October 27, 1964, Reagan delivered one of his most famous addresses, which later became known as "A Time for Choosing." Although Goldwater went on to lose in a landslide, the speech propelled Reagan to the forefront of the conservative wing of the Republican Party. At this time a group of wealthy Californians who would become known as the kitchen cabinet—Justin Dart, Henry Salvatori, Holmes Tuttle,

Leonard Firestone, Cy Rubel, and others—urged Reagan to run for governor of California in 1966. Although Reagan had exceptionally high name recognition, the race was an uphill battle, for he faced a strong Republican primary challenge from San Francisco mayor George Christopher, and later from incumbent Democratic governor EDMUND (PAT) BROWN.

Both of Reagan's opponents underestimated him, something that would play to his advantage throughout his political career. Brown attempted to undermine Reagan's credibility by dismissing him as an actor (Brown ran a television commercial during the election that showed him speaking to a group of schoolchildren and saying, "I'm running against an actor, and you know who killed Abe Lincoln, don't you?"), while his primary opponent George Christopher sought to portray him as a right-wing extremist. Reagan skillfully deflected both charges with his reassuring manner and by running a folksy campaign that took advantage of a rising sense of unease among the middle class, particularly regarding racial matters and student unrest.

Reagan was an effective campaigner who learned how to connect with an audience from years of speaking on behalf of General Electric Corporation. As an actor, a corporate spokesman, and a politician, Reagan studied each of these crafts carefully and knew his strengths and weaknesses. He listened to advice and never assumed he knew what was best. While it would be incorrect to say that Reagan was a "puppet" of his handlers, he frequently deferred to their advice and was happy to delegate a wide range of his authority to "the fellas," his name for his entourage of advisers. But in certain areas, particularly in dealing with the public, he had great confidence in his ability. Coupled with this was his genuine belief that government had become an intrusive presence in the lives of many Americans, and that taxation was impeding economic growth and threatening personal freedom. He defeated both Christopher and Brown, the latter by a landslide margin of 58 to 42 percent. At the height of Lyndon Johnson's "Great Society," Ronald Reagan became one of the most prominent critics of big government within the emerging Republican majority.

His years as governor were marked by battles over taxes and spending cuts, confronting student revolts at California's major public universities, and tangles with higher education administrators who were inclined to accept many of the demands of the student demon-strators. In a number of high-profile confrontations, particularly at the University of California at Berkeley, Reagan resisted the demands of what he saw as pampered students allied with left-leaning faculty and administrators. His popularity on the state's campuses was further diminished by his vocal support for the Vietnam War. Reagan argued for a more muscular approach to the war in Vietnam, and would later become one of the more prominent supporters of Richard Nixon's Vietnam policies. Nonetheless, Reagan approved of a last-minute campaign in 1968 for him to win the Republican nomination for president by defeating Richard Nixon and New York governor Nelson Rockefeller. This last-ditch effort

Ronald Reagan with his horse Little Man at Rancho Del Cielo, February 1977

failed, but nevertheless it boosted Reagan's reputation as the spokesman for the right wing of the Republican Party.

Reagan won reelection in 1970 against Jesse Unruh, the Speaker of the California Assembly, by a margin of 53 to 45 percent. During that election Reagan portrayed himself as the guardian of the taxpayers' money against a "typical tax and spend liberal." His final four years in Sacramento were marked by a successful effort to reform welfare, elements of which would become national policy almost two decades later. Reagan also continued his fight against "excessive" government spending, and frequently exercised his line-item veto power—a total of 943 times during his tenure in Sacramento.

In the fall of 1975, Reagan decided to challenge the incumbent Republican president GERALD R. FORD for his party's nomination. He perceived Ford to be an accidental and somewhat ineffectual president, and he considered his policy of détente with the Soviet Union and his plan to "give away" the Panama Canal as defeatist. Reagan proved to be a tenacious candidate in the 1976 campaign; after having lost the opening series of primaries to President Ford and running out of money at a critical juncture, he turned around and defeated Ford in the North Carolina primary and went on to beat him in Texas, Alabama, Georgia, California, and many other states, ultimately losing the nomination by only 70 votes. Reagan delivered an impromptu speech at the Republican National Convention in Kansas City, Missouri, that inspired the party faithful, and caused many delegates to believe that he would be their candidate in 1980.

Following his defeat for the nomination Reagan renewed a practice he began after he left the governorship of writing a newspaper column and delivering a syndicated weekly radio address on current issues. His radio addresses proved very popular and kept him in touch with his conservative base around the country, and his star quality made him a much sought-after fund-raiser for the party. He was, in the minds of many, the Republican front-runner for 1980. Reagan's nomination campaign got off to a rocky start when he lost the Iowa caucus to former CIA director GEORGE H. W. BUSH, but he came roaring back with a decisive win over Bush in the critical New Hampshire primary.

At the Republican National Convention in Detroit in July 1980, Reagan toyed with the idea of selecting former president Ford as his running mate, in an unusual arrangement that would have allowed Ford to handle the foreign policy portfolio of the administration. He ultimately rejected the idea, and turned to his chief adversary of the 1980 primary elections, Bush. Candidate Reagan capitalized on the so-called misery index—the unemployment and inflation rates, which at times exceeded 20 percent during the 1980 campaign. He asked Americans if they were "better off now" than they were four years ago, and a week later a majority of Americans answered "no." Reagan brought a Republican majority into the U.S. Senate for the first time since the Eisenhower years, and held that majority until the 1986 elections.

President Reagan was just weeks shy of his 70th birthday when he took the oath of office, making him the nation's oldest president at the time of his inauguration. He had three priorities for his first term: reducing income tax rates, balancing the budget, and increasing defense spending. Many critics were skeptical that Reagan could simultaneously achieve all three goals, but he persisted in his belief that reduced tax rates would spur enough economic growth to offset the lost revenue from tax rate cuts and would also provide the revenue for increased defense spending. He was also committed to restraining domestic spending and believed that his proposals to spur economic growth through tax cuts, in concert with reduced government regulations, would unleash American productivity and break the back of the 1970s "stagflation." Less than a month after an assassination attempt on Reagan's life on March 30, 1981, Reagan delivered a dramatic address to Congress urging its members to pass his economic agenda, which became commonly referred to as "Reaganomics." The emotional response to Reagan's shooting, coupled with his skillful appeal for public support, helped to secure passage later that summer of a substantial tax cut along with sizable reductions in the federal budget, delivering an early victory for the administration's domestic agenda.

In foreign affairs Reagan struck an assertive, and in the eyes of some, a belligerent tone. At his first press conference he accused the leadership of the Soviet Union of "reserv[ing] unto themselves the right to commit any crime, to lie, to cheat" and observed that "the only morality they recognize is what will further their cause." Reagan remained on the rhetorical offensive against the Soviet Union for much of his first term, urging the rest of the world to resist "the aggressive impulses of an evil empire." In Central America Reagan approved a covert operation designed to overthrow the Sandinista government of Nicaragua and offered covert and overt assistance to the government of El Salvador in its fight against leftist guerrillas. He was committed to installing intermediate-range missiles in Western Europe to counter a perceived threat from the Soviet Union's recently installed SS-20 missiles in Eastern Europe, although under his zero-option proposal he offered to cancel that deployment if the Soviets withdrew their missiles. He began the largest peacetime buildup of American military forces, including the development of the B-1 bomber and the Stealth bomber, and the construction of naval vessels to equip the United States with a 600-

ship navy. He also worked to restore the Central Intelligence Agency's covert capability, which was downgraded during JIMMY CARTER's presidency. Later, Reagan's admirers would come to see a grand design in what they labeled the "Reagan Doctrine"—the idea of applying pressure through economic, military, and covert means to hasten the collapse of the Soviet Union. One such admirer of Ronald Reagan was British prime minister MARGARET THATCHER, who claimed that Reagan "won the Cold War without firing a shot."

Reagan's domestic agenda on social issues met with perhaps the fiercest resistance from his opponents, particularly his hostility toward affirmative-action programs, his opposition to abortion, and his attempt to pass an amendment to the Constitution that would allow prayer in public schools. Nevertheless, he never placed these issues at the top of his agenda, much to the despair of groups such as Jerry Falwell's "Moral Majority," one of the most prominent groups in the so-called Christian Right.

At the halfway point of his first term in office, it appeared that Reagan might be a vulnerable candidate in the 1984 campaign. A stagnant economy with unemployment hovering at more than 10 percent hurt the Republican Party in the off-year elections of 1982, and Reagan was accused of being indifferent to the plight of the unemployed. He repeatedly urged Congress and the public to "stay the course" with Reaganomics, although he veered off course by agreeing to a tax increase in August 1982, apparently convincing himself that he was approving a tax reform designed to close loopholes in the tax code. Slowly the country began to emerge from the stagflation of the 1970s and early 1980s, in time for the presidential election of 1984. The monetary policies of the Federal Reserve wrung the life out of inflation, and Reagan's opposition to large, "pump priming" programs contributed as well.

Near the close of his first term, Reagan suffered the most deadly foreign policy setback of his presidency. A peacekeeping effort in Lebanon designed to restore some order to that fractured nation led to the deaths of 241 marines, the victims of a terrorist attack on their barracks on October 23, 1983. Reagan cut his losses and withdrew the American forces a short time later. Just days after the Lebanon barracks attack, Reagan ordered an attack on the Caribbean island of Grenada, which was governed by a Marxist regime allied with Cuba and the Soviet Union. The American attack, while somewhat poorly executed, was successful in dislodging the Marxist government. While a relatively minor event in terms of the military challenge presented by the Grenadans and a small Cuban contingent of soldier-engineers, it was the first successful exercise of force by the United States since the failure in Vietnam and the disastrous hostage rescue mission in Iran in 1980. It boosted Reagan's image as a leader who was determined to restore American pride and conduct a more assertive foreign policy.

In Western Europe President Reagan faced massive opposition to the placement of Pershing II and Cruise missiles to counter the Soviet SS-20 missiles deployed in Eastern Europe. A worldwide "nuclear freeze" movement organized large protests in major European and American cities, and the fear of a nuclear exchange between the two superpowers was at its highest level since the Cuban missile crisis. Reagan, buoyed by the support of Margaret Thatcher, German chancellor HELMUT KOHL, and French President FRANÇOIS MITTERRAND, "stayed the course" and proceeded with the deployment throughout the month of November 1983.

By the time of the 1984 presidential election, the nation's economy was back on track, and Reagan could argue that he had bolstered America's prestige through the economic comeback and the rebuilding of the nation's armed forces—it was, according to the Reagan campaign, "morning in America." He easily defeated former vice president WALTER MONDALE in the general election, carrying 49 states, although a shaky performance by a seemingly aged president in the first presidential debate caused much consternation in the Reagan camp.

Reagan's second term was characteristic of other two-term presidencies, in that it was marked by drift and scandal. Despite his landslide victory in 1984, some of the steam had gone out of the Reagan Revolution. The most important second-term domestic policy initiative was tax reform, and although the president's proposal met with some success, it was hardly an issue that served as a rallying cry for the faithful. While his popularity remained high well into 1986, by November of that year news reports of a secret initiative to win the release of American hostages in Lebanon and at the same time covertly support the Nicaraguan "contras" (or "Freedom Fighters" as Reagan called them) threatened to undermine his presidency. Reagan offered conflicting explanations of his understanding of this opening to Iran, but frequently suggested that it was intended to strengthen the hand of moderate Iranians who hoped for improved relations with the West. The profits from the Iranian arms sales were transferred into Swiss bank accounts set aside for use by the contras. While many Americans disagreed with Reagan's conservative stance on the issues, his integrity had rarely been questioned in the past, but throughout the Iran-contra affair his reputation as a leader who could be trusted was severely tested. In a nationally televised address delivered in March 1987, Reagan admitted that "a few months ago I told the American people I did not trade arms for hostages. My heart and my best intentions still tell me that's true, but the facts and the evidence tell me it is not. . . . It was a mistake." With this address, Reagan began a slow but steady recovery in public opinion polls that lasted until his departure from office.

The final years of the Reagan presidency saw significant improvement in relations between the United States and the Soviet Union. The summit in Geneva led to significant breakthroughs in arms control and other areas, though Reagan's commitment to the Strategic Defense Initiative remained a stumbling block to a proposal to eliminate all nuclear weapons, a position both leaders claimed to share. Reagan's previously derided zero-option proposal was accepted by Soviet leader MIKHAIL GORBACHEV, and the man who once referred to the Soviet Union as an "evil empire" visited Moscow in the spring of 1988, met with Soviet dissidents, spoke to students at Moscow State University, and toured Red Square where he and Gorbachev displayed a genuine affection for one another.

By the end of his eight years in office, the 78-year-old president was showing signs of his age, but his upbeat personality and his gentlemanly demeanor remained intact. He once remarked in 1987, "since I came to the White House, I've gotten two hearing aids, had a colon operation, a prostate operation, skin cancer, and I've been shot . . . damn thing is, I never felt better." His vice president, GEORGE H. W. BUSH, easily defeated his Democratic challenger Michael Dukakis in the 1988 election, and Reagan eagerly awaited the day when he could return to his California ranch. In his farewell address he modestly credited his accomplishments in office to the American people, and endorsed the idea that he had presided over a Reagan revolution that restored common sense to the workings of the federal government and left his "shining city upon a hill" a stronger and freer place.

Reagan generally kept a low profile in his postpresidential years, appearing at Republi-

can Party events in Washington and at a tribute to Margaret Thatcher in the nation's capital. In November 1994 he released a written statement announcing that he was suffering from Alzheimer's disease, ending the statement in his usual buoyant way by proclaiming, "when the Lord calls me home, whenever that may be, I will leave with the greatest love for this country of ours and eternal optimism for its future. I now begin the journey that will lead me into the sunset of my life. I know that for America there will always be a bright dawn ahead."

Ronald Reagan died on June 5, 2004, at the age of 93. His wife, Nancy, and his three surviving children were at his side. Reagan was laid to rest at a private ceremony at the Reagan Library on June 11, 2004, as the sun set over the Pacific Ocean. His epitaph reflected his undying optimism and faith in human nature: "I know in my heart that man is good. That what is right will always eventually triumph. And there's purpose and worth to each and every life."

Regan, Donald T.
(1918–2003) *secretary of the Treasury, chief of staff*

President Reagan's first secretary of the Treasury and second White House chief of staff left Washington under a cloud following revelations of the Iran-contra affair. While never directly linked to the scandal, Regan was blamed by many Reagan loyalists, including NANCY REAGAN, for failing to control the National Security Council staff. A tough-talking marine corps veteran who rose from obscurity to become a major corporate executive and a loyal Reagan cabinet officer, he and the president by all accounts enjoyed each other's company, but their relationship became yet another casualty of the Iran-contra affair.

Following his graduation from high school, Donald Regan stayed in his hometown of Cambridge, Massachusetts, to attend Harvard University, receiving his B.A. in English in 1940. Regan went on to seek a law degree, but decided to leave law school after less than a year to join the marine corps. He served throughout the Pacific theater and participated in such famous battles as Guadalcanal and Okinawa, reaching the rank of lieutenant colonel by the time he left the service in 1946.

Regan entered the business world after the war, joining Merrill, Lynch, Pierce, Fenner, and Smith, America's largest investment firm, as an account executive trainee. He served as an account executive in Washington, D.C., and in New York City for six years before being promoted to a department manager in 1952. Just two years later, at the age of 35, Regan became the youngest partner in the history of Merrill Lynch. He continued to climb the corporate ladder at Merrill Lynch, taking over the Philadelphia office in 1955, then serving as director of the administrative division in New York from 1960 to 1964. Regan was promoted to executive vice president in 1964. Four years later, he became president of Merrill Lynch. Finally in 1971, Regan reached the pinnacle of the corporate world by taking over as chairman and CEO of the firm, a position he held until the election of Ronald Reagan in 1980.

Reagan and his team were impressed with the record Regan amassed at Merrill Lynch, and in December 1980 he was asked to head the Treasury Department. He played a key role in the development and passage of Reagan's fiscal package in 1981, but it was not until his second year in office that he became the clear spokesman for Reagan's economic team. His support for free markets and tax cuts, his competence as treasury secretary, and his loyalty to the president earned him the respect of many conservatives, including Reagan. In an odd personnel move, Regan exchanged posts with Chief of Staff JAMES BAKER at the start of Reagan's second term in office. He was a strong chief of staff who brought a corporate managerial style to the White House that drew the ire of many of Reagan's associates.

As Reagan became mired in the Iran-contra scandal in late 1986, Regan was criticized in the press for not protecting the president from the political firestorm. In the words of columnist Fred Barnes, he became "the administration's designated scapegoat." Regan resigned his post in February 1987 and was replaced by former senator HOWARD BAKER. In his memoir, *For the Record: From Wall Street to Washington*, Regan offered an unflattering portrait of Nancy Reagan as a heavy-handed first lady whom he held responsible for his ouster. After he left the White House, he became president of Regdon Associates. He died in Virginia in June 2003.

S

Scalia, Antonin
(1936–) *associate justice, U.S. Supreme Court*

A Reagan appointee to the U.S. Supreme Court, Antonin Scalia fulfilled the expectations of conservatives in the Reagan administration who lobbied for his nomination and became something of a scourge to liberal law professors who favored a more activist judiciary. Scalia developed a reputation for writing blunt and sometimes acerbic opinions, reportedly alienating some of his colleagues on the bench with what they see as his tendency toward heavy-handed criticism when they diverge from his opinions. Scalia consistently opposed extending privacy rights to homosexuals and is an outspoken foe of abortion rights and the movement to legalize gay marriage. He has surprised his critics on occasion, voting to strike down statutes outlawing flag burning and writing a lone but powerful dissent on a decision that upheld the independent counsel law; years later, after the excesses of Kenneth Starr's investigation of President Bill Clinton, many of the latter's supporters expressed the view that Scalia was right.

Antonin Scalia graduated summa cum laude from Georgetown University in 1957. Following graduation, he was admitted to Har-

vard Law School, where he became editor of the *Harvard Law Review* and received his LL.B. in 1960. After receiving a Sheldon Fellowship, he remained at Harvard until 1961, then took a position with Jones, Day, Cockley, and Reavis, a Cleveland-based law firm. After six years in private practice, Scalia discovered an interest in teaching law, and in 1967 he took a faculty position at the University of Virginia. He served as an associate professor until 1970, when he was promoted to full professor.

Scalia accepted his first government position in 1971 when he became general counsel in the Office of Telecommunications Policy. In 1972, he was appointed chairman of the Administrative Conference of the United States, where he remained until 1974. He then joined the Justice Department as an assistant attorney general in the office of legal counsel. In 1977, Scalia decided to leave government service, taking a scholar-in-residence position at the conservative American Enterprise Institute. After a brief stint at the AEI, he returned to academia full time with a job at the University of Chicago as a professor of law. He taught at Chicago until 1982, leaving briefly in 1980 for a one-year visiting professorship at Stanford University. During his time in Chicago and Stanford, Scalia remained associated with the AEI as the editor of their journal, *Regulation*. This position allowed him to gain notoriety in conservative circles and establish himself as a leading thinker on issues of law and judicial power.

Scalia's zealous support of judicial restraint was noticed by the Reagan administration, and in 1982 he was named to the U.S. Circuit Court of Appeals in Washington, D.C. He remained true to his principles during his time on the circuit court, resisting the judicial activism of his peers and advocating a strict adherence to the Constitution. In 1986, following the retirement of Warren Burger, President Reagan elevated William Rehnquist as the chief justice of the Supreme Court. He then nominated Scalia to fill the vacancy left by Rehnquist, and on September 26, 1986, after unanimous consent by the Senate, Scalia became an associate justice on the Supreme Court.

In his nearly 20 years on the Court, Scalia has become something of a hero to conservatives, ardently opposing abortion rights, affirmative action, hate speech laws, gay rights, and the strict separation of church and state, all of which are issues dear to conservatives. He has also continued to strongly resist any attempts at legislating from the bench, preferring instead to leave that to the legislative branch. In 1996, he gave a lecture at Princeton University on his judicial methodology. Subsequently published under the title *A Matter of Interpretation: Federal Courts and the Law*, Scalia rejects the common-law approach which too often leads to judicial activism and instead advocates a process of examining the Constitution as well as historical precedents, a method he calls "textualism."

Along with Associate Justice Clarence Thomas, who is his most consistent voting partner, Scalia is widely regarded as the most conservative member currently on the Supreme Court. His popularity among conservatives has led to some talk of his entering national politics,

perhaps even as a presidential candidate, but Scalia has dismissed any notion that he will vacate his seat on the Court any time in the near future.

Schweiker, Richard S.
(1926–) *secretary of health and human services*

During his second term in the U.S. Senate, Richard Schweiker, a liberal Republican from Pennsylvania, agreed to join the ticket with Ronald Reagan as a candidate for vice president in the campaign for the 1976 GOP presidential nomination. Incumbent president GERALD FORD eventually won the nomination, but when Reagan became president in January 1981, Schweiker became his first secretary of health and human services, serving at this post until 1983.

Schweiker joined the U.S. Navy after high school and served aboard an aircraft carrier until the end of World War II. When he returned from the war, he entered Pennsylvania State University, earning his degree Phi Beta Kappa in 1950. He then joined his father's business, Olean Tile Company, near his home town of Norristown, Pennsylvania, where he remained until 1960. Schweiker soon became involved in local politics and in 1960 he won in his first bid for public office, defeating conservative incumbent John A. Lafore for a seat in the U.S. House of Representatives. During his eight years of service in the House, he was known as a liberal Republican, earning higher marks from groups like Americans for Democratic Action than from conservative organizations. In 1968, Schweiker was elected to the U.S. Senate, winning reelection in 1974.

Less than two years into his second term, Schweiker was asked to join the presidential ticket of former California governor Ronald Reagan in his campaign against incumbent president GERALD FORD. The race between Reagan and Ford was close leading into the party convention, and Reagan believed that naming a running mate like Schweiker would win votes from the moderate wing of the Republican Party, particularly among the 103 delegates from Schweiker's Pennsylvania. After an intense fight at the convention, the Reagan-Schweiker ticket lost narrowly to Ford, and Schweiker returned to his seat in the Senate. In the final four years of his term, his voting record underwent a major shift to the right; the liberal Americans for Democratic Action dropped his rating from 89 percent in 1975 to 15 percent in 1977. He did not seek reelection when his Senate term expired in January 1981.

Schweiker again supported Reagan's candidacy for the GOP nomination in 1980, serving as the northeast states campaign chairman. When Reagan defeated President JIMMY CARTER in the general election, Schweiker was rewarded with the post of secretary of health and human services (HHS). Schweiker had been the ranking Republican on the Senate Labor and Human Resources Committee, the Health Subcommittee, and the Appropriations Subcommittee on Labor, Health, Education, and Welfare during his second Senate term, posts which gave him intimate knowledge of health and welfare policy. Early in his Senate career, he cosponsored a national health insurance bill with Senator Edward Kennedy (D-Mass.), but by 1977 he was calling for deregulation and privatization in the health care sector. In 1979, he introduced a bill forcing businesses to give their employees flexibility in choosing health insurance plans, further strengthening his reputation as a conservative on health care policy.

Schweiker offered little in concrete proposals during his confirmation hearings, indicating only his desire to cut departmental waste and fraud, and encouraging greater preventive health care measures such as exercise and good

nutrition. After becoming HHS secretary, he pushed for more state control and various cuts in federal welfare programs. His proposed cuts caused a great deal of resentment among many of his former liberal and moderate colleagues in Congress. In health care policy, Schweiker played a significant role in the creation of the Medicare prospective-payment system, a price control system that sought to shift hospital costs to other parts of Medicare.

In 1983, Schweiker stepped down as HHS secretary and returned to the business world as president of the American Council of Life Insurance in McLean, Virginia. He was succeeded by MARGARET HECKLER.

Shevardnadze, Eduard
(1928–   ) *foreign minister of the Soviet Union*

In July 1985 Eduard Shevardnadze replaced longtime foreign minister ANDREI GROMYKO, and established a pragmatic "new thinking" direction in Soviet foreign policy. Following the collapse of the Soviet Union in December 1991, he returned to his native Georgia and became his country's first freely elected president.

As a youth, Shevardnadze was strongly influenced by his older brother to devote his career to the Communist Party organization. He began working for the Communist Youth League (Komsomol) when he was 18, and two years later joined the Communist Party of the Soviet Union (CPSU). He also attended the Georgian Communist's Higher Party School for his formal education, where he graduated in 1951. Shevardnadze worked for the Komsomol until 1961, rising to the Central Committee of the All-Union Komsomol and, in 1957, to first secretary of the Komsomol of Georgia. In 1965, he moved to the center of the Georgian Communist Party apparatus when he was appointed interior minister. Corruption was a serious issue in Georgia under party leader Vassily Mzhevandze, and, as interior minister, Shevardnadze launched an effort to eliminate this problem. The effort ultimately led to the ouster of Mzhevandze in 1972 and the rise of Shevardnadze as first secretary of the Georgian Communist Party.

Shevardnadze served for the next 13 years as leader of the party and continued to battle corruption in the bureaucracy; 75 percent of the party leadership was removed in just his first 18 months in power. He also initiated economic reforms that led to mild improvements in the Georgian economy, earning him a reputation as a progressive thinker within the Communist Party. His leadership in Georgia led to his appointment to the Central Committee of the CPSU in 1976 and as a candidate member of the Politburo two years later.

On July 1, 1985, the new Soviet general secretary, MIKHAIL GORBACHEV, surprised everyone when he named Shevardnadze foreign minister, replacing 28-year veteran ANDREI GROMYKO. He was also given full membership in the Politburo, becoming the first Georgian to sit in this body since Joseph Stalin. Shevardnadze had little experience in international affairs prior to his appointment, but Gorbachev was attracted to his pragmatic approach to politics and his desire to seek a new direction in Soviet foreign policy. The two leaders brought a different direction to foreign policy, called "new thinking," which focused on reducing the strain the high military budget was placing on the ailing Soviet economy. Gorbachev had long preached the need for such reforms, but with Shevardnadze as foreign minister he now had the power to move in this direction.

The Soviet Union steadily reduced its commitments abroad over the next several years. The country quickly disengaged from Eastern Europe, where Gorbachev repudiated the Brezhnev Doctrine in the face of growing opposition to communist governments in the region.

The most costly, and as a result, most pressing military expenditure was the arms race with the United States. Shevardnadze worked closely with his American counterparts, Secretaries of State GEORGE SHULTZ and JAMES BAKER III, to negotiate meaningful arms reductions and put an end to the arms race. The results of "new thinking" were revolutionary for the international community. After nearly a decade fighting in Afghanistan, the Red Army withdrew its forces in February 1989, eliminating a costly operation from the Soviet budget. Between September and December 1989, communism collapsed throughout Eastern Europe and was replaced by free, democratic governments. And the United States and Soviet Union took substantial steps to reduce the threat of nuclear weapons, most notably with the signing of the Intermediate Nuclear Force (INF) Treaty in December 1987, which eliminated all nuclear missiles with ranges of 300 to 3,400 miles.

Following the collapse of the Eastern bloc and the reunification of Germany, Shevardnadze came under heavy pressure from conservatives in the party who charged him with betraying the Soviet Union. He surprised everyone by resigning from office on December 20, 1990, and warned that the Soviet Union was heading toward "dictatorship" once again. He left the CPSU six months later and became the leader of the Movement for Democratic Reform. Three months after the failed coup attempt against Gorbachev by party hard-liners in August 1991, Shevardnadze was persuaded to resume his old post; he remained at the job for just another month before the Soviet Union officially dissolved in December 1991.

Shevardnadze returned to his native Georgia to another political crisis involving the government of Georgian president Zviad Gamsakhurdia, whose regime had taken on an increasingly authoritarian nature in recent years and plunged the nation into civil war. Over the next several years, Shevardnadze was appointed to top leadership positions in the new democratic Georgia, first as chairman of the State Council then chairman of the parliament. In 1995, he was elected president of Georgia by popular vote, and four years later was reelected with over 70 percent of the vote. However, his regime was toppled by a popular uprising in November 2003 amid accusations of corruption and election fraud.

Shultz, George P.
(1920–   ) *secretary of state*

George Shultz had one of the longest records of service as secretary of state in modern times, and was a critical player in forging the breakthrough agreements reached by Ronald Reagan and MIKHAIL GORBACHEV. Shultz believed in the idea that patient diplomacy, like a well-tended garden, often takes years to bear fruit. In an administration in which diplomats and diplomatic institutions were sometimes sneered at, Shultz's initiatives were frequently opposed by the more ideological members of the administration, including his longtime colleague CASPAR WEINBERGER, the secretary of defense. Interestingly, despite his belief in the importance of diplomacy, Shultz was often the most hawkish member of Reagan's foreign policy team, advocating the use of force on a number of occasions, in particular in response to

Secretary of State George Shultz meets with President Reagan at Camp David, Maryland, December 31, 1982.

terrorist attacks on U.S. interests in the Middle East. His warning about the long-term effect of the American withdrawal from Lebanon in 1984 seems particularly prescient in light of the encouragement that this event provided to Osama Bin Laden and some members of his inner circle, who cited this retreat as evidence that if you killed Americans, the U.S. government would recoil and withdraw.

George Shultz graduated cum laude from Princeton University in 1942 with a degree in economics. Soon after his graduation, he joined the U.S. Marine Corps and served in the Pacific theater in World War II. He left active duty in 1945 and returned to school for graduate studies at the Massachusetts Institute of Technology. Shultz earned his Ph.D. from MIT in 1949 in industrial economics, focusing largely on labor relations and employment issues.

Upon receiving his doctorate, Shultz decided to remain at MIT as an instructor in the industrial relations department. He was promoted to assistant professor in 1949, then in 1955 became associate professor of industrial relations. Shultz also got his first experience in politics during his time at MIT, serving on arbitration boards for worker-management disputes, and as a senior staff economist to President Eisenhower's Council of Economic Advisors. In 1957, Shultz moved to Illinois and took a position as professor of industrial relations at the University of Chicago. He stayed in Chicago until 1968, adding the job of dean of the Graduate Business School in 1962. Shultz gained notoriety in both industry and government during his tenure at Chicago as he joined several independent committees on unemployment, labor, and industry issues, along with several task forces on the same issues created by the Kennedy and Johnson administrations.

After the 1968 presidential election, Shultz was appointed to his first cabinet post as secretary of labor in the Nixon administration. He worked diligently at the Labor Department to implement Nixon's affirmative-action programs and achieve union reforms. He also played a major role in several labor disputes, most notably the 1970 postal employees strike when the National Guard was called into New York City to organize the mail. He was at this job for less than two years before accepting the position as the first director of the Office of Management and Budget, where he continued to deal with the issues of wage and price controls and labor disputes. In May 1972 Shultz became the first economist appointed as secretary of the Treasury, and he dealt with a number of difficult issues including inflation and federal debt, currency and trade issues, and the growing concern over OPEC's impact on the international economy. Shultz earned high praise and respect from his peers as a highly competent official with a firm grasp on a number of policy issues and with power rivaling that of Henry Kissinger.

Shultz left the Nixon administration in March 1974, to teach and enter the business world; he taught courses at Stanford University and joined the San Francisco firm Bechtel Corporation as an executive vice president. In 1975, Shultz became president and a member of the board of directors of Bechtel. He returned to public service after the election of Ronald Reagan in 1980. For the first year and a half of the Reagan administration, while still president of Bechtel, Shultz served on the president's Economic Advisory Board. Then, following the resignation of ALEXANDER HAIG, Shultz was asked to become secretary of state.

Shultz joined the administration in July 1982 amid conflicts in the Middle East and Central America, and a growing tension with the Soviet Union. Shultz was a proponent of a strong defense and holding a firm line against terrorism and the Soviet Union. The negotiating skills he developed over the previous 20 years proved invaluable in his dealings with world leaders. This was clearly seen in his frequent meetings with Soviet ambassador Anatoly Dobrynin and Foreign Minister EDUARD SHE-VARDNADZE, and later with Secretary-General Mikhail Gorbachev on issues such as human rights, Soviet intervention in the Third World, and arms control. Shultz was a key force in the eventual success of arms reductions and the improvement in U.S.–Soviet relations. Throughout much of the Reagan presidency, he clashed repeatedly with secretary of defense Caspar Weinberger over a number of issues, including the placement of peacekeeping forces in Lebanon, fashioning an appropriate response to terrorism, and arms control negotiations with the Soviet Union. His distinguished public service in the Reagan administration was marred only by his propensity to threaten to resign on numerous occasions. Some of these resignation threats were principled responses to decisions he disagreed with, while others, according to media reports, involved his sense of feeling slighted over an aircraft assigned to him, and other such petty issues.

Shultz left government service at the end of the Reagan administration and returned to the Bechtel Corporation. He also joined Stanford University's Hoover Institution as a Distinguished Fellow in 1989. In 1993, Shultz released his memoir of the Reagan years, *Turmoil and Triumph*, where he offered a comprehensive and balanced view of the president, blaming him for the Iran-contra scandal (Shultz vigorously opposed the president's decision to sell arms to Iran) while crediting him with achieving victory in the cold war. Shultz currently lives in California and continues to work at the Bechtel Corporation and the Hoover Institution.

Smith, William French
(1917–1990)   *attorney general*

Ronald Reagan's personal attorney and a member of Reagan's California kitchen cabinet,

William French Smith served as the nation's attorney general from 1981–85. Smith was an integral player in the process that led President Reagan in 1981 to appoint the first woman to the U.S. Supreme Court, SANDRA DAY O'CON-NOR. A low-key person who was somewhat media-averse, Smith nonetheless recruited a number of talented young conservatives who went on to have a major impact on the law and in other policy areas in the succeeding decades.

Smith graduated with a bachelor's degree from UCLA in 1939, then moved East to begin graduate studies at Harvard Law School. After receiving his LL.B. in 1942, Smith joined the naval reserve, where he remained until the end of World War II, serving in the Pacific theater. He returned to California and began working on labor law in 1946 for a prominent Los Angeles corporate law firm, Gibson, Dunn, and Crutcher. Smith became a partner of the firm in 1951 and eventually senior partner and head of the company's labor department.

During the 1960s, Smith became involved in conservative politics in California. He supported Republican Barry Goldwater in his 1964 bid for the presidency, and it was during this time that Smith befriended one of Goldwater's most famous supporters, actor Ronald Reagan. Smith was impressed by Reagan's communication skills and his conservative ideology, and he began urging Reagan to run for governor of California. Reagan won the governorship in 1966, and two years later he appointed Smith to the Board of Regents of the University of California. Smith stayed on the board for several years, acting as chairman from 1970 to 1972 and 1974 to 1976. He remained one of Reagan's closest friends and advisers throughout his political career.

Smith became a leading fund-raiser for Reagan in his 1980 presidential election campaign. Following Reagan's landslide victory, the president asked his old friend to become the nation's 74th attorney general. During his years as attorney general, Smith took a hands-off approach to policymaking, but he was an outspoken advocate of judicial restraint, and criticized mandatory busing and affirmative action programs as examples of judicial activism. He also played a key role in Reagan's War on Drugs and fought for stronger criminal penalties.

Smith announced his intention to leave the Reagan administration after three years in office, although he remained attorney general for 13 more months due to confirmation problems with his successor, EDWIN MEESE III. After he left his post at the Justice Department, Smith went back to work for his law firm in Los Angeles. He continued to work for the Reagan legacy as chairman of the board of trustees of the Reagan Presidential Foundation, the organization responsible for the creation of the Reagan Library in Simi Valley, California. In October 1990 Smith died of cancer in Los Angeles.

Spencer, Stuart K.
(1927–   ) *campaign strategist*

Stuart Spencer has served as a political consultant for more than 40 years for some of the top Republican leaders in the nation, including Nelson Rockefeller, GERALD FORD, and Ronald Reagan. Although he never held an official post in the Reagan administration, he served as a top strategist to the president for the 1980 and 1984 presidential elections and as an unofficial adviser during the Iran-contra affair. Spencer holds the distinction of being the only man to direct a campaign that defeated Ronald Reagan. In 1976, while managing the Ford campaign, Spencer took advantage of the insight he gained from directing Reagan's gubernatorial races and ran a campaign that kept Reagan on the defensive for much of the race. This slight was not forgotten by NANCY REAGAN, but she managed to forgive Spencer in 1980 when her husband's presidential campaign ran into trou-

ble. Spencer went back to work for the Reagans and was a key factor in their successful race for the White House in 1980.

Spencer joined the U.S. Navy at the age of 18 for the final months of World War II, then in 1946 returned to California and earned his associate's degree from East Los Angeles Junior College. He continued his education at California State University at Los Angeles, completing his degree in sociology in 1951. Spencer worked as the director of parks and recreation for the city of Alhambra, California, for most of the decade, but his real love during this time was politics. He first registered as a Democrat in 1948, but after being turned off by the liberal wing of his party and attracted to the leadership of President Dwight Eisenhower, he joined the Republican Party.

Spencer took his first political job in 1958 as a field organizer with the Los Angeles County Republican Committee. In 1960, he left his position at the parks service and started a political consulting firm, Spencer-Roberts, with friend Bill Roberts. They focused on state and local campaigns for the first few years, earning a reputation as an effective consulting firm after a series of election victories. In 1964, the firm was hired by New York governor Nelson Rockefeller to run his California primary campaign against Arizona senator Barry Goldwater. Although Rockefeller's bid was unsuccessful, the reputation of Spencer-Roberts was further enhanced by the campaign, and in 1966 Ronald Reagan hired the firm to help with his run for governor of California. Spencer and Roberts framed Reagan as a moderate during the campaign, helping Reagan defeat incumbent governor EDMUND G. BROWN by nearly a million votes. Four years later, the firm was commissioned to run Reagan's reelection campaign, when Reagan defeated Jesse Unruh, Speaker of the California State Assembly.

In October 1975 Spencer joined President GERALD FORD's campaign for the Republican nomination against Reagan, and was credited by many in the party for Ford's narrow victory at the national convention. He rejoined the Reagan team after a disastrous beginning in the 1980 primary battle and played a critical role in getting the campaign back on track. He encouraged Reagan to select GEORGE H. W. BUSH as his running mate and also to accept the challenge from JIMMY CARTER to participate in two debates. He went back to work in California following Reagan's victory in the general election, but in late 1982, following the midterm elections, he began planning with other White House aides for Reagan's reelection campaign. He returned to Washington in 1984 to coordinate the broad re-election strategy, which concentrated on the new feeling of patriotism and prosperity in America contrasted with the tax-and-spend policies of Democratic challenger Walter Mondale. In 1986 Spencer became a special political aide to the president to help Reagan deal with the fallout from the Iran-contra affair. He was among many top aides who recommended that Reagan fire White House chief of staff DONALD REGAN and publicly admit to making a mistake in selling arms to Iran, which Reagan agreed to do.

Widely recognized as a top political strategist, he was inducted in the American Association of Political Consultants' Hall of Fame in 1993. He is still active in the California office of Spencer-Roberts.

Stockman, David A.
(1946–   ) *director, Office of Management and Budget*

A controversial figure from Ronald Reagan's first term as president, David Stockman was the most prominent director of the Office of Management and Budget in the history of that office. His failed attempts to reduce government spending and control the federal deficit left him disillusioned with President Reagan and despairing about the ability of the American government to engage in a coherent budget process. Upon leaving the administration, he wrote a bitter memoir of his time in power that left many in the Reagan White House seething. This visceral response was due to the fact that the president had allowed him to stay in his OMB position despite the embarrassment Stockman caused with an interview he gave to a reporter from the *Atlantic Monthly* where he claimed, among other things, that supply-side economics was a rehashed version of trickle-down economics. Reagan's kindness, it was held, had not been repaid. Nonetheless, even his most ardent foes confessed that Stockman possessed a remarkable mastery of the intricacies of the federal budget, which most mortals found to be beyond understanding.

Stockman's family moved to Michigan shortly after his birth and David remained in the state until he completed his undergraduate studies at Michigan State University. He graduated from Michigan State in 1968 with a B.A. in American history, and then began graduate studies at Harvard University's Divinity School. He stayed in Cambridge until 1970, switching from theology to politics and never completing either degree. He then took a job as special assistant to Illinois congressman John Anderson. Two years later, Stockman became executive director of the House Republican Conference.

In 1976 Stockman ran for and won a seat in the U.S. Congress from the fourth district of Michigan. He served two terms in the House of Representatives, chairing the Republican Economic Policy Task Force throughout his entire four years in office. In 1981, Stockman became president Reagan's first Office of Management and Budget director at the age of 35, the youngest cabinet member during the 20th century.

Stockman was known in Washington as a boy genius and an eccentric who preferred spending time crunching numbers to interacting with people. He was a leading proponent of

OMB director David A. Stockman briefs President Reagan in the Oval Office, October 6, 1981.

supply-side economics, and his opinions had a major influence on fiscal policy in the early years of the Reagan administration. Many have credited Stockman with the early success of Reagan's economic policy.

However, shortly after the administration's proposals passed Congress and the nation fell into a recession, Stockman began to publicly disparage Reaganomics and the effects the president's policies were having on the economy. During a series of interviews with reporter William Greider, Stockman questioned the credibility of Reagan's economic program by attacking the trickle-down theory and blaming the growing deficits on vast miscalculations and rosy economic forecasts. These comments were made public in the December 1981 issue of the *Atlantic Monthly*, and caused a political firestorm that prompted many calls for Stockman's ouster.

Reagan resisted these calls and kept Stockman in the administration until his return to the private sector in the summer of 1985. A year later, Stockman released his memoir of the Reagan years, *The Triumph of Politics: How the Reagan Revolution Failed*, in which he criticized the entire administration, including himself, for failing to balance the budget and for abandoning the conservative goals Reagan campaigned for in 1980. He also offered unflattering profiles of Reagan and many members of his administration. Since his exit from the administration, Stockman has been a managing director at Salomon Brothers in New York City.

T

Thatcher, Margaret H.
(Baroness Thatcher of Kesteven)
(1925–) *prime minister of Great Britain*

Ronald Reagan and Margaret Thatcher were cut from the same ideological cloth. The "special relationship" between the United Kingdom and the United States was at its cold war zenith during the 1980s when Thatcher was prime minister and Reagan was in the White House. These two leaders had a profound impact on each of their nations, moving their societies in a free-market direction and leading the Western alliance in an assertive stance toward the Soviet Union. Not since the days of Franklin Roosevelt and Winston Churchill had the Anglo-American relationship been so close. Only on one occasion did this partnership come close to failing, and that was during the October 1983 American attack on Grenada, a British Commonwealth nation. Thatcher was furious at Reagan for waiting to inform her as the attack was about to occur, and used unusually strong language to condemn it. Beyond this incident, the two worked in concert on the major issues of the day. It was Mrs. Thatcher who paved the way for the famous Reagan-Gorbachev summits of the 1980s, through her early endorsement of Gorbachev's bona fides.

In 1943, Margaret Thatcher was accepted into Oxford's Somerville College, yet instead of studying in her desired field of law she was forced to study chemistry. She graduated from Somerville in 1947 with a B.Sc. in chemistry. Thatcher immediately became involved in politics while at Oxford, joining the Oxford University Conservative Association and campaigning for Conservative Party candidate Quentin Hogg in a local election. Yet upon graduation, she fell back on her chemistry degree and took a job as a research chemist for a plastics company in Essex, outside of London. She quickly realized that chemistry was not her preferred career choice, so in 1950 she began her studies in law.

A life in politics, however, remained the real goal for Thatcher. In 1950, she attempted to enter the political arena in her own right, but lost her bid for a seat in the House of Commons from the industrial town of Dartford. She then returned to studying law at night, passing the bar exam in December 1953, and going on to practice tax and patent law for the next several years. She made a second bid for Parliament in 1959, this time from her district in Finchley. Her campaign was successful and at 34, Margaret Thatcher became the youngest woman in Parliament.

Thatcher served her district in the House of Commons for the next 20 years before becoming party leader in 1979. Although she worked only in junior parliamentary positions for her first 10 years in office, she earned a reputation as a competent and dedicated party official. She received her first senior post with the victory of the Tories and Edward Heath in 1970, becoming secretary of state for education and science, and the only woman in the Heath cabinet.

By 1974, the Conservative Party in Britain was in a state of disarray. The Heath government, bowing to pressure from the trade unions and the Labour Party, had all but abandoned its conservative policies in favor of Keynesian fiscal policy and monetary expansion, a practice chided as the "U-Turn" by the opposition and disgruntled Tories alike. After failing to bring a recovery to the British economy, in March 1974 the Tories were voted out of power. In 1975, frustrated at the direction of the Tory Party and the leadership's seeming lack of commitment to conservative values, Thatcher decided to challenge Heath for the position of party leader. In a stunning vote on the second ballot, Thatcher defeated Heath and became the new leader of the Conservative Party. The next four years marked a dark period in British history, encompassing labor unrest, high unemployment, and even a loan from the International Monetary Fund. A series of paralyzing labor strikes in late 1978, dubbed the "Winter of Discontent," exposed the impotence of the Callaghan government in confronting union power, and led to a vote of "no confidence" in Parliament on March 28, 1979.

Thatcher's conservative philosophy developed a large following during the Wilson and Callaghan governments, and in May 1979, after the Tory victory in the general election, she became Britain's first woman prime minister. She came into office with specific goals in both foreign and domestic policy. Thatcher believed in a strong defense, the importance of nuclear deterrence, and a close relationship with the United States. She was also a steadfast proponent of Britain's sovereignty and independence; thus, she approached the growing debate on European integration with skepticism and unease. At home, Thatcher sought to dramatically reform the welfare state, curb union power, and bring privatization to many British industries.

Thatcher's first two years in office were difficult, as unemployment continued to rise at home, and after her retreat and compromise on Rhodesia policy, she had yet to earn respect as a competent leader abroad. By 1982 it looked as though Thatcher's tenure would be a short one, but following her decisive and popular leader-

President Reagan and Prime Minister Margaret Thatcher on the South Lawn during her arrival ceremony, February 26, 1981

ship in the Falklands War she easily won reelection in 1983. Her second term was the most successful, as she aggressively pursued her agenda for privatization, ending union power, and restoring the British economy. She was largely successful in her efforts, privatizing more than 30 industries, defeating the National Union of Mineworkers' strike, and bringing inflation from 21 percent in 1980 down to 3 percent in 1986. She also earned a reputation as a strong world leader with her key involvement in the cold war and her forceful opposition to the growth of the European Community. In addition, she forged an unusually close relationship with President Reagan, exceeded only by the wartime alliance of Franklin Roosevelt and Winston Churchill.

In June 1987, the Tories won their third consecutive election, and Thatcher continued to push for her conservative agenda. Yet after the economy began to falter with increasing unemployment and inflation returned to double digits, her popularity faded and a rising tide of anti-Thatcher sentiment grew in Britain. After the massive outcry from the British public in April 1990 over the poll tax, many senior Tories felt it was time for a change in leadership. Thatcher failed to win the party leadership after a challenge by her former defense minister, Michael Heseltine, and on November 22, 1990, Thatcher resigned as leader of the Tories. John Major, former chancellor of the Exchequer, succeeded Thatcher as prime minister after the Conservative victory in the next general election.

After leaving office, Thatcher wrote several books, including two volumes of memoirs, *The Downing Street Years* and *The Path to Power*, and other political commentaries such as *Statecraft*. She now sits in the House of Lords as Baroness Thatcher of Kesteven. The central tenets of what is now known as "Thatcherism" have left an imprint on the British political landscape that is still apparent today. Her

efforts at privatization, reducing the role of the national government, and ending the imposing power of trade unions have all become ingrained in British society. Her belief in a strong defense, a close relationship with the United States, and a cautious approach to European integration have also remained central themes in British foreign and defense policy.

Thornburgh, Richard L.
(1932–) *attorney general*

After two terms as governor of Pennsylvania, Richard Thornburgh joined the Reagan administration as attorney general in 1988 and was charged with restoring confidence in an office tarnished by years of investigations into the conduct of former attorney general EDWIN MEESE. Leaving the Justice Department in 1991, he was defeated in a special election for a vacant Senate seat in Pennsylvania, which served as something of a trial run for the presidential election of 1992.

Thornburgh earned a degree in engineering from Yale University in 1954, then moved to the University of Pittsburgh to study law. After receiving his law degree, he worked for several firms before settling down at Kirkpatrick, Lockhart, and Johnson, a prestigious Pittsburgh law firm, in 1959. From 1967 to 1969, Thornburgh was appointed to the boards of several major organizations, including the Urban League of Pittsburgh and the American Civil Liberties Union of Pittsburgh.

In 1969 President Nixon named Thornburgh the U.S. attorney for western Pennsylvania. He stayed at this post until 1975 when he became assistant attorney general for the criminal division of the U.S. Department of Justice. President GERALD FORD selected Thornburgh for this position due to his reputation for honesty and asked him to initiate a series of ethical reforms in the Justice Department in the wake of the Watergate scandal. His most lasting achievement was the creation of the public integrity office, established to investigate ethical violations within the department.

When Ford left office in 1977, Thornburgh returned to Pittsburgh and became a partner in his old law firm. A year later, he decided to make a bid for public office, running for and winning the governorship of Pennsylvania. When he entered office, Pennsylvania had one of the 10 highest unemployment rates of any state in the nation. By the time he left in 1987, the rate had dropped dramatically and Pennsylvania was in the top 10 states with the lowest unemployment. He also succeeded in balancing the state budget all of his eight years in office, reforming education and welfare programs, and leaving a $350 million surplus. He left the governor's office after two terms and moved into academia as director of the Institute of Politics at Harvard's John F. Kennedy School of Government.

In 1988, Thornburgh was named attorney general for the Reagan administration after the resignation of EDWIN MEESE. Serving only the remaining six months of the Reagan administration, Thornburgh focused largely on white-collar crime and the war on drugs. In 1989 President GEORGE H. W. BUSH retained Thornburgh as attorney general where he remained until 1991. He continued to work on the issues of drugs and white-collar crime, as well as legislation dealing with hate crimes, terrorism, and environmental issues. His most important work as attorney general was in securing the passage of the Americans with Disabilities Act in July 1990, an accomplishment he called "one of the proudest moments" of his life.

Thornburgh left the Justice Department in July 1991 to run for the U.S. Senate. He lost the election to Harris Wofford, but a year later he was named Under-Secretary-General of the United Nations, where he remained until 1993. While at the UN, he urged the U.S.

government to act like a superpower and pay over 1 billion in past dues to the organization. After leaving this position, he returned to his old law firm, where he currently serves as a counsel in the Washington office.

Tower, John G.
(1926–1991) U.S. senator

John Tower left a decade-long career in academia in 1961 to enter national politics, enjoying four terms as a U.S. senator from Texas and becoming known as a leading expert on arms control and national defense policy. After retiring from the Senate in 1985, Tower served in a number of important positions, including chief U.S. negotiator for the START II arms control talks with the Soviet Union, and chairman of the President's Special Review Board investigating the Iran-contra affair, commonly known as the Tower Commission. His nomination to serve as secretary of defense in the first Bush administration was rejected after a bitter fight with his former colleagues, a setback he found particularly difficult to accept. He died shortly thereafter in a plane crash in Georgia.

Tower grew up in Texas, and following military service in World War II, he returned to his home state to attend Southwestern University. He earned his B.A. in 1948, then began working in radio for the next two years. He entered graduate studies at the London School of Economics and Political Science, and Southern Methodist University, receiving a master's degree in 1953. He had begun a career in teaching two years earlier, serving as an assistant professor of political science at Midwestern State University in Wichita Falls, Texas. He stayed at this job until 1960 when he decided to leave academia for a career in politics.

Still very young at just 35 years of age, Tower surprised many when he won a seat in the U.S. Senate, becoming the first Republican senator in Texas since 1877. He immediately became associated with the rising conservative wing of the GOP when he wrote *A Program for Conservatives* in 1962. The book contained a foreword by the most visible leader of the conservative movement, Barry Goldwater, whom Tower ardently supported in his 1964 run for the White House. As the war in Vietnam progressed, Tower earned a reputation as a hawk on military affairs. He eventually became known as one of the Senate's foremost experts on defense policy. He also became a staunch supporter for several issues that affected his home state, including agriculture, fishing, and energy. He won reelection to the Senate three more times, in 1966, 1972, and 1978, slowly rising in seniority and gaining key committee appointments.

Tower was named chairman of the Senate Armed Services Committee in 1980 at a critical time in the cold war. After the election of Ronald Reagan in 1980, Tower became one of the president's key allies in the Senate, providing unwavering support for Reagan's defense buildup and advocating funding for new military technologies. In 1984, after nearly 25 years in the Senate, Tower decided not to seek a fifth term. Following his departure from the Senate, President Reagan named Tower his chief negotiator at the Strategic Arms Reduction Talks with the Soviet Union in Geneva. He served at this post for the next 15 months during one of the most critical times in U.S.-Soviet arms control negotiations.

Tower returned to Texas in 1986 and accepted a position as a political science lecturer at Southern Methodist University. Shortly after he began at SMU, he was called back to Washington to chair the board investigating the Iran-contra scandal. The President's Special Review Board, commonly known as the Tower Commission, delivered a strong rebuke to President Reagan and many administration officials, but the report absolved the president from any criminal charges. Tower remained in Washington after the investigation and took a job as chairman of Tower, Eggers, and Greene Consulting.

In 1989, President Bush nominated Tower to head the Department of Defense, but his nomination ran into fierce opposition from both sides of the aisle, including Senate Armed Services Committee Chairman Sam Nunn (D-Ga.). He endured five weeks of congressional hearings in which his reputation was called into question by stories of womanizing and heavy drinking. His nomination was ultimately rejected; nonetheless, President Bush, appreciating Tower's expertise on defense policy, selected him to serve as chairman of his Foreign Intelligence Advisory Board.

Tower went back to his consulting firm after the rejection and in 1991 he released a memoir, titled *Consequences: A Personal and Political Memoir.* The book offered a candid look at the humiliation and anger that came from the failed nomination, and Tower was openly critical of several sitting senators. During a book publicity tour, Tower, one of his daughters, and 21 other passengers died when their plane crashed near Brunswick, Georgia.

V–W

Verity, C. William, Jr.
(1917–   ) *secretary of commerce*

By the early 1980s Armco chairman C. William Verity, Jr., had established himself as a major figure in the business community, earning appointments as chairman of the U.S. Chamber of Commerce and chairman of President Reagan's Task Force on Private Sector Initiatives. Following the tragic death of MALCOLM BALDRIGE in 1987, Verity served as Reagan's commerce secretary until the end of his second term.

Verity earned his B.A. in economics from Yale University in 1939. He worked in a number of industries over the next few years, including the advertising firm Young and Rubicam and as manager of the Hapsburg House restaurant. In 1942 he joined the U.S. Navy to fight in World War II, serving in the Pacific theater until 1946. Following the war, he took a job with Armco in his hometown of Middletown, Ohio. He started off working in the personnel department, but moved quickly up the corporate ladder to become vice president in 1965, then chairman of the board just six years later.

Verity's ascension to the top of Armco Corporation, earned him a great deal of respect in the business world and he was selected to serve on several major boards and commissions. From 1979 to 1984, he served as cochairman of the U.S.–USSR Trade Economic Council. In 1980 and 1981, he was chairman of the U.S. Chamber of Commerce. Also in 1981, he was named chairman of President Reagan's Task Force on Private Sector Initiatives, the bipartisan group organized to foster greater cooperation between government and private business and industry. In October 1987 Verity joined Reagan's cabinet as secretary of commerce, succeeding Malcolm Baldrige, who had recently died in a rodeo accident. He remained in the Reagan administration until the end of the term in January 1989.

Walesa, Lech
(1943–   ) *president of Poland*

Lech Walesa led the Polish Solidarity movement in its struggle for better economic and working conditions throughout the 1980s. Solidarity eventually grew to more than 10 million members and brought the first collapse of a communist government in Eastern Europe in 1989, and a year later, Walesa became the first freely elected Polish president since World War II. Walesa's movement was supported both rhetorically and in a substantive way by the Reagan administration through covert assistance provided by the Central Intelligence Agency.

Walesa went to work as an electrician at the Lenin Shipyard in the Baltic port city of Gdansk immediately after finishing his mandatory three year military service in the Polish army in 1965. The plight of Polish workers under the communist government made an immediate impression on Walesa, leading him to become an active member of the communist-controlled labor union organization. Over the next several years, he pursued the normal avenues of arbitration with government authorities, but it was apparent that the government only paid lip service to the union's demands and any changes that were made were largely symbolic. In December 1970 rising prices and harsh economic conditions led to a series of workers strikes on the Baltic coast, prompting a violent response from the government, which sent in military units and killed dozens of shipyard workers in quelling the demonstrations. Walesa then became chairman of the Strike Committee at the Lenin Shipyard and negotiated an agreement with Edward Gierek, first secretary of the Polish Communist Party, gaining a number of concessions by the government on behalf of Polish workers.

As the government failed to honor the provisions of the agreement over the next few years, Walesa became an outspoken advocate of workers' rights and a leader in the growing trade union movement. On April 29, 1978, he joined with other leading union activists in Gdansk to draft the Charter of Workers' Rights and form the underground Baltic Committee of Independent Trade Unions. Walesa continued in his post on the government-sanctioned trade union while secretly meeting with the Baltic committee. In December 1978 he joined with other union activists and organized a memorial service at the Lenin Shipyard for the 45 workers killed in the December 1970

strikes. They organized a second service commemorating the 1970 strikes a year later at the Lenin Shipyard, along with a massive demonstration in which Walesa called for the legal formation of independent trade unions. Walesa and several of his colleagues lost their jobs as a result of the demonstration, but they continued their efforts to legalize independent unions.

Workers at the Lenin Shipyard organized another series of strikes in August 1980 in response to rising food prices. Walesa, no longer an employee at the shipyard, climbed the 12-foot fence surrounding the shipyard and took control of the demonstration. After three days of negotiations with government officials, he widened the strike to included sympathy strikers in the Gdansk area, forcing Deputy Prime Minister Mieczyslaw Jagielski to begin talks with Walesa. On August 23, the government agreed to recognize workers' right to strike and to elect members to their own independent trade unions, and a week later he signed the Gdansk Agreement ending the strike and beginning a new era in the Polish union movement. Shortly after the agreement, the Strike Committee was transformed into Solidarity, the first free workers' union in Eastern Europe, and Walesa was elected leader of the union.

The next six months were a period of calm in Poland, as Solidarity and the Communist Party showed signs of peaceful coexistence, yet behind this public facade the government was working on ways to dismantle the new trade union. They initiated a massive propaganda campaign against Solidarity and violently suppressed several local chapters of the union, leading to a breakdown of talks between Walesa and the government in August 1981, on the eve of Solidarity's first national congress, when Walesa was reelected chairman of the union. After several more months of strikes and demonstrations, Archbishop Jozef Glemp and

First Secretary General WOJCIECH JARUZEL-SKI organized a summit with Walesa. The government proposed the formation of a Council for National Agreement to foster a workable relationship between the Communist Party, the Catholic Church, and Solidarity, but Walesa rejected the proposal after realizing that the church and Solidarity would have only symbolic power.

After losing its bid to peacefully limit union power, the Polish military cracked down on Solidarity on December 13, 1981, imprisoning most of its leaders, including Walesa, and declaring martial law throughout the country. The Reagan administration responded by choosing not to continue a host of U.S.-Polish agreements expiring that year, and levying sanctions against the Polish government. In June 1982 Reagan had a meeting with POPE JOHN PAUL II in which both leaders pledged to undertake clandestine operations to maintain Solidarity and destabilize the Polish Communists. Later that summer the United States, in association with the Vatican, the AFL-CIO, and the National Endowment for Democracy, began clandestine activities against the Polish government. Bolstered by international support, Solidarity, declared illegal by the government in October 1982, built a broad clandestine network that kept a close relationship with Walesa during his 11 months in prison.

Walesa was released from prison in November 1982 and returned to work at the Lenin Shipyard shortly after the lifting of martial law in August 1983. For his efforts at improving working conditions and human rights in Poland, he was awarded the 1983 Nobel Peace Prize, which he dedicated to the millions of members of the outlawed Solidarity. Over the next five years, Walesa urged the government to resume talks with the trade unions, but little progress was made toward an acceptable agreement until widespread strikes occurred in the summer of 1988. The Polish government, now facing a potential revolution as a result of a worsening social and economic situation in the country, agreed to meet with leaders of Solidarity and construct a power-sharing agreement.

Partially free elections took place in June 1989, in which every Solidarity candidate won election to the Polish parliament. After the Communists failed to form a government, a new coalition, led by Solidarity, consolidated power in August, and Tadeusz Mazowiecki was named the first noncommunist prime minister of Poland since World War II. Walesa refused any government post, instead running for reelection as leader of Solidarity at its second national congress in April 1990. As relations worsened between Solidarity and the new Mazowiecki government, Walesa began calling for full legislative and presidential elections, which were eventually held in December 1990. Walesa won in the final round of voting by a 3 to 1 margin, and became president of Poland on December 22, 1990.

Walesa's popularity steadily declined during his presidency, as Poland struggled to cope with the difficult transition from communism to democracy. His government initiated a "shock therapy" approach that dismantled the fiscal policies of the communist government all at once and replaced them with free-market principles. There were signs of improvement in the overall health of the economy after just one year, with the trade deficit turning into a surplus and the growth rate around 6 percent, but the general public only noticed the drop in wages and output, and the rise in unemployment and food prices. As a result, Walesa was defeated by Communist Aleksander Kwasniewski in the 1995 presidential election.

Since his fall from power, Walesa's popularity in Poland has continued to fall. He ran for president again in 2000, but received only 1 percent of the popular vote, prompting his resignation as chairman of the Christian Democratic Party. He currently serves as vice president of the Lech Walesa Institute Foundation and speaks frequently on political issues around the world.

Walsh, Lawrence E.
(1912–) *independent counsel, Iran-contra investigation*

In December 1986 Lawrence Walsh was named an independent counsel to investigate the illegal sale of arms to Iran and the diversion of the funds to the Nicaraguan contras, known as the Iran-contra affair. After a six-year investigation, Walsh brought indictments against several Reagan administration officials and won a number of convictions, only to see these officials pardoned by President GEORGE H. W. BUSH in the final weeks of his presidency.

When Walsh was two years old, his family emigrated to the United States from Nova Scotia, and Walsh became a naturalized U.S. citizen at the age of 10. He attended Columbia University and earned an A.B. in 1932, then continued on to complete a law degree three years later. After passing the New York bar exam he was named deputy assistant district attorney under Thomas Dewey. In 1941 he entered private practice as an associate at Davis, Polk, Wardwell, Sunderland, and Kiendl in New York. Walsh moved to Albany to continue working under Dewey when Dewey won the New York governor's race in 1942, serving as Dewey's assistant counsel, then counsel to the governor, and also as counsel to the New York Public Service Commission. In 1954, Walsh was named to the federal district court for the southern district of New York by President Dwight Eisenhower. Although this was a lifetime appointment, after just three years on the bench he resigned to become deputy attorney general, working under his longtime friend, Attorney General William Rogers.

In 1960 Walsh left public service and returned to his old law firm, this time as a partner, where he stayed for the next 10 years and developed a reputation as a successful corporate lawyer. He returned to political life again in 1969 as President Richard Nixon's personal representative at the Paris peace talks after recommendation by William Rogers, then secretary of state. He left Paris after less than a year and returned to his law firm. He continued with this firm until 1981, also serving in a number of organizations and commissions, including president of the American Bar Association from 1975 to 1976. In 1981, he moved to Oklahoma City and joined the law firm of Crowe and Dunlevy, where he remained for the duration of his career.

In December 1986, Walsh took his most prominent appointment when he was named as the independent counsel for the Iran-contra investigation. He conducted a thorough, six-year investigation of everyone involved in the scandal, up to and including President Reagan. He also convicted several members of the administration, including Lt. Col. OLIVER NORTH and former National Security Advisor JOHN POINDEXTER, although these convictions were later overturned by an appeals court when a judge ruled that immunized congressional testimony had been used in their trials. Walsh also indicted former defense secretary CASPAR WEINBERGER after it was alleged that he knew more about the operation than he had acknowledged. In December 1992 President Bush pardoned Weinberger along with several other administration officials. A frustrated Walsh resigned shortly after the pardons and returned to his law practice in Oklahoma City. There he wrote two books on the investigation, *Final Report of the Independent Counsel* and *Firewall: The Iran-Contra Conspiracy and Cover-up.*

Watt, James G.
(1938–   ) *secretary of the interior*

Ronald Reagan's first secretary of the interior had a penchant for controversy, and left office in 1983, to the great relief of the president's more politically sensitive advisers. James Watt personified the so-called sagebrush rebellion, a movement in the western United States that sought to reverse the federal government's proclivity to acquire vast quantities of land and restrict ranching and mining and lumber interests from using those lands.

Watt attended the University of Wyoming and received his B.S. in 1960, then continued on at Wyoming to receive his law degree in 1962. He passed the Wyoming bar exam in the same year, but instead of entering a legal career, Watt chose a job in politics, becoming a legislative assistant to Wyoming senator Milward L. Simpson. He stayed in this position until 1966, when he became secretary to the U.S. Chamber of Commerce Natural Resources Committee and Environmental Pollution Advisory Panel. In 1969 Watt joined the Nixon administration as the Interior Department's deputy assistant secretary of water and power development. Three years later, he became director of the Bureau of Outdoor Recreation in Washington, D.C. Watt became vice chairman of the Federal Power Commission in 1975.

In 1977, Watt became president and chief legal officer for the Mountain States Legal Foundation, a Denver-based advocacy group that frequently challenged the nation's leading environmental organizations. His work for this group caught the attention of Reagan administration officials and in 1981 Watt was confirmed as secretary of the interior.

Almost immediately after his confirmation, Watt became the target of sharp criticism and fierce opposition. He was a passionate conservative who overwhelmingly supported industry and development over environmental concerns. Policy initiatives such as deregulation of mining, oil drilling along the Pacific coast, and the development of wilderness lands led to attacks from every major environmental group, all of whom Watt gladly confronted. He also drew criticism for some off-the-cuff remarks that offended, among others, Jews, African Americans, and handicapped Americans. By 1983 he had become a lightning rod for criticism, and the administration's environmental and deregulation agendas were suffering greatly from Watt's presence in the cabinet. On October 9, 1983, Watt resigned his post and was replaced by William Clark.

Following his resignation from the Reagan administration, Watt remained in Washington, D.C., and worked as a business consultant. In 1985, he and coauthor Doug Wead wrote *The Courage of a Conservative*, which examined the decline in conservative values in America and the danger of a secularized society. Watt joined the faculty at the University of Wyoming's College of Commerce and Industry in 1986.

Webster, William H.
(1924–   ) *FBI director, CIA director*

In less than 25 years in law, William Webster rose to the top of his field, earning appointments to the U.S. District Court and the U.S. Court of Appeals. He moved to the executive branch in 1978, serving as director of the Federal Bureau of Investigation, then director of Central Intelligence for President Reagan, restoring confidence in both agencies in the wake of the Watergate and Iran-contra scandals.

Webster joined the student body at Amherst College in Massachusetts after high school, but left shortly after to join the U.S. Navy and serve in World War II. Following the war, he returned to Amherst and earned his B.A. in 1947. He moved back to his home state of Missouri to study law at Washington

University Law School, completing his J.D. in 1949. He began a career in law immediately, passing the Missouri bar exam and joining a private practice in St. Louis, although his career was interrupted once again when he chose to serve in the Korean War for two years. He returned to his firm after the war and remained in private practice until 1960.

Webster was appointed to his first government post in 1960, serving as the U.S. attorney for the Eastern District of Missouri. After four years as U.S. attorney, he went back to private practice while also serving on the Missouri Board of Law Examiners until 1969. Webster was named to the U.S. District Court in 1970 by President Nixon and three years later was appointed to the U.S. Court of Appeals for the Eighth Circuit, a stepping-stone for many Supreme Court justices.

In 1978, Webster left the bench to become director of the FBI. The FBI was a damaged agency when Webster took over; under the leadership of J. Edgar Hoover, it had come under fire for its involvement in disrupting the antiwar and civil rights movements of the 1960s. More recently, the FBI had been implicated in the Watergate coverup, and new improprieties by the bureau came to light during the congressional intelligence investigations of 1975 and 1976, further eroding public confidence in the agency. When President JIMMY CARTER selected Webster in 1978, he purposely brought in a man known for his integrity to restore public confidence in the FBI. During his 10 years as FBI director, Webster succeeded in creating a more positive image of the FBI through his efforts in battling political corruption, white-collar crime, and drug trafficking.

In 1987 President Reagan called on Webster to restore confidence to another ailing agency, the CIA. Much like the FBI, public confidence in the CIA had been severely damaged during the Pike and Church congres-

sional intelligence hearings in the 1970s. During the 1980s, under the directorship of WILLIAM CASEY, the CIA's reputation further declined as a result of several questionable covert operations coming to light, most notably the Iran contra affair. When Webster took over as DCI, he worked hard to establish a relationship with Congress and keep members of the intelligence committees adequately informed of the agency's operations. He was praised for bringing a greater degree of cooperation and transparency to the CIA when he retired in 1991.

Following his retirement, Webster was appointed to several important investigative commissions, including the President's Advisory Council on Homeland Security, the National Commission on the Future of DNA Evidence, and the Statutory Commission on the Advancement of Federal Law Enforcement. In October 2002 he was named chairman of the Securities and Exchange Commission's Public Company Accounting Oversight Board. However, questions arose about his ties to big business and his lack of financial expertise, and after two weeks of strong opposition Webster resigned his post.

Weinberger, Caspar
(1917–) *secretary of defense*

A longtime Reagan ally from his service in Governor Reagan's cabinet in California, Caspar Weinberger presided over the largest defense buildup in American history. Deeply loyal to the president throughout his nearly seven years as secretary of defense, Weinberger was a zealous foe of communism and shared the president's view that the Soviet Union was an evil empire. He quietly left his Defense post in 1987, concerned that Reagan's arms agreements with Soviet leader MIKHAIL GORBACHEV were detrimental to American security

Secretary of Defense Caspar Weinberger presents a Department of Defense publication "Soviet Military Power" to President Reagan in the Oval Office, March 8, 1983.

and undermining the resolve of the West. Nonetheless, despite his hawkish views toward the Soviet Union, Weinberger frequently counseled against the use of force, often to the dismay of his longtime colleague, Secretary of State GEORGE SHULTZ.

Caspar Weinberger left his home in San Francisco to attend Harvard University in 1934, graduating magna cum laude in 1938. Concerned about the growing threat of Nazi Germany, he attempted to join the Royal Canadian Air Force in 1940 to fight in the Battle of Britain alongside other American volunteers. Weinberger was not allowed to join the air force due to his poor depth perception, so he went back to Harvard to study law. In 1941 he completed his law degree, then, with America's entry into World War II, he immediately enlisted in the U.S. Army. Weinberger fought with the 41st Infantry in the South Pacific, then joined General Douglas MacArthur's

intelligence staff toward the end of the war. He received a Bronze Star for his service and reached the rank of captain by the time he left the army in 1945.

After the war, Weinberger returned to California with his family and got a job as a law clerk to U.S. Court of Appeals judge William E. Orr. Two years later, he entered private law practice with San Francisco-based Heller, Ehrman, White, and McAuliffe. He stayed with this firm for the next 22 years, becoming a partner in 1959. Weinberger became actively involved in California politics during this time. In 1952, he won a seat in the California state legislature, a post he held until 1958. He was very successful in this post, being selected in 1958 as the most effective member of the legislature in a California poll.

Weinberger was a major figure in the California Republican Party by the 1960s. During his service as vice chairman of the California GOP, he helped to recruit a B-movie actor named Ronald Reagan to speak on conservative issues. He and Reagan became good friends, and Weinberger joined his administration as director of finance in 1968. After the election of Richard Nixon in 1968, Weinberger moved to Washington, to become chairman of the Federal Trade Commission. He was then appointed as deputy director of the Office of Management and Budget. In 1972, Weinberger took over as director of the OMB, where his penchant for budget cutting earned him the nickname "Cap the Knife." After less than two years as head of OMB, Weinberger was appointed as secretary of health, education, and welfare.

After he left HEW, Weinberger accepted senior positions in several major corporations, including director of PepsiCo in New York and director of Quaker Oats Company in Chicago. In 1975, he moved back to California and joined Bechtel Corporation as a vice president and general counsel. It was not long, however, before he was back in Washington, accepting the appointment as defense secretary in the Reagan administration in 1981. Weinberger was one of the chief architects of Reagan's defense policy, which doubled the military budget and led to the largest peacetime arms buildup in the nation's history. He believed strongly in the restoration of American military superiority as a necessary check on the Soviet Union and other communist governments. As a result, he opposed many arms control agreements, particularly in the early years of the Reagan administration, that he believed would hinder America's ability to defeat the Soviets in an arms race.

Weinberger left the Reagan administration in November 1987 and stayed in Washington as counsel at Rogers and Wells international law firm. He also continued to work with the Reagan administration as a member of the president's Foreign Intelligence Advisory Board and the National Economic Commission. In January 1989, he became the publisher of *Forbes* magazine in New York City. He released two memoirs that covered his experiences in the Reagan administration, *Fighting for Peace: Seven Critical Years in the Pentagon* and *In the Arena: A Memoir of the Twentieth Century*. Weinberger currently lives in Washington and is chairman of *Forbes* magazine.

Wright, James C., Jr.
(1922–) *Speaker, U.S. House of Representatives*

In 1987, after 32 years in the U.S. House of Representatives, James C. Wright, Jr., succeeded THOMAS (TIP) O'NEILL as Speaker of the House, but retired from politics less than three years later after becoming implicated in a series of financial scandals. As House majority leader during the Reagan administration, he served as a forceful opponent of the Reagan

agenda, almost single-handedly derailing the administration's policy in Central America.

Wright studied for two years at Weatherford College and the University of Texas after high school before entering the U.S. Army in December 1941 to fight in World War II. He served for six years as a pilot in the U.S. Army Air Force, flying combat missions in the South Pacific and earning a Distinguished Flying Cross. Following the war, Wright went directly into politics, winning a seat in the Texas state legislature. He quickly established himself as a liberal Democrat with his support of civil rights legislation. His voting record on this issue contributed to the loss of his seat in the state House of Representatives after just one term. The following year he became mayor of Weatherford, Texas, serving at this post until 1954. He also became president of the League of Texas Municipalities in 1953.

In 1955, after defeating incumbent Wingate Lucas in the Democratic primary, Wright entered national politics with a seat in the U.S. House of Representatives from the 12th District of Texas. He would stay at this position for the next 34 years, winning reelection 17 times and becoming one of the most powerful members of Congress. In 1977 Wright became the House majority leader for the Democratic Party. When Ronald Reagan took over the White House in 1981, Wright and Speaker of the House Tip O'Neill were strongly opposed to the president's policies, particularly regarding aid to the contras in Central America and supply-side economics.

In 1987 Wright became Speaker of the House, taking over from the retiring O'Neill. Shortly after his appointment, allegations of improper financial dealings were directed at the new Speaker. The watchdog group Common Cause charged Wright with taking royalty checks inflated from his book, *Reflections of a Public Man* (disguised to evade congressional regulations), and asked the House Ethics Committee to investigate the charges. He was also implicated in a second scandal, this one involving ties to federal regulators involved in failing savings and loan companies. House Republicans, led by Georgia congressman Newt Gingrich, pressed the Speaker for more than a year to answer his accusers, forcing Wright's retirement after just one term at the top of the House leadership. Although he was never convicted on any of the charges, on May 31, 1989, after more than three decades in the House, Wright retired from political life and returned to Texas.

APPENDICES

CHRONOLOGY

1911

February 6—Reagan is born to John and Nelle Reagan in Tampico, Illinois.

1928

August—Reagan enters Eureka College for studies in economics.

1932

Reagan gets his first job out of college, working for WOC radio in Davenport, Iowa.

1937

Warner Brothers signs Reagan to a seven-year studio contract.

1940

January 26—Reagan is married to fellow actress, Jane Wyman. Reagan stars in *Knute Rockne, All American* as Notre Dame football player George Gipp, gaining the nickname "the Gipper."

1941

January 4—Maureen, Reagan's first daughter, is born.

December—Reagan is drafted into the army but because of poor vision joins the Motion Picture Army Unit to produce training and propaganda films.

1945

March—Reagan and Wyman adopt a son, Michael Edward Reagan.

1946

November—While mediating between unions for the Screen Actors Guild, Reagan's exposure to communist activity in the unions leads to a lifelong disdain for their methods and ideology.

1947

June 26—Jane Wyman gives birth four months prematurely to a baby girl. Their third child, Christine, dies the following day. Reagan is elected president of the Screen Actors Guild. During his tenure, he testifies as a friendly witness before the House Un-American Activities Committee. The committee pressures Hollywood to blacklist suspected communists in the movie industry.

1948

June 6—Reagan and Jane Wyman are divorced.

1950

Reagan campaigns for California Democrat Helen Gahagan Douglas in her bid for the U.S. Senate against Richard Nixon.

1952

Reagan urges fellow Democrats to vote for Dwight D. Eisenhower in the 1952 election.

March 4—Reagan marries actress Nancy Davis.

October 22—Nancy gives birth to Patricia (Patti) Ann, the Reagans' first child.

1954

January—General Electric hires Reagan to host the Sunday evening television program, *G.E. Theater.*

1956

Reagan stumps again as a Democrat for President Eisenhower.

1958

May 28—Nancy gives birth to Ronald (Ron) Prescott, their second and last child.

1960

Reagan, still a Democrat, campaigns for former vice president Richard Nixon in the 1960 election against John F. Kennedy. He gives more than 200 speeches during the campaign in support of Nixon.

1962

Reagan is fired from his job with General Electric after giving a political speech labeling the Tennessee Valley Authority, a major source of business for G.E., an example of "big government." Reagan becomes a registered Republican. Reagan's mother, Nelle, dies of what is later suspected to be Alzheimer's disease.

1964

Reagan stars as a villain in the last film of his acting career, *The Killers*. Reagan is hired to become the host of Death Valley Days.

October 27—Stumping for Arizona senator Barry Goldwater in his presidential campaign, Reagan delivers his most important political speech to date. The speech, entitled "A Time for Choosing," criticizes big government and the massive spending of the Johnson administration. After Goldwater's defeat in the general election, many begin to look at Reagan as the new leader of the conservative movement.

1965

Reagan writes his autobiography, *Where's the Rest of Me?*

1966

January 1—Reagan announces his candidacy for governor of California.

November 8—After campaigning on a platform of reducing waste in government and confronting the student movement, Reagan defeats incumbent governor Edmund G. (Pat) Brown by nearly 1 million votes.

1967

January 3—Reagan is sworn in as governor of California. Facing a $200 million deficit in the state budget, and constitutionally required to balance the budget, Reagan proposes a 10 percent across-the-board spending cut.

February 2—Responding to proposed budget cuts in the University of California system, students organize a demonstration in front of the Capitol Building in Sacramento. Two days later, a larger demonstration occurs in the same place.

June 15—Reagan signs the Therapeutic Abortion Act. He later expresses his regret over signing this law because it made it easier for a woman in California to get an abortion.

October 25—Reagan calls on the government to take a tougher approach to protestors of the Vietnam War.

1968

May 2—Lyn Nofziger, a Reagan aide, and a group of wealthy California friends begin a campaign to draft Reagan for the 1968 GOP presidential nomination.

August 5—At the Republican Convention in Miami, Reagan announces his candidacy for the party's presidential nomination. The effort fails, and Reagan endorses Richard Nixon's candidacy.

1969

Reagan sends the National Guard to the University of California at Berkeley to quell a massive student strike. They remain at the campus for 17 days. This event greatly polarizes opinion on Reagan. Reports indicate that California's budget increased during Reagan's first term in office, contrary to his promise to reduce the budget by this month.

1970

Reagan defeats Jesse Unruh, Democratic leader of the California Assembly, and earns a second term as California governor. Reagan continues his attack on the excesses of welfare spending by characterizing the program as the biggest drain on state and local budgets.

1971

August 11—The California legislature passes a compromise welfare bill, which is seen by many as a success for Reagan.

1973

January 18—After submitting a budget with a $1.1 billion surplus, Reagan gives a rebate to all of the state's taxpayers.

May 1—Reagan publicly defends President Nixon during the Watergate scandal.

1974

August 6—Three days before Nixon's resignation, Reagan finally admits the president deceived the nation.

August 9—President Nixon resigns; Gerald Ford becomes the 38th president.

November 5—Jerry Brown, son of former governor Pat Brown, wins the California governor's election.

1975

November 20—Reagan officially begins his campaign for the 1976 Republican presidential nomination against incumbent president Gerald Ford.

1976

February 24—Reagan loses a close contest to Ford in the New Hampshire primary.

February 27—Reagan receives the endorsement of only one former Republican National Committee chairman. The other 11 endorse President Ford.

March 17—Reagan is under pressure to withdraw from the election by the National Republican Conference of Mayors. Three days later, a group of Republican governors call on Reagan to leave the race.

March 23—After Reagan runs out of campaign funds, his advisers suggest that he withdraw from the race. Reagan insists he will stay in until the convention, and after giving a national speech attacking Ford's policy of détente, he wins the North Carolina primary by seven percentage points.

August 18—At the Republican National Convention in Kansas City, Reagan narrowly loses the nomination to Ford, winning 47.4 percent of the delegates.

August 19—Following Ford's acceptance speech, Reagan is asked to come to the stage and address the convention. He delivers one of his most memorable speeches, stressing the need to fight for the preservation of freedom.

November—President Ford loses the presidential election to Democrat Jimmy Carter.

1978

Islamic fundamentalists, under the leadership of Ayatollah Khomeini, overthrow the U.S.-backed Iranian government of Mohammad Reza Pahlavi and declare martial law to prevent protests against the new government. The change of power comes as a shock to the U.S. government and the public.

1979

July 15—President Carter delivers his so-called malaise speech to the American public; although he never uses that word, the president argues that a "crisis of spirit" is impairing the nation's ability to solve its domestic problems.

July 19—Nicaraguan president Anastasio Somoza is overthrown and the Sandinista National Liberation Front (FSLN), a Marxist-Leninist group backed by Cuba, comes to power.

July 31—Reagan visits the North American Aerospace Defense Command (NORAD). During the visit, he discovers that the United States has no defense against nuclear weapons. This visit influences Reagan's later decision to seek a national missile defense program.

November 4—The U.S. embassy in Tehran, Iran, is seized by student militants and 52 Americans are taken as hostages.

November 13—Reagan officially announces his candidacy for the 1980 GOP presidential nomination.

December 29—The Soviet Union invades neighboring Afghanistan. The era of détente with Moscow comes to an abrupt halt.

1980

February 26—Reagan takes 51 percent of the vote in the New Hampshire primary, easily defeating six other GOP candidates. That same day, John Sears is fired as campaign manager and replaced by William Casey.

July 16—Reagan accepts the GOP presidential nomination at the convention in Detroit and selects George H. W. Bush as his running mate.

July 19–August 3—The United States takes part in a 50-nation boycott of the 1980 Olympics in Moscow to protest the Soviet invasion of Afghanistan.

September 9—In a speech to the International Business Council in Chicago, Reagan outlines his vision of a balanced budget, lower taxes, and a stronger national defense.

September 22—Poland's Solidarity trade union forms under the leadership of Lech Walesa.

October 28—Reagan debates President Carter. During the debate, Reagan coins his famous phrase, "There you go again," in response to Carter's attack on Reagan's policy proposals. Following the debate, Reagan's lead steadily increases.

November 4—Reagan defeats Carter in the general election, winning 44 states and 489 electoral votes. The GOP also takes control of the Senate for the first time in 16 years.

November 5—One day after Reagan's victory, the Dow Jones Industrial Average increases dramatically, particularly defense, oil, and technology stocks.

1981

January 6—Reagan and Secretary of State-designate Alexander Haig have their first real discussion, and Haig tells Reagan he wants to be given exclusive responsibility on foreign policy matters and serve as the administration's spokesman on foreign policy.

January 10—Communist rebels in El Salvador launch an offensive against the U.S.-backed government.

January 20—Reagan is inaugurated as the 40th U.S. president. Later that day, Iran releases the 52 hostages taken in November 1979.

January 22—Reagan establishes the Presidential Task Force on Regulatory Relief to address the burden of overregulation in America.

January 23—The Labor Department reports a 12.4 percent inflation rate in 1980, marking the second double-digit increase in two years.

January 26—Lech Walesa leads the workers of Poland on an "illegal" strike and calls for a five-day workweek. In a tribute to the hostages, Reagan signs his first formal act as president, making January 29 "A Day of Thanksgiving to Honor Our Safely Returned Hostages."

January 29—Reagan gives his first press conference as president. He says détente has been a one-way street and accuses the Soviet Union of lying, cheating, and stealing to achieve their goals.

February—Brezhnev indicates interest in a summit meeting, but Reagan and Haig have no interest. They want to see a change in Soviet behavior before agreeing to such a meeting.

February 5—Reagan addresses the nation on the economy and outlines his program for economic recovery.

February 18—Reagan presents his economic recovery program to a joint session of Congress, calling for a $41.4 billion budget cut, a three-year, 30 percent tax cut, and an increase in the defense budget.

February 23—The State Department claims that communist rebels in El Salvador are being aided by Cuba, the Soviet Union, and other communist nations. The White House lobbies hard for the passage of Reagan's economic package. Reagan himself meets with 467 legislators in his first 100 days in office.

February 26—The Cabinet Councils are formed by the administration. (In addition to the National Security Council, the Reagan administration created five "Cabinet Councils" designed to shape policy in five major areas. The new councils were economic affairs; commerce and trade; natural resources and environment; food and agriculture; and human resources).

March—Polls show two-thirds of the public support Reagan's economic program.

March 6—The Reagan administration says it will sell AWACS (Airborne Warning and Control Systems) aircraft and other weapons to Saudi Arabia.

March 10—Reagan submits his 1982 budget to Congress. Although it proposes cutting 200 more programs than was suggested by President Carter, it still projects a deficit of $45 billion.

March 17—Senators Pete Domenici and Fritz Hollings produce a bipartisan agreement to keep an ailing Social Security system solvent by freezing Social Security cost of living adjustment (COLA) increases. The package, which would include spending reductions, is rejected

by Reagan after the OMB, and his closest aides convince him not to break a campaign promise and cut Social Security.

March 18—Secretary of State Alexander Haig publicly accuses the Soviet leadership of supporting terrorism and trying to establish a beachhead in Central America.

March 20—The Solidarity trade union declares a nationwide workers' strike in Poland in protest of the communist government.

March 26—Reagan signs Executive Order 12301, establishing a presidential council on integrity and efficiency.

March 30—John Hinckley, Jr., attempts to assassinate President Reagan outside the Washington Hilton Hotel. Reagan suffers a wound to the chest and Press Secretary James Brady is shot in the head. Brady survives, but with severe brain damage. Haig says "As of now, I am in control of the White House" after the assassination attempt on Reagan. Additional comments that appear to misinterpret the line of presidential succession produce widespread criticism of Haig.

April—During a speech in Europe, Defense Secretary Caspar Weinberger upsets many with comments critical of détente. Secretary of State Haig is said to be displeased.

April 1—The United States suspends $15 million in aid to Nicaragua due to the Sandinista government's support of communist rebels in El Salvador. Nancy Reagan consults astrologer Joan Quigley for the first time about which days are safe for the president and which are not.

April 11—Reagan leaves the hospital and returns to the White House to continue his recovery.

April 24—Reagan lifts the grain embargo placed on the Soviet Union during the Carter administration. Haig disagrees with the decision, as does Weinberger, but for different reasons.

April 28—Reagan speaks to a joint session of Congress for the first time since the assassination attempt. He is warmly received by all of the legislators, and his economic package gains strong support.

May 2—The largest antiwar demonstration since the Vietnam War takes place in Washington to protest Reagan's Central America policy and his proposed cuts in social programs.

May 4—In an effort to reduce inflation rates, the Federal Reserve Board raises the discount rate to 14 percent.

May 6—The United States expels Libyan diplomats and shuts down Libya's Washington mission.

May 7—The House of Representatives passes Reagan's budget bill, 270-154.

May 13—Pope John Paul II survives an assassination attempt at the Vatican. There are rumors of a "Bulgarian connection" and possible KGB involvement in the attack.

May 17—Reagan gives an impassioned anticommunist speech during the commencement at the University of Notre Dame.

June 3—Supreme Court Justice Potter Stewart announces he will retire on July 3, 1981.

June 25—Reagan's budget proposal, Graham-Latta II, is passed by Congress.

July 7—To fill the spot on the Supreme Court vacated by Potter Stewart, Reagan nominates the first woman to the highest bench, Sandra Day O'Connor.

July 16—The Reagan administration announces its preference for a political solution to the problems in El Salvador.

July 19–21—Reagan travels to Ottawa, Canada, for his first G-7 economic summit.

July 27—Reagan addresses the nation on federal tax reduction legislation.

July 29—Reagan's tax bill is approved by the House, 238-195. In order to assure passage, he had to compromise on his original offer of a three-year, 30 percent tax cut and agree to a 25 percent cut instead.

August 3–5—Reagan gives the air traffic controllers union (PATCO) 48 hours to return to work after they strike, vowing to fire the holdouts. When many refuse to return, Reagan follows through on his promise and fires the workers.

August 13—Reagan signs his tax cut bill into law.

September—The first high-level direct contact between the United States and USSR in the Reagan administration takes place when Haig meets with Soviet foreign minister Andrei Gromyko. The meeting is basically a sparring exchange, but Haig does express U.S. readiness to talk about limiting intermediate nuclear forces.

September 9—Facing a choice between a balanced budget and an increase in the defense budget, Reagan chooses to increase defense spending. OMB director David Stockman wanted a 7 percent increase over Carter's budget, while Defense Secretary Caspar Weinberger, whom Reagan ultimately sided with, suggested 10 percent.

September 19—Labor union members demonstrate against the Reagan administration in Washington, D.C. Estimates put the number of people participating in the protest at over 250,000.

September 24—Reagan gives a speech to the nation on the economy and Social Security.

September 25—Sandra Day O'Connor is sworn in as an associate justice of the Supreme Court.

October—Members of the nuclear freeze movement stage demonstrations in Britain and West Germany to protest the American deployment of Pershing II missiles in Europe. Reagan infuriates Europeans when, in impromptu remarks, he seems to envision a possible nuclear war limited to Europe.

October 2—Reagan announces the United States will build the B-1 bomber and the MX missile as part of his defense buildup.

October 5—Reagan launches his Voluntarism Initiative.

October 6—Egyptian president Anwar Sadat is assassinated in Cairo. He is succeeded by Hosni Mubarak.

October 15—Reagan gives a speech to the World Affairs Council on free enterprise in the Third World.

October 18—As the economy gets worse, Reagan admits that there is "a slight recession," but he predicts it will rebound by the spring. Days later, he says there is not a good chance

the budget will be balanced in 1984. Reagan celebrates the 200th anniversary of the Battle of Yorktown with French president François Mitterrand.

October 21–24—Reagan attends the summit on international cooperation and development in Cancún, Mexico.

October 28—The U.S. Senate approves the sale of AWACS weapons to Saudi Arabia.

November—The NATO INF deployment attracts 400,000 protesters in Amsterdam.

November 6—Unemployment increases to a six-year high, 8 percent, sparking talk that the economy is in recession.

November 10—In the November issue of *Atlantic Monthly*, OMB director David Stockman says Reagan's economic program was based on "rosy scenario" forecasts and that "supply-side" economics was really a Trojan horse to benefit the rich. Against the advice of many in the administration, Reagan allows Stockman to keep his job at OMB.

November 18—In a speech to the National Press Club, Reagan proposes a "zero option" in Europe while at the same time setting a date for the deployment of Pershing IIs in Europe. He says that the deployment will be canceled if the Soviet Union dismantles all intermediate-range nuclear missiles pointed at Western Europe. Reagan's daughter, Patti, publicly calls for her father to halt deployment of nuclear missiles in Europe at the Hollywood Bowl on "Survival Sunday."

November 23—Reagan exercises his first veto as president on the 1982 Continuing Budget Resolution.

November 30—The United States and Soviet Union begin arms control negotiations in Geneva, Switzerland.

December 10—Reagan calls on all American nationals to leave Libya due to a deterioration of relations between the two countries.

December 13—General Wojciech Jaruzelski imposes martial law in Poland after the trade union Solidarity threatens the future of his government.

December 14—Israel officially annexes the Golan Heights, land they seized during the Seven Days' War in 1967.

December 18—The United Nations issues a resolution condemning Israel's annexation; the United States supports the resolution.

December 22—Reagan meets with Polish ambassador Romuald Spasowski, who has defected to the United States.

December 23—The Reagan administration announces limited sanctions against the Polish government in response to their crackdown on the Solidarity trade union.

December 28—In a speech to the nation, Reagan publicly blames the Soviet leadership for the crackdown on Solidarity in Poland. He places economic sanctions on the Soviet Union.

1982

January—The second meeting between Haig and Gromyko takes place but is shortened to one brief session because of the Polish situation.

January 4—After being engulfed in a scandal over a gift to the first lady from Japanese jour-

nalists, National Security Advisor Richard V. Allen resigns his post. William P. Clark becomes the new NSA.

January 6—Reagan submits his 1983 budget to Congress. The budget, which proposes major cuts in all areas except defense, still projects a $91.5 billion deficit.

January 8—The Justice Department drops its antitrust lawsuit against IBM. Telecommunications giant AT&T is broken into 22 smaller corporations, called Baby Bells.

January 26—Reagan gives his State of the Union address, calling for a "new federalism" where social programs will be run by the states, not the federal government.

January 28—Media reports of human rights violations by the U.S.-backed government of El Salvador call into question Reagan's support for that regime. Some reports indicate that entire villages were destroyed.

February 9—Reagan gives a speech in Indianapolis reiterating his call for a "new federalism" that would return power to the states.

February 22—Reagan commemorates the 250th anniversary of George Washington's birthday.

February 24—Reagan recommends an economic and military plan for the Caribbean region called the Caribbean Basin Initiative at a meeting of the Organization of American States.

March—The top secret "Fiscal Year 1984–1988 Defense Guidance" report is completed, outlining the strategic design for the administration. The report emphasizes new areas in fighting the Soviet Union such as covert aid to the developing world, economic warfare, an arms race with the most technologically advanced weapons, and calls for the ability to wage a protracted nuclear or conventional war with the Soviets. It is considered the first strategic design of the Reagan administration. It was promptly leaked. Soviet premier Leonid Brezhnev announces a unilateral moratorium on further deployment of SS-20 missiles in Europe.

March 4—General John Vessey, Jr., is appointed chairman of the Joint Chiefs of Staff.

March 10—Reagan announces an embargo against Libya.

March 23—Reagan unveils his Enterprise Zone Initiative.

March 31—Reagan publicly denounces the nuclear freeze movement.

April 2–3—War between Great Britain and Argentina in the Falkland Islands begins after Argentina claims the "Malvinas" Islands as Argentinean territory and invades the islands.

April 14—The White House establishes the Presidential Commission on Drunk Driving.

April 15—The Department of Education proposes a school voucher plan called the Tuition Tax Credit plan.

April 22—Robert d'Aubuisson, a right-wing leader in El Salvador, is elected president. He is thought to be connected to death squads in El Salvador.

April 23—The inflation rate drops 0.3 percent, signaling the first decrease in the rate in a year.

April 29—Reagan addresses the nation on the budget and calls for a balanced budget amendment to the Constitution.

April 30—The United States publicly announces its support of Great Britain in their war with Argentina over the Falkland Islands.

May—A Soviet Central Committee plenum says the most pressing issues facing the USSR are economic problems. Specifically highlighted are the effect of sanctions from the crackdown in Poland, too many Third World commitments, high military expenditures, and the new arms race.

May 7—The unemployment rate rises to 9.4 percent in April, the worst rate since World War II.

May 9—Reagan unveils his Strategic Arms Reduction Treaty (START) in a speech at Eureka College.

June 4–6—Reagan travels to Versailles, France, for a G-7 economic summit.

June 6—Israel invades Lebanon.

June 7—Reagan meets with Pope John Paul II. They agree to undertake efforts to assist Solidarity and destabilize the Polish Communist regime.

June 8—In a speech in front of the British parliament, Reagan predicts the defeat of communism and calls for a "crusade for freedom."

June 12—Close to 1 million people gather in New York City's Central Park for a peaceful nuclear freeze demonstration.

June 15—Brezhnev announces a unilateral Soviet pledge not to be the first to use nuclear weapons.

June 21—A court finds John Hinckley, Jr., not guilty by reason of insanity.

Summer—Reagan authorizes a major covert action program to support Solidarity and destabilize the Communist government of Poland. Similar actions are taken in Czechoslovakia and Hungary. The AFL-CIO, the Vatican, and the CIA all play major roles in the operation.

June 25—Alexander Haig resigns as secretary of state and is replaced by George Shultz.

June 29—Negotiations on the START treaty between the United States and the Soviet Union open in Geneva.

June 30—The proposed Equal Rights Amendment dies after lack of support in Congress. Reagan signs Executive Order 12369, establishing the President's Private Sector Survey on Cost Control, also known as the Grace Commission after its chairman, Peter Grace.

July 6—Reagan agrees to send a small contingent of U.S. troops to Beirut, Lebanon, as part of a peacekeeping force.

July 19—The poverty rate reaches 14 percent, marking the highest rate of poverty since 1967. A rally is held at the Capitol in support of the Balanced Budget Amendment.

July 22—Council of Economic Advisers chairman Murray L. Weidenbaum resigns.

July 27—The Reagan administration announces that El Salvador is making progress in the area of human rights.

August—Reagan issues National Security Decision Directive (NSDD) 54, initiating his first formal policy on Eastern Europe.

August 1—Martin S. Feldstein is appointed the new chairman of the Council of Economic Advisers.

August 9—John Hinckley, Jr., is sentenced to an indefinite stay in a mental hospital.

August 20—Reagan unveils his Middle East initiative, dubbed "Fresh Start."

August 25—The first group of U.S. Marines arrives in Lebanon as part of an international peacekeeping force.

August 28—The U.S. embassy in El Salvador and the Catholic Church contest the administration's claim that human rights are improving in El Salvador. They say the human rights situation is deteriorating.

September 1—Reagan delivers a speech to the nation on the Middle East.

September 3—Reagan signs the Tax Equity and Fiscal Responsibility Act at his ranch in California.

September 13—A special prosecutor exonerates Labor Secretary Raymond Donovan from criminal charges.

September 20—Reagan speaks to the nation about the formation of a multinational force for Lebanon.

September–early October—Secretary of State George Shultz meets for the first time with Andrei Gromyko in New York. Shultz presents a list of U.S. complaints, mostly regarding human rights and Soviet involvement in the Third World.

October 1—The House of Representatives rejects the Balanced Budget Amendment.

October 14—The administration launches the Organized Crime and Drug Trafficking Initiatives.

October 15—The administration announces a grain sale agreement with the Soviet Union.

October 28—Soviet general secretary Leonid Brezhnev criticizes the Reagan arms buildup and claims the U.S. president is threatening to lead the world to nuclear war.

November—The U.S. economy plunges into its worst recession since the Great Depression. More than 9 million Americans are unemployed.

November 2—The Democratic Party gains 26 seats in the House in the 1982 midterm elections. The GOP maintains control of the Senate as neither party gains seats.

November 5—At the height of the recession, the official unemployment rate rises to 10.4 percent.

November 10—Leonid Brezhnev dies and is succeeded by former KGB head Yuri Andropov.

November 13—The United States lifts sanctions on the construction of the Soviet natural gas pipeline.

November 22—Yuri Andropov delivers his first major speech to the Soviet Central Committee where he shows optimism about improved relations with the United States and rejects the idea of taking a harder line against Washington. In a speech to the nation, Reagan announces his decision to deploy 100 MX missiles.

December 7—Congress rejects funding for the MX missile.

December 16—The House of Representatives cites EPA administrator Anne Burford for contempt after she refuses to release subpoenaed documents.

1983

January—Reagan's approval rating drops to 35 percent. Reagan signs NSDD-75, the first formal policy dealing with the Soviet Union.

January 1—Unemployment claims 11.5 million people, a rate of 10.8 percent.

January 3—The administration organizes a presidential commission to study new ways to base the MX missile.

January 5—Reagan signs a five-cent-per-gallon gasoline tax increase into law.

January 12—Richard Schweiker resigns as secretary of health and human services; he is replaced by Margaret Heckler. Kenneth Adelman is named director of the Arms Control and Disarmament Agency after the retirement of Eugene Rostow.

January 19—Secretary of State George Shultz sends Reagan a memorandum outlining "U.S.-Soviet Relations in 1983," calling for an intensified dialogue with the Soviets. Reagan, with the military buildup well underway, is responsive to the idea.

January 21—Signs of economic recovery become evident as the inflation rate drops to 3.9 percent, down from 8.9 percent the previous year.

January 25—Reagan continues to press for spending cuts, calling for a freeze in domestic spending during his State of the Union address.

January 31—Reagan sends his 1984 budget to Congress. The budget contains a $189 billion deficit and, despite frequent calls for Reagan to raise taxes or cut defense spending, he rejects the advice.

February 4—The official unemployment rate drops from 10.8 percent in January to 10.4 percent.

February 7—Reagan fires scandal-tarnished EPA official Rita Lavelle.

February 15—Reagan holds his first meeting with a Soviet official, Ambassador Anatoly Dobrynin. Reagan's personal request to allow a Christian family to emigrate to the United States succeeds.

March—Shultz continues urging Reagan to improve relations with the Soviet Union. He submits memorandums to Reagan with names such as "U.S.-Soviet Relations: Where Do We Want to Be and How Do We Get There?" and "Next Steps in U.S.-Soviet Relations."

March 8—Reagan delivers a speech to the National Association of Evangelicals meeting in Orlando, Florida, in which he calls the Soviet Union an "evil empire." The speech draws sharp criticism from many inside America and around the world.

March 9—Anne Burford resigns as EPA administrator; she is succeeded by former EPA chief William Ruckelshaus. In response to Reagan's "evil empire" speech, the Soviet news agency TASS says Reagan is guided by a "bellicose lunatic anticommunism."

March 10—Reagan addresses the nation on Central America.

March 23—In a nationally televised speech from the Oval Office, Reagan unveils his plans to create a national missile defense system, dubbed the Strategic Defense Initiative (SDI).

March 25—Shultz, Reagan, and William Clark meet to discuss Soviet policy. The president gives Shultz his approval to pursue negotiations.

April—After several meetings, Shultz tells Dobrynin that the United States is ready to negotiate a long-term grain settlement.

April 6—The Scowcroft Commission releases its report calling for the modernization of U.S. strategic weapons while at the same time seeking arms control agreements with the Soviet Union that includes meaningful, verifiable reductions in nuclear weapons.

April 11—The presidential commission studying the MX missile recommends the production of 100 MX missiles to be based in existing silos.

April 18—Sixty people, including 17 Americans, are killed when a bomb explodes at the U.S. embassy in Beirut.

April 20—Reagan signs the 1983 Social Security Amendments. The government reports a rise in the gross national product in the first quarter of 1983, indicating the end of the recession.

April 27—Reagan speaks to Congress on El Salvador.

May 25—Congress approves funds for the MX missile project.

May 27–29—Reagan hosts his first G-7 summit in Williamsburg, Virginia.

June 3—The administration unveils its Excellence in Education campaign.

June 7—The United States responds to the expulsion of diplomats from Nicaragua by ordering 21 Nicaraguan officials to leave the United States immediately. This event symbolizes the deteriorating relations between Washington and Managua.

June 15—Shultz gives his new comprehensive statement on Soviet policy before a congressional committee. The plan calls for negotiations with the Soviets if they modify their behavior at home and in Eastern Europe and restrain their actions in the developing world.

June 18—Reagan nominates Paul Volcker to another term as chairman of the Federal Reserve Bank.

July 1—The last phase of Reagan's tax cut goes into effect.

July 4—In a congratulatory Independence Day letter to Reagan, Soviet leader Yuri Andropov suggests eliminating the threat of nuclear weapons. Reagan conveys his desire that both nations work towards this goal in Geneva.

July 18—The administration creates the Commission on Central America, chaired by former secretary of state Henry Kissinger.

July 19—Captive Nations Week is designated by the Reagan administration.

July 21—The Polish government ends martial law.

July 28—The United States and Soviet Union agree to a new, five-year grain agreement. The administration creates the Commission on Organized Crime.

August 21—Benigno Aquino, Filipino opposition leader, is assassinated upon his return to Manila from a self-imposed exile.

August 24—Reagan replies to Andropov's July 4 letter and suggests intensified dialogue but with no concrete proposals.

August 27—A massive civil rights demonstration takes place in Washington for the 30-year anniversary of the 1963 March on Washington.

September 1—The Soviet Union shoots down a commercial Korean airliner (KAL 007), killing all 269 passengers aboard, including 61 Americans.

September 5—In a speech to the nation regarding the downing of KAL 007, Reagan reacts sharply, calling the event a "crime against humanity."

September 7—Reagan presents his Adult Literacy Initiative.

September 8—Shultz and Gromyko have a tense meeting in Madrid. Soon after, the United States refuses to allow Gromyko's plane to land in New York. A long chill in U.S.-Soviet relations follows.

September 21—The federal government reports a 9.7 percent growth in the gross national product in the second quarter, signaling a strong economic recovery.

September 24—Reagan delivers an address for the Voice of America and presents his broad vision for negotiations with the Soviet Union.

September 26—Reagan speaks to the United Nations General Assembly about the Soviet Union.

September 28—As relations deteriorate in the wake of the KAL 007 incident, Yuri Andropov accuses Reagan of risking a nuclear war.

October 5—The AFL-CIO endorses Democrat Walter Mondale for president in 1984. The administration unveils the Job Training Partnership Program.

October 6—Solidarity leader Lech Walesa is awarded the Nobel Peace Prize.

October 9—Controversial interior secretary James Watt resigns.

October 13—National Security Advisor William Clark is nominated as the new interior secretary.

October 17—Deputy National Security Advisor Robert McFarlane succeeds Clark as National Security Advisor. Reagan forms an exploratory reelection campaign committee.

October 23—A suicide truck bomb explodes at a U.S. Marine barracks in Beirut, Lebanon, killing 241 American soldiers.

October 25—Five thousand U.S. troops invade the Caribbean island of Grenada.

October 27—Reagan speaks about Lebanon and Grenada in a nationally televised address. During the address, he also criticizes the Soviet Union for its conduct in international affairs.

November—NATO conducts a nuclear exercise named Able Archer. Although such exercises are common, this one comes at a tense time in East-West relations and includes high-level leaders for the first time.

November 8–9—The KGB center in Moscow sends flash telegrams asking for all information relating to possible U.S. preparations for an imminent nuclear strike on the Soviet Union.

November 11—Reagan addresses the Japanese Diet on the issue of trade policy.

November 18—Congress approves aid to the contras in Nicaragua.

November 20—*The Day After,* a television movie showing the effects of a nuclear war, is watched by 100 million Americans, including Reagan.

November 23—The first shipment of Pershing II missiles arrives in West Germany. In response to the delivery, the Soviet Union walks out of the Intermediate-Range Nuclear Forces talks in Geneva.

December—Reagan and Yuri Andropov are named Men of the Year by *Time* magazine. The Soviet Union halts START treaty talks.

December 4—The United States conducts an air strike on Syrian military sites in Lebanon.

December 8—Terrorists attack the embassies of the United States, France, and several other nations in Kuwait.

December 15—Under Operation Staunch, the United States advises other nations not to sell weapons to Iran to assist them in their war with Iraq.

December 28—The United States withdraws from the United Nations Educational, Scientific, and Cultural Organization (UNESCO) due to alleged mismanagement and political bias.

1984

January 11—The Kissinger Commission releases a report supporting the administration's goals in Central America and recommending increased military and economic aid to El Salvador.

January 16—Reagan delivers a speech on the Soviet Union expressing a new tone of willingness to seek negotiations with Moscow. He calls for a return to negotiations on nuclear arms and proposes talks on reducing conventional forces in Europe.

January 17—Shultz follows with a similar speech in Stockholm. He meets privately with Gromyko to renew the dialogue halted at Madrid by the KAL 007 incident.

January 20—Secretary of State George Shultz labels Iran a sponsor of international terrorism.

January 23—Following the resignation of William French Smith, Reagan nominates the counsellor to the president, Edwin Meese, as attorney general.

January 25—In his State of the Union address, Reagan asks Congress to cooperate in reducing the budget deficit.

January 29—Reagan formally announces his intention to seek reelection.

February 2—Reagan submits his 1985 budget to Congress. Despite rhetoric in favor of reducing the deficit, the budget includes a $180.4 billion deficit.

February 7—The administration announces the withdrawal of U.S. Marines from Lebanon by the end of the month.

February 9—Soviet leader Yuri Andropov dies and is succeeded by Konstantin Chernenko. Public opinion polls show only 38 percent of Americans approve of Reagan's foreign policy, while 49 percent disapprove.

February 23—Chernenko sends a private letter to Reagan.

March 3—CIA station chief William Buckley is kidnapped and held hostage by terrorists in Lebanon.

March 7—Reagan responds to Chernenko's letter, marking the first dialogue between Reagan and the new Soviet leader. Shultz meets with Ambassador Dobrynin. The meeting is productive and indicates a thaw in the cold relations since the downing of KAL 007.

March 8—A Reagan-Schultz attempt at back-channel diplomacy with the Soviets fails after Brent Scowcroft is denied a meeting with Chernenko and instead is asked to meet with one of Gromyko's deputies.

March 19—Chernenko sends a second letter to Reagan, responding to Reagan's reply.

March 20—Congress fails to pass a proposed constitutional amendment in support of school prayer.

April 9—Nicaragua files a lawsuit against the United States in the World Court over the mining of Nicaraguan harbors and covert aid to the contras.

April 10—The U.S. Senate passes a nonbinding resolution condemning the mining of Nicaragua's harbors.

April 16—Reagan signs National Security Decision Directive 138, calling for a more aggressive policy toward terrorism. Reagan responds to Chernenko's second letter. After this letter, the two do not communicate again until June.

April 30—During a six-day trip to China, Reagan signs a scientific and cultural exchange agreement with the Chinese leadership.

May 6—Napoleón Duarte is elected president of El Salvador.

May 9—In a nationally televised speech, Reagan makes his case for aiding the Nicaraguan contras in their fight with the Sandinista government. In the speech, Reagan calls the contras "freedom fighters."

May 24—Reagan gives a speech honoring the Vietnam War's Unknown Soldier.

May 29—The United States ships 400 Stinger missiles to Saudi Arabia for defense if the Iran-Iraq war should escalate.

June—After a public appeal by Republican Senate leaders to hold a summit meeting with the Soviets, Reagan says he's willing "to meet and talk any time" with Chernenko.

June 1—Secretary of State George Shultz meets secretly with Nicaraguan president Daniel Ortega in Managua. Ortega tells Shultz that the United States has no business interfering with matters in Nicaragua.

June 4—Reagan delivers a speech to the Irish parliament.

June 6—Reagan travels to Pointe du Hoc, France, and delivers a speech to U.S. veterans on the 40th anniversary of the Normandy landing. Chernenko writes a third letter to Reagan. Dobrynin follows the correspondence with a meeting with Shultz and the two agree to take minor steps to improving bilateral relations. They agree to exchange delegations of journalists in the summer.

June 7–9—Reagan travels to London for a G-7 economic summit.

June 10—The U.S. Army runs a successful test of an interceptor missile, emboldening proponents of SDI.

June 16—Reagan observes Captive Nations Week by denouncing the "Communist totalitarianism" of the USSR as the "single greatest challenge to human rights in the world today."

June 25—The U.S. Senate follows the lead of the House of Representatives and votes to cut all aid to the Nicaraguan contras.

July—Wealthy Saudis begin secretly funding the Nicaraguan contras $1 million per month through a Cayman Islands account.

July 17—Reagan signs into law the Minimum Drinking Age Bill.

July 18—Reagan signs the Deficit Reduction Bill.

July 18–19—Walter Mondale wins the Democratic Party's presidential nomination and selects Congresswoman Geraldine Ferraro as his running mate at the party's national convention in San Francisco.

July 28–August 12—Reciprocating the 1980 boycott of the Olympic games in Moscow, the Soviet Union boycotts the 1984 Summer Olympics in Los Angeles.

August 11—Reagan makes a joke about bombing the Soviet Union during a sound check for his weekly radio address: "My fellow Americans, I am pleased to tell you today that I've signed legislation that will outlaw Russia forever. We begin bombing in five minutes." The gaffe is greeted with fear and outrage from many who claim it as proof of Reagan's militarist tendencies.

August 22—Reagan and Vice President George H. W. Bush are nominated to head the 1984 GOP ticket at the Republican National Convention in Dallas, Texas.

August 23—Reagan gives his acceptance speech at the Republican National Convention.

September 20—Terrorists bomb the U.S. embassy in Beirut, killing 12 people.

September 21—The Reagan administration works out a compromise with Congress over funding for the MX missile.

September 23—Reagan meets briefly with Gromyko in New York City and expresses his desire for improved relations with the Soviet Union.

September 24—In a speech to the U.N. General Assembly, Reagan proposes a broad framework for U.S.-Soviet arms talks.

September 28—Reagan and Soviet Foreign Minister Andrei Gromyko meet at the White House. Gromyko leaves the meeting believing that Reagan is serious about improving U.S.-Soviet relations.

October 7—Reagan takes part in his first presidential debate with Walter Mondale in Louisville, Kentucky. Reagan's poor performance leads many to name Mondale the winner of the debate and causes the "age" issue to resurface.

October 10—Congress passes the second Boland Amendment, prohibiting the United States from "supporting, directly or indirectly, military or paramilitary operations in Nicaragua by any nation, group, organization or individual."

October 16—In a rare interview with the *Washington Post*, Chernenko reaffirms his desire for good relations with the United States.

October 21—Abandoning his reliance on numbers and policy details, Reagan turns in a more natural, and successful, performance in his second debate with Mondale. He diffuses the "age" issue by noting that he will not make his opponent's "youth and inexperience" an issue in the election.

October 30—Indian prime minister Indira Gandhi is assassinated.

November 6—Reagan easily wins reelection over Mondale, taking 49 states and 59 percent of the vote in the largest electoral vote landslide ever. Republicans maintain control of the Senate while Democrats maintain control of the House.

November 22—The United States and Soviet Union agree to new talks on nuclear and space issues in Geneva in January 1985.

1985

January—The United States announces it will boycott the World Court proceedings.

January 5—Counsellor to the president Edwin Meese is again nominated to be attorney general.

January 7–8—Shultz and Gromyko meet in Geneva and agree on a formula for the upcoming nuclear and space arms control talks.

January 8—Chief of Staff James Baker and Treasury Secretary Donald Regan swap positions in the administration.

January 20—Reagan is inaugurated for a second term as president, the oldest president ever sworn in, at the age of 73.

January 27—Shultz and Gromkyo agree to start arms control negotiations in Geneva on March 12.

January 30—UN ambassador Jeanne J. Kirkpatrick announces her resignation.

February 3—A Gallup poll shows a dramatic increase in Reagan's popularity from a year earlier; his approval rating jumps to 62 percent while his disapproval rating drops to 29 percent.

February 5—On the 40th anniversary of the Yalta Conference, Reagan says, "the freedom of Eastern Europe is unfinished business."

February 6—Reagan delivers his State of the Union address. He focuses on urging Congress to pass a comprehensive tax reform bill.

February 25—After a difficult confirmation, Edwin Meese is sworn in as attorney general.

March 10—Soviet premier Konstantin Chernenko dies. Mikhail Gorbachev is named the new general secretary of the Soviet Union.

March 12—The United States and the Soviet Union resume arms control talks in Geneva.

March 15—Labor Secretary Raymond Donovan resigns after he is indicted on charges of fraud and larceny.

March 19—The Senate approves funding for MX missiles.

March 21—The first Politburo meeting after Gorbachev's succession takes place. The members declare Soviet readiness to pursue détente with the West.

March 24—Gorbachev writes the first of many letters to Reagan. Major Arthur D. Nicolson, Jr., of the military liaison mission in East Germany, is shot and killed, heightening U.S.-Soviet tensions. Many minor retaliatory measures are taken, including an April 28 House vote of 394-2 condemning the Soviet "murder."

March 25—The administration presents the Youth Employment Opportunity Wage Initiative.

April 4—Reagan announces his Nicaraguan peace plan.

April 7—Gorbachev announces a Soviet moratorium on the deployment of medium-range nuclear missiles.

April 10—A congressional delegation led by Tip O'Neill goes to Moscow. O'Neill delivers a letter to Gorbachev from Reagan asking for a summit.

April 11—The administration establishes the Domestic Policy Council and the Economic Policy Council.

April 23—Gorbachev addresses a plenary session of the Central Committee, outlining for the first time his foreign and domestic policy.

Late April—The United States conducts an unprecedented overall review of Soviet policy, due mostly to changed priorities in the White House.

May 1—The Reagan administration places a trade embargo on Nicaragua.

May 4—Reagan attends the G-7 economic summit in Bonn, West Germany.

May 5—During his trip to Europe, Reagan visits Bitburg Cemetery in West Germany. The visit is controversial because it has been discovered that former Nazi officers are buried in the cemetery. Reagan also visits Bergen-Belsen concentration camp and delivers a speech honoring the victims of the Holocaust. The Reagan administration acknowledges the Reagan Doctrine is a policy designed to aid anticommunist insurgencies in the developing world.

May 8—Reagan speaks to the European Parliament about the Soviet military threat.

May 14—Shultz and Gromyko meet, but neither side budges on arms control issues, especially Shultz on SDI.

May 20—The administration launches the Summer Jobs for Youth Program.

May 28—Reagan delivers a speech to the nation on tax reform.

June 3—CIA agent William Buckley dies in Lebanon, and his death is kept secret. Buckley had been a hostage in Lebanon since March 1984.

June 6—The U.S. Senate votes 55-42 to approve $38 million over two years in nonmilitary aid to the Nicaraguan contras.

June 10—Reagan announces the United States will continue to comply with SALT II, but refuses to make any long-term commitment to the treaty.

June 12—The House of Representatives approves U.S. aid to the contras.

June 14—Terrorists hijack TWA Flight 847, holding 153 passengers, including 135 Americans, hostage. One American is killed and 113 passengers are released, but 39 are still held hostage in Lebanon.

June 18—During a press conference, Reagan promises he will never give in to the demands of terrorists.

June 20—Reagan presents Mother Teresa with the Medal of Freedom.

June 30—The remaining 39 hostages from TWA Flight 847 are released. Reagan addresses the nation on the release.

July 1—Soviet premier Mikhail Gorbachev agrees to a summit meeting with Reagan in the near future.

July 2—Eduard A. Shevardnadze is named to succeed Gromyko as Soviet foreign minister.

July 9—Office of Management and Budget director David Stockman announces his retirement.

July 13—Reagan undergoes surgery for cancer of his large intestine.

July 18—Recovering from cancer surgery, Reagan approves National Security Advisor Robert McFarlane's proposal to open a channel with Iranian foreign minister Ghorbanifar.

July 20—Reagan leaves Bethesda Navy Medical Center and returns to the White House. The government of South Africa declares martial law.

July 25—Ghorbanifar meets with Israeli officials for the first time on an arms deal.

August 8—A suicide car bomb attack at a U.S. air base in West Germany kills two Americans.

August 20—Israel ships 96 antitank missiles to Iran. The transaction fails to have the desired effect; no American hostages are released.

August 30—Israel sends another 508 antitank missiles to Iran.

September 9—Reagan announces the United States will place limited economic sanctions on South Africa.

September 13—The United States conducts its first antisatellite test in space.

September 17—Reagan says in a televised news conference that he will not use SDI as a bargaining chip in Geneva.

September 26—Shultz and Eduard Shevard- nadze hold meetings on arms control before the Geneva summit.

September 27—Shevardnadze meets Reagan and gives him a letter from Gorbachev that goes beyond earlier Soviet offers—50 percent reductions in strategic offensive arms, to 6,000 warheads, with an agreement not to continue SDI. Reagan is adamant in rejecting the pro- posals.

September 28—Shultz and Shevardnadze meet a second time to discuss arms control.

September 30—The Soviet Union presents its START proposal, calling for deep cuts in strategic offensive forces for the first time.

October 2—Actor Rock Hudson, a longtime friend of the Reagans, dies of AIDS. The death causes Reagan to take notice of the growing epidemic and declare AIDS research a "top priority." Spending levels on research, however, remain low. Six former secretaries of defense write Reagan a letter asking him to abide by a strict interpretation of the Anti- Ballistic Missile (ABM) treaty.

October 3—Gorbachev visits Paris and pro- poses direct talks with Britain and France over nuclear weapons. He also announces a unilat- eral reduction of deployed SS-20s to 243, the number that existed before the NATO deployment of Pershing and cruise missiles in 1983.

October 7–11—After a group of Palestinian ter- rorists hijack the cruise ship Achille Lauro and kill one American, the U.S. Air Force inter- cepts the EgyptAir jetliner carrying them to a safe haven and arrests the terrorists. The plane is forced to land at a military airbase in Sicily, but the group's ringleader is allowed to go free by Italian authorities despite strenuous appeals from the United States not to release him.

October 18—The Pentagon announces it will begin mandatory blood tests for all military personnel to prevent the spread of the AIDS virus.

October 24—Reagan speaks to the United Nations at its 40th-anniversary celebration and talks of a fresh start in U.S.-Soviet relations.

November 1—The United States presents its START proposal to the Soviet Union. This counterproposal also includes deep cuts but maintains SDI.

November 5—Shultz and Gorbachev have a chilly meeting together, dampening both sides' expectations at Geneva.

November 14—Reagan speaks to the United States and Soviet Union over the Voice of America service on the upcoming Geneva summit.

November 16—Reagan travels to Geneva for his first summit with Mikhail Gorbachev.

November 17—Lt. Col. Oliver North takes over the arms shipment operation with Iran.

November 18—Defense Secretary Caspar Wein- berger publishes an open letter to Reagan in the *Washington Post* urging Reagan not to com- promise on SDI at the Geneva summit.

November 19–20—Reagan meets with Gor- bachev for the start of the Geneva summit. No major breakthroughs occur, but Reagan gets Gorbachev to agree to a future visit to Wash- ington. In addition, both nations issue a joint statement on their desire to achieve a 50 per- cent reduction in nuclear arms.

November 21—Reagan returns to the United States following the Geneva summit and is warmly received by the public for his efforts to reduce nuclear arms. He addresses Congress on the progress made in Geneva.

December 2—National Security Advisor Robert McFarlane resigns and is succeeded by Deputy NSA John Poindexter.

December 7—Secretary of State Shultz, Secretary of Defense Weinberger, and Chief of Staff Regan all advise Reagan to end the sale of arms to Iran.

December 10—The International Physicians for the Prevention of Nuclear War, a group of Soviet and American doctors, wins the Nobel Peace Prize.

December 12—Reagan signs the Gramm-Rudman-Hollings bill aimed at reducing the budget deficit. A U.S. military plane crashes in Newfoundland, Canada, killing 248 soldiers.

1986

January 1—Reagan delivers a televised New Year's Day address to the people of the Soviet Union, while Gorbachev addresses the American people on U.S. television.

January 7—The administration levies economic sanctions on Libya.

January 15—Mikhail Gorbachev announces a plan to eliminate all nuclear weapons by the year 2000 but only if the United States will abandon its SDI program. Reagan replies that he will not budge on SDI and that he is still in support of the 50 percent reduction agreed to at the Geneva summit. Reagan signs a bill making the birthday of civil rights leader Martin Luther King, Jr., a national holiday.

January 17—Reagan undergoes colon surgery.

January 28—The space shuttle *Challenger* explodes shortly after takeoff, killing all seven astronauts on board and stunning the nation.

February 3—The administration creates a special commission to investigate the *Challenger* disaster.

February 4—Reagan delivers his State of the Union address and talks about family values and reducing the deficit.

February 5—Reagan sends his 1987 budget to Congress. With a deficit of $143.6 billion, the overall deficit would surpass $1 trillion.

February 6—Reagan resumes contact with Gorbachev in a personal letter, responding to Gorbachev's December letter.

February 7—Ousted Haitian president François (Papa Doc) Duvalier seeks safe asylum in France.

February 11—Reagan publicly vows to veto any tax increase passed by Congress.

February 16—The United States sends 1,000 missiles to Iran.

February 22—Reagan sends another letter to Gorbachev, this one advancing some new arms control proposals but not moving closer to Gorbachev's demands on nuclear testing or SDI.

February 22–25—A rebellion breaks out in the Philippines, and Ferdinand Marcos is removed from power.

February 25—Reagan asks for $100 million in aid for the Nicaraguan contras. The House of Representatives rejects the request, but the Senate

approves it. The United States recognizes the new Philippine government under Corazon Aquino.

February 26—Reagan addresses the nation on the issue of national security.

March 7—The United States, concerned about Soviet espionage, orders the Soviet UN diplomatic staff cut from 275 to 170 members over two years.

March 13—The USS *Yorktown* enters Soviet territorial waters despite Soviet warnings.

March 15—At the funeral of Swedish prime minister Olof Palme, Shultz meets with Soviet prime minister Nikolai Ryzhkov in Stockholm. The meeting is frank, but no progress is made.

March 16—Reagan addresses the nation on Nicaragua.

March 18–19—Reagan meets with Canadian prime minister Brian Mulroney to talk about how the two nations can work together to reduce acid rain.

March 24–25—Libya shoots surface-to-air missiles at U.S. carrier aircraft over the Gulf of Sidra, but no Americans are harmed. Reagan responds by bombing Libyan military targets, killing 37 people.

April 2—Terrorists bomb a TWA flight, killing four Americans.

April 5—Terrorists detonate a bomb at a West Berlin nightclub frequented by U.S. military personnel, killing one serviceman and one civilian and injuring 230 others.

April 14—In response to the terrorist attack in West Berlin, Reagan orders an attack against Libyan military and government sites, killing about 100 people, allegedly including the adopted daughter of Libyan leader Muammar Gadhafi.

April 15—Due to U.S. raids in Libya, the Soviets cancel the planned May 14–16 meeting between Shevardnadze and Shultz.

April 26—An explosion occurs at the Soviet Union's Chernobyl nuclear power station, killing several people and spreading radiation as far west as France.

May 2—Reagan attends a G-7 economic summit in Japan.

May 29—A special prosecutor begins investigating former deputy chief of staff Michael Deaver. Oliver North tells National Security Advisor Robert McFarlane that the money from the arms sales to Iran is being given to the contras in Nicaragua.

June—Reagan declares SALT II officially "dead." Gorbachev gives a major address to the Soviet Central Committee with several new ideas. Reagan responds favorably to all except the SDI restrictions, calling the speech a turning point.

June 9—The *Challenger* disaster commission releases its report to the administration.

June 17—Supreme Court Chief Justice Warren Burger announces his retirement. Reagan nominates Associate Justice William Rehnquist to replace Burger. He then chooses conservative judge Antonin Scalia to fill the remaining vacancy on the bench.

June 24—Reagan addresses the nation on the importance of aiding the contras in Nicaragua.

June 25—The House of Representatives approves aid to the contras by 12 votes after five months of debate. Reagan lauds the effort by Congress to support the "freedom fighters" in Central America.

June 27—The International Court of Justice votes 12-3 that the United States broke international law by supporting contra forces in Nicaragua.

July 3–6—Independence Day celebrations are held at the Statue of Liberty in New York City. Reagan enjoys the festivities with a 68 percent approval rating, the highest since he has taken office.

July 7—The Supreme Court strikes down major portions of the Gramm-Rudman deficit reduction bill.

July 26—After 16 months, Father Lawrence Jenco is released from captivity in Beirut, Lebanon.

August 16—Congress passes Reagan's 1986 Tax Reform Bill.

August 23—The FBI arrests Soviet spy Gennady F. Zakharov.

August 27—Reagan signs an antiterrorism bill banning arms sales to any nation supporting terrorism.

September—In response to the arrest of Gennady F. Zakharov, the Soviet Union arrests U.S. journalist Nicholas Daniloff. A deal is reached on September 29 whereby Daniloff is released without being tried. Zakharov is released on September 30 after pleading *nolo contendere*. The United States also wins the release of dissidents from the USSR.

September 9—American Frank Reed is kidnapped by terrorists in Beirut.

September 14—Ronald and Nancy Reagan deliver an unprecedented joint address to the nation in which they call for a national crusade against drugs in America.

September 18—Philippines president Corazon Aquino delivers a speech to a joint session of the U.S. Congress.

September 22—Reagan speaks to the United Nations on progress in nuclear arms reductions with the Soviet Union.

September 26—Following confirmation by the Senate, William Rehnquist is sworn in as chief justice of the Supreme Court, and Antonin Scalia is sworn in as associate justice.

September 30—Reagan announces he will attend a summit with Mikhail Gorbachev in Reykjavik, Iceland.

October—The first Soviet aircraft is shot down over Afghanistan by U.S. Stinger missiles.

October 11–12—Reagan meets Gorbachev for the two-day Reykjavik summit. A sweeping arms reduction agreement is dashed at the end of the summit when Gorbachev insists on the United States abandoning SDI, a proposal that Reagan firmly rejects.

October 17—Congress approves an antidrug bill and the Simpson-Mazzoli immigration bill, two legislative victories for the administration.

October 21—American Edward Tracy is kidnapped by terrorists and held hostage in Lebanon.

October 22—Reagan signs the 1986 tax reform bill.

October 30—The United States sends another 500 antitank missiles to Iran.

November 2—American hostage David Jacobson is released from captivity.

November 3—The U.S. arms sale to Iran is made public for the first time in a report from the Lebanese magazine *Al Shiraa*. After Tehran confirms the story, the Iran-contra scandal begins to accelerate quickly.

November 4—The Democratic Party takes back control of the Senate and increases its lead in the House with a major victory in the midterm elections.

November 5–6—Shultz and Eduard Shevardnadze meet in Vienna to try to restore the U.S.-Soviet relationship after the Reykjavik summit.

November 6—Reagan signs the Immigration Reform and Control Act.

November 10–11—After a routine meeting of the Eastern European states, Gorbachev declares an end to the Brezhnev Doctrine.

November 13—Reagan delivers a speech to the nation admitting sending some defensive weapons to Iran but denying the sale was made in exchange for the release of hostages. Polls show the public does not believe Reagan, and his approval ratings plummet.

November 21—Attorney General Edwin Meese is pressed by Congress to order an inquiry into the Iran-contra affair to bring the facts to light.

November 22—The Attorney General's Office discovers the connection between the sale of arms to Iran and the funding of the contras.

November 24—According to Meese, Reagan seems surprised and shaken when he is told by Meese of the diversion of funds to the contras.

November 25—Meese holds a press conference on Iran-contra and says $10 million to $30 million from arms sales to Iran was diverted to the contras. National Security Advisor John Poindexter resigns. Oliver North is fired.

December 1—Reagan appoints a commission headed by Senator John Tower to examine Iran-contra and offer recommendations for reforming the administration's national security decision-making process.

December 2—Frank Carlucci is named the new National Security Advisor. Reagan's approval rating plummets 21 points, from 67 percent to 46 percent, in just one month, according to a poll from the *New York Times*.

December 6—Reagan publicly admits to making a "mistake" in judgment in trying to gain the release of hostages with the sale of arms to Iran.

December 18—Director of Central Intelligence William Casey enters the hospital for brain cancer surgery.

December 19—E. Lawrence Walsh is named as a special prosecutor to investigate the Iran-contra affair.

December 31—Reagan speaks to the Soviet people in a New Year's Eve radio address.

1987

January 5—Reagan sends his 1988 budget to Congress. It is the first budget in history to exceed $1 trillion. Reagan enters the hospital for prostate surgery.

January 27—Reagan delivers his State of the Union address.

January 30—Reagan vetoes the Water Quality Control Act.

February 2—William Casey resigns as DCI. In his second appearance before the Tower board, Reagan appears confused and contradicts some of his earlier statements.

February 3–4—Congress overrides Reagan's veto of the Water Quality Control Act.

February 6—The administration unveils its "Up from Dependency" welfare initiative.

February 9—Former National Security Advisor Robert McFarlane attempts suicide.

February 16—Gorbachev begins an international forum in Moscow called "For a Nuclear Free World, for the Survival of Humanity."

February 19—The United States lifts economic sanctions against Poland.

February 20—Reagan sends a memo to the Tower board saying he doesn't remember ever approving the sale of arms to Iran. "I don't remember, period."

February 26—The Tower Commission releases its report on Iran-contra. It is critical of the administration but finds no criminal wrongdoing. Reagan's approval rating drops to 42 percent. Soviets resume nuclear testing for the first time since their unilateral ban in July 1985.

February 27—Chief of Staff Donald Regan resigns and is succeeded by former Senate majority leader Howard Baker.

February 28—Gorbachev delivers a speech proposing the elimination of all Soviet and American intermediate-range nuclear missiles in Europe, with no strings attached.

March 3—Reagan welcomes Gorbachev's arms reduction proposal in his first White House press conference since the Iran-contra scandal broke.

March 4—In a nationally televised address, Reagan accepts responsibility for Iran-contra. His approval rating jumps to 51 percent after the speech.

March 23—The administration decides to "reflag" and escort tankers in the Persian Gulf to protect them from attack by both Iran and Iraq, who are locked in a grinding war.

March 25—The Supreme Court upholds an affirmative-action law.

March 31—The House of Representatives overrides Reagan's veto of a public works program bill.

April 2—The Senate joins the House in overriding Reagan's veto.

April 13–14—Shultz meets with Shevardnadze, then Gorbachev. Gorbachev proposes the "double-zero" proposal, designed to eliminate intermediate and short-range missiles, but Shultz rejects this because of concerns expressed by some NATO allies.

May 5—Congressional hearings begin on the Iran-contra scandal. The administration launches the White House Conference for a Drug-Free America.

May 8—Gary Hart drops his bid for the Democratic presidential nomination after reports surface that he had an affair with model Donna Rice.

May 17—Thirty-seven U.S. soldiers are killed when an Iraqi missile hits the USS *Stark* in the Persian Gulf.

May 19—William Webster succeeds William Casey as director of central intelligence.

May 25—Former labor secretary Raymond Donovan is exonerated of all criminal charges.

May 31—Reagan delivers his first speech on the AIDS virus, calling for widespread testing.

June 2—Alan Greenspan is nominated as chairman of the Federal Reserve Board following the resignation of Paul Volcker.

June 8—Reagan attends a G-7 economic summit in Venice, Italy. At the summit, the United States agrees to lift tariffs against Japan.

June 12—Reagan delivers a speech at the Brandenberg Gate in West Germany. During the speech, Reagan, referring to the Berlin Wall, says, "Mr. Gorbachev, tear down this wall!" NATO formally accepts the "double-zero" proposal, supported by Reagan and Kohl and opposed by Thatcher.

June 26—Supreme Court Associate Justice Lewis Powell retires from the bench.

July 1—Reagan nominates Robert Bork to the Supreme Court.

July 16—British prime minister Margaret Thatcher travels to the United States and publicly praises the Reagan administration. Her remarks are an important boost to the administration's confidence after the damaging Iran-contra affair.

July 23—Gorbachev proposes a global double-zero, eliminating all intermediate and short-range missiles from Asia and Europe. Reagan names a national commission to study the AIDS virus.

July 25—Commerce Secretary Malcolm Baldrige is killed during rodeo practice.

August 5—The administration launches the Central American Peace Initiative.

August 25—The Dow Jones Industrial Average reaches an all-time high at 2,722.42.

August 26—German chancellor Helmut Kohl announces his intention to destroy West Germany's Pe-IA missiles after the U.S. and Soviet INFs and SRINFs are eliminated.

August 28—An attempted coup in the Philippines fails, and the United States reiterates its support for the government of Corazon Aquino.

September 15—Shevardnadze arrives for three days of intensive talks in Washington. He brings Reagan a letter from Gorbachev asking one final time for a compromise on SDI, which Reagan declines. Both sides announce in principle an INF treaty and a summit in the fall. Shevardnadze also tells Shultz the Soviet Union plans on withdrawing from Afghanistan soon.

September 16—Reagan participates in the bicentennial celebration of the Constitution in Philadelphia.

September 21—The U.S. military fires at Iranian ships laying mines in the Persian Gulf. Reagan speaks to the United Nations on the INF treaty and on Iran.

October 1—Transportation Secretary Elizabeth Dole resigns to work on her husband's 1988 presidential campaign.

October 3—The United States and Canada reach a trade agreement.

October 6—The Senate Judiciary Committee rejects the nomination of Robert Bork to the Supreme Court.

October 7—Reagan addresses the Organization of American States on his Central American Peace Initiative.

October 14—Reagan speaks to the nation about the upcoming Washington summit.

October 16—Iran launches a successful missile strike against a U.S.-flagged tanker in the Persian Gulf.

October 17—First Lady Nancy Reagan undergoes a mastectomy to remove a cancerous tumor.

October 19—The U.S. stock market suffers the worst one-day drop in its history. The Dow Jones falls 508 points.

October 23—The Senate rejects the nomination of Robert Bork to the Supreme Court. During a meeting with Shultz, Gorbachev, under pressure from conservatives in the Politburo, pushes for an end to SDI and says an INF treaty is not a compelling reason to hold a summit.

October 29—Reagan chooses Douglas Ginsburg as his next Supreme Court nominee.

October 30—Gorbachev gives in on SDI and sends Shevardnadze to Washington to announce a summit date of December 7.

November 2—New FBI director William Sessions is sworn into office.

November 4—Reagan speaks to the European public over the United States Information Agency's "Worldnet" about progress in U.S.-Soviet relations.

November 5—Caspar Weinberger resigns as secretary of defense and is replaced by Frank Carlucci.

November 7—Douglas Ginsburg withdraws his name from consideration for the Supreme Court due to revelations of marijuana use.

November 11—Reagan nominates Anthony Kennedy to the Supreme Court.

November 18—Congress releases its report on the Iran-contra affair, laying the "ultimate responsibility" for the affair on Reagan.

November 23–24—Shultz and Shevardnadze meet in Geneva and resolve most of the remaining issues regarding the INF Treaty. Also, progress is made on a START agreement.

November 24—Reagan announces the details of the INF Treaty in a speech in Denver.

December 4—Reagan reluctantly signs legislation mandating continued strict interpretation of the ABM treaty.

December 8—Reagan and Gorbachev hold their third summit in Washington, D.C. During the summit, they sign the INF Treaty, the first treaty to eliminate an entire class of nuclear weapons. They also agree to work for a START agreement before the end of Reagan's term.

December 10—Reagan addresses the nation on the results of the Washington summit. The U.S. trade deficit reaches a one-month high of $17.3 billion. Former deputy chief of staff Michael Deaver is found guilty of perjury.

1988

January 1—Reagan addresses the Soviet Union, and Gorbachev speaks to the United States.

January 25—Reagan delivers his State of the Union address and assures the public that his administration is "not finished yet."

February 3—The Senate approves the nomination of Anthony Kennedy as an associate justice of the Supreme Court. Congress votes down a proposal for contra aid.

February 4—Panamanian leader Manuel Noriega is indicted by a U.S. grand jury on drug charges.

February 8—Vice President George Bush is defeated by Senator Bob Dole in the Iowa caucus.

February 16—George Bush and Democratic hopeful Michael Dukakis both win their party's primary election in New Hampshire.

February 18—Anthony Kennedy is sworn in as an associate justice of the Supreme Court.

February 25—Reagan tells the *Washington Post* that time is too short to reach a START agreement before the Moscow summit.

February 29—The White House Conference for a Drug Free America takes place.

March 11—Gorbachev says a START agreement is still possible before the summit.

March 13—Nina Andreyeva publishes an article entitled "I Cannot Waive Principles" in the conservative Soviet paper *Sovetskaya Rossiya*, blasting Gorbachev's policies.

March 16—Oliver North, John Poindexter, and two other government officials are indicted by a federal grand jury for their roles in the Iran-contra affair. U.S. soldiers are sent to Honduras to prevent any possible incursion by the Nicaraguan military.

March 23—The contra forces in Nicaragua sign a cease-fire agreement with the Sandinista government.

April 5—*Pravda* publishes a full-page attack on the Nina Andreyeva article in support of the Gorbachev government.

April 8—Former Reagan aide Lyn Nofziger is convicted of breaking ethics laws and sentenced to jail.

April 14—The Soviet Union agrees on a troop withdrawal plan from Afghanistan. The withdrawal will begin on May 15, 1988, and be completed by February 15, 1989.

April 24—Education Secretary William Bennett reports improvements in the public school system but says it is still at risk.

May 5—Former chief of staff Donald Regan publishes his memoir, *For the Record*. In the book, he reveals Nancy Reagan's frequent consultations with astrologer Joan Quigley.

May 11—Reagan officially endorses the candidacy of Vice President George Bush for president.

May 16—Surgeon General C. Everett Koop labels cigarettes as addictive drugs.

May 27—The Senate ratifies the INF Treaty 93-5, making it the first arms control treaty approved by the Senate since the 1972 SALT I treaty.

May 29–June 1—Reagan travels to Moscow for his fourth and final summit with Gorbachev.

Although they have failed to reach a new arms agreement, they pledge to continue working toward one. They also laud the improvements in U.S.-Soviet relations in recent years.

May 30—Reagan visits the Russian Orthodox Danilov Monastery. That evening, he hosts a dinner at the U.S. embassy in Moscow for Soviet dissidents.

May 31—Reagan speaks to students at Moscow State University on the virtues of freedom.

June—The official unemployment rate drops to a 14-year low.

June 3—Reagan gives a speech to the Royal Institute of International Affairs in London.

June 19—Reagan attends the G-7 economic summit in Toronto, Canada.

June 29—Reagan stumps for Vice President Bush for the first time.

July 1—Reagan signs the Medicare Catastrophic Coverage Act.

July 3—The USS *Vincennes* accidentally shoots down Iran Air Flight 655 over the Persian Gulf, killing 290 civilians.

July 5—Edwin Meese resigns his post as attorney general.

July 7—Reports begin to surface about the gravity of the savings and loan crisis in America. The collapse of S&Ls in Texas alone is estimated at $152 billion.

July 12—Richard Thornburgh is nominated to replace Meese in the Justice Department.

July 18–21—The Democratic National Convention is held in Atlanta, and Michael Dukakis and Lloyd Bentsen are selected as the presidential and vice presidential nominees.

August 2—Reagan announces his HIV Action Plan.

August 3—Reagan vetoes the National Defense Authorization Act.

August 10—Reagan signs a bill awarding reparations payments to Japanese-Americans interned during World War II.

August 11—The Senate confirms Richard Thornburgh as the new attorney general. Reagan signs the Disaster Assistance Act.

August 15–18—George Bush and Indiana senator Dan Quayle are nominated as the GOP presidential and vice presidential candidates at the Republican National Convention in New Orleans. Reagan delivers a farewell address to the convention.

September—Gorbachev sends Shevardnadze to Washington to emphasize the importance of continuing the dialogue for the transition to the next administration.

September 13—Reagan signs the Fair Housing Act Amendments.

September 25—Bush and Dukakis hold their first presidential debate.

September 26—Reagan addresses the UN General Assembly on the issue of disarmament.

September 28—The U.S.-Canada Free Trade Agreement is signed.

September 30—Gorbachev addresses the United Nations and announces a unilateral reduction of Soviet forces by 500,000 men over the next two years, mostly in Eastern Europe.

October 5—Reagan attends the cornerstone-laying ceremony at the Holocaust Memorial Museum.

October 13—Bush and Dukakis hold their second presidential debate. Reagan signs the Family Support Act.

October 22—Congress passes a sweeping anti-drug bill.

October 25—Reagan signs the Department of Veteran Affairs Act, creating a new cabinet-level department.

November 8—Bush defeats Dukakis by a large margin in the presidential election. The Democratic Party keeps control of the House and Senate.

November 18—Reagan signs the Anti-Drug Abuse Act.

November 21—A groundbreaking ceremony is held at the site of the Reagan Presidential Library in Simi Valley, California.

December 1—The Supreme Soviet approves new election procedures, the creation of the Congress of Peoples Deputies, and enhanced authority for the president. This signifies a major step toward political reform in the Soviet Union.

December 7—Reagan and Gorbachev meet for the last time on Governor's Island in New York Harbor. Gorbachev seems more interested in speaking with President-elect Bush and continuing progress on arms reductions. Reagan speaks to the conservative American Enterprise Institute.

December 8—Reagan gives his final press conference as president.

December 14—The administration drops its ban on conducting talks with the Palestine Liberation Organization.

December 16—Reagan gives a speech on foreign policy at the University of Virginia.

December 21—Terrorists bomb Pan Am Flight 103 over Lockerbie, Scotland, killing all 259 passengers and 11 civilians on the ground. Libya is suspected in the attack.

1989

January—Shultz and Shevardnadze meet for the 13th and final time when they attend a conference in Paris on banning chemical weapons.

January 1—Reagan addresses the Soviet Union, and Gorbachev addresses the United States.

January 4—U.S. military planes shoot down two Libyan fighter jets over the Mediterranean Sea after the Libyan pilots fly directly at the American jets.

January 11—Reagan delivers his farewell address to the nation.

January 20—George H. W. Bush succeeds Reagan as the 41st president of the United States. Reagan leaves office with the highest approval rating of any president since Franklin Delano Roosevelt. The Reagans move to a home in Bel-Air, California.

March—Soviet citizens are given the right to vote in nationwide elections for the first time in Soviet history.

April 5—The government in Poland agrees to legalize Solidarity.

June—Solidarity leader Lech Walesa is elected president of Poland.

September–December—Over a span of four months, every Eastern European nation cuts its ties with Moscow and leaves the Soviet bloc.

November—Britain's Queen Elizabeth II presents Reagan with an honorary knighthood, the Knights Grand Cross of the Most Honourable Order of the Bath. Reagan publishes his autobiography, *An American Life*.

November 9—The Berlin Wall, a symbol of division between East and West, is opened after nearly 30 years.

1990

February—The Sandinista government is voted out of power after free elections in Nicaragua.

1991

November 4—The Ronald Reagan Library and Museum is dedicated in Simi Valley, California.

December 25—Mikhail Gorbachev officially dissolves the Soviet Union. The cold war ends less than three years after Reagan leaves the White House.

1992

July 24—Reagan appears for questioning in an Iran-contra trial one day after former defense secretary Caspar Weinberger is questioned. Reagan has trouble remembering names and facts from his days as president.

1993

Doctors at the Mayo Clinic diagnose Reagan with Alzheimer's disease.

1994

February 6—In a public appearance for his 83rd birthday, Reagan is visibly confused, confirming his affliction with Alzheimer's.

November 5—Reagan writes a letter to the American people announcing he has Alzheimer's disease. He tells the American people, "I now begin the journey that will lead me into the sunset of my life. I know that for America there will always be a bright dawn ahead." Reagan never appears in public again.

Principal U.S. Government Officials of the Reagan Years

Supreme Court

Warren Earl Burger, Chief Justice, 1969–1986
William Hubbs Rehnquist, Chief Justice
 (appointed 1986), 1972–
Potter Stewart, 1958–1981
Byron Raymond White, 1962–1993
Thurgood Marshall, 1967–1991

Harry Andrew Blackman, 1970–1994
Lewis Franklin Powell, Jr., 1972–1987
John Paul Stevens, 1975–
Sandra Day O'Connor, 1981–
Antonin Scalia, 1986–
Anthony M. Kennedy, 1988–

Executive Departments

Department of Agriculture
Secretary of Agriculture
 John Rusling Block, 1981–1986
 Richard Lyng, 1986–1989

Department of Commerce
Secretary of Commerce
 Philip M. Klutznick, 1980–1981
 Malcolm Baldrige, 1981–1987
 C. William Verity, 1987–1989

Department of Defense
Secretary of Defense
 Caspar Weinberger, 1981–1987
 Frank C. Carlucci, 1987–1989

Department of Education
Secretary of Education
 Terrell H. Bell, 1981–1984
 William J. Bennett, 1985–1988
 Lauro F. Cavazos, 1988–1989

Department of Energy
Secretary of Energy
 James Edwards, 1981–1982
 Donald Hodel, 1982–1985
 John Herrington, 1985–1989

Department of Health and Human Services (HHS)
Secretary of Health and Human Services
 Richard Schweiker, 1981–1983
 Margaret Heckler, 1983–1985
 Otis R. Bowen, 1985–1989

Department of Housing and Urban Development (HUD)
Secretary of Housing and Urban Development
Samuel Pierce, 1981–1989

Department of the Interior
Secretary of the Interior
James Watt, 1981–1983
William Clark, 1983–1985
Donald Hodel, 1985–1989

Department of Justice
Attorney General
William French Smith, 1981–1985
Edwin Meese, 1985–1988
Richard Thornburgh, 1988–1989

Department of Labor
Secretary of Labor
Raymond J. Donovan, 1981–1985
William E. Brock, 1985–1987
Ann Dore McLaughlin, 1987–1989

Department of State
Secretary of State
Alexander Haig, Jr., 1981–1982
George Schultz, 1982–1989

Department of Transportation
Secretary of Transportation
Andrew Lewis, 1981 1983
Elizabeth Dole, 1983–1987
James Burnley, 1987–1989

Department of the Treasury
Secretary of the Treasury
Donald Regan, 1981–1985
James Baker, 1985–1988
Nicholas F. Brady, 1988–1989

REGULATORY COMMISSION AND INDEPENDENT AGENCIES

Central Intelligence Agency (CIA)
William J. Casey, Director, 1981–1987
William Webster, Director, 1987–1991

Environmental Protection Agency (EPA)
Anne M. Gorsuch, 1981–1983
William D. Ruckelchauss, 1983–1985
Lee M. Thomas, 1985–1989

Federal Emergency Management Agency (FEMA)
John Macy, 1979–1981
Bernard Gallagher, Jan 1981–Apr 1981
John W. McConnell, Apr 1981–May 1981
Louis O. Giufridda, 1981–1985
Robert H. Morris, Sept 1985–Nov 1985
Julius W. Becton, Jr., 1985–1989

Federal Reserve System
Paul A. Volcker, 1979–1987
Alan Greenspan, 1987–

National Endowment for the Arts
Livingston L. Biddle, 1977–1981
Frank Hodsoll, 1982–1989

National Aeronautic and Space Administration (NASA)
James M. Beggs, Administrator, 1981–1985
James C. Fletcher, Administrator, 1986–1989

Securities and Exchange Commission
John Shad (R), Chair 1981–1987
David S. Ruder (R), Chair 1987–1989
Bevis Longstreth (D), 1981–1984
James C. Treadway, Jr. (R), 1982–1985
Charles C. Cox (R), 1983–1989
Charles L. Marinaccio (D), 1984–1985
Aulana L. Peters (D), 1984–1988
Joseph A. Grundfest (D), 1985–1990
Edward H. Fleischman (R), 1986–1992

UNITED STATES HOUSE OF REPRESENTATIVES

97th Congress (1981–1983)

Speaker of the House
Thomas P. O'Neill, Jr. (D-Massachusetts)

Majority Leader
James C. Wright, Jr. (D-Texas)

Republican Leader
Robert H. Michel (R-Illinois)

Majority Whip
Thomas S. Foley (D-Washington)

Republican Whip
Trent Lott (R-Mississippi)

98th Congress (1983–1985)

Speaker of the House
Thomas P. O'Neill, Jr. (D-Massachusetts)

Majority Leader
James C. Wright, Jr. (D-Texas)

Republican Leader
Robert H. Michel (R-Illinois)

Majority Whip
Thomas S. Foley (D-Washington)

Republican Whip
Trent Lott (R-Mississippi)

99th Congress (1985–1987)

Speaker of the House
Thomas P. O'Neill, Jr. (D-Massachusetts)

Majority Leader
James C. Wright, Jr. (D-Texas)

Republican Leader
Robert H. Michel (R-Illinois)

Majority Whip
Thomas S. Foley (D-Washington)

Republican Whip
Trent Lott (R-Mississippi)

100th Congress (1987–1989)

Speaker of the House
Thomas P. O'Neill, Jr. (D-Massachusetts)

Majority Leader
Thomas S. Foley (D-Washington)

Republican Leader
Robert H. Michel (R-Illinois)

Majority Whip
Tony Coelho (D-California)

Republican Whip
Trent Lott (R-Mississippi)

UNITED STATES SENATE

97th Senate (1981–1983)

President
George H. W. Bush

President Pro Tempore
Strom Thurmond (R-South Carolina)

Majority Leader
Howard H. Baker (R-Tennessee)

Democratic Leader
Robert C. Byrd (D-West Virginia)

Majority Whip
Theodore F. Stevens (R-Arkansas)
1977–1985

Democratic Whip
Alan Cranston (D-California), 1977–1991

98th Senate (1983–1985)

President
George H. W. Bush

President Pro Tempore
Strom Thurmond (R-South Carolina)

Majority Leader
Howard H. Baker (R-Tennessee)

Democratic Leader
Robert C. Byrd (D-West Virginia)

Majority Whip
Theodore F. Stevens (R-Arkansas),
1977–1985

Democratic Whip
Alan Cranston (D-California), 1977–1991

99th Senate (1985–1987)

President
George H. W. Bush

President Pro Tempore
Strom Thurmond (R-South Carolina)

Majority Leader
Robert Dole (R-Kansas)

Democratic Leader
Robert C. Byrd (D-West Virginia)

Majority Whip
Alan K. Simpson (R-Wyoming), 1985–1995

Democratic Whip
Alan Cranston (D-California), 1977–1991

100th Senate (1987–1989)

President
George H. W. Bush

President Pro Tempore
John C. Stennis (D-Mississippi)

Majority Leader
Robert C. Byrd (D-West Virginia)

Republican Leader
Robert Dole (R-Kansas)

Majority Whip
Alan Cranston (D-California), 1977–1991

Republican Whip
Alan K. Simpson (R-Wyoming), 1985–1995

SELECTED PRIMARY DOCUMENTS

22. "Star Wars" Address to the Nation on Defense and National Security, March 23, 1983

23. Address Before a Joint Session of the Congress on Central America, April 27, 1983

24. Address on Soviet Attack on Korean Flight 007, September 5, 1983

25. Address to the Nation on Events in Lebanon and Grenada, October 27, 1983

26. Remarks on Signing the Bill Making the Birthday of Martin Luther King, Jr., a National Holiday, November 2, 1983

27. Address to the Nation Announcing the Reagan-Bush Candidacies for Reelection, January 29, 1984

28. Remarks at Memorial Day Ceremonies Honoring an Unknown Serviceman of the Vietnam Conflict, Arlington, Virginia, May 28, 1984

29. Remarks to the Citizens of Ballyporeen, Ireland, June 3, 1984

30. Remarks at a Ceremony Commemorating the 40th Anniversary of the Normandy Invasion, D day, June 6, 1984

31. Remarks Accepting the Presidential Nomination at the Republican National Convention in Dallas, Texas, August 23, 1984

32. Second Inaugural Address, January 21, 1985

33. 1985 State of the Union Address, February 6, 1985

34. Remarks at a Commemorative Ceremony at Bergen-Belsen Concentration Camp in the Federal Republic of Germany, May 5, 1985

35. *Challenger* Disaster Speech, January 28, 1986

36. Address to the Nation on the United States Air Strike against Libya, April 14, 1986

37. On the Campaign against Drug Abuse, the President and Mrs. Reagan, from the White House, September 14, 1986

38. Address to the Nation on the Iran-Contra Affair, March 4, 1987

39. "Tear Down This Wall" Speech at the Brandenburg Gate, West Berlin, June 12, 1987

40. Remarks at Signing of INF Treaty, December 8, 1987

41. Address to Students at Moscow State University, May 31, 1988

42. Reagan's Farewell Speech, January 11, 1989

43. Remarks at the Dedication of the Cold War Memorial at Westminster College, November 10, 1990

44. 1992 Republican National Convention Speech, Houston, Texas, August 17, 1992

45. Announcement of Alzheimer's Disease, Letter to the Nation, November 5, 1994

1. Reagan's Commencement Address at Eureka College
June 7, 1957

This speech, delivered at Reagan's alma mater, incorporates many of the themes he honed while serving as a spokesman for General Electric Corporation during the 1950s. Reagan would emphasize these same themes 30 years later as president; in fact, one of Reagan's greatest strengths was his unwavering allegiance to a consistent set of beliefs. These principles included the idea that the United States was a divinely inspired nation, a "city upon a hill" as Reagan would later call it, and that the great political question of modern times involved the struggle between those who believed in the "sanctity of individual freedom" and those inclined to defer to "the supremacy of the state." The former, Reagan contended, allowed human creativity to flourish, while the latter descended into regimentation and conformity. Like many conservatives of that era, Reagan feared that the system of limited government and individual rights created by the Founding Fathers was gradually being replaced by an overbearing administrative state with an insatiable appetite for growth. The reader will also note Reagan's condemnation of communist activity in Hollywood, and around the globe, as an "evil force."

I'm sure you all must know the depth of my gratitude for this honor you have done me. What you can't know is how great is my feeling of unworthiness. For some 25 years I have nursed a feeling of guilt about the degree given me here upon the occasion of my own graduation. It was, I feel, more honorary than earned and for all these years I have carefully refrained from referring to myself as a "student" here. My very instinct is to mumble a modest "thanks" and sit down, but that retreat is denied me. Inherent in my invitation is the obligation to make some remarks appropriate to this occasion which shall climax your years of academic endeavor. I do not take this responsibility lightly. Realizing there are many present who are better qualified to perform this function, I have inquired right down to the start of the Processional as to an appropriate theme.

There was a temptation of course to beg your favor by citing the mistakes of my generation, dwelling on the awful state of the world and suggesting that you would bring order out of chaos and set things right. I'm not that pessimistic, however, and would be less than honest and sincere if I chose such a course. With your permission I would rather speak of something very close to my heart. You members of the graduating class of 1957 are today coming into your inheritance. You are taking your adult places in a society unique in the history of man's tribal relations. I would like to play the role of a "legal light" in the reading of the will, and to discuss with you the terms and conditions of your legacy.

Looming large in your inheritance is this country, this land America, placed as it is between two great oceans. Those who discovered and pioneered it had to have rare qualities of courage and imagination nor did these qualities stop there. Even the modern-day immigrants have been possessed of courage beyond that of their neighbors. The courage to tear up centuries-old roots and leave their homelands, to come to this land where even the language was strange. Such courage is part of our inheritance, all of us spring from these special people and these qualities have contributed to the make-up of the American personality.

There are conditions to this "will" of which I speak. There are terms the heirs must meet in order to qualify for the legacy. But, I have never been able to believe that America is just a reward for those of extra courage and resourcefulness. This is a land of destiny and our forefathers found their way here by some Divine system of selective service gathered here to fulfill a mission to advance man a further step in his climb from the swamps.

Almost two centuries ago a group of disturbed men met in the small Pennsylvania State House. They gathered to decide on a course of action. Behind the locked and guarded doors they debated for hours whether or not to sign the Declaration which had been presented for their consideration. For hours the talk was treason and its price the headsman's axe, the gallows and noose. The talk went on and decision was not forthcoming. Then, Jefferson writes, a voice was heard coming from the balcony:

> They may stretch our necks on all the gibbets in the land. They may turn every tree into a gallows, every home into a grave, and yet the words of that parchment can never die. They may pour our blood on a thousand scaffolds and yet from every drop that dyes the axe a new champion of freedom will spring into birth. The words of this declaration will live long after our bones are dust.
>
> To the mechanic in his workshop they will speak hope; to the slave in the mines, freedom; but to the coward rulers, these words will speak in tones of warning they cannot help but hear. Sign that parchment. Sign if the next moment the noose is around your neck. Sign if the next minute this hall rings with the clash of falling axes! Sign by all your hopes in life or death, not only for yourselves but for all ages, for that parchment will be the textbook of freedom, the bible of the rights of man forever.
>
> Were my soul trembling on the verge of eternity, my hand freezing in death, I would still implore you to remember this truth, God has given America to be free.

As he finished, the speaker sank back in his seat exhausted. Inspired by his eloquence the delegates rushed forward to sign the Declaration of Independence. When they turned to thank the speaker for his timely words he couldn't be found and to this day no one knows who he was or how he entered or left the guarded room.

Here was the first challenge to the people of this new land, the charging of this nation with a responsibility to all mankind. And down through the years with but few lapses the people of America have fulfilled their destiny. Almost a century and a half after that day in Philadelphia, this nation entered a great world conflict in Europe. Volumes of cynical words have been written about that war and our part in it. Our motives have been questioned and there has been talk of ulterior motives in high places, of world markets and balance of power. But all the words of all the cynics cannot erase the fact that millions of Americans sacrificed, fought and many died in the sincere and selfless belief that they were making the world safe for democracy and advancing the cause of freedom for all men.

A quarter of a century later America went into World War II, and never in the history of man had the issues of right and wrong been so clearly defined, so much so that it makes one question how anyone could have remained neutral. And again in the greatest mass undertaking the world has ever seen, America fulfilled her destiny.

A short time after that war was concluded a plane was winging its way across the Pacific Ocean. It contained dignitaries of the Philippines and of our own government. Landing at a naval installation a short distance from Manila, the plane was held there while those people listened by radio to the first detonation of an experimental atomic weapon at the Bikini Atoll. Then the plane took to the air again and soon landed in Manila. There these people, together with our vice president, senators, generals and admirals, met with 250,000 Filipinos in the Grand Concourse, where they watched the American flag come down and the flag of the Philippine independence take its place.

I was privileged to sit in an auditorium one night and hear one of the passengers on that plane, a great man of the Philippines, describe this scene, General Carlos Romulo, whose father was killed by American soldiers in the Philippine insurrection. As a boy, the General was taught to be a guerrilla and to fight Americans and hate them. But I saw him, with tears in his eyes, tell us how he turned to his wife that day in Manila and said, a hundred years from now will our children's children learn in their schoolrooms that on this day an atomic weapon was detonated for the first time on a Pacific Island, or will they learn that on another Pacific Island a great and powerful nation, which had bled the flower of its youth into the sands of the island's beaches reconquering them from a savage enemy, had on this day turned to the people of that island and for the first time in the history of man's relationship to man had said, "Here, we've taken your country back for you. It's yours." As we heard him, I think most of us realized once again the magnitude of the challenge of our destiny, that here indeed is "the last best hope of man on earth."

And now today we find ourselves involved in another struggle, this time called a cold war. This cold war between great sovereign nations isn't really a new struggle at all. It is the oldest struggle of humankind, as old as man himself. This is a simple struggle between those of us who believe that man has the dignity and sacred right and the ability to choose and shape his own destiny and those who do not so believe. This irreconcilable conflict is between those who believe in the sanctity of individual freedom and those who believe in the supremacy of the state.

In a phase of this struggle not widely known, some of us came toe to toe with this enemy, this evil force in our own community in Hollywood, and make no mistake about it, this is an evil force. Don't be deceived because you are not hearing the sound of gunfire, because even so you are fighting for your lives. And you're fighting against the best organized and the most capable enemy of freedom and of

right and decency that has ever been abroad in the world. Some years ago, back in the thirties, a man who was apparently just a technician came to Hollywood to take a job in our industry, an industry whose commerce is in tinsel and colored lights and make-believe. He went to work in the studios, and there were few to know he came to our town on direct orders from the Kremlin. When he quietly left our town a few years later the cells had been formed and planted in virtually all of our organizations, our guilds and unions. The framework for the Communist front organizations had been established.

It was some time later, under the guise of a jurisdictional strike involving a dispute between two unions, that we saw war come to Hollywood. Suddenly there were 5,000 tin-hatted, club-carrying pickets outside the studio gates. We saw some of our people caught by these hired henchmen; we saw them open car doors and put their arms across them and break them until they hung straight down the side of the car, and then these tin-hatted men would send our people on into the studio. We saw our so-called glamour girls, who certainly had to be conscious of what a scar on the face or a broken nose could mean careerwise going through those picket lines day after day without complaint. Nor did they falter when they found the bus which they used for transportation to and from work in flames from a bomb that had been thrown into it just before their arrival. Two blocks from the studio everyone would get down on hands and knees on the floor to avoid the bricks and stones coming through the windows. And the 5,000 pickets out there in their tin hats weren't even motion picture workers. They were maritime workers from the waterfront, members of Mr. Harry Bridges' union.

We won our fight in Hollywood—cleared them out after seven long months in which even homes were broken, months in which many of us carried arms that were granted us by the police, and in which policemen lived in our homes, guarding our children at night. And what of the quiet film technician who had left our town before the fighting started? Well, in 1951 he turned up on the Monterey Peninsula where he was involved in a union price-fixing conspiracy. Two years ago he appeared on the New York waterfront where he was Harry Bridges' righthand man in an attempt to establish a liaison between the New York and West Coast waterfront workers. And a few months ago he was mentioned in the speech of a U.S. Congresswoman who was thanking him for his help in framing labor legislation. He is a registered lobbyist in Washington for Harry Bridges.

Now that the first flush of victory is over we in Hollywood find ourselves blessed with a newly developed social awareness. We have allowed ourselves to become a sort of a village idiot on the fringe of the industrial scene, fair game for any demagogue or bigot who wants to stand up in the pulpit or platform and attack us. We are also fair game for those people, well-meaning though they may be, who believe that the answer to the world's ills is more government and more restraint and more regimentation. Suddenly we find that we are a group of second-class citizens subject to discriminatory taxation, government interference and harassment.

This harassment reaches its peak, of course, in censorship. Here in this great land of the free exchange of ideas, our section of the communications industry is subjected to political censorship in more than 200 cities and 11 states, and it's spreading every day. But are we the only victims of these restraints and restrictions on our personal freedom? Is censorship really a restriction on us who already have a voluntary censorship code of good taste, or is this an invasion of your freedom? Isn't this the case of a few of your neighbors taking upon themselves the right to tell you what you are

capable of seeing and hearing on a motion picture screen?

So we worry a little about the class of '57, we who are older and have known another day. We worry that perhaps someday you might not resist as strongly as we would if someone decides to tell you what you can read in a newspaper, or hear on the radio, or hear from a speaker's platform, or what you can say or what you can think. So there are terms and conditions to the will, and one of the terms is your own eternal vigilance guarding against restrictions on our American freedom.

You today are smarter than we were. You are better educated and better informed than we were twenty-five years ago. And that is part of your heritage. You enjoy these added benefits because, more than 100 years ago near this very spot, a man plunged an ax into a tree and said, here we will build a school for our children." And for over 100 years people have contributed to the endowment and support of this college. Their contributions were of the utmost in generosity because they could never know the handclasp of gratitude in return for their contributions. Their gifts were to generations yet unborn.

Many of us here share this heritage with you, and some of us shared it under different circumstances. I recall my own days on this campus in the depths of the depression. Even with study and reading I don't think you can quite understand what it was like to live in an America where the Illinois National Guard, with fixed bayonets, paraded down Michigan Avenue in Chicago as a warning to the more than half million unemployed men who slept every night in alleys and doorways under newspapers. On this campus many of us came who brought not one cent to help this school and pay for our education. The college, of course, had suffered and lost much of its endowment in the stock crash, had seen its revenue not only from endowment but from gifts curtailed because of the great financial chaos. But we heard none of that. We attended a college that made it possible for us to attend regardless of our lack of means, that created jobs for us, so that we could eat and sleep, and that allowed us to defer our tuition and trusted that they could get paid some day long after we had gone. And the professors, God bless them, on this campus, the most dedicated group of men and women whom I have ever known, went long months without drawing any pay. Sometimes the college, with a donation of a little money or produce from a farm, would buy groceries and dole them out to the teachers to at least try and provide them with food. We know something of your heritage, but even if we had been able to pay as many of you have paid for your education, we, and you, must realize that the total price paid by any student of this college is far less than it costs this college to educate you. This is true not only of Eureka, but of the hundreds of schools and universities across the land.

Now today as you prepare to leave your Alma Mater, you go into a world in which, due to our carelessness and apathy, a great many of our freedoms have been lost. It isn't that an outside enemy has taken them. It's just that there is something inherent in government which makes it, when it isn't controlled, continue to grow. So today for every seven of us sitting here in this lovely outdoor theater, there is one public servant, and 31 cents of every dollar earned in America goes in taxes. To support the multitudinous and gigantic functions of government, taxation is levied which tends to dry up the very sources of contributions and donations to colleges like Eureka. So in this time of prosperity we find these church schools, these small independent colleges and even the larger universities, hard put to maintain themselves and to continue doing the job they have done so unselfishly and well for all these years. Observe the contrast between

these small church colleges and our government, because, as I have said before, these have always given far more than was ever given to them in return.

Class of 1957, it will be part of the terms of the will for you to take stock in the days to come, because we enjoy a form of government in which mistakes can be rectified. The dictator can never admit he was wrong, but we are blessed with a form of government where we can call a halt, and say, "Back up. Let's take another look." Remember that every government service, every offer of government-financed security, is paid for in the loss of personal freedom. I am not castigating government and business for those many areas of normal cooperation, for those services that we know we must have and that we do willingly support. It is very easy to give up our personal freedom to drive 90 miles an hour down a city street in return for the safety that we will get for ourselves and our loved ones. Of course, that might not be a good example. It seems sometimes that this is a thing we have paid for in advance and the merchandise hasn't yet been delivered. But in the days to come whenever a voice is raised telling you to let the government do it, analyze very carefully to see whether the suggested service is worth the personal freedom which you must forego in return for such service.

There are many well-meaning people today who work at placing an economic floor beneath all of us so that no one shall exist below a certain level or standard of living, and certainly we don't quarrel with this. But look more closely and you may find that all too often these well-meaning people are building a ceiling above which no one shall be permitted to climb and between the two are pressing us all into conformity, into a mold of standardized mediocrity. The tendency toward assembly-line education in some of our larger institutions, where we are not teaching but training to fulfill certain specific jobs in the economic life of our nation, is a part of this same pattern.

We have a vast system of public education in this country, a network of great state universities and colleges and none of us would have it otherwise. But there are those among us who urge expansion of this system until all education is by way of tax-supported institutions. Today we enjoy academic freedom in America as it is enjoyed nowhere else in the world. But this pattern was established by the independent secular and church colleges of our land, schools like Eureka. Down through the years these colleges and universities have maintained intellectual freedom because they were beholden to no political group, for when politics control the purse strings, they also control the policy. No one advocates the elimination of our tax-supported universities, but we should never forget that their academic freedom is assured only so long as we have the leavening influence of hundreds of privately endowed colleges and universities throughout the land.

So you should resolve, here and now, that you will not only accept your heritage but abide by the terms and conditions of the will. You should firmly resolve that these schools will not just be a part of America's past, but that they will continue to be a part of America's great future. Democracy with the personal freedoms that are ours we hold literally in trust for that day when we shall have fulfilled our destiny and brought mankind a great and long step from the swamps. Can we deliver it to our children? Democracy depends upon service voluntarily rendered, money voluntarily contributed. These institutions which have contributed so much to us, from which we have received so much of our heritage, were here for our benefit only because our forefathers preferred voluntarily to support institutions of their choice in addition to sharing taxation for the support of governmental institutions. The will provides, class of 1957, not only that you receive

this heritage and cherish it, but that you voluntarily tax your own time and your own money and contribute to these free institutions so that generations not yet born in this country and in the rest of the world, may benefit from this same heritage of freedom. It will be very easy for you to say, "Well, I will do something, some day. When I can afford it, I am going to." But would you let an old "grad" tell you one thing now? Giving is a habit. Get into the habit now, because you will never be able to afford to give and contribute, thus to repay the obligation you owe to those people who made this college possible, if you wait until you think you can afford it. Start now regardless of how small, and in the days to come when you are confronted with demands for many worthwhile causes and charities I think you will find that you will give dutifully to all the worthy ones. But here and there you will pick one or two that will be favorites, and you can do no better than to pick this, your Alma Mater, because you will not only be repaying your own personal obligations, you will be making your contribution to the very process which has made and continues to keep America great.

This democracy of ours which sometimes we've treated so lightly, is more than ever a comfortable cloak, so let us not tear it asunder, for no man knows once it is destroyed where or when he will find its protective warmth again.

Source: "Eureka College Class of '57," June 7, 1957, The President Reagan Information Page. Available online. URL: http://www.presidentreagan. info/speeches/eureka.cfm

2. "A Time for Choosing" October 27, 1964

This is arguably the most important speech of Ronald Reagan's political career. Broadcast on the NBC television network, the speech raised more than $8 million for the presidential campaign of

Barry Goldwater and propelled Reagan into the forefront of the conservative movement. The title of the speech was applied after the fact, but it is an accurate label, since Reagan believed Goldwater offered the American people "a choice, not an echo." In certain ways, the speech reads better than it was delivered, for Reagan's genial smile and relaxed manner is not as apparent here as it would be in later addresses. There is more of an angry tone to his delivery, leading one to wonder if Reagan learned an important lesson from Goldwater's experience—that snarling conservatives frighten the American voter, and that a sunny disposition is the only effective method of delivering a conservative message to a society devoted to progress and the pursuit of happiness.

I am going to talk of controversial things. I make no apology for this. It's time we asked ourselves if we still know the freedoms intended for us by the Founding Fathers. James Madison said, "We base all our experiments on the capacity of mankind for self government." This idea that government was beholden to the people, that it had no other source of power, is still the newest, most unique idea in all the long history of man's relation to man. This is the issue of this election: Whether we believe in our capacity for self-government or whether we abandon the American Revolution and confess that a little intellectual elite in a far-distant capital can plan our lives for us better than we can plan them ourselves.

You and I are told we must choose between a left and right, but I suggest there is no such thing as a left or right. There is only an up or down. Up to man's age-old dream—the maximum of individual freedom consistent with order—or down to the ant heap of totalitarianism. Regardless of their sincerity, their humanitarian motives, those who would sacrifice freedom for security have embarked on this downward path. Plutarch warned, "The real destroyer of the liberties of the people is he who spreads among them bounties, donations

and benefits." The Founding Fathers knew a government can't control the economy without controlling people. And they knew when a government sets out to do that, it must use force and coercion to achieve its purpose. So we have come to a time for choosing. Public servants say, always with the best of intentions, "What greater service we could render if only we had a little more money and a little more power." But the truth is that outside of its legitimate function, government does nothing as well or as economically as the private sector. Yet any time you and I question the schemes of the do-gooders, we're denounced as being opposed to their humanitarian goals. It seems impossible to legitimately debate their solutions with the assumption that all of us share the desire to help the less fortunate. They tell us we're always "against," never "for" anything. We are for a provision that destitution should not follow unemployment by reason of old age, and to that end we have accepted Social Security as a step toward meeting the problem. However, we are against those entrusted with this program when they practice deception regarding its fiscal shortcomings, when they charge that any criticism of the program means that we want to end payments. . . . We are for aiding our allies by sharing our material blessings with nations which share our fundamental beliefs, but we are against doling out money government to government, creating bureaucracy, if not socialism, all over the world. We need true tax reform that will at least make a start toward restoring for our children the American Dream that wealth is denied to no one, that each individual has the right to fly as high as his strength and ability will take him. . . . But we can not have such reform while our tax policy is engineered by people who view the tax as a means of achieving changes in our social structure. . . .

Have we the courage and the will to face up to the immorality and discrimination of the progressive tax, and demand a return to traditional proportionate taxation? . . . Today in our country the tax collector's share is 37 cents of every dollar earned. Freedom has never been so fragile, so close to slipping from our grasp. Are you willing to spend time studying the issues, making yourself aware, and then conveying that information to family and friends? Will you resist the temptation to get a government handout for your community? Realize that the doctor's fight against socialized medicine is your fight. We can't socialize the doctors without socializing the patients. Recognize that government invasion of public power is eventually an assault upon your own business. If some among you fear taking a stand because you are afraid of reprisals from customers, clients, or even government, recognize that you are just feeding the crocodile hoping he'll eat you last.

If all of this seems like a great deal of trouble, think what's at stake. We are faced with the most evil enemy mankind has known in his long climb from the swamp to the stars. There can be no security anywhere in the free world if there is no fiscal and economic stability within the United States. Those who ask us to trade our freedom for the soup kitchen of the welfare state are architects of a policy of accommodation.

They say the world has become too complex for simple answers. They are wrong. There are no easy answers, but there are simple answers. We must have the courage to do what we know is morally right. Winston Churchill said that "the destiny of man is not measured by material computation. When great forces are on the move in the world, we learn we are spirits—not animals." And he said, "There is something going on in time and space, and beyond time and space, which, whether we like it or not, spells duty."

You and I have a rendezvous with destiny. We will preserve for our children this, the last best hope of man on earth, or we will sentence them to take the first step into a thousand years of darkness. If we fail, at least let our children and our children's children say of us we justified our brief moment here. We did all that could be done.

Source: "'The Speech,'" October 27, 1964. Ronald Reagan Presidential Foundation and Library. Available online. URL: http://www.reaganfoundation.com/reagan/speeches/rendezvous.asp

3. "The Creative Society" April 19, 1966

This speech summarizes the major themes of Ronald Reagan's campaign for governor of California in 1966. Reagan committed himself to creating an alternative to Lyndon Johnson's "Great Society," whereby power would devolve to the lowest possible levels of society, essentially in this order of importance: to the individual, the family, local governments, state government, and as a last resort, the federal government. The "Great Society," according to Reagan, meant greater tax burdens for average Americans, and increasingly intrusive and inefficient central government. The theme of this speech, while somewhat unusual in 1960s America, was rooted in the antifederalist and Jeffersonian tradition dating back to the founding of the nation. The extent to which Reagan studied early American history is open to question, but the place of his thinking within the contours of American political thought is not.

Each generation is critical of its predecessor. And as the day nears when the classroom and playing field must give way to that larger arena with its problems of inequity and human misunderstanding, it's easy to look at those of us already in that arena and demand to know why the problems remain unsolved. We, who preceded you, asked that question of those who preceded us, and another generation will ask it of you. I hope there will be less justification for the question when it becomes your turn to answer. Don't get me wrong! When the generation of which I'm a part leaves the stage, I think that history will record that seldom has any generation fought harder and paid a higher price for freedom. We have known three wars in our lifetime, cataclysmic, worldwide depression—and these events toppled governments and reshaped the map. At the same time, as a result of this, perhaps just because of human frailty, we have downgraded our performance with an attitude sometimes apathetic—sometimes cynical—toward the conduct of public affairs.

We are confused and we have confused you with a double standard of morality. We try to keep alive a moral code for our individual conduct—"Don't cheat," "Promises are sacred." "Your word is your bond," "Serve your fellow men"—but at the same time, we accept double-dealing at government levels, and we've lost our capacity to get angry when decisions are not based on moral truth, but on political expediency. When small men are granted great rewards for political favors, we excuse it with the expression: "Well, that's politics."

I've already established myself now as not of your generation, but I'm aware there are those who go even farther and place me as far back as the Ice Age, or even farther than that—in the period of McKinley. I realize that modern political dialogue concerns itself largely with false image-making, rather than with legitimate debate over differing viewpoints; and no candidate can hope to engage in a political contest without experiencing the deliberate distortions of his positions and his beliefs. But I sometimes wonder if we haven't reached one of those moments in time when the stakes are much too high for this kind of middle-aged juvenile delinquency.

Public officials are elected primarily for one purpose—to solve public problems. You have a right to ask any candidate about his understanding of the problems facing us, his acceptance of responsibility for solving those problems, and whether he has a fresh approach or just offers the same old bargain-basement politics—"We'll do everything the other fellow's been doing, only we'll do it cheaper and better." You have a right to know—and I am obligated to tell you—where I stand and what I believe.

To begin with—I am not a politician. I am an ordinary citizen with a deep-seated belief that much of what troubles us has been brought about by politicians; and it's high time that more ordinary citizens brought the fresh air of common sense thinking to bear on these problems. We've had enough of the wheeling and dealing, and enough of schemers and schemes. I think it's time now for dreamers—practical dreamers—willing to re-implement the original dream which became this nation—that idea that has never fully been tried before in the world—that you and I have the capacity for self-government—the dignity and the ability and the God-given freedom to make our own decisions, to plan our own lives and to control our own destiny.

Now it has been said that nothing is more powerful than an idea whose time has come. This took place some 200 years ago in this country. But there is another such idea abroad in the land today. Americans, divided in so many ways, are united in their determination that no area of human need should be ignored. A people that can reach out to the stars has decided that the problems of human misery can be solved and they'll settle for nothing less.

The big question is not whether—but how, and at what price. We can't accept the negative philosophy of those who close their eyes, hoping the problems will disappear, or that questions of unemployment, inequality of opportunity, or the needs of the elderly and the sick will take care of themselves. But, neither should we unquestioningly follow those others who pass the problems along to the federal government, abdicating their personal and local responsibility.

The trouble with that solution is that for every ounce of federal help we get, we surrender an ounce of personal freedom. The Great Society grows greater every day—greater in cost, greater in inefficiency and greater in waste. Now this is not to quarrel with its humanitarian goals or deny that it can achieve those goals. But, I do deny that it offers the only—or even the best—method of achieving those goals.

The administration in Sacramento is guilty of a leadership gap. Unwilling, or unable, to solve the problems of California, it has reduced this state to virtually an administrative district of the federal government. This isn't to deny the rightful place of the federal government; but state sovereignty is an integral part of the checks and balances designed to restrain power and to restrain one group from destroying the freedom of another. We can do more by keeping California tax dollars in California than we can by running them through those puzzle palaces on the Potomac only to get them back minus a carrying charge.

Federal help has neither reduced the size of the burden of our state government, nor has it solved our problems. In California, government is larger in proportion to the population than in any other state and it is increasing twice as fast as the increase in population. Our tax burden, local and state, is $100 higher per capita than it is in the rest of the nation, and the local property tax is increasing twice as fast as our increase in personal income.

What is obviously needed is not more government, but better government, seeking a solution to the problems that will not add to bureaucracy, or unbalance the budget, or further centralize power. Therefore, I propose a constructive alternative to the Great Society, which I have chosen to call "A Creative Soci-ety." While leadership and initiative for this Creative Society should begin in the governor's office, it would be the task of the entire state government to discover, enlist and mobilize the incredibly rich human resources of California, calling on the best in every field to review and revise our governmental structure and present plans for streamlining it and making it more efficient and more effective.

There is no major problem that cannot be resolved by a vigorous and imaginative state administration willing to utilize the tremendous potential of our people. We have the greatest concentration of industrial and scientific research facilities of any state in the Union. Tens of thousands of successful and highly talented men and women are in our business communities; colleges and universities are rich in possibilities for study and research; charities and philanthropic enterprises are many, and there are innumerable people of creative talent in the professions.

We have attracted the most youthful, the brightest and the best trained people from every state and every nation. We have untapped resources in the retired men and women with lifetime records of achievement in every conceivable area of endeavor. Probably there is more talent prematurely retired in California than in any other state; and these people, I believe, would welcome a chance for meaningful personal fulfillment in community service—if only someone would ask them.

And that is the basis of the Creative Society—government no longer substituting for the people, but recognizing that it cannot possibly match the great potential of the people, and thus, must coordinate the creative energies of the people for the good of the whole.

Now this isn't some glorified program for passing the buck and telling the people to play Samaritan and solve the problems on their own, while government stands by to hand out Good Conduct ribbons. There is a definite and active role for government, but as our numbers increase and society grows more complex, the idea of an economy planned or controlled by government just doesn't make sense. No matter how talented the government is, it is incapable of making the multitudinous decisions that must be made every day in the market place and in our community living. Big business has already replaced autocratic rule from the top with decentralization, and government must do the same thing.

This means the Creative Society must return authority to the local communities—give them the right to run their own affairs. The people in San Francisco know better than anyone in Sacramento where a freeway in San Francisco should go.

A skyrocketing crime rate has given California almost double its proportionate share of crime—crimes of violence—simply because the state, as a result of certain judicial decisions, denies local governments the right to pass ordinances for the protection of the people. Time after time, legislation has been introduced to correct this. Much of it died in committee in Sacramento; but eventually, when it did pass the Assembly or the Senate it was vetoed by the governor. The legislation will, and must, be reintroduced and signed into law to give our police the power to make our streets safe again. At the same time, government must call upon the best minds in the field of human relations and law and penology for a creative study of our penal and our parole systems.

I propose and urge the adoption of a plan whereby a joint committee of laymen and members of the Bar Association will choose a panel of individuals, based on their personal character and on their legal experience and ability. And then the governor would be forced to appoint all judges from this panel, taking judicial appointments once and for all out of politics.

A confidential survey of industry reveals that by all the criteria used to establish economic health, California comes off looking like that fellow on TV before he takes the pill. We lead the nation in population increase, but we lag far behind the national average in growth of personal income, retail sales and gross product. When home construction fell off last year in the country, it declined five times more in California than it did in the rest of the nation. Five years ago, we were sixth among the states in our ability to attract new industries; today we have fallen to 13th. And running like a thread through this survey are the reports of government's unfriendly attitude toward business, evidenced by the harassing regulations, needless paper work and regressive tax policies.

The present administration's approach to our deteriorating business climate is always another pill out of the same old bottle. Build another bureau, add another tax, and put the unemployed on the public payroll. The Creative Society will, instead, turn to those who truly have the capacity to create jobs and prosperity. Ask the best brains of industry and the community: What is needed to make California once again attractive to industry? Ask them to evolve the plans for creating job opportunities and a program of on-the-job training—because in the last analysis, employment and prosperity are the function and responsibility of private enterprise. It is government's responsibility to end the harassment, roadblocks, regressive taxation and to offer, wherever practical, tax incentives that will help to provide jobs and a friendly business climate.

No small part of the heavy tax load that is borne by the working men and women of our state is a welfare load, which doubled in the last five years, and is increasing faster than our spending on education. Those who administer welfare at the county and local levels have their hands tied by excessive regulations and red tape imposed by both Washington and Sacramento. A Creative Society would call upon their experience and the thinking of the campus researchers and others experienced in philanthropy and public service to make a study to establish that we are doing all we can, first of all, for those who are disabled, aged and who, through no fault of their own, must depend on the rest of us. Our goal should be not only to provide the necessities of life, but those comforts such as we can afford that will make their life worth living.

Then, such a commission must turn and investigate that part of welfare having to do with those who need temporary help—who are being helped through an emergency period only until they can again play a productive role. We must determine that this is still our purpose and that we have not, instead, settled on a program of perpetuating poverty with a permanent dole. We see today a second generation, and even a third generation of citizens, growing up, marrying, having children, accepting public welfare for three generations as a way of life. The 11th century Hebrew physician and philosopher, Maimonides, said there are eight steps in helping the needy. The lowest of these is the handout; the highest is to teach them to help themselves. By contract, our State Department of Public Welfare has a book out and they explain the guiding philosophy of welfare at the state administration level is redistribution of income. Well, this is a reversal of the carrot and stick philosophy, penalizing the industrious and rewarding the unproductive. Redistributing income does not increase purchasing power or prosperity—only increased productivity can accomplish that. Much of welfare spending could become invested, if we would direct some of that spending toward education and training to prevent people from becoming public dependents in the first place.

I have been told there is work in our public institutions, some of which could be performed by unemployables, even illiterates—enough to give jobs to 50,000. Such work should be part of a welfare rehabilitation program. Somewhere,

every problem that faces us is being solved economically and efficiently by citizens who didn't wait for the slow growth of bureaucracy. The Creative Society would encourage the expansion of these voluntary efforts instead of competing them out of existence with free federal handouts which turn out not to be very free at all.

A Californian concerned with needy college students and their problems aroused the interest of bankers and other interested citizens and today, through the United Student Loan Fund, some 65,000 students, on 700 campuses, have borrowed $35 million from banks which will be repaid after graduation. Private citizens underwrite every dollar voluntarily with government playing no part whatsoever.

Following the tragic disturbance in Watts last summer, the Los Angeles Chamber of Commerce mobilized hundreds of industrial concerns in this area and they agreed that unemployment was their responsibility. Working with a committee of fine, responsible Negro businessmen in that area, they set out to establish an employment and job training program and so far, they have put 5,000 of the citizens in that area to work or in on-the-job training spots. This is almost as many people as there are poverty program administrators in the area.

A businessman in Texas brought up in poverty—now successful—founded a boys ranch. He and his wife worked tirelessly—just the two of them—and they have developed what J. Edgar Hoover has called a "blue print for the prevention of crime." Three hundred boys, ranging in age from 4 to 17, are cared for at a per capita cost of about $1,600 a year. Compare this with the $3,600 a year it costs us to maintain a boy in Juvenile Hall.

Here in California, a B'nai B'rith Lodge adopted one of our youth probation camps. Just by lending a helping hand—showing an interest—being willing to listen to these young men, they have reduced the period of time the boys must stay in this camp by a full one-third. It would be easy to establish what that means to the taxpayer in dollars and cents. And all it took was a little time and a little human compassion.

Have we in America forgotten our own accomplishments? For 200 years we've been fighting the most successful war on poverty the world has ever seen. We built the West without waiting for an area redevelopment plan. San Francisco, destroyed by fire, was rebuilt by Californians who didn't wait for urban renewal. We have fought our wars with citizen-soldiers and dollar-a-year men.

At the end of World War I, American citizens cooperated with government in a voluntary program of Belgian Relief that saved millions of lives. As World War II drew to a close, Jesse Jones, Secretary of Commerce, alarmed at the plans he saw on bureaucratic drawing boards in Washington, appealed to corporation heads and businessmen and asked them, instead, to plan the transition from a war- to a peace-time economy. The Council of Economic Advisors was born. Fifty thousand business leaders, through 2,000 community organizations, performed what is still viewed as an economic miracle—and no tax dollars changed hands.

Farming is California's greatest industry, responsible, directly or indirectly, for one-third of our employment and 70 percent of all the cash business transactions that take place in the state. We produce a greater variety on California farms than any other state—some 200 crops—and 98% of our farming is out on the free market, unsubsidized by the federal farm program. But our farmers have very little voice in our state capital of Sacramento. Last year they were made into guinea pigs for a sociological experiment by the federal government, aided and abetted by our state government. They, and representatives of associated industries, should be called in and they should be asked, in a Creative Society, for common sense

answers to their problems and the voice of California government should be raised in their behalf.

Control of education should remain, as much as possible, at the level of the local school boards and unwanted unification should not be imposed from above, but should only take place if it represents the will of the people directly involved. Increased autonomy should be granted to our state colleges and universities and the management of the people's affairs should be kept, as much as possible, at the local level.

The Creative Society, in other words, is simply a return to the people of the privilege of self-government, as well as a pledge for more efficient representative government—citizens of proven ability in their fields, serving where their experience qualifies them, proposing common sense answers for California's problems, reviewing governmental structure itself and bringing it into line with the most advanced, modern business practices. Those who talk of complex problems, requiring more government planning and more control, in reality are taking us back in time to the acceptance of rule of the many by the few. Time to look to the future. We've had enough talk—disruptive talk—in America of left and right, dividing us down the center. There is really no such choice facing us. The only choice we have is up or down—up, to the ultimate in individual freedom consistent with law and order, or down, to the deadly dullness of totalitarianism.

Do we still have the courage and the capacity to dream? If so, I wish you'd join me in a dream. Join me in a dream of a California whose government isn't characterized by political hacks and cronies and relatives—an administration that doesn't make its decisions based on political expediency but on moral truth. Together, let us find men to match our mountains. We can have a government administered by men and women who are appointed on the basis of ability and dedication—not as a reward for political favors. If we must have a double standard of morality, then let it be one which demands more of those in government, not less.

This is a practical dream—it's a dream you can believe in—it's a dream worthy of your generation. Better yet, it's a dream that can come true and all we have to do is want it badly enough.

Source: "The Creative Society," April 19, 1966, The Ronald Reagan Presidential Foundation and Library. Available online. URL: http://www.reaganfoundation.com/reagan/speeches/creative.asp

4. "California and the Problem of Government Growth" January 5, 1967

Ronald Reagan's landslide 1966 win over Edmund G. (Pat) Brown made him a figure to be reckoned with in national politics. In his first inaugural address as governor of California, Reagan remained faithful to the message he had delivered for some time: the importance of cutting taxes, reforming welfare, restoring respect for law and order, cutting government spending and balancing the state's budget. The speech also included two concise lines which drove many of his opponents to distraction, and which Reagan would repeat on many occasions in the future: "For many years now, you and I have been shushed like children and told there are no simple answers to the complex problems which are beyond our comprehension. Well the truth is, there are simple answers, they just are not easy ones."

To a number of us, this is a first and hence a solemn and momentous occasion, and yet, on the broad page of state and national history, what is taking place here is almost commonplace routine. We are participating in the orderly transfer of administrative authority by

direction of the people. And this is the simple magic which makes a commonplace routine a near miracle to many of the world's inhabitants: the continuing fact that the people, by democratic process, can delegate this power, yet retain custody of it.

Perhaps you and I have lived with this miracle too long to be properly appreciative. Freedom is a fragile thing and is never more than one generation away from extinction, It is not ours by inheritance; it must be fought for and defended constantly by each generation, for it comes only once to a people. Those who have known freedom and then lost it have never known it again. Knowing this, it is hard to explain those who even today would question the people's capacity for self-rule. Will they answer this: if no one among us is capable of governing himself, then who among us has the capacity to govern someone else? Using the temporary authority granted by the people, an increasing number lately have sought to control the means of production, as if this could be done without eventually controlling those who produce. Always this is explained as necessary to the people's welfare. But, "The deterioration of every government begins with the decay of the principle upon which it was founded" [Montesquieu]. This is as true today as it was when it was written in 1748.

Government is the people's business, and every man, woman and child becomes a shareholder with the first penny of tax paid. With all the profound wording of the Constitution, probably the most meaningful words are the first three: "We, the People." Those of us here today who have been elected to constitutional office or legislative position are in that three-word phrase. We are of the people, chosen by them to see that no permanent structure of government ever encroaches on freedom or assumes a power beyond that freely granted by the people. We stand between the taxpayer and the tax-spender.

It is inconceivable to me that anyone could accept this delegated authority without asking God's help. I pray that we who legislate and administer will be granted wisdom and strength beyond our own limited power; that with Divine guidance we can avoid easy expedients, as we work to build a state where liberty under law and justice can triumph, where compassion can govern, and wherein the people can participate and prosper because of their government and not in spite of it.

The path we will chart is not an easy one. It demands much of those chosen to govern, but also from those who did the choosing. And let there be no mistake about this: We have come to a crossroad, a time of decision, and the path we follow turns away from any idea that government and those who serve it are omnipotent. It is a path impossible to follow unless we have faith in the collective wisdom and genius of the people. Along this path government will lead but not rule, listen but not lecture. It is the path of a Creative Society.

A number of problems were discussed during the campaign, and I see no reason to change the subject now. Campaign oratory on the issues of crime, pollution of air and water, conservation, welfare, and expanded educational facilities does not mean the issues will go away because the campaign has ended. Problems remain to be solved and they challenge all of us. Government will lead, of course, but the answer must come from all of you.

We will make specific proposals and we will solicit other ideas. In the area of crime, where we have double our proportionate share, we will propose legislation to give back to local communities the right to pass and enforce ordinances which will enable the police to more adequately protect these communities. Legislation already drafted will be submitted, calling upon the Legislature clearly to state in the future whether newly adopted laws are intended to preempt the right of local governments to legislate in the same field. Hopefully, this will free judges from having to guess the intent of those who passed the legislation in the first place.

At the same time, I pledge my support and fullest effort to a plan which will remove from politics, once and for all, the appointment of judges . . . not that I believe I'll be overburdened with making judicial appointments in the immediate future.

Just as we assume a responsibility to guard our young people up to a certain age from the possible harmful effects of alcohol and tobacco, so do I believe we have a right and a responsibility to protect them from the even more harmful effects of exposure to smut and pornography. We can and must frame legislation that will accomplish this purpose without endangering freedom of speech and the press.

When fiscally feasible, we hope to create a California crime technological foundation utilizing both public and private resources in a major effort to employ the most scientific techniques to control crime. At such a time, we should explore the idea of a state police academy to assure that police from even the smallest communities can have the most advanced training. We lead the nation in many things; we are going to stop leading in crime. Californians should be able to walk our streets safely day or night. The law-abiding are entitled to at least as much protection as the lawbreakers.

While on the subject of crime . . . those with a grievance can seek redress in the courts or legislature, but not in the streets. Lawlessness by the mob, as with the individual, will not be tolerated. We will act firmly and quickly to put down riot or insurrection wherever and whenever the situation requires.

Welfare is another of our major problems. We are a humane and generous people and we accept without reservation our obligation to help the aged, disabled, and those unfortunates who, through no fault of their own, must depend on their fellow man. But we are not going to perpetuate poverty by substituting a permanent dole for a paycheck. There is no humanity or charity in destroying self-reliance, dignity, and self-respect . . . the very substance of moral fiber.

We seek reforms that will, wherever possible, change relief check to paycheck. Spencer Williams, Administrator of Health and Welfare, is assessing the amount of work that could be done in public installations by welfare recipients. This is not being done in any punitive sense, but as a beginning step in rehabilitation to give the individual the self-respect that goes with performing a useful service.

But this is not the ultimate answer. Only private industry in the last analysis can provide jobs with a future. Lieutenant Governor Robert Finch will be liaison between government and the private sector in an all-out program of job training and education leading to real employment.

A truly great citizen of our state and a fine American, Mr. H. C. McClellan, has agreed to institute a statewide program patterned after the one he directed so successfully in the "curfew area" of Los Angeles. There, in the year and a half since the tragic riots, fully half of the unemployed have been channeled into productive jobs in private industry, and more than 2,600 businesses are involved. Mr. McClellan will be serving without pay and the entire statewide program will be privately financed. While it will be directed at all who lack opportunity, it offers hope especially to those minorities who have a disproportionate share of poverty and unemployment.

In the whole area of welfare, everything will be done to reduce administrative overhead, cut red tape, and return control as much as possible to the county level. And the goal will be investment in, and salvage of, human beings.

This Administration will cooperate with the State Superintendent of Public Instruction in his expressed desires to return more control of curriculum and selection of textbooks to local school districts. We will support his efforts to make recruitment of out-of-state teachers less difficult.

In the subject of education . . . hundreds of thousands of young men and women will receive an education in our state colleges and universities. We are proud of our ability to provide this opportunity for our youth and we believe it is no denial of academic freedom to provide this education within a framework of reasonable rules and regulations. Nor is it a violation of individual rights to require obedience to these rules and regulations or to insist that those unwilling to abide by them should get their education elsewhere.

It does not constitute political interference with intellectual freedom for the taxpaying citizens who support the college and university systems to ask that, in addition to teaching, they build character on accepted moral and ethical standards.

Just as a man is entitled to a voice in government, so he should certainly have that right in the very personal matter of earning a living. I have always supported the principle of the union shop, even though that includes a certain amount of compulsion with regard to union membership. For that reason it seems to me that government must accept a responsibility for safeguarding each union member's democratic rights within his union. For that reason we will submit legislative proposals to guarantee each union member a secret ballot in his union on policy matters and the use of union dues.

There is also need for a mediation service in labor management disputes not covered by existing law. There are improvements to be made in workmen's compensation in death benefits and benefits to the permanently dis-

abled. At the same time, a tightening of procedures is needed to free business from some unjust burdens.

A close liaison with our congressional representatives in Washington, both Democratic and Republican, is needed so that we can help bring about beneficial changes in Social Security, secure less restrictive controls on federal grants, and work for a tax retention plan that will keep some of our federal taxes here for our use with no strings attached. We should strive also to get tax credits for our people to help defray the cost of sending their children to college.

We will support a bipartisan effort to lift the archaic 160-acre limitation imposed by the federal government on irrigated farms. Restrictive labor policies should never again be the cause of crops rotting in the fields for lack of harvesters.

Here in our own Capitol, we will seek solutions to the problems of unrealistic taxes which threaten economic ruin to our biggest industry. We will work with the farmer as we will with business, industry, and labor to provide a better business climate so that they may prosper and we all may prosper.

There are other problems and possible problems facing us. One such is now pending before the United States Supreme Court. I believe it would be inappropriate to discuss that matter now. We will, however, be prepared with remedial legislation we devoutly hope will be satisfactory to all of our citizens if court rulings make this necessary.

This is only a partial accounting of our problems and our dreams for the future. California, with its climate, its resources, and its wealth of young, aggressive, talented people, must never take second place. We can provide jobs for all our people who will work, and we can have honest government at a price we can afford. Indeed, unless we accomplish this, our problems will go unsolved, our dreams unfulfilled and we will know the taste of ashes.

I have put off until last what is by no means least among our problems. Our fiscal situation has a sorry similarity to the situation of a jetliner out over the North Atlantic, Paris-bound. The pilot announced he had news; some good, some bad, and he would give the bad news first. They had lost radio contact; their compass and altimeter were not working; they didn't know their altitude, direction or where they were headed. Then he gave the good news they had a 100-mile-an-hour tail-wind and they were ahead of schedule.

Our fiscal year began July 1st and will end on the coming June 30th six months from now. The present budget for this twelve-month period is $4.6 billion, an all-time high for any of the fifty states. When this budget was presented, it was admittedly in excess of the estimated tax revenues for the year. It was adopted with the assurance that a change in bookkeeping procedures would solve this imbalance.

With half the year gone, and faced now with the job of planning next year's budget, we have an estimate provided by the experienced personnel of the Department of Finance. We have also an explanation of how a change i bookkeeping could seemingly balance a budg that called for spending $400 million m than we would take in.

Very simply, it was just another one-t windfall a gimmick that solved nothing only postponed the day of reckoning. W financing the twelve-month spending wi teen-month income. All the tax reven the first quarter of next year—July, Aug September—will be used to finance th expenses up to June 30th. And inci even that isn't enough, because we have a deficit of some $63 million.

Now, with the budget establi present level, we are told that it. must be increased next year to me problems of population growth a

But the magic of the changed bookkeeping is all used up. We are back to only twelve months' income for twelve months' spending. Almost automatically we are being advised of all the new and increased taxes which, if adopted, will solve the problem. Curiously enough, another one-time windfall is being urged. If we switch to withholding of personal income tax, we will collect two years' taxes the first year and postpone our moment of truth perhaps until everyone forgets we did not cause the problem we only inherited it. Or maybe we are to stall, hoping a rich uncle will remember us in his will.

If we accept the present budget as absolutely necessary and add on projected increases plus funding for property tax relief (which I believe is absolutely essential and for which we are preparing a detailed and comprehensive program), our deficit in the coming year would reach three-quarters of a billion dollars.

But Californians are already burdened with combined state and local taxes $113 per capita higher than the national average. Our property tax contributes to a slump in the real estate and building trades industries and makes it well-nigh impossible for many citizens to continue owning their own homes.

For many years now, you and I have been shushed like children and told there are no simple answers to the complex problems which are beyond our comprehension.

Well the truth is, there are simple answers, they just are not easy ones. The time has come for us to decide whether collectively we can afford everything and anything we think of simply because we think of it. The time has come to run a check to see if all the services government provides were in answer to demands or were just goodies dreamed up for our supposed betterment. The time has come to match outgo to income, instead of always doing it the other way around.

The cost of California's government is so high; it adversely affects our business cli-mate. We have a phenomenal growth with hundreds of thousands of people joining us each year. Of course, the overall cost of government must go up to provide necessary services for these newcomers, but growth should mean increased prosperity and thus a lightening of the load each individual must bear. If this isn't true, then you and I should be planning how we can put up a fence along the Colorado River and seal our borders. Well, we aren't going to do that. We are going to squeeze and cut and trim until we reduce the cost of government. It won't be easy, nor will it be pleasant, and it will involve every department of government, starting with the governor's office. I have already informed the legislature of the reorganization we hope to effect with their help in the executive branch and I have asked for their cooperation and support.

The new director of finance is in complete agreement that we turn to additional sources of revenue only if it becomes clear that economies alone cannot balance the budget.

Disraeli said: "Man is not a creature of circumstances. Circumstances are the creatures of men." You and I will shape our circumstances to fit our needs.

Let me reaffirm a promise made during the months of campaigning. I believe in your right to know all the facts concerning the people's business. Independent firms are making an audit of state finances. When it is completed, you will have that audit. You will have all the information you need to make the decisions which must be made. This is not just a problem for the administration; it is a problem for all of us to solve together. I know that you can face any prospect and do anything that has to be done as long as you know the truth of what you are up against.

We will put our fiscal house in order. And as we do, we will build those things we need to make our state a better place in which to live

and we will enjoy them more, knowing we can afford them and they are paid for.

If, in glancing aloft, some of you were puzzled by the small size of our state flag . . . there is an explanation. That flag was carried into battle in Vietnam by young men of California. Many will not be coming home. One did, Sergeant Robert Howell, grievously wounded. He brought that flag back. I thought we would be proud to have it fly over the Capitol today. It might even serve to put our problems in better perspective. It might remind us of the need to give our sons and daughters a cause to believe in and banners to follow.

If this is a dream, it is a good dream, worthy of our generation and worth passing on to the next.

Let this day mark the beginning.

Source: "The Problems Facing California (1967)," January 5, 1967, The President Reagan Information Page. Available online. URL: http://www.presidentreagan.info/speeches/california_government.cfm

5. "City Upon a Hill"
Conservative Political Action Conference
January 25, 1974

This address to the Conservative Political Action Conference is classic Reagan. Beginning with a tribute to recently released prisoners of war from Vietnam (including future senator and presidential aspirant John McCain), Reagan compares the Vietnam POWs with the heroes of the American founding, and sprinkles his address with numerous folksy anecdotes belittling the capability of the federal government and hailing the wisdom and virtue of the "common" man. The spontaneous action of individuals has served the nation well, and a meddlesome central government threatens to undermine this tradition of individual initiative. As always, Reagan's America is a land inhabited by heroes and guided by a providential hand; the
United States is an exceptional nation destined to accomplish great things.

There are three men here tonight I am very proud to introduce. It was a year ago this coming February when this country had its spirits lifted as they have never been lifted in many years. This happened when planes began landing on American soil and in the Philippines, bringing back men who had lived with honor for many miserable years in North Vietnam prisons. Three of those men are here tonight, John McCain, Bill Lawrence and Ed Martin. It is an honor to be here tonight. I am proud that you asked me and I feel more than a little humble in the presence of this distinguished company.

There are men here tonight who, through their wisdom, their foresight and their courage, have earned the right to be regarded as prophets of our philosophy. Indeed they are prophets of our times. In years past when others were silent or too blind to the facts, they spoke up forcefully and fearlessly for what they believed to be right. A decade has passed since Barry Goldwater walked a lonely path across this land reminding us that even a land as rich as ours can't go on forever borrowing against the future, leaving a legacy of debt for another generation and causing a runaway inflation to erode the savings and reduce the standard of living. Voices have been raised trying to rekindle in our country all of the great ideas and principles which set this nation apart from all the others that preceded it, but louder and more strident voices utter easily sold clichés.

Cartoonists with acid-tipped pens portray some of the reminders of our heritage and our destiny as old-fashioned. They say that we are trying to retreat into a past that actually never existed. Looking to the past in an effort to keep our country from repeating the errors of history is termed by them as "taking the country back to McKinley." Of course I never found that was so bad—under McKinley we freed Cuba. On the span of history, we are still thought of as a young upstart country celebrating soon only our second century as a nation, and yet we are the oldest continuing republic in the world.

I thought that tonight, rather than talking on the subjects you are discussing, or trying to find something new to say, it might be appropriate to reflect a bit on our heritage.

You can call it mysticism if you want to, but I have always believed that there was some divine plan that placed this great continent between two oceans to be sought out by those who were possessed of an abiding love of freedom and a special kind of courage.

This was true of those who pioneered the great wilderness in the beginning of this country, as it is also true of those later immigrants who were willing to leave the land of their birth and come to a land where even the language was unknown to them. Call it chauvinistic, but our heritage does not set us apart. Some years ago a writer, who happened to be an avid student of history, told me a story about that day in the little hall in Philadelphia where honorable men, hard-pressed by a King who was flouting the very law they were willing to obey, debated whether they should take the fateful step of declaring their independence from that king. I was told by this man that the story could be found in the writings of Jefferson. I confess, I never researched or made an effort to verify it. Perhaps it is only legend. But story, or legend, he described the atmosphere, the strain, the debate, and that as men for the first time faced the consequences of such an irretrievable act, the walls resounded with the dread word of treason and its price—the gallows and the headman's axe. As the day wore on the issue hung in the balance, and then, according to the story, a man rose in the small gallery. He was not a young man and was obviously calling on all the energy he could muster. Citing the

grievances that had brought them to this moment he said, "Sign that parchment. They may turn every tree into a gallows, every home into a grave and yet the words of that parchment can never die. For the mechanic in his workshop, they will be words of hope, to the slave in the mines—freedom." And he added, "If my hands were freezing in death, I would sign that parchment with my last ounce of strength. Sign, sign if the next moment the noose is around your neck, sign even if the hall is ringing with the sound of the headman's axe, for that parchment will be the textbook of freedom, the bible of the rights of man forever." And then it is said he fell back exhausted. But 56 delegates, swept by his eloquence, signed the Declaration of Independence, a document destined to be as immortal as any work of man can be. And according to the story, when they turned to thank him for his timely oratory, he could not be found nor were there any who knew who he was or how he had come in or gone out through the locked and guarded doors.

Well, as I say, whether story or legend, the signing of the document that day in Independence Hall was miracle enough. Fifty-six men, a little band so unique—we have never seen their like since—pledged their lives, their fortunes and their sacred honor. Sixteen gave their lives, most gave their fortunes and all of them preserved their sacred honor. What manner of men were they? Certainly they were not an unwashed, revolutionary rabble, nor were they adventurers in a heroic mood. Twenty-four were lawyers and jurists, 11 were merchants and tradesmen, nine were farmers. They were men who would achieve security but valued freedom more.

And what price did they pay? John Hart was driven from the side of his desperately ill wife. After more than a year of living almost as an animal in the forest and in caves, he returned to find his wife had died and his children had vanished. He never saw them again, his property was destroyed and he died of a broken heart—but with no regret, only pride in the part he had played that day in Independence Hall. Carter Braxton of Virginia lost all his ships—they were sold to pay his debts. He died in rags. So it was with Ellery, Clymer, Hall, Walton, Gwinnett, Rutledge, Morris, Livingston, and Middleton. Nelson, learning that Cornwallis was using his home for a headquarters, personally begged Washington to fire on him and destroy his home—he died bankrupt. It has never been reported that any of these men ever expressed bitterness or renounced their action as not worth the price. Fifty-six rank-and-file, ordinary citizens had founded a nation that grew from sea to shining sea, five million farms, quiet villages, cities that never sleep—all done without an area re-development plan, urban renewal or a rural legal assistance program.

Now we are a nation of 211 million people with a pedigree that includes blood lines from every corner of the world. We have shed that American-melting-pot blood in every corner of the world, usually in defense of someone's freedom. Those who remained of that remarkable band we call our Founding Fathers tied up some of the loose ends about a dozen years after the Revolution. It had been the first revolution in all man's history that did not just exchange one set of rulers for another. This had been a philosophical revolution. The culmination of men's dreams for 6,000 years were formalized with the Constitution, probably the most unique document ever drawn in the long history of man's relation to man. I know there have been other constitutions, new ones are being drawn today by newly emerging nations. Most of them, even the one of the Soviet Union, contains many of the same guarantees as our own Constitution, and still there is a difference. The difference is so subtle that we often overlook it, but is so great that it tells the

whole story. Those other constitutions say, "Government grants you these rights" and ours says, "You are born with these rights, they are yours by the grace of God, and no government on earth can take them from you."

Lord Acton of England, who once said, "Power corrupts, and absolute power corrupts absolutely," would say of that document, "They had solved with astonishing ease and unduplicated success two problems which had heretofore baffled the capacity of the most enlightened nations. They had contrived a system of federal government which prodigiously increased national power and yet respected local liberties and authorities, and they had founded it on a principle of equality without surrendering the securities of property or freedom." Never in any society has the preeminence of the individual been so firmly established and given such a priority.

In less than twenty years we would go to war because the God-given rights of the American sailors, as defined in the Constitution, were being violated by a foreign power. We served notice then on the world that all of us together would act collectively to safeguard the rights of even the least among us. But still, in an older, cynical world, they were not convinced. The great powers of Europe still had the idea that one day this great continent would be open again to colonizing and they would come over and divide us up. In the meantime, men who yearned to breathe free were making their way to our shores. Among them was a young refugee from the Austro-Hungarian Empire. He had been a leader in an attempt to free Hungary from Austrian rule. The attempt had failed and he fled to escape execution. In America, this young Hungarian, Koscha by name, became an importer by trade and took out his first citizenship papers. One day, business took him to a Mediterranean port. There was a large Austrian warship under the command of an admiral in the harbor. He had a manservant with him. He had described to this manservant what the flag of his new country looked like. Word was passed to the Austrian warship that this revolutionary was there and in the night he was kidnapped and taken aboard that large ship. This man's servant, desperate, walking up and down the harbor, suddenly spied a flag that resembled the description he had heard. It was a small American war sloop. He went aboard and told Captain Ingraham, of that war sloop, his story. Captain Ingraham went to the American Consul. When the American Consul learned that Koscha had only taken out his first citizenship papers, the consul washed his hands of the incident. Captain Ingraham said, "I am the senior officer in this port and I believe, under my oath of my office, that I owe this man the protection of our flag."

He went aboard the Austrian warship and demanded to see their prisoner, our citizen. The Admiral was amused, but they brought the man on deck. He was in chains and had been badly beaten. Captain Ingraham said, "I can hear him better without those chains," and the chains were removed. He walked over and said to Koscha, "I will ask you one question; consider your answer carefully. Do you ask the protection of the American flag?" Koscha nodded dumbly "Yes," and the Captain said, "You shall have it." He went back and told the frightened consul what he had done. Later in the day three more Austrian ships sailed into harbor. It looked as though the four were getting ready to leave. Captain Ingraham sent a junior officer over to the Austrian flag ship to tell the Admiral that any attempt to leave that harbor with our citizen aboard would be resisted with appropriate force. He said that he would expect a satisfactory answer by four o'clock that afternoon. As the hour neared they looked at each other through the glasses. As it struck four he had them roll the cannons into the ports and had then light the tapers with which they would set off the cannons—one little sloop.

Suddenly the lookout tower called out and said, "They are lowering a boat," and they rowed Koscha over to the little American ship.

Captain Ingraham then went below and wrote his letter of resignation to the United States Navy. In it he said, "I did what I thought my oath of office required, but if I have embarrassed my country in any way, I resign." His resignation was refused in the United States Senate with these words: "This battle that was never fought may turn out to be the most important battle in our Nation's history." Incidentally, there is to this day, and I hope there always will be, a USS *Ingraham* in the United States Navy.

I did not tell that story out of any desire to be narrowly chauvinistic or to glorify aggressive militarism, but it is an example of government meeting its highest responsibility.

In recent years we have been treated to a rash of noble-sounding phrases. Some of them sound good, but they don't hold up under close analysis. Take for instance the slogan so frequently uttered by the young senator from Massachusetts, "The greatest good for the greatest number." Certainly under that slogan, no modern day Captain Ingraham would risk even the smallest craft and crew for a single citizen. Every dictator who ever lived has justified the enslavement of his people on the theory of what was good for the majority.

We are not a warlike people. Nor is our history filled with tales of aggressive adventures and imperialism, which might come as a shock to some of the placard painters in our modern demonstrations. The lesson of Vietnam, I think, should be that never again will young Americans be asked to fight and possibly die for a cause unless that cause is so meaningful that we, as a nation, pledge our full resources to achieve victory as quickly as possible.

I realize that such a pronouncement, of course, would possibly be laying one open to the charge of warmongering—but that would also be ridiculous. My generation has paid a higher price and has fought harder for freedom that any generation that had ever lived. We have known four wars in a single lifetime. All were horrible, all could have been avoided if at a particular moment in time we had made it plain that we subscribed to the words of John Stuart Mill when he said that "war is an ugly thing, but not the ugliest of things."

The decayed and degraded state of moral and patriotic feeling which thinks nothing is worth a war is worse. The man who has nothing which he cares about more than his personal safety is a miserable creature and has no chance of being free unless made and kept so by the exertions of better men than himself.

The widespread disaffection with things military is only a part of the philosophical division in our land today. I must say to you who have recently, or presently are still receiving an education, I am awed by your powers of resistance. I have some knowledge of the attempts that have been made in many classrooms and lecture halls to persuade you that there is little to admire in America. For the second time in this century, capitalism and free enterprise are under assault. Privately owned business is blamed for spoiling the environment, exploiting the worker and seducing, if not outright raping, the customer. Those who make the charge have the solution, of course—government regulation and control. We may never get around to explaining how citizens who are so gullible that they can be suckered into buying cereal or soap that they don't need and would not be good for them, can at the same time be astute enough to choose representatives in government to which they would entrust the running of their lives.

Not too long ago, a poll was taken on 2,500 college campuses in this country. Thousands and thousands of responses were obtained. Overwhelmingly, 65, 70, and 75 percent of the students found business responsible, as I have said before, for the things that were wrong in this country. That same number said that government was the solution and should take over the management and the control of private business. Eighty percent of the respondents said they wanted government to keep its paws out of their private lives.

We are told every day that the assembly-line worker is becoming a dull-witted robot and that mass production results in standardization. Well, there isn't a socialist country in the world that would not give its copy of Karl Marx for our standardization. Standardization means production for the masses and the assembly line means more leisure for the worker—freedom from backbreaking and mind-dulling drudgery that man had known for centuries past. Karl Marx did not abolish child labor or free the women from working in the coal mines in England, the steam engine and modern machinery did that.

Unfortunately, the disciples of the new order have had a hand in determining too much policy in recent decades. Government has grown in size and power and cost through the New Deal, the Fair Deal, the New Frontier and the Great Society. It costs more for government today than a family pays for food, shelter and clothing combined. Not even the Office of Management and Budget knows how many boards, commissions, bureaus and agencies there are in the federal government, but the federal registry, listing their regulations, is just a few pages short of being as big as the Encyclopedia Britannica. During the Great Society we saw the greatest growth of this government. There were eight cabinet departments and 12 independent agencies to administer the federal health program. There were 35 housing programs and 20 transportation projects. Public utilities had to cope with 27 different agencies on just routine business. There were 192 installations and nine departments with 1,000 projects having to do with the field of pollution.

and opera companies, non-profit theaters, and publish more books than all the other nations of the world put together.

Somehow America has bred a kindliness into our people unmatched anywhere, as has been pointed out in that best-selling record by a Canadian journalist. We are not a sick society. A sick society could not produce the men that set foot on the moon, or who are now circling the earth above us in the Skylab. A sick society bereft of morality and courage did not produce the men who went through those year of torture and captivity in Vietnam. Where did we find such men? They are typical of this land as the Founding Fathers were typical. We found them in our streets, in the offices, the shops and the working places of our country and on the farms.

We cannot escape our destiny, nor should we try to do so. The leadership of the free world was thrust upon us two centuries ago in that little hall of Philadelphia. In the days following World War II, when the economic strength and power of America was all that stood between the world and the return to the dark ages, Pope Pius XII said, "The American people have a great genius for splendid and unselfish actions. Into the hands of America God has placed the destinies of an afflicted mankind."

We are indeed, and we are today, the last best hope of man on earth.

Source: "City Upon a Hill (1974)," January 25, 1974, The President Reagan Information Page. Available online. URL: http://www.presidentreagan.info/speeches/city_upon_a_hill.cfm

6. "To Restore America"
March 31, 1976

This speech was delivered in the midst of Reagan's 1976 fight for the Republican presidential nomination against Gerald Ford. The contest became bitter at times, as some of the rhetoric in this speech indi-cates. For a man who generally liked everyone he met, something about Gerald Ford seemed to particularly irk Ronald Reagan. It was more than his status as an "accidental" president; Ford's propensity to rely on the old Eastern wing of the GOP (as seen in his selection of Nelson Rockefeller as his vice president) convinced Reagan that Ford was not a serious, principled conservative. Reagan criticized Ford over his handling of the economy, his budget deficits, his "Whip Inflation Now" campaign, his status as a Washington insider due to his lengthy career in Congress, and also for his policy of détente, which Reagan contended allowed the Soviet Union to gain the upper hand in the cold war. Reagan also condemned the treaty negotiations with Panama designed to facilitate a peaceful transfer of the Panama Canal to the Panamanian government. The latter issue ignited the conservative wing of the GOP, and contributed to Reagan's win in the North Carolina primary and to successive wins thereafter. Reagan fought all the way to the Republican National Convention in Kansas City that summer, losing by a narrow margin to Ford but positioning himself as the heir to the Republican nomination in 1980.

Good evening to all of you from California. Tonight, I'd like to talk to you about issues. Issues which I think are involved—or should be involved in this primary election season. I'm a candidate for the Republican nomination for president. But I hope that you who are Independents and Democrats will let me talk to you also tonight because the problems facing our country are problems that just don't bear any party label.

In this election season the White House is telling us a solid economic recovery is taking place. It claims a slight drop in unemployment. It says that prices aren't going up as fast, but they are still going up, and that the stock market has shown some gains. But, in fact, things seem just about as they were back in the 1972 election year. Remember, we were also coming out of a recession then. Inflation had been running at round 6 percent. Unemployment about 7 [percent]. Remember, too, the upsurge and the optimism lasted through the election year and into 1973. And then the roof fell in. Once again we had unemployment. Only this time not 7 percent, more than 10. And inflation wasn't 6 percent, it was 12 percent. Now, in this election year 1976, we're told we're coming out of this recession just because inflation and unemployment rates have fallen, to what they were at the worst of the previous recession. If history repeats itself, will we be talking recovery four years from now merely because we've reduced inflation from 25 percent to 12 percent?

The fact is, we'll never build a lasting economic recovery by going deeper into debt at a faster rate than we ever have before. It took this nation 166 years until the middle of World War II to finally accumulate a debt of $95 billion. It took this administration just the last 12 months to add $95 billion to the debt. And this administration has run up almost one-fourth of the total national debt in just these short 19 months.

Inflation is the cause of recession and unemployment. And we're not going to have real prosperity or recovery until we stop fighting the symptoms and start fighting the disease. There's only one cause for inflation—government spending more than government takes in. The cure is a balanced budget. Ah, but they tell us, 80 percent of the budget is uncontrollable. It's fixed by laws passed by Congress. Well, laws passed by Congress can be repealed by Congress. And, if Congress is unwilling to do this, then isn't it time we elect a Congress that will?

Soon after he took office, Mr. Ford promised he would end inflation. Indeed, he declared war on inflation. And, we all donned those WIN buttons to "Whip Inflation Now." Unfortunately the war—if it ever really started—was soon over. Mr. Ford, without WIN button,

appeared on TV, and promised he absolutely would not allow the Federal deficit to exceed $60 billion (which incidentally was $5 billion more than the biggest previous deficit we'd ever had). Later he told us it might be as much as $70 billion. Now we learn it's 80 billion or more.

Then came a White House proposal for a $28 billion tax cut, to be matched by a $28 billion cut in the proposed spending—not in present spending, but in the proposed spending in the new budget. Well, my question then and my question now is, if there was $28 billion in the new budget that could be cut, what was it doing there in the first place?

Unfortunately, Washington doesn't feel the same pain from inflation that you and I do. As a matter of fact, government makes a profit on inflation. For instance, last July Congress vaccinated itself against that pain. It very quietly passed legislation (which the president signed into law) which automatically now gives a pay increase to every Congressman every time the cost of living goes up.

It would have been nice if they'd thought of some arrangement like that for the rest of us. They could, for example, correct a great unfairness that now exists in our tax system. Today, when you get a cost of living pay raise—one that just keeps you even with purchasing power—it often moves you up into a higher tax bracket. This means you pay a higher percentage in tax, but you reduce your purchasing power. Last year, because of this inequity, the government took in $7 billion in undeserved profit in the income tax alone, and this year they'll do even better.

Now isn't it time that Congress looked after your welfare as well as its own? Those whose spending policies cause inflation to begin with should be made to feel the painful effect just as you and I do.

Repeal of Congress' automatic pay raise might leave it with more incentive to do something to curb inflation. Now, let's look at

Social Security. Mr. Ford says he wants to "preserve the integrity of Social Security." Well, I differ with him on one word. I would like to restore the integrity of Social Security. Those who depend on it see a continual reduction in their standard of living. Inflation strips the increase in their benefits. The maximum benefit today buys 80 fewer loaves of bread than it did when that maximum payment was only $85 a month. In the meantime, the Social Security payroll tax has become the most unfair tax any worker pays. Women are discriminated against, particularly working wives. And, people who reach Social Security age and want to continue working, should be allowed to do so without losing their benefits. I believe a presidential commission of experts should be appointed to study and present a plan to strengthen and improve Social Security while there's still time—so that no person who has contributed to Social Security will ever lose a dime.

Before leaving this subject of our economic problems, let's talk about unemployment. Ending inflation is the only long range and lasting answer to the problem of unemployment. The Washington Establishment is not the answer. It's the problem. Its tax policies, its harassing regulation, its confiscation of investment capital to pay for its deficits keeps business and industry from expanding to meet your needs and to provide the jobs we all need.

No one who lived through the Great Depression can ever look upon an unemployed person with anything but compassion. To me, there is no greater tragedy than a breadwinner willing to work, with a job skill but unable to find a market for that job skill. Back in those dark depression days I saw my father on a Christmas Eve open what he thought was a Christmas greeting from his boss. Instead, it was the blue slip telling him he no longer had a job. The memory of him sitting there holding that slip of paper and then saying in a half whisper, "That's quite a Christmas present"; it will stay with me as long as I live.

Other problems go unsolved. Take energy. Only a short time ago we were lined up at the gas station—turned our thermostats down as Washington announced "Project Independence." We were going to become self-sufficient, able to provide for our own energy needs. At the time, we were only importing a small percentage of our oil. Yet, the Arab boycott caused half a million Americans to lose their jobs when plants closed down for lack of fuel. Today, it's almost three years later and "Project Independence" has become "Project Dependence." Congress has adopted an energy bill so bad we were led to believe Mr. Ford would veto it. Instead, he signed it. And, almost instantly, drilling rigs all over our land started shutting down. Now, for the first time in our history we are importing more oil than we produce. How many Americans will be laid off if there's another boycott? The energy bill is a disaster that never should have been signed.

An effort has been made in this campaign to suggest that there aren't any real differences between Mr. Ford and myself. Well, I believe there are, and these differences are fundamental. One of them has to do with our approach to government. Before Richard Nixon appointed him Vice President, Mr. Ford was a Congressman for 25 years. His concern, of necessity, was the welfare of his congressional district. For most of his adult life he has been a part of the Washington Establishment. Most of my adult life has been spent outside of government. My experience in government was the eight years I served as governor of California. If it were a nation, California would be the 7th-ranking economic power in the world today.

When I became governor, I inherited a state government that was in almost the same situation as New York City. The state payroll had been growing for a dozen years at a rate of from five to seven thousand new employees each year. State government was spending from a million to a million-and-a-half dollars more each day than it was taking in. The State's great water project was unfinished and under-funded by a half a billion dollars. My predecessor had spent the entire year's budget for Medicaid in the first six months of the fiscal year. And, we learned that the teacher's retirement fund was unfunded—a $4 billion liability hanging over every property owner in the state. I didn't know whether I'd been elected governor or appointed receiver. California was faced with insolvency and on the verge of bankruptcy. We had to increase taxes. Well, this came very hard for me because I felt taxes were already too great a burden. I told the people the increase in my mind was temporary and that, as soon as we could, we'd return their money to them.

I had never in my life thought of seeking or holding public office and I'm still not quite sure how it all happened. In my own mind, I was a citizen representing my fellow citizens against the institution of government. I turned to the people, not to politicians for help. Instead of a committee to screen applicants for jobs, I had a citizens' recruiting committee, and I told this committee I wanted an administration made up of men and women who did not want government careers and who'd be the first to tell me if their government job was unnecessary. And I had that happen. [A] young man from the aerospace industry dissolved his department in four months, handed me the key to this office, and told me we'd never needed the department. And to this day, I not only have never missed it—I don't know where it was.

There was a reason for my seeking people who didn't want government careers. Dr. Parkinson summed it all up in his book on bureaucracy. He said, "Government hires a rat-catcher and the first thing you know, he's become a rodent control officer." In those entire eight years, most of us never lost that feeling that we were there representing the

people against what Cicero once called the "arrogance of officialdom." We had a kind of watchword we used on each other. "When we begin thinking of government as we instead of they, we've been here too long." Well, I believe that attitude would be beneficial in Washington.

We didn't stop just with getting our administration from the ranks of the people. We also asked for help from expert people in a great many fields, and more than 250 of our citizens volunteered to form into task forces. They went into every department and agency of state government to see how modern business practices could make government more efficient, economical and responsive. They gave an average of 117 days apiece full time, away from their own jobs and careers at no cost to the taxpayers. They made eighteen hundred specific recommendations. We implemented more than sixteen hundred of those recommendations.

This was government-by-the-people, proving that it works when the people work at it. When we ended our eight years, we turned over to the incoming administration a balanced budget, a $500 million surplus, and virtually the same number of employees we'd started with eight years before—even though the increase in population had given some departments a two-thirds increase in work load. The water project was completed with $165 million left over. Our bonds had a triple A rating, the highest credit rating you can get. And the teachers' retirement program was fully funded on a sound actuarial basis. And, we kept our word to the taxpayers—we returned to them in rebates and tax cuts $5 billion 761 million.

I believe that what we did in California can be done in Washington if government will have faith in the people and let them bring their common sense to bear on the problems bureaucracy hasn't solved. I believe in the people. Now, Mr. Ford places his faith in the Washington Establishment. This has been evident in his appointment of former Congressmen and longtime government workers to positions in his Administration. Well, I don't believe that those who have been part of the problem are necessarily the best qualified to solve those problems.

The truth is, Washington has taken over functions that don't truly belong to it. In almost every case it has been a failure. Now, understand, I'm speaking of those programs which logically should be administered at state and local levels. Welfare is a classic example. Voices that are raised now and then urging a federalization of welfare don't realize that the failure of welfare is due to federal interference. Washington doesn't even know how many people are on welfare—how many cheaters are getting more than one check. It only knows how many checks it's sending out. Its own rules keep it from finding out how many are getting more than one check.

Well, California had a welfare problem. Sixteen percent of all welfare recipients in the country were drawing their checks in our state. We were sending welfare checks to families who decided to live abroad. One family was receiving its check in Russia. Our caseload was increasing by 40,000 people a month. Well, after a few years of trying to control this runaway program and being frustrated by bureaucrats here in California and in Washington, we turned again to a citizens' task force. The result was the most comprehensive welfare reform ever attempted. And in less than three years we reduced the rolls by more than 300,000 people, saved the taxpayers $2 billion, and increased the grants to the truly deserving needy by an average of 43 percent. We also carried out a successful experiment which I believe is an answer to much of the welfare problem in the nation. We put able-bodied welfare recipients to work at useful community projects in return for their welfare grants.

Now, let's look at housing. Washington has tried to solve this problem for the poor by building low-cost houses. So far it's torn down three and a half homes for every one it's built.

Schools—in America we created at the local level and administered at the local level for many years the greatest public school system in the world. Now through something called federal aid to education, we have something called federal interference, and education has been the loser. Quality has declined as federal intervention has increased. Nothing has created more bitterness, for example, than forced busing to achieve racial balance. It was born of a hope that we could increase understanding and reduce prejudice and antagonism. And I'm sure we all approved of that goal. But busing has failed to achieve the goal. Instead, it has increased the bitterness and animosity it was supposed to reduce. California's Superintendent of Public Instruction, Wilson Riles (himself a Black), says, "The concept that Black children can't learn unless they are sitting with white children is utter and complete nonsense." Well, I agree. The money now being wasted on this social experiment could be better spent to provide the kind of school facilities every child deserves. Forced busing should be ended by legislation if possible—by constitutional amendment if necessary. And, control of education should be returned to local school districts.

The other day Mr. Ford came out against gun control. But back in Washington, D.C., his Attorney General has proposed a seven-point program that amounts to just that: gun control. I don't think that making it difficult for law-abiding citizens to obtain guns will lower the crime rate—not when the criminals will always find a way to get them. In California I think we found an answer. We put into law what is practical gun control. Anyone convicted of having a gun in his possession while he committed a crime: add five to fifteen years to the prison sentence.

Sometimes bureaucracy's excesses are so great that we laugh at them. But they are costly laughs. Twenty-five years ago the Hoover Commission discovered that Washington files a million reports a year just reporting there is nothing to report. Independent business people, shopkeepers and farmers file billions of reports every year required of them by Washington. It amounts to some 10 billion pieces of paper each year, and it adds $50 billion a year to the cost of doing business. Now, Washington has been loud in its promise to do something about this blizzard of paperwork. And they made good. Last year they increased it by 20 percent.

But there is one problem which must be solved or everything else is meaningless. I am speaking of the problem of our national security. Our nation is in danger, and the danger grows greater with each passing day. Like an echo from the past, the voice of Winston Churchill's grandson was heard recently in Britain's House of Commons warning that the spread of totalitarianism threatens the world once again and the democracies are "wandering without aim."

"Wandering without aim" describes the United States' foreign policy. Angola is a case in point. We gave just enough support to one side to encourage it to fight and die, but too little to give them a chance of winning. And while we're disliked by the winner, distrusted by the loser, and viewed by the world as weak and unsure. If détente were the two-way street it's supposed to be, we could have told the Soviet Union to stop its trouble-making and leave Angola to the Angolans. But it didn't work out that way.

Now, we are told Washington is dropping the word "détente," but keeping the policy. But whatever it's called, the policy is what's at fault. What is our policy? Mr. Ford's new Ambassador to the United Nations attacks our long-time ally, Israel. In Asia, our new relationship

with mainland China can have practical benefits for both sides. But that doesn't mean it should include yielding to demands by them, as the administration has, to reduce our military presence on Taiwan where we have a long-time friend and ally, the Republic of China.

And, it's also revealed now that we seek to establish friendly relations with Hanoi. To make it more palatable, we're told that this might help us learn the fate of the men still listed as Missing in Action. Well, there's no doubt our government has an obligation to end the agony of parents, wives and children who've lived so long with uncertainty. But, this should have been one of our first demands of Hanoi's patron saint, the Soviet Union, if détente had any meaning at all. To present it now as a reason for friendship with those who have already violated their promise to provide such information is hypocrisy.

In the last few days, Mr. Ford and Dr. Kissinger have taken us from hinting at invasion of Cuba, to laughing it off as a ridiculous idea. Except, that it was their ridiculous idea. No one else suggested it. Once again—what is their policy? During this last year, they carried on a campaign to befriend Castro. They persuaded the Organization of American States to lift its trade embargo, lifted some of the U.S. trade restrictions. They engaged in cultural exchanges. And then, on the eve of the Florida primary election, Mr. Ford went to Florida, called Castro an outlaw and said he'd never recognize him. But he hasn't asked our Latin American neighbors to reimpose a single sanction, nor has he taken any action himself. Meanwhile, Castro continues to export revolution to Puerto Rico, to Angola, and who knows where else?

As I talk to you tonight, negotiations with another dictator go forward—negotiations aimed at giving up our ownership of the Panama Canal Zone. Apparently, everyone knows about this except the rightful owners of the Canal Zone—you, the people of the United States. General Omar Torrijos, the dictator of Panama, seized power eight years ago by ousting the duly elected government. There have been no elections since. No civil liberties. The press is censored. Torrijos is a friend and ally of Castro and, like him, is pro-Communist. He threatens sabotage and guerrilla attacks on our installations if we don't yield to his demands. His foreign minister openly claims that we have already agreed in principle to giving up the Canal Zone.

Well, the Canal Zone is not a colonial possession. It is not a long-term lease. It is sovereign United States Territory every bit the same as Alaska and all the states that were carved from the Louisiana Purchase. We should end those negotiations and tell the General: We bought it, we paid for it, we built it, and we intend to keep it.

Mr. Ford says détente will be replaced by "peace through strength." Well now, that slogan has a nice ring to it, but neither Mr. Ford nor his new Secretary of Defense will say that our strength is superior to all others. In one of the dark hours of the Great Depression, Franklin Delano Roosevelt said, "It is time to speak the truth frankly and boldly." Well, I believe former Secretary of Defense James Schlesinger was trying to speak the truth frankly and boldly to his fellow citizens. And that's why he is no longer Secretary of Defense.

The Soviet Army outnumbers ours more than two-to-one and in reserves four-to-one. They out-spend us on weapons by 50 percent. Their Navy outnumbers ours in surface ships and submarines two-to-one. We're outgunned in artillery three-to-one and their tanks outnumber ours four-to-one. Their strategic nuclear missiles are larger, more powerful and more numerous than ours. The evidence mounts that we are Number Two in a world where it's dangerous, if not fatal, to be second best. Is this why Mr. Ford refused to invite

Alexander Solzhenitsyn to the White House? Or, why Mr. Ford traveled halfway 'round the world to sign the Helsinki Pact, putting our stamp of approval on Russia's enslavement of the captive nations? We gave away the freedom of millions of people—freedom that was not ours to give.

Now we must ask if someone is giving away our own freedom. Dr. Kissinger is quoted as saying that he thinks of the United States as Athens and the Soviet Union as Sparta. "The day of the U.S. is past and today is the day of the Soviet Union." And he added, ". . . My job as Secretary of State is to negotiate the most acceptable second-best position available." Well, I believe in the peace of which Mr. Ford spoke—as much as any man. But peace does not come from weakness or from retreat. It comes from the restoration of American military superiority.

Ask the people of Latvia, Estonia, Lithuania, Czechoslovakia, Poland, Hungary—all the others: East Germany, Bulgaria, Romania—ask them what it's like to live in a world where the Soviet Union is Number One. I don't want to live in that kind of world; and I don't think you do either. Now we learn that another high official of the State Department, Helmut Sonnenfeldt, whom Dr. Kissinger refers to as his "Kissinger," has expressed the belief that, in effect, the captive nations should give up any claim of national sovereignty and simply become a part of the Soviet Union. He says, "their desire to break out of the Soviet straitjacket" threatens us with World War III. In other words, slaves should accept their fate.

Well, I don't believe the people I've met in almost every State of this Union are ready to consign this, the last island of freedom, to the dust bin of history, along with the bones of dead civilizations of the past. Call it mysticism, if you will, but I believe God had a divine purpose in placing this land between the two great oceans to be found by those who had a special love of freedom and the courage to leave the countries of their birth. From our forefathers to our modern-day immigrants, we've come from every corner of the earth, from every race and every ethnic background, and we've become a new breed in the world. We're Americans and we have a rendezvous with destiny. We spread across this land, building farms and towns and cities, and we did it without any federal land planning program or urban renewal.

Indeed, we gave birth to an entirely new concept in man's relation to man. We created government as our servant, beholden to us and possessing no powers except those voluntarily granted to it by us. Now a self-anointed elite in our nation's capital would have us believe we are incapable of guiding our own destiny. They practice government by mystery, telling us it's too complex for our understanding. Believing this, they assume we might panic if we were to be told the truth about our problems.

Why should we become frightened? No people who have ever lived on this earth have fought harder, paid a higher price for freedom, or done more to advance the dignity of man than the living Americans—the Americans living in this land today. There isn't any problem we can't solve if government will give us the facts. Tell us what needs to be done. Then, get out of the way and let us have at it.

Recently on one of my campaign trips I was doing a question-and-answer session, and suddenly I received a question from a little girl—couldn't have been over six or seven years old—standing in the very front row. I'd heard the question before but somehow in her asking it, she threw me a little bit. She said, why do you want to be president? Well, I tried to tell her about giving government back to the people; I tried to tell her about turning authority back to the states and local communities, and so forth; winding down the bureaucracy. [It] might have been an answer for adults, but I knew that it wasn't what that little girl wanted,

and I left very frustrated. It was on the way to the next stop that I turned to Nancy and I said I wish I had it to do over again because I'd like to answer her question.

Well, maybe I can answer it now. I would like to go to Washington. I would like to be president, because I would like to see this country become once again a country where a little six-year old girl can grow up knowing the same freedom that I knew when I was six years old, growing up in America. If this is the America you want for yourself and your children; if you want to restore government not only of and for but by the people; to see the American spirit unleashed once again; to make this land a shining, golden hope God intended it to be, I'd like to hear from you. Write, or send a wire. I'd be proud to hear your thoughts and your ideas.

Thank you, and good night.

Source: "To Restore America (1976)," March 31, 1976, The President Reagan Information Page. Available online. URL: http://www.presidentreagan.info/speeches/restore_america.cfm

7. Concession Speech at 1976 Republican National Convention August 19, 1976

At the close of the 1976 Republican Convention, Ronald and Nancy Reagan were called to the podium by Gerald Ford, who had accepted his party's nomination only hours before. Reagan offered these off-the-cuff remarks (it is unclear whether he prepared for the possibility of speaking to the convention; nonetheless, portions of these remarks were taken from earlier speeches). Many delegates in the convention hall were moved to tears, and some were left wondering if the party had nominated the wrong man. The speech reveals in no uncertain terms Reagan's disgust with nuclear weapons, a position he consistently held—no one should have been surprised at the radical proposals

Reagan offered during his presidency to reduce if not outright abolish nuclear weapons.

Thank you very much. Mr. President, Mrs. Ford, Mr. Vice President, Mr. Vice President to be—(Applause and laughter)—the distinguished guests here, and you ladies and gentlemen: I am going to say fellow Republicans here, but also those who are watching from a distance, all of those millions of Democrats and Independents who I know are looking for a cause around which to rally and which I believe we can give them. (Applause)

Mr. President, before you arrived tonight, these wonderful people here when we came in gave Nancy and myself a welcome. That, plus this, and plus your kindness and generosity in honoring us by bringing us down here will give us a memory that will live in our hearts forever. (Applause)

Watching on television these last few nights, and I have seen you also with the warmth that you greeted Nancy, and you also filled my heart with joy when you did that. (Applause)

May I just say some words. There are cynics who say that a party platform is something that no one bothers to read and it doesn't very often amount to much. Whether it is different this time than it has ever been before, I believe the Republican Party has a platform that is a banner of bold, unmistakable colors, with no pastel shades. (Applause)

We have just heard a call to arms based on that platform, and a call to us to really be successful in communicating and reveal to the American people the difference between this platform and the platform of the opposing party, which is nothing but a revamp and a reissue and a running of a late, late show of the thing that we have been hearing from them for the last 40 years. (Applause)

If I could just take a moment; I had an assignment the other day. Someone asked me to write a letter for a time capsule that is going to be opened in Los Angeles a hundred years from now, on our Tricentennial. It sounded like an easy assignment. They suggested I write something about the problems and the issues today. I set out to do so, riding down the coast in an automobile, looking at the blue Pacific out on one side and the Santa Ynez Mountains on the other, and I couldn't help but wonder if it was going to be that beautiful a hundred years from now as it was on that summer day.

Then as I tried to write—let your own minds turn to that task. You are going to write for people a hundred years from now, who know all about us. We know nothing about them. We don't know what kind of a world they will be living in.

And suddenly I thought to myself if I write of the problems, they will be the domestic problems the President spoke of here tonight; the challenges confronting us, the erosion of freedom that has taken place under Democratic rule in this country, the invasion of private rights, the controls and restrictions on the vitality of the great free economy that we enjoy. These are our challenges that we must meet.

And then again there is that challenge of which he spoke that we live in a world in which the great powers have poised and aimed at each other horrible missiles of destruction, nuclear weapons that can in a matter of minutes arrive at each other's country and destroy, virtually, the civilized world we live in.

And suddenly it dawned on me, those who would read this letter a hundred years from now will know whether those missiles were fired. They will know whether we met our challenge. Whether they have the freedoms that we have known up until now will depend on what we do here.

Will they look back with appreciation and say, "Thank God for those people in 1976 who headed off that loss of freedom, who kept us now 100 years later free, who kept our world from nuclear destruction"?

And if we failed, they probably won't get to read the letter at all because it spoke of individual freedom, and they won't be allowed to talk of that or read of it.

This is our challenge; and this is why here in this hall tonight, better than we have ever done before, we have got to quit talking to each other and about each other and go out and communicate to the world that we may be fewer in numbers than we have ever been, but we carry the message they are waiting for.

We must go forth from here united, determined that what a great general said a few years ago is true: There is no substitute for victory, Mr. President. (Applause)

Source: "'76 Convention Closer," August 19, 1976, The Ronald Reagan Presidential Foundation and Library. Available online. URL: http://www.reaganfoundation.com/reagan/speeches/convention.asp

8. "A New Republican Party" Conservative Political Action Conference February 6, 1977

Reagan kept his political prospects alive by writing a syndicated newspaper column and delivering daily radio broadcasts that were distributed nationwide. He also continued to speak around the nation on the "mashed potato circuit" as he referred to it, and frequently dropped in on gatherings of the conservative faithful at the National Review *and the Conservative Political Action Conference. This address is the strongest statement ever made by Ronald Reagan in defining modern American conservatism. He rejected the calls from some of his brethren to form a third party, and made it clear that he expected to remain in the Republican Party, and transform that party's reputation as a haven for country-club businessmen*

into a populist conservative party. Reagan was successful in doing this, building the modern Republican Party with defectors from the Democratic Party (the so-called Reagan Democrats), both in blue-collar wards in the urban North, and among disaffected southern Democrats disturbed by their party's position on race, social issues, and national defense.

I'm happy to be back with you in this annual event after missing last year's meeting. I had some business in New Hampshire that wouldn't wait.

Three weeks ago here in our nation's capital I told a group of conservative scholars that we are currently in the midst of a re-ordering of the political realities that have shaped our time. We know today that the principles and values that lie at the heart of conservatism are shared by the majority.

Despite what some in the press may say, we who are proud to call ourselves "conservative" are not a minority of a minority party; we are part of the great majority of Americans of both major parties and of most of the independents as well.

A Harris poll released September 7, 1975 showed 18 percent identifying themselves as liberal and 31 percent as conservative, with 41 percent as middle of the road; a few months later, on January 5, 1976, by a 43-19 plurality those polled by Harris said they would "prefer to see the country move in a more conservative direction than a liberal one."

Last October 24th, the Gallup organization released the result of a poll taken right in the midst of the presidential campaign. Respondents were asked to state where they would place themselves on a scale ranging from "right-of-center" (which was defined as "conservative") to left-of-center (which was defined as "liberal").

- Thirty-seven percent viewed themselves as left-of-center or liberal

- Twelve percent placed themselves in the middle

- Fifty-one percent said they were right-of-center, that is, conservative.

What I find interesting about this particular poll is that it offered those polled a range of choices on a left-right continuum. This seems to me to be a more realistic approach than dividing the world into strict left and rights. Most of us, I guess, like to think of ourselves as avoiding both extremes, and the fact that a majority of Americans chose one or the other position on the right end of the spectrum is really impressive.

Those polls confirm that most Americans are basically conservative in their outlook. But once we have said this, we conservatives have not solved our problems, we have merely stated them clearly. Yes, conservatism can and does mean different things to those who call themselves conservatives.

You know, as I do, that most commentators make a distinction between what they call "social" conservatism and "economic" conservatism. The so-called social issues—law and order, abortion, busing, quota systems—are usually associated with blue-collar, ethnic and religious groups themselves traditionally associated with the Democratic Party. The economic issues—inflation, deficit spending and big government—are usually associated with Republican Party members and independents who concentrate their attention on economic matters.

Now I am willing to accept this view of two major kinds of conservatism—or, better still, two different conservative constituencies. But at the same time let me say that the old lines that once clearly divided these two kinds of conservatism are disappearing.

In fact, the time has come to see if it is possible to present a program of action based on political principle that can attract those inter-ested in the so-called social issues and those interested in "economic" issues. In short, isn't it possible to combine the two major segments of contemporary American conservatism into one politically effective whole?

I believe the answer is: Yes, it is possible to create a political entity that will reflect the views of the great hitherto conservative majority. We went a long way toward doing it in California. We can do it in America. This is not a dream, a wistful hope. It is and has been a reality. I have seen the conservative future and it works.

Let me say again what I said to our conservative friends from the academic world: What I envision is not simply a melding together of the two branches of American conservatism into a temporary uneasy alliance, but the creation of a new, lasting majority.

This will mean compromise. But not a compromise of basic principle. What will emerge will be something new: something open and vital and dynamic, something the great conservative majority will recognize as its own, because at the heart of this undertaking is principled politics.

I have always been puzzled by the inability of some political and media types to understand exactly what is meant by adherence to political principle. All too often in the press and the television evening news it is treated as a call for "ideological purity." Whatever ideology may mean—and it seems to mean a variety of things, depending upon who is using it—it always conjures up in my mind a picture of a rigid, irrational clinging to abstract theory in the face of reality. We have to recognize that in this country "ideology" is a scare word. And for good reason. Marxist-Leninism is, to give but one example, an ideology. All the facts of the real world have to be fitted to the Procrustean bed of Marx and Lenin. If the facts don't happen to fit the ideology, the facts are chopped off and discarded.

principles we espouse are universal and cut across traditional lines. In every Congressional district there should be a search made for young men and women who share these principles and they should be brought into positions of leadership in the local Republican Party groups. We can find attractive, articulate candidates if we look, and when we find them, we will begin to change the sorry state of affairs that has led a Democratic-controlled Congress for more than 40 years. I need not remind you that you can have the soundest principles in the world, but if you don't have candidates who can communicate those principles, candidates who are articulate as well as principled, you are going to lose election after election. I refuse to believe that the good Lord divided this world into Republicans who defend basic values and Democrats who win elections. We have to find tough, bright young men and women who are sick and tired of cliches and the pomposity and the mind-numbing economic idiocy of the liberals in Washington.

It is at this point, however, that we come across a question that is really the essential one: What will be the basis of this New Republican Party? To what set of values and principles can our candidates appeal? Where can Americans who want to know where we stand look for guidance?

Fortunately, we have an answer to that question. That answer was provided last summer by the men and women of the Republican Party—not just the leadership, but the ones who have built the party on local levels all across the country.

The answer was provided in the 1976 platform of the Republican Party.

This was not a document handed down from on high. It was hammered out in free and open debate among all those who care about our party and the principles it stands for.

The Republican platform is unique. Unlike any other party platform I have ever seen, it answers not only programmatic questions for the immediate future of the party but also provides a clear outline of the underlying principles upon which those programs are based.

The New Republican Party can and should use the Republican platform of 1976 as the major source from which a Declaration of Principles can be created and offered to the American people.

Tonight I want to offer to you my own version of what such a declaration might look like. I make no claim to originality. This declaration I propose is relatively short, taken, for the most part, word for word from the Republican platform. It concerns itself with basic principles, not with specific solutions.

We, the members of the New Republican Party, believe that the preservation and enhancement of the values that strengthen and protect individual freedom, family life, communities and neighborhoods and the liberty of our beloved nation should be at the heart of any legislative or political program presented to the American people. Toward that end, we, therefore, commit ourselves to the following propositions and offer them to each American believing that the New Republican Party, based on such principles, will serve the interest of all the American people.

We believe that liberty can be measured by how much freedom Americans have to make their own decisions, even their own mistakes. Government must step in when one's liberties impinge on one's neighbor's. Government must protect constitutional rights, deal with other governments, protect citizens from aggressors, assure equal opportunity, and be compassionate in caring for those citizens who are unable to care for themselves.

Our federal system of local-state-national government is designed to sort out on what level these actions should be taken. Those concerns of a national character—such as air and water pollution that do not respect state boundaries, or the national transportation system, or efforts to safeguard your civil liberties—must, of course, be handled on the national level.

As a general rule, however, we believe that government action should be taken first by the government that resides as close to you as possible.

We also believe that Americans, often acting through voluntary organizations, should have the opportunity to solve many of the social problems of their communities. This spirit of freely helping others is uniquely American and should be encouraged in every way by government.

Families must continue to be the foundation of our nation.

Families—not government programs—are the best way to make sure our children are properly nurtured, our elderly are cared for, our cultural and spiritual heritages are perpetuated, our laws are observed and our values are preserved. It is imperative that our government's programs, actions, officials and social welfare institutions never be allowed to jeopardize the family. We fear the government may be powerful enough to destroy our families; we know that it is not powerful enough to replace them. The New Republican Party must be committed to working always in the interest of the American family.

Every dollar spent by government is a dollar earned by individuals. Government must always ask: Are your dollars being wisely spent? Can we afford it? Is it not better for the country to leave your dollars in your pocket?

Elected officials, their appointees, and government workers are expected to perform their public acts with honesty, openness, diligence, and special integrity.

Government must work for the goal of justice and the elimination of unfair practices, but no government has yet designed a more productive economic system or one which benefits as many people as the American market system.

The beauty of our land is our legacy to our children. It must be protected by us so that they can pass it on intact to their children.

The United States must always stand for peace and liberty in the world and the rights of the individual. We must form sturdy partnerships with our allies for the preservation of freedom. We must be ever willing to negotiate differences, but equally mindful that there are American ideals that cannot be compromised. Given that there are other nations with potentially hostile design, we recognize that we can reach our goals only while maintaining a superior national defense, second to none.

In his inaugural speech President Carter said that he saw the world "dominated by a new spirit." He said, and I quote: "The passion for freedom is on the rise."

Well, I don't know how he knows this, but if it is true, then it is the most unrequited passion in human history. The world is being dominated by a new spirit, all right, but it isn't the spirit of freedom.

It isn't very often you see a familiar object that shocks and frightens you. But the other day I came across a map of the world created by Freedom House, an organization monitoring the state of freedom in the world for the past 25 years. It is an ordinary map, with one exception: it shows the world's nations in white for free, shaded for partly free and black for not free.

Almost all of the great Eurasian land mass is completely colored black, from the western border of East Germany, through middle and eastern Europe, through the awesome spaces of the Soviet Union, on to the Bering Strait in the north, down past the immensity of China, still further down to Vietnam and the South China Sea—in all that huge, sprawling, inconceivably immense area not a single political or personal or religious freedom exists. The entire continent of Africa, from the Mediterranean to the Cape of Good Hope, from the Atlantic to the Indian Ocean, all that vastness is almost totally unfree. In the tiny nation of Tanzania alone, according to a report in the *New York Times*, there are 3,000 people in detention for political crimes—that is more than the total being held in South Africa! The Mideast has only one free state: Israel. If a visitor from another planet were to approach earth, and if this planet showed free nations in light and unfree nations in darkness, the pitifully small beacons of light would make him wonder what was hidden in that terrifying, enormous blackness.

We know what is hidden: gulag. Torture. Families—and human beings—broken apart. No free press, no freedom of religion. The ancient forms of tyranny revived and made even more hideous and strong through what Winston Churchill once called "a perverted science." Men rotting for years in solitary confinement because they have different political and economic beliefs, solitary confinement that drives the fortunate ones insane and makes the survivors wish for death.

Only now and then do we in the West hear a voice from out of that darkness. Then there is silence—the silence of human slavery. There is no more terrifying sound in human experience, with one possible exception. Look at that map again. The very heart of the darkness is the Soviet Union and from that heart comes a different sound. It is the whirring sound of machinery and the whisper of the computer technology we ourselves have sold them. It is the sound of building, building of the strongest military machine ever devised by man. Our military strategy is designed to hopefully prevent a war. Theirs is designed to win one. A group of eminent scientists, scholars and intelligence experts offer a survey showing that the Soviet Union is driving for military superiority and are derided as hysterically making, quote, "a worst case," unquote, concerning Soviet intentions and capabilities.

But is it not precisely the duty of the national government to be prepared for the worst case? Two senators, after studying the North Atlantic Treaty Organization, have reported to the Armed Forces committee that Soviet forces in Eastern Europe have the capability to launch, with little warning, a "potentially devastating" attack in Central Europe from what is termed a "standing alert."

Reading their report, one can almost see the enormous weight of the parts of the earth that are under tyranny shifting in an irresistible tilt toward that tiny portion of land in freedom's light. Even now in Western Europe we have Communists in the government of Italy. France appeasing terrorists, and England—for centuries the model or the sword of freedom in Western Europe—weak, dispirited, turning inward.

A "worst case?" How could you make a good case out of the facts as they are known? The Soviet Union, poised on the edge of free Europe, capable of striking from a standing start, has modern tanks in far greater numbers than the outmoded vehicles of NATO. We have taken comfort from NATO's superiority in the air, but now the Soviet Union has made a dramatic swing away from its historic defensive air posture to one capable of supporting offensive action. NATO's southern flank is described in the Senate report with a single word: shambles.

The report is simply reality as it was, with different names and faces, in Europe in the late 1930s when so many refused to believe and thought if we don't look the threat will go away.

We don't want hysteria. We don't want distortion of Soviet power. We want truth. And above all we want peace. And to have that the United States has to immediately re-examine its entire view of the world and develop a strategy of freedom. We cannot be the second-best super-power for the simple reason that he who is second is last. In this deadly game, there are no silver medals for second.

President Carter, as a candidate, said he would cut five to seven billion dollars from the defense budget. We must let him know that, while we agree there must be no fat in our armed forces, those armed forces must be capable of coping with the new reality presented to us by the Russians, and cutting seven billion dollars out of our defense budget is not the way to accomplish this. Some years ago, a young President said we will make any sacrifice, bear any burden, and we will, to preserve our freedom.

Our relationship with mainland China is clouded. The so-called "gang of four" are up one day and down the next and we are seeing the pitfalls of making deals with charismatic personalities and living legends. The charisma fades as the living legends die, and those who take their place are interested not in our best wishes but in power. The keyword for China today is turmoil. We should watch and observe and analyze as closely and rationally as we can.

But in our relationships with the mainland of China we should always remember that the conditions and possibilities for, and the realities of, freedom exist to an infinitely greater degree with our Chinese friends in Taiwan. We can never go wrong if we do what is morally right, and the moral way—the honorable way—is to keep our commitment, our solemn promise to the people of Taiwan.

Our liberal friends have made much of the lack of freedom in some Latin American countries. Senator Edward Kennedy and his colleagues here in Washington let no opportunity pass to let us know about horrors in Chile. Well, I think when the United States of America is considering a deal with a country that hasn't had an election in almost eight years, where the press is under the thumb of a dictatorship, where ordinary citizens are abducted in the night by secret police, where military domination of the country is known to be harsh on dissenters and when these things are documented, we should reject overtures from those who rule such a country.

But the country I'm describing is not Chile—it is Panama.

We are negotiating with a dictatorship that comes within the portion of that map colored black for no freedom. No civil rights. One-man rule. No free press.

Candidate Carter said he would never relinquish "actual control" of the Panama Canal. President Carter is negotiating with a dictatorship whose record on civil and human rights is as I have just described and the negotiations concern the rights guaranteed to us by treaty which we will give up under a threat of violence. In only a few weeks we will mark the second anniversary of the death of freedom for the Vietnamese. An estimated 300,000 of them are being "re-educated" in concentration camps to forget about freedom.

There is only one major question on the agenda of national priorities and that is the state of our national security. I refer, of course, to the state of our armed forces—but also to our state of mind, to the way we perceive the world. We cannot maintain the strength we need to survive, no matter how many missiles we have, no matter how many tanks we build, unless we are willing to reverse:

- The trend of deteriorating faith in and continuing abuse of our national intelligence agencies. Let's stop the sniping and the propaganda and the historical revisionism and let the CIA and the other intelligence agencies do their job!

- Let us reverse the trend of public indifference to problems of national security. In every congressional district citizens should join together, enlist and educate neighbors and make certain that congressmen know we care. The front pages of major newspapers on the East Coast recently headlined and told in great detail of a takeover, the takeover of a magazine published in New York—not a nation losing its freedom. You would think, from the attention it received in the media, that it was a matter of blazing national interest whether the magazine lived or died. The tendency of much of the media to ignore the state of our national security is too well documented for me to go on.

My friends, the time has come to start acting to bring about the great conservative majority party we know is waiting to be created.

And just to set the record straight, let me say this about our friends who are now Republicans but who do not identify themselves as conservatives: I want the record to show that I do not view the new revitalized Republican Party as one based on a principle of exclusion. After all, you do not get to be a majority party by searching for groups you won't associate or work with. If we truly believe in our principles, we should sit down and talk. Talk with anyone, anywhere, at any time if it means talking about the principles for the Republican Party. Conservatism is not a narrow ideology, nor is it the exclusive property of conservative activists.

We've succeeded better than we know. Little more than a decade ago more than two-thirds of Americans believed the federal government could solve all our problems, and do so without restricting our freedom or bankrupting the nation.

We warned of things to come, of the danger inherent in unwarranted government involvement in things not its proper province. What we warned against has come to pass. And today more than two-thirds of our citizens are telling us, and each other, that social engineering by the federal government has failed. The Great Society is great only in power, in size and in cost. And so are the problems it set out to solve. Freedom has been diminished and we stand on the brink of economic ruin.

Our task now is not to sell a philosophy, but to make the majority of Americans, who already share that philosophy, see that modern

conservatism offers them a political home. We are not a cult, we are members of a majority. Let's act and talk like it.

The job is ours and the job must be done. If not by us, who? If not now, when?

Our party must be the party of the individual. It must not sell out the individual to cater to the group. No greater challenge faces our society today than ensuring that each one of us can maintain his dignity and his identity in an increasingly complex, centralized society.

Extreme taxation, excessive controls, oppressive government competition with business, galloping inflation, frustrated minorities and forgotten Americans are not the products of free enterprise. They are the residue of centralized bureaucracy, of government by a self-anointed elite.

Our party must be based on the kind of leadership that grows and takes its strength from the people. Any organization is in actuality only the lengthened shadow of its members. A political party is a mechanical structure created to further a cause. The cause, not the mechanism, brings and holds the members together. And our cause must be to rediscover, reassert and reapply America's spiritual heritage to our national affairs.

Then with God's help we shall indeed be as a city upon a hill with the eyes of all people upon us.

Source: "A New Republican Party (1977)," February 6, 1977, The President Reagan Information Page. Available online. URL: http://www.presidentreagan.info/speeches/new_republican_party.cfm

9. Announcing for President New York Hilton, New York City November 13, 1979

Reagan faced some formidable opponents in the 1980 Republican primaries, including Ambassador

George H. W. Bush, Senator Howard Baker, former Texas governor (and ex-Democrat) John Connally, Senator Robert Dole, and Congressmen Philip Crane and John Anderson. After losing the Iowa caucuses, Reagan rebounded in New Hampshire and went on to dispatch his opponents one by one, Bush being the last to fall. Reagan focused on the sagging economy and on the decline of the American spirit in the wake of gasoline shortages, high inflation, and foreign policy setbacks. Reagan claimed that the nation's best days lay ahead and that America's greatness could be restored if the government got out of the way of the American people.

Good evening. I am here tonight to announce my intention to seek the Republican nomination for President of the United States.

I'm sure that each of us has seen our country from a number of viewpoints depending on where we've lived and what we've done. For me it has been as a boy growing up in several small towns in Illinois, as a young man in Iowa trying to get a start in the years of the Great Depression, and later in California for most of my adult life.

I've seen America from the stadium press box as a sportscaster, as an actor, officer of my labor union, soldier, officeholder and as both a Democrat and Republican. I've lived in America where those who often had too little to eat outnumbered those who had enough. There have been four wars in my lifetime and I've seen our country face financial ruin in the Depression. I have also seen the great strength of this nation as it pulled itself up from that ruin to become the dominant force in the world.

To me our country is a living, breathing presence, unimpressed by what others say is impossible, proud of its own success, generous, yes and naive, sometimes wrong, never mean and always impatient to provide a better life for its people in a framework of a basic fairness and freedom.

Someone once said that the difference between an American and any other kind of person is that an American lives in anticipation of the future because he knows it will be a great place. Other people fear the future as just a repetition of past failures. There's a lot of truth in that. If there is one thing we are sure of it is that history need not be relived; that nothing is impossible, and that man is capable of improving his circumstances beyond what we are told is fact.

There are those in our land today, however, who would have us believe that the United States, like other great civilizations of the past, has reached the zenith of its power; that we are weak and fearful, reduced to bickering with each other and no longer possessed of the will to cope with our problems.

Much of this talk has come from leaders who claim that our problems are too difficult to handle. We are supposed to meekly accept their failures as the most which humanly can be done. They tell us we must learn to live with less, and teach our children that their lives will be less full and prosperous than ours have been; that the America of the coming years will be a place where—because of our past excesses—it will be impossible to dream and make those dreams come true.

I don't believe that. And, I don't believe you do either. That is why I am seeking the presidency. I cannot and will not stand by and see this great country destroy itself. Our leaders attempt to blame their failures on circumstances beyond their control, on false estimates by unknown, unidentifiable experts who rewrite modern history in an attempt to convince us our high standard of living, the result of thrift and hard work, is somehow selfish extravagance which we must renounce as we join in sharing scarcity. I don't agree that our nation must resign itself to inevitable decline, yielding its proud position to other hands. I am totally unwilling to see this country fail in its obligation to itself and to the other free peoples of the world.

The crisis we face is not the result of any failure of the American spirit; it is failure of our leaders to establish rational goals and give our people something to order their lives by. If I am elected, I shall regard my election as proof that the people of the United States have decided to set a new agenda and have recognized that the human spirit thrives best when goals are set and progress can be measured in their achievement.

During the next year I shall discuss in detail a wide variety of problems which a new administration must address. Tonight I shall mention only a few.

No problem that we face today can compare with the need to restore the health of the American economy and the strength of the American dollar. Double-digit inflation has robbed you and your family of the ability to plan. It has destroyed the confidence to buy and it threatens the very structure of family life itself as more and more wives are forced to work in order to help meet the ever-increasing cost of living. At the same time, the lack of real growth in the economy has introduced the justifiable fear in the minds of working men and women who are already overextended that soon there will be fewer jobs and no money to pay for even the necessities of life. And tragically as the cost of living keeps going up, the standard of living which has been our great pride keeps going down.

The people have not created this disaster in our economy; the federal government has. It has overspent, overestimated, and over-regulated. It has failed to deliver services within the revenues it should be allowed to raise from taxes. In the 34 years since the end of World War II, it has spent $448 billion more than it has collected in taxes—$448 billion of printing-press money, which has made every dollar you earn worth less and less. At the same time,

the federal government has cynically told us that high taxes on business will in some way "solve" the problem and allow the average taxpayer to pay less. Well, business is not a taxpayer; it is a tax collector. Business has to pass its tax burden on to the customer as part of the cost of doing business. You and I pay taxes imposed on business every time we go to the store. Only people pay taxes and it is political demagoguery or economic illiteracy to try and tell us otherwise.

The key to restoring the health of the economy lies in cutting taxes. At the same time, we need to get the waste out of federal spending. This does not mean sacrificing essential services, nor do we need to destroy the system of benefits which flow to the poor, elderly, the sick and the handicapped. We have long since committed ourselves, as a people, to help those among us who cannot take care of themselves. But the federal government has proven to be the costliest and most inefficient provider of such help we could possibly have.

We must put an end to the arrogance of a federal establishment which accepts no blame for our condition, cannot be relied upon to give us a fair estimate of our situation and utterly refuses to live within its means. I will not accept the supposed "wisdom" which has it that the federal bureaucracy has become so powerful that it can no longer be changed or controlled by any administration. As President I would use every power at my command to make the federal establishment respond to the will and the collective wishes of the people.

We must force the entire federal bureaucracy to live in the real world of reduced spending, streamlined function and accountability to the people it serves. We must review the function of the federal government to determine which of those are the proper province of levels of government closer to the people.

The 10th article of the Bill of Rights is explicit in pointing out that the federal gov-

ernment should do only those things specifically called for in the Constitution. All others
shall remain with the states or the people. We
haven't been observing that 10th article of late.
The federal government has taken on functions
it was never intended to perform and which it
does not perform well. There should be a
planned, orderly transfer of such functions to
states and communities and a transfer with
them of the sources of taxation to pay for them.

The savings in administrative overhead
would be considerable and certainly there would
be increased efficiency and less bureaucracy.

By reducing federal tax rates where they
discourage individual initiative—especially personal income tax rates—we can restore incentives, invite greater economic growth and at the
same time help give us better government
instead of bigger government. Proposals such
as the Kemp-Roth bill would bring about this
kind of realistic reductions in tax rates.

In short, a punitive tax system must be
replaced by one that restores incentive for the
worker and for industry; a system that rewards
initiative and effort and encourages thrift.

All these things are possible; none of them
will be easy. But the choice is clear. We can go
on letting the country slip over the brink to
financial ruin with the disaster that it means for
the individual or we can find the will to work
together to restore confidence in ourselves and
to regain the confidence of the world. I have
lived through one Depression. I carry with me
the memory of a Christmas Eve when my
brother and I and our parents exchanged our
modest gifts—there was no lighted tree as
there had been on Christmases past. I remember watching my father open what he thought
was a greeting from his employer. We all
watched and yes, we were hoping it was a
bonus check. It was notice that he no longer
had a job. And in those days the government
ran the radio announcements telling workers
not to leave home looking for jobs—there were
no jobs. I'll carry with me always the memory
of my father sitting there holding that enve-
lope, unable to look at us. I cannot and will not
stand by while inflation and joblessness destroy
the dignity of our people.

Another serious problem which must be
discussed tonight is our energy situation. Our
country was built on cheap energy. Today,
energy is not cheap and we face the prospect
that some forms of energy may soon not be
available at all.

Last summer you probably spent hours sitting in gasoline lines. This winter, some will
be without heat and everyone will be paying
much more simply to keep home and family
warm. If you ever had any doubt of the government's inability to provide for the needs of
the people, just look at the utter fiasco we now
call "the energy crisis." Not one straight
answer nor any realistic hope of relief has
come from the present administration in
almost three years of federal treatment of the
problem. As gas lines grew, the administration
again panicked and now has proposed to put
the country on a wartime footing; but for this
"war" there is no victory in sight. And, as
always, when the federal bureaucracy fails, all
it can suggest is more of the same. This time
it's another bureau to untangle the mess by the
ones we already have.

But, this just won't work. Solving the
energy crisis will not be easy, but it can be
done. First we must decide that "less" is not
enough. Next, we must remove government
obstacles to energy production. And, we must
make use of those technological advantages we
still possess.

It is no program simply to say "use less
energy." Of course waste must be eliminated
and efficiently promoted, but for the government simply to tell people to conserve is not
an energy policy. At best it means we will run
out of energy a little more slowly. But a day will
come when the lights will dim and the wheels

of industry will turn more slowly and finally stop. As President I will not endorse any course which has this as its principal objective.

We need more energy and that means diversifying our sources of supply away from the OPEC countries. Yes, it means more efficient automobiles. But it also means more exploration and development of oil and natural gas here in our own country. The only way to free ourselves from the monopoly pricing power of OPEC is to be less dependent on outside sources of fuel.

The answer, obvious to anyone except those in the administration it seems, is more domestic production of oil and gas. We must also have wider use of nuclear power within strict safety rules, of course. There must be more spending by the energy industries on research and development of substitutes for fossil fuels.

In years to come solar energy may provide much of the answer but for the next two or three decades we must do such things as master the chemistry of coal. Putting the market system to work for these objectives is an essential first step for their achievement. Additional multi-billion-dollar federal bureaus and programs are not the answer.

In recent weeks there has been much talk about "excess" oil company profits. I don't believe we've been given all the information we need to make a judgment about this. We should have that information. Government exists to protect us from each other. It is not government's function to allocate fuel or impose unnecessary restrictions on the marketplace. It is government's function to determine whether we are being unfairly exploited and if so to take immediate and appropriate action. As President I would do exactly that.

On the foreign front, the decade of the 1980s will place severe pressures upon the United States and its allies. We can expect to be tested in ways calculated to try our patience, to confound our resolve and to erode our belief in ourselves. During a time when the Soviet Union may enjoy nuclear superiority over this country, we must never waver in our commitment to our allies nor accept any negotiation which is not clearly in the national interest. We must judge carefully. Though we should leave no initiative untried in our pursuit of peace, we must be clear-voiced in our resolve to resist any unpeaceful act wherever it may occur. Negotiation with the Soviet Union must never become appeasement.

For the most of the last 40 years, we have been preoccupied with the global struggle—the competition—with the Soviet Union and with our responsibilities to our allies. But too often in recent times we have just drifted along with events, responding as if we thought of ourselves as a nation in decline. To our allies we seem to appear to be a nation unable to make decisions in its own interests, let alone in the common interest. Since the Second World War we have spent large amounts of money and much of our time protecting and defending freedom all over the world. We must continue this, for if we do not accept the responsibilities of leadership, who will? And if no one will, how will we survive?

The 1970s have taught us the foolhardiness of not having a long-range diplomatic strategy of our own. The world has become a place where, in order to survive, our country needs more than just allies—it needs real friends. Yet, in recent times we often seem not to have recognized who our friends are. This must change. It is now time to take stock of our own house and to resupply its strength.

Part of that process involves taking stock of our relationship with Puerto Rico. I favor statehood for Puerto Rico and if the people of Puerto Rico vote for statehood in their coming referendum I would, as President, initiate the enabling legislation to make this a reality.

We live on a continent whose three countries possess the assets to make it the strongest, most prosperous and self-sufficient area on Earth. Within the borders of this North American continent are the food, resources, technology and undeveloped territory which, properly managed, could dramatically improve the quality of life of all its inhabitants.

It is no accident that this unmatched potential for progress and prosperity exists in three countries with such long-standing heritages of free government. A developing closeness among Canada, Mexico and the United States—a North American accord—would permit achievement of that potential in each country beyond that which I believe any of them—strong as they are—could accomplish in the absence of such cooperation. In fact, the key to our own future security may lie in both Mexico and Canada becoming much stronger countries than they are today.

No one can say at this point precisely what form future cooperation among our three countries will take. But if I am elected President, I would be willing to invite each of our neighbors to send a special representative to our government to sit in on high level planning sessions with us, as partners, mutually concerned about the future of our continent. First, I would immediately seek the views and ideas of Canadian and Mexican leaders on this issue, and work tirelessly with them to develop closer ties among our peoples. It is time we stopped thinking of our nearest neighbors as foreigners.

By developing methods of working closely together, we will lay the foundations for future cooperation on a broader and more significant scale. We will put to rest any doubts of those cynical enough to believe that the United States would seek to dominate any relationship among our three countries, or foolish enough to think that the governments and peoples of Canada and Mexico would ever permit such domination to occur. I for one am confident that we can show the world by example that the nations of North America are ready, within the context of an unswerving commitment to freedom, to see new forms of accommodation to meet a changing world. A developing closeness between the United States, Canada and Mexico would serve notice on friends and foe alike that we were prepared for a long haul, looking outward again and confident of our future; that together we are going to create jobs, to generate new fortunes of wealth for many and provide a legacy for the children of each of our countries. Two hundred years ago, we taught the world that a new form of government, created out of the genius of man to cope with his circumstances, could succeed in bringing a measure of quality to human life previously thought impossible.

Now let us work toward the goal of using the assets of this continent, its resources, technology, and foodstuffs in the most efficient ways possible for the common good of all its people. It may take the next 100 years but we can dare to dream that at some future date a map of the world might show the North American continent as one in which the people's commerce of its three strong countries flow more freely across their present borders than they do today.

In recent months leaders in our government have told us that we, the people, have lost confidence in ourselves; that we must regain our spirit and our will to achieve our national goals. Well, it is true there is a lack of confidence, an unease with things the way they are. But the confidence we have lost is confidence in our government's policies. Our unease can almost be called bewilderment at how our defense strength has deteriorated. The great productivity of our industry is now surpassed by virtually all the major nations who compete with us for world markets, and our currency is no longer the stable measure of value it once was.

But there remains the greatness of our people, our capacity for dreaming up fantastic deeds and bringing them off to the surprise of an unbelieving world. When Washington's men were freezing at Valley Forge, Tom Paine told his fellow Americans: "We have it in our power to begin the world over again." We still have that power.

We—today's living Americans—have in our lifetime fought harder, paid a higher price for freedom and done more to advance the dignity of man than any people who have ever lived on this Earth. The citizens of this great nation want leadership—yes—but not a "man on a white horse" demanding obedience to his commands. They want someone who believes they can "begin the world over again." A leader who will unleash their great strength and remove the roadblocks government has put in their way. I want to do that more than anything I've ever wanted. And it's something that I believe with God's help I can do.

I believe this nation hungers for a spiritual revival; hungers to once again see honor placed above political expediency; to see government once again the protector of our liberties, not the distributor of gifts and privilege. Government should uphold and not undermine those institutions which are custodians of the very values upon which civilization is founded—religion, education and, above all, family. Government cannot be clergyman, teacher and patriot. It is our servant, beholden to us.

We who are privileged to be Americans have had a rendezvous with destiny since the moment in 1630 when John Winthrop, standing on the deck of the tiny *Arbella* off the coast of Massachusetts, told the little band of Pilgrims, "We shall be a city upon a hill. The eyes of all people are upon us so that if we shall deal falsely with our God in this work we have undertaken and so cause Him to withdraw His present help from us, we shall be made a story and a byword throughout the world."

A troubled and afflicted mankind looks to us, pleading for us to keep our rendezvous with destiny; that we will uphold the principles of self-reliance, self-discipline, morality, and—above all—responsible liberty for every individual that we will become that shining city on a hill.

I believe that you and I together can keep this rendezvous with destiny.

Thank you and good night.

Source: "Intent to Run for President," November 13, 1979, The Ronald Reagan Presidential Foundation and Library. Available online. URL: http://www.reaganfoundation.com/reagan/speeches/intent.asp

10. 1980 Republican National Convention Acceptance Speech
July 1, 1980

Reagan accepted his party's nomination in the unlikely location of Detroit, Michigan, a traditionally Democratic stronghold. It was a wise decision on the part of the Republican Party, for the nation's automobile capital was hurting, along with much of the country's economy. Reagan toyed with the idea of selecting former president Gerald Ford as his running mate, but dropped that notion and selected his primary opponent George H. W. Bush. In his acceptance speech, Reagan again reached out to disgruntled Democrats and Independents, hammering on the theme that the Carter administration and the Democrats in Congress had presided over a period of American decline: "Can anyone look at our reduced standing in the world today and say, 'Let's have four more years of this?'"

Mr. Chairman, Mr. Vice President to be, this convention, my fellow citizens of this great nation: With a deep awareness of the responsibility conferred by your trust, I accept your nomination for the presidency of the United States. I do so with deep gratitude, and I think also I might interject on behalf of all of us, our thanks to Detroit and the people of Michigan and to this city for the warm hospitality they have shown. And I thank you for your whole-hearted response to my recommendation in regard to George Bush as a candidate for vice president.

I am very proud of our party tonight. This convention has shown to all America a party united, with positive programs for solving the nation's problems; a party ready to build a new consensus with all those across the land who share a community of values embodied in these words: family, work, neighborhood, peace and freedom.

I know we have had a quarrel or two, but only as to the method of attaining a goal. There was no argument about the goal. As president, I will establish a liaison with the 50 governors to encourage them to eliminate, wherever it exists, discrimination against women. I will monitor federal laws to insure their implementation and to add statutes if they are needed.

More than anything else, I want my candidacy to unify our country; to renew the American spirit and sense of purpose. I want to carry our message to every American, regardless of party affiliation, who is a member of this community of shared values.

Never before in our history have Americans been called upon to face three grave threats to our very existence, any one of which could destroy us. We face a disintegrating economy, a weakened defense and an energy policy based on the sharing of scarcity.

The major issue of this campaign is the direct political, personal and moral responsibility of Democratic Party leadership—in the White House and in Congress—for this unprecedented calamity which has befallen us. They tell us they have done the most that humanly could be done. They say that the United States has had its day in the sun; that our nation has passed its zenith. They expect you to tell your children that the American people no longer have the will to cope with

their problems; that the future will be one of sacrifice and few opportunities.

My fellow citizens, I utterly reject that view. The American people, the most generous on earth, who created the highest standard of living, are not going to accept the notion that we can only make a better world for others by moving backwards ourselves. Those who believe we can have no business leading the nation.

I will not stand by and watch this great country destroy itself under mediocre leadership that drifts from one crisis to the next, eroding our national will and purpose. We have come together here because the American people deserve better from those to whom they entrust our nation's highest offices, and we stand united in our resolve to do something about it.

We need a rebirth of the American tradition of leadership at every level of government and in private life as well. The United States of America is unique in world history because it has a genius for leaders—many leaders—on many levels. But, back in 1976, Mr. Carter said, "Trust me." And a lot of people did. Now, many of those people are out of work. Many have seen their savings eaten away by inflation. Many others on fixed incomes, especially the elderly, have watched helplessly as the cruel tax of inflation wasted away their purchasing power. And, today, a great many who trusted Mr. Carter wonder if we can survive the Carter policies of national defense.

"Trust me" government asks that we concentrate our hopes and dreams on one man; that we trust him to do what's best for us. My view of government places trust not in one person or one party, but in those values that transcend persons and parties. The trust is where it belongs—in the people. The responsibility to live up to that trust is where it belongs, in their elected leaders. That kind of relationship, between the people and their elected leaders, is a special kind of compact.

Three hundred and sixty years ago, in 1620, a group of families dared to cross a mighty ocean to build a future for themselves in a new world. When they arrived at Plymouth, Massachusetts, they formed what they called a "compact," an agreement among themselves to build a community and abide by its laws.

The single act—the voluntary binding together of free people to live under the law—set the pattern for what was to come.

A century and a half later, the descendants of those people pledged their lives, their fortunes and their sacred honor to found this nation. Some forfeited their fortunes and their lives; none sacrificed honor.

Four score and seven years later, Abraham Lincoln called upon the people of all America to renew their dedication and their commitment to a government of, for and by the people.

Isn't it once again time to renew our compact of freedom; to pledge to each other all that is best in our lives; all that gives meaning to them—for the sake of this, our beloved and blessed land?

Together, let us make this a new beginning. Let us make a commitment to care for the needy; to teach our children the values and the virtues handed down to us by our families; to have the courage to defend those values and the willingness to sacrifice for them.

Let us pledge to restore, in our time, the American spirit of voluntary service, of cooperation, of private and community initiative; a spirit that flows like a deep and mighty river through the history of our nation.

As your nominee, I pledge to restore to the federal government the capacity to do the people's work without dominating their lives. I pledge to you a government that will not only work well, but wisely; its ability to act tempered by prudence, and its willingness to do good balanced by the knowledge that government is never more dangerous than when our desire to have it help us blinds us to its great power to harm us.

The first Republican president once said, "While the people retain their virtue and their vigilance, no administration by any extreme of wickedness or folly can seriously injure the government in the short space of four years."

If Mr. Lincoln could see what's happened in these last three-and-a-half years, he might hedge a little on that statement. But, with the virtues that are our legacy as a free people and with the vigilance that sustains liberty, we still have time to use our renewed compact to overcome the injuries that have been done to America these past three-and-a-half years.

First, we must overcome something the present administration has cooked up: a new and altogether indigestible economic stew, one part inflation, one part high unemployment, one part recession, one part runaway taxes, one part deficit spending and seasoned by an energy crisis. It's an economic stew that has turned the national stomach.

Ours are not problems of abstract economic theory. Those are problems of flesh and blood; problems that cause pain and destroy the moral fiber of real people who should not suffer the further indignity of being told by the government that it is all somehow their fault. We do not have inflation because as Mr. Carter says, we have lived too well.

The head of a government which has utterly refused to live within its means and which has, in the last few days, told us that this year's deficit will be $60 billion, dares to point the finger of blame at business and labor, both of which have been engaged in a losing struggle just trying to stay even.

High taxes, we are told, are somehow good for us, as if, when government spends our money it isn't inflationary, but when we spend it it is.

Those who preside over the worst energy shortage in our history tell us to use less, so that we will run out of oil, gasoline and natural gas a little more slowly. Conservation is desirable, of course, for we must not waste energy. But conservation is not the sole answer to our energy needs.

America must get to work producing more energy. The Republican program for solving economic problems is based on growth and productivity.

Large amounts of oil and natural gas lay beneath our land and off our shores, untouched because the present administration seems to believe the American people would rather see more regulation, taxes and controls than more energy.

Coal offers great potential. So does nuclear energy produced under rigorous safety standards. It could supply electricity for thousands of industries and millions of jobs and homes. It must not be thwarted by a tiny minority opposed to economic growth which often finds friendly ears in regulatory agencies for its obstructionist campaigns.

Make no mistake. We will not permit the safety of our people or our environmental heritage to be jeopardized, but we are going to reaffirm that the economic prosperity of our people is a fundamental part of our environment.

Our problems are both acute and chronic, yet all we hear from those in positions of leadership are the same tired proposals for more government tinkering, more meddling and more control—all of which led us to this state in the first place.

Can anyone look at the record of this administration and say, "Well done"? Can anyone compare the state of our economy when the Carter administration took office with where we are today and say, "Keep up the good work"? Can anyone look at our reduced standing in the world today and say, "Let's have four more years of this"?

I believe the American people are going to answer these questions the first week of November and their answer will be, "No—we've had enough." And, then it will be up to us—beginning next January 20th—to offer an administration and congressional leadership of competence and more than a little courage.

We must have the clarity of vision to see the difference between what is essential and what is merely desirable, and then the courage to bring our government back under control and make it acceptable to the people.

It is essential that we maintain both the forward momentum of economic growth and the strength of the safety net beneath those in society who need help. We also believe it is essential that the integrity of all aspects of Social Security be preserved.

Beyond these essentials, I believe it is clear our federal government is overgrown and overweight. Indeed, it is time for our government to go on a diet. Therefore, my first act as chief executive will be to impose an immediate and thorough freeze on federal hiring. Then, we are going to enlist the very best minds from business, labor and whatever quarter to conduct a detailed review of every department, bureau and agency that lives by federal appropriations. We are also going to enlist the help and ideas of many dedicated and hard-working government employees at all levels who want a more efficient government as much as the rest of us do. I know that many are demoralized by the confusion and waste they confront in their work as a result of failed and failing policies.

Our instructions to the groups we enlist will be simple and direct. We will remind them that government programs exist at the sufferance of the American taxpayer and are paid for with money earned by working men and women. Any program that represents a waste of their money—a theft from their pocketbooks—must have that waste eliminated or the program must go—by executive order where possible, by congressional action where necessary. Everything that can be run more effectively by state and local government we shall turn over to state and local government, along with the funding sources to pay for it. We are going to put an end to the money merry-go-round where our money becomes Washington's money, to be spent by the states and cities exactly the way the federal bureaucrats tell them to.

I will not accept the excuse that the federal government has grown so big and powerful that it is beyond the control of any president, any administration or Congress. We are going to put an end to the notion that the American taxpayer exists to fund the federal government. The federal government exists to serve the American people. On January 20th, we are going to re-establish that truth.

Also on that date we are going to initiate action to get substantial relief for our taxpaying citizens and action to put people back to work. None of this will be based on any new form of monetary tinkering or fiscal sleight-of-hand. We will simply apply to government the common sense we all use in our daily lives.

Work and family are at the center of our lives, the foundation of our dignity as a free people. When we deprive people of what they have earned, or take away their jobs, we destroy their dignity and undermine their families. We cannot support our families unless there are jobs; and we cannot have jobs unless people have both money to invest and the faith to invest it.

These are concepts that stem from an economic system that for more than two hundred years has helped us master a continent, create a previously undreamed of prosperity for our people and has fed millions of others around the globe. That system will continue to serve us in the future if our government will stop ignoring the basic values on which it was built and stop betraying the trust and good will of the American workers who keep it going.

The American people are carrying the heaviest peacetime tax burden in our nation's history—and it will grow even heavier, under present law, next January. We are taxing ourselves into economic exhaustion and stagnation, crushing our ability and incentive to save, invest and produce.

This must stop. We must halt this fiscal self-destruction and restore sanity to our economic system.

I have long advocated a 30 percent reduction in income tax rates over a period of three years. This phased tax reduction would begin with a 10 percent "down payment" tax cut in 1981, which the Republicans and Congress and I have already proposed.

A phased reduction of tax rates would go a long way toward easing the heavy burden on the American people. But, we should not stop here.

Within the context of economic conditions and appropriate budget priorities during each fiscal year of my presidency, I would strive to go further. This would include improvement in business depreciation taxes so we can stimulate investment in order to get plants and equipment replaced, put more Americans back to work and put our nation back on the road to being competitive in world commerce. We will also work to reduce the cost of government as a percentage of our gross national product.

The first task of national leadership is to set honest and realistic priorities in our policies and our budget and I pledge that my administration will do that.

When I talk of tax cuts, I am reminded that every major tax cut in this century has strengthened the economy, generated renewed productivity and ended up yielding new revenues for the government by creating new investment, new jobs and more commerce among our people.

The present administration has been forced by us Republicans to play follow-the-leader with regard to a tax cut. But, in this election year we must take with the proverbial "grain of salt" any tax cut proposed by those who have given us the greatest tax increase in our history.

When those in leadership give us tax increases and tell us we must also do with less, have they thought about those who have always had less—especially the minorities? This is like telling them that just as they step on the first rung of the ladder of opportunity, the ladder is being pulled out from under them. That may be the Democratic leadership's message to the minorities, but it won't be ours. Our message will be: we have to move ahead, but we're not going to leave anyone behind.

Thanks to the economic policies of the Democratic Party, millions of Americans find themselves out of work. Millions more have never even had a fair chance to learn new skills, hold a decent job, or secure for themselves and their families a share in the prosperity of this nation.

It is time to put America back to work; to make our cities and towns resound with the confident voices of men and women of all races, nationalities and faiths bringing home to their families a decent paycheck they can cash for honest money.

For those without skills, we'll find a way to help them get skills.

For those without job opportunities we'll stimulate new opportunities, particularly in the inner cities where they live.

For those who have abandoned hope, we'll restore hope and we'll welcome them into a great national crusade to make America great again!

When we move from domestic affairs and cast our eyes abroad, we see an equally sorry chapter on the record of the present administration.

A Soviet combat brigade trains in Cuba, just 90 miles from our shores.

A Soviet army of invasion occupies Afghanistan, further threatening our vital interests in the Middle East.

America's defense strength is at its lowest ebb in a generation, while the Soviet Union is vastly outspending us in both strategic and conventional arms.

Our European allies, looking nervously at the growing menace from the East, turn to us for leadership and fail to find it.

And, incredibly more than 50 of our fellow Americans have been held captive for over eight months by a dictatorial foreign power that holds us up to ridicule before the world.

Adversaries large and small test our will and seek to confound our resolve, but we are given weakness when we need strength, vacillation when the times demand firmness.

The Carter administration lives in the world of make-believe, every day drawing up a response to that day's problems, troubles, regardless of what happened yesterday and what will happen tomorrow.

The rest of us, however, live in the real world. It is here that disasters are overtaking our nation without any real response from Washington.

This is make-believe, self-deceit and—above all—transparent hypocrisy. For example, Mr. Carter says he supports the volunteer army, but he lets military pay and benefits slip so low that many of our enlisted personnel are actually eligible for food stamps. Re-enlistment rates drop and, just recently, after he fought all week against a proposal to increase the pay of our men and women in uniform, he helicoptered out to our carrier, the U.S.S. *Nimitz*, which was returning from long months of duty. He told the crew that he advocated better pay for them and their comrades! Where does he really stand, now that he's back on shore?

I'll tell you where I stand. I do not favor a peacetime draft or registration, but I do favor pay and benefit levels that will attract and keep highly motivated men and women in our volunteer forces and an active reserve trained and ready for an instant call in case of an emergency.

There may be a sailor at the helm of the ship of state, but the ship has no rudder. Critical decisions are made at times almost in comic fashion, but who can laugh? Who was not embarrassed when the administration handed a major propaganda victory in the United Nations to the enemies of Israel, our staunch Middle East ally for three decades, and then claim that the American vote was a "mistake," the result of a "failure of communication" between the president, his secretary of state and his U.N. ambassador?

Who does not feel a growing sense of unease as our allies, facing repeated instances of an amateurish and confused administration, reluctantly conclude that America is unwilling or unable to fulfill its obligations as leader of the free world?

Who does not feel rising alarm when the question in any discussion of foreign policy is no longer. "Should we do something?" but "Do we have the capacity to do anything?"

The administration which has brought us to this state is seeking your endorsement for four more years of weakness, indecision, mediocrity and incompetence. No American should vote until he or she has asked, is the United States stronger and more respected now than it was three-and-a-half years ago? Is the world today a safer place in which to live?

It is the responsibility of the president of the United States, in working for peace, to insure that the safety of our people cannot successfully be threatened by a hostile foreign power. As president, fulfilling that responsibility will be my number one priority.

We are not a warlike people. Quite the opposite. We always seek to live in peace. We resort to force infrequently and with great reluctance—and only after we have determined that it is absolutely necessary. We are awed—and rightly so—by the forces of destruction loose in the world in this nuclear era. But neither can we be naive or foolish. Four times in my lifetime America has gone to war, bleeding the lives of its young men into the sands of beachheads, the fields of Europe and the jungles and rice paddies of Asia. We know only too well that war comes not when the forces of freedom are strong, but when they are weak. It is then that tyrants are tempted.

We simply cannot learn these lessons the hard way again without risking our destruction.

Of all the objectives we seek, first and foremost is the establishment of lasting world peace. We must always stand ready to negotiate in good faith, ready to pursue any reasonable avenue that holds forth the promise of lessening tensions and furthering the prospects of peace. But let our friends and those who may wish us ill take note: the United States has an obligation to its citizens and to the people of the world never to let those who would destroy freedom dictate the future course of human life on this planet. I would regard my election as proof that we have renewed our resolve to preserve world peace and freedom. This nation will once again be strong enough to do that.

This evening marks the last step—save one—of a campaign that has taken Nancy and me from one end of this great land to the other, over many months and thousands of miles. There are those who question the way we choose a president, who say that our process imposes difficult and exhausting burdens on those who seek the office. I have not found it so.

It is impossible to capture in words the splendor of this vast continent which God has granted as our portion of his creation. There are no words to express the extraordinary strength and character of this breed of people we call Americans.

Everywhere we have met thousands of Democrats, Independents and Republicans from all economic conditions and walks of life bound together in that community of shared values of family, work, neighborhood, peace and freedom. They are concerned, yes, but they are not frightened. They are disturbed, but not dismayed. They are the kind of men and women Tom Paine had in mind when he wrote—during the darkest days of the American Revolution—"We have it in our power to begin the world over again."

Nearly one-hundred-and-fifty years after Tom Paine wrote those words, an American president told the generation of the Great Depression that it had a "rendezvous with destiny." I believe this generation of Americans today has a rendezvous with destiny.

Tonight, let us dedicate ourselves to renewing the American compact. I ask you not simply to "Trust me," but to trust your values—our values—and to hold me responsible for living up to them. I ask you to trust that American spirit which knows no ethnic, religious, social, political, regional or economic boundaries; the spirit that burned with zeal in the hearts of millions of immigrants from every corner of the earth who came here in search of freedom.

Some say that spirit no longer exists. But I have seen it—I have felt it—all across the land; in the big cities, the small towns and in rural America. The American spirit is still there, ready to blaze into life if you and I are willing to do what has to be done; the practical, down-to-earth things that will stimulate our economy, increase productivity and put America back to work.

The time is now to resolve that the basis of a firm and principled foreign policy is one that takes the world as it is and seeks to change it by leadership and example, not by harangue, harassment or wishful thinking.

The time is now to say that while we shall seek new friendships and expand and improve others, we shall not do so by breaking our word or casting aside old friends and allies.

And, the time is now to redeem promises once made to the American people by another candidate, in another time and other place. He said, ". . . For three long years I have been going up and down this country preaching that government—federal, state and local—costs too much. I shall not stop that preaching. As an immediate program of action, we must abolish useless offices. We must eliminate unnecessary functions of government. . . . we must consolidate subdivisions of government and, like the private citizen, give up luxuries which we can no longer afford.

"I propose to you, my friends, and through you that government of all kinds, big and little, be made solvent and that the example be set by the president of the United States and his Cabinet."

So said Franklin Delano Roosevelt in his acceptance speech to the Democratic National Convention in July 1932.

The time is now, my fellow Americans, to recapture our destiny, to take it into our own hands. But, to do this will take many of us, working together. I ask you tonight to volunteer your help in this cause so we can carry our message throughout the land.

Yes, isn't now the time that we, the people, carried out these unkept promises? Let us pledge to each other and to all America on this July day 48 years later, we intend to do just that.

I have thought of something that is not part of my speech and I'm worried over whether I should do it.

Can we doubt that only a Divine Providence placed this land, this island of freedom, here as a refuge for all those people in the world who yearn to breathe freely: Jews and Christians enduring persecution behind the Iron Curtain, the boat people of Southeast Asia, of Cuba and Haiti, the victims of drought and famine in Africa, the freedom fighters of Afghanistan and our own countrymen held in savage captivity.

I'll confess that I've been a little afraid to suggest what I'm going to suggest—I'm more afraid not to—that we begin our crusade joined together in a moment of silent prayer.

God bless America.

Source: "Time to Recapture our Destiny," July 1, 1980, The Ronald Reagan Presidential Foundation and Library. Available online. URL: http://www.reaganfoundation.com/reagan/speeches/time_to.asp

11. First Inaugural Address
January 20, 1981

Ronald Reagan's inauguration took place in the midst of fast-breaking developments over the fate of the American hostages in Iran. Shortly after delivering this speech, word arrived that the hostages had been released and were leaving Iranian airspace. This event, coupled with the normal excitement surrounding any change of government, got the administration off to a fast start. Reagan's inaugural address, written with the assistance of former Nixon aide Kenneth Khachigian, restated many of the principles he embraced in the 1950s during his General Electric days. Reagan once again identified himself with the antifederalist tradition: "All of us need to be reminded that the federal government did not create the states; the states created the federal government." The most memorable line from the speech, "in this present crisis, government is not the solution to our problem; government is the problem," sent a chill down the spine of any unreconstructed New Dealer or New Frontiersman who happened to be listening. And in a veiled reference to President Carter's hostage problem, Reagan vowed to do things differently: "Our reluctance for conflict should not be misjudged as a failure of will. When action is required to preserve our national security, we will act." These words, and others, would come back to haunt him later in his presidency.

Senator Hatfield, Mr. Chief Justice, Mr. President, Vice President Bush, Vice President Mondale, Senator Baker, Speaker O'Neill, Reverend Moomaw, and my fellow citizens: To a few of us here today, this is a solemn and most momentous occasion; and yet, in the history of our nation, it is a commonplace occurrence. The orderly transfer of authority as called for in the Constitution routinely takes place as it has for almost two centuries and few of us stop to think how unique we really are. In the eyes of many in the world, this every-4-year ceremony we accept as normal is nothing less than a miracle.

Mr. President, I want our fellow citizens to know how much you did to carry on this tradition. By your gracious cooperation in the transition process, you have shown a watching world that we are a united people pledged to maintaining a political system which guarantees individual liberty to a greater degree than any other, and I thank you and your people for all your help in maintaining the continuity which is the bulwark of our Republic.

The business of our nation goes forward. These United States are confronted with an economic affliction of great proportions. We suffer from the longest and one of the worst sustained inflations in our national history. It distorts our economic decisions, penalizes thrift, and crushes the struggling young and the fixed-income elderly alike. It threatens to shatter the lives of millions of our people.

Idle industries have cast workers into unemployment, causing human misery and personal indignity. Those who do work are denied a fair return for their labor by a tax system which penalizes successful achievement and keeps us from maintaining full productivity.

But great as our tax burden is, it has not kept pace with public spending. For decades, we have piled deficit upon deficit, mortgaging our future and our children's future for the temporary convenience of the present. To continue this long trend is to guarantee tremendous social, cultural, political, and economic upheavals.

You and I, as individuals, can, by borrowing, live beyond our means, but for only a limited period of time. Why, then, should we think that collectively, as a nation, we are not bound by that same limitation?

We must act today in order to preserve tomorrow. And let there be no misunderstanding—we are going to begin to act, beginning today.

The economic ills we suffer have come upon us over several decades. They will not go away in days, weeks, or months, but they will go away. They will go away because we, as Americans, have the capacity now, as we have had in the past, to do whatever needs to be done to preserve this last and greatest bastion of freedom.

In this present crisis, government is not the solution to our problem; government is the problem.

From time to time, we have been tempted to believe that society has become too complex to be managed by self-rule, that government by an elite group is superior to government for, by, and of the people. But if no one among us is capable of governing himself, then who among us has the capacity to govern someone else? All of us together, in and out of government, must bear the burden. The solutions we seek must be equitable, with no one group singled out to pay a higher price.

We hear much of special interest groups. Our concern must be for a special interest group that has been too long neglected. It knows no sectional boundaries or ethnic and racial divisions, and it crosses political party lines. It is made up of men and women who raise our food, patrol our streets, man our mines and our factories, teach our children, keep our homes, and heal us when we are sick—professionals, industrialists, shopkeepers, clerks, cabbies, and truckdrivers. They are,

in short, "We the people," this breed called Americans.

Well, this administration's objective will be a healthy, vigorous, growing economy that provides equal opportunity for all Americans, with no barriers born of bigotry or discrimination. Putting America back to work means putting all Americans back to work. Ending inflation means freeing all Americans from the terror of runaway living costs. All must share in the productive work of this "new beginning" and all must share in the bounty of a revived economy. With the idealism and fair play which are the core of our system and our strength, we can have a strong and prosperous America at peace with itself and the world.

So, as we begin, let us take inventory. We are a nation that has a government—not the other way around. And this makes us special among the nations of the Earth. Our government has no power except that granted it by the people. It is time to check and reverse the growth of government which shows signs of having grown beyond the consent of the governed.

It is my intention to curb the size and influence of the Federal establishment and to demand recognition of the distinction between the powers granted to the Federal Government and those reserved to the States or to the people. All of us need to be reminded that the Federal Government did not create the States; the States created the Federal Government.

Now, so there will be no misunderstanding, it is not my intention to do away with government. It is, rather, to make it work—work with us, not over us; to stand by our side, not ride on our back. Government can and must provide opportunity, not smother it; foster productivity, not stifle it.

If we look to the answer as to why, for so many years, we achieved so much, prospered as no other people on Earth, it was because here, in this land, we unleashed the energy and individual genius of man to a greater extent than has ever been done before. Freedom and the dignity of the individual have been more available and assured here than in any other place on Earth. The price for this freedom at times has been high, but we have never been unwilling to pay that price.

It is no coincidence that our present troubles parallel and are proportionate to the intervention and intrusion in our lives that result from unnecessary and excessive growth of government. It is time for us to realize that we are too great a nation to limit ourselves to small dreams. We are not, as some would have us believe, doomed to an inevitable decline. I do not believe in a fate that will fall on us no matter what we do. I do believe in a fate that will fall on us if we do nothing. So, with all the creative energy at our command, let us begin an era of national renewal. Let us renew our determination, our courage, and our strength. And let us renew our faith and our hope.

We have every right to dream heroic dreams. Those who say that we are in a time when there are no heroes just don't know where to look. You can see heroes every day going in and out of factory gates. Others, a handful in number, produce enough food to feed all of us and then the world beyond. You meet heroes across a counter—and they are on both sides of that counter. There are entrepreneurs with faith in themselves and faith in an idea who create new jobs, new wealth and opportunity. They are individuals and families whose taxes support the Government and whose voluntary gifts support church, charity, culture, art, and education. Their patriotism is quiet but deep. Their values sustain our national life.

I have used the words "they" and "their" in speaking of these heroes. I could say "you" and "your" because I am addressing the heroes of whom I speak—you, the citizens of this blessed land. Your dreams, your hopes, your goals are going to be the dreams, the hopes, and the goals of this administration, so help me God.

We shall reflect the compassion that is so much a part of your makeup. How can we love our country and not love our countrymen, and loving them, reach out a hand when they fall, heal them when they are sick, and provide opportunities to make them self-sufficient so they will be equal in fact and not just in theory?

Can we solve the problems confronting us? Well, the answer is an unequivocal and emphatic "yes." To paraphrase Winston Churchill, I did not take the oath I have just taken with the intention of presiding over the dissolution of the world's strongest economy.

In the days ahead I will propose removing the roadblocks that have slowed our economy and reduced productivity. Steps will be taken aimed at restoring the balance between the various levels of government. Progress may be slow—measured in inches and feet, not miles—but we will progress. It is time to reawaken this industrial giant, to get government back within its means, and to lighten our punitive tax burden. And these will be our first priorities, and on these principles, there will be no compromise.

On the eve of our struggle for independence a man who might have been one of the greatest among the Founding Fathers, Dr. Joseph Warren, president of the Massachusetts Congress, said to his fellow Americans, "Our country is in danger, but not to be despaired of. . . . On you depend the fortunes of America. You are to decide the important questions upon which rests the happiness and the liberty of millions yet unborn. Act worthy of yourselves."

Well, I believe we, the Americans of today, are ready to act worthy of ourselves, ready to do what must be done to ensure happiness and liberty for ourselves, our children and our children's children.

And as we renew ourselves here in our own land, we will be seen as having greater strength throughout the world. We will again be the exemplar of freedom and a beacon of hope for those who do not now have freedom.

To those neighbors and allies who share our freedom, we will strengthen our historic ties and assure them of our support and firm commitment. We will match loyalty with loyalty. We will strive for mutually beneficial relations. We will not use our friendship to impose on their sovereignty, for our own sovereignty is not for sale.

As for the enemies of freedom, those who are potential adversaries, they will be reminded that peace is the highest aspiration of the American people. We will negotiate for it, sacrifice for it; we will not surrender for it—now or ever.

Our forbearance should never be misunderstood. Our reluctance for conflict should not be misjudged as a failure of will. When action is required to preserve our national security, we will act. We will maintain sufficient strength to prevail if need be, knowing that if we do so we have the best chance of never having to use that strength.

Above all, we must realize that no arsenal, or no weapon in the arsenals of the world, is so formidable as the will and moral courage of free men and women. It is a weapon our adversaries in today's world do not have. It is a weapon that we as Americans do have. Let that be understood by those who practice terrorism and prey upon their neighbors.

I am told that tens of thousands of prayer meetings are being held on this day, and for that I am deeply grateful. We are a nation under God, and I believe God intended for us to be free. It would be fitting and good, I think, if on each Inauguration Day in future years it should be declared a day of prayer.

This is the first time in history that this ceremony has been held, as you have been told, on this West Front of the Capitol. Standing here, one faces a magnificent vista, opening up on this city's special beauty and history. At the end of this open mall are those shrines to the giants on whose shoulders we stand.

Directly in front of me, the monument to a monumental man: George Washington, Father of our country. A man of humility who came to greatness reluctantly. He led America out of revolutionary victory into infant nationhood. Off to one side, the stately memorial to Thomas Jefferson. The Declaration of Independence flames with his eloquence.

And then beyond the Reflecting Pool the dignified columns of the Lincoln Memorial. Whoever would understand in his heart the meaning of America will find it in the life of Abraham Lincoln.

Beyond those monuments to heroism is the Potomac River, and on the far shore the sloping hills of Arlington National Cemetery with its row on row of simple white markers bearing crosses or Stars of David. They add up to only a tiny fraction of the price that has been paid for our freedom.

Each one of those markers is a monument to the kinds of hero I spoke of earlier. Their lives ended in places called Belleau Wood, The Argonne, Omaha Beach, Salerno and halfway around the world on Guadalcanal, Tarawa, Pork Chop Hill, the Chosin Reservoir, and in a hundred rice paddies and jungles of a place called Vietnam.

Under one such marker lies a young man—Martin Treptow—who left his job in a small town barbershop in 1917 to go to France with the famed Rainbow Division. There, on the western front, he was killed trying to carry a message between battalions under heavy artillery fire.

We are told that on his body was found a diary. On the flyleaf under the heading, "My Pledge," he had written these words: "America must win this war. Therefore, I will work, I will save, I will sacrifice, I will endure, I will fight cheerfully and do my utmost, as if the issue of the whole struggle depended on me alone."

The crisis we are facing today does not require of us the kind of sacrifice that Martin Treptow and so many thousands of others were called upon to make. It does require, however, our best effort, and our willingness to believe in ourselves and to believe in our capacity to perform great deeds; to believe that together, with God's help, we can and will resolve the problems which now confront us.

And, after all, why shouldn't we believe that? We are Americans. God bless you, and thank you.

Source: "Inaugural Address," January 20, 1981, The Ronald Reagan Presidential Library. Available online. URL: http://www.reagan.utexas.edu/resource/speeches/1981/12081a.htm

12. First Presidential News Conference January 29, 1981

Ronald Reagan was never a master of detail when it came to handling reporters' questions, but he was quite capable of uttering a quip that would defuse a touchy subject or at least allow him to emerge somewhat unscathed. This press conference was notable for the president's response to a question about the intentions of the leaders of the Soviet Union. Reagan depicted the Soviet leadership as thoroughly immoral, and used rhetoric rarely heard from an American president, at least since the early days of the cold war. It was words such as these that caused many in the East and the West to believe that the prospect for peaceful relations between the Soviet Union and the United States had reached its lowest point since the Cuban missile crisis of 1962. Soviet rhetoric toward Reagan was even more disdainful, comparing the president to Adolf Hitler and accusing him of plotting to launch World War III.

The President. How do you do? I have a brief opening statement here before I take your questions.

The National Economy

Yesterday Secretary of the Treasury Donald Regan sent to the Congress a request to raise the debt ceiling to $985 billion. This represents a dramatic jump of $50 billion over the previous debt ceiling. The administration took this action with great regret, because it's clear that the massive deficits our government runs is one of the root causes of our profound economic problems, and for too many years this process has come too easily for us. We've lived beyond our means and then financed our extravagance on the backs of the American people.

The clear message I received in the election campaign is that we must gain control of this inflationary monster.

Let me briefly review for the American people what we've already done. Within moments of taking the oath of office, I placed a freeze on the hiring of civilian employees in the Federal Government. Two days later I issued an order to cut down on government travel, reduce the number of consultants to the government, stopped the procurement of certain items, and called on my appointees to exercise restraint in their own offices. Yesterday I announced the elimination of remaining Federal controls on U.S. oil production and marketing.

Today I'm announcing two more actions to reduce the size of the Federal Government.

First, I'm taking major steps toward the elimination of the Council on Wage and Price Stability. This Council has been a failure. It has been totally ineffective in controlling inflation, and it's imposed unnecessary burdens on labor and business. Therefore, I am now ending the wage and price program of the Council. I am eliminating the staff that carries out its wage/pricing activities, and I'm asking Congress to rescind its budget, saving the taxpayers some $1 million a year.

My second decision today is a directive ordering key Federal agencies to freeze pending regulations for 60 days. This action gives my administration time to start a new regulatory oversight process and also prevents certain last-minute regulatory decisions of the previous administration, the so-called midnight regulations, from taking effect without proper review and approval.

All of us should remember that the Federal Government is not some mysterious institution comprised of buildings, files, and paper. The people are the government. What we create we ought to be able to control. I do not intend to make wildly skyrocketing deficits and runaway government simple facts of life in this administration. As I've said, our ills have come upon us over several decades, and they will not go away in days or weeks or months. But I want the American people to know that we have begun.

Now I'll be happy to take your questions. Helen [Helen Thomas, United Press International].

U.S. Relations with Iran

Q. Mr. President, will your policy toward Iran be one of revenge or reconciliation? And will the United States honor the recent commitments to Iran, especially since you approved of most of them during the campaign?

The President. Well, I'm certainly not thinking of revenge, and I don't know whether reconciliation would be possible with the present government, or absence of a government, in Iran.

I think that the United States will honor the obligations. As a matter of fact, the most important of those were already put into effect by the preceding administration in negotiating the release. We are, however, studying, because there were four major

agreements and there were nine Executive orders, and we are studying thoroughly what is a pretty complex matter, we've discovered, with regard to whether they are in keeping with international and our own national laws. And so, I won't be able to really answer your questions on specifics until we've completed that study.

Reductions in Federal Spending

Q. Mr. President, the Treasury Secretary said Monday that your budget cuts will be of a much higher magnitude than most people thought they would be. You said they would be across the board. Now that you've had some time to study the budget, can you say where these cuts will be made, what program will feel the cuts the most?

The President. They'll be made every place. Maybe across the board was the wrong decision, although it describes it. What I meant was that no one is exempt from being looked at for areas in which we can make cuts in spending.

And yes, they probably are going to be bigger than anyone has ever attempted, because this administration did not come here to be a caretaker government and just hope we could go along the same way and maybe do it a little better. We think the time has come where there has to be a change of direction of this country, and it's going to begin with reducing government spending.

U.S. Response to Terrorist Acts

Q. Mr. President, in your welcoming address to the freed Americans, you sounded a warning of swift and effective retribution in future terrorist situations. What kind of action are you prepared to take to back up this hard rhetoric?

The President. Well, that's a question that I don't think you can or should answer as to specifics. This is a big and it's a powerful nation. It has a lot of options open to it, and to try and specify now just particularly what you should do I think is one of the things that's been wrong.

People have gone to bed in some of these countries that have done these things to us in the past confident that they can go to sleep, wake up in the morning, and the United States wouldn't have taken any action. What I meant by that phrase was that anyone who does these things, violates our rights in the future, is not going to be able to go to bed with that confidence.

Walt [Walter Rodgers, Associated Press Radio].

Strategic Arms Limitation

Q. Mr. President, you campaigned rather vociferously against the SALT II treaty, saying it was slightly toward the Soviet Union. Yet I noticed your Secretary of State, Mr. Haig, now seems to suggest that for the time being, at least, the United States will abide by the limits of the SALT II treaty and he hopes the Soviet Union will, too. How long do you intend that the United States should abide by the terms of a SALT agreement which you consider inequitable, and what do you consider its greatest inequities to be?

The President. Well, the SALT treaty, first of all, I think, permits a continued buildup on both sides of strategic nuclear weapons but, in the main thing, authorizes an immediate increase in large numbers of Soviet warheads. There is no verification as to the number of warheads on the missile, no method for us to do this.

I don't think that a treaty—SALT means strategic arms limitation—that actually permits a buildup, on both sides, of strategic nuclear weapons can properly be called that.

And I have said that when we can—and I am willing for our people to go in to negotiate or, let me say, discussions leading to negotiations—that we should start negotiating on the basis of trying to effect an actual reduction in the numbers of nuclear weapons. That would then be real strategic arms limitation.

And I happen to believe, also, that you can't sit down at a table and just negotiate that unless you take into account, in consideration at that table all the other things that are going on. In other words, I believe in linkage.

Sam [Sam Donaldson, ABC News].

Goals of the Soviet Union

Q. Mr. President, what do you see as the long-range intentions of the Soviet Union? Do you think, for instance, the Kremlin is bent on world domination that might lead to a continuation of the cold war, or do you think that under other circumstances détente is possible?

The President. Well, so far détente's been a one-way street that the Soviet Union has used to pursue its own aims. I don't have to think of an answer as to what I think their intentions are; they have repeated it. I know of no leader of the Soviet Union since the revolution, and including the present leadership, that has not more than once repeated in the various Communist congresses they hold their determination that their goal must be the promotion of world revolution and a one-world Socialist or Communist state, whichever word you want to use.

Now, as long as they do that and as long as they, at the same time, have openly and publicly declared that the only morality they recognize is what will further their cause, meaning they reserve unto themselves the right to commit any crime, to lie, to cheat, in order to attain that, and that is moral, not immoral, and we operate on a different set of standards, I think when you do business with them, even at a détente, you keep that in mind.

American Businesses and Iran

Q. Mr. President, what's your opinion of American companies that now want to resume business with Iran?

The President. My opinion of American companies that want to resume business with Iran? I hope they're going to do it by long distance. [Laughter] We wouldn't want to go back to having just a different cast of characters, but the same show going on. [Laughter]

I can understand that, particularly in the field of energy, their wanting to do that, but we are urging the people to think long and hard before they travel to Iran, because we don't think their safety can be guaranteed there.

American Prisoners in Vietnam

Q. Mr. President, three Americans are still incarcerated in Vietnam. Can you tell us the status of their cases and whether the administration is doing anything to get them back?

The President. I have told our people about those three. They knew about them, of course, but I've told them that, yes, we continue and we want to get them back, also.

Now, I know I've been staying down front here too much. I've got to prove I can look at the back rows there. You, sir.

Affirmative Action Programs

Q. Okay. Mr. President, some administrative officials have promised adherence to the civil rights laws which are on the books, but there has been considerable discussion about dismantling the affirmative action aspect that gives those laws, to some people, greater meaning. And I'm wondering, Mr. President, that if there will be a retreat in the Federal Government on the government's advocacy of affirmative action programs generally and in Federal hiring of blacks and Hispanics specifically?

The President. No, there will be no retreat. This administration is going to be dedicated to equality. I think we've made great progress in the civil rights field. I think there are some things, however, that may not be as useful as they once were or that may even be distorted in the practice, such as some affirmative action programs becoming quota systems. And I'm old enough to remember when quotas existed in the United States for the purpose of discrimination, and I don't want to see that happen again.

Decontrol of Natural Gas Prices

Q. Mr. President, when and how will you seek the decontrol of natural gas prices?

The President. Well, we haven't dealt with that problem yet. We thought oil would do for a starter. But I can't really answer your question. That will be a matter for discussion in future cabinet meetings.

Lou [Lou Cannon, Washington Post].

Soviet Grain Embargo

Q. Mr. President, during the campaign you repeatedly talked about the unfairness of the grain embargo, as you saw it. Do you have second thoughts now, or will you lift the grain embargo?

The President. Well, with the grain embargo, my quarrel with it from the first was that I thought it was asking only one group of Americans to participate, the farmers.

You only have two choices with an embargo: You either lift it, or you broaden it. And we have not made a decision except that, at the request of Secretary of Agriculture John Block, I have taken the matter of the embargo out of, you might say, the discussions of the National Security Council, and it, next week, is on the agenda for a full Cabinet meeting as to what our course will be. So, I can't answer what we do about it until next week.

As I say, it was asking one group of Americans to bear the burden and, I have always thought, was more of a kind of gesture than it was something real.

Yes, ma'am.

Atlanta Murders

Q. Mr. President, what will you do to honor the request from Atlanta officials for you and the Federal Government to intercede in the Atlanta case of 17 missing black children?

The President. Just a few minutes before I came in here, that message was handed to me that the Atlanta mayor wanted to talk, and we are going to get someone in touch with him immediately. Now, you recognize, of course, that possibly civil rights would be the only basis upon which we could have any jurisdiction down there in this. For FBI, for example, on any other thing, there's been no evidence of crossing State lines or anything. And yet we want to be helpful, because that is a most tragic case, and so we will be meeting on that very shortly.

U.S. Policy toward the Caribbean

Q. Mr. President, when the Jamaican Prime Minister was here yesterday, Mr. Seaga, he suggested publicly that now might be a good time for you, as the new President, to have a

foreign policy initiative for Latin America and for the Caribbean. Do you intend to follow that suggestion, and if so, how would your policies differ from those of former President Carter?

The President. Well, I think we've seen a great reverse in the Caribbean situation, and it came about through Prime Minister Seaga's election. It was the turnover or turn-around of a nation that had gone, certainly, in the direction of the Communist movement; it was a protégé of Castro. And his election was greeted by me with great enthusiasm, because it represented the people by their vote, having experienced that kind of government, turned another direction.

And I think this opens the door for us to have a policy in the Mediterranean [Caribbean] of bringing them back in—those countries that might have started in that direction—or keeping them in the Western World, in the free world. And so, we are looking forward to cooperation with Prime Minister Seaga.

Registration for the Draft

Q. Mr. President, I think you meant "Caribbean" in that last answer rather than "Mediterranean."

The President. What'd I say?

Q. "Mediterranean."

The President. Oh. I meant "Caribbean." I'm sorry.

Q. What do you intend to do, Mr. President, about the draft registration law that was passed during President Carter's administration? And in view of your opposition to it in the campaign, how is that consistent with your avowed intention to strengthen our national defenses?

The President. Well, to answer the last part first, I just didn't feel that the advance registration, on all the evidence we could get, would materially speed up the process if an emergency required the draft. It did create a bureaucracy. It caused, certainly, some unrest and dissatisfaction. And we were told that it would only be a matter of several days if we had to call up in a draft, that we could do that several days earlier with the registration than we would be able if there was no registration at all.

This is one that's something to be looked at further down. I've only been here 9 days, and most of these 9 days have been spent in Cabinet meetings on the economy, getting ready to send our package up to the Hill. And so, I just have to tell you that we will be dealing with that, meet with that, and make a decision on what to do with it down the road someplace.

Gary [Gary Schuster, Detroit News].

Tax Reductions

Q. Mr. President, speaking of your economic package, can you give us your thoughts on an effective date for the tax cuts that you plan to recommend in your economic recovery plan, and specifying whether you prefer one effective date for business and another for personal cuts or whether you'd like to combine them?

The President. I'd like to see it all go forward all at once. As to date, I know there's been talk about whether it should be retroactive back or whether it should be as of that minute. That, to me, isn't as important as getting for individuals the principle of a 10-percent cut for each of 3 years in place and the business taxes, also, so that we can all look forward with some confidence of stability in the program. And we're going to strive for that. And I can't really answer you

about what the date will be until we submit the package.

U.S. Relations with Iran

Q. Mr. President, I know you said earlier that you were not thinking of revenge toward Iran. But does that preclude any punishment whatsoever for what they've done?

The President. Well, again, I have to ask your forbearance and wait until we've finished our study of this whole situation as to what we're going to do. I don't think any of us have a friendly feeling toward the people that have done what they have done. But I think it's too complex for me to answer until we've had time to really study this.

Q. Mr. President, just one follow-up. Would you go so far as to encourage American businesses to resume commercial trade with Iran?

The President. At this point, no.

Departments of Energy and Education

Q. Mr. President, do you intend to follow through with your campaign pledges to abolish the Departments of Energy and Education?

The President. I have not retreated from that at all. Yes. The process, however, that I have asked for is for both Secretary Bell of Education and Secretary Jim Edwards of Energy to reorganize, to produce the most effective streamlining of their Departments that they can—in Education, to look at the appropriate role of the Federal Government in education, if there is one, and to report back. And then we will decide, making our recommendations. Much the same thing holds true with the Department of Energy. The reason for this being that while they were new Cabinet-level agencies, they incorporated government functions and programs that had been going on in them, and they came under that umbrella. And we have to find out which of those functions that have been a Federal Government function continue and where they would best fit.

But, yes, I'm determined, and I believe that it was wrong to have created the two agencies to begin with.

Dairy Price Supports

Q. Mr. President, during the campaign your chief farm spokesman put you on record as favoring, for the time being, continuation of the dairy price support level where it had been. Within the last couple of days, your budget director and your Secretary of Agriculture have indicated that the dairy program is too expensive and should be cut back. Could you reconcile those differences of approach for us?

The President. Well, I could only tell you that this, again, is something to wait for the next Cabinet meeting. All of these things are worked out between the appropriate Cabinet members and our Director of OMB, and then they come to the Cabinet for full discussion so that others who have an interest in this can have their input. And so, I can't answer you, because that has not yet come to the Cabinet.

Stability in Persian Gulf Region

Q. Mr. President, Iran and the Soviet Union share a long border in a region vital to the future stability of the world. Given the anti-U.S. sentiment there, how do you best think the United States can ensure the stability of the region, the Persian Gulf region?

The President. Of the—you said Iran, the border between Iran and the Soviet Union.

Well, I think one of the first things that has to happen for stability, has got to be, in

Iran itself, to establish a government that can speak as a government for Iran. And part of our problem in all these long 444 days has been the inability of anyone seemingly to speak for that nation, to have a government. Now, I think that any country would want to help another if they really showed an intent to have a government that would abide by international law and do what they could to help them in that regard. But until such a thing appears apparent there, I don't know that there's anything we can do.

U.S. Relations with Iran

Q. Mr. President, if it's your intention to signal the world that this country will respond with swift retribution in cases of international terrorism in the future, why is it your policy not to retaliate against Iran?

The President. Well, what good would just revenge do, and what form would that take? I don't think revenge is worthy of us. On the other hand, I don't think we act as if this never happened. And I'd rather wait until, as I say, we complete this study.

Who said—I know I've been on this side too long, but someone said, "Por favor." [Laughter]

Hispanics in Reagan Administration

Q. Mr. President, still I am impressed when I listened the other day, "Viva la roja, la blanca, y azul."

Mr. President, it is true that when Hispanics are given the opportunity to serve this country, they serve the country with diligence and dispatch. In view of this undisputed fact, when are you going to appoint Hispanic Americans to serve in your administration in policymaking positions?

The President. We are definitely recruiting and definitely trying to do that. I want an administration that will be representative of the country as a whole, and please don't judge us on the fact that we have only picked a hundred. There will be 1,700 positions to fill in the executive branch and the White House senior staff and staff. And the personnel committee in our administration that is talent hunting and looking for these people contains members of the minorities, Hispanics, and even a majority of women, and we want that very much. So, don't judge us now by the tip of the iceberg. Wait till it's all in.

Interest Rates and the Federal Reserve System

Q. Mr. President? Yes, thank you.

Mr. President, Paul Volcker, the Chairman of the Federal Reserve Board, has been implementing policies that are exactly opposite in basic thrust from what you recommend. He has been squeezing the productive sector of the economy in favor of the speculative sector. Now, I mean frankly, Mr. President, there are important sections of the American economy that are about to go under and won't even have an opportunity to benefit from the programs that you're putting forward because of the Federal Reserve policy.

I have a two-part question. First of all, do you think that objective economic conditions justify the interest rate levels that we now have? And I don't mean for your answer to imply criticism of the Fed; it's just an objective question. And the second question is, are you concerned that there might be a sabotage, so to speak, of your policies by programs that the Federal Reserve might be putting forward?

The President. No, I'm not concerned that there would be sabotage. I've met with Mr. Volcker, and not with the intention of trying

to dictate, because it is an independent agency, and I respect that.

But I think that we have to face the fact that interest rates are not in themselves a cause of inflation; they're a consequence. And when you have, as we have had, double-digit inflation back to back for 2 solid years now—the last time that happened was in World War I—and when you have double-digit inflation there, that way there is no question that interest rates are going to have to go up and follow that inflation rate.

And so, the answer to the interest rates is going to be our program of reducing government spending, tied to the reduction of the tax rates that we've spoken of to bring down inflation, and you'll find that interest rates come down. We do want from the Fed and would ask for a moderate policy of money supply increasing relative to legitimate growth. All of these things have to work together. But I don't think that the Fed just deliberately raises interest rates.

The reason that we've got to tie taxes and we have to tie spending together is we, for all these decades, we've talked and we've talked about solving these problems, and we've acted as if the two were separate. So, one year we fight inflation and then unemployment goes up, and then the next year we fight unemployment and inflation goes up. It's time to keep the two together where they belong, and that's what we're going to do.

Yes, sir.

Reagan Administration Appointees

Q. Mr. President, a number of conservative leaders, among them some of your staunchest and most durable supporters, such as senator Jesse Helms, are very concerned about some of your appointments.

The basis of the concern is that many people who have been longtime Reaganites and supporters of yours do not seem to be able to get jobs, like Bill Van Cleave, who played a key role on your defense transition team, whereas other individuals who have not supported you throughout the years or your philosophy, like Mr. Terrel Bell, the secretary of education, who was for the establishment of the Department which you've said you're going to abolish, when Mr. Frank Carlucci, deputy secretary of defense, who was not a supporter of yours, that they have gotten jobs.

My question is, why are these individuals in your administration? Why isn't Mr. Van Cleave? And how much of a problem do you think this conservative dissatisfaction with your appointments is?

The President. The only problem that I've had that is more difficult than knowing which hand raised to point to here—and believe me, it bothers me; I go home feeling guilty for all the hands that I couldn't point to. [Laughter] The only problem greater I've had is in the selection of personnel.

Now, in many instances some of the people that have been mentioned, whose names that have been mentioned by others did not want a position in the administration—helped, worked very hard, and wanted nothing for it. But you also have to recognize there aren't that many positions. After all, look how many votes I had. You can't reward them all.

Ms. Thomas. Thank you, Mr. President.

The President. Thank you. All right. Thank you all very much.

Source: "The President's News Conference," January 29, 1981, The Ronald Reagan Presidential Library. Available online. URL: http://www.reagan.utexas.edu/resource/speeches/1981/12981b.htm

13. Address Before a Joint Session of the Congress on the Program for Economic Recovery April 28, 1981

Just weeks after being struck by an assassin's bullet, Ronald Reagan addressed a joint session of Congress to appeal for passage of his economic package. Reagan received something of a hero's welcome, for the nation, and Congress, was impressed by his gallant and jocular response to the attack on his life. Reagan loved to read letters sent to him from American citizens, particularly from young people, and he began this address referring to one such letter he received after being shot. This speech, and others, generated a massive amount of mail to the Congress urging support for the president's proposals, which ultimately passed and began the era of "Reaganomics."

You wouldn't want to talk me into an encore, would you? [Laughter]

Mr. Speaker, Mr. President, distinguished Members of the Congress, honored guests, and fellow citizens:

I have no words to express my appreciation for that greeting.

I have come to speak to you tonight about our economic recovery program and why I believe it's essential that the Congress approve this package, which I believe will lift the crushing burden of inflation off of our citizens and restore the vitality to our economy and our industrial machine.

First, however, and due to events of the past few weeks, will you permit me to digress for a moment from the all-important subject of why we must bring government spending under control and reduce tax rates. I'd like to say a few words directly to all of you and to those who are watching and listening tonight, because this is the only way I know to express to all of you on behalf of Nancy and myself our appreciation for your messages and flowers and, most of all, your prayers, not only for me but for those others who fell beside me.

The warmth of your words, the expression of friendship and, yes, love, meant more to us than you can ever know. You have given us a memory that we'll treasure forever. And you've provided an answer to those few voices that were raised saying that what happened was evidence that ours is a sick society.

The society we heard from is made up of millions of compassionate Americans and their children, from college age to kindergarten. As a matter of fact, as evidence of that I have a letter with me. The letter came from Peter Sweeney. He's in the second grade in the Riverside School in Rockville Centre, and he said, "I hope you get well quick or you might have to make a speech in your pajamas." [Laughter] He added a postscript. "P.S. If you have to make a speech in your pajamas, I warned you." [Laughter]

Well, sick societies don't produce men like the two who recently returned from outer space. Sick societies don't produce young men like Secret Service agent Tim McCarthy, who placed his body between mine and the man with the gun simply because he felt that's what his duty called for him to do. Sick societies don't produce dedicated police officers like Tom Delahanty or able and devoted public servants like Jim Brady. Sick societies don't make people like us so proud to be Americans and so very proud of our fellow citizens.

Now, let's talk about getting spending and inflation under control and cutting your tax rates.

Mr. Speaker and Senator Baker, I want to thank you for your cooperation in helping to arrange this joint session of the Congress. I won't be speaking to you very long tonight, but I asked for this meeting because the urgency of our joint mission has not changed.

Thanks to some very fine people, my health is much improved. I'd like to be able to say that with regard to the health of the economy.

It's been half a year since the election that charged all of us in this Government with the task of restoring our economy. Where have we come in this 6 months? Inflation, as measured by the Consumer Price Index, has continued at a double-digit rate. Mortgage interest rates have averaged almost 15 percent for these 6 months, preventing families across America from buying homes. There are still almost 8 million unemployed. The average worker's hourly earnings after adjusting for inflation are lower today than they were 6 months ago, and there have been over 6,000 business failures.

Six months is long enough. The American people now want us to act and not in half-measures. They demand and they've earned a full and comprehensive effort to clean up our economic mess. Because of the extent of our economy's sickness, we know that the cure will not come quickly and that even with our package, progress will come in inches and feet, not in miles. But to fail to act will delay even longer and more painfully the cure which must come. And that cure begins with the Federal budget. And the budgetary actions taken by the Congress over the next few days will determine how we respond to the message of last November 4th. That message was very simple. Our government is too big, and it spends too much.

For the last few months, you and I have enjoyed a relationship based on extraordinary cooperation. Because of this cooperation we've come a long distance in less than 3 months. I want to thank the leadership of the Congress for helping in setting a fair timetable for consideration of our recommendations. And committee chairmen on both sides of the aisle have called prompt and thorough hearing.

We have also communicated in a spirit of candor, openness, and mutual respect. Tonight, as our decision day nears and as the House of Representatives weighs its alternatives, I wish to address you in that same spirit.

The Senate Budget Committee, under the leadership of Pete Domenici, has just today voted out a budget resolution supported by Democrats and Republicans alike that is in all major respects consistent with the program that we have proposed. Now we look forward to favorable action on the Senate floor, but an equally crucial test involves the House of Representatives.

The House will soon be choosing between two different versions or measures to deal with the economy. One is the measure offered by the House Budget Committee. The other is a bipartisan measure, a substitute introduced by Congressmen Phil Gramm of Texas and Del Latta of Ohio.

On behalf of the administration, let me say that we embrace and fully support that bipartisan substitute. It will achieve all the essential aims of controlling government spending, reducing the tax burden, building a national defense second to none, and stimulating economic growth and creating millions of new jobs.

At the same time, however, I must state our opposition to the measure offered by the House Budget Committee. It may appear that we have two alternatives. In reality, however, there are no more alternatives left. The committee measure quite simply falls far too short of the essential actions that we must take.

For example, in the next 3 years, the committee measure projects spending $141 billion more than does the bipartisan substitute. It regrettably cuts over $14 billion in essential defense spending, funding required to restore America's national security. It adheres to the failed policy of trying to balance the budget on the taxpayer's back. It would increase tax payments by over a third, adding up to a staggering quarter of a trillion dollars. Federal taxes would increase 12 percent each year. Taxpayers would be paying a larger share of their income to government in 1984 than they do at present.

In short, that measure reflects an echo of the past rather than a benchmark for the future. High taxes and excess spending growth created our present economic mess; more of the same will not cure the hardship, anxiety, and discouragement it has imposed on the American people.

Let us cut through the fog for a moment. The answer to a government that's too big is to stop feeding its growth. Government spending has been growing faster than the economy itself. The massive national debt which we accumulated is the result of the government's high spending diet. Well, it's time to change the diet and to change it in the right way.

I know the tax portion of our package is of concern to some of you. Let me make a few points that I feel have been overlooked. First of all, it should be looked at as an integral part of the entire package, not something separate and apart from the budget reductions, the regulatory relief, and the monetary restraints. Probably the most common misconception is that we are proposing to reduce Government revenues to less than what the Government has been receiving. This is not true. Actually, the discussion has to do with how much of a tax increase should be imposed on the taxpayer in 1982.

Now, I know that over the recess in some informal polling some of your constituents have been asked which they'd rather have, a balanced budget or a tax cut, and with the common sense that characterizes the people of this country, the answer, of course, has been a balanced budget. But may I suggest, with no inference that there was wrong intent on the part of those who asked the question, the question was inappropriate to the situation.

Our choice is not between a balanced budget and a tax cut. Properly asked, the question is, "Do you want a great big raise in your taxes this coming year or, at the worst, a very little increase with the prospect of tax reduction and a balanced budget down the road a ways." With the common sense that the people have already shown, I'm sure we all know what the answer to that question would be.

A gigantic tax increase has been built into the system. We propose nothing more than a reduction of that increase. The people have a right to know that even with our plan they will be paying more in taxes, but not as much more as they will without it.

The option, I believe, offered by the House Budget Committee, will leave spending too high and tax rates too high. At the same time, I think it cuts the defense budget too much, and by attempting to reduce the deficit through higher taxes, it will not create the kind of strong economic growth and the new jobs that we must have.

Let us not overlook the fact that the small, independent business man or woman creates more than 80 percent of all the new jobs and employs more than half of our total workforce. Our across-the-board cut in tax rates for a 3-year period will give them much of the incentive and promise of stability they need to go forward with expansion plans calling for additional employees.

Tonight, I renew my call for us to work as a team, to join in cooperation so that we find answers which will begin to solve all our economic problems and not just some of them. The economic recovery package that I've outlined to you over the past weeks is, I deeply believe, the only answer that we have left.

Reducing the growth of spending, cutting marginal tax rates, providing relief from over-regulation, and following a noninflationary and predictable monetary policy are interwoven measures which will ensure that we have addressed each of the severe dislocations which threaten our economic future. These policies will make our economy stronger, and the stronger economy will balance the budget which we're committed to do by 1984.

When I took the oath of office, I pledged loyalty to only one special interest group—"We the people." Those people—neighbors and friends, shopkeepers and laborers, farmers and craftsmen—do not have infinite patience. As a matter of fact, some 80 years ago, Teddy Roosevelt wrote these instructive words in his first message to the Congress: "The American people are slow to wrath, but when their wrath is once kindled, it burns like a consuming flame." Well, perhaps that kind of wrath will be deserved if our answer to these serious problems is to repeat the mistakes of the past.

The old and comfortable way is to shave a little here and add a little there. Well, that's not acceptable anymore. I think this great and historic Congress knows that way is no longer acceptable. [Applause]

Thank you very much.

I think you've shown that you know the one sure way to continue the inflationary spiral is to fall back into the predictable patterns of old economic practices. Isn't it time that we tried something new?

When you allowed me to speak to you here in these chambers a little earlier, I told you that I wanted this program for economic recovery to be ours—yours and mine. I think the bipartisan substitute bill has achieved that purpose. It moves us toward economic vitality.

Just 2 weeks ago, you and I joined millions of our fellow Americans in marveling at the magic historical moment that John Young and Bob Crippen created in their space shuttle, Columbia. The last manned effort was almost 6 years ago, and I remembered on this more recent day, over the years, how we'd all come to expect technological precision of our men and machines. And each amazing achievement became commonplace, until the next new challenge was raised.

With the space shuttle we tested our ingenuity once again, moving beyond the accomplishments of the past into the promise and uncertainty of the future. Thus, we not only planned to send up a 122-foot aircraft 170 miles into space, but we also intended to make it maneuverable and return it to Earth, landing 98 tons of exotic metals delicately on a remote, dry lakebed. The space shuttle did more than prove our technological abilities. It raised our expectations once more. It started us dreaming again.

The poet Carl Sandburg wrote, "The republic is a dream. Nothing happens unless first a dream." And that's what makes us, as Americans, different. We've always reached for a new spirit and aimed at a higher goal. We've been courageous and determined, unafraid and bold. Who among us wants to be first to say we no longer have those qualities, that we must limp along, doing the same things that have brought us our present misery?

I believe that the people you and I represent are ready to chart a new course. They look to us to meet the great challenge, to reach beyond the commonplace and not fall short for lack of creativity or courage.

Someone you know has said that he who would have nothing to do with thorns must never attempt to gather flowers. Well, we have much greatness before us. We can restore our economic strength and build opportunities like none we've ever had before.

As Carl Sandburg said, all we need to begin with is a dream that we can do better than before. All we need to have is faith, and that dream will come true. All we need to do is act, and the time for action is now.

Thank you. Good night.

Source: "Address Before a Joint Session of the Congress on the Program for Economic Recovery," April 28, 1981, The Ronald Reagan Presidential Library. Available online. URL: http://www.reagan.utexas.edu/resource/speeches/1981/42881c.htm

14. Address at Commencement Exercises at the University of Notre Dame May 17, 1981

Ronald Reagan had no real ties to Notre Dame University, but few of the "Fighting Irish" who attended this speech in May 1981 would have believed that after hearing these remarks. Reagan played the character of the dying Notre Dame half-back George Gipp in Knute Rockne—All American *(1940), and seemed at times to have displaced the real George Gipp in the minds of many. "Win one for the Gipper" became a battle cry for Reagan's campaigns, quite fitting for a man who believed that heroes, real or imagined, were part of what made life worth living.*

Father Hesburgh, I thank you very much and for so many things. The distinguished honor that you've conferred upon me here today, I must say, however, compounds a sense of guilt that I have nursed for almost 50 years. I thought the first degree I was given was honorary. [Laughter] But it's wonderful to be here today with Governor Orr, Governor Bowen, Senators Lugar and Quayle, and Representative Hiler, these distinguished honorees, the trustees, administration, faculty, students, and friends of Notre Dame and, most important, the graduating class of 1981.

Nancy and I are greatly honored to share this day with you, and our pleasure has been more than doubled because I am also sharing the platform with a longtime and very dear friend, Pat O'Brien.

Pat and I haven't been able to see much of each other lately, so I haven't had a chance to tell him that there is now another tie that binds us together. Until a few weeks ago I knew very little about my father's ancestry. He had been orphaned at age 6. But now I've learned that his grandfather, my great-grandfather, left Ireland to come to America, leaving his home in Ballyporeen, a village in County Tipperary in

Ireland, and I have learned that Ballyporeen is the ancestral home of the O'Briens.

Now, if I don't watch out, this may turn out to be less of a commencement than a warm bath in nostalgic memories. Growing up in Illinois, I was influenced by a sports legend so national in scope, it was almost mystical. It is difficult to explain to anyone who didn't live in those times. The legend was based on a combination of three elements: a game, football; a university, Notre Dame; and a man, Knute Rockne. There has been nothing like it before or since.

My first time to ever see Notre Dame was to come here as a sports announcer, 2 years out of college, to broadcast a football game. You won or I wouldn't have mentioned it. [Laughter]

A number of years later I returned here in the company of Pat O'Brien and a galaxy of Hollywood stars for the world premiere of *Knute Rockne—All American* in which I was privileged to play George Gipp. I've always suspected that there might have been many actors in Hollywood who could have played the part better, but no one could have wanted to play it more than I did. And I was given the part largely because the star of that picture, Pat O'Brien, kindly and generously held out a helping hand to a beginning young actor.

Having come from the world of sports, I'd been trying to write a story about Knute Rockne. I must confess that I had someone in mind to play the Gipper. On one of my sports broadcasts before going to Hollywood, I had told the story of his career and tragic death. I didn't have very many words on paper when I learned that the studio that employed me was already preparing a story treatment for that film. And that brings me to the theme of my remarks.

I'm the fifth President of the United States to address a Notre Dame commencement. The temptation is great to use this forum as an address on a great international or national issue that has nothing to do with this occasion. Indeed, this is somewhat traditional. So, I wasn't surprised when I read in several reputable journals that I was going to deliver an address on foreign policy or on the economy. I'm not going to talk about either.

But, by the same token, I'll try not to belabor you with some of the standard rhetoric that is beloved of graduation speakers. For example, I'm not going to tell you that "You know more today than you've ever known before or than you will ever know again." [Laughter] The other standby is, "When I was 14, I didn't think my father knew anything. By the time I was 21, I was amazed at how much the old gentleman had learned in 7 years." And then, of course, the traditional and the standby is that "A university like this is a storehouse of knowledge because the freshmen bring so much in and the seniors take so little away." [Laughter]

You members of the graduating class of 18—or 1981—[laughter]—I don't really go back that far—[laughter]—are what behaviorists call achievers. And while you will look back with warm pleasure on your memories of these years that brought you here to where you are today, you are also, I know, looking at the future that seems uncertain to most of you but which, let me assure you, offers great expectations.

Take pride in this day. Thank your parents, as one on your behalf has already done here. Thank those who've been of help to you over the last 4 years. And do a little celebrating; you're entitled. This is your day, and whatever I say should take cognizance of that fact. It is a milestone in life, and it marks a time of change.

Winston Churchill, during the darkest period of the "Battle of Britain" in World War II said: "When great causes are on the move in the world . . . we learn we are spirits, not animals, and that something is going on in space and time, and beyond space and time, which, whether we like it or not, spells duty."

Now, I'm going to mention again that movie that Pat and I and Notre Dame were in, because it says something about America. First, Knute Rockne as a boy came to America with his parents from Norway. And in the few years it took him to grow up to college age, he became so American that here at Notre Dame, he became an All American in a game that is still, to this day, uniquely American.

As a coach, he did more than teach young men how to play a game. He believed truly that the noblest work of man was building the character of man. And maybe that's why he was a living legend. No man connected with football has ever achieved the stature or occupied the singular niche in the Nation that he carved out for himself, not just in a sport, but in our entire social structure.

Now, today I hear very often, "Win one for the Gipper," spoken in a humorous vein. Lately I've been hearing it by Congressmen who are supportive of the programs that I've introduced. [Laughter] But let's look at the significance of that story. Rockne could have used Gipp's dying words to win a game any time. But 8 years went by following the death of George Gipp before Rock revealed those dying words, his deathbed wish.

And then he told the story at halftime to a team that was losing, and one of the only teams he had ever coached that was torn by dissension and jealousy and factionalism. The seniors on that team were about to close out their football careers without learning or experiencing any of the real values that a game has to impart. None of them had known George Gipp. They were children when he played for Notre Dame. It was to this team that Rockne told the story and so inspired them that they rose above their personal animosities. For someone they had never known, they joined together in a common cause and attained the unattainable.

We were told when we were making the picture of one line that was spoken by a player during that game. We were actually afraid to put it in the picture. The man who carried the ball over for the winning touchdown was injured on the play. We were told that as he was lifted on the stretcher and carried off the field he was heard to say, "That's the last one I can get for you, Gipper."

Now, it's only a game. And maybe to hear it now, afterward—and this is what we feared—it might sound maudlin and not the way it was intended. But is there anything wrong with young people having an experience, feeling something so deeply, thinking of someone else to the point that they can give so completely of themselves? There will come times in the lives of all of us when we'll be faced with causes bigger than ourselves, and they won't be on a playing field.

This Nation was born when a band of men, the Founding Fathers, a group so unique we've never seen their like since, rose to such selfless heights. Lawyers, tradesmen, merchants, farmers—56 men achieved security and standing in life but valued freedom more. They pledged their lives, their fortunes, and their sacred honor. Sixteen of them gave their lives. Most gave their fortunes. All preserved their sacred honor.

They gave us more than a nation. They brought to all mankind for the first time the concept that man was born free, that each of us has inalienable rights, ours by the grace of God, and that government was created by us for our convenience, having only the powers that we choose to give it. This is the heritage that you're about to claim as you come out to join the society made up of those who have preceded you by a few years, or some of us by a great many.

This experiment in man's relation to man is a few years into its third century. Saying that may make it sound quite old. But let's look at it from another viewpoint or perspective. A few years ago, someone figured out that if you could condense the entire history of life on Earth into a motion picture that would run for

24 hours a day, 365 days—maybe on leap years we could have an intermission—[laughter]—this idea that is the United States wouldn't appear on the screen until 3 1/2 seconds before midnight on December 31st. And in those 3 1/2 seconds not only would a new concept of society come into being, a golden hope for all mankind, but more than half the activity, economic activity in world history, would take place on this continent. Free to express their genius, individual Americans, men and women, in 3 1/2 seconds, would perform such miracles of invention, construction, and production as the world had never seen.

As you join us out there beyond the campus, you know there are great unsolved problems. Federalism, with its built in checks and balances, has been distorted. Central government has usurped powers that properly belong to local and State governments. And in so doing, in many ways that central government has begun to fail to do the things that are truly the responsibility of a central government.

All of this has led to the misuse of power and preemption of the prerogatives of people and their social institutions. You are graduating from a great private, or, if you will, independent university. Not too many years ago, such schools were relatively free from government interference. In recent years, government has spawned regulations covering virtually every facet of our lives. The independent and church-supported colleges and universities have found themselves enmeshed in that network of regulations and the costly blizzard of paperwork that government is demanding. Thirty-four congressional committees and almost 80 subcommittees have jurisdiction over 439 separate laws affecting education at the college level alone. Almost every aspect of campus life is now regulated—hiring, firing, promotions, physical plant, construction, recordkeeping, fundraising and, to some extent, curriculum and educational programs.

I hope when you leave this campus that you will do so with a feeling of obligation to your alma mater. She will need your help and support in the years to come. If ever the great independent colleges and universities like Notre Dame give way to and are replaced by tax-supported institutions, the struggle to preserve academic freedom will have been lost.

We're troubled today by economic stagnation, brought on by inflated currency and prohibitive taxes and burdensome regulations. The cost of stagnation in human terms, mostly among those least equipped to survive it, is cruel and inhuman.

Now, after those remarks, don't decide that you'd better turn your diploma back in so you can stay another year on the campus. I've just given you the bad news. The good news is that something is being done about all this because the people of America have said, "Enough already." You know, we who had preceded you had just gotten so busy that we let things get out of hand. We forgot that we were the keepers of the power, forgot to challenge the notion that the state is the principal vehicle of social change, forgot that millions of social interactions among free individuals and institutions can do more to foster economic and social progress than all the careful schemes of government planners.

Well, at last we're remembering, remembering that government has certain legitimate functions which it can perform very well, that it can be responsive to the people, that it can be humane and compassionate, but that when it undertakes tasks that are not its proper province, it can do none of them as well or as economically as the private sector.

For too long government has been fixing things that aren't broken and inventing miracle cures for unknown diseases.

We need you. We need your youth. We need your strength. We need your idealism to help us make right that which is wrong. Now,

I know that this period of your life, you have been and are critically looking at the mores and customs of the past and questioning their value. Every generation does that. May I suggest, don't discard the time-tested values upon which civilization was built simply because they're old. More important, don't let today's doomcriers and cynics persuade you that the best is past, that from here on it's all downhill. Each generation sees farther than the generation that preceded it because it stands on the shoulders of that generation. You're going to have opportunities beyond anything that we've ever known.

The people have made it plain already. They want an end to excessive government intervention in their lives and in the economy, an end to the burdensome and unnecessary regulations and a punitive tax policy that does take "from the mouth of labor the bread it has earned." They want a government that cannot only continue to send men across the vast reaches of space and bring them safely home, but that can guarantee that you and I can walk in the park of our neighborhood after dark and get safely home. And finally, they want to know that this Nation has the ability to defend itself against those who would seek to pull it down.

And all of this, we the people can do. Indeed, a start has already been made. There's a task force under the leadership of the Vice President, George Bush, that is to look at those regulations I've spoken of. They have already identified hundreds of them that can be wiped out with no harm to the quality of life. And the cancellation of just those regulations will leave billions and billions of dollars in the hands of the people for productive enterprise and research and development and the creation of jobs.

The years ahead are great ones for this country, for the cause of freedom and the spread of civilization. The West won't contain communism, it will transcend communism. It won't bother to dismiss or denounce it, it will dismiss it as some bizarre chapter in human history whose last pages are even now being written.

William Faulkner, at a Nobel Prize ceremony some time back, said man "would not only [merely] endure: he will prevail" against the modern world because he will return to "the old verities and truths of the heart." And then Faulkner said of man, "He is immortal because he alone among creatures . . . has a soul, a spirit capable of compassion and sacrifice and endurance."

One can't say those words—compassion, sacrifice, and endurance—without thinking of the irony that one who so exemplifies them, Pope John Paul II, a man of peace and goodness, an inspiration to the world, would be struck by a bullet from a man towards whom he could only feel compassion and love. It was Pope John Paul II who warned in last year's encyclical on mercy and justice against certain economic theories that use the rhetoric of class struggle to justify injustice. He said, "In the name of an alleged justice the neighbor is sometimes destroyed, killed, deprived of liberty or stripped of fundamental human rights."

For the West, for America, the time has come to dare to show to the world that our civilized ideas, our traditions, our values, are not—like the ideology and war machine of totalitarian societies—just a facade of strength. It is time for the world to know our intellectual and spiritual values are rooted in the source of all strength, a belief in a Supreme Being, and a law higher than our own.

When it's written, history of our time won't dwell long on the hardships of the recent past. But history will ask—and our answer determine the fate of freedom for a thousand years—Did a nation born of hope lose hope? Did a people forged by courage find courage wanting? Did a generation steeled by hard war and a harsh peace forsake honor at the moment of great climactic struggle for the human spirit?

If history asks such questions, it also answers them. And the answers are to be found in the heritage left by generations of Americans before us. They stand in silent witness to what the world will soon know and history someday record: that in the [its] third century, the American Nation came of age, affirmed its leadership of free men and women serving self-lessly a vision of man with God, government for people, and humanity at peace.

A few years ago, an Australian Prime Minister, John Gorton, said, "I wonder if anybody ever thought what the situation for the comparatively small nations in the world would be if there were not in existence the United States, if there were not this giant country prepared to make so many sacrifices." This is the noble and rich heritage rooted in great civil ideas of the West, and it is yours.

My hope today is that in the years to come—and come it shall—when it's your time to explain to another generation the meaning of the past and thereby hold out to them their promise of the future, that you'll recall the truths and traditions of which we've spoken. It is these truths and traditions that define our civilization and make up our national heritage. And now, they're yours to protect and pass on.

I have one more hope for you: when you do speak to the next generation about these things, that you will always be able to speak of an America that is strong and free, to find in your hearts an unbounded pride in this much-loved country, this once and future land, this bright and hopeful nation whose generous spirit and great ideals the world still honors.

Congratulations, and God bless you.

Source: "Address at Commencement Exercises at the University of Notre Dame," May 17, 1981, The Ronald Reagan Presidential Library. Available online. URL: http://www.reagan.utexas.edu/resource/speeches/1981/51781a.htm

15. Remarks in Denver, Colorado, at the Annual Convention of the National Association for the Advancement of Colored People June 29, 1981

Throughout his tenure in office, Ronald Reagan struggled to convince African Americans that he believed in equal rights for all. While most of the president's friends and associates attested to his belief in racial equality, and Reagan himself bristled at any suggestion to the contrary, his stance on affirmative action and on tax breaks for religious colleges that practiced segregation caused many African Americans to view him with suspicion. This address to the NAACP in June 1981, was one of Reagan's rare appearances at a meeting of a civil rights organization. After receiving a frosty reception at this event and in meetings with the Congressional Black Caucus, Reagan curtailed his contacts with these groups.

Chairwoman Margaret Bush Wilson, I thank you very much for that introduction and that explanation also of my year's tardiness in getting here.

I remember a year ago I was in California when I received your invitation at the same time that I received a clipping that I had not answered your invitation. Now, at that moment it was almost impossible for me—well, it was impossible to find a way—not even Air Force One could have bridged from California to Florida. But I'm delighted that this time, as you say, there was better staff work and I was able to get the invitation in plenty of time.

President Cobb, Vice Chairman Kelly Alexander, and Executive Director Benjamin Hooks, the ladies and gentlemen here on the platform, the members of the board of directors, and you, ladies and gentlemen, representatives to this convention:

I'm very happy to be talking to the NAACP's 72d annual convention.

There are many things that we need to discuss, and I thank you for the invitation to do so. Let us talk today about the needs of the future, not the misunderstandings of the past; about new ideas, not old ones; about what must become a continuing dialog, not a dialog that flows only at intermittent conventions that we both attend.

Part of that continuing dialog took place last Tuesday when I met with Ben Hooks and Margaret Bush Wilson in the Oval Office. Our discussion was candid and useful. The wide range of our conversation showed that there is a great deal to be gained when we take time to share our views. And while our communication should always deal with current issues of importance, it must never stray far from our national commitment to battle against discrimination and increase our knowledge of each other.

A few isolated groups in the backwater of American life still hold perverted notions of what America is all about. Recently in some places in the nation there's been a disturbing reoccurrence of bigotry and violence. If I may, from the platform of this organization, known for its tolerance, I would like to address a few remarks to those groups who still adhere to senseless racism and religious prejudice, to those individuals who persist in such hateful behavior.

If I were speaking to them instead of to you, I would say to them, "You are the ones who are out of step with our society. You are the ones who willfully violate the meaning of the dream that is America. And this country, because of what it stands for, will not stand for your conduct." My administration will vigorously investigate and prosecute those who, by violence or intimidation, would attempt to deny Americans their constitutional rights.

Another kind of terror has recently plagued the city of Atlanta. Not long ago in a speech before the Congress I read the now famous "pajama letter" from Peter Sweeney. If only my letters from children could all be as lighthearted as Peter's. Other letters are more poignant. When little girls in Atlanta write asking that I make things right so they won't be scared anymore, even a President of the United States can feel a little helpless.

We committed the resources of the FBI and a number of Federal agencies to help Mayor Jackson. I appointed Vice President Bush to head this Federal task force, and its work will continue until this tragic episode is over. Not counting manpower and equipment, we've provided over $4 million to this cause. I know that all of us wish we could tell the children of Atlanta that they need no longer fear, and until we can say that, however, we will not be satisfied until those children can once again play safely in their schoolyards and parks.

Our dialog must also include discussions on how we can best protect the rights and privileges of all our citizens. My administration will root out any case of government discrimination against minorities and uphold and enforce the laws that protect them. I emphasize that we will not retreat on the nation's commitment to equal treatment of all citizens. Now, that, in my view, is the primary responsibility of National Government. The Attorney General is now carefully studying the decennial redistricting plans being submitted under the current Voting Rights Act. As soon as we have all the information there will be a decision regarding extension of the act.

Until a decision is announced, you should know this: I regard voting as the most sacred right of free men and women. We have not sacrificed and fought and toiled to protect that right so that now we can sit back and permit a barrier to come between a secret ballot and any citizen who makes a choice to cast it. Nothing—nothing will change that as long as I am in a position to uphold the Constitution of the United States.

In the months ahead, our dialog also will include tough and realistic questions about the role of the Federal Government in the black community. I'm not satisfied with its results, and I don't think you are either. And the failures of the past have been particularly hard on the minority poor, because their hopes have failed as surely as the Federal programs that built those hopes. But I must not be the only one who questions about government policies.

Can the black teenager who faces a staggering unemployment rate feel that government policies are a success? Can the black wage earner who sees more and more of his take-home pay shrinking because of government taxes feel satisfied? Can black parents say, despite a massive influx of Federal aid, that educational standards in our schools have improved appreciably? Can the woman I saw on television recently—whose family had been on welfare for three generations and who feared that her children might be the fourth—can she believe that current government policies will save her children from such a fate?

We ask these tough questions, because we share your concerns about the future of the black community. We ask these questions, because the blacks of America should not be patronized as just one more voting bloc to be wooed and won. You are individuals as we all are. Some have special needs. I don't think the Federal Government has met those needs.

I've been listening to the specific needs of many people—blacks, farmers, refugees, union members, women, small business men and women, and other groups—they're commonly referred to as special-interest groups. Well, in reality they're all members of the interest group that I spoke of the day I took the oath of office. They are the people of America. And I'm pleased to serve that special-interest group.

The people of the inner cities will be represented by this administration every bit as much as the citizens of Flagstaff, Arizona,

Ithaca, New York, or Dixon, Illinois, where I grew up. Anyone who becomes President realizes he must represent all the people of the land, not just those of a home State or a particular party. Nor can he be just President of those who voted for him.

But it doesn't matter what groups we belong to, what area we live in, how much or how little we earn; the economy affects every single one of us regardless of our other interests and affiliations. We have proceeded full throttle on our economic recovery program, because a strong, growing economy without inflation is the surest, most equitable way to ease the pressures on all the segments of our society.

The well-being of blacks, like the well-being of every other American, is linked directly to the health of the economy. For example, industries in which blacks had made sufficient gains in employment—substantial gains, like autos and steel—have been particularly hard hit. And "last hired, first fired" is a familiar refrain to too many black workers. And I don't need to tell this group what inflation has done to those who can least afford it. A declining economy is a poisonous gas that claims its first victims in poor neighborhoods, before floating out into the community at large.

Therefore, in our national debate over budget and tax proposals, we shall not concede the moral high ground to the proponents of those policies that are responsible in the first place for our economic mess—a mess which has injured all Americans. We will not concede the moral high ground to those who show more concern for Federal programs than they do for what really determines the income and financial health of blacks—the nation's economy.

Now, I know you've been told that my proposal for economic recovery is designed to discriminate against all who are economically deprived. Now, those who say that could be confused by the misstatements that have been made by some who are either ignorant of the facts or those who are practicing, for political reasons, pure demagoguery.

Rebuilding America's economy is an absolute moral imperative if we're to avoid splitting this society in two with class against class. I do not intend to let America drift further toward economic segregation. We must change the economic direction of this country to bring more blacks into the mainstream, and we must do it now.

And 1938, before we had the equality we know today, Langston Hughes wrote "Let America Be America Again." And he wrote:

Oh, yes, I see [say] it plain
America never was America to me.
And yet I swear this oath—
America will be!

America will be. That is the philosophy the people proclaimed in last November's election. America will be. And this time, she will be for everyone. Together, we can recreate for every citizen the same economic opportunities that we saw lift up a land of immigrant people, the kind of opportunities that have swept the hungry and the persecuted into the mainstream of our life since the American experiment began.

To a number of black Americans, the U.S. economy has been something of an underground railroad; it has spirited them away from poverty to middle-class prosperity and beyond. But too many blacks still remain behind. A glance at the statistics will show that a large proportion of the black people have not found economic freedom. Nationwide, for example, 43 percent of black families in 1979 had money incomes under $10,000.

Harriet Tubman, who was known as the "conductor" of that earlier underground railroad, said on her first escape from slavery, "When I found I had crossed that line, I looked at my hands to see if I was the same person.

There was such a glory over everything." Even after a century the beauty of her words is powerful. We can only imagine the soaring of her soul, what a feeling that must have been when she crossed into freedom and the physical and mental shackles fell from her person.

Harriet Tubman's glory was the glory of the American experience. It was a glory which had no color or religious preference or nationality. It was simply, eloquently, the universal thirst that all people have for freedom.

Well, there are poor people in this country who should experience just such an elation if they found the economic freedom of a solid job, a productive job—not one concocted by government and dependent on Washington winds; a real job where they could put in a good day's work, complain about the boss, and then go home with confidence and self-respect. Why has this Nation been unable to fill such a basic, admirable need?

The government can provide subsistence, yes, but it seldom moves people up the economic ladder. And as I've said before, you have to get on the ladder before you can move up on it. I believe many in Washington, over the years, have been more dedicated to making needy people government-dependent rather than independent. They've created a new kind of bondage, because regardless of how honest their intention in the beginning, those they set out to help soon became clients essential to the well-being of those who administered the programs.

An honest program would be dedicated to making people independent, no longer in need of government assistance. But then what would happen to those who made a career of helping? Well, Americans have been very generous, with good intentions and billions of dollars, toward those they believed were living in hardship. And yet, in spite of the hopes, the government has never lived up to the dreams of poor people. Just as the Emancipation Proclamation freed black people 118 years ago, today we need to declare an economic emancipation.

I genuinely and deeply believe the economic package we've put forth will move us toward black economic freedom, because it's aimed at lifting an entire country and not just parts of it. There's a truth to the words spoken by John F. Kennedy that a rising tide lifts all boats. Yes, I know it's been said, "What about the fellow without a boat who can't swim?" Well, I believe John Kennedy's figure of speech was referring to the benefits which accrue to all when the economy is flourishing.

Now, much has been said and written—not all of it flattering—about the savings I've proposed in the budget which were adopted by the House last Friday. I can assure you that the budget savings we've advocated are much more equitable than the tremendous cuts in social programs, made by inflation and the declining economy, which can't find jobs for almost 8 million men and women who are unemployed.

Those cuts are exacted without regard to need or age. Let me give some examples. In the prosperity of the 1960's, an era of only a few Federal programs costing very little, the number of people living in poverty was reduced by nearly 50 percent. During the "stagflation" of the 1970's with many Federal programs with huge budgets, the number living in poverty was reduced by only 6 percent.

In the 1960's black unemployment fell from 10.7 percent to 6.4 percent. In the 1970's it increased from 6.4 percent to 11.3 percent. What is more, relative to the white unemployment rate, black unemployment fell more in the 1960's but rose more in the 1970's. The declining economy has cut black family income. From 1959 to 1969, the median family income of blacks, after adjusting for inflation, rose at 5 percent per year, but from 1969 to 1979, income actually dropped.

Now, these are hard economic facts which are hard to take, because they show massive amounts of government aid and intervention have failed to produce the desired results. A strong economy returns the greatest good to the black population. It returns a benefit greater than that provided by specific Federal programs. By slowing the growth of government and by limiting the tax burden and thus stimulating investment, we will also be reducing inflation and unemployment. We will be creating jobs, nearly 3 million additional new jobs by 1986. We will be aiding minority businesses, which have been particularly hard hit by the scarcity of capital and the prohibitive interest rates. And these concerns are what the bipartisan tax cut proposal currently before the Congress is all about.

I said the other day in our conversation in the Oval Office that the income a year or two ago—I don't have the most recent figure—for the black community was something like $140 billion. Now, in most neighborhoods what really brings prosperity is when the income of that neighborhood is then multiplied by turning over several times within that community. I must tell you that in the black communities in America the turnover is less than once before the dollars, those $140 billion, go out into the community at large. And that has to be changed.

In the convention last summer Benjamin Hooks—the one that I missed—well, no, this was the Republican Convention; I made that one—[laughter]—Benjamin Hooks said to the assembled delegates, "we must decide as a nation if we're to become prisoners of our past or possessors of an enlightened and progressive future." Those are the very words I want to say to you today.

We cannot be tied to the old ways of solving our economic and racial problems. But it is time we looked to new answers and new ways of thinking that will accomplish the very ends the New Deal and the Great Society anticipated. We're not repealing the gains of black people. We're solidifying those gains and making them safe for your children and grandchildren.

It's time that we found ways to make the American economic pie bigger instead of just cutting an ever smaller pie into more but smaller slices. It's time we welcomed those Americans into the circle of prosperity to let them share in the wonders of our society, and it's time to break the cycle of dependency that has become the legacy of so many Federal programs that no longer work—indeed, some of which never did work.

Let me give you an idea of how bountiful this famous economic pie could have been by now. If productivity had not stopped growing and then started downhill after 1965, the gross national product today would be $850 billion bigger—enough to balance the budget, cut personal and social security taxes in half, and still provide every American with an extra $2,500 in spending money. And all of this would have happened with the compliments of the private sector.

Now, you wisely learned to harness the Federal Government in the hard pull toward equality, and that was right, because guaranteeing equality of treatment is government's proper function. But as the last decade of statistics I just read indicated, government is no longer the strong draft horse of minority progress, because it has attempted to do too many things it's not equipped to do. I ask you if it isn't time to hitch up a fresh horse to finish the task. Free enterprise is a powerful workhorse that can solve many problems of the black community that government alone can no longer solve.

The black leadership of this Nation has shown tremendous courage, both physical and intellectual, and great creativity as it sought to bring equality to its people. You in this audience are the inheritors of that proud black heritage. You are the black leaders of today, and I believe you possess the very same courage and creativity. I ask you to use that courage and cre-

ativity to examine the challenges that are facing not just blacks but all of America.

I ask you to question the status quo as your predecessors did and look for new and imaginative ways to overcome minority problems. I'm talking about the kind of courage and questioning your chairman, Margaret Bush Wilson, showed in taking the heat for the NAACP's controversial 1978 energy statement—a statement which shook the elitists of our country back into the real world, at least for a time. What I'm asking you to consider requires not so much a leap of faith, but a realization that the Federal Government alone is just not capable of doing the job we all want done for you or any other Americans.

In the months ahead, as the administration is free to turn attention from the economic program to other needs of America, we'll be advancing proposals on a number of issues of concern to this convention. The inner cities, for example, should be communities, neighborhoods, not warehouses of despair where children are bused out and ineffectual Federal funds are bused in. I believe that with the aid of commonsense government assistance and the use of free enterprise zones, with less reliance on busing and more reliance on better, basic education, and with an emphasis on local activism, such as you represent, communities can be reinvigorated.

Certainly, we're all inspired by the wonderful example of Marva Collins in Chicago, the gallant lady who has the educational grit to make Shakespeare admirers out of inner-city children. She just proves to me what a friend of mine, Wilson Riles, California's superintendent of education, used to say: "The concept that black children can't learn unless they're sitting among white children is utter and complete nonsense." Now, Dr. Riles was not suggesting that integration isn't a good and proper thing; it is. And it's good for all of us when it's brought about with commonsense and attention to what is best for the children.

We plan to take a look, a comprehensive look, at the education of blacks from primary school upward and strengthen the base of black colleges, which are a sound educational investment. They are more than that. They're a proud tradition, a symbol of black determination and accomplishment, and I feel deeply they must be preserved. We've increased the share of Department of Education Title III funds spent on black colleges, and that trend will continue.

We have equal concern for the black business leaders of today. Minority business development, as I indicated earlier, is a key to black economic progress. Black-owned businesses are especially important in neighborhood economies where the dollars, as I said, spent have a beneficial multiplier effect.

We want your input. I expect my domestic advisers to be in regular touch with you as our policies evolve. We may not always agree, but new ideas are often sparked by opinions clashing.

I didn't come here today bearing the promises of government handouts, which others have brought and which you've rightly learned to mistrust. Instead, I ask you to join me to build a coalition for change.

Seventy-two years ago the famous call went forth, the call for a conference emphasizing the civil and political rights of blacks. And the result of that call, of course, was the National Association for the Advancement of Colored People. Well, today let us issue a call for new perspectives on the economic challenges facing black Americans. Let us issue a call for exciting programs to spring America forward toward the next century, an America full of new solutions to old problems.

We will link hands to build an era where we can put fear behind us and hope in front of us. It can be an era in which programs are less important than opportunities. It can be an era where we all reach out in reconciliation instead of anger and dispute.

In the war in Vietnam several years ago, a live grenade fell among a group of American soldiers. They were frozen with horror knowing they were only seconds away from death. Then one young soldier, a black, threw himself on the grenade, covering it with his helmet and his body. He died to save his comrades. Greater glory hath no man. Congressional Medal of Honor winner, posthumously presented, Garfield Langhorn's last whispered words were, "You have to care."

Let us care. Let us work to build a nation that is free of racism, full of opportunity, and determined to loosen the creative energies of every person of every race, of every station, to make a better life. It will be my honor to stand alongside you to answer this call.

Thank you.

Source: "Remarks in Denver, Colorado, at the Annual Convention of the National Association for the Advancement of Colored People," June 29, 1981, The Ronald Reagan Presidential Library. Available online. URL: http://www.reagan.utexas.edu/resource/speeches/1981/62981a.htm

16. Remarks and a Question-and-Answer Session with Reporters on the Air Traffic Controllers Strike August 3, 1981

The strike by members of PATCO (the Professional Air Traffic Controllers Organization) confronted Ronald Reagan with a difficult choice; PATCO had endorsed his bid for the presidency in 1980, and Reagan was proud of the fact that he had once been the president of a union (the Screen Actors Guild). However, Reagan was determined not to allow a strike by federal employees who had a no-strike provision in their contracts, and whose strike had the potential to harm the American economy. Reagan gave the striking controllers 48 hours to return to work, and terminated those who did not. His deci-

sive action sent a strong message around the world at a time when labor unrest was commonplace and often crippling, and may have helped break the back of inflation in the United States by signaling that organized labor's best days were behind it. Perhaps more important, it solidified Reagan's image as a decisive leader for whom the term "angst-ridden" was a completely alien concept.

The President. This morning at 7 A.M. the union representing those who man America's air traffic control facilities called a strike. This was the culmination of 7 months of negotiations between the Federal Aviation Administration and the union. At one point in these negotiations agreement was reached and signed by both sides, granting a $40 million increase in salaries and benefits. This is twice what other government employees can expect. It was granted in recognition of the difficulties inherent in the work these people perform. Now, however, the union demands are 17 times what had been agreed to—$681 million. This would impose a tax burden on their fellow citizens which is unacceptable.

I would like to thank the supervisors and controllers who are on the job today, helping to get the nation's air system operating safely. In the New York area, for example, four supervisors were scheduled to report for work, and 17 additionally volunteered. At National Airport a traffic controller told a newsperson he had resigned from the union and reported to work because "How can I ask my kids to obey the law if I don't?" This is a great tribute to America.

Let me make one thing plain. I respect the right of workers in the private sector to strike. Indeed, as president of my own union, I led the first strike ever called by that union. I guess I'm maybe the first one to ever hold this office who is a lifetime member of an AFL-CIO union. But we cannot compare labor-management relations in the private sector with government.

Government cannot close down the assembly line. It has to provide without interruption the protective services which are government's reason for being.

It was in recognition of this that the Congress passed a law forbidding strikes by government employees against the public safety. Let me read the solemn oath taken by each of these employees, a sworn affidavit, when they accepted their jobs: "I am not participating in any strike against the Government of the United States or any agency thereof, and I will not so participate while an employee of the Government of the United States or any agency thereof."

It is for this reason that I must tell those who fail to report for duty this morning they are in violation of the law, and if they do not report for work within 48 hours, they have forfeited their jobs and will be terminated.

Source: "Remarks and a Question-and-Answer Session with Reporters on the Air Traffic Controllers Strike," August 3, 1981, The Ronald Reagan Presidential Library. Available online. URL: http://www.reagan.utexas.edu/resource/speeches/1981/80381a.htm

17. "Zero-Option"Speech to National Press Club November 18, 1981

This speech, widely derided at the time as a ploy on Reagan's part, outlined a vision to eliminate an entire class of nuclear weapons, a truly radical proposal dismissed as "non-negotiable" by pundits and the Politburo. It later became the basis of the U.S.-Soviet Intermediate-range Nuclear Forces (INF) Treaty signed at the White House by President Reagan and Mikhail Gorbachev in December 1987.

Officers, ladies and gentlemen of the National Press Club and, as of a very short time ago, fellow members:

Back in April while in the hospital I had, as you can readily understand, a lot of time for reflection. And one day I decided to send a personal, handwritten letter to Soviet President Leonid Brezhnev reminding him that we had met about 10 years ago in San Clemente, California, as he and President Nixon were concluding a series of meetings that had brought hope to all the world. Never had peace and good will seemed closer at hand.

I'd like to read you a few paragraphs from that letter. "Mr. President: When we met, I asked if you were aware that the hopes and aspirations of millions of people throughout the world were dependent on the decisions that would be reached in those meetings. You took my hand in both of yours and assured me that you were aware of that and that you were dedicated with all your heart and soul and mind to fulfilling those hopes and dreams."

I went on in my letter to say: "The people of the world still share that hope. Indeed, the peoples of the world, despite differences in racial and ethnic origin, have very much in common. They want the dignity of having some control over their individual lives, their destiny. They want to work at the craft or trade of their own choosing and to be fairly rewarded. They want to raise their families in peace without harming anyone or suffering harm themselves. Government exists for their convenience, not the other way around.

"If they are incapable, as some would have us believe, of self-government, then where among them do we find any who are capable of governing others?

"Is it possible that we have permitted ideology, political and economic philosophies, and governmental policies to keep us from considering the very real, everyday problems of our peoples? Will the average Soviet family be better off or even aware that the Soviet Union has imposed a government of its own choice on the people of Afghanistan? Is life better for the people of Cuba because the Cuban military dictate who shall govern the people of Angola?

"It is often implied that such things have been made necessary because of territorial ambitions of the United States; that we have imperialistic designs, and thus constitute a threat to your own security and that of the newly emerging nations. Not only is there no evidence to support such a charge, there is solid evidence that the United States, when it could have dominated the world with no risk to itself, made no effort whatsoever to do so.

"When World War II ended, the United States had the only undamaged industrial power in the world. Our military might was at its peak, and we alone had the ultimate weapon, the nuclear weapon, with the unquestioned ability to deliver it anywhere in the world. If we had sought world domination then, who could have opposed us?

"But the United States followed a different course, one unique in all the history of mankind. We used our power and wealth to rebuild the war-ravished economies of the world, including those of the nations who had been our enemies. May I say, there is absolutely no substance to charges that the United States is guilty of imperialism or attempts to impose its will on other countries, by use of force."

I continued my letter by saying—or concluded my letter, I should say—by saying, "Mr. President, should we not be concerned with eliminating the obstacles which prevent our people, those you and I represent, from achieving their most cherished goals?"

Well, it's in the same spirit that I want to speak today to this audience and the people of the world about America's program for peace and the coming negotiations which begin November 30th in Geneva, Switzerland. Specifically, I want to present our program for preserving peace in Europe and our wider program for arms control.

Twice in my lifetime, I have seen the peoples of Europe plunged into the tragedy of war. Twice in my lifetime, Europe has suffered destruction and military occupation in wars that statesmen proved powerless to prevent, soldiers unable to contain, and ordinary citizens unable to escape. And twice in my lifetime, young Americans have bled their lives into the soil of those battlefields not to enrich or enlarge our domain, but to restore the peace and independence of our friends and Allies.

All of us who lived through those troubled times share a common resolve that they must never come again. And most of us share a common appreciation of the Atlantic Alliance that has made a peaceful, free, and prosperous Western Europe in the post-war era possible.

But today, a new generation is emerging on both sides of the Atlantic. Its members were not present at the creation of the North Atlantic Alliance. Many of them don't fully understand its roots in defending freedom and rebuilding a war-torn continent. Some young people question why we need weapons, particularly nuclear weapons, to deter war and to assure peaceful development. They fear that the accumulation of weapons itself may lead to conflagration. Some even propose unilateral disarmament.

I understand their concerns. Their questions deserve to be answered. But we have an obligation to answer their questions on the basis of judgment and reason and experience. Our policies have resulted in the longest European peace in this century. Wouldn't a rash departure from these policies, as some now suggest, endanger that peace?

From its founding, the Atlantic Alliance has preserved the peace through unity, deterrence, and dialog. First, we and our Allies have stood united by the firm commitment that an attack upon any one of us would be considered an attack upon us all. Second, we and our Allies have deterred aggression by maintaining forces strong enough to ensure that any aggressor would lose more from an attack than he could possibly gain. And third, we and our Allies have engaged the Soviets in a dialog about mutual restraint and arms limitations, hoping to reduce the risk of war and the burden of armaments and to lower the barriers that divide East from West.

These three elements of our policy have preserved the peace in Europe for more than a third of a century. They can preserve it for generations to come, so long as we pursue them with sufficient will and vigor.

Today, I wish to reaffirm America's commitment to the Atlantic Alliance and our resolve to sustain the peace. And from my conversations with allied leaders, I know that they also remain true to this tried and proven course.

NATO's policy of peace is based on restraint and balance. No NATO weapons, conventional or nuclear, will ever be used in Europe except in response to attack. NATO's defense plans have been responsible and restrained. The Allies remain strong, united, and resolute. But the momentum of the continuing Soviet military buildup threatens both the conventional and the nuclear balance.

Consider the facts. Over the past decade, the United States reduced the size of its Armed Forces and decreased its military spending. The Soviets steadily increased the number of men under arms. They now number more than double those of the United States. Over the same period, the Soviets expanded their real military spending by about one-third. The Soviet Union increased its inventory of tanks to some 50,000, compared to our 11,000. Historically a land power, they transformed their navy from a coastal defense force to an open ocean fleet, while the United States, a sea power with transoceanic alliances, cut its fleet in half.

During a period when NATO deployed no new intermediate-range nuclear missiles and actually withdrew 1,000 nuclear warheads, the Soviet Union deployed more than 750 nuclear warheads on the new SS-20 missiles alone.

Our response to this relentless buildup of Soviet military power has been restrained but firm. We have made decisions to strengthen all three legs of the strategic triad: sea-, land-, and air-based. We have proposed a defense program in the United States for the next 5 years which will remedy the neglect of the past decade and restore the eroding balance on which our security depends.

I would like to discuss more specifically the growing threat to Western Europe which is posed by the continuing deployment of certain Soviet intermediate-range nuclear missiles. The Soviet Union has three different types of such missile systems: the SS-20, the SS-4, and the SS-5, all with the range capable of reaching virtually all of Western Europe. There are other Soviet weapon systems which also represent a major threat.

Now, the only answer to these systems is a comparable threat to Soviet threats, to Soviet targets; in other words, a deterrent preventing the use of these Soviet weapons by the counterthreat of a like response against their own territory. At present, however, there is no equivalent deterrent to these Soviet intermediate missiles. And the Soviets continue to add one new SS-20 a week.

To counter this, the Allies agreed in 1979, as part of a two-track decision, to deploy as a deterrent land-based cruise missiles and Pershing II missiles capable of reaching targets in the Soviet Union. These missiles are to be deployed in several countries of Western Europe. This relatively limited force in no way serves as a substitute for the much larger strategic umbrella spread over our NATO Allies. Rather, it provides a vital link between conventional shorter-range nuclear forces in Europe and intercontinental forces in the United States.

Deployment of these systems will demonstrate to the Soviet Union that this link cannot be broken. Deterring war depends on the perceived ability of our forces to perform effectively. The more effective our forces are, the less likely it is that we'll have to use them. So, we and our allies are proceeding to modernize NATO's nuclear forces of intermediate range to meet increased Soviet deployments of nuclear systems threatening Western Europe.

Let me turn now to our hopes for arms control negotiations. There's a tendency to make this entire subject overly complex. I want to be clear and concise. I told you of the letter I wrote to President Brezhnev last April. Well, I've just sent another message to the Soviet leadership. It's a simple, straightforward, yet, historic message. The United States proposes the mutual reduction of conventional intermediate-range nuclear and strategic forces. Specifically, I have proposed a four-point agenda to achieve this objective in my letter to President Brezhnev.

The first and most important point concerns the Geneva negotiations. As part of the 1979 two-track decision, NATO made a commitment to seek arms control negotiations with the Soviet Union on intermediate range nuclear forces. The United States has been preparing for these negotiations through close consultation with our NATO partners.

We're now ready to set forth our proposal. I have informed President Brezhnev that when our delegation travels to the negotiations on intermediate range, land-based nuclear missiles in Geneva on the 30th of this month, my representatives will present the following proposal: The United States is prepared to cancel its deployment of Pershing II and ground-launch cruise missiles if the Soviets will dismantle their SS-20, SS-4, and SS-5 missiles. This would be an historic step. With Soviet agreement, we could together substantially reduce the dread threat of nuclear war which hangs over the people of Europe. This, like the first footstep on the Moon, would be a giant step for mankind.

Now, we intend to negotiate in good faith and go to Geneva willing to listen to and consider the proposals of our Soviet counterparts, but let me call to your attention the background against which our proposal is made.

During the past 6 years while the United States deployed no new intermediate-range missiles and withdrew 1,000 nuclear warheads from Europe, the Soviet Union deployed 750 warheads on mobile, accurate ballistic missiles. They now have 1,100 warheads on the SS-20s, SS-4s and 5s. And the United States has no comparable missiles. Indeed, the United States dismantled the last such missile in Europe over 15 years ago.

As we look to the future of the negotiations, it's also important to address certain Soviet claims, which left unrefuted could become critical barriers to real progress in arms control.

The Soviets assert that a balance of intermediate range nuclear forces already exists. That assertion is wrong. By any objective measure, as this chart indicates, the Soviet Union has developed an increasingly overwhelming advantage. They now enjoy a superiority on the order of six to one. The red is the Soviet buildup; the blue is our own. That is 1975, and that is 1981.

Now, Soviet spokesmen have suggested that moving their SS-20s behind the Ural Mountains will remove the threat to Europe. Well, as this map demonstrates, the SS-20s, even if deployed behind the Urals, will have a range that puts almost all of Western Europe—the great cities—Rome, Athens, Paris, London, Brussels, Amsterdam, Berlin, and so many more—all of Scandinavia, all of the Middle East, all of northern Africa, all within range of these missiles which, incidentally, are mobile and can be moved on shorter notice. These little images mark the present location which would give them a range clear out into the Atlantic.

The second proposal that I've made to President Brezhnev concerns strategic weapons. The United States proposes to open negotiations on strategic arms as soon as possible next year.

I have instructed Secretary Haig to discuss the timing of such meetings with Soviet representatives. Substance, however, is far more important than timing. As our proposal for the Geneva talks this month illustrates, we can make proposals for genuinely serious reductions, but only if we take the time to prepare carefully.

The United States has been preparing carefully for resumption of strategic arms negotiations because we don't want a repetition of past disappointments. We don't want an arms control process that sends hopes soaring only to end in dashed expectations.

Now, I have informed President Brezhnev that we will seek to negotiate substantial reductions in nuclear arms which would result in levels that are equal and verifiable. Our approach to verification will be to emphasize openness and creativity, rather than the secrecy and suspicion which have undermined confidence in arms control in the past.

While we can hope to benefit from work done over the past decade in strategic arms negotiations, let us agree to do more than simply begin where these previous efforts left off. We can and should attempt major qualitative and quantitative progress. Only such progress can fulfill the hopes of our own people and the rest of the world. And let us see how far we can go in achieving truly substantial reductions in our strategic arsenals.

To symbolize this fundamental change in direction, we will call these negotiations START—Strategic Arms Reduction Talks.

The third proposal I've made to the Soviet Union is that we act to achieve equality at lower levels of conventional forces in Europe. The defense needs of the Soviet Union hardly call for maintaining more combat divisions in

East Germany today than were in the whole Allied invasion force that landed in Normandy on D-Day. The Soviet Union could make no more convincing contribution to peace in Europe, and in the world, than by agreeing to reduce its conventional forces significantly and constrain the potential for sudden aggression.

Finally, I have pointed out to President Brezhnev that to maintain peace we must reduce the risks of surprise attack and the chance of war arising out of uncertainty or miscalculation.

I am renewing our proposal for a conference to develop effective measures that would reduce these dangers. At the current Madrid meeting of the Conference on Security and Cooperation in Europe, we're laying the foundation for a Western-proposed conference on disarmament in Europe. This conference would discuss new measures to enhance stability and security in Europe. Agreement in this conference is within reach. I urge the Soviet Union to join us and many other nations who are ready to launch this important enterprise.

All of these proposals are based on the same fair-minded principles—substantial, militarily significant reduction in forces, equal ceilings for similar types of forces, and adequate provisions for verification.

My administration, our country, and I are committed to achieving arms reductions agreements based on these principles. Today I have outlined the kinds of bold, equitable proposals which the world expects of us. But we cannot reduce arms unilaterally. Success can only come if the Soviet Union will share our commitment, if it will demonstrate that its often-repeated professions of concern for peace will be matched by positive action.

Preservation of peace in Europe and the pursuit of arms reduction talks are of fundamental importance. But we must also help to bring peace and security to regions now torn by conflict, external intervention, and war.

The American concept of peace goes well beyond the absence of war. We foresee a flowering of economic growth and individual liberty in a world at peace.

At the economic summit conference in Cancun, I met with the leaders of 21 nations and sketched out our approach to global economic growth. We want to eliminate the barriers to trade and investment which hinder these critical incentives to growth, and we're working to develop new programs to help the poorest nations achieve self-sustaining growth.

And terms like "peace" and "security," we have to say, have little meaning for the oppressed and the destitute. They also mean little to the individual whose state has stripped him of human freedom and dignity. Wherever there is oppression, we must strive for the peace and security of individuals as well as states. We must recognize that progress and the pursuit of liberty is a necessary complement to military security. Nowhere has this fundamental truth been more boldly and clearly stated than in the Helsinki Accords of 1975. These accords have not yet been translated into living reality.

Today I've announced an agenda that can help to achieve peace, security, and freedom across the globe. In particular, I have made an important offer to forego entirely deployment of new American missiles in Europe if the Soviet Union is prepared to respond on an equal footing.

There is no reason why people in any part of the world should have to live in permanent fear of war or its specter. I believe the time has come for all nations to act in a responsible spirit that doesn't threaten other states. I believe the time is right to move forward on arms control and the resolution of critical regional disputes at the conference table. Nothing will have a higher priority for me and for the American people over the coming months and years.

Addressing the United Nations 20 years ago, another American President described the goal that we still pursue today. He said, "If we all can persevere, if we can look beyond our shores and ambitions, then surely the age will dawn in which the strong are just and the weak secure and the peace preserved."

He didn't live to see that goal achieved. I invite all nations to join with America today in the quest for such a world.

Thank you.

Source: "Remarks to Members of the National Press Club on Arms Reduction and Nuclear Weapons," November 18, 1981, The Ronald Reagan Presidential Library. Available online. URL: http://www.reagan.utexas.edu/resource/speeches/1981/111881a.htm

18. Address to the Nation about Christmas and the Situation in Poland
December 23, 1981

President Reagan disappointed some of his conservative supporters by not responding more aggressively to the crackdown on the first genuine free trade union in the Eastern bloc—the Solidarity Movement in Poland. Reagan's friend, conservative columnist George Will, claimed that the president's lifting of the grain embargo and his reluctance to apply strict economic sanctions against the Soviet Union in retaliation for the crackdown revealed that the administration "loves commerce more than it loathes communism." Reagan's rhetoric regarding "the courageous Polish people" who were "betrayed by their own government" was nonetheless moving, and in fact, behind the scenes, the Central Intelligence Agency, in concert with the Vatican, was covertly keeping Solidarity alive.

Good evening.

At Christmas time, every home takes on a special beauty, a special warmth, and that's certainly true of the White House, where so many famous Americans have spent their Christmases over the years. This fine old home, the people's house, has seen so much, been so much a part of all our lives and history. It's been humbling and inspiring for Nancy and me to be spending our first Christmas in this place.

We've lived here as your tenants for almost a year now, and what a year it's been. As a people we've been through quite a lot—moments of joy, of tragedy, and of real achievement— moments that I believe have brought us all closer together. G. K. Chesterton once said that the world would never starve for wonders, but only for the want of wonder.

At this special time of year, we all renew our sense of wonder in recalling the story of the first Christmas in Bethlehem, nearly 2,000 year ago.

Some celebrate Christmas as the birthday of a great and good philosopher and teacher. Others of us believe in the divinity of the child born in Bethlehem, that he was and is the promised Prince of Peace. Yes, we've questioned why he who could perform miracles chose to come among us as a helpless babe, but maybe that was his first miracle, his first great lesson that we should learn to care for one another.

Tonight, in millions of American homes, the glow of the Christmas tree is a reflection of the love Jesus taught us. Like the shepherds and wise men of that first Christmas, we Americans have always tried to follow a higher light, a star, if you will. At lonely campfire vigils along the frontier, in the darkest days of the Great Depression, through war and peace, the twin beacons of faith and freedom have brightened the American sky. At times our footsteps may have faltered, but trusting in God's help, we've never lost our way.

Just across the way from the White House stand the two great emblems of the holiday season: a Menorah, symbolizing the Jewish festival of Hanukkah, and the National Christmas

Tree, a beautiful towering blue spruce from Pennsylvania. Like the National Christmas Tree, our country is a living, growing thing planted in rich American soil. Only our devoted care can bring it to full flower. So, let this holiday season be for us a time of rededication.

Even as we rejoice, however, let us remember that for some Americans, this will not be as happy a Christmas as it should be. I know a little of what they feel. I remember one Christmas Eve during the Great Depression, my father opening what he thought was a Christmas greeting. It was a notice that he no longer had a job.

Over the past year, we've begun the long, hard work of economic recovery. Our goal is an America in which every citizen who needs and wants a job can get a job. Our program for recovery has only been in place for 12 weeks now, but it is beginning to work. With your help and prayers, it will succeed. We're winning the battle against inflation, runaway government spending and taxation, and that victory will mean more economic growth, more jobs, and more opportunity for all Americans.

A few months before he took up residence in this house, one of my predecessors, John Kennedy, tried to sum up the temper of the times with a quote from an author closely tied to Christmas, Charles Dickens. We were living, he said, in the best of times and the worst of times. Well, in some ways that's even more true today. The world is full of peril, as well as promise. Too many of its people, even now, live in the shadow of want and tyranny.

As I speak to you tonight, the fate of a proud and ancient nation hangs in the balance. For a thousand years, Christmas has been celebrated in Poland, a land of deep religious faith, but this Christmas brings little joy to the courageous Polish people. They have been betrayed by their own government.

The men who rule them and their totalitarian allies fear the very freedom that the Polish people cherish. They have answered the stirrings of liberty with brute force, killings, mass arrests, and the setting up of concentration camps. Lech Walesa and other Solidarity leaders are imprisoned, their fate unknown. Factories, mines, universities, and homes have been assaulted.

The Polish Government has trampled underfoot solemn commitments to the UN Charter and the Helsinki accords. It has even broken the Gdansk agreement of August 1980, by which the Polish Government recognized the basic right of its people to form free trade unions and to strike.

The tragic events now occurring in Poland, almost 2 years to the day after the Soviet invasion of Afghanistan, have been precipitated by public and secret pressure from the Soviet Union. It is no coincidence that Soviet Marshal Kulikov, chief of the Warsaw Pact forces, and other senior Red Army officers were in Poland while these outrages were being initiated. And it is no coincidence that the martial law proclamations imposed in December by the Polish Government were being printed in the Soviet Union in September.

The target of this depression [repression] is the Solidarity Movement, but in attacking Solidarity its enemies attack an entire people. Ten million of Poland's 36 million citizens are members of Solidarity. Taken together with their families, they account for the overwhelming majority of the Polish nation. By persecuting Solidarity the Polish Government wages war against its own people.

I urge the Polish Government and its allies to consider the consequences of their actions. How can they possibly justify using naked force to crush a people who ask for nothing more than the right to lead their own lives in freedom and dignity? Brute force may intimidate, but it cannot form the basis of an enduring society, and the ailing Polish economy cannot be rebuilt with terror tactics.

Poland needs cooperation between its government and its people, not military oppression. If the Polish Government will honor the commitments it has made to human rights in documents like the Gdansk agreement, we in America will gladly do our share to help the shattered Polish economy, just as we helped the countries of Europe after both World Wars.

It's ironic that we offered, and Poland expressed interest in accepting, our help after World War II. The Soviet Union intervened then and refused to allow such help to Poland. But if the forces of tyranny in Poland, and those who incite them from without, do not relent, they should prepare themselves for serious consequences. Already, throughout the Free World, citizens have publicly demonstrated their support for the Polish people. Our government, and those of our allies, have expressed moral revulsion at the police state tactics of Poland's oppressors. The Church has also spoken out, in spite of threats and intimidation. But our reaction cannot stop there.

I want emphatically to state tonight that if the outrages in Poland do not cease, we cannot and will not conduct "business as usual" with the perpetrators and those who aid and abet them. Make no mistake, their crime will cost them dearly in their future dealings with America and free peoples everywhere. I do not make this statement lightly or without serious reflection.

We have been measured and deliberate in our reaction to the tragic events in Poland. We have not acted in haste, and the steps I will outline tonight and others we may take in the days ahead are firm, just, and reasonable.

In order to aid the suffering Polish people during this critical period, we will continue the shipment of food through private humanitarian channels, but only so long as we know that the Polish people themselves receive the food. The neighboring country of Austria has opened her doors to refugees from Poland. I have therefore directed that American assistance, including supplies of basic foodstuffs, be offered to aid the Austrians in providing for these refugees.

But to underscore our fundamental opposition to the repressive actions taken by the Polish Government against its own people, the administration has suspended all government-sponsored shipments of agricultural and dairy products to the Polish Government. This suspension will remain in force until absolute assurances are received that distribution of these products is monitored and guaranteed by independent agencies. We must be sure that every bit of food provided by America goes to the Polish people, not to their oppressors.

The United States is taking immediate action to suspend major elements of our economic relationships with the Polish Government. We have halted the renewal of the Export-Import Bank's line of export credit insurance to the Polish Government. We will suspend Polish civil aviation privileges in the United States. We are suspending the right of Poland's fishing fleet to operate in American waters. And we're proposing to our allies the further restriction of high technology exports to Poland.

These actions are not directed against the Polish people. They are a warning to the Government of Poland that free men cannot and will not stand idly by in the face of brutal repression. To underscore this point, I've written a letter to General Jaruzelski, head of the Polish Government. In it, I outlined the steps we're taking and warned of the serious consequences if the Polish Government continues to use violence against its populace. I've urged him to free those in arbitrary detention, to lift martial law, and to restore the internationally recognized rights of the Polish people to free speech and association.

The Soviet Union, through its threats and pressures, deserves a major share of blame for the developments in Poland. So, I have also sent a letter to President Brezhnev urging him to permit the restoration of basic human rights in Poland provided for in the Helsinki Final Act. In it, I informed him that if this repression continues, the United States will have no choice but to take further concrete political and economic measures affecting our relationship.

When 19th century Polish patriots rose against foreign oppressors, their rallying cry was, "For our freedom and yours." Well, that motto still rings true in our time. There is a spirit of solidarity abroad in the world tonight that no physical force can crush. It crosses national boundaries and enters into the hearts of men and women everywhere. In factories, farms, and schools, in cities and towns around the globe, we the people of the Free World stand as one with our Polish brothers and sisters. Their cause is ours, and our prayers and hopes go out to them this Christmas.

Yesterday, I met in this very room with Romuald Spasowski, the distinguished former Polish Ambassador who has sought asylum in our country in protest of the suppression of his native land. He told me that one of the ways the Polish people have demonstrated their solidarity in the face of martial law is by placing lighted candles in their windows to show that the light of liberty still glows in their hearts.

Ambassador Spasowski requested that on Christmas Eve a lighted candle will burn in the White House window as a small but certain beacon of our solidarity with the Polish people. I urge all of you to do the same tomorrow night, on Christmas Eve, as a personal statement of your commitment to the steps we're taking to support the brave people of Poland in their time of troubles.

Once, earlier in this century, an evil influence threatened that the lights were going out all over the world. Let the light of millions of candles in American homes give notice that the light of freedom is not going to be extinguished. We are blessed with a freedom and abundance denied to so many. Let those candles remind us that these blessings bring with them a solid obligation, an obligation to the God who guides us, an obligation to the heritage of liberty and dignity handed down to us by our forefathers and an obligation to the children of the world, whose future will be shaped by the way we live our lives today.

Christmas means so much because of one special child. But Christmas also reminds us that all children are special, that they are gifts from God, gifts beyond price that mean more than any presents money can buy. In their love and laughter, in our hopes for their future lies the true meaning of Christmas.

So, in a spirit of gratitude for what we've been able to achieve together over the past year and looking forward to all that we hope to achieve together in the years ahead, Nancy and I want to wish you all the best of holiday seasons. As Charles Dickens, whom I quoted a few moments ago, said so well in "A Christmas Carol," "God bless us, every one."

Good night.

Source: "Address to the Nation about Christmas and the Situation in Poland," December 23, 1981, The Ronald Reagan Presidential Library. Available online. URL: http://www.reagan.utexas.edu/resource/speeches/1981/122381e.htm

19. "The Crusade for Freedom" Address to British Parliament June 8, 1982

Once again Ronald Reagan shocked many observers with his stark condemnation of Soviet totalitarianism, and his unmitigated faith in the ability of the West to prevail in the cold war. In the face of a growing "nuclear freeze" movement, Reagan persisted in arguing for the deployment of American

Pershing II and cruise missiles in Europe to counter the Soviets' SS-20s and other intermediate range missiles. Many members of the nuclear freeze movement considered both sides equally culpable for the arms race and saw the United States and the USSR as morally equivalent, while Reagan continued to argue for the superiority of the Western world. In this address to the British parliament, Reagan offered a more elegant description of what he would later call "the evil empire," and vowed to win the cold war: "What I am describing now is a plan and a hope for the long term—the march of freedom and democracy which will leave Marxism-Leninism on the ash heap of history as it has left other tyrannies which stifle the freedom and muzzle the self-expression of the people."

We're approaching the end of a bloody century plagued by a terrible political invention—totalitarianism. Optimism comes less easily today, not because democracy is less vigorous, but because democracy's enemies have refined their instruments of repression. Yet optimism is in order because day by day democracy is proving itself to be a not at all fragile flower. From Stettin on the Baltic to Varna on the Black Sea, the regimes planted by totalitarianism have had more than thirty years to establish their legitimacy. But none—not one regime—has yet been able to risk free elections. Regimes planted by bayonets do not take root.

The strength of the Solidarity movement in Poland demonstrates the truth told in an underground joke in the Soviet Union. It is that the Soviet Union would remain a one-party nation even if an opposition party were permitted because everyone would join the opposition party. . . .

Historians looking back at our time will note the consistent restraint and peaceful intentions of the West. They will note that it was the democracies who refused to use the threat of their nuclear monopoly in the forties and early fifties for territorial or imperial gain.

Had that nuclear monopoly been in the hands of the Communist world, the map of Europe—indeed, the world—would look very different today. And certainly they will note it was not the democracies that invaded Afghanistan or suppressed Polish Solidarity or used chemical and toxin warfare in Afghanistan and Southeast Asia.

If history teaches anything, it teaches self-delusion in the face of unpleasant facts is folly. We see around us today the marks of our terrible dilemma—predictions of doomsday, anti-nuclear demonstrations, an arms race in which the West must, for its own protection, be an unwilling participant. At the same time we see totalitarian forces in the world who seek subversion and conflict around the globe to further their barbarous assault on the human spirit. What, then, is our course? Must civilization perish in a hail of fiery atoms? Must freedom wither in a quiet, deadening accommodation with totalitarian evil?

Sir Winston Churchill refused to accept the inevitability of war or even that it was imminent. He said, "I do not believe that Soviet Russia desires war. What they desire is the fruits of war and the indefinite expansion of their power and doctrines. But what we have to consider here today while time remains is the permanent prevention of war and the establishment of conditions of freedom and democracy as rapidly as possible in all countries."

Well, this is precisely our mission today: to preserve freedom as well as peace. It may not be easy to see; but I believe we live now at a turning point.

In an ironic sense Karl Marx was right. We are witnessing today a great revolutionary crisis, a crisis where the demands of the economic order are conflicting directly with those of the political order. But the crisis is happening not in the free, non-Marxist West but in the home of Marxism-Leninism, the Soviet Union. It is the Soviet Union that runs against the tide of history by denying human freedom and human dignity to its citizens. It also is in deep economic difficulty. The rate of growth in the national product has been steadily declining since the fifties and is less than half of what it was then.

The dimensions of this failure are astounding: a country which employs one-fifth of its population in agriculture is unable to feed its own people. Were it not for the private sector, the tiny private sector tolerated in Soviet agriculture, the country might be on the brink of famine. These private plots occupy a bare 3 percent of the arable land but account for nearly one-quarter of Soviet farm output and nearly one-third of meat products and vegetables. Overcentralized, with little or no incentives, year after year the Soviet system pours its best resources into the making of instruments of destruction. The constant shrinkage of economic growth combined with the growth of military production is putting a heavy strain on the Soviet people. What we see here is a political structure that no longer corresponds to its economic base, a society where productive forces are hampered by political ones.

The decay of the Soviet experiment should come as no surprise to us. Wherever the comparisons have been made between free and closed societies—West Germany and East Germany, Austria and Czechoslovakia, Malaysia and Vietnam—it is the democratic countries that are prosperous and responsive to the needs of their people. And one of the simple but overwhelming facts of our time is this: of all the millions of refugees we've seen in the modern world, their flight is always away from, not toward the Communist world. Today on the NATO line, our military forces face east to prevent a possible invasion. On the other side of the line, the Soviet forces also face east to prevent their people from leaving.

The hard evidence of totalitarian rule has caused in mankind an uprising of the intellect and will. Whether it is the growth of the new schools of economics in America or England or the appearance of the so-called new philosophers in France, there is one unifying thread running through the intellectual work of these groups—rejection of the arbitrary power of the state, the refusal to subordinate the rights of the individual to the superstate, the realization that collectivism stifles all the best human impulses. . . .

Chairman Brezhnev repeatedly has stressed that the competition of ideas and systems must continue and that this is entirely consistent with relaxation of tensions and peace.

Well, we ask only that these systems begin by living up to their own constitutions, abiding by their own laws, and complying with the international obligations they have undertaken. We ask only for a process, a direction, a basic code of decency, not for an instant transformation.

We cannot ignore the fact that even without our encouragement there has been and will continue to be repeated explosion against repression and dictatorships. The Soviet Union itself is not immune to this reality. Any system is inherently unstable that has no peaceful means to legitimize its leaders. In such cases, the very repressiveness of the state ultimately drives people to resist it, if necessary, by force.

While we must be cautious about forcing the pace of change, we must not hesitate to declare our ultimate objectives and to take concrete actions to move toward them. We must be staunch in our conviction that freedom is not the sole prerogative of a lucky few but the inalienable and universal right of all human beings. So states the United Nations Universal Declaration of Human Rights, which, among other things, guarantees free elections.

The objective I propose is quite simple to state: to foster the infrastructure of democracy, the system of a free press, unions, political parties, universities, which allows a people to choose their own way to develop their own culture, to reconcile their own differences through peaceful means.

This is not cultural imperialism; it is providing the means for genuine self-determination and protection for diversity. Democracy already flourishes in countries with very different cultures and historical experiences. It would be cultural condescension, or worse, to say that any people prefer dictatorship to democracy. Who would voluntarily choose not to have the right to vote, decide to purchase government propaganda handouts instead of independent newspapers, prefer government to worker-controlled unions, opt for land to be owned by the state instead of those who till it, want government repression of religious liberty, a single political party instead of a free choice, a rigid cultural orthodoxy instead of democratic tolerance and diversity.

Since 1917 the Soviet Union has given covert political training and assistance to Marxist-Leninists in many countries. Of course, it also has promoted the use of violence and subversion by these same forces. Over the past several decades, West European and other social democrats, Christian democrats, and leaders have offered open assistance to fraternal, political, and social institutions to bring about peaceful and democratic progress. Appropriately, for a vigorous new democracy, the Federal Republic of Germany's political foundations have become a major force in this effort.

We in America now intend to take additional steps, as many of our allies have already done, toward realizing this same goal. The chairmen and other leaders of the national Republican and Democratic party organizations are initiating a study with the bipartisan American Political Foundation to determine how the United States can best contribute as a nation to the global campaign for democracy now gathering force. They will have the cooperation of congressional leaders of both parties, along with representatives of business, labor,

and other major institutions in our society. I look forward to receiving their recommendations and to working with these institutions and the Congress in the common task of strengthening democracy throughout the world.

It is time that we committed ourselves as a nation—in both the public and private sectors—to assisting democratic development. . . .

What I am describing now is a plan and a hope for the long term—the march of freedom and democracy which will leave Marxism-Leninism on the ash heap of history as it has left other tyrannies which stifle the freedom and muzzle the self-expression of the people. And that's why we must continue our efforts to strengthen NATO even as we move forward with our zero-option initiative in the negotiations on intermediate-range forces and our proposal for a one-third reduction in strategic ballistic missile warheads.

Our military strength is a prerequisite to peace, but let it be clear we maintain this strength in the hope it will never be used, for the ultimate determinant in the struggle that's now going on in the world will not be bombs and rockets but a test of wills and ideas, a trial of spiritual resolve, the values we hold, the beliefs we cherish, the ideals to which we are dedicated.

The British people know that, given strong leadership, time, and a little bit of hope, the forces of good ultimately rally and triumph over evil. Here among you is the cradle of self-government, the Mother of Parliaments. Here is the enduring greatness of the British contribution to mankind, the great civilized ideas: individual liberty, representative government, and the rule of law under God.

I've often wondered about the shyness of some of us in the West about standing for these ideals that have done so much to ease the plight of man and the hardships of our imperfect world. This reluctance to use those vast resources at our command reminds me of the elderly lady whose home was bombed in the blitz. As the rescuers moved about, they found a bottle of brandy she'd stored behind the staircase, which was all that was left standing. And since she was barely conscious, one of the workers pulled the cork to give her a taste of it. She came around immediately and said, "Here now—there now, put it back. That's for emergencies."

Well, the emergency is upon us. Let us be shy no longer. Let us go to our strength. Let us offer hope. Let us tell the world that a new age is not only possible but probable.

During the dark days of the Second World War, when this island was incandescent with courage, Winston Churchill exclaimed about Britain's adversaries, "What kind of people do they think we are?" Well, Britain's adversaries found out what extraordinary people the British are. But all the democracies paid a terrible price for allowing the dictators to underestimate us. We dare not make that mistake again. So, let us ask ourselves, "What kind of people do we think we are?" And let us answer, "Free people, worthy of freedom and determined not only to remain so but to help others gain their freedom as well."

Sir Winston led his people to great victory in war and then lost an election just as the fruits of victory were about to be enjoyed. But he left office honorably and, as it turned out, temporarily, knowing that the liberty of his people was more important than the fate of any single leader. History recalls his greatness in ways no dictator will ever know. And he left us a message of hope for the future, as timely now as when he first uttered it, as opposition leader in the Commons nearly twenty-seven years ago, when he said, "When we look back on all the perils through which we have passed and at the mighty foes that we have laid low and all the dark and deadly designs that we have frustrated, why should we fear for our future? We have," he said, "come safely through the worst."

Well, the task I've set forth will long outlive our own generation. But together, we too have come through the worst. Let us now begin a major effort to secure the best—a crusade for freedom that will engage the faith and fortitude of the next generation. For the sake of peace and justice, let us move toward a world in which all people are at last free to determine their own destiny.

Source: "Address to Members of the British Parliament," June 8, 1982, The Ronald Reagan Presidential Library. Available online. URL: http://www.reagan.utexas.edu/resource/speeches/1982/60882a.htm

20. "We Will Not Be Turned Back" CPAC Conference February 18, 1983

This address to the conservative faithful at CPAC was in some ways a practice run for the 1984 presidential election. Utilizing a mix of humor, anecdotes, and statistics, Reagan celebrates the upturn in the economy after the recession of the early 1980s begins to recede. His opponents claimed that the flat economy of 1981–1982 was a result of "Reaganomics;" now that the economy is rebounding Reagan is more than happy to embrace that label. He also renewed his commitment to the conservative social agenda, particularly restoring prayer in the public schools and restricting abortion rights. The latter issue was a sore point of sorts throughout his presidency, with some conservatives convinced that Reagan had not given the issue the attention it deserved.

Ladies and gentlemen, Mr. Chairman [Representative Mickey Edwards, ACU Chairman], reverend clergy, I thank you very much for those very kind words, and I thank you all for certainly a most hearty and warm welcome.

I'm grateful to the American Conservative Union, Young Americans for Freedom,

National Review and Human Events for organizing this third annual memorial service for the Democratic platform of 1980. Someone asked me why I wanted to make it three in a row. Well, you know how the Irish love wakes. [Laughter]

But I'm delighted to be back here with you, at your 10th annual conference. In my last two addresses, I've talked about our common perceptions and goals, and I thought I might report to you here tonight on where we stand in achieving those goals—a sort of "State of the Reagan Report," if you will.

Now, I'm the first to acknowledge that there's a good deal left unfinished on the conservative agenda. Our cleanup crew will need more than two years to deal with the mess left by others for over half a century. But I'm not disheartened. In fact, my attitude about that unfinished agenda isn't very different from that expressed in an anecdote about one of my favorite Presidents, Calvin Coolidge. [Laughter]

Some of you may know that after Cal Coolidge was introduced to the sport of fishing by his Secret Service detail, it got to be quite a passion with him, if you can use that word about "Silent Cal." Anyway, he was once asked by reporters how many fish were in one of his favorite angling places, the River Brule. And Coolidge said the waters were estimated to carry 45,000 trout. And then he said: "I haven't caught them all yet, but I sure have intimidated them."

Well, it's true we haven't brought about every change important to the conscience of a conservative, but we conservatives can take a great deal of honest pride in what we have achieved. In a few minutes I want to talk about just how far we've come and what we need to do to win further victories. But right now, I think a word or two on strategy is in order. You may remember that in the past, I mentioned that it was not our task as conservatives to just point out the mistakes made over all the decades of liberal government, not just to form

an able opposition, but to govern, to lead a nation. And I noted this would make new demands upon our movement, upon all of us.

For the first time in half a century, we've developed a whole new cadre of young conservatives in government. We've shown that conservatives can do more than criticize; we've shown that we can govern and move our legislation through the Congress.

Now, I know there's concern over attempts to roll back some of the gains that we've made. And it seems to me that here we ought to give some thought to strategy—to making sure that we stop and think before we act. For example, some of our critics have been saying recently that they want to take back the people's third-year tax cut and abolish tax indexing. And some others, including members of my staff, wanted immediately to open up a verbal barrage against them. Well, I hope you know that sometimes it's better if a President doesn't say exactly what's on his mind. There's an old story about a farmer and a lawyer that illustrates my point.

It seems that these two got into a pretty bad collision, a traffic accident. They both got out of their cars. The farmer took one look at the lawyer, and walked back to his car, got a package, brought it back. There was a bottle inside, and he said, "Here, you look pretty shook up. I think you ought to take a nip of this, it'll steady your nerves." Well, the lawyer did. And the farmer said, "You still look a bit pale. How about another?" And the lawyer took another swallow. And under the urging of the farmer, he took another and another and another. And then, finally, he said he was feeling pretty good and asked the farmer if he didn't think that he ought to have a little nip, too. And the farmer said, "Not me, I'm waiting for the state trooper."

I wonder if we can't learn something from that farmer. If our liberal friends really want to head into the next election under the banner of taking away from the American people their first real tax cut in nearly 20 years; if, after peering into their heart of hearts, they feel they must tell the American people that over the next six years they want to reduce the income of the average family by $3,000; and if they want to voice these deeply held convictions in an election year—well, fellow conservatives, who are we to stifle the voices of conscience?

Now, in talking about our legislative agenda, I know that some of you have been disturbed by the notion of standby tax increases in the so-called "out years." Well, I wasn't wild about the idea myself. But the economy is getting better, and I believe these improvements are only the beginning. And with some luck, and if the American people respond with the kind of energy and initiative they've always shown in the past, well, maybe it's time we started thinking about some standby tax cuts, too.

But you know, with regard to the economy, I wonder if our political adversaries haven't once again proved that they're our best allies. They spent the last 16 months or so placing all the responsibility for the state of the economy on our shoulders. And with some help from the media, it's been a pretty impressive campaign. They've created quite an image—we're responsible for the economy.

Well, I assume that we're responsible then for inflation which, after back-to-back years in double digits before we got here, has now been reduced to 3.9 percent in 1982. And for the last three months of the year, it ran at only 1.1 percent. In 1982 real wages increased for the first time in three years. Interest rates, as you've already been told, have dropped dramatically, with the prime rate shrinking by nearly 50 percent. And in December, the index of leading indicators was a full 6.3 percent above last March's low point and has risen in eight of the last nine months. Last month housing starts were up 95 percent and building permits 88 percent over the last year at this time. New

home sales are up too by 54 percent since April, and inventories of unsold homes are at the lowest levels in more than a decade. Auto production this quarter is scheduled to increase by 22 percent, and General Motors alone is putting 21,400 of their workers back on the jobs. Last month's sharp decline in the unemployment rate was the most heartening sign of all. It would have taken a $5 billion jobs bill to reduce unemployment by the same amount—and it didn't cost us anything.

It's time to admit our guilt, time we admitted that our liberal critics have been right all the time. And they should go right on telling the American people that the state of economy is precisely the fault of that wicked creature, Kemp-Roth and its havoc-wreaking twin, Reaganomics.

Let's confess, let's admit that we've turned the corner on the economy. And we're especially proud of one thing: when we hit heavy weather, we didn't panic, we didn't go for fast bromides and quick fixes, the huge tax increases or wage and price controls recommended by so many. And our stubbornness, if you want to call it that, will quite literally pay off for every American in the years ahead.

So, let me pledge to you tonight: Carefully, we have set out on the road to recovery. We will not be deterred. We will not be turned back. I reject the policies of the past, the policies of tax and tax, spend and spend, elect and elect. The lesson of these failed policies is clear; I've said this before: you can't drink yourself sober or spend yourself rich, and you can't prime the pump without pumping the prime—as somebody did, like to 21 1/2 percent in 1980.

And a word is in order here on the most historic of all the legislative reforms we've achieved in the last two years—that of tax indexing. You can understand the terror that strikes in the heart of those whose principal constituency is big government. Bracket creep is government's hidden incentive to inflate the currency and bring on inflation, and indexing will end that. It will end those huge, hidden subsidies for bigger and bigger government. In the future, if we get indexing planted firmly as a law of the land, the advocates of big government who want money, more money for their social spending, their social engineering schemes, will have to go to the people and say right out loud: "We want more money from your weekly paycheck, so we're raising your taxes." Do that instead of sneaking it out by way of inflation, which they have helped bring on.

So, all the professional Washingtonians, from bureaucrats to lobbyists to the special interest groups, are frightened—plain scared—and they're working overtime to take this one back. Well, I think I speak for all conservatives when I say tax indexing is non-negotiable. It's a fight we'll take to the people, and we'll win.

But I think you can see how even this debate shows things are changing for the better. It highlights the essential differences between two philosophies now contending for power in American political life. One is the philosophy of the past—a philosophy that has as its constituents an ill-assorted mix of elitists and special-interest groups who see government as the principal vehicle of social change, who believe that the only thing we have to fear is the people, who must be watched and regulated and superintended from Washington.

On the other hand, our philosophy is at the heart of the new political consensus that emerged in America at the beginning of this decade, one that I believe all—well, I believe it will dominate American politics for many decades. The economic disasters brought about by too much government were the catalysts for this consensus. During the '70s, the American people began to see misdirected, overgrown government as the source of many of our social problems—not the solution.

This new consensus has a view of government that's essentially that of our Founding Fathers—that government is the servant, not the master; that it was meant to maintain order, to protect our nation's safety, but otherwise, in the words of that noted political philosopher, schnozzle Jimmy Durante: "Don't put no constrictions on da people. Leave 'em da heck alone."

The overriding goal during the past two years has been to give the government back to the American people, to make it responsive again to their wishes and desires, to do more than bring about a healthy economy or a growing gross national product. We've truly brought about a quiet revolution in American government.

For too many years, bureaucratic self-interest and political maneuvering held sway over efficiency and honesty in government. Federal dollars were treated as the property of bureaucrats, not taxpayers. Those in the federal establishment who pointed to the misuse of those dollars were looked upon as malcontents or troublemakers.

Well, this administration has broken with what was a kind of a buddy system. There have been dramatic turnabouts in some of the more scandal-ridden and wasteful federal agencies and programs. Only a few years ago, the General Service Administration was racked by indictments and report after report of inefficiency and waste. Today at GSA, Jerry Carmen has not only put the whistleblowers back in charge, he's promoted them and given them new responsibilities. Just listen to this little set of figures. Today, General Service Administration work-in-progress time is down from 30 days to seven, even while the agency has sustained budget cuts of 20 percent, office space reductions of 20 percent, and the attrition of 7,000 employees.

At the Government Printing Office, under Dan Sawyer, losses of millions of dollars have suddenly been ended as the workforce was cut through attrition and a hiring freeze, and overtime pay was cut by $6 million in one year alone. The government publication program, which ran a cumulative loss of $20 million over a three-year period, registered a $4.9 million profit, and the GPO as a whole has experienced a profit of $4.1 million last year.

It is said by some that this administration has turned a blind eye to waste and fraud at the Pentagon while overzealously concentrating on the social programs. Well, at the Pentagon, under Cap Weinberger's leadership and our superb service Secretaries, Jack Marsh, John Lehman, and Verne Orr, we have identified more than a billion dollars in savings on waste and fraud, and, over the next seven years, multiyear procurement and other acquisition initiatives will save us almost $30 billion.

Now, these are only three examples of what we're attempting to do to make government more efficient. The list goes on. We have wielded our inspectors general as a strike force accounting for nearly $17 billion in savings in 18 months. With Peter Grace's help, we've called on top management executives and experts from the private sector to suggest modern management techniques for every aspect of government operations. And with an exciting new project called Reform 88, we're going to streamline and reorganize the processes that control the money, information, personnel, and property of the Federal bureaucracy—the maze through which nearly $2 trillion passes each year and which includes 350 different payroll systems and 1,750 personnel offices.

There is more, much more—from cutting down wasteful travel practices to reducing paperwork, from aggressively pursuing the $40 billion in bad debts owed the federal government to reducing publication of more than 70 million copies of wasteful or unnecessary government publications.

But, you know, making government responsive again to the people involves more than eliminating waste and fraud and inefficiency. During the decades when government was intruding into areas where it's neither competent nor needed, it was also ignoring its legitimate and constitutional duties such as preserving the domestic peace and providing for the common defense.

I'll talk about that in a moment. I know you've already heard about that today, some of you. But on the matter of domestic order, a few things need to be said. First of all, it is abundantly clear that much of our crime problem was provoked by a social philosophy that saw man as primarily a creature of his material environment. The same liberal philosophy that saw an era of prosperity and virtue ushered in by changing man's environment through massive federal spending programs also viewed criminals as the unfortunate products of poor socioeconomic conditions or an underprivileged upbringing. Society, not the individual, they said, was at fault for criminal wrongdoing. We are to blame.

Now, we conservatives have been warning about the crime problem for many years, about that permissive social philosophy that did so much to foster it, about a legal system that seemed to specialize in letting hardened criminals go free. And now we have the means and the power to do something. Let's get to work.

Drug pusher after drug pusher, mobster after mobster has escaped justice by taking advantage of our flawed bail and parole system. Criminals who have committed atrocious acts have cynically utilized the technicalities of the exclusionary rule, a miscarriage of justice unique to our legal system. Indeed, one National Institute of Justice study showed that of those arrested for drug felonies in Los Angeles County in 1981, 32 percent were back out on the streets because of perceived problems with the exclusionary rule.

Now, the exclusionary rule—that isn't a law that was passed by Congress or a state legislature, it's what is called case law, the result of judicial decisions. If a law enforcement officer obtains evidence as the result of a violation of the laws regarding search and seizure, that evidence cannot be introduced in a trial even if it proves the guilt of the accused. Now, this is hardly punishment of the officer for his violation of legal procedures, and its only effect, in many cases, is to free someone patently guilty of a crime.

I don't know, maybe I've told you this before, but I have to give you a glaring example of what I've taken too much time to explain here. [In] San Bernardino, California, several years ago, two narcotics agents, based on the evidence they had, obtained a legal warrant to search the home of a man and woman suspected of peddling heroin. They searched the home. They didn't find anything. But as they were leaving, just on a hunch, they turned back to the baby in the crib and took down the diapers, and there was the stash of heroin. The evidence was thrown out of court and the couple went free because the baby hadn't given permission for the violation of its constitutional rights.

Well, this administration has proposed vital reforms of our bail and parole systems and criminal forfeiture and sentencing statutes. These reforms were passed by the Senate 95 to 1 last year. Our anti-crime package never got out of committee in the House of Representatives. Do you see a target there? The American people want these reforms, and they want them now. I'm asking tonight that you mobilize all the powerful resources of this political movement to get these measures passed by the Congress.

On another front, all of you know how vitally important it is for us to reverse the decline in American education, to take responsibility for the education of our children out of the hands of parents and teachers. That's why the Congress must stop dithering. We need those tuition tax credits. We need a voucher system for the parents of disadvan-

taged children. We need education savings accounts, a sort of IRA for college. And finally—and don't think for a moment I've given up—we need to eliminate that unnecessary and politically engendered Department of Education.

There are other steps we're taking to restore government to its rightful duties, to restore the political consensus upon which this nation was founded. Our Founding Fathers prohibited a federal establishment of religion, but there is no evidence that they intended to set up a wall of separation between the state and religious belief itself.

The evidence of this is all around us. In the Declaration of Independence, alone, there are no fewer than four mentions of a Supreme Being. "In God We Trust" is engraved on our coinage. The Supreme Court opens its proceedings with a religious invocation. And the Congress opens each day with prayer from its chaplains. The schoolchildren of the United States are entitled to the same privileges as Supreme Court Justices and Congressmen. Join me in persuading the Congress to accede to the overwhelming desire of the American people for a constitutional amendment permitting prayer in our schools.

And finally, on our domestic agenda, there is a subject that weighs heavily on all of us—the tragedy of abortion on demand. This is a grave moral evil and one that requires the fullest discussion on the floors of the House and Senate. As we saw in the last century with the issue of slavery, any attempt by the Congress to stifle or compromise away discussion of important moral issues only further inflames emotions on both sides and leads ultimately to even more social disruption and disunity.

So, tonight, I would ask that the Congress discuss the issue of abortion openly and freely on the floors of the House and Senate. Let those who believe the practice of abortion to be a moral evil join us in taking this case to our fellow Americans. And let us do so rationally, calmly, and with an honest regard for our fellow Americans.

Speaking for myself, I believe that once implications of abortion on demand are fully aired and understood by the American people, they will resolutely seek its abolition. Now, I know there are many who sincerely believe that limiting the right of abortion violates the freedom of choice of the individual. But if the unborn child is a living entity, then there are two individuals, each with the right to life, liberty, and the pursuit of happiness. Unless and until someone can prove the unborn is not alive—and all medical evidence indicates it is—then we must concede the benefit of the doubt to the unborn infant.

But whether it's cutting spending and taxing, shrinking the size of the deficit, ending overregulation, inefficiency, fraud and waste in government, cracking down on career criminals, revitalizing American education, pressing for prayer and abortion legislation, I think you can see that the agenda we've put before America these past two years has been a conservative one. Oh, and there are two other matters that I think you'd be interested in. First, as part of our federalism effort, next week we will be sending to the Congress our proposal for four mega-block grants that will return vital prerogatives to the states where they belong. And second, the Office of Management and Budget will press ahead with new regulations prohibiting the use of federal tax dollars for purposes of political advocacy.

And these important domestic initiatives have been complemented by the conservative ideas we've brought to the pursuit of foreign policy. In the struggle now going on for the world, we have not been afraid to characterize our adversaries for what they are. We have focused world attention on forced labor on the Soviet pipeline and Soviet repression in Poland and all the other nations that make up what is called the "fourth world"—those living under totalitarian rule who long for freedom.

We publicized the evidence of chemical warfare and other atrocities in Cambodia, which we're now supposed to call Kampuchea, and Afghanistan. We pointed out that totalitarian powers hold a radically different view of morality and human dignity than we do. We must develop a forward strategy for freedom, one based on our hope that someday representative government will be enjoyed by all the people and all the nations of the earth.

We've been striving to give the world the facts about the international arms race. Ever since our nearly total demobilization after World War II, we in the West have been playing catchup. Yes, there's been an international arms race, as some of the declared Democratic candidates for the Presidency tell us. But let them also tell us, there's only been one side doing the racing.

Those of you in the frontline of the conservative movement can be of special assistance in furthering our strategy for freedom, our fight against totalitarianism. First of all, there is no more important foreign policy initiative in this administration, and none that frightens our adversaries more, than our attempts through our international radios to build constituencies for peace in nations dominated by totalitarian, militaristic regimes. We've proposed to the Congress modest but vitally important expenditures for the Voice of America, Radio Free Europe/Radio Liberty and Radio Marti. These proposals stalled last year, but with your help we can get them through the Congress this year. And believe me, nothing could mean more to the Poles, Lithuanians, Cubans, and all the millions of others living in that fourth world.

Now, it would be also unconscionable during any discussion of the need for candor in our foreign policy not to mention here the tragic event that last year shocked the world—the attack on His Holiness, Pope John Paul II—an act of unspeakable evil, an assault on man and God. It was an international outrage and merits the fullest possible investigation. Tonight, I want to take this opportunity to applaud the courage and resourcefulness of the government of Italy in bringing this matter to the attention of the world. And, contrary to what some have suggested, you can depend on it, there is no one on our side that is acting embarrassed or feeling embarrassed because they're going ahead with that investigation. We mean to help them.

And, now, Cap, you can breathe easy, because here we come. We must continue to revitalize and strengthen our Armed Forces. Cap Weinberger's been waging an heroic battle on this front. I'm asking you, the conservative leaders here tonight, to make support for our defense buildup one of your top priorities.

But besides progress in furthering all of these items on the conservative agenda, something else is occurring—something that someday we conservatives may be very proud happened under our leadership. Even with all our recent economic hardships, I believe a feeling of optimism is now entering the American consciousness, a belief that the days of division and discord are behind us and that an era of unity and national renewal is upon us.

A vivid reminder of how our nation has learned and grown and transcended the tragedies of the past was given to us here in Washington only a few months ago. Last November, on the Mall, between the Lincoln Memorial and the Washington Monument, a new memorial was dedicated—one of dark, low lying walls inscribed with the names of those who gave their lives in the Vietnam conflict. Soon, there will be added a sculpture of three infantrymen representing different racial and ethnic backgrounds.

During the dedication ceremonies, the rolls of the missing and dead were read for three days, morning till night, in a candlelight ceremony at the National Cathedral. And those veterans of Vietnam who never were welcomed home with speeches and bands, but who were defeated in battle and were heroes as surely as any who ever fought in a noble cause, staged their own parade on Constitution Avenue.

As America watched them, some in wheelchairs, all of them proud, there was a feeling that as a nation we were coming together, coming together again, and that we had at long last brought the boys home. "A lot of healing . . . went on," said Jan Scruggs, the wounded combat veteran who helped organize support for the memorial. And then there was this newspaper account that appeared after the ceremonies. I'd like to read it to you.

"Yesterday, crowds returned to the memorial. Among them was Herbie Petit, a machinist and former marine from New Orleans. 'Last night,' he said, standing near the wall, 'I went out to dinner with some ex-marines. There was also a group of college students in the restaurant. We started talking to each other, and before we left, they stood up and cheered. The whole week,' Petit said, his eyes red, 'it was worth it just for that.'"

It has been worth it. We Americans have learned again to listen to each other, to trust each other. We've learned that government owes the people an explanation and needs their support for its actions at home and abroad. And we've learned—and pray this time for good—that we must never again send our young men to fight and die in conflicts that our leaders are not prepared to win.

Yet, the most valuable lesson of all, the preciousness of human freedom, has been relearned not just by Americans but all the people of the world. It is the "stark lesson" that Truong Nhu Tang, one of the founders of the National Liberation Front, a former Viet Cong minister and vice-minister of the postwar Vietnamese Communist government, spoke of recently when he explained why he fled Vietnam for freedom. "No previous regime in my country," he wrote about the concentration camps and boat people of Vietnam, "brought such numbers of people to such desperation. Not the military dictators, not the colonialists, not even the ancient Chinese warlords. It is a lesson that my compatriots and I learned through witnessing and through suffering in our own lives the fate of our countrymen. It is a lesson that must eventually move the conscience of the world." This man who had fought on the other side learned the value of freedom only after helping to destroy it and seeing those who had had to give it up.

The task that has fallen to us as Americans is to move the conscience of the world, to keep alive the hope and dream of freedom. For if we fail or falter, there'll be no place for the world's oppressed to flee to. This is not a role we sought. We preach no manifest destiny. But like the Americans who brought a new nation into the world 200 years ago, history has asked much of us in our time. Much we've already given; much more we must be prepared to give.

This is not a task we shrink from; it's a task we welcome. For with the privilege of living in this kindly, pleasant, greening land called America, this land of generous spirit and great ideals, there is also a destiny and a duty, a call to preserve and hold in sacred trust mankind's age-old aspirations of peace and freedom and a better life for generations to come.

God bless you all, and thank you for what you're doing.

Source: "Remarks at the Conservative Political Action Conference Dinner," February 18, 1983, The Ronald Reagan Presidential Library. Available online. URL: http://www.reagan.utexas.edu/resource/speeches/1983/21883e.htm

21. "Evil Empire" March 8, 1983

One of the most noted addresses of Reagan's two terms in office, the so-called Evil Empire speech was delivered at the 41st Annual Convention of the National Association of Evangelicals in Orlando, Florida. The speech, written in concert with one of Reagan's most conservative speechwriters, Tony Dolan, urged the adoption of a constitutional amendment permitting prayer in public schools and the passage of "human life legislation" in Congress. In a clause frequently overlooked due to the controversy surrounding Reagan's statements about the Soviet Union, the President reminded his audience that the United States "has a legacy of evil with which it must deal . . . the long struggle of minority citizens for equal rights." But it was Reagan's comments on the nuclear freeze movement and his description of the Soviet Union as an "evil empire" that grabbed the headlines, and reinforced for some the image of Reagan as a Neanderthal intent on provoking a nuclear war. Interestingly, the speech concludes with a quotation from Thomas Paine that Reagan cited repeatedly throughout his presidency. The most radical revolutionary of the American founding was an unlikely role model for a self-described conservative, but Reagan's conservatism was of a different stripe—his eternal faith in progress and in the wisdom of the common man set him apart from many of his ideological brethren.

Reverend Clergy all, Senator Hawkins, distinguished members of the Florida congressional delegation, and all of you:

I can't tell you how you have warmed my heart with your welcome. I'm delighted to be here today.

Those of you in the National Association of Evangelicals are known for your spiritual and humanitarian work. And I would be especially remiss if I didn't discharge right now one personal debt of gratitude. Thank you for your prayers. Nancy and I have felt their presence many times in many years. And believe me, for us they've made all the difference.

The other day in the East Room of the White House at a meeting there, someone asked me whether I was aware of all the people out there who were praying for the President. And I had to say, "Yes, I am. I've felt it. I believe in intercessionary prayer." But I couldn't help but say to that questioner after he'd asked the question that—or at least say to them that if sometimes when he was praying he got a busy signal, it was just me in there ahead of him. [Laughter] I think I understand how Abraham Lincoln felt when he said, "I have been driven many times to my knees by the overwhelming conviction that I had nowhere else to go." From the joy and the good feeling of this conference, I go to a political reception. [Laughter] Now, I don't know why, but that bit of scheduling reminds me of a story—[Laughter]—which I'll share with you.

An evangelical minister and a politician arrived at Heaven's gate one day together. And St. Peter, after doing all the necessary formalities, took them in hand to show them where their quarters would be. And he took them to a small, single room with a bed, a chair, and a table and said this was for the clergyman. And the politician was a little worried about what might be in store for him. And he couldn't believe it then when St. Peter stopped in front of a beautiful mansion with lovely grounds, many servants, and told him that these would be his quarters.

And he couldn't help but ask, he said, "But wait, how—there's something wrong—how do I get this mansion while that good and holy man only gets a single room?" And St. Peter said, "You have to understand how things are up here. We've got thousands and thousands of clergy. You're the first politician who ever made it." [Laughter]

But I don't want to contribute to a stereotype. [Laughter] So I tell you there are a great many God-fearing, dedicated, noble men and women in public life, present company included. And yes, we need your help to keep us ever mindful of the ideas and the principles that brought us into the public arena in the first place. The basis of those ideals and principles is a commitment to freedom and personal liberty that, itself, is grounded in the much deeper realization that freedom prospers only where the blessings of God are avidly sought and humbly accepted.

The American experiment in democracy rests on this insight. Its discovery was the great triumph of our Founding Fathers, voiced by William Penn when he said: "If we will not be governed by God, we must be governed by tyrants." Explaining the inalienable rights of men, Jefferson said, "The God who gave us life, gave us liberty at the same time." And it was George Washington who said that "of all the disposition and habits which lead to political prosperity, religion and morality are indispensable supporters."

And finally, that shrewdest of all observers of American democracy, Alexis de Tocqueville, put it eloquently after he had gone on a search for the secret of America's greatness and genius—and he said: "Not until I went into the churches of America and heard her pulpits aflame with righteousness did I understand the greatness and the genius of America . . . America is good. And if America ever ceases to be good, America will cease to be great."

Well, I'm pleased to be here today with you who are keeping America great by keeping her good. Only through your work and prayers and those of millions of others can we hope to survive this perilous century and keep alive this experiment in liberty, this last, best hope of man.

I want you to know that this administration is motivated by a political philosophy that sees the greatness of America in you, her people, and in your families, churches, neighborhoods, communities—the Institutions that foster and nourish values like concern for others and respect for the rule of law under God.

Now, I don't have to tell you that this puts us in opposition to, or at least out of step with, a prevailing attitude of many who have turned to a modern-day secularism, discarding the tried and time-tested values upon which our very civilization is based. No matter how well intentioned, their value system is radically different from that of most Americans. And while they proclaim that they're freeing us from superstitions of the past, they've taken upon themselves the job of superintending us by government rule and regulation. Sometimes their voices are louder than ours, but they are not yet a majority.

An example of that vocal superiority is evident in a controversy now going on in Washington. And since I'm involved I've been waiting to hear from the parents of young America. How far are they willing to go in giving to government their prerogatives as parents?

Let me state the case as briefly and simply as I can. An organization of citizens, sincerely motivated and deeply concerned about the increase in illegitimate births and abortions involving girls well below the age of consent, some time ago established a nationwide network of clinics to offer help to these girls and, hopefully, alleviate this situation. Now, again, let me say, I do not fault their intent. However, in their well-intentioned effort, these clinics have decided to provide advice and birth control drugs and devices to underage girls without the knowledge of their parents.

For some years now, the federal government has helped with funds to subsidize these clinics. In providing for this, the Congress decreed that every effort would be made to maximize parental participation. Nevertheless, the drugs and devices are prescribed without getting parental consent or giving notification after they've done so. Girls termed *sexually active*—and that has replaced the word "promiscuous"—are given this help in order to prevent illegitimate birth or abortion.

Well, we have ordered clinics receiving federal funds to notify the parents such help has been given. One of the nation's leading newspapers has created the term "squeal rule" in editorializing against us for doing this, and we're being criticized for violating the privacy of young people. A judge has recently granted an injunction against an enforcement of our rule. I've watched TV panel shows discuss the issue, seen columnists pontificating on our error, but no one seems to mention morality as playing a part in the subject of sex.

Is all of Judeo-Christian tradition wrong? Are we to believe that something so sacred can be looked upon as a purely physical thing with no potential for emotional and psychological harm? And isn't it the parents' right to give counsel and advice to keep their children from making mistakes that may affect their entire lives?

Many of us in government would like to know what parents think about this intrusion in their family by government. We're going to fight in the courts. The right of parents and the rights of family take precedence over those of Washington-based bureaucrats and social engineers.

But the fight against parental notification is really only one example of many attempts to water down traditional values and even abrogate the original terms of American democracy. Freedom prospers when religion is vibrant and the rule of law under God is acknowledged. When our Founding Fathers passed the First Amendment, they sought to protect churches from government interference. They never intended to construct a wall of hostility between government and the concept of religious belief itself.

The evidence of this permeates our history and our government. The Declaration of Independence mentions the Supreme Being no less than four times. "In God We Trust" is engraved on our coinage. The Supreme Court opens its proceedings with a religious invocation. And the members of Congress open their sessions with a prayer. I just happen to believe the schoolchildren of the United States are entitled to the same privileges as Supreme Court justices and congressmen.

Last year, I sent the Congress a constitutional amendment to restore prayer to public schools. Already this session, there's growing bipartisan support for the amendment, and I am calling on the Congress to act speedily to pass it and to let our children pray.

Perhaps some of you read recently about the Lubbock school case, where a judge actually ruled that it was unconstitutional for a school district to give equal treatment to religious and nonreligious student groups, even when the group meetings were being held during the students' own time. The First Amendment never intended to require government to discriminate against religious speech.

Senators Denton and Hatfield have proposed legislation in the Congress on the whole question of prohibiting discrimination against religious forms of student speech. Such legislation could go far to restore freedom of religious speech for public school students. And I hope the Congress considers these bills quickly. And with your help, I think it's possible we could also get the constitutional amendment through the Congress this year.

More than a decade ago, a Supreme Court decision literally wiped off the books of fifty states statutes protecting the rights of unborn children. Abortion on demand now takes the lives of up to one and a half million unborn children a year. Human life legislation ending this tragedy will someday pass the Congress, and you and I must never rest until it does. Unless and until it can be proven that the unborn child is not a living entity, then its right

to life, liberty, and the pursuit of happiness must be protected.

You may remember that when abortion on demand began, many, and indeed, I'm sure many of you, warned that the practice would lead to a decline in respect for human life, that the philosophical premises used to justify abortion on demand would ultimately be used to justify other attacks on the sacredness of human life—infanticide or mercy killing. Tragically enough, those warnings proved all too true. Only last year a court permitted the death by starvation of a handicapped infant.

I have directed the Health and Human Services Department to make clear to every health care facility in the United States that the Rehabilitation Act of 1973 protects all handicapped persons against discrimination based on handicaps, including infants. And we have taken the further step of requiring that each and every recipient of federal funds who provides health care services to infants must post and keep posted in a conspicuous place a notice stating that "discriminatory failure to feed and care for handicapped infants in this facility is prohibited by federal law." It also lists a twenty-four-hour, toll-free number so that nurses and others may report violations in time to save the infant's life.

In addition, recent legislation introduced in the Congress by Representative Henry Hyde of Illinois not only increases restrictions on publicly financed abortions, it also addresses this whole problem of infanticide. I urge the Congress to begin hearings and to adopt legislation that will protect the right of life to all children, including the disabled or handicapped.

Now, I'm sure that you must get discouraged at times, but you've done better than you know, perhaps. There's a great spiritual awakening in America, a renewal of the traditional values that have been the bedrock of America's goodness and greatness.

One recent survey by a Washington-based research council concluded that Americans were far more religious than the people of other nations; 95 percent of those surveyed expressed a belief in God and a huge majority believed the Ten Commandments had real meaning in their lives. And another study has found that an overwhelming majority of Americans disapprove of adultery, teenage sex, pornography, abortion, and hard drugs. And this same study showed a deep reverence for the importance of family ties and religious belief.

I think the items that we've discussed here today must be a key part of the nation's political agenda. For the first time the Congress is openly and seriously debating and dealing with the prayer and abortion issues—and that's enormous progress right there. I repeat: America is in the midst of a spiritual awakening and a moral renewal. And with your biblical keynote, I say today, "Yes, let justice roll on like a river, righteousness like a never-failing stream."

Now, obviously, much of this new political and social consensus I've talked about is based on a positive view of American history, one that takes pride in our country's accomplishments and record. But we must never forget that no government schemes are going to perfect man. We know that living in this world means dealing with what philosophers would call the phenomenology of evil or, as theologians would put it, the doctrine of sin.

There is sin and evil in the world, and we're enjoined by Scripture and the Lord Jesus to oppose it with all our might. Our nation, too, has a legacy of evil with which it must deal. The glory of this land has been its capacity for transcending the moral evils of our past. For example, the long struggle of minority citizens for equal rights, once a source of disunity and civil war, is now a point of pride for all Americans. We must never go back. There is no room for racism, anti-Semitism, or other forms of ethnic and racial hatred in this country.

I know that you've been horrified, as have I, by the resurgence of some hate groups preaching bigotry and prejudice. Use the mighty voice of your pulpits and the powerful standing of your churches to denounce and isolate these hate groups in our midst. The commandment given us is clear and simple: "Thou shalt love thy neighbor as thyself."

But whatever sad episodes exist in our past, any objective observer must hold a positive view of American history, a history that has been the story of hopes fulfilled and dreams made into reality. Especially in this century, America has kept alight the torch of freedom, but not just for ourselves but for millions of others around the world.

And this brings me to my final point today. During my first press conference as president, in answer to a direct question, I point out that, as good Marxist-Leninists, the Soviet leaders have openly and publicly declared that the only morality they recognize is that which will further their cause, which is world revolution. I think I should point out I was only quoting Lenin, their guiding spirit, who said in 1920 that they repudiate all morality that proceeds from supernatural ideas—that's their name for religion—or ideas that are outside class conceptions. Morality is entirely subordinate to the interests of class war. And everything is moral that is necessary for the annihilation of the old, exploiting social order and for uniting the proletariat.

Well, I think the refusal of many influential people to accept this elementary fact of Soviet doctrine illustrates a historical reluctance to see totalitarian powers for what they are. We saw this phenomenon in the 1930s. We see it too often today.

This doesn't mean we should isolate ourselves and refuse to seek an understanding with them. I intend to do everything I can to persuade them of our peaceful intent, to remind them that it was the West that refused to use its nuclear monopoly in the forties and fifties for territorial gain and which now proposes a 50-percent cut in strategic ballistic missiles and the elimination of an entire class of land-based, intermediate-range nuclear missiles.

At the same time, however, they must be made to understand we will never compromise our principles and standards. We will never give away our freedom. We will never abandon our belief in God. And we will never stop searching for a genuine peace. But we can assure none of these things America stands for through the so-called nuclear freeze solutions proposed by some.

The truth is that a freeze now would be a very dangerous fraud, for that is merely the illusion of peace. The reality is that we must find peace through strength.

I would agree to freeze if only we could freeze the Soviets' global desires. A freeze at current levels of weapons would remove any incentive for the Soviets to negotiate seriously in Geneva and virtually end our chances to achieve the major arms reductions which we have proposed. Instead, they would achieve their objectives through the freeze.

A freeze would reward the Soviet Union for its enormous and unparalleled military buildup. It would prevent the essential and long overdue modernization of United States and allied defenses and would leave our aging forces increasingly vulnerable. And an honest freeze would require extensive prior negotiations on the systems and numbers to be limited and on the measures to ensure effective verification and compliance. And the kind of a freeze that has been suggested would be virtually impossible to verify. Such a major effort would divert us completely from our current negotiations on achieving substantial reductions.

A number of years ago, I heard a young father, a very prominent young man in the entertainment world, addressing a tremendous gathering in California. It was during the time of the cold war, and communism and our own way of life were very much on people's minds. And he was speaking to that subject. And suddenly, though, I heard him saying, "I love my little girls more than anything—" And I said to myself, "Oh, no, don't. You can't—don't say that." But I had underestimated him. He went on: "I would rather see my little girls die now, still believing in God, than have them grow up under communism and one day die no longer believing in God."

There were thousands of young people in that audience. They came to their feet with shouts of joy. They had instantly recognized the profound truth in what he had said, with regard to the physical and the soul and what was truly important.

Yes, let us pray for the salvation of all of those who live in that totalitarian darkness— pray they will discover the joy of knowing God. But until they do, let us be aware that while they preach the supremacy of the state, declare its omnipotence over individual man, and predict its eventual domination of all peoples on the earth, they are the focus of evil in the modern world.

It was C. S. Lewis who, in his unforgettable *Screwtape Letters*, wrote: "The greatest evil is not done now in those sordid 'dens of rime' that Dickens loved to paint. It is not even done in concentration camps and labor camps. In those we see its final result. But it is conceived and ordered (moved, seconded, carried and minuted) in clean, carpeted, warmed, and well-lighted offices, by quiet men with white collars and cut fingernails and smooth-shaven cheeks who do no need to raise their voice."

Well, because these "quiet men" do not "raise their voices," because they sometimes speak in soothing tones of brotherhood and peace, because, like other dictators before them, they're always making "their final territorial demand," some would have us accept them at their word and accommodate ourselves to their aggressive impulses. But if history teaches anything, it teaches that simpleminded appeasement or wishful thinking about our adversaries is folly. It means the betrayal of our past, the squandering of our freedom.

So, I urge you to speak out against those who would place the United States in a position of military and moral inferiority. You know, I've always believed that old Screwtape reserved his best efforts for those of you in the church. So, in your discussions of the nuclear freeze proposals, I urge you to beware the temptation of pride—the temptation of blithely declaring yourselves above it all and label both sides equally at fault, to ignore the facts of history and the aggressive impulses of an evil empire, to simply call the arms race a giant misunderstanding and thereby remove yourself from the struggle between right and wrong and good and evil.

I ask you to resist the attempts of those who would have you withhold your support for our efforts, this administration's efforts, to keep America strong and free, while we negotiate real and verifiable reductions in the world's nuclear arsenals and one day, with God's help, their total elimination.

While America's military strength is important, let me add here that I've always maintained that the struggle now going on for the world will never be decided by bombs or rockets, by armies or military might. The real crisis we face today is a spiritual one; at root, it is a test of moral will and faith.

Whittaker Chambers, the man whose own religious conversion made him a witness to one of the terrible traumas of our time, the Hiss-Chambers case, wrote that the crisis of the Western world exists to the degree in which the West is indifferent to God, the degree to which it collaborates in communism's attempt to make man stand alone without God. And then he said, for Marxism-Leninism is actually the

second-oldest faith, first proclaimed in the Garden of Eden with the words of temptation, "Ye shall be as gods."

The Western world can answer this challenge, he wrote, "but only provided that its faith in God and the freedom He enjoins is as great as communism's faith in Man."

I believe we shall rise to the challenge. I believe that communism is another sad, bizarre chapter in human history whose last pages even now are being written. I believe this because the source of our strength in the quest for human freedom is not material, but spiritual. And because it knows no limitation, it must terrify and ultimately triumph over those who would enslave their fellow man. For in the words of Isaiah: "He giveth power to the faint; and to them that have no might He increased strength . . . But they that wait upon the Lord shall renew their strength; they shall mount up with wings as eagles; they shall run, and not be weary . . ."

Yes, change your world. One of our Founding Fathers, Thomas Paine, said, "We have it within our power to begin the world over again." We can do it, doing together what no one church could do by itself.

God bless you, and thank you very much.

Source: "Remarks at the Annual Convention of the National Association of Evangelicals in Orlando, Florida," March 8, 1983, The Ronald Reagan Presidential Library. Available online. URL: http://www.reagan.utexas.edu/resource/speeches/1983/30883b.htm

22. "Star Wars" Address to the Nation on Defense and National Security March 23, 1983

Delivered just days after his "evil empire" speech, Reagan's televised address urging the development of a defensive system to intercept incoming intercontinental ballistic missiles generated an equal

amount of controversy. Reagan's announcement surprised much of the world, including some members of his own national security and foreign policy team. A visit to NORAD (North American Air Defense Command) headquarters in Colorado in July 1979 reinforced notions he had held for some time about the risk and amorality of the doctrine of mutual assured destruction, whereby both superpowers held the other's population hostage in order to maintain the peace. Reagan hoped to find a way around the "balance of terror" and believed that America's best minds could provide the technological fix to do so. His dream of "intercept[ing] and destroy[ing] strategic ballistic missiles before they reached our own soil or that of our allies" remained a highly charged issue decades later, with many members of his own party determined to deploy such a system, and members of the opposition convinced as ever that "star wars" was pure fantasy.

My fellow Americans, thank you for sharing your time with me tonight.

The subject I want to discuss with you, peace and national security, is both timely and important. Timely, because I've reached a decision which offers a new hope for our children in the 21st century, a decision I'll tell you about in a few minutes. And important because there's a very big decision that you must make for yourselves. This subject involves the most basic duty that any President and any people share, the duty to protect and strengthen the peace.

At the beginning of this year, I submitted to the Congress a defense budget which reflects my best judgment of the best understanding of the experts and specialists who advise me about what we and our allies must do to protect our people in the years ahead. That budget is much more than a long list of numbers, for behind all the numbers lies America's ability to prevent the greatest of human tragedies and preserve our free way of life in a sometimes dangerous world. It is part of a careful, long-term plan to

make America strong again after too many years of neglect and mistakes.

Our efforts to rebuild America's defenses and strengthen the peace began 2 years ago when we requested a major increase in the defense program. Since then, the amount of those increases we first proposed has been reduced by half, through improvements in management and procurement and other savings.

The budget request that is now before the Congress has been trimmed to the limits of safety. Further deep cuts cannot be made without seriously endangering the security of the Nation. The choice is up to the men and women you've elected to the Congress, and that means the choice is up to you.

Tonight, I want to explain to you what this defense debate is all about and why I'm convinced that the budget now before the Congress is necessary, responsible, and deserving of your support. And I want to offer hope for the future.

But first, let me say what the defense debate is not about. It is not about spending arithmetic. I know that in the last few weeks you've been bombarded with numbers and percentages. Some say we need only a 5-percent increase in defense spending. The so-called alternate budget backed by liberals in the House of Representatives would lower the figure to 2 to 3 percent, cutting our defense spending by $163 billion over the next 5 years. The trouble with all these numbers is that they tell us little about the kind of defense program America needs or the benefits and security and freedom that our defense effort buys for us.

What seems to have been lost in all this debate is the simple truth of how a defense budget is arrived at. It isn't done by deciding to spend a certain number of dollars. Those loud voices that are occasionally heard charging that the Government is trying to solve a security problem by throwing money at it are nothing more than noise based on ignorance. We start by considering what must be done to maintain peace and review all the possible threats against our security. Then a strategy for strengthening peace and defending against those threats must be agreed upon. And, finally, our defense establishment must be evaluated to see what is necessary to protect against any or all of the potential threats. The cost of achieving these ends is totaled up, and the result is the budget for national defense.

There is no logical way that you can say, let's spend x billion dollars less. You can only say, which part of our defense measures do we believe we can do without and still have security against all contingencies? Anyone in the Congress who advocates a percentage or a specific dollar cut in defense spending should be made to say what part of our defenses he would eliminate and he should be candid enough to acknowledge that his cuts mean cutting our commitments to allies or inviting greater risk or both.

The defense policy of the United States is based on a simple premise: The United States does not start fights. We will never be an aggressor. We maintain our strength in order to deter and defend against aggression—to preserve freedom and peace.

Since the dawn of the atomic age, we've sought to reduce the risk of war by maintaining a strong deterrent and by seeking genuine arms control. "Deterrence" means simply this: making sure any adversary who thinks about attacking the United States, or our allies, or our vital interests, concludes that the risks to him outweigh any potential gains. Once he understands that, he won't attack. We maintain the peace through our strength; weakness only invites aggression.

This strategy of deterrence has not changed. It still works. But what it takes to maintain deterrence has changed. It took one kind of military force to deter an attack when

we had far more nuclear weapons than any other power; it takes another kind now that the Soviets, for example, have enough accurate and powerful nuclear weapons to destroy virtually all of our missiles on the ground. Now, this is not to say that the Soviet Union is planning to make war on us. Nor do I believe a war is inevitable—quite the contrary. But what must be recognized is that our security is based on being prepared to meet all threats.

There was a time when we depended on coastal forts and artillery batteries, because, with the weaponry of that day, any attack would have had to come by sea. Well, this is a different world, and our defenses must be based on recognition and awareness of the weaponry possessed by other nations in the nuclear age.

We can't afford to believe that we will never be threatened. There have been two world wars in my lifetime. We didn't start them and, indeed, did everything we could to avoid being drawn into them. But we were ill-prepared for both. Had we been better prepared, peace might have been preserved.

For 20 years the Soviet Union has been accumulating enormous military might. They didn't stop when their forces exceeded all requirements of a legitimate defensive capability. And they haven't stopped now. During the past decade and a half, the Soviets have built up a massive arsenal of new strategic nuclear weapons—weapons that can strike directly at the United States.

As an example, the United States introduced its last new intercontinental ballistic missile, the Minute Man III, in 1969, and we're now dismantling our even older Titan missiles. But what has the Soviet Union done in these intervening years? Well, since 1969 the Soviet Union has built five new classes of ICBM's, and upgraded these eight times As a result, their missiles are much more powerful and accurate than they were several years ago, and they continue to develop more, while ours are increasingly obsolete.

The same thing has happened in other areas. Over the same period, the Soviet Union built 4 new classes of submarine-launched ballistic missiles and over 60 new missile submarines. We built 2 new types of submarine missiles and actually withdrew 10 submarines from strategic missions. The Soviet Union built over 200 new Backfire bombers, and their brand new Blackjack bomber is now under development. We haven't built a new long-range bomber since our B-52's were deployed about a quarter of a century ago, and we've already retired several hundred of those because of old age. Indeed, despite what many people think, our strategic forces only cost about 15 percent of the defense budget.

Another example of what's happened: in 1978 the Soviets had 600 intermediate-range nuclear missiles based on land and were beginning to add the SS-20—a new, highly accurate, mobile missile with 3 warheads. We had none. Since then the Soviets have strengthened their lead. By the end of 1979, when Soviet leader Brezhnev declared "a balance now exists," the Soviets had over 800 warheads. We still had none. A year ago this month, Mr. Brezhnev pledged a moratorium, or freeze, on SS-20 deployment. But by last August, their 800 warheads had become more than 1,200. We still had none. Some freeze. At this time Soviet Defense Minister Ustinov announced "approximate parity of forces continues to exist." But the Soviets are still adding an average of 3 new warheads a week, and now have 1,300. These warheads can reach their targets in a matter of a few minutes. We still have none. So far, it seems that the Soviet definition of parity is a box score of 1,300 to nothing, in their favor.

So, together with our NATO allies, we decided in 1979 to deploy new weapons, beginning this year, as a deterrent to their SS-20s and as an incentive to the Soviet Union to meet us in serious arms control negotiations. We will begin that deployment late this year. At the same time, however, we're willing to cancel our program if the Soviets will dismantle theirs. This is what we've called a zero-zero plan. The Soviets are now at the negotiating table—and I think it's fair to say that without our planned deployments, they wouldn't be there.

Now let's consider conventional forces. Since 1974 the United States has produced 3,050 tactical combat aircraft. By contrast, the Soviet Union has produced twice as many. When we look at attack submarines, the United States has produced 27 while the Soviet Union has produced 61. For armored vehicles, including tanks, we have produced 11,200. The Soviet Union has produced 54,000—nearly 5 to 1 in their favor. Finally, with artillery, we've produced 950 artillery and rocket launchers while the Soviets have produced more than 13,000—a staggering 14-to-1 ratio.

There was a time when we were able to offset superior Soviet numbers with higher quality, but today they are building weapons as sophisticated and modern as our own.

As the Soviets have increased their military power, they've been emboldened to extend that power. They're spreading their military influence in ways that can directly challenge our vital interests and those of our allies.

The following aerial photographs, most of them secret until now, illustrate this point in a crucial area very close to home: Central America and the Caribbean Basin. They're not dramatic photographs. But I think they help give you a better understanding of what I'm talking about.

This Soviet intelligence collection facility, less than a hundred miles from our coast, is the largest of its kind in the world. The acres and acres of antennae fields and intelligence monitors are targeted on key U.S. military installations and sensitive activities. The installation in Lourdes, Cuba, is manned by 1,500 Soviet technicians. And the satellite ground station allows instant communications with Moscow. This 28 square-mile facility has grown by more than 60 percent in size and capability during the past decade.

In western Cuba, we see this military airfield and its complement of modern, Soviet-built Mig-23 aircraft. The Soviet Union uses this Cuban airfield for its own long-range reconnaissance missions. And earlier this month, two modern Soviet antisubmarine warfare aircraft began operating from it. During the past 2 years, the level of Soviet arms exports to Cuba can only be compared to the levels reached during the Cuban missile crisis 20 years ago.

This third photo, which is the only one in this series that has been previously made public, shows Soviet military hardware that has made its way to Central America. This airfield with its Ml-8 helicopters, anti-aircraft guns, and protected fighter sites is one of a number of military facilities in Nicaragua which has received Soviet equipment funneled through Cuba, and reflects the massive military buildup going on in that country.

On the small island of Grenada, at the southern end of the Caribbean chain, the Cubans, with Soviet financing and backing, are in the process of building an airfield with a 10,000-foot runway. Grenada doesn't even have an air force. Who is it intended for? The Caribbean is a very important passageway for our international commerce and military lines of communication. More than half of all American oil imports now pass through the Caribbean. The rapid buildup of Grenada's military potential is unrelated to any conceivable threat to this island country of under 110,000 people and totally at odds with the pattern of other eastern Caribbean States, most of which are unarmed.

The Soviet-Cuban militarization of Grenada, in short, can only be seen as power projection into the region. And it is in this important economic and strategic area that we're trying to help the Governments of El Salvador, Costa Rica, Honduras, and others in their struggles for democracy against guerrillas supported through Cuba and Nicaragua.

These pictures only tell a small part of the story. I wish I could show you more without compromising our most sensitive intelligence sources and methods. But the Soviet Union is also supporting Cuban military forces in Angola and Ethiopia. They have bases in Ethiopia and South Yemen, near the Persian Gulf oil fields. They've taken over the port that we built at Cam Ranh Bay in Vietnam. And now for the first time in history, the Soviet Navy is a force to be reckoned with in the South Pacific.

Some people may still ask: Would the Soviets ever use their formidable military power? Well, again, can we afford to believe they won't? There is Afghanistan. And in Poland, the Soviets denied the will of the people and in so doing demonstrated to the world how their military power could also be used to intimidate.

The final fact is that the Soviet Union is acquiring what can only be considered an offensive military force. They have continued to build far more intercontinental ballistic missiles than they could possibly need simply to deter an attack. Their conventional forces are trained and equipped not so much to defend against an attack as they are to permit sudden, surprise offensives of their own.

Our NATO allies have assumed a great defense burden, including the military draft in most countries. We're working with them and our other friends around the world to do more. Our defensive strategy means we need military forces that can move very quickly, forces that are trained and ready to respond to any emergency.

Every item in our defense program—our ships, our tanks, our planes, our funds for training and spare parts—is intended for one all-important purpose: to keep the peace.

Unfortunately, a decade of neglecting our military forces had called into question our ability to do that.

When I took office in January 1981, I was appalled by what I found: American planes that couldn't fly and American ships that couldn't sail for lack of spare parts and trained personnel and insufficient fuel and ammunition for essential training. The inevitable result of all this was poor morale in our Armed Forces, difficulty in recruiting the brightest young Americans to wear the uniform, and difficulty in convincing our most experienced military personnel to stay on.

There was a real question then about how well we could meet a crisis. And it was obvious that we had to begin a major modernization program to ensure we could deter aggression and preserve the peace in the years ahead.

We had to move immediately to improve the basic readiness and staying power of our conventional forces, so they could meet—and therefore help deter—a crisis. We had to make up for lost years of investment by moving forward with a long-term plan to prepare our forces to counter the military capabilities our adversaries were developing for the future.

I know that all of you want peace, and so do I. I know too that many of you seriously believe that a nuclear freeze would further the cause of peace. But a freeze now would make us less, not more, secure and would raise, not reduce, the risks of war. It would be largely unverifiable and would seriously undercut our negotiations on arms reduction. It would reward the Soviets for their massive military buildup while preventing us from modernizing our aging and increasingly vulnerable forces. With their present margin of superiority, why should they agree to arms reductions knowing that we were prohibited from catching up?

Believe me, it wasn't pleasant for someone who had come to Washington determined to reduce government spending, but we had to move forward with the task of repairing our defenses or we would lose our ability to deter conflict now and in the future. We had to demonstrate to any adversary that aggression could not succeed, and that the only real solution was substantial, equitable, and effectively verifiable arms reduction—the kind we're working for right now in Geneva.

Thanks to your strong support, and bipartisan support from the Congress, we began to turn things around. Already, we're seeing some very encouraging results. Quality recruitment and retention are up dramatically—more high school graduates are choosing military careers, and more experienced career personnel are choosing to stay. Our men and women in uniform at last are getting the tools and training they need to do their jobs.

Ask around today, especially among our young people, and I think you will find a whole new attitude toward serving their country. This reflects more than just better pay, equipment, and leadership. You the American people have sent a signal to these young people that it is once again an honor to wear the uniform. That's not something you measure in a budget, but it's a very real part of our nation's strength.

It'll take us longer to build the kind of equipment we need to keep peace in the future, but we've made a good start.

We haven't built a new long-range bomber for 21 years. Now we're building the B-1. We hadn't launched one new strategic submarine for 17 years. Now we're building one Trident submarine a year. Our land-based missiles are increasingly threatened by the many huge, new Soviet ICBM's. We're determining how to solve that problem. At the same time, we're working in the START and INF negotiations with the goal of achieving deep reductions in the strategic and intermediate nuclear arsenals of both sides.

We have also begun the long-needed modernization of our conventional forces. The Army is getting its first new tank in 20 years.

The Air Force is modernizing. We're rebuilding our Navy, which shrank from about a thousand ships in the late 1960's to 453 during the 1970's. Our nation needs a superior navy to support our military forces and vital interests overseas. We're now on the road to achieving a 600-ship navy and increasing the amphibious capabilities of our marines, who are now serving the cause of peace in Lebanon. And we're building a real capability to assist our friends in the vitally important Indian Ocean and Persian Gulf region.

This adds up to a major effort, and it isn't cheap. It comes at a time when there are many other pressures on our budget and when the American people have already had to make major sacrifices during the recession. But we must not be misled by those who would make defense once again the scapegoat of the Federal budget.

The fact is that in the past few decades we have seen a dramatic shift in how we spend the taxpayer's dollar. Back in 1955, payments to individuals took up only about 20 percent of the Federal budget. For nearly three decades, these payments steadily increased and, this year, will account for 49 percent of the budget. By contrast, in 1955 defense took up more than half of the Federal budget. By 1980 this spending had fallen to a low of 23 percent. Even with the increase that I am requesting this year, defense will still amount to only 28 percent of the budget.

The calls for cutting back the defense budget come in nice, simple arithmetic. They're the same kind of talk that led the democracies to neglect their defenses in the 1930's and invited the tragedy of World War II. We must not let that grim chapter of history repeat itself through apathy or neglect.

This is why I'm speaking to you tonight to urge you to tell your Senators and Congressmen that you know we must continue to restore our military strength. If we stop in midstream, we will send a signal of decline, of less-ened will, to friends and adversaries alike. Free people must voluntarily, through open debate and democratic means, meet the challenge that totalitarians pose by compulsion. It's up to us, in our time, to choose and choose wisely between the hard but necessary task of preserving peace and freedom and the temptation to ignore our duty and blindly hope for the best while the enemies of freedom grow stronger day by day.

The solution is well within our grasp. But to reach it, there is simply no alternative but to continue this year, in this budget, to provide the resources we need to preserve the peace and guarantee our freedom.

Now, thus far tonight I've shared with you my thoughts on the problems of national security we must face together. My predecessors in the Oval Office have appeared before you on other occasions to describe the threat posed by Soviet power and have proposed steps to address that threat. But since the advent of nuclear weapons, those steps have been increasingly directed toward deterrence of aggression through the promise of retaliation.

This approach to stability through offensive threat has worked. We and our allies have succeeded in preventing nuclear war for more than three decades. In recent months, however, my advisers, including in particular the Joint Chiefs of Staff, have underscored the necessity to break out of a future that relies solely on offensive retaliation for our security.

Over the course of these discussions, I've become more and more deeply convinced that the human spirit must be capable of rising above dealing with other nations and human beings by threatening their existence. Feeling this way, I believe we must thoroughly examine every opportunity for reducing tensions and for introducing greater stability into the strategic calculus on both sides.

One of the most important contributions we can make is, of course, to lower the level of all arms, and particularly nuclear arms. We're engaged right now in several negotiations with the Soviet Union to bring about a mutual reduction of weapons. I will report to you a week from tomorrow my thoughts on that score. But let me just say, I'm totally committed to this course.

If the Soviet Union will join with us in our effort to achieve major arms reduction we will have succeeded in stabilizing the nuclear balance. Nevertheless, it will still be necessary to rely on the specter of retaliation, on mutual threat. And that's a sad commentary on the human condition. Wouldn't it be better to save lives than to avenge them? Are we not capable of demonstrating our peaceful intentions by applying all our abilities and our ingenuity to achieving a truly lasting stability? I think we are. Indeed, we must.

After careful consultation with my advisers, including the Joint Chiefs of Staff, I believe there is a way. Let me share with you a vision of the future which offers hope. It is that we embark on a program to counter the awesome Soviet missile threat with measures that are defensive. Let us turn to the very strengths in technology that spawned our great industrial base and that have given us the quality of life we enjoy today.

What if free people could live secure in the knowledge that their security did not rest upon the threat of instant U.S. retaliation to deter a Soviet attack, that we could intercept and destroy strategic ballistic missiles before they reached our own soil or that of our allies?

I know this is a formidable, technical task, one that may not be accomplished before the end of this century. Yet, current technology has attained a level of sophistication where it's reasonable for us to begin this effort. It will take years, probably decades of effort on many fronts. There will be failures and setbacks, just as there will be successes and breakthroughs. And as we proceed, we must remain constant in preserving the nuclear deterrent and maintaining a solid capability for flexible response. But isn't it worth every investment necessary to free the world from the threat of nuclear war? We know it is.

In the meantime, we will continue to pursue real reductions in nuclear arms, negotiating from a position of strength that can be ensured only by modernizing our strategic forces. At the same time, we must take steps to reduce the risk of a conventional military conflict escalating to nuclear war by improving our nonnuclear capabilities.

America does possess now the technologies to attain very significant improvements in the effectiveness of our conventional, nonnuclear forces. Proceeding boldly with these new technologies, we can significantly reduce any incentive that the Soviet Union may have to threaten attack against the United States or its allies.

As we pursue our goal of defensive technologies, we recognize that our allies rely upon our strategic offensive power to deter attacks against them. Their vital interests and ours are inextricably linked. Their safety and ours are one. And no change in technology can or will alter that reality. We must and shall continue to honor our commitments.

I clearly recognize that defensive systems have limitations and raise certain problems and ambiguities. If paired with offensive systems, they can be viewed as fostering an aggressive policy, and no one wants that. But with these considerations firmly in mind, I call upon the scientific community in our country, those who gave us nuclear weapons, to turn their great talents now to the cause of mankind and world peace, to give us the means of rendering these nuclear weapons impotent and obsolete.

Tonight, consistent with our obligations of the ABM treaty and recognizing the need for closer consultation with our allies, I'm taking an important first step. I am directing a comprehensive and intensive effort to define a long-term research and development program to begin to achieve our ultimate goal of eliminating the threat posed by strategic nuclear missiles. This could pave the way for arms control measures to eliminate the weapons themselves. We seek neither military superiority nor political advantage. Our only purpose—one all people share—is to search for ways to reduce the danger of nuclear war.

My fellow Americans, tonight we're launching an effort which holds the promise of changing the course of human history. There will be risks, and results take time. But I believe we can do it. As we cross this threshold, I ask for your prayers and your support.

Thank you, good night, and God bless you.

Source: "Address to the Nation on Defense and National Security," March 23, 1983, The Ronald Reagan Presidential Library. Available online. URL: http://www.reagan.utexas.edu/resource/speeches/1983/32383d.htm

23. Address Before a Joint Session of the Congress on Central America April 27, 1983

One of Reagan's toughest "sells" as president was convincing Congress and the American people that the Sandinista government of Nicaragua was a threat to the nation's security, and that the government of El Salvador deserved the country's support. A majority of congressional Democrats saw U.S. intervention in Central America as yet another episode in a long history of imperialism, and were dismayed at reports of human rights abuses by the CIA-backed contras and the right-wing death squads operating in El Salvador. Reagan tended to view Central America through the prism of the cold war, and saw ominous signs in the assistance provided to the Sandinistas and the rebels in El Salvador by the Soviet Union and Cuba. Reagan considered the contras to be the moral equivalent of America's founding fathers, and through his CIA director William

Casey, engaged in a pitched, six-year struggle to maintain that force in the field. In the end, Reagan and Casey lost the struggle for control of American policy in Central America, and came perilously close to jeopardizing his presidency as well.

Mr. Speaker, Mr. President, distinguished Members of the Congress, honored guests, and my fellow Americans:

A number of times in past years, Members of Congress and a President have come together in meetings like this to resolve a crisis. I have asked for this meeting in the hope that we can prevent one.

It would be hard to find many Americans who aren't aware of our stake in the Middle East, the Persian Gulf, or the NATO line dividing the free world from the Communist bloc. And the same could be said for Asia.

But in spite of, or maybe because of, a flurry of stories about places like Nicaragua and El Salvador and, yes, some concerted propaganda, many of us find it hard to believe we have a stake in problems involving those countries. Too many have thought of Central America as just that place way down below Mexico that can't possibly constitute a threat to our well-being. And that's why I've asked for this session. Central America's problems do directly affect the security and the well-being of our own people. And Central America is much closer to the United States than many of the world troublespots that concern us. So, as we work to restore our own economy, we cannot afford to lose sight of our neighbors to the south.

El Salvador is nearer to Texas than Texas is to Massachusetts. Nicaragua is just as close to Miami, San Antonio, San Diego, and Tucson as those cities are to Washington, where we're gathered tonight.

But nearness on the map doesn't even begin to tell the strategic importance of Central America, bordering as it does on the

Caribbean—our lifeline to the outside world. Two-thirds of all our foreign trade and petroleum pass through the Panama Canal and the Caribbean. In a European crisis at least half of our supplies for NATO would go through these areas by sea. It's well to remember that in early 1942, a handful of Hitler's submarines sank more tonnage there than in all of the Atlantic Ocean. And they did this without a single naval base anywhere in the area. And today, the situation is different. Cuba is host to a Soviet combat brigade, a submarine base capable of servicing Soviet submarines, and military air bases visited regularly by Soviet military aircraft.

Because of its importance, the Caribbean Basin is a magnet for adventurism. We're all aware of the Libyan cargo planes refueling in Brazil a few days ago on their way to deliver "medical supplies" to Nicaragua. Brazilian authorities discovered the so-called medical supplies were actually munitions and prevented their delivery.

You may remember that last month, speaking on national television, I showed an aerial photo of an airfield being built on the island of Grenada. Well, if that airfield had been completed, those planes could have refueled there and completed their journey.

If the Nazis during World War II and the Soviets today could recognize the Caribbean and Central America as vital to our interests, shouldn't we, also? For several years now, under two administrations, the United States has been increasing its defense of freedom in the Caribbean Basin. And I can tell you tonight, democracy is beginning to take root in El Salvador, which, until a short time ago, knew only dictatorship.

The new government is now delivering on its promises of democracy, reforms, and free elections. It wasn't easy, and there was resistance to many of the attempted reforms, with assassinations of some of the reformers. Guerrilla bands and urban terrorists were portrayed in a worldwide propaganda campaign as freedom fighters, representative of the people. Ten days before I came into office, the guerrillas launched what they called "a final offensive" to overthrow the government. And their radio boasted that our new administration would be too late to prevent their victory.

Well, they learned that democracy cannot be so easily defeated. President Carter did not hesitate. He authorized arms and munitions to El Salvador. The guerrilla offensive failed, but not America's will. Every President since this country assumed global responsibilities has known that those responsibilities could only be met if we pursued a bipartisan foreign policy.

As I said a moment ago, the Government of El Salvador has been keeping its promises, like the land reform program which is making thousands of farm tenants, farm owners. In a little over 3 years, 20 percent of the arable land in El Salvador has been redistributed to more than 450,000 people. That's one in ten Salvadorans who have benefited directly from this program.

El Salvador has continued to strive toward an orderly and democratic society. The government promised free elections. On March 28th, a little more than a year ago, after months of campaigning by a variety of candidates, the suffering people of El Salvador were offered a chance to vote, to choose the kind of government they wanted. And suddenly, the so-called freedom fighters in the hills were exposed for what they really are—a small minority who want power for themselves and their backers, not democracy for the people. The guerrillas threatened death to anyone who voted. They destroyed hundreds of buses and trucks to keep the people from getting to the polling places. Their slogan was brutal: "Vote today, die tonight." But on election day, an unprecedented 80 percent of the electorate braved ambush and gunfire and trudged for miles, many of them, to vote for freedom. Now, that's truly fighting for freedom. We can never turn our backs on that.

Members of this Congress who went there as observers told me of a woman who was wounded by rifle fire on the way to the polls, who refused to leave the line to have her wound treated until after she had voted. Another woman had been told by the guerrillas that she would be killed when she returned from the polls, and she told the guerrillas, "You can kill me, you can kill my family, you can kill my neighbors. You can't kill us all." The real freedom fighters of El Salvador turned out to be the people of that country—the young, the old, the in-between—more than a million of them out of a population of less than 5 million. The world should respect this courage and not allow it to be belittled or forgotten. And again I say, in good conscience, we can never turn our backs on that.

The democratic political parties and factions in El Salvador are coming together around the common goal of seeking a political solution to their country's problems. New national elections will be held this year, and they will be open to all political parties. The government has invited the guerrillas to participate in the election and is preparing an amnesty law. The people of El Salvador are earning their freedom, and they deserve our moral and material support to protect it.

Yes, there are still major problems regarding human rights, the criminal justice system, and violence against noncombatants. And, like the rest of Central America, El Salvador also faces severe economic problems. But in addition to recession-depressed prices for major agricultural exports, El Salvador's economy is being deliberately sabotaged.

Tonight in El Salvador—because of ruthless guerrilla attacks—much of the fertile land cannot be cultivated; less than half the rolling stock of the railways remains operational; bridges, water facilities, telephone and electric

systems have been destroyed and damaged. In one 22-month period, there were 5,000 interruptions of electrical power. One region was without electricity for a third of the year.

I think Secretary of State Shultz put it very well the other day: "Unable to win the free loyalty of El Salvador's people, the guerrillas," he said, "are deliberately and systematically depriving them of food, water, transportation, light, sanitation, and jobs. And these are the people who claim they want to help the common people." They don't want elections because they know they'd be defeated. But, as the previous election showed, the Salvadoran people's desire for democracy will not be defeated.

The guerrillas are not embattled peasants, armed with muskets. They're professionals, sometimes with better training and weaponry than the government's soldiers. The Salvadoran battalions that have received U.S. training have been conducting themselves well on the battlefield and with the civilian population. But so far, we've only provided enough money to train one Salvadoran soldier out of ten, fewer than the number of guerrillas that are trained by Nicaragua and Cuba.

And let me set the record straight on Nicaragua, a country next to El Salvador. In 1979 when the new government took over in Nicaragua, after a revolution which overthrew the authoritarian rule of Somoza, everyone hoped for the growth of democracy. We in the United States did, too. By January of 1981, our emergency relief and recovery aid to Nicaragua totaled $118 million—more than provided by any other developed country. In fact, in the first 2 years of Sandinista rule, the United States directly or indirectly sent five times more aid to Nicaragua than it had in the 2 years prior to the revolution. Can anyone doubt the generosity and the good faith of the American people?

These were hardly the actions of a nation implacably hostile to Nicaragua. Yet, the Government of Nicaragua has treated us as an enemy. It has rejected our repeated peace efforts. It has broken its promises to us, to the Organization of American States and, most important of all, to the people of Nicaragua.

No sooner was victory achieved than a small clique ousted others who had been part of the revolution from having any voice in the government. Humberto Ortega, the Minister of Defense, declared Marxism-Leninism would be their guide, and so it is.

The Government of Nicaragua has imposed a new dictatorship. It has refused to hold the elections it promised. It has seized control of most media and subjects all media to heavy prior censorship. It denied the bishops and priests of the Roman Catholic Church the right to say Mass on radio during Holy Week. It insulted and mocked the Pope. It has driven the Miskito Indians from their homelands, burning their villages, destroying their crops, and forcing them into involuntary internment camps far from home. It has moved against the private sector and free labor unions. It condoned mob action against Nicaragua's independent human rights commission and drove the director of that commission into exile.

In short, after all these acts of repression by the government, is it any wonder that opposition has formed? Contrary to propaganda, the opponents of the Sandinistas are not diehard supporters of the previous Somoza regime. In fact, many are anti-Somoza heroes and fought beside the Sandinistas to bring down the Somoza government. Now they've been denied any part in the new government because they truly wanted democracy for Nicaragua and they still do. Others are Miskito Indians fighting for their homes, their lands, and their lives.

The Sandinista revolution in Nicaragua turned out to be just an exchange of one set of autocratic rulers for another, and the people still have no freedom, no democratic rights, and more poverty. Even worse than its predecessor,

it is helping Cuba and the Soviets to destabilize our hemisphere.

Meanwhile, the Government of El Salvador, making every effort to guarantee democracy, free labor unions, freedom of religion, and a free press, is under attack by guerrillas dedicated to the same philosophy that prevails in Nicaragua, Cuba, and, yes, the Soviet Union. Violence has been Nicaragua's most important export to the world. It is the ultimate in hypocrisy for the unelected Nicaraguan Government to charge that we seek their overthrow, when they're doing everything they can to bring down the elected Government of El Salvador. [Applause] Thank you. The guerrilla attacks are directed from a headquarters in Managua, the capital of Nicaragua.

But let us be clear as to the American attitude toward the Government of Nicaragua. We do not seek its overthrow. Our interest is to ensure that it does not infect its neighbors through the export of subversion and violence. Our purpose, in conformity with American and international law, is to prevent the flow of arms to El Salvador, Honduras, Guatemala, and Costa Rica. We have attempted to have a dialog with the Government of Nicaragua, but it persists in its efforts to spread violence.

We should not, and we will not, protect the Nicaraguan Government from the anger of its own people. But we should, through diplomacy, offer an alternative. And as Nicaragua ponders its options, we can and will—with all the resources of diplomacy—protect each country of Central America from the danger of war.

Even Costa Rica, Central America's oldest and strongest democracy—a government so peaceful it doesn't even have an army—is the object of bullying and threats from Nicaragua's dictators.

Nicaragua's neighbors know that Sandinista promises of peace, nonalliance, and nonintervention have not been kept. Some 36 new military bases have been built. There were only 13 during the Somoza years. Nicaragua's new army numbers 25,000 men, supported by a militia of 50,000. It is the largest army in Central America, supplemented by 2,000 Cuban military and security advisers. It is equipped with the most modern weapons—dozens of Soviet-made tanks, 800 Soviet-bloc trucks, Soviet 152-millimeter howitzers, 100 anti-aircraft guns, plus planes and helicopters. There are additional thousands of civilian advisers from Cuba, the Soviet Union, East Germany, Libya, and the PLO. And we're attacked because we have 55 military trainers in El Salvador.

The goal of the professional guerrilla movements in Central America is as simple as it is sinister: to destabilize the entire region from the Panama Canal to Mexico. And if you doubt beyond this point, just consider what Cayetano Carpio, the now-deceased Salvadoran guerrilla leader, said earlier this month. Carpio said that after El Salvador falls, El Salvador and Nicaragua would be "arm-in-arm and struggling for the total liberation of Central America."

Nicaragua's dictatorial junta, who themselves made war and won power operating from bases in Honduras and Costa Rica, like to pretend that they are today being attacked by forces based in Honduras. The fact is, it is Nicaragua's government that threatens Honduras, not the reverse. It is Nicaragua who has moved heavy tanks close to the border, and Nicaragua who speaks of war. It was Nicaraguan radio that announced on April 8th the creation of a new, unified, revolutionary coordinating board to push forward the Marxist struggle in Honduras.

Nicaragua, supported by weapons and military resources provided by the Communist bloc, represses its own people, refuses to make peace, and sponsors a guerrilla war against El Salvador.

President Truman's words are as apt today as they were in 1947 when he, too, spoke before a joint session of the Congress:

"At the present moment in world history, nearly every nation must choose between alternate ways of life. The choice is not too often a free one. One way of life is based upon the will of the majority and is distinguished by free institutions, representative government, free elections, guarantees of individual liberty, freedom of speech and religion, and freedom from political oppression. The second way of life is based upon the will of a minority forcibly imposed upon the majority. It relies upon terror and oppression, a controlled press and radio, fixed elections, and the suppression of personal freedoms.

"I believe that it must be the policy of the United States to support free peoples who are resisting attempted subjugation by armed minorities or by outside pressures. I believe that we must assist free peoples to work out their own destinies in their own way. I believe that our help should be primarily through economic and financial aid which is essential to economic stability and orderly political processes.

"Collapse of free institutions and loss of independence would be disastrous not only for them but for the world. Discouragement and possibly failure would quickly be the lot of neighboring peoples striving to maintain their freedom and independence."

The countries of Central America are smaller than the nations that prompted President Truman's message. But the political and strategic stakes are the same. Will our response—economic, social, military—be as appropriate and successful as Mr. Truman's bold solutions to the problems of postwar Europe?

Some people have forgotten the successes of those years and the decades of peace, prosperity, and freedom they secured. Some people talk as though the United States were incapable of acting effectively in international affairs without risking war or damaging those we seek to help.

Are democracies required to remain passive while threats to their security and prosperity accumulate? Must we just accept the destabilization of an entire region from the Panama Canal to Mexico on our southern border? Must we sit by while independent nations of this hemisphere are integrated into the most aggressive empire the modern world has seen? Must we wait while Central Americans are driven from their homes like the more than a million who've sought refuge out of Afghanistan, or the 1 1/2 million who have fled Indochina, or the more than a million Cubans who have fled Castro's Caribbean utopia? Must we, by default, leave the people of El Salvador no choice but to flee their homes, creating another tragic human exodus?

I don't believe there's a majority in the Congress or the country that counsels passivity, resignation, defeatism, in the face of this challenge to freedom and security in our own hemisphere. [Applause] Thank you. Thank you.

I do not believe that a majority of the Congress or the country is prepared to stand by passively while the people of Central America are delivered to totalitarianism and we ourselves are left vulnerable to new dangers.

Only last week, an official of the Soviet Union reiterated Brezhnev's threat to station nuclear missiles in this hemisphere, 5 minutes from the United States. Like an echo, Nicaragua's Commandante Daniel Ortega confirmed that, if asked, his country would consider accepting those missiles. I understand that today they may be having second thoughts.

Now, before I go any further, let me say to those who invoke the memory of Vietnam, there is no thought of sending American combat troops to Central America. They are not needed—[applause]—

Thank you. And, as I say, they are not needed and, indeed, they have not been requested there. All our neighbors ask of us is assistance in training and arms to protect themselves while they build a better, freer life.

We must continue to encourage peace among the nations of Central America. We must support the regional efforts now underway to promote solutions to regional problems.

We cannot be certain that the Marxist-Leninist bands who believe war is an instrument of politics will be readily discouraged. It's crucial that we not become discouraged before they do. Otherwise, the region's freedom will be lost and our security damaged in ways that can hardly be calculated.

If Central America were to fall, what would the consequences be for our position in Asia, Europe, and for alliances such as NATO? If the United States cannot respond to a threat near our own borders, why should Europeans or Asians believe that we're seriously concerned about threats to them? If the Soviets can assume that nothing short of an actual attack on the United States will provoke an American response, which ally, which friend will trust us then?

The Congress shares both the power and the responsibility for our foreign policy. Tonight, I ask you, the Congress, to join me in a bold, generous approach to the problems of peace and poverty, democracy and dictatorship in the region. Join me in a program that prevents Communist victory in the short run, but goes beyond, to produce for the deprived people of the area the reality of present progress and the promise of more to come.

Let us lay the foundation for a bipartisan approach to sustain the independence and freedom of the countries of Central America. We in the administration reach out to you in this spirit.

We will pursue four basic goals in Central America:

First, in response to decades of inequity and indifference, we will support democracy, reform, and human freedom. This means using our assistance, our powers of persuasion, and our legitimate leverage to bolster humane democratic systems where they already exist and to help countries on their way to that goal complete the process as quickly as human institutions can be changed. Elections in El Salvador and also in Nicaragua must be open to all, fair and safe. The international community must help. We will work at human rights problems, not walk away from them.

Second, in response to the challenge of world recession and, in the case of El Salvador, to the unrelenting campaign of economic sabotage by the guerrillas, we will support economic development. And by a margin of 2 to 1 our aid is economic now, not military. Seventy-seven cents out of every dollar we will spend in the area this year goes for food, fertilizers, and other essentials for economic growth and development. And our economic program goes beyond traditional aid. The Caribbean Initiative introduced in the House earlier today will provide powerful trade and investment incentives to help these countries achieve self-sustaining economic growth without exporting U.S. jobs. Our goal must be to focus our immense and growing technology to enhance health care, agriculture, industry, and to ensure that we who inhabit this interdependent region come to know and understand each other better, retaining our diverse identities, respecting our diverse traditions and institutions.

And, third, in response to the military challenge from Cuba and Nicaragua—to their deliberate use of force to spread tyranny—we will support the security of the region's threatened nations. We do not view security assistance as an end in itself, but as a shield for democratization, economic development, and diplomacy. No amount of reform will bring peace so long as guerrillas believe they will win by force. No amount of economic help will suffice if guerrilla units can destroy roads and bridges and power stations and crops, again and again, with impunity. But with better training and material help, our neighbors can hold off the guerrillas and give democratic reform time to take root.

And, fourth, we will support dialog and negotiations both among the countries of the region and within each country. The terms and conditions of participation in elections are negotiable. Costa Rica is a shining example of democracy. Honduras has made the move from military rule to democratic government. Guatemala is pledged to the same course. The United States will work toward a political solution in Central America which will serve the interests of the democratic process.

To support these diplomatic goals, I offer these assurances: The United States will support any agreement among Central American countries for the withdrawal, under fully verifiable and reciprocal conditions, of all foreign military and security advisers and troops. We want to help opposition groups join the political process in all countries and compete by ballots instead of bullets. We will support any verifiable, reciprocal agreement among Central American countries on the renunciation of support for insurgencies on neighbors' territory. And, finally, we desire to help Central America end its costly arms race and will support any verifiable, reciprocal agreements on the nonimportation of offensive weapons.

To move us toward these goals more rapidly, I am tonight announcing my intention to name an Ambassador at Large as my special envoy to Central America. He or she will report to me through the Secretary of State. The Ambassador's responsibilities will be to lend U.S. support to the efforts of regional governments to bring peace to this troubled area and to work closely with the Congress to assure the fullest possible, bipartisan coordination of our policies toward the region.

What I'm asking for is prompt congressional approval for the full reprogramming of funds for key current economic and security programs so that the people of Central America can hold the line against externally supported aggression. In addition, I am asking for prompt action on the supplemental request in these same areas to carry us through the current fiscal year and for early and favorable congressional action on my requests for fiscal year 1984.

And finally, I am asking that the bipartisan consensus, which last year acted on the trade and tax provisions of the Caribbean Basin Initiative in the House, again take the lead to move this vital proposal to the floor of both Chambers. And, as I said before, the greatest share of these requests is targeted toward economic and humanitarian aid, not military.

What the administration is asking for on behalf of freedom in Central America is so small, so minimal, considering what is at stake. The total amount requested for aid to all of Central America in 1984 is about $600 million. That's less than one-tenth of what Americans will spend this year on coin-operated video games.

In summation, I say to you that tonight there can be no question: The national security of all the Americas is at stake in Central America. If we cannot defend ourselves there, we cannot expect to prevail elsewhere. Our credibility would collapse, our alliances would crumble, and the safety of our homeland would be put in jeopardy.

We have a vital interest, a moral duty, and a solemn responsibility. This is not a partisan issue. It is a question of our meeting our moral responsibility to ourselves, our friends, and our posterity. It is a duty that falls on all of us—the President, the Congress, and the people. We must perform it together. Who among us would wish to bear responsibility for failing to meet our shared obligation?

Thank you, God bless you, and good night.

Source: "Address Before a Joint Session of the Congress on Central America," April 27, 1983, The Ronald Reagan Presidential Library. Available online. URL: http://www.reagan.utexas.edu/resource/speeches/1983/42783d.htm

24. Address on Soviet Attack on Korean Flight 007 September 5, 1983

Reagan's characterization of the Soviet Union as an "evil empire" was bolstered by the attack on Korean Airlines Flight 007, which drifted over Soviet airspace and was shot down on September 1, 1983. The Soviet account of the events surrounding flight 007 was both evasive and belligerent, and the incident deepened the gulf between the United States and the Kremlin. Reagan was disgusted by the attack and cited it as evidence of the brutality of the communist regime. In a dramatic moment at the United Nations, Ambassador Jeane Kirkpatrick played clandestinely acquired recordings of the exchanges between the Soviet pilot who shot down the plane and his commanders on the ground. Reagan's response was far too muted in the eyes of many of his conservative supporters who advocated an end to arms talks, tighter economic sanctions (particularly grain sales), and the expulsion of every suspected KGB agent in the United States. Reagan was convinced that the Soviets had done irreparable harm to their image internationally, even among supporters of the nuclear freeze, and that it would be best to let them wallow in a crisis of their own making rather than convert it into a tit-for-tat U.S.-Soviet quarrel.

My fellow Americans: I'm coming before you tonight about the Korean airline massacre, the attack by the Soviet Union against 269 innocent men, women, and children aboard an unarmed Korean passenger plane. This crime against humanity must never be forgotten, here or throughout the world.

Our prayers tonight are with the victims and their families in their time of terrible grief. Our hearts go out to them—to brave people like Kathryn McDonald, the wife of a Congressman whose composure and eloquence on the day of her husband's death moved us all. He will be sorely missed by all of us here in government. The parents of one slain couple wired me: "Our daughter . . . and her husband . . . died on Korean Airline Flight 007. Their deaths were the result of the Soviet Union violating every concept of human rights." The emotions of these parents—grief, shock, anger—are shared by civilized people everywhere. From around the world press accounts reflect an explosion of condemnation by people everywhere.

Let me state as plainly as I can: There was absolutely no justification, either legal or moral, for what the Soviets did. One newspaper in India said, "If every passenger plane . . . is fair game for home air forces . . . it will be the end to civil aviation as we know it."

This is not the first time the Soviet Union has shot at and hit a civilian airliner when it overflew its territory. In another tragic incident in 1978, the Soviets shot down an unarmed civilian airliner after having positively identified it as such. In that instance, the Soviet interceptor pilot clearly identified the civilian markings on the side of the aircraft, repeatedly questioned the order to fire on a civilian airliner, and was ordered to shoot it down anyway. The aircraft was hit with a missile and made a crash landing. Several innocent people lost their lives in this attack, killed by shrapnel from the blast of a Soviet missile.

Is this a practice of other countries in the world? The answer is no. Commercial aircraft from the Soviet Union and Cuba on a number of occasions have overflown sensitive United States military facilities. They weren't shot down. We and other civilized countries believe in the tradition of offering help to mariners and pilots who are lost or in distress on the sea or in the air. We believe in following procedures to prevent a tragedy, not to provoke one.

But despite the savagery of their crime, the universal reaction against it, and the evidence of their complicity, the Soviets still refuse to tell the truth. They have persistently refused to admit that their pilot fired on the Korean aircraft. Indeed, they've not even told their own people that a plane was shot down. They have spun a confused tale of tracking the plane by radar until it just mysteriously disappeared from their radar screens, that no one fired a shot of any kind. But then they coupled this with charges that it was a spy plane sent by us and that their planes fired tracer bullets past the plane as a warning that it was in Soviet airspace.

Let me recap for a moment and present the incontrovertible evidence that we have. The Korean airliner, a Boeing 747, left Anchorage, Alaska, bound for Seoul, Korea, on a course south and west which would take it across Japan. Out over the Pacific, in international waters, it was for a brief time in the vicinity of one of our reconnaissance planes, an RC-135, on a routine mission. At no time was the RC-135, in Soviet airspace. The Korean airliner flew on, and the two planes were soon widely separated.

The 747 is equipped with the most modern computerized navigation facilities, but a computer must respond to input provided by human hands. No one will ever know whether a mistake was made in giving the computer the course or whether there was a malfunction. Whichever, the 747 was flying a course further to the west than it was supposed to fly—a course which took it into Soviet airspace. The Soviets tracked this plane for two and a half hours while it flew a straight-line course at 30 to 35,000 feet. Only civilian airliners fly in such a manner. At one point, the Korean pilot gave Japanese air control his position as east of Hokkaido, Japan, showing that he was unaware they were off course by as much or more than a hundred miles.

The Soviets scrambled jet interceptors from a base in Sakhalin Island. Japanese ground sites recorded the interceptor planes' radio transmissions—their conversations with their own ground control. We only have the voices from the pilots; the Soviet ground-to-air transmissions were not recorded. It's plain, however, from the pilot's words that he's responding to orders and queries from his own ground control. Here is a brief segment of the tape which we're going to play in its entirety for the United Nations Security Council tomorrow. [At this point, an audiotape of Soviet military pilots speaking in Russian was played for 22 seconds.]

Those were the voices of the Soviet pilots. In this tape, the pilot who fired the missile describes his search for what he calls the target. He reports he has it in sight; indeed, he pulls up to within about a mile of the Korean plane, mentions its flashing strobe light and that its navigation lights are on. He then reports he's reducing speed to get behind the airliner, gives his distance from the plane at various points in this maneuver, and finally announces what can only be called the Korean airline massacre. He says he has locked on the radar, which aims his missiles, has launched those missiles, the target has been destroyed, and he is breaking off the attack.

Let me point out something here having to do with his closeup view of the airliner on what we know was a clear night with a half moon. The 747 has a unique and distinctive silhouette, unlike any other plane in the world. There is no way a pilot could mistake this for anything other than a civilian airliner. And if that isn't enough, let me point out our RC-135 that I mentioned earlier had been back at its base in Alaska, on the ground for an hour, when the murderous attack took place over the Sea of Japan.

And make no mistake about it, this attack was not just against ourselves or the Republic of Korea. This was the Soviet Union against the world and the moral precepts which guide human relations among people everywhere. It was an act of barbarism, born of a society which wantonly disregards individual rights and the value of human life and seeks constantly to expand and dominate other nations. They deny the deed, but in their conflicting and misleading protestations, the Soviets reveal that, yes, shooting down a plane—even one with hundreds of innocent men, women, children, and babies—is a part of their normal procedure if that plane is in what they claim as their airspace.

They owe the world an apology and an offer to join the rest of the world in working out a system to protect against this ever happening again. Among the rest of us there is one protective measure: an international radio wavelength on which pilots can communicate with planes of other nations if they are in trouble or lost. Soviet military planes are not so equipped, because that would make it easier for pilots who might want to defect.

Our request to send vessels into Soviet waters to search for wreckage and bodies has received no satisfactory answer. Bereaved families of the Japanese victims were harassed by Soviet patrol boats when they tried to get near where the plane is believed to have gone down in order to hold a ceremony for their dead. But we shouldn't be surprised by such inhuman brutality. Memories come back of Czechoslovakia, Hungary, Poland, the gassing of villages in Afghanistan. If the massacre and their subsequent conduct is intended to intimidate, they have failed in their purpose. From every corner of the globe the word is defiance in the face of this unspeakable act and defiance of the system which excuses it and tries to cover it up. With our horror and our sorrow, there is a righteous and terrible anger. It would be easy to think in terms of vengeance, but that is not a proper answer. We want justice and action to see that this never happens again.

Our immediate challenge to this atrocity is to ensure that we make the skies safer and that we seek just compensation for the families of those who were killed. Since my return to

Washington, we've held long meetings, the most recent yesterday with the congressional leadership. There was a feeling of unity in the room, and I received a number of constructive suggestions. We will continue to work with the Congress regarding our response to this massacre. As you know, we immediately made known to the world the shocking facts as honestly and completely as they came to us.

We have notified the Soviets that we will not renew our bilateral agreement for cooperation in the field of transportation so long as they threaten the security of civil aviation. Since 1981 the Soviet airline Aeroflot has been denied the right to fly to the United States. We have reaffirmed that order and are examining additional steps we can take with regard to Aeroflot facilities in this country. We're cooperating with other countries to find better means to ensure the safety of civil aviation and to join us in not accepting Aeroflot as a normal member of the international civil air community unless and until the Soviets satisfy the cries of humanity for justice. I am pleased to report that Canada today suspended Acroflot's landing and refueling privileges for 60 days.

We have joined with other countries to press the International Civil Aviation Organization to investigate this crime at an urgent special session of the Council. At the same time, we're listening most carefully to private groups, both American and international, airline pilots, passenger associations, and others, who have a special interest in civil air safety. I am asking the Congress to pass a joint resolution of condemnation of this Soviet crime. We have informed the Soviets that we're suspending negotiations on several bilateral arrangements we had under consideration.

Along with Korea and Japan, we called an emergency meeting of the U.N. Security Council which began on Friday. On that first day, Korea, Japan, Canada, Australia, the Netherlands, Pakistan, France, China, the United Kingdom, Zaire, New Zealand, and West Germany all joined us in denouncing the Soviet action and expressing our horror. We expect to hear from additional countries as debate resumes tomorrow.

We intend to work with the 13 countries who had citizens aboard the Korean airliner to seek reparations for the families of all those who were killed. The United States will be making a claim against the Soviet Union within the next week to obtain compensation for the benefit of the victims' survivors. Such compensation is an absolute moral duty which the Soviets must assume. In the economic area in general, we're redoubling our efforts with our allies to end the flow of military and strategic items to the Soviet Union.

Secretary Shultz is going to Madrid to meet with representatives of 35 countries who, for three years, have been negotiating an agreement having to do with, among other things, human rights. Foreign Minister Gromyko of the Soviet Union is scheduled to attend that meeting. If he does come to the meeting, Secretary Shultz is going to present him with our demands for disclosure of the facts, corrective action, and concrete assurances that such a thing will not happen again and that restitution be made.

As we work with other countries to see that justice is done, the real test of our resolve is whether we have the will to remain strong, steady, and united. I believe more than ever— as evidenced by your thousands and thousands of wires and phone calls in these last few days— that we do. I have outlined some of the steps we're taking in response to the tragic massacre. There's something I've always believed in, but which now seems more important than ever. The Congress will be facing key national security issues when it returns from recess. There has been legitimate difference of opinion on this subject, I know, but I urge the members of that distinguished body to ponder long and hard the Soviets' aggression as they consider the security and safety of our people—indeed, all people who believe in freedom.

Senator Henry Jackson, a wise and revered statesman and one who probably understood the Soviets as well as any American in history, warned us, "the greatest threat the United States now faces is posed by the Soviet Union." But Senator Jackson said, "If America maintains a strong deterrent—and only if it does—this nation will continue to be a leader in the crucial quest for enduring peace among nations."

The late Senator made those statements in July on the Senate floor, speaking in behalf of the MX missile program he considered vital to restore America's strategic parity with the Soviets.

When John F. Kennedy was president, defense spending as a share of the Federal budget was 70 percent greater than it is today. Since then, the Soviet Union has carried on the most massive military buildup the world has ever seen. Until they're willing to join the rest of the world community, we must maintain the strength to deter their aggression.

But while we do so, we must not give up our effort to bring them into the world community of nations. Peace through strength as long as necessary, but never giving up our effort to bring peace closer through mutual, verifiable reduction in the weapons of war. I've told you of negotiations we've suspended as a result of the Korean airline massacre, but we cannot, we must not give up our effort to reduce the arsenals of destructive weapons threatening the world. Ambassador Nitze has returned to Geneva to resume the negotiations on intermediate-range nuclear weapons in Europe. Equally, we will continue to press for arms reductions in the START talks that resume in October. We are more determined than ever to reduce and, if possible, eliminate the threat hanging over mankind.

We know it will be hard to make a nation that rules its own people through force to cease using force against the rest of the world. But we must try. This is not a role we sought. We preach no manifest destiny. But like Americans who began this country and brought forth this last, best hope of mankind, history has asked much of the Americans of our own time. Much we have already given; much more we must be prepared to give.

Let us have faith, in Abraham Lincoln's words, "that right makes might, and in that faith let us, to the end dare to do our duty as we understand it." If we do, if we stand together and move forward with courage, then history will record that some good did come from this monstrous wrong that we will carry with us and remember for the rest of our lives.

Thank you. God bless you, and good night.

Source: Address to the Nation on the Soviet Attack on a Korean Civilian Airliner, September 5, 1983, The Ronald Reagan Presidential Library. Available online.URL: http://www.reagan.utexas.edu/resource/speeches/1983/90583a.htm

25. Address to the Nation on Events in Lebanon and Grenada October 27, 1983

The autumn of 1983 was a period marked by crisis, including the attack on KAL 007 and the placement of Pershing and cruise missiles in Western Europe. But the last week of October 1983 was probably the most stressful week of the Reagan presidency, with the deaths of 241 U.S. Marines on a peacekeeping mission in Lebanon and the U.S. attack on Grenada coming just hours apart. Despite Reagan's stern rhetoric about staying the course in Lebanon, he ended up withdrawing American forces early in 1984. The question that he asks in this speech, "Let me ask those who say we should get out of Lebanon: If we were to leave Lebanon now, what message would that send to those who foment instability and terrorism?" was answered in the years to come after he ordered the marines to "redeploy" offshore. This redeployment, along with later American retreats, may have encouraged terrorist groups, including Al Qaeda, to believe that killing Americans will make the United States withdraw. Regarding Grenada, the president cited Jimmy Carter's experience in Iran in making the case for the U.S. intervention. Hundreds of American medical students were on the island when the regime's hard-liners staged a coup; Reagan believed their lives were in danger and decided to act. Critics argued that this was a cover story for an invasion that had been in the works for some time, and that the attack was designed to divert the nation's attention from the humiliating debacle in Lebanon. While planning an assault on Grenada had been underway for some time, there's little evidence to support the notion that Reagan saw this as a way of distracting the nation from the events in Beirut. As for the medical students, it appeared in retrospect that their lives were never in danger, but that was not necessarily the perception at the time. Images of the students kissing American soil upon their return to the States bolstered Reagan's case and led a majority of the American public to endorse his decision in public opinion polls.

My fellow Americans:

Some 2 months ago we were shocked by the brutal massacre of 269 men, women, and children, more than 60 of them Americans, in the shooting down of a Korean airliner. Now, in these past several days, violence has erupted again, in Lebanon and Grenada.

In Lebanon, we have some 1,600 marines, part of a multinational force that's trying to help the people of Lebanon restore order and stability to that troubled land. Our marines are assigned to the south of the city of Beirut, near the only airport operating in Lebanon. Just a mile or so to the north is the Italian contingent and not far from them, the French and a company of British soldiers.

This past Sunday, at 22 minutes after 6 Beirut time, with dawn just breaking, a truck, looking like a lot of other vehicles in the city, approached the airport on a busy, main road. There was nothing in its appearance to suggest it was any different than the trucks or cars that were normally seen on and around the airport. But this one was different. At the wheel was a young man on a suicide mission.

The truck carried some 2,000 pounds of explosives, but there was no way our marine guards could know this. Their first warning that something was wrong came when the truck crashed through a series of barriers, including a chain-link fence and barbed wire entanglements. The guards opened fire, but it was too late. The truck smashed through the doors of the headquarters building in which our marines were sleeping and instantly exploded. The four-story concrete building collapsed in a pile of rubble.

More than 200 of the sleeping men were killed in that one hideous, insane attack. Many others suffered injury and are hospitalized here or in Europe.

This was not the end of the horror. At almost the same instant, another vehicle on a suicide and murder mission crashed into the headquarters of the French peacekeeping force, an eight-story building, destroying it and killing more than 50 French soldiers.

Prior to this day of horror, there had been several tragedies for our men in the multinational force. Attacks by snipers and mortar fire had taken their toll.

I called bereaved parents and/or widows of the victims to express on behalf of all of us our sorrow and sympathy. Sometimes there were questions. And now many of you are asking: Why should our young men be dying in Lebanon? Why is Lebanon important to us?

Well, it's true, Lebanon is a small country, more than five-and-a-half thousand miles from our shores on the edge of what we call the

Middle East. But every President who has occupied this office in recent years has recognized that peace in the Middle East is of vital concern to our nation and, indeed, to our allies in Western Europe and Japan. We've been concerned because the Middle East is a powderkeg; four times in the last 30 years, the Arabs and Israelis have gone to war. And each time, the world has teetered near the edge of catastrophe.

The area is key to the economic and political life of the West. Its strategic importance, its energy resources, the Suez Canal, and the well-being of the nearly 200 million people living there—all are vital to us and to world peace. If that key should fall into the hands of a power or powers hostile to the free world, there would be a direct threat to the United States and to our allies.

We have another reason to be involved. Since 1948 our Nation has recognized and accepted a moral obligation to assure the continued existence of Israel as a nation. Israel shares our democratic values and is a formidable force an invader of the Middle East would have to reckon with.

For several years, Lebanon has been torn by internal strife. Once a prosperous, peaceful nation, its government had become ineffective in controlling the militias that warred on each other. Sixteen months ago, we were watching on our TV screens the shelling and bombing of Beirut which was being used as a fortress by PLO bands. Hundreds and hundreds of civilians were being killed and wounded in the daily battles.

Syria, which makes no secret of its claim that Lebanon should be a part of a Greater Syria, was occupying a large part of Lebanon. Today, Syria has become a home for 7,000 Soviet advisers and technicians who man a massive amount of Soviet weaponry, including SS-21 ground-to-ground missiles capable of reaching vital areas of Israel.

A little over a year ago, hoping to build on the Camp David accords, which had led to peace between Israel and Egypt, I proposed a peace plan for the Middle East to end the wars between the Arab States and Israel. It was based on U.N. resolutions 242 and 338 and called for a fair and just solution to the Palestinian problem, as well as a fair and just settlement of issues between the Arab States and Israel.

Before the necessary negotiations could begin, it was essential to get all foreign forces out of Lebanon and to end the fighting there. So, why are we there? Well, the answer is straightforward: to help bring peace to Lebanon and stability to the vital Middle East. To that end, the multinational force was created to help stabilize the situation in Lebanon until a government could be established and a Lebanese army mobilized to restore Lebanese sovereignty over its own soil as the foreign forces withdrew. Israel agreed to withdraw as did Syria, but Syria then reneged on its promise. Over 10,000 Palestinians who had been bringing ruin down on Beirut, however, did leave the country.

Lebanon has formed a government under the leadership of President Gemayel, and that government, with our assistance and training, has set up its own army. In only a year's time, that army has been rebuilt. It's a good army, composed of Lebanese of all factions.

A few weeks ago, the Israeli army pulled back to the Awali River in southern Lebanon. Despite fierce resistance by Syrian-backed forces, the Lebanese army was able to hold the line and maintain the defensive perimeter around Beirut.

In the year that our marines have been there, Lebanon has made important steps toward stability and order. The physical presence of the marines lends support to both the Lebanese Government and its army. It allows the hard work of diplomacy to go forward. Indeed, without the peacekeepers from the U.S., France, Italy, and Britain, the efforts to find a peaceful solution in Lebanon would collapse.

As to that narrower question—what exactly is the operational mission of the marines—the answer is, to secure a piece of Beirut, to keep order in their sector, and to prevent the area from becoming a battlefield. Our marines are not just sitting in an airport. Part of their task is to guard that airport. Because of their presence, the airport has remained operational. In addition, they patrol the surrounding area. This is their part—a limited, but essential part—in the larger effort that I've described.

If our marines must be there, I'm asked, why can't we make them safer? Who committed this latest atrocity against them and why?

Well, we'll do everything we can to ensure that our men are as safe as possible. We ordered the battleship *New Jersey* to join our naval forces offshore. Without even firing them, the threat of its 16-inch guns silenced those who once fired down on our marines from the hills, and they're a good part of the reason we suddenly had a cease-fire. We're doing our best to make our forces less vulnerable to those who want to snipe at them or send in future suicide missions.

Secretary Shultz called me today from Europe, where he was meeting with the Foreign Ministers of our allies in the multinational force. They remain committed to our task. And plans were made to share information as to how we can improve security for all our men.

We have strong circumstantial evidence that the attack on the marines was directed by terrorists who used the same method to destroy our Embassy in Beirut. Those who directed this atrocity must be dealt justice, and they will be. The obvious purpose behind the sniping and, now, this attack was to weaken American will and force the withdrawal of U.S. and French forces from Lebanon. The clear intent of the terrorists was to eliminate our support of the Lebanese Government and to destroy the ability of the Lebanese people to determine their own destiny.

To answer those who ask if we're serving any purpose in being there, let me answer a question with a question. Would the terrorists have launched their suicide attacks against the multinational force if it were not doing its job? The multinational force was attacked precisely because it is doing the job it was sent to do in Beirut. It is accomplishing its mission.

Now then, where do we go from here? What can we do now to help Lebanon gain greater stability so that our marines can come home? Well, I believe we can take three steps now that will make a difference.

First, we will accelerate the search for peace and stability in that region. Little attention has been paid to the fact that we've had special envoys there working, literally, around the clock to bring the warring factions together. This coming Monday in Geneva, President Gemayel of Lebanon will sit down with other factions from his country to see if national reconciliation can be achieved. He has our firm support. I will soon be announcing a replacement for Bud McFarlane, who was preceded by Phil Habib. Both worked tirelessly and must be credited for much if not most of the progress we've made.

Second, we'll work even more closely with our allies in providing support for the Government of Lebanon and for the rebuilding of a national consensus.

Third, we will ensure that the multinational peace-keeping forces, our marines, are given the greatest possible protection. Our Commandant of the Marine Corps, General Kelley, returned from Lebanon today and will be advising us on steps we can take to improve security. Vice President Bush returned just last night from Beirut and gave me a full report of his brief visit.

Beyond our progress in Lebanon, let us remember that our main goal and purpose is to achieve a broader peace in all of the Middle East. The factions and bitterness that we see in Lebanon are just a microcosm of the difficulties that are spread across much of that region. A peace initiative for the entire Middle East, consistent with the Camp David accords and U.N. resolutions 242 and 338, still offers the best hope for bringing peace to the region.

Let me ask those who say we should get out of Lebanon: If we were to leave Lebanon now, what message would that send to those who foment instability and terrorism? If America were to walk away from Lebanon, what chance would there be for a negotiated settlement, producing a unified democratic Lebanon?

If we turned our backs on Lebanon now, what would be the future of Israel? At stake is the fate of only the second Arab country to negotiate a major agreement with Israel. That's another accomplishment of this past year, the May 17th accord signed by Lebanon and Israel.

If terrorism and intimidation succeed, it'll be a devastating blow to the peace process and to Israel's search for genuine security. It won't just be Lebanon sentenced to a future of chaos. Can the United States, or the free world, for that matter, stand by and see the Middle East incorporated into the Soviet bloc? What of Western Europe and Japan's dependence on Middle East oil for the energy to fuel their industries? The Middle East is, as I've said, vital to our national security and economic well-being.

Brave young men have been taken from us. Many others have been grievously wounded. Are we to tell them their sacrifice was wasted? They gave their lives in defense of our national security every bit as much as any man who ever died fighting in a war. We must not strip every ounce of meaning and purpose from their courageous sacrifice.

We're a nation with global responsibilities. We're not somewhere else in the world protecting someone else's interests; we're there protecting our own.

I received a message from the father of a marine in Lebanon. He told me, "In a world where we speak of human rights, there is a sad lack of acceptance of responsibility. My son has chosen the acceptance of responsibility for the privilege of living in this country. Certainly in this country one does not inherently have rights unless the responsibility for these rights is accepted." Dr. Kenneth Morrison said that while he was waiting to learn if his son was one of the dead. I was thrilled for him to learn today that his son Ross is alive and well and carrying on his duties in Lebanon.

Let us meet our responsibilities. For longer than any of us can remember, the people of the Middle East have lived from war to war with no prospect for any other future. That dreadful cycle must be broken. Why are we there? Well, a Lebanese mother told one of our Ambassadors that her little girl had only attended school 2 of the last 8 years. Now, because of our presence there, she said her daughter could live a normal life.

With patience and firmness, we can help bring peace to that strife torn region—and make our own lives more secure. Our role is to help the Lebanese put their country together, not to do it for them.

Now, I know another part of the world is very much on our minds, a place much closer to our shores: Grenada. The island is only twice the size of the District of Columbia, with a total population of about 110,000 people.

Grenada and a half dozen other Caribbean islands here were, until recently, British colonies. They're now independent states and members of the British Commonwealth. While they respect each other's independence, they also feel a kinship with each other and think of themselves as one people.

In 1979 trouble came to Grenada. Maurice Bishop, a protégé of Fidel Castro, staged a military coup and overthrew the government which had been elected under the constitution left to the people by the British. He sought the help of Cuba in building an airport, which he claimed was for tourist trade, but which looked suspiciously suitable for military aircraft, including Soviet-built long-range bombers.

The six sovereign countries and one remaining colony are joined together in what they call the Organization of Eastern Caribbean States. The six became increasingly alarmed as Bishop built an army greater than all of theirs combined. Obviously, it was not purely for defense.

In this last year or so, Prime Minister Bishop gave indications that he might like better relations with the United States. He even made a trip to our country and met with senior officials of the White House and the State Department. Whether he was serious or not, we'll never know. On October 12th, a small group in his militia seized him and put him under arrest. They were, if anything, more radical and more devoted to Castro's Cuba than he had been.

Several days later, a crowd of citizens appeared before Bishop's home, freed him, and escorted him toward the headquarters of the military council. They were fired upon. A number, including some children, were killed, and Bishop was seized. He and several members of his cabinet were subsequently executed, and a 24-hour shoot-to-kill curfew was put in effect. Grenada was without a government, its only authority exercised by a self-proclaimed band of military men.

There were then about 1,000 of our citizens on Grenada, 800 of them students in St. George's University Medical School. Concerned that they'd be harmed or held as hostages, I ordered a flotilla of ships, then on its way to Lebanon with marines, part of our regular rotation program, to circle south on a course that would put them somewhere in the vicinity of Grenada in case there should be a need to evacuate our people.

Last weekend, I was awakened in the early morning hours and told that six members of the Organization of Eastern Caribbean States, joined by Jamaica and Barbados, had sent an urgent request that we join them in a military operation to restore order and democracy to Grenada. They were proposing this action under the terms of a treaty, a mutual assistance pact that existed among them.

These small, peaceful nations needed our help. Three of them don't have armies at all, and the others have very limited forces. The legitimacy of their request, plus my own concern for our citizens, dictated my decision. I believe our government has a responsibility to go to the aid of its citizens, if their right to life and liberty is threatened. The nightmare of our hostages in Iran must never be repeated.

We knew we had little time and that complete secrecy was vital to ensure both the safety of the young men who would undertake this mission and the Americans they were about to rescue. The Joint Chiefs worked around the clock to come up with a plan. They had little intelligence information about conditions on the island.

We had to assume that several hundred Cubans working on the airport could be military reserves. Well, as it turned out, the number was much larger, and they were a military force. Six hundred of them have been taken prisoner, and we have discovered a complete base with weapons and communications equipment, which makes it clear a Cuban occupation of the island had been planned.

Two hours ago we released the first photos from Grenada. They included pictures of a warehouse of military equipment—one of three we've uncovered so far. This warehouse contained weapons and ammunition stacked almost to the ceiling, enough to supply thousands of terrorists. Grenada, we were told, was a friendly island paradise for tourism. Well, it wasn't. It was a Soviet-Cuban colony, being readied as a major military bastion to export terror and undermine democracy. We got there just in time.

I can't say enough in praise of our military—Army rangers and paratroopers, Navy, Marine, and Air Force personnel—those who planned a brilliant campaign and those who carried it out. Almost instantly, our military seized the two airports, secured the campus where most of our students were, and are now in the mopping-up phase.

It should be noted that in all the planning, a top priority was to minimize risk, to avoid casualties to our own men and also the Grenadian forces as much as humanly possible. But there were casualties, and we all owe a debt to those who lost their lives or were wounded. They were few in number, but even one is a tragic price to pay.

It's our intention to get our men out as soon as possible. Prime Minister Eugenia Charles of Dominica—I called that wrong; she pronounces it Dominica—she is Chairman of OECS. She's calling for help from Commonwealth nations in giving the people their right to establish a constitutional government on Grenada. We anticipate that the Governor General, a Grenadian, will participate in setting up a provisional government in the interim.

The events in Lebanon and Grenada, though oceans apart, are closely related. Not only has Moscow assisted and encouraged the violence in both countries, but it provides direct support through a network of surrogates and terrorists. It is no coincidence that when the thugs tried to wrest control over Grenada, there were 30 Soviet advisers and hundreds of Cuban military and paramilitary forces on the island. At the moment of our landing, we communicated with the Governments of Cuba and the Soviet Union and told them we would offer shelter and security to their people on Grenada. Regrettably, Castro ordered his men

to fight to the death, and some did. The others will be sent to their homelands.

You know, there was a time when our national security was based on a standing army here within our own borders and shore batteries of artillery along our coasts, and, of course, a navy to keep the sea lanes open for the shipping of things necessary to our well-being. The world has changed. Today, our national security can be threatened in faraway places. It's up to all of us to be aware of the strategic importance of such places and to be able to identify them.

Sam Rayburn once said that freedom is not something a nation can work for once and win forever. He said it's like an insurance policy; its premiums must be kept up to date. In order to keep it, we have to keep working for it and sacrificing for it just as long as we live. If we do not, our children may not know the pleasure of working to keep it, for it may not be theirs to keep.

In these last few days, I've been more sure than I've ever been that we Americans of today will keep freedom and maintain peace. I've been made to feel that by the magnificent spirit of our young men and women in uniform and by something here in our Nation's Capital. In this city, where political strife is so much a part of our lives, I've seen Democratic leaders in the Congress join their Republican colleagues, send a message to the world that we're all Americans before we're anything else, and when our country is threatened, we stand shoulder to shoulder in support of our men and women in the Armed Forces.

May I share something with you I think you'd like to know? It's something that happened to the Commandant of our Marine Corps, General Paul Kelley, while he was visiting our critically injured marines in an Air Force hospital. It says more than any of us could ever hope to say about the gallantry and heroism of these young men, young men who serve so willingly so that others might have a chance at peace and freedom in their own lives and in the life of their country.

I'll let General Kelley's words describe the incident. He spoke of a "young marine with more tubes going in and out of his body than I have ever seen in one body."

"He couldn't see very well. He reached up and grabbed my four stars, just to make sure I was who I said I was. He held my hand with a firm grip. He was making signals, and we realized he wanted to tell me something. We put a pad of paper in his hand—and he wrote 'Semper Fi.'"

Well, if you've been a marine or if, like myself, you're an admirer of the marines, you know those words are a battlecry, a greeting, and a legend in the Marine Corps. They're marine shorthand for the motto of the Corps—"Semper Fidelis"—"always faithful."

General Kelley has a reputation for being a very sophisticated general and a very tough marine. But he cried when he saw those words, and who can blame him?

That marine and all those others like him, living and dead, have been faithful to their ideals. They've given willingly of themselves so that a nearly defenseless people in a region of great strategic importance to the free world will have a chance someday to live lives free of murder and mayhem and terrorism. I think that young marine and all of his comrades have given every one of us something to live up to.

They were not afraid to stand up for their country or, no matter how difficult and slow the journey might be, to give to others that last, best hope of a better future. We cannot and will not dishonor them now and the sacrifices they've made by failing to remain as faithful to the cause of freedom and the pursuit of peace as they have been.

I will not ask you to pray for the dead, because they're safe in God's loving arms and beyond need of our prayers. I would like to ask you all—wherever you may be in this blessed land—to pray for these wounded young men and to pray for the bereaved families of those who gave their lives for our freedom.

God bless you, and God bless America.

Source: "Address to the Nation on Events in Lebanon and Grenada," October 27, 1983, The Ronald Reagan Presidential Library. Available online. URL: http://www.reagan.utexas.edu/resource/speeches/1983/102783b.htm

26. Remarks on Signing the Bill Making the Birthday of Martin Luther King, Jr., a National Holiday
November 2, 1983

President Reagan's relations with leaders of the African-American community were always strained, and he did not help matters with his comments at a press conference where he implicitly endorsed Senator Jesse Helms's suggestion that Martin Luther King, Jr., may have been a communist. When asked to comment on Helms's remarks, Reagan replied, "We'll know in about 35 years, won't we?"—a reference to the opening of sealed wiretap information illegally gathered by the Federal Bureau of Investigation. Reagan ultimately signed legislation creating the King holiday, and attempted to repair relations with King's family and African Americans with the following remarks.

The President. Mrs. King, members of the King family, distinguished Members of the Congress, ladies and gentlemen, honored guests, I'm very pleased to welcome you to the White House, the home that belongs to all of us, the American people.

When I was thinking of the contributions to our country of the man that we're honoring today, a passage attributed to the American poet John Greenleaf Whittier comes to mind. "Each crisis brings its word and deed." In America, in the fifties and sixties, one of the important crises we faced was racial discrimination. The man whose words and deeds in that crisis stirred our nation to the very depths of its soul was Dr. Martin Luther King, Jr.

Martin Luther King was born in 1929 in an America where, because of the color of their skin, nearly 1 in 10 lived lives that were separate and unequal. Most black Americans were taught in segregated schools. Across the country, too many could find only poor jobs, toiling for low wages. They were refused entry into hotels and restaurants, made to use separate facilities. In a nation that proclaimed liberty and justice for all, too many black Americans were living with neither.

In one city, a rule required all blacks to sit in the rear of public buses. But in 1955, when a brave woman named Rosa Parks was told to move to the back of the bus, she said, "No." A young minister in a local Baptist church, Martin Luther King, then organized a boycott of the bus company—a boycott that stunned the country. Within 6 months the courts had ruled the segregation of public transportation unconstitutional.

Dr. King had awakened something strong and true, a sense that true justice must be colorblind, and that among white and black Americans, as he put it, "Their destiny is tied up with our destiny, and their freedom is inextricably bound to our freedom; we cannot walk alone."

In the years after the bus boycott, Dr. King made equality of rights his life's work. Across the country, he organized boycotts, rallies, and marches. Often he was beaten, imprisoned, but he never stopped teaching nonviolence. "Work with the faith," he told his followers, "that unearned suffering is redemptive." In 1964 Dr. King became the youngest man in history to win the Nobel Peace Prize.

Dr. King's work brought him to this city often. And in one sweltering August day in 1963, he addressed a quarter of a million people at the Lincoln Memorial. If American history grows from two centuries to twenty, his words that day will never be forgotten. "I have a dream that one day on the red hills of Georgia, the sons of former slaves and the sons of former slave owners will be able to sit down together at the table of brotherhood."

In 1968 Martin Luther King was gunned down by a brutal assassin, his life cut short at the age of 39. But those 39 short years had changed America forever. The Civil Rights Act of 1964 had guaranteed all Americans equal use of public accommodations, equal access to programs financed by Federal funds, and the right to compete for employment on the sole basis of individual merit. The Voting Rights Act of 1965 had made certain that from then on black Americans would get to vote. But most important, there was not just a change of law; there was a change of heart. The conscience of America had been touched. Across the land, people had begun to treat each other not as blacks and whites, but as fellow Americans.

And since Dr. King's death, his father, the Reverend Martin Luther King, Sr., and his wife, Coretta King, have eloquently and forcefully carried on his work. Also his family have joined in that cause.

Now our nation has decided to honor Dr. Martin Luther King, Jr., by setting aside a day each year to remember him and the just cause he stood for. We've made historic strides since Rosa Parks refused to go to the back of the bus. As a democratic people, we can take pride in the knowledge that we Americans recognized a grave injustice and took action to correct it. And we should remember that in far too many countries, people like Dr. King never have the opportunity to speak out at all.

But traces of bigotry still mar America. So, each year on Martin Luther King Day, let us not only recall Dr. King, but rededicate ourselves to the Commandments he believed in and sought to live every day: Thou shall love thy God with all thy heart, and thou shall love thy neighbor as thyself. And I just have to believe that all of us—if all of us, young and old, Republicans and Democrats, do all we can to live up to those Commandments, then we will see the day when Dr. King's dream comes true, and in his words, "All of God's children will be able to sing with new meaning, '. . . land where my fathers died, land of the pilgrim's pride, from every mountainside, let freedom ring.'"

Thank you, God bless you, and I will sign it.

Mrs. King. Thank you, Mr. President, Vice President Bush, Majority Leader Baker and the distinguished congressional and senatorial delegations, and other representatives who've gathered here, and friends.

All right-thinking people, all right-thinking Americans are joined in spirit with us this day as the highest recognition which this nation gives is bestowed upon Martin Luther King, Jr., one who also was the recipient of the highest recognition which the world bestows, the Nobel Peace Prize.

In his own life's example, he symbolized what was right about America, what was noblest and best, what human beings have pursued since the beginning of history. He loved unconditionally. He was in constant pursuit of truth, and when he discovered it, he embraced it. His nonviolent campaigns brought about redemption, reconciliation, and justice. He taught us that only peaceful means can bring about peaceful ends, that our goal was to create the love community.

America is a more democratic nation, a more just nation, a more peaceful nation because Martin Luther King, Jr., became her preeminent nonviolent commander.

Martin Luther King, Jr., and his spirit live within all of us. Thank God for the blessing of his life and his leadership and his commitment. What manner of man was this? May we make ourselves worthy to carry on his dream and create the love community.

Thank you.

Source: "Remarks on Signing the Bill Making the Birthday of Martin Luther King, Jr., a National Holiday," November 2, 1983, The Ronald Reagan Presidential Library. Available online. URL: http://www.reagan.utexas.edu/resource/speeches/1983/110283a.htm

27. Address to the Nation Announcing the Reagan-Bush Candidacies for Reelection
January 29, 1984

Ronald Reagan apparently seriously considered not running for reelection in 1984, and at least one of his closest advisers, William Clark, suggested that he contemplate leaving after one term. In the end, Reagan decided to run, and put any retirement rumors to rest with this announcement.

My fellow Americans:

It's been nearly 3 years since I first spoke to you from this room. Together we've faced many difficult problems, and I've come to feel a special bond of kinship with each one of you. Tonight I'm here for a different reason. I've come to a difficult personal decision as to whether or not I should seek reelection.

When I first addressed you from here, our national defenses were dangerously weak, we had suffered humiliation in Iran, and at home we were adrift, possibly because of a failure here in Washington to trust the courage and character of you, the people. But worst of all, we were on the brink of economic collapse from years of government overindulgence and abusive overtaxation. Thus, I had to report that we were "in the worst economic mess since the Great Depression."

Inflation had risen to over 13 percent in 1979 and to 19 percent in March of 1980. Those back-to-back years of price explosions were the highest in more than 60 years. In the 5 years before I came here, taxes had actually doubled. Your cost-of-living pay raises just bumped you into higher tax brackets.

Interest rates over 21 percent, the highest in 120 years; productivity, down 2 consecutive years; industrial production down; actual wages and earnings down—the only things going up were prices, unemployment, taxes, and the size of government. While you tightened your belt, the Federal Government tightened its grip.

Well, things have changed. This past year inflation dropped down to 3.2 percent. Interest rates, cut nearly in half. Retail sales are surging. Homes are being built and sold. Auto assembly lines are opening up. And in just the last year, 4 million people have found jobs—the greatest employment gain in 33 years. By beginning to rebuild our defenses, we have restored credible deterrence and can confidently seek a secure and lasting peace, as well as a reduction in arms.

As I said Wednesday night, America is back and standing tall. We've begun to restore great American values—the dignity of work, the warmth of family, the strength of neighborhood, and the nourishment of human freedom.

But our work is not finished. We have more to do in creating jobs, achieving control over government spending, returning more autonomy to the States, keeping peace in a more settled world, and seeing if we can't find room in our schools for God.

At my inaugural, I quoted words that had been spoken over 200 years ago by Dr. Joseph Warren, president of the Massachusetts Congress. "On you depend the fortunes of America," he told his fellow Americans. "You are to decide the important question on which rests the happiness and liberty of millions yet unborn." And he added, "Act worthy of yourselves."

Over these last 3 years, Nancy and I have been sustained by the way you, the real heroes of American democracy, have met Dr. Warren's challenge. You were magnificent as we pulled the Nation through the long night of our national calamity. You have, indeed, acted worthy of yourselves.

Your high standards make us remember the central question of public service: Why are we here? Well, we're here to see that government continues to serve you, not the other way around.

We're here to lift the weak and to build the peace, and most important, we're here, as Dr. Warren said, to act today for the happiness and liberty of millions yet unborn, to seize the future so that every new child of this beloved Republic can dream heroic dreams. If we do less, we betray the memory of those who have given so much.

This historic room and the Presidency belong to you. It is your right and responsibility every 4 years to give someone temporary custody of this office and of the institution of the Presidency. You so honored me, and I'm grateful—grateful and proud of what, together, we have accomplished.

We have made a new beginning. Vice President Bush and I would like to have your continued support and cooperation in completing what we began 3 years ago. I am, therefore, announcing that I am a candidate and will seek reelection to the office I presently hold.

Thank you for the trust you've placed in me. God bless you, and good night.

Source: "Address to the Nation Announcing the Reagan-Bush Candidacies for Reelection," January 29, 1984, The Ronald Reagan Presidential Library. Available online. URL: http://www.reagan.utexas.edu/resource/speeches/1984/12984a.htm

28. Remarks at Memorial Day Ceremonies Honoring an Unknown Serviceman of the Vietnam Conflict Arlington, Virginia May 28, 1984

President Reagan often had difficulty restraining his emotions whenever he paid tribute to fallen soldiers or civilian heroes. He viewed these ceremonies as an integral part of his presidency, not a distraction from his job. In these brief remarks, Reagan honored the Unknown Soldier of the Vietnam War, a war which Reagan once described as a "noble cause." The president also awarded the Congressional Medal of Honor to the Unknown Soldier, the highest military award given for service above and beyond the call of duty while in action against the enemy. Years later, through advances in the science of DNA identification, the identity of the Unknown Soldier from the Vietnam War was determined to be Air Force Lieutenant Michael Blassie of St. Louis, Missouri, whose aircraft was shot down over South Vietnam in 1972. His remains were removed from the tomb at Arlington National Cemetery in 1998 and returned to his family for burial.

My fellow Americans:

Memorial Day is a day of ceremonies and speeches. Throughout America today, we honor the dead of our wars. We recall their valor and their sacrifices. We remember they gave their lives so that others might live.

We're also gathered here for a special event—the national funeral for an unknown soldier who will today join the heroes of three other wars.

When he spoke at a ceremony at Gettysburg in 1863, President Lincoln reminded us that through their deeds, the dead had spoken more eloquently for themselves than any of the living ever could, and that we living could only honor them by rededicating ourselves to the cause for which they so willingly gave a last full measure of devotion.

Well, this is especially so today, for in our minds and hearts is the memory of Vietnam and all that that conflict meant for those who sacrificed on the field of battle and for their loved ones who suffered here at home.

Not long ago, when a memorial was dedicated here in Washington to our Vietnam veterans, the events surrounding that dedication were a stirring reminder of America's resilience, of how our nation could learn and grow and transcend the tragedies of the past.

During the dedication ceremonies, the rolls of those who died and are still missing were read for three days in a candlelight ceremony at the National Cathedral. And the veterans of Vietnam who were never welcomed home with speeches and bands, but who were never defeated in battle and were heroes as surely as any who have ever fought in a noble cause, staged their own parade on Constitution Avenue. As America watched them—some in wheelchairs, all of them proud—there was a feeling that this nation—that as a nation we were coming together again and that we had, at long last, welcomed the boys home.

"A lot of healing went on," said one combat veteran who helped organize support for the memorial. And then there was this newspaper account that appeared after the ceremonies. I'd like to read it to you. "Yesterday, crowds returned to the Memorial. Among them was Herbie Petit, a machinist and former Marine from New Orleans. 'Last night,' he said, standing near the wall, 'I went out to dinner with some other ex-Marines. There was also a group of college students in the restaurant. We started talking to each other. And before we left, they stood up and cheered us. The whole week,' Petit said, his eyes red, 'it was worth it just for that.'"

It has been worth it. We Americans have learned to listen to each other and to trust each other again. We've learned that government owes the people an explanation and needs their support for its actions at home and abroad. And we have learned, and I pray this time for good, the most valuable lesson of all—the preciousness of human freedom.

It has been a lesson relearned not just by Americans but by all the people of the world. Yet, while the experience of Vietnam has given us a stark lesson that ultimately must move the conscience of the world, we must remember that we cannot today, as much as some might want to, close this chapter in our history, for the war in Southeast Asia still haunts a small but brave group of Americans—the families of those still missing in the Vietnam conflict.

They live day and night with uncertainty, with an emptiness, with a void that we cannot fathom. Today some sit among you. Their feelings are a mixture of pride and fear. They're proud of their sons or husbands, fathers or brothers who bravely and nobly answered the call of their country. But some of them fear that this ceremony writes a final chapter, leaving those they love forgotten.

Well, today then, one way to honor those who served or may still be serving in Vietnam is to gather here and rededicate ourselves to securing the answers for the families of those missing in action. I ask the members of Congress, the leaders of veterans groups, and the citizens of an entire nation present or listening, to give these families your help and your support, for they still sacrifice and suffer.

Vietnam is not over for them. They cannot rest until they know the fate of those they loved and watched march off to serve their country. Our dedication to their cause must be strengthened with these events today. We write no last chapters. We close no books. We put away no final memories. An end to America's involvement in Vietnam cannot come before we've achieved the fullest possible accounting of those missing in action.

This can only happen when their families know with certainty that this nation discharged her duty to those who served nobly and well. Today a united people call upon Hanoi with one voice: Heal the sorest wound of this conflict. Return our sons to America. End the grief of those who are innocent and undeserving of any retribution.

The Unknown Soldier who is returned to us today and whom we lay to rest is symbolic of all our missing sons, and we will present him with the Congressional Medal of Honor, the highest military decoration that we can bestow.

About him we may well wonder, as others have: As a child, did he play on some street in a great American city? Or did he work beside his father on a farm out in America's heartland? Did he marry? Did he have children? Did he look expectantly to return to a bride?

We'll never know the answers to these questions about his life. We do know, though, why he died. He saw the horrors of war but bravely faced them, certain his own cause and his country's cause was a noble one; that he was fighting for human dignity, for free men everywhere. Today we pause to embrace him and all who served us so well in a war whose end offered no parades, no flags, and so little thanks. We can be worthy of the values and ideals for which our sons sacrificed—worthy of their courage in the face of a fear that few of us will ever experience—by honoring their commitment and devotion to duty and country.

Many veterans of Vietnam still serve in the Armed Forces, work in our offices, on our farms, and in our factories. Most have kept their experiences private, but most have been strengthened by their call to duty. A grateful nation opens her heart today in gratitude for their sacrifice, for their courage, and for their noble service. Let us, if we must, debate the lessons learned at some other time. Today, we simply say with pride, "Thank you, dear son. May God cradle you in His loving arms."

We present to you our nation's highest award, the Congressional Medal of Honor, for service above and beyond the call of duty in action with the enemy during the Vietnam era.

Thank you.

Source: "Remarks at Memorial Day Ceremonies Honoring an Unknown Serviceman of the Vietnam Conflict," May 28, 1984, The Ronald Reagan Presidential Library. Available online. URL: http://www.reagan.utexas.edu/resource/speeches/1984/52884a.htm

29. Remarks to the Citizens of Ballyporeen, Ireland June 3, 1984

Reagan was proud of his Irish heritage and loved to tell stories involving his ancestral homeland and of the many Irish immigrants, including his great-grandfather, who came to the United States seeking a better life. The tiny town of Ballyporeen was never quite the same after the "Gipper" arrived for a visit in June 1984.

In the business that I formerly was in, I would have to say this is a very difficult spot—to be introduced to you who have waited so patiently—following this wonderful talent that we've seen here. And I should have gone on first, and then you should have followed—[laughter]—to close the show. But thank you very much.

Nancy and I are most grateful to be with you here today, and I'll take a chance and say, *muintir na hEireann* [people of Ireland]. Did I get it right? [Applause] All right. Well, it's difficult to express my appreciation to all of you.

I feel like I'm about to drown everyone in a bath of nostalgia. Of all the honors and gifts that have been afforded me as President, this visit is the one that I will cherish dearly. You see, I didn't know much about my family background—not because of a lack of interest, but because my father was orphaned before he was 6 years old. And now thanks to you and the efforts of good people who have dug into the history of a poor immigrant family, I know at last whence I came. And this has given my soul a new contentment. And it is a joyous feeling. It is like coming home after a long journey.

You see, my father, having been orphaned so young, he knew nothing of his roots also. And, God rest his soul, I told the Father, I think he's here, too, today, and very pleased and happy to know that this is whence he came.

Robert Frost, a renowned American poet, once said, "Home is the place where, when you have to go there, they have to take you in." [Laughter] Well, it's been so long since my great-grandfather set out that you don't have to take me in. So, I'm certainly thankful for this wonderful homecoming today. I can't think of a place on the planet I would rather claim as my roots more than Ballyporeen, County Tipperary.

My great-grandfather left here in a time of stress, seeking to better himself and his family. From what I'm told, we were a poor family. But my ancestors took with them a treasure, an indomitable spirit that was cultivated in the rich soil of this county.

And today I come back to you as a descendant of people who are buried here in paupers' graves. Perhaps this is God's way of reminding us that we must always treat every individual, no matter what his or her station in life, with dignity and respect. And who knows? Someday that person's child or grandchild might grow up to become the Prime Minister of Ireland or President of the United States.

Looking around town today, I was struck by the similarity between Ballyporeen and the small town in Illinois where I was born, Tampico. Of course, there's one thing you have that we didn't have in Tampico. We didn't have a Ronald Reagan Lounge in town. [Laughter] Well, the spirit is the same, this spirit of warmth, friendliness, and openness in Tampico and Ballyporeen, and you make me feel very much at home.

What unites us is our shared heritage and the common values of our two peoples. So many Irish men and women from every walk of life played a role in creating the dream of America. One was Charles Thompson, Secretary of the Continental Congress, and who designed the first Great Seal of the United States. I'm certainly proud to be part of that great Irish American tradition. From the time of our revolution when Irishmen filled the ranks of the Continental Army, to the building of the railroads, to the cultural contributions of individuals like the magnificent tenor John McCormack and the athletic achievements of the great heavyweight boxing champion John L. Sullivan—all of them are part of a great legacy.

Speaking of sports, I'd like to take this opportunity to congratulate an organization of which all Irish men and women can be proud, an organization that this year is celebrating its 100th anniversary: the Gaelic Athletic Association. I understand it was formed a hundred years ago in Tipperary to foster the culture and games of traditional Ireland. Some of you may be aware that I began my career as a sports announcer—a sports broadcaster, so I had an early appreciation for sporting competition. Well, congratulations to all of you during this GAA centennial celebration.

I also understand that not too far from here is the home of the great Irish novelist Charles Joseph Kickham. The Irish identity flourished in the United States. Irish men and women proud of their heritage can be found in every walk of life. I even have some of them in my Cabinet. One of them traces his maternal roots to Mitchellstown, just down the road from Ballyporeen. And he and I have almost the same name. I'm talking about Secretary of the Treasury Don Regan.

He spells it R-e-g-a-n. We're all of the same clan, we're all cousins. I tried to tell the Secretary one day that his branch of the family spelled it that way because they just couldn't handle as many letters as ours could. [Laughter] And then I received a paper from Ireland that told me that the clan to which we belong, that in it those who said "Regan" and spelled it that way were the professional people and the educators, and only the common laborers called it "Reagan." [Laughter] So, meet a common laborer.

The first job I ever got—I was 14 years old, and they put a pick and a shovel in my hand and my father told me that that was fitting and becoming to one of our name.

The bond between our two countries runs deep and strong, and I'm proud to be here in recognition and celebration of our ties that bind. My roots in Ballyporeen, County Tipperary, are little different than millions of other Americans who find their roots in towns and counties all over the Isle of Erin. I just feel exceptionally lucky to have this chance to visit you.

Last year a member of my staff came through town and recorded some messages from you. It was quite a tape, and I was moved deeply by the sentiments that you expressed. One of your townsmen sang me a bit of a tune about Sean Tracy, and a few lines stuck in my mind. They went like this—not that I'll sing—"And I'll never more roam, from my own native home, in Tipperary so far away."

Well, the Reagans roamed to America, but now we're back. And Nancy and I thank you from the bottom of our hearts for coming out to welcome us, for the warmth of your welcome. God bless you all.

Source: "Remarks to the Citizens of Ballyporeen, Ireland," June 3, 1984, The Ronald Reagan Presidential Library. Available online. URL: http://www.reagan.utexas.edu/resource/speeches/1984/84jun.htm

30. Remarks at a Ceremony Commemorating the 40th Anniversary of the Normandy Invasion, D day June 6, 1984

Ronald Reagan served as a captain in the Army Air Corps during World War II making training films and war documentaries. While he was of the so-called greatest generation, his poor vision kept him from a combat role. On the 40th anniversary of D day, he paid tribute to those who fell during the Allied invasion of Europe. In a beautifully choreographed event on the cliffs of Pointe du Hoc, Reagan delivered a memorable speech, one that set the standard for his successors at similar commemorations. One particularly moving passage brought tears to the eyes of the audience gathered to hear the address, mainly veterans of the Army Ranger unit which assaulted the German redoubt perched atop the cliffs: "These are the boys of Pointe du Hoc. These are the men who took the cliffs. These are the champions who helped free a continent. These are the heroes who helped end a war." Reagan also used the occasion to reach out to a former ally, the Soviet Union. "In truth, there is no reconciliation we would welcome more than a reconciliation with the Soviet Union, so, together, we can lessen the risks of war, now and forever. It's fitting to remember here the great losses also suffered by the Russian people during World War II: 20 million perished, a terrible price that testifies to all the world the necessity of ending war."

We're here to mark that day in history when the Allied armies joined in battle to reclaim this continent to liberty. For 4 long years, much of Europe had been under a terrible shadow. Free nations had fallen, Jews cried out in the camps, millions cried out for liberation. Europe was enslaved, and the world prayed for its rescue. Here in Normandy the rescue began. Here the Allies stood and fought against tyranny in a giant undertaking unparalleled in human history.

We stand on a lonely, windswept point on the northern shore of France. The air is soft, but 40 years ago at this moment, the air was dense with smoke and the cries of men, and the air was filled with the crack of rifle fire and the roar of cannon. At dawn, on the morning of the 6th of June, 1944, 225 Rangers jumped off the British landing craft and ran to the bottom of these cliffs. Their mission was one of the most difficult and daring of the invasion: to climb these sheer and desolate cliffs and take out the enemy guns. The Allies had been told that some of the mightiest of these guns were here and they would be trained on the beaches to stop the Allied advance.

The Rangers looked up and saw the enemy soldiers—the edge of the cliffs shooting down at them with machineguns and throwing grenades. And the American Rangers began to climb. They shot rope ladders over the face of these cliffs and began to pull themselves up. When one Ranger fell, another would take his place. When one rope was cut, a Ranger would grab another and begin his climb again. They climbed, shot back, and held their footing. Soon, one by one, the Rangers pulled themselves over the top, and in seizing the firm land at the top of these cliffs, they began to seize back the continent of Europe. Two hundred and twenty-five came here. After 2 days of fighting, only 90 could still bear arms.

Behind me is a memorial that symbolizes the Ranger daggers that were thrust into the top of these cliffs. And before me are the men who put them there.

These are the boys of Pointe du Hoc. These are the men who took the cliffs. These are the champions who helped free a continent. These are the heroes who helped end a war.

Gentlemen, I look at you and I think of the words of Stephen Spender's poem. You are men who in your "lives fought for life . . . and left the vivid air signed with your honor."

I think I know what you may be thinking right now—thinking "we were just part of a bigger effort; everyone was brave that day." Well, everyone was. Do you remember the story of Bill Millin of the 51st Highlanders? Forty years ago today, British troops were pinned down near a bridge, waiting desperately for help. Suddenly, they heard the sound of bagpipes, and some thought they were dreaming. Well, they weren't. They looked up and saw Bill Millin with his bagpipes, leading the reinforcements and ignoring the smack of the bullets into the ground around him.

Lord Lovat was with him—Lord Lovat of Scotland, who calmly announced when he got to the bridge, "Sorry I'm a few minutes late," as if he'd been delayed by a traffic jam, when in truth he'd just come from the bloody fighting on Sword Beach, which he and his men had just taken.

There was the impossible valor of the Poles who threw themselves between the enemy and the rest of Europe as the invasion took hold, and the unsurpassed courage of the Canadians who had already seen the horrors of war on this coast. They knew what awaited them there, but they would not be deterred. And once they hit Juno Beach, they never looked back.

All of these men were part of a rollcall of honor with names that spoke of a pride as bright as the colors they bore: the Royal Winnipeg Rifles, Poland's 24th Lancers, the Royal Scots Fusiliers, the Screaming Eagles, the Yeomen of England's armored divisions, the forces of Free France, the Coast Guard's "Matchbox Fleet" and you, the American Rangers.

Forty summers have passed since the battle that you fought here. You were young the day you took these cliffs; some of you were hardly more than boys, with the deepest joys of life before you. Yet, you risked everything here. Why? Why did you do it? What impelled you to put aside the instinct for self-preservation and risk your lives to take these cliffs? What inspired all the men of the armies that met here? We look at you, and somehow we know the answer. It was faith and belief; it was loyalty and love.

The men of Normandy had faith that what they were doing was right, faith that they fought for all humanity, faith that a just God would grant them mercy on this beachhead or on the next. It was the deep knowledge—and pray God we have not lost it—that there is a profound, moral difference between the use of force for liberation and the use of force for conquest. You were here to liberate, not to conquer, and so you and those others did not doubt your cause. And you were right not to doubt.

You all knew that some things are worth dying for. One's country is worth dying for, and democracy is worth dying for, because it's the most deeply honorable form of government ever devised by man. All of you loved liberty. All of you were willing to fight tyranny, and you knew the people of your countries were behind you.

The Americans who fought here that morning knew word of the invasion was spreading through the darkness back home. They fought—or felt in their hearts, though they couldn't know in fact, that in Georgia they were filling the churches at 4 A.M., in Kansas they were kneeling on their porches and praying, and in Philadelphia they were ringing the Liberty Bell.

Something else helped the men of D-day: their rockhard belief that Providence would have a great hand in the events that would unfold here; that God was an ally in this great cause. And so, the night before the invasion, when Colonel Wolverton asked his parachute troops to kneel with him in prayer he told them: Do not bow your heads, but look up so you can see God and ask His blessing in what we're about to do. Also that night, General Matthew Ridgway on his cot, listening in the darkness for the promise God made to Joshua: "I will not fail thee nor forsake thee."

These are the things that impelled them; these are the things that shaped the unity of the Allies.

When the war was over, there were lives to be rebuilt and governments to be returned to the people. There were nations to be reborn. Above all, there was a new peace to be assured. These were huge and daunting tasks. But the Allies summoned strength from the faith, belief, loyalty, and love of those who fell here. They rebuilt a new Europe together.

There was first a great reconciliation among those who had been enemies, all of whom had suffered so greatly. The United States did its part, creating the Marshall plan to help rebuild our allies and our former enemies. The Marshall plan led to the Atlantic alliance—a great alliance that serves to this day as our shield for freedom, for prosperity, and for peace.

In spite of our great efforts and successes, not all that followed the end of the war was happy or planned. Some liberated countries were lost. The great sadness of this loss echoes down to our own time in the streets of Warsaw, Prague, and East Berlin. Soviet troops that came to the center of this continent did not leave when peace came. They're still there, uninvited, unwanted, unyielding, almost 40 years after the war. Because of this, allied forces still stand on this continent. Today, as 40 years ago, our armies are here for only one purpose—to protect and defend democracy. The

only territories we hold are memorials like this one and graveyards where our heroes rest.

We in America have learned bitter lessons from two World Wars: It is better to be here ready to protect the peace, than to take blind shelter across the sea, rushing to respond only after freedom is lost. We've learned that isolationism never was and never will be an acceptable response to tyrannical governments with an expansionist intent.

But we try always to be prepared for peace; prepared to deter aggression; prepared to negotiate the reduction of arms; and, yes, prepared to reach out again in the spirit of reconciliation. In truth, there is no reconciliation we would welcome more than a reconciliation with the Soviet Union, so, together, we can lessen the risks of war, now and forever.

It's fitting to remember here the great losses also suffered by the Russian people during World War II: 20 million perished, a terrible price that testifies to all the world the necessity of ending war. I tell you from my heart that we in the United States do not want war. We want to wipe from the face of the Earth the terrible weapons that man now has in his hands. And I tell you, we are ready to seize that beachhead. We look for some sign from the Soviet Union that they are willing to move forward, that they share our desire and love for peace, and that they will give up the ways of conquest. There must be a changing there that will allow us to turn our hope into action.

We will pray forever that some day that changing will come. But for now, particularly today, it is good and fitting to renew our commitment to each other, to our freedom, and to the alliance that protects it.

We are bound today by what bound us 40 years ago, the same loyalties, traditions, and beliefs. We're bound by reality. The strength of America's allies is vital to the United States, and the American security guarantee is essential to the continued freedom of Europe's democracies. We were with you then; we are with you now. Your hopes are our hopes, and your destiny is our destiny.

Here, in this place where the West held together, let us make a vow to our dead. Let us show them by our actions that we understand what they died for. Let our actions say to them the words for which Matthew Ridgway listened: "I will not fail thee nor forsake thee."

Strengthened by their courage, heartened by their value [valor], and borne by their memory, let us continue to stand for the ideals for which they lived and died.

Thank you very much, and God bless you all.

Source: "Remarks at a Ceremony Commemorating the 40th Anniversary of the Normandy Invasion, D-day," June 6, 1984, The Ronald Reagan Presidential Library. Available online. URL: http://www.reagan.utexas.edu/resource/speeches/1984/60684a.htm

31. Remarks Accepting the Presidential Nomination at the Republican National Convention in Dallas, Texas
August 23, 1984

Reagan's acceptance speech was delivered to an elated crowd of Republicans who sensed they were on the verge of a landslide victory. Reagan struggled while delivering the address, since the giddy delegates were determined to participate in the speech. The president hoped to convince Americans that the "San Francisco" Democrats would take the nation back to the days of Jimmy Carter (whose vice president, Walter Mondale, was the Democratic nominee) and back to high inflation, high interest rates, and high taxes. Reagan's address was filled with patriotic references: to the Olympic games held in Los Angeles that summer, to the Statue of Liberty, to the rescue of American students on the "imprisoned" island of Grenada, and finally, to the nation itself, that "shining city on a hill," where it was "morning again" in 1984.

The President. Mr. Chairman, Mr. Vice President, delegates to this convention, and fellow citizens: In 75 days, I hope we enjoy a victory that is the size of the heart of Texas. Nancy and I extend our deep thanks to the Lone Star State and the "Big D"—the city of Dallas—for all their warmth and hospitality.

Four years ago I didn't know precisely every duty of this office, and not too long ago, I learned about some new ones from the first graders of Corpus Christi School in Chambersburg, Pennsylvania. Little Leah Kline was asked by her teacher to describe my duties. She said: "The President goes to meetings. He helps the animals. The President gets frustrated. He talks to other Presidents." How does wisdom begin at such an early age?

Tonight, with a full heart and deep gratitude for your trust, I accept your nomination for the Presidency of the United States. I will campaign on behalf of the principles of our party which lift America confidently into the future.

America is presented with the clearest political choice of half a century. The distinction between our two parties and the different philosophy of our political opponents are at the heart of this campaign and America's future.

I've been campaigning long enough to know that a political party and its leadership can't change their colors in 4 days. We won't, and no matter how hard they tried, our opponents didn't in San Francisco. We didn't discover our values in a poll taken a week before the convention. And we didn't set a weathervane on top of the Golden Gate Bridge before we started talking about the American family.

The choices this year are not just between two different personalities or between two political parties. They're between two different visions of the future, two fundamentally different ways of governing—their government of pessimism, fear, and limits, or ours of hope, confidence, and growth.

Their government sees people only as members of groups; ours serves all the people of America as individuals. Theirs lives in the past, seeking to apply the old and failed policies to an era that has passed them by. Ours learns from the past and strives to change by boldly charting a new course for the future. Theirs lives by promises, the bigger, the better. We offer proven, workable answers.

Our opponents began this campaign hoping that America has a poor memory. Well, let's take them on a little stroll down memory lane. Let's remind them of how a 4.8-percent inflation rate in 1976 became back-to-back years of double-digit inflation—the worst since World War I—punishing the poor and the elderly, young couples striving to start their new lives, and working people struggling to make ends meet.

Inflation was not some plague borne on the wind; it was a deliberate part of their official economic policy, needed, they said, to maintain prosperity. They didn't tell us that with it would come the highest interest rates since the Civil War. As average monthly mortgage payments more than doubled, home building nearly ground to a halt; tens of thousands of carpenters and others were thrown out of work. And who controlled both Houses of the Congress and the executive branch at that time? Not us, not us.

Campaigning across America in 1980, we saw evidence everywhere of industrial decline. And in rural America, farmers' costs were driven up by inflation. They were devastated by a wrongheaded grain embargo and were forced to borrow money at exorbitant interest rates just to get by. And many of them didn't get by. Farmers have to fight insects, weather, and the marketplace; they shouldn't have to fight their own government.

The high interest rates of 1980 were not talked about in San Francisco. But how about taxes? They were talked about in San Francisco. Will Rogers once said he never met a man he didn't like. Well, if I could paraphrase Will, our friends in the other party have never met a tax they didn't like or hike.

Under their policies, tax rates have gone up three times as much for families with children as they have for everyone else over these past three decades. In just the 5 years before we came into office, taxes roughly doubled.

Some who spoke so loudly in San Francisco of fairness were among those who brought about the biggest single, individual tax increase in our history in 1977, calling for a series of increases in the Social Security payroll tax and in the amount of pay subject to that tax. The bill they passed called for two additional increases between now and 1990, increases that bear down hardest on those at the lower income levels.

The Census Bureau confirms that, because of the tax laws we inherited, the number of households at or below the poverty level paying Federal income tax more than doubled between 1980 and 1982. Well, they received some relief in 1983, when our across-the-board tax cut was fully in place. And they'll get more help when indexing goes into effect this January.

Our opponents have repeatedly advocated eliminating indexing. Would that really hurt the rich? No, because the rich are already in the top brackets. But those working men and women who depend on a cost-of-living adjustment just to keep abreast of inflation would find themselves pushed into higher tax brackets and wouldn't even be able to keep even with inflation because they'd be paying a higher income tax. That's bracket creep; and our opponents are for it, and we're against it.

It's up to us to see that all our fellow citizens understand that confiscatory taxes, costly social experiments, and economic tinkering were not just the policies of a single administration. For the 26 years prior to January of 1981, the opposition party controlled both Houses of Congress. Every spending bill and every tax for more than a quarter of a century has been of their doing.

About a decade ago, they said Federal spending was out of control, so they passed a budget control act and, in the next 5 years, ran up deficits of $260 billion. Some control.

In 1981 we gained control of the Senate and the executive branch. With the help of some concerned Democrats in the House we started a policy of tightening the Federal budget instead of the family budget.

A task force chaired by Vice President George Bush—the finest Vice President this country has ever had—it eliminated unnecessary regulations that had been strangling business and industry.

And while we have our friends down memory lane, maybe they'd like to recall a gimmick they designed for their 1976 campaign. As President Ford told us the night before last, adding the unemployment and inflation rates, they got what they called a misery index. In '76 it came to 12 1/2 percent. They declared the incumbent had no right to seek reelection with that kind of a misery index. Well, 4 years ago, in the 1980 election, they didn't mention the misery index, possibly because it was then over 20 percent. And do you know something? They won't mention it in this election either. It's down to 11.6 and dropping.

By nearly every measure, the position of poor Americans worsened under the leadership of our opponents. Teenage drug use, out-of-wedlock births, and crime increased dramatically. Urban neighborhoods and schools deteriorated. Those whom government intended to help discovered a cycle of dependency that could not be broken. Government became a drug, providing temporary relief, but addiction as well.

And let's get some facts on the table that our opponents don't want to hear. The biggest annual increase in poverty took place between 1978 and 1981—over 9 percent each year, in the first 2 years of our administration. Well, I should—pardon me—I didn't put a period in there. In the first 2 years of our administration, that annual increase fell to 5.3 percent. And 1983 was the first year since 1978 that there was no appreciable increase in poverty at all.

Pouring hundreds of billions of dollars into programs in order to make people worse off was irrational and unfair. It was time we ended this reliance on the government process and renewed our faith in the human process.

In 1980 the people decided with us that the economic crisis was not caused by the fact that they lived too well. Government lived too well. It was time for tax increases to be an act of last resort, not of first resort.

The people told the liberal leadership in Washington, "Try shrinking the size of government before you shrink the size of our paychecks."

Our government was also in serious trouble abroad. We had aircraft that couldn't fly and ships that couldn't leave port. Many of our military were on food stamps because of meager earnings, and reenlistments were down. Ammunition was low, and spare parts were in short supply.

Many of our allies mistrusted us. In the 4 years before we took office, country after country fell under the Soviet yoke. Since January 20th, 1981, not 1 inch of soil has fallen to the Communists.

Audience. 4 more years! 4 more years! 4 more years!

The President. All right.

Audience. 4 more years! 4 more years! 4 more years!

The President. But worst of all, Americans were losing the confidence and optimism about the future that has made us unique in the world. Parents were beginning to doubt that their children would have the better life that has been the dream of every American generation.

We can all be proud that pessimism is ended. America is coming back and is more confident than ever about the future. Tonight, we thank the citizens of the United States whose faith and unwillingness to give up on themselves or this country saved us all.

Together, we began the task of controlling the size and activities of the government by reducing the growth of its spending while passing a tax program to provide incentives to increase productivity for both workers and industry. Today, a working family earning $25,000 has about $2,900 more in purchasing power than if tax and inflation rates were still at the 1980 level.

Today, of all the major industrial nations of the world, America has the strongest economic growth; one of the lowest inflation rates; the fastest rate of job creation—6 1/2 million jobs in the last year and a half—a record 600,000 business incorporations in 1983; and the largest increase in real, after-tax personal income since World War II. We're enjoying the highest level of business investment in history, and America has renewed its leadership in developing the vast new opportunities in science and high technology. America is on the move again and expanding toward new eras of opportunity for everyone.

Now, we're accused of having a secret. Well, if we have, it is that we're going to keep the mighty engine of this nation revved up. And that means a future of sustained economic growth without inflation that's going to create for our children and grandchildren a prosperity that finally will last.

Today our troops have newer and better equipment; their morale is higher. The better armed they are, the less likely it is they will have to use that equipment. But if, heaven forbid, they're ever called upon to defend this nation, nothing would be more immoral than asking them to do so with weapons inferior to those of any possible opponent.

We have also begun to repair our valuable alliances, especially our historic NATO alliance. Extensive discussions in Asia have enabled us to start a new round of diplomatic progress there.

In the Middle East, it remains difficult to bring an end to historic conflicts, but we're not discouraged. And we shall always maintain our pledge never to sell out one of our closest friends, the State of Israel.

Closer to home, there remains a struggle for survival for free Latin American States, allies of ours. They valiantly struggle to prevent Communist takeovers fueled massively by the Soviet Union and Cuba. Our policy is simple: We are not going to betray our friends, reward the enemies of freedom, or permit fear and retreat to become American policies—especially in this hemisphere.

None of the four wars in my lifetime came about because we were too strong. It's weakness that invites adventurous adversaries to make mistaken judgments. America is the most peaceful, least warlike nation in modern history. We are not the cause of all the ills of the world. We're a patient and generous people. But for the sake of our freedom and that of others, we cannot permit our reserve to be confused with a lack of resolve.

Ten months ago, we displayed this resolve in a mission to rescue American students on the imprisoned island of Grenada. Democratic candidates have suggested that this could be likened to the Soviet invasion of Afghanistan—

Audience. Boo-o-o!

The President.—the crushing of human rights in Poland or the genocide in Cambodia.

Audience. Boo-o-o!

The President. Could you imagine Harry Truman, John Kennedy, Hubert Humphrey, or Scoop Jackson making such a shocking comparison?

Audience. No!

The President. Nineteen of our fine young men lost their lives on Grenada, and to even remotely compare their sacrifice to the murderous actions taking place in Afghanistan is unconscionable.

There are some obvious and important differences. First, we were invited in by six East Caribbean States. Does anyone seriously believe the people of Eastern Europe or Afghanistan invited the Russians?

Audience. No!

The President. Second, there are hundreds of thousands of Soviets occupying captive nations across the world. Today, our combat troops have come home. Our students are safe, and freedom is what we left behind in Grenada.

There are some who've forgotten why we have a military. It's not to promote war; it's to be prepared for peace. There's a sign over the entrance to Fairchild Air Force Base in Washington State, and that sign says it all: "Peace is our profession."

Our next administration—

Audience. 4 more years! 4 more years! 4 more years!

The President. All right.

Audience. 4 more years! 4 more years! 4 more years!

The President. I heard you. And that administration will be committed to completing the unfinished agenda that we've placed before the Congress and the Nation. It is an agenda which calls upon the national Democratic leadership to cease its obstructionist ways.

We've heard a lot about deficits this year from those on the other side of the aisle. Well, they should be experts on budget deficits. They've spent most of their political careers creating deficits. For 42 of the last 50 years, they have controlled both Houses of the Congress.

Audience. Boo-o-o!

The President. And for almost all of those 50 years, deficit spending has been their deliberate policy. Now, however, they call for an end to deficits. They call them ours. Yet, at the same time, the leadership of their party resists our every effort to bring Federal spending under control. For 3 years straight, they have prevented us from adopting a balanced budget amendment to the Constitution. We will continue to fight for that amendment, mandating that government spend no more than government takes in.

And we will fight, as the Vice President told you, for the right of a President to veto items in appropriations bills without having to veto the entire bill. There is no better way than the line item veto, now used by Governors in 43 States to cut out waste in government. I know. As Governor of California, I successfully made such vetos over 900 times.

Now, their candidate, it would appear, has only recently found deficits alarming. Nearly 10 years ago he insisted that a $52 billion deficit should be allowed to get much bigger in order to lower unemployment, and he said that sometimes "we need a deficit in order to stimulate the economy."

Audience. Boo-o-o!

The President. As a Senator, he voted to override President Ford's veto of billions of dollars in spending bills and then voted no on a proposal to cut the 1976 deficit in half.

Audience. Boo-o-o!

The President. Was anyone surprised by his pledge to raise your taxes next year if given the chance?

Audience. No!

The President. In the Senate, he voted time and again for new taxes, including a 10-percent income tax surcharge, higher taxes on certain consumer items. He also voted against cutting the excise tax on automobiles. And he was part and parcel of that biggest single, individual tax increase in history—the Social Security payroll tax of 1977. It tripled the maximum tax and still didn't make the system solvent.

Audience. Boo-o-o!

The President. If our opponents were as vigorous in supporting our voluntary prayer amendment as they are in raising taxes, maybe we could get the Lord back in the schoolrooms and drugs and violence out.

Something else illustrates the nature of the choice Americans must make. While we've been hearing a lot of tough talk on crime from our opponents, the House Democratic leadership continues to block a critical anticrime bill that passed the Republican Senate by a 91-to-1 vote. Their burial of this bill means that you and your families will have to wait for even safer homes and streets.

There's no longer any good reason to hold back passage of tuition tax credit legislation. Millions of average parents pay their full share of taxes to support public schools while choosing to send their children to parochial or other independent schools. Doesn't fairness dictate that they should have some help in carrying a double burden?

When we talk of the plight of our cities, what would help more than our enterprise zones bill, which provides tax incentives for private industry to help rebuild and restore decayed areas in 75 sites all across America? If they really wanted a future of boundless new opportunities for our citizens, why have they buried enterprise zones over the years in committee?

Our opponents are openly committed to increasing our tax burden.

Audience. Boo-o-o!

The President. We are committed to stopping them, and we will.

They call their policy the new realism, but their new realism is just the old liberalism. They will place higher and higher taxes on small businesses, on family farms, and on other working families so that government may once again grow at the people's expense. You know, we could say they spend money like drunken sailors, but that would be unfair to drunken sailors—[laughter]—

Audience. 4 more years! 4 more years! 4 more years!

The President. All right. I agree.

Audience. 4 more years! 4 more years! 4 more years!

The President. I was going to say, it would be unfair, because the sailors are spending their own money. [Laughter]

Our tax policies are and will remain prowork, progrowth, and profamily. We intend to simplify the entire tax system—to make taxes more fair, easier to understand, and, most important, to bring the tax rates of every American further down, not up. Now, if we bring them down far enough, growth will continue strong; the underground economy will shrink; the world will beat a path to our door; and no one will be able to hold America back; and the future will be ours.

Audience. U.S.A.! U.S.A.! U.S.A.!

The President. All right. Another part of our future, the greatest challenge of all, is to reduce the risk of nuclear war by reducing the levels of nuclear arms. I have addressed parliaments, have spoken to parliaments in Europe and Asia during these last 3 1/2 years, declaring that a nuclear war cannot be won and must never be fought. And those words, in those assemblies, were greeted with spontaneous applause.

There are only two nations who by their agreement can rid the world of those doomsday weapons—the United States of America and the Soviet Union. For the sake of our children and the safety of this Earth, we ask the Soviets—who have walked out of our negotiations—to join us in reducing and, yes, ridding the Earth of this awful threat.

When we leave this hall tonight, we begin to place those clear choices before our fellow citizens. We must not let them be confused by those who still think that GNP stands for gross national promises. [Laughter] But after the debates, the position papers, the speeches, the conventions, the television

commercials, primaries, caucuses, and slogans—after all this, is there really any doubt at all about what will happen if we let them win this November?

Audience. No!

The President. Is there any doubt that they will raise our taxes?

Audience. No!

The President. That they will send inflation into orbit again?

Audience. No!

The President. That they will make government bigger then ever?

Audience. No!

The President. And deficits even worse?

Audience. No!

The President. Raise unemployment?

Audience. No!

The President. Cut back our defense preparedness?

Audience. No!

The President. Raise interest rates?

Audience. No!

The President. Make unilateral and unwise concessions to the Soviet Union?

Audience. No!

The President. And they'll do all that in the name of compassion.

Audience. Boo-o-o!

The President. It's what they've done to America in the past. But if we do our job right, they won't be able to do it again.

Audience. Reagan! Reagan! Reagan!

The President. It's getting late.

Audience. Reagan! Reagan! Reagan!

The President. All right. In 1980 we asked the people of America, "Are you better off than you were 4 years ago?" Well, the people answered then by choosing us to bring about a change. We have every reason now, 4 years later, to ask that same question again, for we have made a change.

The American people joined us and helped us. Let us ask for their help again to renew the mandate of 1980, to move us further forward on the road we presently travel, the road of common sense, of people in control of their own destiny; the road leading to prosperity and economic expansion in a world at peace.

As we ask for their help, we should also answer the central question of public service: Why are we here? What do we believe in? Well for one thing, we're here to see that government continues to serve the people and not the other way around. Yes, government should do all that is necessary, but only that which is necessary.

We don't lump people by groups or special interests. And let me add, in the party of Lincoln, there is no room for intolerance and not even a small corner for anti-Semitism or bigotry of any kind. Many people are welcome in our house, but not the bigots.

We believe in the uniqueness of each individual. We believe in the sacredness of human life. For some time now we've all fallen into a pattern of describing our choice as left or right. It's become standard rhetoric in discussions of political philosophy. But is that really an accurate description of the choice before us?

Go back a few years to the origin of the terms and see where left or right would take us if we continued far enough in either direction. Stalin. Hitler. One would take us to Communist totalitarianism; the other to the totalitarianism of Hitler.

Isn't our choice really not one of left or right, but of up or down? Down through the welfare state to statism, to more and more government largesse accompanied always by more government authority, less individual liberty and, ultimately, totalitarianism, always advanced as for our own good. The alternative is the dream conceived by our Founding Fathers, up to the ultimate in individual freedom consistent with an orderly society.

We don't celebrate dependence day on the Fourth of July. We celebrate Independence Day.

Audience. U.S.A.! U.S.A.! U.S.A.!

The President. We celebrate the right of each individual to be recognized as unique, possessed of dignity and the sacred right to life, liberty, and the pursuit of happiness. At the same time, with our independence goes a generosity of spirit more evident here than in almost any other part of the world. Recognizing the equality of all men and women, we're willing and able to lift the weak, cradle those who hurt, and nurture the bonds that tie us together as one nation under God.

Finally, we're here to shield our liberties, not just for now or for a few years but forever.

Could I share a personal thought with you tonight, because tonight's kind of special to me. It's the last time, of course, that I will address you under these same circumstances. I hope you'll invite me back to future conventions. Nancy and I will be forever grateful for the honor you've done us, for the opportunity to serve, and for your friendship and trust.

I began political life as a Democrat, casting my first vote in 1932 for Franklin Delano Roosevelt. That year, the Democrats called for a 25-percent reduction in the cost of government by abolishing useless commissions and offices and consolidating departments and bureaus, and giving more authority to State governments. As the years went by and those promises were forgotten, did I leave the Democratic Party, or did the leadership of that party leave not just me but millions of patriotic Democrats who believed in the principles and philosophy of that platform?

One of the first to declare this was a former Democratic nominee for President—Al Smith, the Happy Warrior, who went before the Nation in 1936 to say, on television—or on radio that he could no longer follow his party's leadership and that he was "taking a walk." As Democratic leaders have taken their party further and further away from its first principles, it's no surprise that so many responsible Democrats feel that our platform is closer to their views, and we welcome them to our side.

Four years ago we raised a banner of bold colors—no pale pastels. We proclaimed a dream of an America that would be "a shining city on a hill."

We promised that we'd reduce the growth of the Federal Government, and we have. We said we intended to reduce interest rates and inflation, and we have. We said we would reduce taxes to provide incentives for individuals and business to get our economy moving again, and we have. We said there must be jobs with a future for our people, not government make-work programs, and, in the last 19 months, as I've said, 6 1/2 million new jobs in the private sector have been created. We said we would once again be respected throughout the world, and we are. We said we would restore our ability to protect our freedom on land, sea, and in the air, and we have.

We bring to the American citizens in this election year a record of accomplishment and the promise of continuation.

We came together in a national crusade to make America great again, and to make a new beginning. Well, now it's all coming together. With our beloved nation at peace, we're in the midst of a springtime of hope for America. Greatness lies ahead of us.

Holding the Olympic games here in the United States began defining the promise of this season.

Audience. U.S.A.! U.S.A.! U.S.A.!

The President. All through the spring and summer, we marveled at the journey of the Olympic torch as it made its passage east to west. Over 9,000 miles, by some 4,000 runners, that flame crossed a portrait of our nation.

From our Gotham City, New York, to the Cradle of Liberty, Boston, across the Appalachian springtime, to the City of the Big Shoulders, Chicago. Moving south toward Atlanta, over to St. Louis, past its Gateway Arch, across wheatfields into the stark beauty of the Southwest and then up into the still, snowcapped Rockies. And, after circling the greening Northwest, it came down to California, across the Golden Gate and finally into Los Angeles. And all along the way, that torch became a celebration of America. And we all became participants in the celebration.

Each new story was typical of this land of ours. There was Ansel Stubbs, a youngster of 99, who passed the torch in Kansas to 4-year-old Katie Johnson. In Pineville, Kentucky, it came at 1 a.m., so hundreds of people lined the streets with candles. At Tupelo, Mississippi, at 7 a.m. on a Sunday morning, a robed church choir sang "God Bless America" as the torch went by.

That torch went through the Cumberland Gap, past the Martin Luther King, Jr., Memorial, down the Santa Fe Trail, and alongside Billy the Kid's grave.

In Richardson, Texas, it was carried by a 14 year old boy in a special wheelchair. In West Virginia the runner came across a line of deaf children and let each one pass the torch for a few feet, and at the end these youngsters' hands talked excitedly in their sign language. Crowds spontaneously began singing "America the Beautiful" or "The Battle Hymn of the Republic."

And then, in San Francisco a Vietnamese immigrant, his little son held on his shoulders, dodged photographers and policemen to cheer a 19-year-old black man pushing an 88-year-old white woman in a wheelchair as she carried the torch.

My friends, that's America.

Audience. U.S.A.! U.S.A.! U.S.A.!

The President. We cheered in Los Angeles as the flame was carried in and the giant Olympic torch burst into a billowing fire in front of the teams, the youth of 140 nations assembled on the floor of the Coliseum. And in that moment, maybe you were struck as I was with the uniqueness of what was taking place before a hundred thousand people in the stadium, most of them citizens of our country, and over a billion worldwide watching on television. There were athletes representing 140 countries here to compete in the one country in all the world whose people carry the bloodlines of all those 140 countries and more. Only in the United States is there such a rich mixture of races, creeds, and nationalities—only in our melting pot.

And that brings to mind another torch, the one that greeted so many of our parents and grandparents. Just this past Fourth of July, the torch atop the Statue of Liberty was hoisted down for replacement. We can be forgiven for thinking that maybe it was just worn out from lighting the way to freedom for 17 million new Americans. So, now we'll put up a new one.

The poet called Miss Liberty's torch the "lamp beside the golden door." Well, that was the entrance to America, and it still is. And now you really know why we're here tonight.

The glistening hope of that lamp is still ours. Every promise, every opportunity is still golden in this land. And through that golden door our children can walk into tomorrow with the knowledge that no one can be denied the promise that is America.

Her heart is full; her door is still golden, her future bright. She has arms big enough to comfort and strong enough to support, for the strength in her arms is the strength of her people. She will carry on in the eighties unafraid, unashamed, and unsurpassed.

In this springtime of hope, some lights seem eternal; America's is.

Thank you, God bless you, and God bless America.

Source: "Remarks Accepting the Presidential Nomination at the Republican National Convention in Dallas, Texas," August 23, 1984, The Ronald Reagan Presidential Library. Available online. URL: http://www.reagan.utexas.edu/resource/speeches/1984/82384f.htm

32. Second Inaugural Address January 21, 1985

Reagan trounced his Democratic opponent Walter Mondale in the 1984 election, all the while running a campaign that was devoid of specific policy proposals for the future, beyond tax reform. While presidential inaugural addresses are often recitations of broad principles, this one is especially

noteworthy for its emphasis on generalities. Reagan's second inauguration coincided with one of the worst cold spells in Washington's history, and many events, including this speech, were moved inside to avoid cases of hypothermia.

Senator Mathias, Chief Justice Burger, Vice President Bush, Speaker O'Neill, Senator Dole, Reverend Clergy, members of my family and friends, and my fellow citizens:

This day has been made brighter with the presence here of one who, for a time, has been absent—Senator John Stennis.

God bless you and welcome back.

There is, however, one who is not with us today: Representative Gillis Long of Louisiana left us last night. I wonder if we could all join in a moment of silent prayer. (Moment of silent prayer.) Amen.

There are no words adequate to express my thanks for the great honor that you have bestowed on me. I will do my utmost to be deserving of your trust.

This is, as Senator Mathias told us, the 50th time that we the people have celebrated this historic occasion. When the first President, George Washington, placed his hand upon the Bible, he stood less than a single day's journey by horseback from raw, untamed wilderness. There were 4 million Americans in a union of 13 States. Today we are 60 times as many in a union of 50 States. We have lighted the world with our inventions, gone to the aid of mankind wherever in the world there was a cry for help, journeyed to the Moon and safely returned. So much has changed. And yet we stand together as we did two centuries ago.

When I took this oath four years ago, I did so in a time of economic stress. Voices were raised saying we had to look to our past for the greatness and glory. But we, the present-day Americans, are not given to looking backward. In this blessed land, there is always a better tomorrow.

Four years ago, I spoke to you of a new beginning and we have accomplished that. But in another sense, our new beginning is a continuation of that beginning created two centuries ago when, for the first time in history, government, the people said, was not our master, it is our servant; its only power that which we the people allow it to have.

That system has never failed us, but, for a time, we failed the system. We asked things of government that government was not equipped to give. We yielded authority to the National Government that properly belonged to States or to local governments or to the people themselves. We allowed taxes and inflation to rob us of our earnings and savings and watched the great industrial machine that had made us the most productive people on Earth slow down and the number of unemployed increase.

By 1980, we knew it was time to renew our faith, to strive with all our strength toward the ultimate in individual freedom consistent with an orderly society.

We believed then and now there are no limits to growth and human progress when men and women are free to follow their dreams.

And we were right to believe that. Tax rates have been reduced, inflation cut dramatically, and more people are employed than ever before in our history.

We are creating a nation once again vibrant, robust, and alive. But there are many mountains yet to climb. We will not rest until every American enjoys the fullness of freedom, dignity, and opportunity as our birthright. It is our birthright as citizens of this great Republic, and we'll meet this challenge.

These will be years when Americans have restored their confidence and tradition of progress; when our values of faith, family, work, and neighborhood were restated for a modern age; when our economy was finally freed from government's grip; when we made sincere efforts at meaningful arms reduction, rebuilding our defenses, our economy, and developing new technologies, and helped preserve peace in a troubled world; when Americans courageously supported the struggle for liberty, self-government, and free enterprise throughout the world, and turned the tide of history away from totalitarian darkness and into the warm sunlight of human freedom.

My fellow citizens, our Nation is poised for greatness. We must do what we know is right and do it with all our might. Let history say of us, "These were golden years—when the American Revolution was reborn, when freedom gained new life, when America reached for her best."

Our two-party system has served us well over the years, but never better than in those times of great challenge when we came together not as Democrats or Republicans, but as Americans united in a common cause.

Two of our Founding Fathers, a Boston lawyer named Adams and a Virginia planter named Jefferson, members of that remarkable group who met in Independence Hall and dared to think they could start the world over again, left us an important lesson. They had become political rivals in the Presidential election of 1800. Then years later, when both were retired, and age had softened their anger, they began to speak to each other again through letters. A bond was reestablished between those two who had helped create this government of ours.

In 1826, the 50th anniversary of the Declaration of Independence, they both died. They died on the same day, within a few hours of each other, and that day was the Fourth of July.

In one of those letters exchanged in the sunset of their lives, Jefferson wrote: "It carries me back to the times when, beset with difficulties and dangers, we were fellow laborers in the same cause, struggling for what is most valuable to man, his right to self-government. Laboring always at the same oar, with some

wave ever ahead threatening to overwhelm us, and yet passing harmless . . . we rode through the storm with heart and hand."

Well, with heart and hand, let us stand as one today: One people under God determined that our future shall be worthy of our past. As we do, we must not repeat the well-intentioned errors of our past. We must never again abuse the trust of working men and women, by sending their earnings on a futile chase after the spiraling demands of a bloated Federal Establishment. You elected us in 1980 to end this prescription for disaster, and I don't believe you reelected us in 1984 to reverse course.

At the heart of our efforts is one idea vindicated by 25 straight months of economic growth: Freedom and incentives unleash the drive and entrepreneurial genius that are the core of human progress. We have begun to increase the rewards for work, savings, and investment; reduce the increase in the cost and size of government and its interference in people's lives.

We must simplify our tax system, make it more fair, and bring the rates down for all who work and earn. We must think anew and move with a new boldness, so every American who seeks work can find work; so the least among us shall have an equal chance to achieve the greatest things—to be heroes who heal our sick, feed the hungry, protect peace among nations, and leave this world a better place.

The time has come for a new American emancipation—a great national drive to tear down economic barriers and liberate the spirit of enterprise in the most distressed areas of our country. My friends, together we can do this, and do it we must, so help me God.

From new freedom will spring new opportunities for growth, a more productive, fulfilled and united people, and a stronger America— an America that will lead the technological revolution, and also open its mind and heart and soul to the treasures of literature, music, and poetry, and the values of faith, courage, and love.

A dynamic economy, with more citizens working and paying taxes, will be our strongest tool to bring down budget deficits. But an almost unbroken 50 years of deficit spending has finally brought us to a time of reckoning. We have come to a turning point, a moment for hard decisions. I have asked the Cabinet and my staff a question, and now I put the same question to all of you: If not us, who? And if not now, when? It must be done by all of us going forward with a program aimed at reaching a balanced budget. We can then begin reducing the national debt.

I will shortly submit a budget to the Congress aimed at freezing government program spending for the next year. Beyond that, we must take further steps to permanently control Government's power to tax and spend. We must act now to protect future generations from Government's desire to spend its citizens' money and tax them into servitude when the bills come due. Let us make it unconstitutional for the Federal Government to spend more than the Federal Government takes in.

We have already started returning to the people and to State and local governments responsibilities better handled by them. Now, there is a place for the Federal Government in matters of social compassion. But our fundamental goals must be to reduce dependency and upgrade the dignity of those who are infirm or disadvantaged. And here a growing economy and support from family and community offer our best chance for a society where compassion is a way of life, where the old and infirm are cared for, the young and, yes, the unborn protected, and the unfortunate looked after and made self-sufficient.

And there is another area where the Federal Government can play a part. As an older American, I remember a time when people of different race, creed, or ethnic origin in our land found hatred and prejudice installed in social custom and, yes, in law. There is no story more heartening in our history than the progress that we have made toward the "brotherhood of man" that God intended for us. Let us resolve there will be no turning back or hesitation on the road to an America rich in dignity and abundant with opportunity for all our citizens.

Let us resolve that we the people will build an American opportunity society in which all of us—white and black, rich and poor, young and old—will go forward together arm in arm. Again, let us remember that though our heritage is one of blood lines from every corner of the Earth, we are all Americans pledged to carry on this last, best hope of man on Earth.

I have spoken of our domestic goals and the limitations which we should put on our National Government. Now let me turn to a task which is the primary responsibility of National Government—the safety and security of our people.

Today, we utter no prayer more fervently than the ancient prayer for peace on Earth. Yet history has shown that peace will not come, nor will our freedom be preserved, by good will alone. There are those in the world who scorn our vision of human dignity and freedom. One nation, the Soviet Union, has conducted the greatest military buildup in the history of man, building arsenals of awesome offensive weapons.

We have made progress in restoring our defense capability. But much remains to be done. There must be no wavering by us, nor any doubts by others, that America will meet her responsibilities to remain free, secure, and at peace.

There is only one way safely and legitimately to reduce the cost of national security, and that is to reduce the need for it. And this we are trying to do in negotiations with the Soviet Union. We are not just discussing limits on a further increase of nuclear weapons. We seek, instead, to reduce their number. We seek the total elimination one day of nuclear weapons from the face of the Earth.

Now, for decades, we and the Soviets have lived under the threat of mutual assured destruction; if either resorted to the use of nuclear weapons, the other could retaliate and destroy the one who had started it. Is there either logic or morality in believing that if one side threatens to kill tens of millions of our people, our only recourse is to threaten killing tens of millions of theirs?

I have approved a research program to find, if we can, a security shield that would destroy nuclear missiles before they reach their target. It wouldn't kill people, it would destroy weapons. It wouldn't militarize space, it would help demilitarize the arsenals of Earth. It would render nuclear weapons obsolete. We will meet with the Soviets, hoping that we can agree on a way to rid the world of the threat of nuclear destruction.

We strive for peace and security, heartened by the changes all around us. Since the turn of the century, the number of democracies in the world has grown fourfold. Human freedom is on the march, and nowhere more so than our own hemisphere. Freedom is one of the deepest and noblest aspirations of the human spirit. People, worldwide, hunger for the right of self-determination, for those inalienable rights that make for human dignity and progress.

America must remain freedom's staunchest friend, for freedom is our best ally.

And it is the world's only hope, to conquer poverty and preserve peace. Every blow we inflict against poverty will be a blow against its dark allies of oppression and war. Every victory for human freedom will be a victory for world peace.

So we go forward today, a nation still mighty in its youth and powerful in its purpose. With our alliances strengthened, with our economy leading the world to a new age of economic expansion, we look forward to a world rich in possibilities. And all this because we have worked and acted together, not as members of political parties, but as Americans.

My friends, we live in a world that is lit by lightning. So much is changing and will change, but so much endures, and transcends time.

History is a ribbon, always unfurling; history is a journey. And as we continue our journey, we think of those who traveled before us. We stand together again at the steps of this symbol of our democracy—or we would have been standing at the steps if it hadn't gotten so cold. Now we are standing inside this symbol of our democracy. Now we hear again the echoes of our past: a general falls to his knees in the hard snow of Valley Forge; a lonely President paces the darkened halls, and ponders his struggle to preserve the Union; the men of the Alamo call out encouragement to each other; a settler pushes west and sings a song, and the song echoes out forever and fills the unknowing air.

It is the American sound. It is hopeful, bighearted, idealistic, daring, decent, and fair. That's our heritage; that is our song. We sing it still. For all our problems, our differences, we are together as of old, as we raise our voices to the God who is the Author of this most tender music. And may He continue to hold us close as we fill the world with our sound—sound in unity, affection, and love—one people under God, dedicated to the dream of freedom that He has placed in the human heart, called up on now to pass that dream on to a waiting and hopeful world.

God bless you and may God bless America.

Source: "Inaugural Address," January 21, 1985, The Ronald Reagan Presidential Library. Available online. URL: http://www.reagan.utexas.edu/resource/speeches/1985/85jan.htm

33. 1985 State of the Union Address February 6, 1985

State of the union addresses are important occasions in the life of any administration. This address was given when Reagan was at the height of his power, having won one of the largest victories in the history of American presidential elections, and with his party still in control of the Senate. Reagan celebrated what had occurred in his four years in office as "the American miracle," and asked Congress to support his agenda of tax reform, increased defense spending, tougher crime legislation, and a conservative social agenda. Delivered on his 74th birthday, the speech includes Reagan's request to Speaker of the House "Tip" O'Neill for a special gift, which the president never received.

I come before you to report on the state of our Union, and I'm pleased to report that after 4 years of united effort, the American people have brought forth a nation renewed, stronger, freer, and more secure than before.

Four years ago we began to change, forever I hope, our assumptions about government and its place in our lives. Out of that change has come great and robust growth—in our confidence, our economy, and our role in the world.

Tonight America is stronger because of the values that we hold dear. We believe faith and freedom must be our guiding stars, for they show us truth, they make us brave, give us hope, and leave us wiser than we were. Our progress began not in Washington, D.C., but in the hearts of our families, communities, workplaces, and voluntary groups which, together, are unleashing the invincible spirit of one great nation under God.

Four years ago we said we would invigorate our economy by giving people greater freedom and incentives to take risks and letting them keep more of what they earned. We did what we promised, and a great industrial giant is reborn.

Tonight we can take pride in 25 straight months of economic growth, the strongest in 34 years; a 3-year inflation average of 3.9 percent, the lowest in 17 years; and 7.3 million new jobs in 2 years, with more of our citizens working than ever before.

New freedom in our lives has planted the rich seeds for future success:

• For an America of wisdom that honors the family, knowing that if [as] the family goes, so goes our civilization;

• For an America of vision that sees tomorrow's dreams in the learning and hard work we do today;

• For an America of courage whose service men and women, even as we meet, proudly stand watch on the frontiers of freedom;

• For an America of compassion that opens its heart to those who cry out for help.

We have begun well. But it's only a beginning. We're not here to congratulate ourselves on what we have done but to challenge ourselves to finish what has not yet been done.

We're here to speak for millions in our inner cities who long for real jobs, safe neighborhoods, and schools that truly teach. We're here to speak for the American farmer, the entrepreneur, and every worker in industries fighting to modernize and compete. And, yes, we're here to stand, and proudly so, for all who struggle to break free from totalitarianism, for all who know in their hearts that freedom is the one true path to peace and human happiness.

Proverbs tell us, without a vision the people perish. When asked what great principle holds our Union together, Abraham Lincoln said, "Something in [the] Declaration giving liberty, not alone to the people of this country, but hope to the world for all future time."

We honor the giants of our history not by going back but forward to the dreams their vision foresaw. My fellow citizens, this nation is poised for greatness. The time has come to proceed toward a great new challenge—a second American Revolution of hope and opportunity; a revolution carrying us to new heights of progress by pushing back frontiers of knowledge and space; a revolution of spirit that taps the soul of America, enabling us to summon greater strength than we've ever known; and a revolution that carries beyond our shores the golden promise of human freedom in a world of peace.

Let us begin by challenging our conventional wisdom. There are no constraints on the human mind, no walls around the human spirit, no barriers to our progress except those we ourselves erect. Already, pushing down tax rates has freed our economy to vault forward to record growth.

In Europe, they're calling it "the American Miracle." Day by day, we're shattering accepted notions of what is possible. When I was growing up, we failed to see how a new thing called radio would transform our marketplace. Well, today, many have not yet seen how advances in technology are transforming our lives.

In the late 1950's workers at the AT&T semiconductor plant in Pennsylvania produced five transistors a day for $7.50 apiece. They now produce over a million for less than a penny apiece.

New laser techniques could revolutionize heart bypass surgery, cut diagnosis time for viruses linked to cancer from weeks to minutes, reduce hospital costs dramatically, and hold out new promise for saving human lives.

Our automobile industry has overhauled assembly lines, increased worker productivity, and is competitive once again.

We stand on the threshold of a great ability to produce more, do more, be more. Our economy is not getting older and weaker; it's getting younger and stronger. It doesn't need rest and supervision; it needs new challenge,

greater freedom. And that word "freedom" is the key to the second American Revolution that we need to bring about.

Let us move together with an historic reform of tax simplification for fairness and growth. Last year I asked Treasury Secretary—then—Regan to develop a plan to simplify the tax code, so all taxpayers would be treated more fairly and personal tax rates could come further down.

We have cut tax rates by almost 25 percent, yet the tax system remains unfair and limits our potential for growth. Exclusions and exemptions cause similar incomes to be taxed at different levels. Low-income families face steep tax barriers that make hard lives even harder. The Treasury Department has produced an excellent reform plan, whose principles will guide the final proposal that we will ask you to enact.

One thing that tax reform will not be is a tax increase in disguise. We will not jeopardize the mortgage interest deduction that families need. We will reduce personal tax rates as low as possible by removing many tax preferences. We will propose a top rate of no more than 35 percent, and possibly lower. And we will propose reducing corporate rates, while maintaining incentives for capital formation.

To encourage opportunity and jobs rather than dependency and welfare, we will propose that individuals living at or near the poverty line be totally exempt from Federal income tax. To restore fairness to families, we will propose increasing significantly the personal exemption. And tonight, I am instructing Treasury Secretary James Baker—I have to get used to saying that—to begin working with congressional authors and committees for bipartisan legislation conforming to these principles. We will call upon the American people for support and upon every man and woman in this Chamber. Together, we can pass, this year, a tax bill for fairness, simplicity, and growth, making this economy the engine of our dreams and America the investment capital of the world. So let us begin.

Tax simplification will be a giant step toward unleashing the tremendous pent-up power of our economy. But a second American Revolution must carry the promise of opportunity for all. It is time to liberate the spirit of enterprise in the most distressed areas of our country.

This government will meet its responsibility to help those in need. But policies that increase dependency, break up families, and destroy self-respect are not progressive; they're reactionary. Despite our strides in civil rights, blacks, Hispanics, and all minorities will not have full and equal power until they have full economic power.

We have repeatedly sought passage of enterprise zones to help those in the abandoned corners of our land find jobs, learn skills, and build better lives. This legislation is supported by a majority of you.

Mr. Speaker, I know we agree that there must be no forgotten Americans. Let us place new dreams in a million hearts and create a new generation of entrepreneurs by passing enterprise zones this year. And, Tip, you could make that a birthday present.

Nor must we lose the chance to pass our youth employment opportunity wage proposal. We can help teenagers, who have the highest unemployment rate, find summer jobs, so they can know the pride of work and have confidence in their futures.

We'll continue to support the Job Training Partnership Act, which has a nearly two-thirds job placement rate. Credits in education and health care vouchers will help working families shop for services that they need.

Our administration is already encouraging certain low-income public housing residents to own and manage their own dwellings. It's time that all public housing residents have that opportunity of ownership.

The Federal Government can help create a new atmosphere of freedom. But States and localities, many of which enjoy surpluses from the recovery, must not permit their tax and regulatory policies to stand as barriers to growth.

Let us resolve that we will stop spreading dependency and start spreading opportunity; that we will stop spreading bondage and start spreading freedom.

There are some who say that growth initiatives must await final action on deficit reductions. Well, the best way to reduce deficits is through economic growth. More businesses will be started, more investments made, more jobs created, and more people will be on payrolls paying taxes. The best way to reduce government spending is to reduce the need for spending by increasing prosperity. Each added percentage point per year of real GNP growth will lead to cumulative reduction in deficits of nearly $200 billion over 5 years.

To move steadily toward a balanced budget, we must also lighten government's claim on our total economy. We will not do this by raising taxes. We must make sure that our economy grows faster than the growth in spending by the Federal Government. In our fiscal year 1986 budget, overall government program spending will be frozen at the current level. It must not be one dime higher than fiscal year 1985, and three points are key.

First, the social safety net for the elderly, the needy, the disabled, and unemployed will be left intact. Growth of our major health care programs, Medicare and Medicaid, will be slowed, but protections for the elderly and needy will be preserved.

Second, we must not relax our efforts to restore military strength just as we near our goal of a fully equipped, trained, and ready professional corps. National security is government's first responsibility; so in past years defense spending took about half the Federal budget. Today it takes less than a third. We've already reduced our planned defense expenditures by nearly a hundred billion dollars over the past 4 years and reduced projected spending again this year.

You know, we only have a military-industrial complex until a time of danger, and then it becomes the arsenal of democracy. Spending for defense is investing in things that are priceless—peace and freedom.

Third, we must reduce or eliminate costly government subsidies. For example, deregulation of the airline industry has led to cheaper airfares, but on Amtrak taxpayers pay about $35 per passenger every time an Amtrak train leaves the station. It's time we ended this huge Federal subsidy.

Our farm program costs have quadrupled in recent years. Yet I know from visiting farmers, many in great financial distress, that we need an orderly transition to a market-oriented farm economy. We can help farmers best not by expanding Federal payments but by making fundamental reforms, keeping interest rates heading down, and knocking down foreign trade barriers to American farm exports.

We're moving ahead with Grace commission reforms to eliminate waste and improve government's management practices. In the long run, we must protect the taxpayers from government. And I ask again that you pass, as 32 States have now called for, an amendment mandating the Federal Government spend no more than it takes in. And I ask for the authority, used responsibly by 43 Governors, to veto individual items in appropriation bills. Senator Mattingly has introduced a bill permitting a 2-year trial run of the line-item veto. I hope you'll pass and send that legislation to my desk.

Nearly 50 years of government living beyond its means has brought us to a time of reckoning. Ours is but a moment in history. But one moment of courage, idealism, and bipartisan unity can change American history forever.

Sound monetary policy is key to long-running economic strength and stability. We will continue to cooperate with the Federal Reserve Board, seeking a steady policy that ensures price stability without keeping interest rates artificially high or needlessly holding down growth.

Reducing unneeded redtape and regulations, and deregulating the energy, transportation, and financial industries have unleashed new competition, giving consumers more choices, better services, and lower prices. In just one set of grant programs we have reduced 905 pages of regulations to 31. We seek to fully deregulate natural gas to bring on new supplies and bring us closer to energy independence. Consistent with safety standards, we will continue removing restraints on the bus and railroad industries, we will soon end up legislation—or send up legislation, I should say—to return Conrail to the private sector where it belongs, and we will support further deregulation of the trucking industry.

Every dollar the Federal Government does not take from us, every decision it does not make for us will make our economy stronger, our lives more abundant, our future more free.

Our second American Revolution will push on to new possibilities not only on Earth but in the next frontier of space. Despite budget restraints, we will seek record funding for research and development.

We've seen the success of the space shuttle. Now we're going to develop a permanently manned space station and new opportunities for free enterprise, because in the next decade Americans and our friends around the world will be living and working together in space.

In the zero gravity of space, we could manufacture in 30 days lifesaving medicines it would take 30 years to make on Earth. We can make crystals of exceptional purity to produce super computers, creating jobs, technologies, and medical breakthroughs beyond anything we ever dreamed possible.

As we do all this, we'll continue to protect our natural resources. We will seek reauthorization and expanded funding for the Superfund program to continue cleaning up hazardous waste sites which threaten human health and the environment.

Now, there's another great heritage to speak of this evening. Of all the changes that have swept America the past 4 years, none brings greater promise than our rediscovery of the values of faith, freedom, family, work, and neighborhood.

We see signs of renewal in increased attendance in places of worship; renewed optimism and faith in our future; love of country rediscovered by our young, who are leading the way. We've rediscovered that work is good in and of itself, that it ennobles us to create and contribute no matter how seemingly humble our jobs. We've seen a powerful new current from an old and honorable tradition—American generosity.

From thousands answering Peace Corps appeals to help boost food production in Africa, to millions volunteering time, corporations adopting schools, and communities pulling together to help the neediest among us at home, we have refound our values. Private sector initiatives are crucial to our future.

I thank the Congress for passing equal access legislation giving religious groups the same right to use classrooms after school that other groups enjoy. But no citizen need tremble, nor the world shudder, if a child stands in a classroom and breathes a prayer. We ask you again, give children back a right they had for a century and a half or more in this country.

The question of abortion grips our nation. Abortion is either the taking of a human life or it isn't. And if it is—and medical technology is increasingly showing it is—it must be stopped. It is a terrible irony that while some turn to abortion, so many others who cannot become

parents cry out for children to adopt. We have room for these children. We can fill the cradles of those who want a child to love. And tonight I ask you in the Congress to move this year on legislation to protect the unborn.

In the area of education, we're returning to excellence, and again, the heroes are our people, not government. We're stressing basics of discipline, rigorous testing, and homework, while helping children become computer-smart as well. For 20 years Scholastic Aptitude Test scores of our high school students went down, but now they have gone up 2 of the last 3 years. We must go forward in our commitment to the new basics, giving parents greater authority and making sure good teachers are rewarded for hard work and achievement through merit pay.

Of all the changes in the past 20 years, none has more threatened our sense of national well-being than the explosion of violent crime. One does not have to be attacked to be a victim. The woman who must run to her car after shopping at night is a victim. The couple draping their door with locks and chains are victims; as is the tired, decent cleaning woman who can't ride a subway home without being afraid.

We do not seek to violate the rights of defendants. But shouldn't we feel more compassion for the victims of crime than for those who commit crime? For the first time in 20 years, the crime index has fallen 2 years in a row. We've convicted over 7,400 drug offenders and put them, as well as leaders of organized crime, behind bars in record numbers.

But we must do more. I urge the House to follow the Senate and enact proposals permitting use of all reliable evidence that police officers acquire in good faith. These proposals would also reform the habeas corpus laws and allow, in keeping with the will of the overwhelming majority of Americans, the use of the death penalty where necessary.

There can be no economic revival in ghettos when the most violent among us are allowed to roam free. It's time we restored domestic tranquility. And we mean to do just that.

Just as we're positioned as never before to secure justice in our economy, we're poised as never before to create a safer, freer, more peaceful world. Our alliances are stronger than ever. Our economy is stronger than ever. We have resumed our historic role as a leader of the free world. And all of these together are a great force for peace.

Since 1981 we've been committed to seeking fair and verifiable arms agreements that would lower the risk of war and reduce the size of nuclear arsenals. Now our determination to maintain a strong defense has influenced the Soviet Union to return to the bargaining table. Our negotiators must be able to go to that table with the united support of the American people. All of us have no greater dream than to see the day when nuclear weapons are banned from this Earth forever.

Each Member of the Congress has a role to play in modernizing our defenses, thus supporting our chances for a meaningful arms agreement. Your vote this spring on the Peacekeeper missile will be a critical test of our resolve to maintain the strength we need and move toward mutual and verifiable arms reductions.

For the past 20 years we've believed that no war will be launched as long as each side knows it can retaliate with a deadly counterstrike. Well, I believe there's a better way of eliminating the threat of nuclear war. It is a Strategic Defense Initiative aimed ultimately at finding a nonnuclear defense against ballistic missiles. It's the most hopeful possibility of the nuclear age. But it's not very well understood.

Some say it will bring war to the heavens, but its purpose is to deter war in the heavens and on Earth. Now, some say the research would be expensive. Perhaps, but it could save millions of lives, indeed humanity itself. And some say if we build such a system, the Soviets will build a defense system of their own. Well, they already have strategic defenses that surpass ours; a civil defense system, where we have almost none; and a research program covering roughly the same areas of technology that we're now exploring. And finally some say the research will take a long time. Well, the answer to that is: "Let's get started."

Harry Truman once said that, ultimately, our security and the world's hopes for peace and human progress "lie not in measures of defense or in the control of weapons, but in the growth and expansion of freedom and self-government."

And tonight, we declare anew to our fellow citizens of the world: Freedom is not the sole prerogative of a chosen few; it is the universal right of all God's children. Look to where peace and prosperity flourish today. It is in homes that freedom built. Victories against poverty are greatest and peace most secure where people live by laws that ensure free press, free speech, and freedom to worship, vote, and create wealth.

Our mission is to nourish and defend freedom and democracy, and to communicate these ideals everywhere we can. America's economic success is freedom's success; it can be repeated a hundred times in a hundred different nations. Many countries in east Asia and the Pacific have few resources other than the enterprise of their own people. But through low tax rates and free markets they've soared ahead of centralized economies. And now China is opening up its economy to meet its needs.

We need a stronger and simpler approach to the process of making and implementing trade policy, and we'll be studying potential changes in that process in the next few weeks. We've seen the benefits of free trade and lived through the disasters of protectionism. Tonight I ask all our trading partners, developed and developing alike, to join us in a new round of trade negotiations to expand trade and competition and strengthen the global economy—and to begin it in this next year.

There are more than 3 billion human beings living in Third World countries with an average per capita income of $650 a year. Many are victims of dictatorships that impoverished them with taxation and corruption. Let us ask our allies to join us in a practical program of trade and assistance that fosters economic development through personal incentives to help these people climb from poverty on their own.

We cannot play innocents abroad in a world that's not innocent; nor can we be passive when freedom is under siege. Without resources, diplomacy cannot succeed. Our security assistance programs help friendly governments defend themselves and give them confidence to work for peace. And I hope that you in the Congress will understand that, dollar for dollar, security assistance contributes as much to global security as our own defense budget.

We must stand by all our democratic allies. And we must not break faith with those who are risking their lives—on every continent, from Afghanistan to Nicaragua—to defy Soviet-supported aggression and secure rights which have been ours from birth.

The Sandinista dictatorship of Nicaragua, with full Cuban-Soviet bloc support, not only persecutes its people, the church, and denies a free press, but arms and provides bases for Communist terrorists attacking neighboring states. Support for freedom fighters is self-defense and totally consistent with the OAS and U.N. Charters. It is essential that the Congress continue all facets of our assistance to Central America. I want to work with you to support the democratic forces whose struggle is tied to our own security.

And tonight, I've spoken of great plans and great dreams. They're dreams we can make come true. Two hundred years of American history should have taught us that nothing is impossible.

Ten years ago a young girl left Vietnam with her family, part of the exodus that fol-lowed the fall of Saigon. They came to the United States with no possessions and not knowing a word of English. Ten years ago— the young girl studied hard, learned English, and finished high school in the top of her class. And this May, May 22d to be exact, is a big date on her calendar. Just 10 years from the time she left Vietnam, she will graduate from the United States Military Academy at West Point. I thought you might like to meet an American hero named Jean Nguyen.

Now, there's someone else here tonight, born 79 years ago. She lives in the inner city, where she cares for infants born of mothers who are heroin addicts. The children, born in withdrawal, are sometimes even dropped on her doorstep. She helps them with love. Go to her house some night, and maybe you'll see her silhouette against the window as she walks the floor talking softly, soothing a child in her arms—Mother Hale of Harlem, and she, too, is an American hero.

Jean, Mother Hale, your lives tell us that the oldest American saying is new again: Anything is possible in America if we have the faith, the will, and the heart. History is asking us once again to be a force for good in the world. Let us begin in unity, with justice, and love.

Thank you, and God bless you.

Source: "Address Before a Joint Session of the Congress on the State of the Union," February 6, 1985, The Ronald Reagan Presidential Library. Available online. URL: http://www.reagan.utexas. edu/resource/speeches/1985/20685e.htm

34. Remarks at a Commemorative Ceremony at Bergen-Belsen Concentration Camp in the Federal Republic of Germany
May 5, 1985

Reagan was embroiled in a controversy over his visit to Germany in May 1985, when he agreed to

accompany German chancellor Helmut Kohl to the Bitburg Cemetery that included gravesites of members of the dreaded SS, Hitler's shock troops. After an emotional appeal from American Jewish leaders asking Reagan to cancel the Bitburg visit and an equally emotional plea from Kohl to proceed with it, Reagan decided to visit Bitburg and added this stop at the Bergen-Belsen concentration camp. Reagan fought back tears as he delivered this moving tribute to the victims of the Holocaust, which included an especially poignant remembrance of Anne Frank.

Chancellor Kohl and honored guests, this painful walk into the past has done much more than remind us of the war that consumed the European Continent. What we have seen makes unforgettably clear that no one of the rest of us can fully understand the enormity of the feelings carried by the victims of these camps. The survivors carry a memory beyond anything that we can comprehend. The awful evil started by one man, an evil that victimized all the world with its destruction, was uniquely destructive of the millions forced into the grim abyss of these camps.

Here lie people—Jews—whose death was inflicted for no reason other than their very existence. Their pain was borne only because of who they were and because of the God in their prayers. Alongside them lay many Christians—Catholics and Protestants.

For year after year, until that man and his evil were destroyed, hell yawned forth its awful contents. People were brought here for no other purpose but to suffer and die—to go unfed when hungry, uncared for when sick, tortured when the whim struck, and left to have misery consume them when all there was around them was misery.

I'm sure we all share similar first thoughts, and that is: What of the youngsters who died at this dark stalag? All was gone for them forever—not to feel again the warmth of life's sunshine and promise, not the laughter and the splendid ache of growing up, nor the consoling embrace of a family. Try to think of being young and never having a day without searing emotional and physical pain—desolate, unrelieved pain.

Today, we've been grimly reminded why the commandant of this camp was named "the Beast of Belsen." Above all, we're struck by the horror of it all—the monstrous, incomprehensible horror. And that's what we've seen but is what we can never understand as the victims did. Nor with all our compassion can we feel what the survivors feel to this day and what they will feel as long as they live. What we've felt and are expressing with words cannot convey the suffering that they endured. That is why history will forever brand what happened as the Holocaust.

Here, death ruled, but we've learned something as well. Because of what happened, we found that death cannot rule forever, and that's why we're here today. We're here because humanity refuses to accept that freedom of the spirit of man can ever be extinguished. We're here to commemorate that life triumphed over the tragedy and the death of the Holocaust—overcame the suffering, the sickness, the testing and, yes, the gassings. We're here today to confirm that the horror cannot outlast hope, and that even from the worst of all things, the best may come forth. Therefore, even out of this overwhelming sadness, there must be some purpose, and there is. It comes to us through the transforming love of God.

We learn from the Talmud that: "It was only through suffering that the children of Israel obtained three priceless and coveted gifts: The Torah, the Land of Israel, and the World to Come." Yes, out of this sickness—as crushing and cruel as it was—there was hope for the world as well as for the world to come. Out of the ashes—hope, and from all the pain—promise.

So much of this is symbolized today by the fact that most of the leadership of free

Germany is represented here today. Chancellor Kohl, you and your countrymen have made real the renewal that had to happen. Your nation and the German people have been strong and resolute in your willingness to confront and condemn the acts of a hated regime of the past. This reflects the courage of your people and their devotion to freedom and justice since the war. Think how far we've come from that time when despair made these tragic victims wonder if anything could survive.

As we flew here from Hanover, low over the greening farms and the emerging springtime of the lovely German countryside, I reflected, and there must have been a time when the prisoners at Bergen-Belsen and those of every other camp must have felt the springtime was gone forever from their lives. Surely we can understand that when we see what is around us—all these children of God under bleak and lifeless mounds, the plainness of which does not even hint at the unspeakable acts that created them. Here they lie, never to hope, never to pray, never to love, never to heal, never to laugh, never to cry.

And too many of them knew that this was their fate, but that was not the end. Through it all was their faith and a spirit that moved their faith.

Nothing illustrates this better than the story of a young girl who died here at Bergen-Belsen. For more than 2 years Anne Frank and her family had hidden from the Nazis in a confined annex in Holland where she kept a remarkably profound diary. Betrayed by an informant, Anne and her family were sent by freight car first to Auschwitz and finally here to Bergen-Belsen.

Just 3 weeks before her capture, young Anne wrote these words: "It's really a wonder that I haven't dropped all my ideals because they seem so absurd and impossible to carry out. Yet I keep them because in spite of everything I still believe that people are good at heart. I simply can't build up my hopes on a foundation consisting of confusion, misery, and death. I see the world gradually being turned into a wilderness. I hear the ever approaching thunder which will destroy us too; I can feel the suffering of millions and yet, if I looked up into the heavens I think that it will all come right, that this cruelty too will end and that peace and tranquility will return again." Eight months later, this sparkling young life ended here at Bergen-Belsen. Somewhere here lies Anne Frank.

Everywhere here are memories—pulling us, touching us, making us understand that they can never be erased. Such memories take us where God intended His children to go—toward learning, toward healing, and, above all, toward redemption. They beckon us through the endless stretches of our heart to the knowing commitment that the life of each individual can change the world and make it better.

We're all witnesses; we share the glistening hope that rests in every human soul. Hope leads us, if we're prepared to trust it, toward what our President Lincoln called the better angels of our nature. And then, rising above all this cruelty, out of this tragic and nightmarish time, beyond the anguish, the pain and the suffering for all time, we can and must pledge: Never again.

Source: "Remarks at a Commemorative Ceremony at Bergen-Belsen Concentration Camp in the Federal Republic of Germany," May 5, 1985, The Ronald Reagan Presidential Library. Available online. URL: http://www.reagan.utexas.edu/resource/speeches/1985/50585a.htm

35. *Challenger* Disaster Speech January 28, 1986

President Reagan was at his best when playing the role of "healer-in-chief." On the morning of January

28, 1986, the space shuttle Challenger *exploded shortly after lifting off from the Kennedy Space Center at Cape Canaveral, Florida. Seven astronauts, including America's first "teacher in space," Christa McAuliffe, were killed as they "slipped the surly bonds of earth." In his address later that evening, Reagan recited this passage and others from the poem "High Flight." The poem was written by John Gillespie Magee, an American who volunteered to serve with the Royal Canadian Air Force in Britain and was killed in 1941. Reagan knew the poem, as did his speechwriter Peggy Noonan, and these passages provided a dramatic climax to the brief address.*

Ladies and Gentlemen, I'd planned to speak to you tonight to report on the state of the Union, but the events of earlier today have led me to change those plans. Today is a day for mourning and remembering. Nancy and I are pained to the core by the tragedy of the shuttle Challenger. We know we share this pain with all of the people of our country. This is truly a national loss.

Nineteen years ago, almost to the day, we lost three astronauts in a terrible accident on the ground. But we've never lost an astronaut in flight; we've never had a tragedy like this. And perhaps we've forgotten the courage it took for the crew of the shuttle. But they, the Challenger Seven, were aware of the dangers, overcame them and did their jobs brilliantly. We mourn seven heroes: Michael Smith, Dick Scobee, Judith Resnik, Ronald McNair, Ellison Onizuka, Gregory Jarvis, and Christa McAuliffe. We mourn their loss as a nation together.

[To] the families of the seven: we cannot bear, as you do, the full impact of this tragedy. But we feel the loss, and we're thinking about you so very much. Your loved ones were daring and brave, and they had that special grace, that special spirit that says, "Give me a challenge, and I'll meet it with joy." They had a hunger to explore the universe and discover its truths.

They wished to serve, and they did. They served all of us. We've grown used to wonders in this century. It's hard to dazzle us. But for 25 years the United States space program has been doing just that. We've grown used to the idea of space, and perhaps we forget that we've only just begun. We're still pioneers. They, the members of the Challenger crew, were pioneers.

And I want to say something to the schoolchildren of America who were watching the live coverage of the shuttle's takeoff. I know it is hard to understand, but sometimes painful things like this happen. It's all part of the process of exploration and discovery. It's all part of taking a chance and expanding man's horizons. The future doesn't belong to the fainthearted; it belongs to the brave. The Challenger crew was pulling us into the future, and we'll continue to follow them.

I've always had great faith in and respect for our space program, and what happened today does nothing to diminish it. We don't hide our space program. We don't keep secrets and cover things up. We do it all up front and in public. That's the way freedom is, and we wouldn't change it for a minute. We'll continue our quest in space. There will be more shuttle flights and more shuttle crews and, yes, more volunteers, more civilians, more teachers in space. Nothing ends here; our hopes and our journeys continue. I want to add that I wish I could talk to every man and woman who works for NASA or who worked on this mission and tell them: "Your dedication and professionalism have moved and impressed us for decades. And we know of your anguish. We share it."

There's a coincidence today. On this day 390 years ago, the great explorer Sir Francis Drake died aboard ship off the coast of Panama. In his lifetime the great frontiers were the oceans, and an historian later said, "He lived by the sea, died on it, and was buried in it." Well today we can say of the Challenger crew: Their dedication was, like Drake's, complete.

The crew of the space shuttle Challenger honored us by the manner in which they lived their lives. We will never forget them, nor the last time we saw them, this morning, as they prepared for their journey and waved goodbye and "slipped the surly bonds of earth" to "touch the face of God."

Thank you.

Source: "Address to the Nation on the Explosion of the Space Shuttle Challenger," January 28, 1986, The Ronald Reagan Presidential Library. Available online. URL: http://www.reagan.utexas.edu/resource/speeches/1986/12886b.htm

36. Address to the Nation on the United States Air Strike against Libya April 14, 1986

Reagan tangled with Libya's unstable leader Muammar al-Gadhafi throughout the 1980s, but this incident was by far the most serious confrontation between the two nations. On April 5, 1986, a Berlin nightclub crowded with American soldiers was bombed, killing one soldier and wounding many others; shortly after this the National Security Agency intercepted communications in which Libyan agents boasted about the bombing to superiors in Tripoli. Reagan decided to retaliate, and ordered the air force and the navy to hit targets in Tripoli and Benghazi, including Gadhafi's own home, which the administration viewed as a terrorist headquarters. The strike was impaired by the refusal of the French to allow Air Force F-111s based in England to fly through their airspace; nevertheless, the attack proceeded and a number of Libyan targets were struck. Reaction among the Democratic leadership and many foreign governments was highly critical, but in the short run the raid prompted Gadhafi to curb his terrorist activities.

My fellow Americans:

At 7 o'clock this evening eastern time air and naval forces of the United States launched a series of strikes against the headquarters, terrorist facilities, and military assets that support Mu'ammar Qadhafi's subversive activities. The attacks were concentrated and carefully targeted to minimize casualties among the Libyan people with whom we have no quarrel. From initial reports, our forces have succeeded in their mission.

Several weeks ago in New Orleans, I warned Colonel Qadhafi we would hold his regime accountable for any new terrorist attacks launched against American citizens. More recently I made it clear we would respond as soon as we determined conclusively who was responsible for such attacks. On April 5th in West Berlin a terrorist bomb exploded in a nightclub frequented by American servicemen. Sergeant Kenneth Ford and a young Turkish woman were killed and 230 others were wounded, among them some 50 American military personnel. This monstrous brutality is but the latest act in Colonel Qadhafi's reign of terror. The evidence is now conclusive that the terrorist bombing of La Belle discotheque was planned and executed under the direct orders of the Libyan regime. On March 25th, more than a week before the attack, orders were sent from Tripoli to the Libyan People's Bureau in East Berlin to conduct a terrorist attack against Americans to cause maximum and indiscriminate casualties. Libya's agents then planted the bomb. On April 4th the People's Bureau alerted Tripoli that the attack would be carried out the following morning. The next day they reported back to Tripoli on the great success of their mission.

Our evidence is direct; it is precise; it is irrefutable. We have solid evidence about other attacks Qadhafi has planned against the United States installations and diplomats and even American tourists. Thanks to close cooperation with our friends, some of these have been prevented. With the help of French authorities, we recently aborted one such attack: a planned massacre, using grenades and small arms, of civilians waiting in line for visas at an American Embassy.

Colonel Qadhafi is not only an enemy of the United States. His record of subversion and aggression against the neighboring States in Africa is well documented and well known. He has ordered the murder of fellow Libyans in countless countries. He has sanctioned acts of terror in Africa, Europe, and the Middle East, as well as the Western Hemisphere. Today we have done what we had to do. If necessary, we shall do it again. It gives me no pleasure to say that, and I wish it were otherwise. Before Qadhafi seized power in 1969, the people of Libya had been friends of the United States. And I'm sure that today most Libyans are ashamed and disgusted that this man has made their country a synonym for barbarism around the world. The Libyan people are a decent people caught in the grip of a tyrant.

To our friends and allies in Europe who cooperated in today's mission, I would only say you have the permanent gratitude of the American people. Europeans who remember history understand better than most that there is no security, no safety, in the appeasement of evil. It must be the core of Western policy that there be no sanctuary for terror. And to sustain such a policy, free men and free nations must unite and work together. Sometimes it is said that by imposing sanctions against Colonel Qadhafi or by striking at his terrorist installations we only magnify the man's importance, that the proper way to deal with him is to ignore him. I do not agree.

Long before I came into this office, Colonel Qadhafi had engaged in acts of international terror, acts that put him outside the company of civilized men. For years, however, he suffered no economic or political or military sanction; and the atrocities mounted in number, as did the innocent dead and wounded. And for us to ignore by inaction the slaughter of American civilians and American soldiers, whether in nightclubs or airline terminals, is simply not in the American tradition. When our citizens are abused or attacked anywhere in the world on the direct orders of a hostile regime, we will respond so long as I'm in this Oval Office. Self-defense is not only our right, it is our duty. It is the purpose behind the mission undertaken tonight, a mission fully consistent with Article 51 of the United Nations Charter.

We believe that this preemptive action against his terrorist installations will not only diminish Colonel Qadhafi's capacity to export terror, it will provide him with incentives and reasons to alter his criminal behavior. I have no illusion that tonight's action will ring down the curtain on Qadhafi's reign of terror. But this mission, violent though it was, can bring closer a safer and more secure world for decent men and women. We will persevere. This afternoon we consulted with the leaders of Congress regarding what we were about to do and why. Tonight I salute the skill and professionalism of the men and women of our Armed Forces who carried out this mission. It's an honor to be your Commander in Chief.

We Americans are slow to anger. We always seek peaceful avenues before resorting to the use of force—and we did. We tried quiet diplomacy, public condemnation, economic sanctions, and demonstrations of military force. None succeeded. Despite our repeated warnings, Qadhafi continued his reckless policy of intimidation, his relentless pursuit of terror. He counted on America to be passive. He counted wrong. I warned that there should be no place on Earth where terrorists can rest and train and practice their deadly skills. I meant it. I said that we would act with others, if possible, and alone if necessary to ensure that terrorists have no sanctuary anywhere. Tonight, we have.

Thank you, and God bless you.

Source: "Address to the Nation on the United States Air Strike against Libya," April 14, 1986,

The Ronald Reagan Presidential Library. Available online. URL: http://www.reagan.utexas.edu/resource/speeches/1986/41486g.htm

37. On the Campaign against Drug Abuse The President and Mrs. Reagan, from the White House, September 14, 1986

Ronald and Nancy Reagan delivered this joint address to the nation, a rare event in the history of the presidency. Mrs. Reagan's devoted the bulk of her public duties as first lady to her "Just Say No" campaign against drug abuse. She adopted a more traditional role as first lady than either Rosalynn Carter or Hillary Clinton, focusing on her antidrug crusade and the Foster Grandparents Program. But her most important role was behind the scenes— ensuring that her husband's staff pursued his agenda, not theirs.

Good evening. Usually, I talk with you from my office in the West Wing of the White House. But tonight there's something special to talk about, and I've asked someone very special to join me. Nancy and I are here in the West Hall of the White House, and around us are the rooms in which we live. It's the home you've provided for us, of which we merely have temporary custody.

Nancy's joining me because the message this evening is not my message but ours. And we speak to you not simply as fellow citizens but as fellow parents and grandparents and as concerned neighbors. It's back-to-school time for America's children. And while drug and alcohol abuse cuts across all generations, it's especially damaging to the young people on whom our future depends. So tonight, from our family to yours, from our home to yours, thank you for joining us.

America has accomplished so much in these last few years, whether it's been re-

building our economy or serving the cause of freedom in the world. What we've been able to achieve has been done with your help—with us working together as a nation united. Now we need your support again. Drugs are menacing our society. They're threatening our values and undercutting our institutions. They're killing our children.

From the beginning of our administration, we've taken strong steps to do something about this horror. Tonight I can report to you that we've made much progress. Thirty-seven Federal agencies are working together in a vigorous national effort, and by next year our spending for drug law enforcement will have more than tripled from its 1981 levels. We have increased seizures of illegal drugs. Shortages of marijuana are now being reported. Last year alone over 10,000 drug criminals were convicted and nearly $250 million of their assets were seized by the DEA, the Drug Enforcement Administration.

And in the most important area, individual use, we see progress. In 4 years the number of high school seniors using marijuana on a daily basis has dropped from 1 in 14 to 1 in 20. The U.S. military has cut the use of illegal drugs among its personnel by 67 percent since 1980. These are a measure of our commitment and emerging signs that we can defeat this enemy. But we still have much to do.

Despite our best efforts, illegal cocaine is coming into our country at alarming levels and 4 to 5 million people regularly use it. Five hundred thousand Americans are hooked on heroin. One in twelve persons smokes marijuana regularly. Regular drug use is even higher among the age group 18 to 25 most likely just entering the workforce. Today there's a new epidemic: smokable cocaine, otherwise known as crack. It is an explosively destructive and often lethal substance which is crushing its users. It is an uncontrolled fire.

And drug abuse is not a so-called victimless crime. Everyone's safety is at stake when drugs and excessive alcohol are used by people on the highways or by those transporting our citizens or operating industrial equipment. Drug abuse costs you and your fellow Americans at least $60 billion a year.

From the early days of our administration, Nancy has been intensely involved in the effort to fight drug abuse. She has since traveled over 100,000 miles to 55 cities in 28 States and 6 foreign countries to fight school-age drug and alcohol abuse. She's given dozens of speeches and scores of interviews and has participated in 24 special radio and TV tapings to create greater awareness of this crisis. Her personal observations and efforts have given her such dramatic insights that I wanted her to share them with you this evening.

Nancy. Thank you. As a mother, I've always thought of September as a special month, a time when we bundled our children off to school, to the warmth of an environment in which they could fulfill the promise and hope in those restless minds. But so much has happened over these last years, so much to shake the foundations of all that we know and all that we believe in. Today there's a drug and alcohol abuse epidemic in this country, and no one is safe from it not you, not me, and certainly not our children, because this epidemic has their names written on it. Many of you may be thinking: "Well, drugs don't concern me." But it does concern you. It concerns us all because of the way it tears at our lives and because it's aimed at destroying the brightness and life of the sons and daughters of the United States.

For 5 years I've been traveling across the country learning and listening. And one of

the most hopeful signs I've seen is the building of an essential, new awareness of how terrible and threatening drug abuse is to our society. This was one of the main purposes when I started, so of course it makes me happy that that's been accomplished. But each time I meet with someone new or receive another letter from a troubled person on drugs, I yearn to find a way to help share the message that cries out from them. As a parent, I'm especially concerned about what drugs are doing to young mothers and their newborn children. Listen to this news account from a hospital in Florida of a child born to a mother with a cocaine habit: "Nearby, a baby named Paul lies motionless in an incubator, feeding tubes riddling his tiny body. He needs a respirator to breathe and a daily spinal tap to relieve fluid buildup on his brain. Only 1 month old, he's already suffered 2 strokes."

Now you can see why drug abuse concerns every one of us—all the American family. Drugs steal away so much. They take and take, until finally every time a drug goes into a child, something else is forced out like love and hope and trust and confidence. Drugs take away the dream from every child's heart and replace it with a nightmare, and it's time we in America stand up and replace those dreams. Each of us has to put our principles and consciences on the line, whether in social settings or in the workplace, to set forth solid standards and stick to them. There's no moral middle ground. Indifference is not an option. We want you to help us create an outspoken intolerance for drug use. For the sake of our children, I implore each of you to be unyielding and inflexible in your opposition to drugs.

Our young people are helping us lead the way. Not long ago, in Oakland, California, I was asked by a group of children what to do if they were offered drugs, and I answered,

"Just say no." Soon after that, those children in Oakland formed a Just Say No club, and now there are over 10,000 such clubs all over the country. Well, their participation and their courage in saying no needs our encouragement. We can help by using every opportunity to force the issue of not using drugs to the point of making others uncomfortable, even if it means making ourselves unpopular.

Our job is never easy because drug criminals are ingenious. They work every day to plot a new and better way to steal our children's lives, just as they've done by developing this new drug, crack. For every door that we close, they open a new door to death. They prosper on our unwillingness to act. So, we must be smarter and stronger and tougher than they are. It's up to us to change attitudes and just simply dry up their markets.

And finally, to young people watching or listening, I have a very personal message for you: There's a big, wonderful world out there for you. It belongs to you. It's exciting and stimulating and rewarding. Don't cheat yourselves out of this promise. Our country needs you, but it needs you to be clear-eyed and clear-minded. I recently read one teenager's story. She's now determined to stay clean but was once strung out on several drugs. What she remembered most clearly about her recovery was that during the time she was on drugs everything appeared to her in shades of black and gray and after her treatment she was able to see colors again.

So, to my young friends out there: Life can be great, but not when you can't see it. So, open your eyes to life: to see it in the vivid colors that God gave us as a precious gift to His children, to enjoy life to the fullest, and to make it count. Say yes to your life. And when it comes to drugs and alcohol just say no.

The President. I think you can see why Nancy has been such a positive influence on all that we're trying to do. The job ahead of us is very clear. Nancy's personal crusade, like that of so many other wonderful individuals, should become our national crusade. It must include a combination of government and private efforts which complement one another. Last month I announced six initiatives which we believe will do just that.

First, we seek a drug-free workplace at all levels of government and in the private sector. Second, we'll work toward drug-free schools. Third, we want to ensure that the public is protected and that treatment is available to substance abusers and the chemically dependent. Our fourth goal is to expand international cooperation while treating drug trafficking as a threat to our national security. In October I will be meeting with key U.S. Ambassadors to discuss what can be done to support our friends abroad. Fifth, we must move to strengthen law enforcement activities such as those initiated by Vice President Bush and Attorney General Meese. And finally, we seek to expand public awareness and prevention.

In order to further implement these six goals, I will announce tomorrow a series of new proposals for a drug-free America. Taken as a whole, these proposals will toughen our laws against drug criminals, encourage more research and treatment and ensure that illegal drugs will not be tolerated in our schools or in our workplaces. Together with our ongoing efforts, these proposals will bring the Federal commitment to fighting drugs to $3 billion. As much financing as we commit, however, we would be fooling ourselves if we thought that massive new amounts of money alone will provide the solution. Let us not forget that in America people solve problems and no national crusade has ever succeeded without human investment. Winning the crusade against drugs will not be achieved by just throwing money at the problem.

Your government will continue to act aggressively, but nothing would be more effective than for Americans simply to quit using illegal drugs. We seek to create a massive change in national attitudes which ultimately will separate the drugs from the customer, to take the user away from the supply. I believe, quite simply, that we can help them quit, and that's where you come in.

My generation will remember how America swung into action when we were attacked in World War II. The war was not just fought by the fellows flying the planes or driving the tanks. It was fought at home by a mobilized nation of men and women alike building planes and ships, clothing sailors and soldiers, feeding marines and airmen; and it was fought by children planting victory gardens and collecting cans. Well, now we're in another war for our freedom, and it's time for all of us to pull together again. So, for example, if your friend or neighbor or a family member has a drug or alcohol problem, don't turn the other way. Go to his help or to hers. Get others involved with your clubs, service groups, and community organizations—and provide support and strength. And, of course, many of you've been cured through treatment and self-help. Well, you're the combat veterans, and you have a critical role to play. You can help others by telling your story and providing a willing hand to those in need. Being friends to others is the best way of being friends to ourselves. It's time, as Nancy said, for America to "just say no" to drugs.

Those of you in union halls and workplaces everywhere: Please make this challenge a part of your job every day. Help us preserve the health and dignity of all workers. To businesses large and small: we need the creativity of your enterprise applied directly to this national problem. Help us. And those of you who are educators: Your wisdom and leadership are indispensable to this cause. From the pulpits of this spirit filled land: we would welcome your reassuring message of redemption and forgiveness and of helping one another. On the athletic fields: You men and women are among the most beloved citizens of our country. A child's eyes fill with your heroic achievements. Few of us can give youngsters something as special and strong to look up to as you. Please don't let them down.

And this camera in front of us: It's a reminder that in Nancy's and my former profession and in the newsrooms and production rooms of our media centers you have a special opportunity with your enormous influence to send alarm signals across the nation. To our friends in foreign countries: We know many of you are involved in this battle with us. We need your success as well as ours. When we all come together, united, striving for this cause, then those who are killing America and terrorizing it with slow but sure chemical destruction will see that they are up against the mightiest force for good that we know. Then they will have no dark alleyways to hide in.

In this crusade, let us not forget who we are. Drug abuse is a repudiation of everything America is. The destructiveness and human wreckage mock our heritage. Think for a moment how special it is to be an American. Can we doubt that only a divine providence placed this land, this island of freedom, here as a refuge for all those people on the world who yearn to breathe free?

The revolution out of which our liberty was conceived signaled an historical call to an entire world seeking hope. Each new arrival of immigrants rode the crest of that hope. They came, millions seeking a safe harbor from the oppression of cruel regimes. They came, to escape starvation and disease. They came, those surviving the Holocaust and the Soviet gulags. They came, the boat people, chancing death for even a glimmer of hope that they could have a new life. They all came to taste the air redolent and rich with the freedom that is ours. What an insult it will be to what we are and whence we came if we do not rise up together in defiance against this cancer of drugs.

And there's one more thing. The freedom that so many seek in our land has not been preserved without a price. Nancy and I shared that remembrance 2 years ago at the Normandy American Cemetery in France. In the still of that June afternoon, we walked together among the soldiers of freedom, past the hundreds of white markers which are monuments to courage and memorials to sacrifice. Too many of these and other such graves are the final resting places of teenagers who became men in the roar of battle.

Look what they gave to us who live. Never would they see another sunlit day glistening off a lake or river back home or miles of corn pushing up against the open sky of our plains. The pristine air of our mountains and the driving energy of our cities are theirs no more. Nor would they ever again be a son to their parents or a father to their own children. They did this for you, for me, for a new generation to carry our democratic experiment proudly forward. Well, that's something I think we're obliged to honor, because what they did for us means that we owe as a simple act of civic stewardship to use our freedom wisely for the common good.

As we mobilize for this national crusade, I'm mindful that drugs are a constant temptation for millions. Please remember this when your courage is tested: You are Americans. You're the product of the freest society

mankind has ever known. No one, ever, has the right to destroy your dreams and shatter your life.

Right down the end of this hall is the Lincoln Bedroom. But in the Civil War that room was the one President Lincoln used as his office. Memory fills that room, and more than anything that memory drives us to see vividly what President Lincoln sought to save. Above all, it is that America must stand for something and that our heritage lets us stand with a strength of character made more steely by each layer of challenge pressed upon the nation. We Americans have never been morally neutral against any form of tyranny. Tonight we're asking no more than that we honor what we have been and what we are by standing together.

Now we go on to the next stop: making a final commitment not to tolerate drugs by anyone, anytime, anyplace. So, won't you join us in this great, new national crusade?

God bless you, and good night.

Source: "The Campaign Against Drug Abuse," September 14, 1986, The President Reagan Information Page. Available online. URL: http://www.presidentreagan.info/speeches/drugs.cfm

38. Address to the Nation on the Iran-Contra Affair March 4, 1987

Ronald Reagan was seen by most of his fellow citizens as a straight-talking person who, for whatever he lacked in terms of mastery of detail, was someone you could trust. This attribute was sorely tested during the Iran-contra crisis, when conflicting accounts were offered regarding the actions of John Poindexter, Oliver North, and others. Reagan seemed at times to defend their actions, and condemn them at other times. Worst of all, he was determined to stick to his script that the opening to Iran was simply an attempt to reach out to moderate elements in that regime, and had nothing to do with freeing the American hostages held in Lebanon. Finally, in this speech, after heavy lobbying by Mrs. Reagan and old associates such as Stuart Spencer and Michael Deaver, Reagan admitted that, "a few months ago I told the American people I did not trade arms for hostages. My heart and my best intentions still tell me that's true, but the facts and the evidence tell me it is not." There were reasons why his "strategic opening" to Iran degenerated into paying ransom for hostages, Reagan explained, but there were "no excuses. It was a mistake." This admission helped Reagan put the scandal behind him, but things would never be quite the same. The Reagan presidency peaked in the fall of 1986 before Iran-contra broke, and Reagan's detached management style, which had been hailed by many as a model of executive leadership, was now routinely derided.

My fellow Americans: I've spoken to you from this historic office on many occasions and about many things. The power of the Presidency is often thought to reside within this Oval Office. Yet it doesn't rest here; it rests in you, the American people, and in your trust. Your trust is what gives a President his powers of leadership and his personal strength, and it's what I want to talk to you about this evening.

For the past 3 months, I've been silent on the revelations about Iran. And you must have been thinking: "Well, why doesn't he tell us what's happening? Why doesn't he just speak to us as he has in the past when we've faced troubles or tragedies?" Others of you, I guess, were thinking: "What's he doing hiding out in the White House?" Well, the reason I haven't spoken to you before now is this: You deserve the truth. And as frustrating as the waiting has been, I felt it was improper to come to you with sketchy reports, or possibly even erroneous statements, which would then have to be corrected, creating even more doubt and confusion. There's been enough of that.

I've paid a price for my silence in terms of your trust and confidence. But I've had to wait, as you have, for the complete story. That's why I appointed ambassador David Abshire as my special counselor to help get out the thousands of documents to the various investigations. And I appointed a special review board, the Tower board, which took on the chore of pulling the truth together for me and getting to the bottom of things. It has now issued its findings.

I'm often accused of being an optimist, and it's true I had to hunt pretty hard to find any good news in the Board's report. As you know, it's well-stocked with criticisms, which I'll discuss in a moment; but I was very relieved to read this sentence: ". . . the Board is convinced that the President does indeed want the full story to be told." And that will continue to be my pledge to you as the other investigations go forward.

I want to thank the members of the panel: former Senator John Tower, former Secretary of State Edmund Muskie, and former National Security Advisor Brent Scowcroft. They have done the Nation, as well as me personally, a great service by submitting a report of such integrity and depth. They have my genuine and enduring gratitude.

I've studied the Board's report. Its findings are honest, convincing, and highly critical; and I accept them. And tonight I want to share with you my thoughts on these findings and report to you on the actions I'm taking to implement the Board's recommendations.

First, let me say I take full responsibility for my own actions and for those of my administration. As angry as I may be about activities undertaken without my knowledge, I am still accountable for those activities. As disappointed as I may be in some who served me, I'm still the one who must answer to the American people for this behavior. And as personally distasteful as I find secret bank accounts and diverted funds—well, as the Navy would say, this happened on my watch.

Let's start with the part that is the most controversial. A few months ago I told the American people I did not trade arms for hostages. My heart and my best intentions still tell me that's true, but the facts and the evidence tell me it is not. As the Tower board reported, what began as a strategic opening to Iran deteriorated, in its implementation, into trading arms for hostages. This runs counter to my own beliefs, to administration policy, and to the original strategy we had in mind. There are reasons why it happened, but no excuses. It was a mistake.

I undertook the original Iran initiative in order to develop relations with those who might assume leadership in a post-Khomeini government. It's clear from the Board's report, however, that I let my personal concern for the hostages spill over into the geo-political strategy of reaching out to Iran. I asked so many questions about the hostages' welfare that I didn't ask enough about the specifics of the total Iran plan.

Let me say to the hostage families: We have not given up. We never will. And I promise you we'll use every legitimate means to free your loved ones from captivity. But I must also caution that those Americans who freely remain in such dangerous areas must know that they're responsible for their own safety.

Now, another major aspect of the Board's findings regards the transfer of funds to the Nicaraguan contras. The Tower board wasn't able to find out what happened to this money, so the facts here will be left to the continuing investigations of the court-appointed Independent Counsel and the two congressional investigating committees. I'm confident the truth will come out about this matter, as well. As I told the Tower board, I didn't know about any diversion of funds to the contras. But as President, I cannot escape responsibility.

Much has been said about my management style, a style that's worked successfully for me during 8 years as governor of California and for most of my Presidency. The way I work is to identify the problem, find the right individuals to do the job, and then let them go to it. I've found this invariably brings out the best in people. They seem to rise to their full capability, and in the long run you get more done.

When it came to managing the NSC staff, let's face it, my style didn't match its previous track record. I've already begun correcting this. As a start, yesterday I met with the entire professional staff of the National Security Council. I defined for them the values I want to guide the national security policies of this country. I told them that I wanted a policy that was as justifiable and understandable in public as it was in secret. I wanted a policy that reflected the will of the Congress as well as of the White House. And I told them that there'll be no more freelancing by individuals when it comes to our national security.

You've heard a lot about the staff of the National Security Council in recent months. Well, I can tell you, they are good and dedicated government employees, who put in long hours for the Nation's benefit. They are eager and anxious to serve their country.

One thing still upsetting me, however, is that no one kept proper records of meetings or decisions. This led to my failure to recollect whether I approved an arms shipment before or after the fact. I did approve it; I just can't say specifically when. Well, rest assured, there's plenty of recordkeeping now going on at 1600 Pennsylvania Avenue.

For nearly a week now, I've been studying the Board's report I want the American people to know that this wrenching ordeal of recent months has not been in vain. I endorse every one of the Tower board's recommendations. In fact, I'm going beyond its recommendations so as to put the house in even better order.

I'm taking action in three basic areas: personnel, national security policy, and the process for making sure that the system works. First, personnel—I've brought in an accomplished and highly respected new team here at the White House. They bring new blood, new energy, and new credibility and experience.

Former Senator Howard Baker, my new chief of staff, possesses a breadth of legislative and foreign affairs skills that's impossible to match. I'm hopeful that his experience as minority and majority leader of the Senate can help us forge a new partnership with the Congress, especially on foreign and national security policies. I'm genuinely honored that he's given up his own Presidential aspirations to serve the country as my Chief of Staff.

Frank Carlucci, my new National Security Advisor, is respected for his experience in government and trusted for his judgment and counsel. Under him, the NSC staff is being rebuilt with proper management discipline. Already, almost half the NSC professional staff is comprised of new people.

Yesterday I nominated William Webster, a man of sterling reputation, to be Director of the Central Intelligence Agency. Mr. Webster has served as Director of the FBI and as a U.S. District Court judge. He understands the meaning of "rule of law."

So that his knowledge of national security matters can be available to me on a continuing basis, I will also appoint John Tower to serve as a member of my Foreign Intelligence Advisory Board. I am considering other changes in personnel, and I'll move more furniture, as I see fit, in the weeks and months ahead.

Second, in the area of national security policy, I have ordered the NSC to begin a comprehensive review of all covert operations. I have also directed that any covert activity be in support of clear policy objectives and in compliance with American values. I expect a covert policy that if Americans saw it on the front page of their newspaper, they'd say, "That makes sense." I have had issued a directive prohibiting the NSC staff itself from undertaking covert operations—no ifs, ands, or buts. I have asked Vice President Bush to reconvene his task force on terrorism to review our terrorist policy in light of the events that have occurred.

Third, in terms of the process of reaching national security decisions, I am adopting in total the Tower report's model of how the NSC process and staff should work. I am directing Mr. Carlucci to take the necessary steps to make that happen. He will report back to me on further reforms that might be needed. I've created the post of NSC legal adviser to assure a greater sensitivity to matters of law.

I am also determined to make the congressional oversight process work. Proper procedures for consultation with the Congress will be followed, not only in letter but in spirit. Before the end of March, I will report to the Congress on all the steps I've taken in line with the Tower board's conclusions.

Now, what should happen when you make a mistake is this: You take your knocks, you learn your lessons, and then you move on. That's the healthiest way to deal with a problem. This in no way diminishes the importance of the other continuing investigations, but the business of our country and our people must proceed. I've gotten this message from Republicans and Democrats in Congress, from allies around the world, and—if we're reading the signals right—even from the Soviets. And of course, I've heard the message from you, the American people. You know, by the time you reach my age, you've made plenty of mistakes. And if you've lived your life properly—so, you learn. You put things in perspective. You pull your energies together. You change. You go forward.

My fellow Americans, I have a great deal that I want to accomplish with you and for you over the next 2 years. And the Lord willing, that's exactly what I intend to do.

Good night, and God bless you.

Source: "Iran-Contra," March 4, 1987, The President Reagan Information Page. Available online. URL: http://www.presidentreagan.info/speeches/drugs.cfm

39. "Tear Down This Wall" Speech at the Brandenburg Gate, West Berlin June 12, 1987

American presidents are often remembered for the words they say, whether it's Abraham Lincoln warning about a house divided, or Franklin Roosevelt proclaiming that the only thing we had to fear was fear itself, or John F. Kennedy asking Americans to do what they could do for their country. Ronald Reagan's emblematic line is likely to be, "Mr. Gorbachev, tear down this wall!"

Thank you very much. Chancellor Kohl, Governing Mayor Diepgen, ladies and gentlemen: Twenty-four years ago, President John F. Kennedy visited Berlin, speaking to the people of this city and the world at the city hall. Well, since then two other presidents have come, each in his turn, to Berlin. And today I, myself, make my second visit to your city.

We come to Berlin, we American Presidents, because it's our duty to speak, in this place, of freedom. But I must confess, we're drawn here by other things as well: by the feeling of history in this city, more than 500 years older than our own nation; by the beauty of the Grunewald and the Tiergarten; most of all, by your courage and determination. Perhaps the composer, Paul Lincke, understood something about American Presidents. You see, like so many Presidents before me, I come here today because wherever I go, whatever I do: *"Ich hab noch einen koffer in Berlin."* [I still have a suitcase in Berlin.]

Our gathering today is being broadcast throughout Western Europe and North America. I understand that it is being seen and heard as well in the East. To those listening throughout Eastern Europe, I extend my warmest greetings and the good will of the American people. To those listening in East Berlin, a special word: Although I cannot be with you, I address my remarks to you just as surely as to those standing here before me. For I join you, as I join your fellow countrymen in the West, in this firm, this unalterable belief: *Es gibt nur ein Berlin.* [There is only one Berlin.]

Behind me stands a wall that encircles the free sectors of this city, part of a vast system of barriers that divides the entire continent of Europe. From the Baltic, south, those barriers cut across Germany in a gash of barbed wire, concrete, dog runs, and guard towers. Farther south, there may be no visible, no obvious wall. But there remain armed guards and checkpoints all the same—still a restriction on the right to travel, still an instrument to impose upon ordinary men and women the will of a totalitarian state. Yet it is here in Berlin where the wall emerges most clearly; here, cutting across your city, where the news photo and the television screen have imprinted this brutal division of a continent upon the mind of the world. Standing before the Brandenburg Gate, every man is a German, separated from his fellow men. Every man is a Berliner, forced to look upon a scar.

President von Weizsacker has said: "The German question is open as long as the Brandenburg Gate is closed." Today I say: As long as this gate is closed, as long as this scar of a wall is permitted to stand, it is not the German question alone that remains open, but the question of freedom for all mankind. Yet I do not come here to lament. For I find in Berlin a message of hope, even in the shadow of this wall, a message of triumph.

In this season of spring in 1945, the people of Berlin emerged from their air-raid shelters to find devastation Thousands of miles away, the people of the United States reached out to help. And in 1947 Secretary of State—as you've been told—George Marshall announced the creation of what would become known as the Marshall plan. Speaking precisely 40 years ago this month, he said: "Our policy is directed not against any country or doctrine, but against hunger, poverty, desperation, and chaos."

In the Reichstag a few moments ago, I saw a display commemorating this 40th anniversary of the Marshall plan. I was struck by the sign on a burnt-out, gutted structure that was being rebuilt. I understand that Berliners of my own generation can remember seeing signs like it dotted throughout the Western sectors of the city. The sign read simply: "The Marshall plan is helping here to strengthen the free world." A strong, free world in the West, that dream became real. Japan rose from ruin to become an economic giant. Italy, France, Belgium—virtually every nation in Western Europe saw political and economic rebirth; the European Community was founded.

In West Germany and here in Berlin, there took place an economic miracle, the Wirtschaftswunder. Adenauer, Erhard, Reuter, and other leaders understood the practical importance of liberty—that just as truth can flourish only when the journalist is given freedom of speech, so prosperity can come about only when the farmer and businessman enjoy economic freedom. The German leaders reduced tariffs, expanded free trade, lowered taxes. From 1950 to 1960 alone, the standard of living in West Germany and Berlin doubled.

Where four decades ago there was rubble, today in West Berlin there is the greatest industrial output of any city in Germany—busy office blocks, fine homes and apartments, proud avenues, and the spreading lawns of park land. Where a city's culture seemed to have been destroyed, today there are two great universities, orchestras and an opera, countless theaters, and museums. Where there was want, today there's abundance—food, clothing, automobiles—the wonderful goods of the Ku'damm. From devastation, from utter ruin, you Berliners have, in freedom, rebuilt a city that once again ranks as one of the greatest on Earth. The Soviets may have had other plans. But, my friends, there were a few things the Soviets didn't count on: *Berliner herz, Berliner humor, ja, und Berliner schnauze.* [Berliner heart, Berliner humor, yes, and a Berliner mouth.] [Laughter]

In the 1950s, Khrushchev predicted: "We will bury you." But in the West today, we see a free world that has achieved a level of prosperity and well-being unprecedented in all human history. In the Communist world, we see failure, technological backwardness, declining standards of health, even want of the most basic kind—too little food. Even today, the Soviet Union still cannot feed itself. After these four decades, then, there stands before the entire world one great and inescapable conclusion: Freedom leads to prosperity. Freedom replaces the ancient hatreds among the nations with comity and peace. Freedom is the victor.

And now the Soviets themselves may, in a limited way, be coming to understand the importance of freedom. We hear much from Moscow about a new policy of reform and openness. Some political prisoners have been released. Certain foreign news broadcasts are no longer being jammed. Some economic enterprises have been permitted to operate with greater freedom from state control. Are these the beginnings of profound changes in the Soviet state? Or are they token gestures, intended to raise false hopes in the West, or to strengthen the Soviet system without changing it? We welcome change and openness; for we believe that freedom and security go together, that the advance of human liberty can only strengthen the cause of world peace.

There is one sign the Soviets can make that would be unmistakable, that would advance dramatically the cause of freedom and peace. General Secretary Gorbachev, if you seek peace, if you seek prosperity for the Soviet Union and Eastern Europe, if you seek liberalization: Come here to this gate! Mr. Gorbachev, open this gate! Mr. Gorbachev, tear down this wall!

I understand the fear of war and the pain of division that afflict this continent, and I pledge to you my country's efforts to help overcome these burdens. To be sure, we in the West must resist Soviet expansion. So we must maintain defenses of unassailable strength. Yet we seek peace; so we must strive to reduce arms on both sides. Beginning 10 years ago, the Soviets challenged the Western alliance with a grave new threat, hundreds of new and more deadly SS-20 nuclear missiles, capable of striking every capital in Europe. The Western alliance responded by committing itself to a counterdeployment unless the Soviets agreed to negotiate a better solution; namely, the elimination of such weapons on both sides. For many months, the Soviets refused to bargain in earnestness. As the alliance, in turn, prepared to go forward with its counterdeployment, there were difficult days—days of protests like those during my 1982 visit to this city—and the Soviets later walked away from the table.

But through it all, the alliance held firm. And I invite those who protested then, I invite those who protest today, to mark this fact: Because we remained strong, the Soviets came back to the table. And because we remained strong, today we have within reach the possibility, not merely of limiting the growth of arms, but of eliminating, for the first time, an entire class of nuclear weapons from the face of the Earth. As I speak, NATO ministers are meeting in Iceland to review the progress of our proposals for eliminating these weapons. At the talks in Geneva, we have also proposed deep cuts in strategic offensive weapons. And the Western allies have likewise made far-reaching proposals to reduce the danger of conventional war and to place a total ban on chemical weapons.

While we pursue these arms reductions, I pledge to you that we will maintain the capacity to deter Soviet aggression at any level at which it might occur. And in cooperation with many of our allies, the United States is pursuing the Strategic Defense Initiative research to base deterrence not on the threat of offensive retaliation, but on defenses that truly defend; on systems, in short, that will not target populations, but shield them. By these means we seek to increase the safety of Europe and all the world. But we must remember a crucial fact: East and West do not mistrust each other because we are armed; we are armed because we mistrust each other—and our differences are not about weapons but about liberty. When President Kennedy spoke at the City Hall those 24 years ago freedom was encircled, Berlin was under siege. And today, despite all the pressures upon this city, Berlin stands secure in its liberty. And freedom itself is transforming the globe.

In the Philippines, in South and Central America, democracy has been given a rebirth. Throughout the Pacific, free markets are working miracle after miracle of economic growth. In the industrialized nations a technological revolution is taking place—a revolution marked by rapid, dramatic advances in computers and telecommunications.

In Europe, only one nation and those it controls refuse to join the community of freedom. Yet in this age of redoubled economic growth, of information and innovation, the Soviet Union faces a choice: It must make fundamental changes, or it will become obsolete. Today thus represents a moment of hope. We in the West stand ready to cooperate with the East to promote true openness, to break down barriers that separate people, to create a safer, freer world.

And surely there is no better place than Berlin, the meeting place of East and West, to make a start. Free people of Berlin: Today, as in the past, the United States stands for the strict observance and full implementation of all parts of the Four Power Agreement of 1971. Let us use this occasion, the 750th anniversary of this city, to usher in a new era, to seek a still fuller, richer life for the Berlin of the future. Together, let us maintain and develop the ties between the Federal Republic and the Western sectors of Berlin, which is permitted by the 1971 agreement. And I invite Mr. Gorbachev: Let us work to bring the Eastern and Western parts of the city closer together, so that all the inhabitants of all Berlin can enjoy the benefits that come with life in one of the great cities of the world. To open Berlin still further to all Europe, East and West, let us expand the vital air access to this city, finding ways of making commercial air service to Berlin more convenient, more comfortable, and more economical. We look to the day when West Berlin can become one of the chief aviation hubs in all central Europe.

With our French and British partners, the United States is prepared to help bring international meetings to Berlin. It would be only fitting for Berlin to serve as the site of United Nations meetings, or world conferences on human rights and arms control or other issues that call for international cooperation. There is no better way to establish hope for the future than to enlighten young minds, and we would be honored to sponsor summer youth exchanges, cultural events, and other programs for young Berliners from the East. Our French and British friends, I'm certain, will do the same. And it's my hope that an authority can be found in East Berlin to sponsor visits from young people of the Western sectors.

One final proposal, one close to my heart: Sport represents a source of enjoyment and ennoblement, and you many have noted that the Republic of Korea (South Korea) has offered to permit certain events of the 1988 Olympics to take place in the North. International sports competitions of all kinds could take place in both parts of this city. And what better way to demonstrate to the world the openness of this city than to offer in some future year to hold the Olympic games here in Berlin, East and West?

In these four decades, as I have said, you Berliners have built a great city. You've done so in spite of threats, the Soviet attempts to impose the East-mark, the blockade. Today the city thrives in spite of the challenges implicit in the very presence of this wall. What keeps you here? Certainly there's a great deal to be said for your fortitude, for your defiant courage. But I believe there's something deeper, something that involves Berlin's whole look and feel and way of life, not mere sentiment. No one could live long in Berlin without being completely disabused of illusions. Something instead, that has seen the difficulties of life in Berlin but chose to accept them, that continues to build this good and proud city in contrast to a surrounding totalitarian presence that refuses to release human energies or aspirations. Something that speaks with a powerful voice of affirmation, that says yes to this city, yes to the future, yes to freedom. In a word, I would submit that what keeps you in Berlin is love both profound and abiding.

Perhaps this gets to the root of the matter, to the most fundamental distinction of all between East and West. The totalitarian world produces backwardness because it does such violence to the spirit, thwarting the human impulse to create, to enjoy, to worship. The totalitarian world finds even symbols of love and of worship an affront. Years ago, before the

East Germans began rebuilding their churches, they erected a secular structure: the television tower at Alexander Platz. Virtually ever since, the authorities have been working to correct what they view as the tower's one major flaw, treating the glass sphere at the top with paints and chemicals of every kind. Yet even today when the Sun strikes that sphere—that sphere that towers over all Berlin the light makes the sign of the cross. There in Berlin, like the city itself, symbols of love, symbols of worship, cannot be suppressed.

As I looked out a moment ago from the Reichstag, that embodiment of German unity, I noticed words crudely spray-painted upon the wall, perhaps by a young Berliner, "This wall will fall. Beliefs become reality." Yes, across Europe, this wall will fall. For it cannot withstand faith; it cannot withstand truth. The wall cannot withstand freedom.

And I would like, before I close, to say one word. I have read, and I have been questioned since I've been here about certain demonstrations against my coming. And I would like to say just one thing, and to those who demonstrate so. I wonder if they have ever asked themselves that if they should have the kind of government they apparently seek, no one would ever be able to do what they're doing again.

Thank you and God bless you all.

Source: "Brandenburg Gate," June 12, 1987, The President Reagan Information Page. Available online. URL: http://www.presidentreagan.info/speeches/brandenburg_gate.cfm

40. Remarks at Signing of INF Treaty December 8, 1987

The INF (Intermediate Nuclear Forces) treaty was a personal triumph for President Reagan in that the treaty followed the outline of a widely criticized proposal he presented six years earlier. The INF breakthrough was somewhat surprising, for little more than a year earlier the United States and the Soviet Union were deadlocked on disarmament issues due to Gorbachev's insistence on restricting the American Strategic Defense Initiative, which Reagan rejected. In the end, Gorbachev and Reagan put their differences aside and ordered their negotiating teams back to the table. In a nationally broadcast event from the East Room of the White House, Reagan and Gorbachev signed the INF treaty, eliminating for the first time an entire class of nuclear weapons. Reagan could not resist reminding his Soviet counterpart, and reassuring his conservative base at home, that his motto in all negotiations with the Soviets was "trust, but verify," a statement Gorbachev had heard perhaps once too often.

President Reagan. Thank you all very much. Welcome to the White House. This ceremony and the treaty we're signing today are both excellent examples of the rewards of patience. It was over 6 years ago, November 18, 1981, that I first proposed what would come to be called the zero option. It was a simple proposal—one might say, disarmingly simple. (*Laughter*) Unlike treaties in the past, it didn't simply codify the status quo or a new arms buildup; it didn't simply talk of controlling an arms race.

For the first time in history, the language of "arms control" was replaced by "arms reduction"—in this case, the complete elimination of an entire class of U.S. and Soviet nuclear missiles. Of course, this required a dramatic shift in thinking, and it took conventional wisdom some time to catch up. Reaction to say the least, was mixed. To some the zero option was impossibly visionary and unrealistic' to others merely a propaganda ploy. Well, with patience, determination, and commitment, we've made this impossible vision a reality.

General Secretary Gorbachev, I'm sure you're familiar with Ivan Krylov's famous tale about the swan, the crawfish, and the pike. It seems that once upon a time these three were trying to move a wagonload together. They hitched and harnessed themselves to the wagon. It wasn't very heavy, but no matter how hard they worked, the wagon just wouldn't move. You see, the swan was flying upward; the crawfish kept crawling backward; the pike kept making for the water. The end result was that they got nowhere, and the wagon is still there to this day. Well, strong and fundamental moral differences continue to exist between our nations. But today, on this vital issue, at least, we've seen what can be accomplished when we pull together.

The numbers alone demonstrate the value of this agreement. On the Soviet side, over 1,500 deployed warheads will be removed, and all ground-launched intermediate-range missiles, including the SS-20's, will be destroyed. On our side, our entire complement of Pershing II and ground-launched cruise missiles, with some 400 deployed warheads, will all be destroyed. Additional backup missiles on both sides will also be destroyed.

But the importance of this treaty transcends numbers. We have listened to the wisdom in an old Russian maxim. And I'm sure you're familiar with it, Mr. General Secretary, though my pronunciation may give you difficulty. The maxim is: *Dovorey no provorey*—trust, but verify.

General Secretary Gorbachev. You repeat that at every meeting. *(Laughter)*

President Reagan. I like it. *(Laughter)*

This agreement contains the most stringent verification regime in history, including provisions for inspection teams actually residing in each other's territory and several other forms of onsite inspection, as well. This treaty protects the interests of America's friends and allies. It also embodies another important principle: the need for *glasnost*, a greater openness in military programs and forces.

We can only hope that this history making agreement will not be an end in itself but the beginning of a working relationship that will enable us to tackle the other urgent issues before us: strategic offensive nuclear weapons, the balance of conventional forces in Europe, the destructive and tragic regional conflicts that beset so many parts of our globe, and respect for the human and natural rights God has granted to all men.

To all here who have worked so hard to make this vision a reality: Thank you, and congratulations—above all to Ambassadors Glitman and Obukhov. To quote another Russian—as you can see, I'm becoming quite an expert—*(Laughter)*—in Russian proverbs: "The harvest comes more from sweat than from dew."

So, I'm going to propose to General Secretary Gorbachev that we issue one last instruction: Get some well-deserved rest. *(Laughter)*

General Secretary Gorbachev. We're not going to do that. *(laughter)*

President Reagan. Well, now, Mr. General Secretary, would you like to say a few words before we sign the treaty?

General Secretary Gorbachev. Mr. President, ladies and gentlemen, comrades, succeeding generations will hand down their verdict on the importance of the events which we are about to witness. But I will venture to say that what we are going to do, the signing of the first-ever agreement eliminating nuclear weapons, has a universal significance for mankind, both from the standpoint of world politics and from the standpoint of humanism.

For everyone, and above all, for our two great powers, the treaty whose text is on this table offers a big chance at last to get onto the road leading away from the threat of catastrophe. It is our duty to take full advantage of that chance and move together toward a nuclear-free world, which holds out for our children and grandchildren and for their children and grandchildren the promise of a fulfilling and happy life without fear and without a senseless waste of resources on weapons of destruction.

We can be proud of planting this sapling, which may one day grow into a mighty tree of peace. But it is probably still too early to bestow laurels upon each other. As the great American poet and philosopher Ralph Waldo Emerson said: "The reward of a thing well done is to have done it."

So, let us reward ourselves by getting down to business. We have covered a 7-year-long road, replete with intense work and debate. One last step towards this table, and the treaty will be signed.

May December 8, 1987, become a date that will be inscribed in the history books, a date that will mark the watershed separating the era of a mounting risk of nuclear war from the era of a demilitarization of human life.

Source: "INF Treaty," December 8, 1987, The President Reagan Information Page. Available online. URL: http://www.presidentreagan.info/speeches/inf_treaty.cfm

41. Address to Students at Moscow State University May 31, 1988

One of the more remarkable events from Reagan's final months in office was his visit to Moscow in May 1988. Scenes of the old cold warrior kissing babies in Red Square and putting his arm around Gorbachev would have been unimaginable just a few years earlier. The cold war for all practical pur- *poses ended at this point, having melted during "this Moscow spring," as Reagan called it. The president used his trip to the Soviet Union to offer encouragement and assistance to religious dissidents, and to also preach the gospel of American democracy and capitalism at every available opportunity. His address to the sons and daughters of the Soviet elite at Moscow State University was vintage Reagan, extolling the virtues of free enterprise and celebrating the creativity emanating from an untidy but vibrant democracy.*

Before I left Washington, I received many heartfelt letters and telegrams asking me to carry here a simple message—perhaps, but also some of the most important business of this summit—it is a message of peace and goodwill and hope for a growing friendship and closeness between our two peoples.

First I want to take a little time to talk to you much as I would to any group of university students in the United States. I want to talk not just of the realities of today, but of the possibilities of tomorrow.

You know, one of the first contacts between your country and mine took place between Russian and American explorers. The Americans were members of Cook's last voyage on an expedition searching for an Arctic passage; on the island of Unalaska, they came upon the Russians, who took them in, and together, with the native inhabitants, held a prayer service on the ice.

The explorers of the modern era are the entrepreneurs, men with vision, with the courage to take risks and faith enough to brave the unknown. These entrepreneurs and their small enterprises are responsible for almost all the economic growth in the United States. They are the prime movers of the technological revolution. In fact, one of the largest personal computer firms in the United States was started by two college students, no older than you, in the garage behind their home.

Some people, even in my own country, look at the riot of experiment that is the free market and see only waste. What of all the entrepreneurs that fail? Well, many do, particularly the successful ones. Often several times. And if you ask them the secret of their success, they'll tell you, it's all that they learned in their struggles along the way—yes, it's what they learned from failing. Like an athlete in competition, or a scholar in pursuit of the truth, experience is the greatest teacher.

We are seeing the power of economic freedom spreading around the world—places such as the Republic of Korea, Singapore, and Taiwan have vaulted into the technological era, barely pausing in the industrial age along the way. Low-tax agricultural policies in the sub-continent mean that in some years India is now a net exporter of food. Perhaps most exciting are the winds of change that are blowing over the People's Republic of China, where one-quarter of the world's population is now getting its first taste of economic freedom.

At the same time, the growth of democracy has become one of the most powerful political movements of our age. In Latin America in the 1970's, only a third of the population lived under democratic government. Today over 90 percent does. In the Philippines, in the Republic of Korea, free, contested, democratic elections are the order of the day. Throughout the world, free markets are the model for growth. Democracy is the standard by which governments are measured.

We Americans make no secret of our belief in freedom. In fact, it's something of a national pastime. Every four years the American people choose a new president, and 1988 is one of those years. At one point there were 13 major candidates running in the two major parties, not to mention all the others, including the Socialist and Libertarian candidates—all trying to get my job.

About 1,000 local television stations, 8,500 radio stations, and 1,700 daily newspapers, each one an independent, private enterprise, fiercely independent of the government, report on the candidates, grill them in interviews, and bring them together for debates. In the end, the people vote—they decide who will be the next president.

But freedom doesn't begin or end with elections. Go to any American town, to take just an example, and you'll see dozens of synagogues and mosques—and you'll see families of every conceivable nationality, worshipping together.

Go into any schoolroom, and there you will see children being taught the Declaration of Independence, that they are endowed by their Creator with certain unalienable rights—among them life, liberty, and the pursuit of happiness—that no government can justly deny—the guarantees in their Constitution for freedom of speech, freedom of assembly, and freedom of religion.

Go into any courtroom and there will preside an independent judge, beholden to no government power. There every defendant has the right to a trial by a jury of his peers, usually 12 men and women—common citizens, they are the ones, the only ones, who weigh the evidence and decide on guilt or innocence. In that court, the accused is innocent until proven guilty, and the word of a policeman, or any official, has no greater legal standing than the word of the accused.

Go to any university campus, and there you'll find an open, sometimes heated discussion of the problems in American society and what can be done to correct them. Turn on the television, and you'll see the legislature conducting the business of government right there before the camera, debating and voting on the legislation that will become the law of the land. March in any demonstrations, and there are many of them—the people's right of assembly is guaranteed in the Constitution and protected by the police.

But freedom is more even than this: Freedom is the right to question, and change the established way of doing things. It is the continuing revolution of the marketplace. It is the understanding that allows us to recognize shortcomings and seek solutions. It is the right to put forth an idea, scoffed at by the experts, and watch it catch fire among the people. It is the right to stick—to dream—to follow your dream, or stick to your conscience, even if you're the only one in a sea of doubters.

Freedom is the recognition that no single person, no single authority of government has a monopoly on the truth, but that every individual life is infinitely precious, that every one of us put on this world has been put there for a reason and has something to offer.

America is a nation made up of hundreds of nationalities. Our ties to you are more than ones of good feeling; they're ties of kinship. In America, you'll find Russians, Armenians, Ukrainians, peoples from Eastern Europe and Central Asia. They come from every part of this vast continent, from every continent, to live in harmony, seeking a place where each cultural heritage is respected, each is valued for its diverse strengths and beauties and the richness it brings to our lives.

Recently, a few individuals and families have been allowed to visit relatives in the West. We can only hope that it won't be long before all are allowed to do so, and Ukrainian-Americans, Baltic-Americans, Armenian-Americans, can freely visit their homelands, just as this Irish-American visits his.

Freedom, it has been said, makes people selfish and materialistic, but Americans are one of the most religious peoples on Earth. Because they know that liberty, just as life itself, is not earned, but a gift from God, they seek to share that gift with the world. "Reason and experience," said George Washington, in his farewell address, "both forbid us to expect that national morality can prevail in exclusion of religious principle. And it is substantially true, that virtue or morality is a necessary spring of popular government."

Democracy is less a system of government than it is a system to keep government limited, unintrusive: A system of constraints on power to keep politics and government secondary to the important things in life, the true sources of value found only in family and faith.

I have often said, nations do not distrust each other because they are armed; they are armed because they distrust each other. If this globe is to live in peace and prosper, if it is to embrace all the possibilities of the technological revolution, then nations must renounce, once and for all, the right to an expansionist foreign policy. Peace between nations must be an enduring goal—not a tactical stage in a continuing conflict.

I've been told that there's a popular song in your country—perhaps you know it—whose evocative refrain asks the question, "Do the Russians want a war?" In answer it says, "Go ask that silence lingering in the air, above the birch and poplar there; beneath those trees the soldiers lie. Go ask my mother, ask my wife; then you will have to ask no more, 'Do the Russians want a war?'"

But what of your one-time allies? What of those who embraced you on the Elbe? What if we were to ask the watery graves of the Pacific, or the European battlefields where America's fallen were buried far from home? What if we were to ask their mothers, sisters, and sons, do Americans want war? Ask us, too, and you'll find the same answer, the same longing in every heart. People do not make wars, governments do—and no mother would ever willingly sacrifice her sons for territorial gain, for economic advantage, for ideology. A people free to choose will always choose peace.

Americans seek always to make friends of old antagonists. After a colonial revolution with Britain we have cemented for all ages the ties of kinship between our nations. After a terrible civil war between North and South, we healed our wounds and found true unity as a nation. We fought two world wars in my lifetime against Germany and one with Japan, but now the Federal Republic of Germany and Japan are two of our closest allies and friends.

Some people point to the trade disputes between us as a sign of strain, but they're the frictions of all families, and the family of free nations is a big and vital and sometimes boisterous one. I can tell you that nothing would please my heart more than in my lifetime to see American and Soviet diplomats grappling with the problem of trade disputes between America and a growing, exuberant, exporting Soviet Union that had opened up to economic freedom and growth.

Is this just a dream? Perhaps. But it is a dream that is our responsibility to have come true.

Your generation is living in one of the most exciting, hopeful times in Soviet history. It is a time when the first breath of freedom stirs the air and the heart beats to the accelerated rhythm of hope, when the accumulated spiritual energies of a long silence yearn to break free.

We do not know what the conclusion of this journey will be, but we're hopeful that the promise of reform will be fulfilled. In this Moscow spring, this May 1988, we may be allowed that hope—that freedom, like the fresh green sapling planted over Tolstoi's grave, will blossom forth at least in the rich fertile soil of your people and culture. We may be allowed to hope that the marvelous sound of a new openness will keep rising through, ringing through, leading to a new world of reconciliation, friendship, and peace.

Thank you all very much and da blagoslovit vas gospod! God bless you.

Source: "Moscow State," May 31, 1988, The President Reagan Information Page. Available online. URL: http://www.presidentreagan.info/speeches/moscow_state.cfm

42. Reagan's Farewell Speech January 11, 1989

Reagan's final remarks to the nation fell somewhat flat, perhaps partly due to his intrinsic inability to take credit for anything, and his general reluctance to talk about himself. Nevertheless, he was convinced that the policies adopted under his watch left the "shining city upon a hill" better off than he found it, and he urged Americans to give their support to the incoming president, George H. W. Bush, the first vice president since Martin Van Buren to make a direct transition to the presidency via an election victory. He expressed one regret regarding his time in office, and that was the increasing deficits that had accumulated on his watch. Reagan also encouraged Americans to teach their children about American history—"an informed patriotism" was essential, for if Americans "forget what we did, we won't know who we are." More than any other modern chief executive, Reagan was happy to leave the White House, and yearned to return to his California ranch and clear brush.

This is the 34th time I'll speak to you from the Oval Office and the last. We've been together 8 years now, and soon it'll be time for me to go. But before I do, I wanted to share some thoughts, some of which I've been saving for a long time.

It's been the honor of my life to be your President. So many of you have written the past few weeks to say thanks, but I could say as much to you. Nancy and I are grateful for the opportunity you gave us to serve.

One of the things about the Presidency is that you're always somewhat apart. You spent a lot of time going by too fast in a car someone else is driving, and seeing the people through tinted glass—the parents holding up a child, and the wave you saw too late and couldn't return. And so many times I wanted to stop and reach out from behind the glass, and connect. Well, maybe I can do a little of that tonight.

People ask how I feel about leaving. And the fact is, "parting is such sweet sorrow." The sweet part is California and the ranch and freedom. The sorrow—the goodbyes, of course, and leaving this beautiful place.

You know, down the hall and up the stairs from this office is the part of the White House where the President and his family live. There are a few favorite windows I have up there that I like to stand and look out of early in the morning. The view is over the grounds here to the Washington Monument, and then the Mall and the Jefferson Memorial. But on mornings when the humidity is low, you can see past the Jefferson to the river, the Potomac, and the Virginia shore. Someone said that's the view Lincoln had when he saw the smoke rising from the Battle of Bull Run. I see more prosaic things: the grass on the banks, the morning traffic as people make their way to work, now and then a sailboat on the river.

I've been thinking a bit at that window. I've been reflecting on what the past 8 years have meant and mean. And the image that comes to mind like a refrain is a nautical one—a small story about a big ship, and a refugee, and a sailor. It was back in the early eighties, at the height of the boat people. And the sailor was hard at work on the carrier *Midway*, which was patrolling the South China Sea. The sailor, like most American servicemen, was young, smart, and fiercely observant. The crew spied on the horizon a leaky little boat. And crammed inside were refugees from Indochina hoping to get to America. The *Midway* sent a small launch to bring them to the ship and safety. As the refugees made their way through the choppy seas, one spied the sailor on deck, and stood up, and called out to him. He yelled, "Hello, American sailor. Hello, freedom man."

A small moment with a big meaning, a moment the sailor, who wrote it in a letter, couldn't get out of his mind. And, when I saw it, neither could I. Because that's what it was to be an American in the 1980's. We stood, again, for freedom. I know we always have, but in the past few years the world again—and in a way, we ourselves—rediscovered it.

It's been quite a journey this decade, and we held together through some stormy seas. And at the end, together, we are reaching our destination.

The fact is, from Grenada to the Washington and Moscow summits, from the recession of '81 to '82, to the expansion that began in late '82 and continues to this day, we've made a difference. The way I see it, there were two great triumphs, two things that I'm proudest of. One is the economic recovery, in which the people of America created—and filled—19 million new jobs. The other is the recovery of our morale. America is respected again in the world and looked to for leadership.

Something that happened to me a few years ago reflects some of this. It was back in 1981, and I was attending my first big economic summit, which was held that year in Canada. The meeting place rotates among the member countries. The opening meeting was a formal dinner of the heads of government of the seven industrialized nations. Now, I sat there like the new kid in school and listened, and it was all François this and Helmut that. They dropped titles and spoke to one another on a first-name basis. Well, at one point I sort of leaned in and said, "My name's Ron." Well, in that same year, we began the actions we felt would ignite an economic comeback—cut taxes and regulation, started to cut spending. And soon the recovery began.

Two years later, another economic summit with pretty much the same cast. At the big opening meeting we all got together, and all of a sudden, just for a moment, I saw that everyone was just sitting there looking at me. And then one of them broke the silence. "Tell us about the American miracle," he said.

Well, back in 1980, when I was running for President, it was all so different. Some pundits said our programs would result in catastrophe. Our views on foreign affairs would cause war. Our plans for the economy would cause inflation to soar and bring about economic collapse. I even remember one highly respected economist saying, back in 1982, that "The engines of economic growth have shut down here, and they're likely to stay that way for years to come." Well, he and the other opinion leaders were wrong. The fact is what they call "radical" was really 'right.' What they called 'dangerous' was just "desperately needed."

And in all of that time I won a nickname, "The Great Communicator." But I never thought it was my style or the words I used that made a difference: it was the content. I wasn't a great communicator, but I communicated great things, and they didn't spring full bloom from my brow, they came from the heart of a great nation—from our experience, our wisdom, and our belief in the principles that have guided us for two centuries. They called it the Reagan revolution. Well, I'll accept that, but for me it always seemed more like the great rediscovery, a rediscovery of our values and our common sense.

Common sense told us that when you put a big tax on something, the people will produce less of it. So, we cut the people's tax rates, and the people produced more than ever before. The economy bloomed like a plant that had been cut back and could now grow quicker and stronger. Our economic program brought about the longest peacetime expansion in our history: real family income up, the

poverty rate down, entrepreneurship booming, and an explosion in research and new technology. We're exporting more than ever because American industry became more competitive and at the same time, we summoned the national will to knock down protectionist walls abroad instead of erecting them at home.

Common sense also told us that to preserve the peace, we'd have to become strong again after years of weakness and confusion. So, we rebuilt our defenses, and this New Year we toasted the new peacefulness around the globe. Not only have the superpowers actually begun to reduce their stockpiles of nuclear weapons—and hope for even more progress is bright—but the regional conflicts that rack the globe are also beginning to cease. The Persian Gulf is no longer a war zone. The Soviets are leaving Afghanistan. The Vietnamese are preparing to pull out of Cambodia, and an American-mediated accord will soon send 50,000 Cuban troops home from Angola.

The lesson of all this was, of course, that because we're a great nation, our challenges seem complex. It will always be this way. But as long as we remember our first principles and believe in ourselves, the future will always be ours. And something else we learned: Once you begin a great movement, there's no telling where it will end. We meant to change a nation, and instead, we changed a world.

Countries across the globe are turning to free markets and free speech and turning away from the ideologies of the past. For them, the great rediscovery of the 1980's has been that, lo and behold, the moral way of government is the practical way of government: Democracy, the profoundly good, is also the profoundly productive.

When you've got to the point when you can celebrate the anniversaries of your 39th birthday you can sit back sometimes, review your life, and see it flowing before you. For me there was a fork in the river, and it was right in the middle of my life. I never meant to go into politics. It wasn't my intention when I was young. But I was raised to believe you had to pay your way for the blessings bestowed on you. I was happy with my career in the entertainment world, but I ultimately went into politics because I wanted to protect something precious.

Ours was the first revolution in the history of mankind that truly reversed the course of government, and with three little words: "We the People." "We the People" tell the government what to do; it doesn't tell us. 'We the People' are the driver; the government is the car. And we decide where it should go, and by what route, and how fast. Almost all the world's constitutions are documents in which governments tell the people what their privileges are. Our Constitution is a document in which "We the People" tell the government what it is allowed to do. "We the People" are free. This belief has been the underlying basis for everything I've tried to do these past 8 years.

But back in the 1960's, when I began, it seemed to me that we'd begun reversing the order of things—that through more and more rules and regulations and confiscatory taxes, the government was taking more of our money, more of our options, and more of our freedom. I went into politics in part to put up my hand and say, "Stop." I was a citizen politician, and it seemed the right thing for a citizen to do.

I think we have stopped a lot of what needed stopping. And I hope we have once again reminded people that man is not free unless government is limited. There's a clear cause and effect here that is as neat and predictable as a law of physics: As government expands, liberty contracts.

Nothing is less free than pure communism—and yet we have, the past few years, forged a satisfying new closeness with the Soviet Union. I've been asked if this isn't a gamble, and my answer is no because we're basing our actions not on words but deeds. The détente of the 1970's was based not on actions but promises. They'd promise to treat their own people and the people of the world better. But the *gulag* was still the *gulag*, and the state was still expansionist, and they still waged proxy wars in Africa, Asia, and Latin America.

Well, this time, so far, it's different. President Gorbachev has brought about some internal democratic reforms and begun the withdrawal from Afghanistan. He has also freed prisoners whose names I've given him every time we've met.

But life has a way of reminding you of big things through small incidents. Once, during the heady days of the Moscow summit, Nancy and I decided to break off from the entourage one afternoon to visit the shops on Arbat Street—that's a little street just off Moscow's main shopping area. Even though our visit was a surprise, every Russian there immediately recognized us and called out our names and reached for our hands. We were just about swept away by the warmth. You could almost feel the possibilities in all that joy. But within seconds, a KGB detail pushed their way toward us and began pushing and shoving the people in the crowd. It was an interesting moment. It reminded me that while the man on the street in the Soviet Union yearns for peace, the government is Communist. And those who run it are Communists, and that means we and they view such issues as freedom and human rights very differently.

We must keep up our guard, but we must also continue to work together to lessen and eliminate tension and mistrust. My view is that President Gorbachev is different from previous Soviet leaders. I think he knows some of the things wrong with his society and is trying to fix them. We wish him well. And we'll continue to work to make sure that the Soviet Union that eventually emerges from this process is a less threatening one. What it all boils down to is this: I want the new closeness to continue. And it will, as long as we make it clear that we will continue to act in a certain way as long as they continue to act in a helpful manner. If and when they don't, at first pull your punches. If they persist, pull the plug. It's still trust by verify. It's still play, but cut the cards. It's still watch closely. And don't be afraid to see what you see.

I've been asked if I have any regrets. Well, I do. The deficit is one. I've been talking a great deal about that lately, but tonight isn't for arguments, and I'm going to hold my tongue. But an observation: I've had my share of victories in the Congress, but what few people noticed is that I never won anything you didn't win for me. They never saw my troops, they never saw Reagan's regiments, the American people. You won every battle with every call you made and letter you wrote demanding action. Well, action is still needed. If we're to finish the job. Reagan's regiments will have to become the Bush brigades. Soon he'll be the chief, and he'll need you every bit as much as I did.

Finally, there is a great tradition of warnings in Presidential farewells, and I've got one that's been on my mind for some time. But oddly enough it starts with one of the things I'm proudest of in the past 8 years: the resurgence of national pride that I called the new patriotism. This national feeling is good, but it won't count for much, and it won't last unless it's grounded in thoughtfulness and knowledge.

An informed patriotism is what we want. And are we doing a good enough job teaching our children what America is and what she represents in the long history of the world? Those of us who are over 35 or so years of age grew up in a different America. We were taught, very directly, what it means to be an American. And we absorbed, almost in the air, a love of country and an appreciation of its

institutions. If you didn't get these things from your family you got them from the neighborhood, from the father down the street who fought in Korea or the family who lost someone at Anzio. Or you could get a sense of patriotism from school. And if all else failed you could get a sense of patriotism from the popular culture. The movies celebrated democratic values and implicitly reinforced the idea that America was special. TV was like that, too, through the mid-sixties.

But now, we're about to enter the nineties, and some things have changed. Younger parents aren't sure that an unambivalent appreciation of America is the right thing to teach modern children. And as for those who create the popular culture, well-grounded patriotism is no longer the style. Our spirit is back, but we haven't reinstitutionalized it. We've got to do a better job of getting across that America is freedom—freedom of speech, freedom of religion, freedom of enterprise. And freedom is special and rare. It's fragile; it needs production [protection].

So, we've got to teach history based not on what's in fashion but what's important—why the Pilgrims came here, who Jimmy Doolittle was, and what those 30 seconds over Tokyo meant. You know, 4 years ago on the 40th anniversary of D-day, I read a letter from a young woman writing to her late father, who'd fought on Omaha Beach. Her name was Lisa Zanatta Henn, and she said, "we will always remember, we will never forget what the boys of Normandy did." Well, let's help her keep her word. If we forget what we did, we won't know who we are. I'm warning of an eradication of the American memory that could result, ultimately, in an erosion of the American spirit. Let's start with some basics: more attention to American history and a greater emphasis on civic ritual.

And let me offer lesson number one about America: All great change in America begins at the dinner table. So, tomorrow night in the kitchen I hope the talking begins. And children, if your parents haven't been teaching you what it means to be an American, let 'em know and nail 'em on it. That would be a very American thing to do.

And that's about all I have to say tonight, except for one thing. The past few days when I've been at that window upstairs, I've thought a bit of the "shining city upon a hill." The phrase comes from John Winthrop, who wrote it to describe the America he imagined. What he imagined was important because he was an early Pilgrim, an early freedom man. He journeyed here on what today we'd call a little wooden boat; and like the other Pilgrims, he was looking for a home that would be free. I've spoken of the shining city all my political life, but I don't know if I ever quite communicated what I saw when I said it. But in my mind it was a tall, proud city built on rocks stronger than oceans, windswept, God-blessed, and teeming with people of all kinds living in harmony and peace; a city with free ports that hummed with commerce and creativity. And if there had to be city walls, the walls had doors and the doors were open to anyone with the will and the heart to get here. That's how I saw it, and see it still.

And how stands the city on this winter night? More prosperous, more secure, and happier than it was 8 years ago. But more than that: After 200 years, two centuries, she still stands strong and true on the granite ridge, and her glow has held steady no matter what storm. And she's still a beacon, still a magnet for all who must have freedom, for all the pilgrims from all the lost places who are hurtling through the darkness, toward home.

We've done our part. And as I walk off into the city streets, a final word to the men and women of the Reagan revolution, the men and women across America who for 8 years did the work that brought America back. My friends: We did it. We weren't just marking time. We

made a difference. We made the city stronger, we made the city freer, and we left her in good hands. All in all, not bad, not bad at all.

And so, goodbye, God bless you, and God bless the United States of America.

Source: "Farewell From the White House," January 11, 1989, The President Reagan Information Page, http://www.presidentreagan.info/speeches/farewell.cfm

43. Remarks at the Dedication of the Cold War Memorial at Westminster College November 10, 1990

Reagan paid tribute to Sir Winston Churchill, the "greatest communicator of our time," at the site of the latter's historic "Iron Curtain Speech" in Fulton, Missouri. Coming just one year after the fall of the Berlin Wall, Reagan used the occasion to remind his audience that democracies must always remain vigilant against the siren call of appeasement. Reagan suggested that his own stand and the stand of some of America's allies toward the Soviet Union echoed Winston Churchill's tenacity in the face of the Nazi threat. He concluded his remarks in much the same way he had for almost 40 years, noting that his "city on a hill" was put here by "a divine plan . . . to be found by people from any corner of the earth . . . Here, is the one spot on earth where we have the brotherhood of man."

I can hardly visit this magnificent setting, so rich in memory and symbolism, without recalling the comment Sir Winston Churchill made when he was congratulated on the size of an audience gathered to hear him speak. Any other politician would have been flattered. Not Churchill. It was no great achievement to draw a crowd, he said. Twice as many would have turned out for a public hanging.

Maybe so, but I am deeply grateful to each of you for your warm welcome. What an honor it is for me to come to Fulton—indelibly stamped with the name and eloquence of Churchill. What a privilege to be on hand to help dedicate Edwina Sandys' sculpture celebrating the triumph of her grandfather's principles. And what a source of pride to receive an honorary degree from this distinguished college, who illustrious past is equaled only by its future promise.

Today we rejoice in the demise of the Berlin Wall that was permanently breached just one year ago.

We remember brave men and women on both sides of the iron curtain who devoted their lives—and sometimes sacrificed them—so that we might inhabit a world without barriers. And we recall with the intensity born of shared struggles the greatest Briton of them all, a child of parliamentary democracy who boasted of an American mother and who therefore claimed to be an English-speaking union all by himself.

Who standing here beside this magnificent 12th Century church that commemorated Sir Winston's 1946 visit can ever forget the indomitable figure with the bulldog expression and the upthrust "V" for victory?

As the greatest communicator of our time, Sir Winston enlisted the English language itself in the battle against Hitler and his hateful doctrines. When the Nazi might prevailed from Warsaw to the Channel Islands and from Egypt to the Arctic Ocean, at a time when the whole cause of human liberty stood trembling and imperiled, he breathed defiance in phrases that will ring down through centuries to come.

And when the guns at last fell silent in the Spring of 1945, no man on earth had done more to preserve civilization during the hour of its greatest trial.

Near the end of World War II, but before the election that everyone knew must follow V-E Day, *The Times* of London prepared an editorial suggesting that Prime Minister Churchill run as a non-partisan fig-

ure, above the fray of parliamentary politics, and that he gracefully retire soon after to rest on his laurels and bask in the glow of yesterday's triumph.

The editor informed Sir Winston of both points he intended to make. Churchill had a ready reply. As for the first suggestion, "Mr. Editor," he said, "I fight for my corner." And as for the second, "Mr. Editor, I leave when the pub closes."

For a while in the Summer of 1945 it looked as if perhaps the pub *had* closed.

We all know that democracy can be a fickle employer. But that does little to ease the pain. It's hard to be philosophical on the day after an elections slips through your fingers. Clementine, trying to think of anything to say that might console her husband, looked at the returns and concluded that it might well be a blessing in disguise.

The old lion turned to his wife and said, "At the moment it seems quite effectively disguised."

"I have no regrets," Churchill told visitors in the aftermath of his defeat. "I leave my name to history." But Winston Churchill rarely did the easy thing.

He could not rest so long as tyranny threatened any part of the globe. So when Harry Truman invited him to speak at Westminster College in the Spring of 1946, Churchill leapt at the chance. He hoped that by traveling to the heartland of America he might reach the heart of America. He would do so in an address whose timeless eloquence would be matched by its indisputable logic. Churchill addressed a nation at the pinnacle of world power—but a nation unaccustomed to wielding such authority and historically reluctant to intrude in the affairs of Europe.

In the exhausted aftermath of World War II, few were prepared to listen to warnings of fresh danger.

But Churchill was undaunted. Once before his had been a voice crying out in the wilderness against the suicidal dogmas of appeasement. Once before he had sounded an alarm against those deluded souls who thought they could go on feeding the crocodile with bits and pieces of other countries and somehow avoid his jaws themselves. His warnings had been ignored by a world more in love with temporary ease than long-term security. Yet time had proven him tragically correct.

His Fulton speech was a firebell in the night, a Paul Revere warning that tyranny was once more on the march.

"From Stettin in the Baltic to Trieste in the Adriatic, an iron curtain has descended across the continent." he said.

Churchill titled his speech "The Sinews of Peace," but the reaction it provoked was anything but peaceful. Newspaper editors on both sides of the Atlantic rushed to brand its author a warmonger. Labor MP's asked Prime Minister Attlee to formally repudiate his predecessor's remarks. From Moscow came a blast of rhetoric labeling Stalin's former wartime ally "false and hypocritical" and claiming that having lost an election in his homeland he had decided to try his luck in the United States. Harry Truman knew better.

The people of Missouri were highly pleased by Churchill's visit, and had enjoyed what their distinguished visitor had to say.

And for those trapped behind the iron curtain spied on and lied to by their corrupt governments, denied their freedoms, their bread, even their faith in a power greater than that of the state—for them Churchill was no warmonger and the western alliance no enemy. For the victims of communist oppression, the iron curtain was made all too real in a concrete wall, surrounded by barbed wire and attack dogs and guards with orders to shoot on sight anyone trying to escape the so-called worker's paradise of East Germany.

Today we come full circle from those anxious times. Ours is a more peaceful planet because of men like Churchill and Truman and countless others who shared their dream of a world where no one wields a sword and no one drags a chain. This is their monument. Here, on a grassy slope between the Church of St. Mary the Virgin and Champ Auditorium, a man and a woman break through the wall and symbolically demolish whatever remaining barriers stand in the way of international peace and the brotherhood of nations.

Out of one man's speech was born a new Western resolve.

Not warlike, not bellicose, not expansionist—but firm and principled in resisting those who would devour territory and put the soul itself into bondage. The road to a free Europe that began there in Fulton led to the Truman Doctrine and The Marshall Plan, to N.A.T.O and The Berlin Airlift, through nine American presidencies and more than four decades of military preparedness.

By the time I came to the White House, a new challenge had arisen. Moscow had decided to deploy intermediate-range nuclear missiles like the SS-20 that would threaten every city in Western Europe.

It never launched those missiles, but fired plenty of trial balloons into the air, and it rained propaganda on the United States and the Federal Republic of Germany in an effort to prevent the modernization of N.A.T.O.'s forces on West German soil.

But the Government in Bonn was not deterred. Neither was the rest of Western Europe deceived. At the same time, we in the United States announced our own intention to develop S.D.I.—the Strategic Defense Initiative, to hasten the day when the nuclear nightmare was ended forever and our children's dreams were no longer marred by the specter of instant annihilation.

Of course, not everyone agreed with such a course.

For years it had been suggested by some opinion-makers that all would be well in the world if only the United States lowered its profile. Some of them would not only have us lower our profile—they would also lower our flag. I disagreed. I thought that the 1980's were a time to stop apologizing for America's legitimate national interest, and start asserting them.

I was by no means alone. Principled leaders like Helmut Kohl and Margaret Thatcher reinforced our message that the West would not be blackmailed and that only rational course was to return to the bargaining table in Geneva and work out real and lasting arms reductions fair to both sides.

A new Soviet leader appeared on the scene, untainted by the past, unwilling to be shackled by crumbling orthodoxies. With the rise of Mikhail Gorbachev came the end of numbing oppression. Glasnost introduced openness to the world's most closed society. Perestroika held out the promise of a better life, achieved through democratic institutions and a market economy. And real arms control came to pass, as an entire class of weapons was eliminated for the first time in the atomic age.

Within months the Soviet Empire began to melt like a snowbank in May.

Once country after another overthrew the privileged cliques that had bled their economies and curbed their freedoms. Last month Germany itself was reunited, in the shadow of The Brandenburg Gate and under the democratic umbrella of N.A.T.O. I know something about that neighborhood. Back in June 1987 I stood in the free city of West Berlin and asked Mr. Gorbachev to tear down the wall.

Was he listening? Whether he was, or not, neither he nor the rulers of Eastern Europe could ignore the much louder chants of demonstrators in the streets of Leipzig and Dresden and dozens of other German cities.

In the churches and the schools, in the factories and on the farms, a once silent people found their voice and with it a battering ram to knock down walls, real and imagined.

Because of them, the political map of Europe has been rewritten. The future has been redefined, even as the veil has been lifted on a cruel and bloody past. Just last week, thousand of Soviet citizens, may of them clutching photographs of relatives who died in Stalin's labor camps, marched to the Moscow headquarters of the K.G.B. to unveil a monument to the victims of Stalinist repression. An aging woman named Alla Krichevskaya held up a photograph of a young man in an old fashioned high collar. She wept softly.

"This was my father," she said, "I never knew him. He was sent to Sologetsky (labor camp) in 1932, a few months before I was born, and they shot him in 1937."

In dedicating this memorial, may we pause and reflect on the heroism and the sacrifice of Alla's father and so many, many others like him. Fifty years after Winston Churchill rallied his people in the Battle of Britain, the world is a very different place. Soviet Russia is coming out of the dark to join the family of nations. Central and Eastern Europe struggle to create both freedom and prosperity through market economies. How pleased Sir Winston would be!

Let me conclude with a special word to the students of Westminster College, the empire builders of the 21st Century. Before you leave this place, do not forget why you came. You came to Westminster to explore the diversity of ideas and experience that we call civilization. Here you discover that so long as books are kept open, then minds can never be closed. Here you develop a sense of self, along with the realization that self alone is never enough for a truly satisfying life. For while we make a living by what we get, we make a life by what we give.

Tragically, many walls still remain to endanger our families and our communities.

Later today the Fulton Optimist Club will join with others in recognizing winners of an essay contest called "Why should I say no to drugs?" Obviously Fulton cares about its future as well as its past—above all, it cares about the children who represent that future.

In Fulton, Missouri as in London, Berlin or Los Angeles, the future is what you make it.

Certainly it was unreasonable for a sixty-five-year-old parliamentarian, his counsel rejected until the emergency was at hand, to believe that he could defy the world's most lethal fighting force and crush Hitler in his Berlin lair.

It was unreasonable to suggest that an ancient church, all but destroyed by enemy bombs, could be reconstructed five thousand miles away as a permanent tribute to the man of the century. It was unreasonable to hope that oppressed men and women behind the iron curtain could one day break through to the sunlight of freedom—and that the Soviet Politburo itself would yield to people in the streets.

All this was unreasonable. But it all came true. My fondest wish is that each of you will be similarly unreasonable in pursuing Churchill's objectives—justice, opportunity, and an end to walls wherever they divide the human race.

Shortly before he died, Sir Winston received a letter from his daughter Mary. "In addition to all the feelings a daughter has for a loving, generous father," she wrote, "I owe you what every Englishman, woman and child does—liberty itself." We owe him nothing less.

In dedicating this magnificent sculpture, may we dedicate ourselves to hastening the day when all God's children live in a world without walls. That would be the greatest empire of all.

And now, let me speak directly to the young people and the students here. I wonder yet if you've appreciated how unusual—terribly unusual—this country of ours is?

I received a letter just before I left office from a man. I don't know why he chose to write it, but I'm glad he did. He wrote that you can go to live in France, but you can't become a Frenchman. You can go to live in Germany or Italy, but you can't become a German, an Italian. He went through Turkey, Greece, Japan and other countries. but he said anyone, from any corner of the world, can come to live in the United States and become an American.

Some may call it mysticism if they will, but I cannot help but feel that there was some divine plan that placed this continent here between the two great oceans to be found by people from any corner of the earth—people who had an extra ounce of desire for freedom and some extra courage to rise up and lead their families, their relatives, their friends, their nations and come here to eventually make this country.

The truth of the matter is, if we take this crowd and if we could go through and ask the heritage, the background of every family represented here, we would probably come up with the names of every country on earth, every corner of the world, and every race. Here, is the one spot on earth where we have the brotherhood of man. And maybe as we continue with this proudly, this brotherhood of man made up from people representative of every corner of the earth, maybe one day boundaries all over the earth will disappear as people cross boundaries and find out that, yes, there is a brotherhood of man in every corner.

Thank you all and God Bless you all.

Source: "Westminster College Cold War Memorial," November 10, 1990, The President Reagan Information Page. Available online. URL: http://www.presidentreagan.info/speeches/westminster.cfm

44. 1992 Republican National Convention Speech
Houston, Texas
August 17, 1992

This was Reagan's farewell to the Republican faithful, although no one knew it at the time. George H. W. Bush would lose the election that fall to Governor

Bill Clinton of Arkansas, in part because many disappointed Reaganites abandoned Bush due to his broken "no new taxes" pledge. Nevertheless, the Republican Party came back with a vengeance in the 1994 mid-term elections, capturing the House of Representatives for the first time since the 1950s, and taking control of the Senate as well. The new Republican congressional leadership adored Ronald Reagan and completed the transformation begun in the 1980s to shape the party around Reagan's principles.

Thank you, Paul for that kind introduction. And Mr. Chairman, delegates, friends, fellow Americans, thank you so very much for that welcome. You've given Nancy and me so many wonderful memories, so much of your warmth and affection, we cannot thank you enough for the honor of your friendship.

Over the years, I've addressed this convention as a private citizen, as a governor, as a presidential candidate, as a president and now, once again tonight, as private citizen Ronald Reagan.

Tonight is a very special night for me. Of course, at my age, every night's a very special night. After all, I was born in 1911. Indeed, according to the experts, I have exceeded my life expectancy by quite a few years. Now this a source of great annoyance to some, especially those in the Democratic party.

But, here's the remarkable thing about being born in 1911. In my life's journey over these past eight decades, I have seen the human race through a period of unparalleled tumult and triumph. I have seen the birth of communism and the death of communism. I have witnessed the bloody futility of two World Wars, Korea, Vietnam and the Persian Gulf. I have seen Germany united, divided and united again. I have seen television grow from a parlor novelty to become the most powerful vehicle of communication in history. As a boy I saw streets filled with model-Ts; as a man I have met men who walked on the moon.

I have not only seen, but lived the marvels of what historians have called the "American Century." Yet, tonight is not a time to look backward. For while I take inspiration from the past, like most Americans, I live for the future. So this evening, for just a few minutes, I hope you will let me talk about a country that is forever young.

There was a time when empires were defined by land mass, subjugated peoples, and military might. But the United States is unique because we are an empire of ideals. For two hundred years we have been set apart by our faith in the ideals of democracy, of free men and free markets, and of the extraordinary possibilities that lie within seemingly ordinary men and women. We believe that no power of government is as formidable a force for good as the creativity and entrepreneurial drive of the American people.

Those are the ideals that invented revolutionary technologies and a culture envied by people everywhere. This powerful sense of energy has made America synonymous for opportunity the world over. And after generations of struggle, America is the moral force that defeated communism and all those who would put the human soul itself into bondage.

Within a few short years, we Americans have experienced the most sweeping changes of this century: the fall of the Soviet Union and the rise of the global economy. No transition is without its problems, but as uncomfortable as it may feel at the moment, the changes of the 1990's will leave America more dynamic and less in danger than at any time in my life.

A fellow named James Allen once wrote in his diary, "many thinking people believe America has seen its best days." He wrote that July 26, 1775. There are still those who believe America is weakening; that our glory was the brief flash of time called the 20th Century; that ours was a burst of greatness too bright and brilliant to sustain; that America's purpose is past.

My friends, I utterly reject those views. That's not the America we know. We were meant to be masters of destiny, not victims of fate. Who among us would trade America's future for that of any other country in the world? And who could possibly have so little faith in our America that they would trade our tomorrows for our yesterdays?

I'll give you a hint. They put on quite a production in New York a few weeks ago. You might even call it slick. A stone's throw from Broadway it was, and how appropriate. Over and over they told us they are not the party they were. They kept telling us with straight faces that they're for family values, they're for a strong America, they're for less intrusive government.

And they call me an actor.

To hear them talk, you'd never know that the nightmare of nuclear annihilation has been lifted from our sleep. You'd never know that our standard of living remains the highest in the world. You'd never know that our air is cleaner than it was 20 years ago. You'd never know that we remain the one nation the rest of the world looks to for leadership.

It wasn't always this way. We mustn't forget—even if they would like to—the very different America that existed just 12 years ago; an America with 21 percent interest rates and back to back years of double digit inflation; an America where mortgage payments doubled, paychecks plunged, and motorists sat in gas lines; an America whose leaders told us it was our own fault; that ours was a future of scarcity and sacrifice; and that what we really needed was another good dose of government control and higher taxes.

It wasn't so long ago that the world was a far more dangerous place as well. It was a world where aggressive Soviet communism was on the rise and American strength was in decline. It was a world where our children came of age under the threat of nuclear holocaust. It was a world where our leaders told us that standing up to aggressors was dangerous—that American might and determination were somehow obstacles to peace.

But we stood tall and proclaimed that communism was destined for the ash heap of history. We never heard so much ridicule from our liberal friends. The only thing that got them more upset was two simple words: "Evil Empire."

But we knew then what the liberal Democrat leaders just couldn't figure out: the sky would not fall if America restored her strength and resolve. The sky would not fall if an American president spoke the truth. The only thing that would fall was the Berlin Wall.

I heard those speakers at that other convention saying "we won the Cold War"—and I couldn't help wondering, just who exactly do they mean by "we"? And to top it off, they even tried to portray themselves as sharing the same fundamental values of our party! What they truly don't understand is the principle so eloquently stated by Abraham Lincoln: "You cannot strengthen the weak by weakening the strong. You cannot help the wage-earner by pulling down the wage-payer. You cannot help the poor by destroying the rich. You cannot help men permanently by doing for them what they could and should do for themselves."

If we ever hear the Democrats quoting that passage by Lincoln and acting like they mean it, then, my friends, we will know that the opposition has really changed.

Until then, we see all that rhetorical smoke, billowing out from the Democrats, well ladies and gentlemen, I'd follow the example of their nominee. Don't inhale.

This fellow they've nominated claims he's the new Thomas Jefferson. Well, let me tell you something. I knew Thomas Jefferson. He was a friend of mine. And governor, you're no Thomas Jefferson.

Now let's not dismiss our current troubles, but where they see only problems, I see possibilities—as vast and diverse as the American family itself. Even as we meet, the rest of the world is astounded by the pundits and finger pointers who are so down on us as a nation.

Well I've said it before and I'll say it again—America's best days are yet to come. Our proudest moments are yet to be. Our most glorious achievements are just ahead. America remains what Emerson called her 150 years ago, "the country of tomorrow." What a wonderful description and how true. And yet tomorrow might never have happened had we lacked the courage in the 1980's to chart a course of strength and honor.

All the more reason no one should underestimate the importance of this campaign and what the outcome will mean. The stakes are high. The presidency is serious business. We cannot afford to take a chance. We need a man of serious purpose, unmatched experience, knowledge and ability. A man who understands government, who understands our country and who understands the world. A man who has been at the table with Gorbachev and Yeltsin. A man whose performance as commander-in-chief of the bravest and most effective fighting force in history left the world in awe and the people of Kuwait free of foreign tyranny. A man who has devoted more than half of his life to serving his country. A man of decency, integrity and honor.

And tonight I come to tell you that I—warmly, genuinely, wholeheartedly support the re-election of George Bush as president of the United States.

We know President Bush. By his own admission, he is a quiet man, not a showman. He is a trustworthy and levelheaded leader who is respected around the world. His is a steady hand on the tiller through the choppy waters of the '90s, which is exactly what we need.

We need George Bush!

Yes, we need Bush.

We also need another fighter, a man who happens to be with us this evening, someone who has repeatedly stood up for his deepest convictions. We need our vice president, Dan Quayle.

Now it's true: a lot of liberal democrats are saying it's time for a change; and they're right; the only trouble is they're pointing to the wrong end of Pennsylvania Avenue. What we should change is a Democratic congress that wastes precious time on partisan matters of absolutely no relevance to the needs of the average American. So to all the entrenched interests along the Potomac—the gavel-wielding chairmen, the bloated staffs, the taxers and takers and congressional rule makers, we have a simple slogan for November 1992: clean house!

For you see, my fellow Republicans, we are the change! For 50 of the last 60 years the Democrats have controlled the Senate. And they've had the House of Representatives for 56 of the last 60 years.

It's time to clean house. Clean out the privileges and perks. Clean out the arrogance and the big egos. Clean out the scandals, the corner-cutting and the foot-dragging.

What kind of job do you think they've done during all those years they've been running the Congress?

You know, I used to say to some of those Democrats who chair every committee in the House: "You need to balance the government's checkbook the same way you balance your own." Then I learned how they ran the House bank, and I realized that was exactly what they had been doing!

Now, just imagine what they would do controlled the executive branch, too!

This is the 21st presidential election in my lifetime, the 16th in which I will cast a ballot. Each of those elections had its shifting moods of the moment, its headlines of one day that were forgotten the next. There have been a few more twists and turns this year than in others, a little more shouting about who was up or down, in or out, as we went about selecting our candidates. But now we have arrived, as we always do, at the moment of truth—the serious business of selecting a president.

Now is the time for choosing.

As it did 12 years ago, and as we have seen many times in history, our country now stands at a crossroads. There is widespread doubt about our public institutions and profound concern, not merely about the economy but about the overall direction of this great country.

And as they did then, the American people are clamoring for change and sweeping reform. The question we had to ask 12 years ago is the question we ask today: What kind of change can we Republicans offer the American people?

Some might believe that the things we have talked about tonight are irrelevant to the choice. These new isolationists claim that the American people don't care about how or why we prevailed in the great defining struggle of our age—the victory of liberty over our adversaries. They insist that our triumph is yesterday's news, part of a past that holds no lessons for the future.

Well nothing could be more tragic, after having come all this way on the journey of renewal we began 12 years ago, than if America herself forgot the lessons of individual liberty that she has taught to a grateful world.

Emerson was right. We are the country of tomorrow. Our revolution did not end at Yorktown. More than two centuries later, America remains on a voyage of discovery, a land that has never become, but is always in the act of becoming.

But just as we have led the crusade for democracy beyond our shores, we have a great task to do together in our own home. Now, I would appeal to you to invigorate democracy in your own neighborhoods.

Whether we come from poverty or wealth; whether we are Afro-American or Irish-American; Christian or Jewish, from big cities or small towns, we are all equal in the eyes of God. But as Americans that is not enough we must be equal in the eyes of each other. We can no longer judge each other on the basis of what we are, but must, instead, start finding out who we are. In America, our origins matter less than our destinations and that is what democracy is all about.

A decade after we summoned America to a new beginning, we are beginning still. Every day brings fresh challenges and opportunities to match. With each sunrise we are reminded that millions of our citizens have yet to share in the abundance of American prosperity. Many languish in neighborhoods riddled with drugs and bereft of hope. Still others hesitate to venture out on the streets for fear of criminal violence. Let us pledge ourselves to a new beginning for them.

Let us apply our ingenuity and remarkable spirit to revolutionize education in America so that everyone among us will have the mental tools to build a better life. And while we do so, let's remember that the most profound education begins in the home.

And let us harness the competitive energy that built America, into rebuilding our inner cities so that real jobs can be created for those who live there and real hope can rise out of despair.

Let us strengthen our health care system so that Americans of all ages can be secure in their futures without the fear of financial ruin.

And my friends, once and for all, let us get control of the federal deficit through a Balanced Budget Amendment and line item veto.

And let us all renew our commitment. Renew our pledge to day by day, person by person, make our country and the world a better place to live. Then when the nations of the world turn to us and say, "America, you are the model of freedom and prosperity." We can turn to them and say, "you ain't seen nothing, yet!"

For me, tonight is the latest chapter in a story that began a quarter of a century ago, when the people of California entrusted me with the stewardship of their dreams.

My fellow citizens—those of you here in this hall and those of you at home—I want you to know that I have always had the highest respect for you, for your common sense and intelligence and for your decency. I have always believed in you and in what you could accomplish for yourselves and for others.

And whatever else history may say about me when I'm gone, I hope it will record that I appealed to your best hopes, not your worst fears, to your confidence rather than your doubts. My dream is that you will travel the road ahead with liberty's lamp guiding your steps and opportunity's arm steadying your way.

My fondest hope for each one of you—and especially for the young people here—is that you will love your country, not for her power or wealth, but for her selflessness and her idealism. May each of you have the heart to conceive, the understanding to direct, and the hand to execute works that will make the world a little better for your having been here.

May all of you as Americans never forget your heroic origins, never fail to seek divine guidance, and never lose your natural, God-given optimism.

And finally, my fellow Americans, may every dawn be a great new beginning for America and every evening bring us closer to that shining city upon a hill.

Before I go, I would like to ask the person who has made my life's journey so meaningful, someone I have been so proud of through the years, to join me. Nancy . . .

My fellow Americans, on behalf of both of us, goodbye, and God bless each and every one of you, and God bless this country we love.

Source: "Republican Convention (1992)," August 17, 1992, The President Reagan Information Page. Available online. URL: http://www.presidentreagan.info/speeches/rnc.cfm

45. Announcement of Alzheimer's Disease Letter to the Nation November 5, 1994

This letter needs no introduction. As Reagan's official biographer, Edmund Morris, noted, "reading it again, I realized that I held in my hands a masterly piece of writing. It had the simplicity of genius, or at least the simplicity of a fundamentally religious nature accepting the inevitable."

My fellow Americans, I have recently been told that I am one of the millions of Americans who will be afflicted with Alzheimer's disease.

Upon learning this news, Nancy and I had to decide whether as private citizens we would keep this a private matter or whether we would make this news known in a public way. In the past, Nancy suffered from breast cancer and I had my cancer surgeries. We found through our open disclosures we were able to raise public awareness. We were happy that as a result, many more people underwent testing. They were treated in early stages and able to return to normal, healthy lives.

So now we feel it is important to share it with you. In opening our hearts, we hope this might promote greater awareness of this condition. Perhaps it will encourage a clearer understanding of the individuals and families who are affected by it.

At the moment I feel just fine. I intend to live the remainder of the years God gives me on this Earth doing the things I have always done. I will continue to share life's journey with my beloved Nancy and my family. I plan to enjoy the great outdoors and stay in touch with my friends and supporters.

Unfortunately, as Alzheimer's disease progresses, the family often bears a heavy burden. I only wish there was some way I could spare Nancy from this painful experience. When the time comes, I am confident that with your help she will face it with faith and courage.

In closing, let me thank you, the American people, for giving me the great honor of allowing me to serve as your president. When the Lord calls me home, whenever that day may be, I will leave with the greatest love for this country of ours and eternal optimism for its future.

I now begin the journey that will lead me into the sunset of my life. I know that for America there will always be a bright dawn ahead.

Thank you, my friends. May God always bless you.

Sincerely,

Ronald Reagan

Source: "Ronald Reagan's public letter announcing his Alzheimer's disease," The Ronald Reagan Presidential Library. Available online. URL: http://www.reagan.utexas.edu/resource/handout/Alzheime.htm

SELECTED BIBLIOGRAPHY

The foremost chronicler of "of all things Reagan" is Lou Cannon, a reporter who covered Ronald Reagan for decades at the *San Jose Mercury News* and later for the *Washington Post*. *The Reagan Years* relies heavily on Cannon's three works listed below, and no account of Reagan's public career is complete without reference to them. Cannon's admiration for Reagan seems to have grown with the passage of time; some of his earlier works, including the first edition of *President Reagan: The Role of a Lifetime*, were more critical of Reagan than a later edition of that same volume. Cannon's admiration for Reagan is quite apparent in his most recent work, *Governor Reagan*.

The most controversial book about President Reagan, *Dutch: A Memoir of Ronald Reagan*, was written by Edmund Morris, the Pulitzer Prize–winning author of *The Rise of Theodore Roosevelt*. Morris was appointed Reagan's official biographer in 1985, and published his book in 1999 after a series of delays. Morris desperately tried to penetrate the "wall" Reagan was notorious for "hiding" behind, and he appears to have engaged in a fruitless search for complexity in Reagan that simply wasn't there. Morris was widely criticized for his use of fictional characters in a work of nonfiction; while that decision was

regrettable, *Dutch* offers many insights into Reagan that were obscured by the controversy surrounding the inclusion of these characters. Additionally, Morris focused on Reagan's personality—consequently many policy issues and political events were neglected. However, Morris is a gifted writer (despite a propensity for littering his text with phrases in various foreign languages designed to impress) who was given remarkable access to the inner workings of the Reagan White House during the second term. His work is a valuable, although incomplete, resource on the Reagan years.

Professor Kiron Skinner, along with Martin and Annelise Anderson, two former Reagan associates now affiliated with the Hoover Institution at Stanford University, have edited two pathbreaking collections of Reagan's writings that provide an unparalled glimpse into Reagan's thinking. Their first work, *Reagan in His Own Hand: The Writings of Ronald Reagan That Reveal His Revolutionary Vision for America*, convinced many skeptics that Reagan thought deeply about the issues closest to his heart. The second collection of Reagan's writings was derived from his personal correspondence. *Reagan: A Life in Letters*, offers perhaps the best view behind the "wall" that Nancy Reagan and many of the president's associates have spoken of; this was a president who kept his distance, and the "what made Reagan tick" question comes closest to being answered in these letters. Ronald Reagan's own memoir, *An American Life*, published in 1990, is somewhat disappointing, partly due to the fact that Reagan disliked talking about himself and recoiled from introspection. Nancy Reagan's memoir, *My Turn*, is at times a petty work of score-settling that does little to enhance the first lady's reputation.

The most impressive memoir to emerge from a member of Reagan's cabinet is Secretary of State George Shultz's *Turmoil and Triumph: My Years as Secretary of State*. Shultz emerges as a patient, strategic thinker who understood the importance of tending to diplomacy as one tends to a garden—sometimes it takes years to bear fruit, but the benefits can be enormous. Shultz's rival in Reagan's cabinet, Caspar Weinberger, has written two accounts of his service as secretary of defense, *Fighting for Peace* and *In the Arena*. These are less thoughtful and detailed works than the Shultz memoir, but Weinberger's devotion to Reagan and his Churchillian commitment to rebuilding the American military comes through in bold relief. Former White House chief of staff Donald Regan used his memoir, *For the Record*, as a vehicle to settle scores with the first lady, including revealing Mrs. Reagan's reliance on an astrologer when arranging the president's schedule. David Stockman's *The Triumph of Politics* and Alexander Haig's *Caveat* both engaged in score settling, while occasionally presenting useful insights into Reagan's first term; the former offered a particularly critical account of Caspar Weinberger, while the latter was dismayed by what he saw as an excessive concern by some White House staff members to husband Reagan's political capital at the expense of good

policy. Longtime Reagan aides Michael Deaver and Edwin Meese both authored memoirs of their time with the Reagans. These are useful accounts for any serious student of the Reagan years; however, it must be said regarding Deaver that he has turned his affiliation with the Reagans into something of a cottage publishing industry, authoring three different books on the president and first lady with few new insights.

A little-known but highly useful analysis of the Reagan presidency can be found in Peter Wallison's *Ronald Reagan: The Power of Conviction and the Success of His Presidency*. Wallison served for a brief period as President Reagan's White House counsel, and he recounts that experience in portions of his book. But the real strength of the work is found in Wallison's analysis of Reagan's leadership style and how it fits into various models offered by Richard Neustadt and other leading scholars of the American presidency. By far the most thoughtful collection of essays on President Reagan and the policies of his administration can be found in *The Reagan Presidency: Pragmatic Conservatism and Its Legacies*, edited by W. Elliot Brownlee and Hugh Davis Graham. The collection contains many of the best papers presented at a conference on the Reagan presidency held at the University of California at Santa Barbara in March 2002. Hugh Heclo's essay on "Ronald Reagan and the American Public Philosophy" is the jewel of the collection.

The following is a comprehensive bibliography of the sources used in compiling *The Reagan Years*. The subject headings are fairly self-explanatory; the first listing is designed to give the reader a sense of the best published material on Ronald Reagan's life and career in general; the remaining lists offer a detailed inventory of the sources available for specific events or policy areas.

Ronald Reagan: General Overview

Anderson, Martin. *Revolution: The Reagan Legacy.* Stanford, Calif.: The Hoover Institution Press, 1990.

Brownlee, W. Elliot, and Hugh Davis Graham, eds. *The Reagan Presidency: Pragmatic Conservatism and Its Legacies.* Lawrence: University Press of Kansas, 2003.

Cannon, Lou. *Governor Reagan: His Rise to Power.* New York: Public Affairs, 2003.

———. *President Reagan: The Role of a Lifetime.* New York: Simon and Schuster, 1991.

———. *Reagan.* New York: G. P. Putnam's Sons, 1982.

Dallek, Matthew. *The Right Moment: Ronald Reagan's First Victory and the Decisive Turning Point in American Politics.* New York: Free Press, 2000.

Deaver, Michael K. *A Different Drummer: My Thirty Years with Ronald Reagan.* New York: Harper-Collins, 2001.

———, *Nancy: A Portrait of My Years with Nancy Reagan.* New York: William Morrow, 2004.

Deaver, Michael K., with Mickey Herskowitz. *Behind the Scenes: In Which the Author Talks about Ronald and Nancy Reagan, and Himself.* New York: William Morrow, 1987.

Dugger, Ronnie. *On Reagan: The Man and His Presidency.* New York: McGraw-Hill. 1983.

Edwards, Anne. *Early Reagan.* New York: William Morrow and Company, 1987.

Haig, Alexander M. Jr. *Caveat: Realism, Reagan, and Foreign Policy.* New York: MacMillan, 1984.

Hannaford, Peter, ed. *Recollections of Reagan: A Portrait of Ronald Reagan.* New York: William Morrow, 1997.

Levy, Peter. *Encyclopedia of the Reagan-Bush Years.* Westport, Conn.: Greenwood Press, 1996.

Meese, Edwin. *With Reagan: The Inside Story.* Washington, D.C.: Regnery-Gateway, 1992.

Morris, Edmund. *Dutch: A Memoir of Ronald Reagan.* New York: Random House, 1999.

Reagan, Nancy, with William Novak. *My Turn: The Memoirs of Nancy Reagan.* New York: Random House, 1989.

Public Papers of the Presidents of the United States, Ronald Reagan, 1981–1989. Washington, D.C.: U.S. Government Printing Office, 1982–1991.

Reagan, Ronald. *Abortion and the Conscience of the Nation.* Sacramento, Calif.: New Regency Publishing, 2000.

———. *An American Life.* New York: Simon and Schuster, 1990.

———. *Speaking My Mind: Selected Speeches.* New York: Simon and Schuster, 1989.

Regan, Donald T. *For the Record: From Wall Street to Washington.* New York: Harcourt Brace Jovanovich, 1988.

Shultz, George P. *Turmoil and Triumph: My Years as Secretary of State.* New York: Charles Scribner's Sons, 1993.

Skinner, Kiron K., Annelise Anderson, and Martin Anderson, eds. *Reagan: A Life in Letters.* New York: Free Press, 2003.

———. *Reagan in His Own Hand: The Writings of Ronald Reagan That Reveal His Revolutionary Vision for America.* New York: Touchstone, 2002.

Stockman, David. *The Triumph of Politics: How the Reagan Revolution Failed.* New York: Harper and Row, 1986.

Strober, Deborah Hart, and Gerald S. Strober. *Reagan: The Man and His Presidency.* Boston: Houghton Mifflin Company, 1998.

Wallison, Peter. *Ronald Reagan: The Power of Conviction and the Success of His Presidency.* Cambridge, Mass.: Westview Press, 2003.

Weinberger, Caspar W. *Fighting for Peace: Seven Critical Years in the Pentagon.* New York: Warner Book, Inc., 1990.

———. *In the Arena: A Memoir of the 20th Century.* Washington, D.C.: Regnery Publishing, 2001.

Agriculture Policy

Drinkard, Jim. "Congress Approves Costly Farm Bill," *Associated Press.* December 18, 1985.

Schwab, Larry M. *The Illusion of a Conservative Reagan Revolution.* New Brunswick, N.J.: Transaction Publishers, 1991.

Skinner, Kiron K., Annelise Anderson, and Martin Anderson, eds. *Reagan in His Own Hand: The Writings of Ronald Reagan That Reveal His Revolutionary Vision for America.* New York: Touchstone, 2002.

Thompson, Robert L. "Agriculture: Growing Government Control." In David Boaz, ed. *Assessing the Reagan Years.* Washington, D.C.: Cato Institute, 1988.

Assassination Attempt

Cannon, Lou. *President Reagan: The Role of a Lifetime.* New York: Simon and Schuster, 1991.

Morris, Edmund. *Dutch: A Memoir of Ronald Reagan.* New York: Random House, 1999.

Raines, Howell. "Left Lung Is Pierced; Coloradan, 25, Arrested—Brady, Press Chief, Is Critically Injured." *New York Times,* March 31, 1981, p. A1.

Reagan, Ronald. *An American Life.* New York: Simon and Schuster, 1990.

Strober, Deborah Hart, and Gerald S. Strober. *Reagan: The Man and His Presidency.* Boston: Houghton Mifflin Company, 1998.

Campaign for President, 1976, 1980, 1984

Cannon, Lou. *President Reagan: The Role of a Lifetime.* New York: Simon and Schuster, 1991.

———. *Reagan.* New York: G. P. Putnam's Sons, 1982.

Greene, John Robert. *The Presidency of Gerald R. Ford.* Lawrence: University Press of Kansas, 1995, pp. 151–52, 164–67.

Kaufman, Burton I. *The Presidency of James Earl Carter, Jr.* Lawrence: University Press of Kansas, 1993, pp. 170–73, 181.

Raine, George. "S.F. Ad Man Riney to Join Hall of Fame." *San Francisco Chronicle.* March 12, 2002, p. B3.

Reagan, Ronald. *An American Life.* New York: Simon and Schuster, 1990.

———. *Speaking My Mind: Selected Speeches.* New York: Simon and Schuster, 1989.

Skinner, Kiron K., Annelise Anderson, and Martin Anderson, eds. *Reagan in His Own Hand: The Writings of Ronald Reagan That Reveal His Revolutionary Vision for America.* New York: Touchstone, 2002.

Strober, Deborah Hart, and Gerald S. Strober. *Reagan: The Man and His Presidency.* Boston: Houghton Mifflin Company, 1998.

Civil Rights, Affirmative Action, and Judicial Appointments

"Bush Pledges 'New Day' for Blacks in U.S." *Houston Chronicle,* July 13, 1988.

Cannon, Lou. *President Reagan: The Role of a Lifetime.* New York: Simon and Schuster, 1991.

Dugger, Ronnie. *On Reagan: The Man and His Presidency.* New York: McGraw-Hill, 1983.

Foxhall, Nene. "Brock Defends Reagan at NAACP Convention." *Houston Chronicle,* June 25, 1985; and "NAACP Chief Hooks Blasts Reagan Civil Rights Stand." *Houston Chronicle,* June 24, 1985.

Jacob, John E. "The Government and Social Problems." In Paul Boyer, ed. *Reagan as President: Contemporary Views of the Man, His Politics, and His Policies.* Chicago: Ivan R. Dee, 1990.

Meese, Edwin. *With Reagan: The Inside Story.* Washington, D.C.: Regnery-Gateway, 1992.

O'Brien, David M. "Federal Judgeships in Retrospect." In W. Elliot Brownlee and Hugh Davis Graham, eds. *The Reagan Presidency: Pragmatic Conservatism and Its Legacies.* Lawrence: University Press of Kansas, 2003.

"Reagan Advisors Say EEOC Has Created 'a New Racism.'" *Wall Street Journal,* January 30, 1981.

Reagan, Ronald. *An American Life.* New York: Simon and Schuster, 1990.

Schwab, Larry. *The Illusion of a Conservative Reagan Revolution.* New Brunswick, N.J.: Transaction Publishers, 1991.

Shenon, Philip. "Job Quotas 'Form of Racism,' Meese Says." *New York Times,* September 18, 1985.

Skrentny, John David. *The Ironies of Affirmative Action: Politics, Culture, and Justice in America.* Chicago: University of Chicago Press, 1996.

Wilkins, Roger. "Smiling Racism." In Paul Boyer, ed. *Reagan as President. Contemporary Views of the Man, His Politics, and His Policies.* Chicago: Ivan R. Dee, 1990.

Education

"Abolition of Education Agency Now 'Moot,' White House Says." *Wall Street Journal*, June 9, 1983.

"A Nation at Risk: The Imperative for Educational Reform," April 1983, U.S. Department of Education. Available online. URL: http://www.ed.gov/pubs/NatAtRisk/index.html. Accessed August 2004.

Boaz, David. "Educational Schizophrenia." In David Boaz, ed. *Assessing the Reagan Years.* Washington, D.C.: Cato Institute, 1988.

Connell, Christopher. "Carnegie Foundation Trustees Criticize Reagan Education Policies." *Associated Press*, June 2, 1985.

———. "Reagan Education." *Associated Press*, January 25, 1988.

Davidson, Joe. "U.S. Lifting Aid for Students, Mostly as Loans." *Wall Street Journal*, October 29, 1986.

Goldberg, Debbie. "Paying for College." *Washington Post*, November 2, 1986.

Johnson, Hayes. "Schools 'Are Still at Risk'." *USA Today*, April 25, 1988.

McCarthy, Colman. "Bennett and Student Loans." *Washington Post*, February 24, 1985.

Mellinkoff, Abe. "A Nation Still at Risk." *San Francisco Chronicle*, April 29, 1988.

Noonan, Peggy. *When Character Was King: A Story of Ronald Reagan.* New York: Viking, 2001.

"The President on Student Aid." *Washington Post*, March 2, 1986.

Raspberry, William. "School Vouchers: Why Not Try Them?" *Washington Post*, November 15, 1985.

Reagan, Ronald. *An American Life.* New York: Simon and Schuster, 1990.

"Reagan Signs Bill to Expand School Services." *Associated Press*, April 29, 1988.

Reeves, Richard. *The Reagan Detour.* New York: Simon and Schuster, 1985.

Richburg, Keith B. "U.S. Seeks Private-School Vouchers for Poor." *Washington Post*, November 9, 1985.

Schwab, Larry M. *The Illusion of a Conservative Reagan Revolution.* New Brunswick: Transaction Publishers, 1991.

Shapiro, Margaret. "House Votes to Extend Student Aid Programs Administration Called Legislation Too Costly." *Washington Post*, December 5, 1985.

Yardley, Jonathan. "What Terrel Bell Learned at The Dept. of Education." *Washington Post*, January 3, 1988.

Deficits, Budget, and Tax Cuts

Anderson, Martin. *Revolution: The Reagan Legacy.* Stanford, Calif.: The Hoover Institution Press, 1990.

Cannon, Lou. *President Reagan: The Role of a Lifetime.* New York: Simon and Schuster, 1991.

———. *Reagan.* New York: G. P. Putnam's Sons, 1982.

D'Souza, Dinesh. *Ronald Reagan: How an Ordinary Man Became an Extraordinary Leader.* New York: Simon and Schuster, 1997.

Hobbs, Charles D. "The Reagan Approach to Welfare and the Homeless." In Kenneth Thompson, ed. *Reagan and the Economy: Nine Intimate Perspectives.* New York: University Press of America, 1994.

Levy, Mickey D. "Origins and Effects of the Deficit." In David Boaz, ed. *Assessing the Reagan Years.* Washington, D.C.: Cato Institute, 1988.

Reagan, Ronald. *An American Life.* New York: Simon and Schuster, 1990.

———. *Speaking My Mind: Selected Speeches.* New York: Simon and Schuster, 1989.

Reagan's First Year. Washington, D.C.: Congressional Quarterly, 1982.

Schwab, Larry. *The Illusion of a Conservative Reagan Revolution.* New Brunswick, N.J.: 1991.

Skinner, Kiron K., Annelise Anderson, and Martin Anderson, eds. *Reagan in His Own Hand: The Writings of Ronald Reagan That Reveal His Revolutionary Vision for America*. New York: Touchstone, 2002.

Sloan, John W. *The Reagan Effect: Economics and Presidential Leadership*. Lawrence: University Press of Kansas, 1999.

Deregulation

Brownlee, W. Elliot. "Revisiting the 'Reagan Revolution,'" In W. Elliot Brownlee and Hugh Davis Graham, eds. *The Reagan Presidency: Pragmatic Conservatism and Its Legacies*. Lawrence: University Press of Kansas, 2003.

Cannon, Lou. *President Reagan: The Role of a Lifetime*. New York: Simon and Schuster, 1991.

Clayton, William E., Jr. "Reagan Still Hoping to Deregulate Gas." *Houston Chronicle*, June 19, 1985.

Crandall, Robert W. "What Ever Happened to Deregulation?" In David Boaz, ed. *Assessing the Reagan Years*. Washington, D.C.: Cato Institute, 1988.

Greenfield, Thomas B. "Reagan's Deregulation Has a Different Meaning." *Globe and Mail*, March 2, 1983.

Henderson, Nell. "Plan Issued for Industrial Regulations." *Washington Post*, August 9, 1985.

Hobbs, Charles D. "The Reagan Approach to Welfare and the Homeless." In Kenneth Thompson, ed. *Reagan and the Economy: Nine Intimate Perspectives*. New York: University Press of America, 1994.

Hoffman, David. "The Long Voyage to Deregulation Nearly Aground." *Washington Post*, January 31, 1984.

Kenworthy, Tom. "Democrats Assail Deregulation Under Reagan; 'Laissez-Faire Attitude' Compromises Safety, House Leaders Say." *Washington Post*, August 10, 1988.

Lee, Jessica. "Deregulation, Arms Cuts to Be Touted." *USA Today*, January 22, 1988.

Levine, Richard. "Unfinished Business: Reagan's Regulatory 'Relief.'" *Management Review*, March 1, 1989.

Mangan, Andrew. "Bush Task Force Recommends Abolishing Fuel Economy Standards." *Associated Press*, December 22, 1986.

Mesce, Deborah. "Reagan Administration Seeks More Deregulation." *Associated Press*, July 22, 1987.

Pierce, Neal R. "Filling the Regulation Gap—If Reagan Won't, the States Will." *Seattle Times*, April 12, 1988.

"Reagan Can Claim Victory in Some Deregulation Efforts." *Wall Street Journal*, December 14, 1983.

Schwab, Larry M. *The Illusion of a Conservative Reagan Revolution*. New Brunswick, N.J.: Transaction Publishers, 1991.

Swoboda, Frank. "The Legacy of Deregulation; Has the Administration's 'Proudest Achievement' Cut Americans' Margin of Safety?" *Washington Post*, October 2, 1988.

Taylor, Robert E., and Andy Pasztor. "Reagan Administration's Deregulation Offensive 'Stopped in Its Tracks' on Environmental Issues." *Wall Street Journal*, January 8, 1985.

Trigaux, Robert. "Reagan Report Urges More Bank Deregulation." *American Banker*, February 7, 1985.

Wermiel, Stephen. "Reagan Administration's Deregulation Drive Often Thwarted by Appeals Court in Washington." *Wall Street Journal*, December 3, 1985.

Yancey, Matt. "Congress To Be Asked to Remove Natural Gas Price Controls." *Associated Press*, December 5, 1985.

Drug Policy

Arieff, Irwin. "Reagan Signs Drug Bill Approving Death Penalty." *Reuters News*, November 18, 1988.

Black, Norman. "Administration Announces New Drug Campaign; American Agent Detained." *Associated Press*, August 14, 1986.

Cannon, Lou. *President Reagan: The Role of a Lifetime.* New York: Simon and Schuster, 1991.

———. "Reagan Launches War on Drugs." *Atlanta Journal-Constitution*, August 2, 1986.

"Congress Clears Massive Anti-Drug Measure." *Congressional Quarterly Almanac* 42 (1986), Congressional Quarterly, Inc., 1987.

De Lama, George. "Reagan Launches Campaign for a 'Drug-Free America.'" *Chicago Tribune*, August 5, 1986.

"Drug Dealing, Terrorism Top Threats, Reagan Says." *Associated Press*, January 3, 1986.

"Election-Year Anti-drug Bill Enacted." *Congressional Quarterly Almanac* 44 (1988), Congressional Quarterly, Inc., 1989.

Hartson, Merrill. "Reagan Heartened by Drug Abuse Report." *Associated Press*, January 16, 1988.

Kempton, Murray. "Reagan's War on Drugs Tells It All." *Newsday*, April 5, 1987.

Leubsdorf, Carl P. "Reagans Press Anti-drug 'Crusade.'" *Dallas Morning News*, September 15, 1986.

Margasak, Larry. "D'Amato Calls Administration's Anti-Drug Effort 'Totally Inept.'" *Associated Press*, May 14, 1985.

Mellinkoff, Abe. "Federal Judge Rules against Reagan." *San Francisco Chronicle*, September 23, 1986.

Nelson, W. Dale. "Reagan Defends Record in Fighting Foreign Drug Trafficking." *Associated Press*, April 16, 1988.

"Reagan Forms Cabinet-Level Drug Panel." *Houston Chronicle*, February 4, 1987.

Schafer, Susanne M. "President Signs Tough New Drug Measure Into Law." *Associated Press*, October 27, 1986.

"Some Gains in the Drug War." *Houston Chronicle*, April 12, 1985.

Taylor, Robert E., and Gary Cohn. "The Drug Trade: War against Narcotics." *Wall Street Journal*, November 27, 1984.

Thornton, Mary. "Administration Attack on Drug's Criticized by DEA Directory." *Washington Post*, May 15, 1984.

Trebach, Arnold S. "Time to Declare a Drug Truce." *Wall Street Journal*, August 2, 1984.

Weinraub, Bernard. "Reagan Plans Broad New Program to Combat Drugs." *Newark Times*, July 29, 1986.

Weissler, Judy. "Mayors Frustrated by Lack of Federal Funding in 'Crusade' against Drugs." *Houston Chronicle*, October 27, 1987.

Weissler, Judy. "Reagan Unveils Plans for Antidrug Crusade." *Houston Chronicle*, August 5, 1986.

Environment

"Administration Opposes Bill on Acid Rain." *San Francisco Chronicle*, April 30, 1986.

Andrews, Robert M. "Reagan's First Term: Conservative Shift at Home, Setbacks Abroad." *Associated Press*, January 20, 1985.

Cannon, Lou *President Reagan: The Role of a Lifetime.* New York: Simon and Schuster, 1991.

"Congress Overrides Clean-Water Bill Veto." *Congressional Quarterly Almanac* 43 (1987), Congressional Quarterly, Inc., 1988.

Dawson, Bill. "Ruckelshaus Wants Overhaul of Toxic Waste Liability System." *Houston Chronicle*, April 19, 1986.

Fuller, Chet. "James Watts of the World Are Symbols of Our Loss of Commitment." *Atlanta Constitution*, December 5, 1988.

Goeller, David. "Congress Makes Little Headway on Environment." *Seattle Times*, December 26, 1987.

Hoffman, David. "Does Not Mention Watt, Burford Controversies President Defends Commitment to Environment." *Washington Post*, June 20, 1984.

———. "Reagan Says Carter Administration Was 'Negligent' With Environment." *Washington Post*, July 13, 1984.

Kilpatrick, James J. "Why Reagan Vetoed the Water-Quality Bill." *Seattle Times*, February 9, 1987.

Lash, Jonathan. "EPA: What Really Happened." *Washington Post*, July 29, 1984.

Marshall

Marshall, Eliot. "EPA's Troubles Reach a Crescendo." *Science*, March 25, 1983.

Moos, Bob. "Reagan's Environmental Record." *Dallas Morning News*, July 30, 1988.

Pasztor, Andy. "EPA to Propose Revised Clean-Air Rules That Will Raise Sulfur Pollution Limits." *Wall Street Journal*, February 14, 1984.

———. "Interior Chief Bars Future Oil Drilling on Wildlife Refuges, Many Scenic Lands." *Wall Street Journal*, January 26, 1984.

Phelps, Charles E. "Any Acid-Rain Controls Sure to Be the Costliest." *Wall Street Journal*, June 3, 1985.

"Pick of Ruckelshaus for EPA Widens Split in Administration." *Wall Street Journal*, March 28, 1983.

"Reagan Defends EPA Chief; Vows Thorough Investigation." *Wall Street Journal*, February 17, 1983.

"Reagan Signs 'Superfund' Waste-Cleanup Bill." *Congressional Quarterly Almanac* 42 (1986), Congressional Quarterly, Inc., 1987.

Schwab, Larry M. *The Illusion of a Conservative Reagan Revolution*. New Brunswick, N.J.: Transaction Publishers, 1991.

Shabecoff, Philip. "House of Representatives Votes to Cite EPA Administrator Anne Gorsuch." *New York Times Abstracts*, December 17, 1982.

Skinner, Kiron K., Annelise Anderson, Martin Anderson, eds. *Reagan in His Own Hand: The Writings of Ronald Reagan That Reveal His Revolutionary Vision for America*. New York: Free Press, 2001.

Smith, Fred L., Jr. "What Environmental Policy?" In David Boaz, ed. *Assessing the Reagan Years*. Washington, D.C.: Cato Institute, 1988.

Stine, Jeffrey K. "Natural Resources and Environmental Policy." In W. Elliot Brownlee and Hugh Davis Graham, eds. *The Reagan Presidency: Pragmatic Conservatism and Its Legacies*. Lawrence: University Press of Kansas, 2003.

Thomas, Fred. "Veto of Water Amendment Seen as Setback." *Omaha World-Herald*, November 9, 1986.

"Watt Resigns Under Pressure as Secretary of Interior." *Wall Street Journal*, October 10, 1983.

Weisskopf, Michael. "President Vetoes Bill to Clean Up Waterways; $18 Billion Measure Called Too Costly." *Washington Post*, November 7, 1986.

Foreign and Defense Policy

Adelman, Kenneth. *The Great Universal Embrace: Arms Summitry—A Skeptics Account*. New York: Simon and Schuster, 1989.

"American Interests Have Long Been Terrorist Targets." *San Francisco Chronicle*, September 12, 2001.

Anderson, Martin. *Revolution: The Reagan Legacy*. Stanford, Calif.: Hoover Institution Press, 1990.

Deutsch, Anthony. "Appeals Court Upholds Conviction of Libyan in Bombing of Pan Am Flight 103." Associated Press Wire Report, March 14, 2002.

D'Souza, Dinesh. *Ronald Reagan: How an Ordinary Man Became an Extraordinary Leader*. New York: Free Press, 1997.

Fitzgerald, Frances. *Way Out There in the Blue*. New York: Simon and Schuster, 2000.

Friedman, Thomas. "Foreign Affairs: Have You Heard?" *New York Times*, April 12, 1995, p. A25.

Knott, Stephen F. "Reagan's Critics." *The National Interest*, Summer, 1996, no. 44.

Haig, Alexander. *Caveat: Realism, Reagan, and Foreign Policy*. New York: Macmillan Publishing Company, 1984.

Hersh, Seymour M. "Target Quaddafi." *New York Times Magazine*, February 22, 1987, p. 17.

Hoag, Christina. "A Murdered Village Comes Back to Life." *Business Week*, March 5, 2001, p. 4.

Levy, Peter. *Encyclopedia of the Reagan-Bush Years*. Westport, Conn.: Greenwood Press, 1996.

Morris, Edmund. *Dutch: A Memoir of Ronald Reagan*. New York: Random House, 1999.

Muir, William K., Jr. "Ronald Reagan's Bully Pulpit: Creating a Rhetoric of Values." In *Presidential*

Speechwriting: From the New Deal to the Reagan Revolution and Beyond. Edited by Kurt Ritter and Martin J. Medhurst. College Station: Texas A & M University Press, 2003.

Nitze, Paul. *From Hiroshima to Glasnost: At the Center of Decision, A Memoir*. New York: Grove-Weidenfeld, 1989.

Reagan, Ronald. *An American Life*. New York: Simon and Schuster, 1990.

———. *Public Papers of the Presidents of the United States, Ronald Reagan, 1981–1989*. Washington, D.C.: U.S. Government Printing Office, 1982–1991.

Saylor, Ryan. Miller Center of Public Affairs, Ronald Reagan Oral History Project. "Briefing Materials, George P. Shultz." Timeline.

Schweizer, Peter. *Reagan's War: The Epic Story of His Forty-Year Struggle and Final Triumph Over Communism*. New York: Doubleday, 2002.

———. *Victory: The Reagan Administration's Secret Strategy That Hastened the Collapse of the Soviet Union*. New York: The Atlantic Monthly Press, 1994.

Scott, James M. *Deciding to Intervene: The Reagan Doctrine and American Foreign Policy*. Durham, N.C.: Duke University Press, 1996, pp. 157–61.

Shultz, George P. *Turmoil and Triumph: My Years as Secretary of State*. New York: Charles Scribner's Sons, 1993.

Slevin, Peter. "Libya Takes Responsibility for Pan Am Flight 103." *Washington Post*, August 16, 2003, p. A-1.

Sloan, John W. *The Reagan Effect: Economics and Presidential Leadership*. Lawrence: University Press of Kansas, 1999.

Steiner, Jessica. Miller Center of Public Affairs, Ronald Reagan Oral History Project. "Briefing Materials, Anthony R. Dolan." Timeline.

Strober, Deborah Hart, and Gerald S. Strober. *Reagan: The Man and His Presidency*. Boston: Houghton Mifflin Company, 1998.

Thatcher, Margaret. *The Downing Street Years*. New York: HarperCollins, 1993.

Walsh, Lawrence E. *Final Report of the Independent Counsel for Iran/Contra Matters, Volume 1: Investigations and Prosecutions*. Washington, D.C., 1993. http://fas.org/irp/offdocs/walsh/chron.htm

Weinberger, Caspar W. *Fighting for Peace: Seven Critical Years in the Pentagon*. New York: Warner Book, Inc., 1990.

———. *In the Arena: A Memoir of the 20th Century*. Washington, D.C.: Regnery Publishing, 2001.

Wills, Garry. *Reagan's America: Innocents at Home*. New York: Penguin Books, 2000.

Winik, Jay. *On the Brink: The Dramatic, Behind-the-Scenes Saga of the Reagan Era and the Men and Women Who Won the Cold War*. New York: Simon and Schuster, 1996.

Woodward, Bob. *Veil: The Secret Wars of the CIA, 1981–1987*. New York: Simon and Schuster, 1987.

Health Care

Feldman, Roger D. "Health Care: The Tyranny of the Budget." In David Boaz, ed. *Assessing the Reagan Years*. Washington, D.C.: Cato Institute, 1988.

Hunt, Terence. "Reagan Proposes Catastrophic Health Insurance for the Elderly." *Associated Press*, February 12, 1987.

Pear, Robert. "Freeze of Medicare Rates Pushed." *Houston Chronicle*, May 30, 1985.

Pierson, Paul. *Dismantling the Welfare State? Reagan, Thatcher, and the Politics of Retrenchment*. Cambridge: Cambridge University Press, 1994.

Rosenblatt, Robert A. "Reagan Signs Major Medicare Expansion." *Los Angeles Times*, July 2, 1988.

Schwab, Larry M. *The Illusion of a Conservative Reagan Revolution*. New Brunswick, N.J.: Transaction Publishers, 1991.

Sorelle, Ruth. "Reagan Is 'Rationing' Health Care to Elderly, AMA Official Charges." *Houston Chronicle*, January 18, 1986.

Immigration

Cannon, Lou. *President Reagan: The Role of a Lifetime*. New York: Simon and Schuster, 1991.

Clayton, William E., Jr. "Reagan Backs Immigration Bill but Hedges on Amnesty Issue." *Houston Chronicle*, June 25, 1985.

Cohodas, Nadine. "Reagan Urged to Take Lead: Immigration Reform Battle Starting Up Again in House." *Congressional Quarterly Weekly Report*, February 1, 1986.

DelVecchio, Rick. "U.S. Says Aliens Need Not Fear New Law." *San Francisco Chronicle*, November 26, 1986.

Fessenden, Ford. "$185 Fee Asked to Document Aliens." *Newsday*, March 17, 1987.

Gerber, Robin. "Labor's Welcome Change of Course on Immigration." The James MacGregor Burns Academy of Leadership website, February 29, 2000. Available online. URL: http://www.academy.umd.edu/AboutUs/news/articles/2-29-00.htm Downloaded August 2004.

Graham, Otis L. "Failing the Test: Immigration Reform." In W. Elliot Brownlee and Hugh Davis Graham, eds. *The Reagan Presidency: Pragmatic Conservatism and Its Legacies.* Lawrence: University Press of Kansas, 2003.

Helton, Arthur C. "A Gap in the Immigration Law." *Washington Post*, August 19, 1987.

Hess, Jennie. "Critics: Amnesty Program Misses Many Eligible Aliens." *Atlanta Journal-Constitution*, April 24, 1988.

Leubsdorf, Carl P. "Reagan Sounds Different Notes on Immigration." *Dallas Morning News*, October 2, 1984.

Lewis, Holden. "INS Official Says No Amnesty Extension Needed." *Dallas Morning News*, April 22, 1988.

McDermott, Terry. "Bill Pardons Some Aliens, Fines Offending Employers." *Seattle Times*, November 2, 1986.

Moore, Stephen, and Aaron Harris. "Still the Pro-Immigration Party?" The Cato Institute Website Available online. URL: http://www.cato.org/dailys/8-26-96.html. Posted August 26, 1996.

Padgett, Tim. "Illegal Aliens 'Scared' by New Law." *Chicago Sun-Times*, January 26, 1987.

Pear, Robert. "Congress, Winding Up Work, Votes Sweeping Aliens Bill; Reagan Expected to Sign It." *New York Times*, October 18, 1986.

———. "U.S. Plans to Expand Amnesty for Illegal Aliens." *New York Times*, April 6, 1987.

"Reagan Proposes Sanctions against Hiring Illegal Aliens." *Dow Jones News Service*, July 30, 1981.

Shapiro, Margaret. "House Passes Immigration Bill." *Washington Post*, June 21, 1984.

Wiessler, Judy. "Immigration Bill Heads to Reagan After Senate OK." *Houston Chronicle*, October 18, 1986.

PATCO Strike

Cannon, Lou. *President Reagan: The Role of a Lifetime.* New York: Simon and Schuster, 1991.

Levy, Peter B. *Encyclopedia of the Reagan-Bush Years.* Westport, Conn.: Greenwood Press, 1996.

Morris, Edmund. *Dutch: A Memoir of Ronald Reagan.* New York: Random House, 1999.

Reagan, Ronald. *An American Life.* New York: Simon and Schuster, 1990.

Skinner, Kiron K. Annelise Anderson, Martin Anderson, eds. *Reagan in His Own Hand: The Writings of Ronald Reagan That Reveal His Revolutionary Vision for America.* New York: Free Press, 2001.

Strober, Deborah Hart, and Gerald S. Strober. *Reagan: The Man and His Presidency.* Boston: Houghton Mifflin Company, 1998.

Social Issues

Boodman, Sandra G., and Michael Specter. "64 Demonstrators Arrested in Protest of AIDS Policy." *Washington Post*, June 2, 1987.

Briggs, Michael. "Reagan Perils Funds for Abortion Advice." *Chicago Sun-Times*, July 31, 1987.

"Bush Booed as He Reiterates Reagan's AIDS Testing Comments." *Associated Press*, June 1, 1987.

Cannon, Lou. *President Reagan: The Role of a Lifetime.* New York: Simon and Schuster, 1991.

———. "Reagan Renews Appeal for Anti-abortion Action." *Washington Post*, January 31, 1984.

Connolly, Mike. "AIDS Policy Punted to Next President." *Houston Chronicle*, August 7, 1988.

Dolman, Joe. "The Right's Crusaders March On." *Atlanta Journal-Constitution*, July 23, 1986.

Dugger, Ronnie. *On Reagan: The Man and His Presidency.* New York: McGraw Hill, 1983.

Fain, Jim. "After Porn, Maybe Meese Will Go After Witchcraft." *Atlanta Journal-Constitution*, June 2, 1986.

Fisher, Patricia. "Reagan-Meese Manifesto—Report on Porn: A Study in Bias." *Seattle Times*, October 29, 1986.

Grabowski, Gene. "Tens of Thousands Hear Reagan Denounce Abortion." *Associated Press*, January 22, 1985.

Hall, Henry Boyd. "U.S. to Deny Funds to World Groups Promoting Abortion." *Wall Street Journal*, July 16, 1984.

Hartson, Merrill. "Reagan Hopes Abortion Decision Will Be Overturned." *Associated Press*, January 13, 1989.

———. "Reagan Unveils Anti-pornography Legislation." *Associated Press*, November 10, 1987.

Hefner, Hugh M. "Porn Doesn't Cause Crime." *Chicago Sun-Times*, December 8, 1985.

Hentoff, Nat. "'Civil Rights' and Pornography—U.S. Judge's Wise Words." *Seattle Times*, December 10, 1984.

Hoffman, David. "On Social Issues, Gains 'Far Short' of Right's Hopes." *Washington Post*, January 31, 1984.

Jaroslovsky, Rich. "Reagan Woos Fundamentalists in Ohio, Criticizes Political Opponents in New York." *Wall Street Journal*, March 7, 1984.

Jones, Malcolm. "Meese Commission Set Back the Cause of Free Speech." *St. Petersburg Times*, August 28, 1988.

Leon, Darren. "Reagan Boosts Anti-abortion Rally with Phone Call." *Associated Press*, June 9, 1985.

McGee, Kevin T. "AIDS Policy Called a National 'Wake-Up Call.'" *USA Today*, June 3, 1988.

"Meese Plans to Step Up Fight against Porn." *Houston Chronicle*, November 2, 1987.

"Meese Pledges New Attacks on Obscenity: Legislation Is Planned to Fight 'Epidemic,' He Says." *Associated Press*, November 1, 1987.

Mower, Joan. "Congressman Seeks Support for Stronger Anti-AIDS Measures." *Associated Press*, October 2, 1985.

Reagan, Ronald. "Abortion and the Conscience of a Nation." *Human Life Review*, Spring 1983, http://www.humanlifereview.com/reagan/reagan_conscience.html.

———. "Remarks at the Annual Convention of the National Association of Evangelicals." In *The Public Papers of President Ronald W. Reagan.* March 8, 1983. http://www.reagan.utexas.edu/resource/speeches/1983/30883b.htm.

"Reagan Not Likely to Put High Priority on Abortion." *Seattle Times*, January 23, 1985.

"Reagan Pledges Effort to End Abortions." *Houston Chronicle*, June 13, 1986.

"Reagan Signs Tough Bill in Crackdown on Child Porn." *San Francisco Chronicle*, November 8, 1986.

"Reagan to Back Constitutional Amendment for School Prayer." *Wall Street Journal*, May 5, 1982.

"Reagan to Sign Bill Toughening Drug Penalties." *Baton Rouge State Times*, November 18, 1988.

Reid, T. R. "Reagan Lobbies Senators on School Prayer." *Washington Post*, March 17, 1984.

Rogers, David. "School Prayer Loses in Senate on 56-44 Vote—Constitutional Amendment Fails to Get Necessary Two-Thirds Majority." *Wall Street Journal*, March 21, 1984.

Rosenberg, Sandra S. "Reagan and Abortion." *Newsday*, February 14, 1986.

Rovner, Julie. "A 'Leave It to the States' Approach: Administration AIDS Policy Comes Under Fire in House." *Congressional Quarterly Weekly Report*, September 26, 1987.

Schwab, Larry M. *The Illusion of a Conservative Reagan Revolution.* London: Transaction Publishers, 1991.

Sternberg, Steve. "Confusion Surrounds Official AIDS Policy." *Atlanta Journal-Constitution*, October 29, 1987.

"Supreme Court Cases, 1965–1990." Hunter College Website. Available online. URL: http://maxweber.hunter.cuny.edu/socio/kuechler/309/absc6590.html. Accessed October 19, 2003.

Tanner, Lindsey "Reagan Addresses Anti-porn Leaders Via Satellite." *Associated Press*, October 25, 1986.

Vicini, James. "Reagan Administration Defends Strict Anti-abortion Law." *Reuters News*, November 10, 1988.

Weiner, Cindy. "U.S. Pornography Law Advocated as a Model." *Globe and Mail*, May 21, 1984.

Wermiel, Stephen. "White House Urges Justices to Overrule '73 Decision Allowing Right to Abortion." *Wall Street Journal*, July 16, 1985.

Williams, Juan. "Reagan Stresses Advocacy of Prayer and Crime Bills." *Washington Post*, February 23, 1984.

Yardley, Jonathan. "The Porn Commission's Hidden Agenda." *Washington Post*, July 14, 1986.

Zimmerman, David R. "The Pornography Issue." *Newsday*, January 28, 1986.

Social Security

Blustein, Paul, and Rich Jaroslovsky. "White House Backs Away from Regan's Suggestions for Change in Social Security." *Wall Street Journal*, May 8, 1984.

Cannon, Lou. *President Reagan: The Role of a Lifetime*. New York: Simon and Schuster, 1991.

Connell, Christopher. "Reagan Accused of Undermining Social Security." *Associated Press*, October 30, 1985.

Derthick, Martha, and Steven M. Teles. "Riding the Third Rail: Social Security Reform." In W. Elliot Brownlee and Hugh Davis Graham, eds. *The Reagan Presidency: Pragmatic Conservatism and Its Legacies*. Lawrence: University Press of Kansas, 2003.

Ferrara, Peter J. "Social Security: Look at Your Pay Stub." In David Boaz, ed. *Assessing the Reagan Years*. Washington, D.C.: Cato Institute, 1988.

Haas, Cliff. "O'Neill Suggests Higher Taxes on Some Social Security Recipients." *Associated Press*, June 26, 1985.

Hoffman, David. "Reagan Pledges Safeguarding of Old-Age Benefits." *Washington Post*, March 1, 1984.

Hoffman, David, and Milton Coleman. "President Denies He Plans to Reduce Social Security." *Washington Post*, October 10, 1984.

Komarow, Steven. "Social Security Budget Cuts Denied." *Associated Press*, November 2, 1987.

Lee, Jessica. "'Budget Summit' Aims at Deficit; Reagan's Advisers to Meet Congress Group." *USA Today*, October 27, 1987.

Lemann, Nicholas. "What's Stockman Really Up To?" *The Record*, Northern New Jersey, December 12, 1984.

Morris, Edmund. *Dutch*. New York: Random House, 1999.

Olofson, Darwin. "President Might Not Veto Cutback in Social Security." *Omaha World-Herald*, December 17, 1984.

Pierson, Paul. *Dismantling the Welfare State? Reagan, Thatcher, and the Politics of Retrenchment*. Cambridge: Cambridge University Press, 1994.

Putzel, Michael. "Reagan Favors Liberalizing Social Security Hikes Keyed to Inflation." *Associated Press*, July 15, 1986.

Rabun, Carl. "Social Security." *Seattle Times*, April 3, 1988.

"Reagan Names Alan Greenspan to Chair Social Security Panel." *Dow Jones News Service*, December 16, 1981.

"Reagan Unveils Plan to Reduce Social Security Taxes." *Dow Jones News Service*, May 2, 1981.

Rogers, David. "Senate Rejects, 65-34, Proposal to Cut Social Security Living-Cost Increases." *Wall Street Journal*, May 2, 1985.

Schwab, Larry M. *The Illusion of a Conservative Reagan Revolution*. New Brunswick, N.J.: Transaction Publishers, 1991.

"Social Security/Reagan Turnabout Angers Republicans." *San Francisco Chronicle*, July 12, 1985.

"Social Security, the Stock Market, and the Elections." *Monthly Review* 52, no. 5 (October 1, 2000).

Wills, Garry. *Reagan's America: Innocents at Home.* New York: Penguin Books, 2000.

Welfare

"A Qualified 'Message of Hope'—Reagan Signs Bill to Overhaul Welfare." *San Francisco Chronicle,* October 14, 1988.

Cannon, Lou. *President Reagan: The Role of a Lifetime.* New York: Simon and Schuster, 1991.

———. *Reagan.* New York: G. P. Putnam's Sons, 1982.

Hobbs, Charles D. "The Reagan Approach to Welfare and the Homeless." Kenneth Thompson, ed. *Reagan and the Economy: Nine Intimate Perspectives.* New York: University Press of America, 1994.

Hopkins, Kevin R. "Social Welfare Policy: A Failure of Vision." In David Boaz, ed. *Assessing the Reagan Years.* Washington, D.C.: Cato Institute, 1988.

McNamee, Mike. "Welfare System Reform an Uphill Struggle." *Dallas Morning News,* February 5, 1986.

Milloy, Marilyn. "Reagan Welfare Plan Doubted." *Newsday,* February 9, 1986.

Morris, Edmund. *Dutch.* New York: Random House, 1999.

Pierson, Paul. *Dismantling the Welfare State? Reagan, Thatcher, and the Politics of Retrenchment.* Cambridge: Cambridge University Press, 1994.

Reagan, Ronald. *An American Life.* New York: Simon and Schuster, 1990.

Schwab, Larry M. *The Illusion of a Conservative Reagan Revolution.* New Brunswick: N.J.: Transaction Publishers, 1991.

Skinner, Kiron K. Annelise Anderson, and Martin Anderson, eds. *Reagan: A Life in Letters.* New York: Free Press, 2003.

———. *Reagan in His Own Hand: The Writings of Ronald Reagan That Reveal His Revolutionary Vision for America.* New York: Touchstone, 2002.

INDEX

Boldface page numbers indicate primary discussions. *Italic* page numbers indicate illustrations.

Muskie, Edmund 74, 75
Mutual Assured Destruction (MAD) 85–86, 93, 252c
MX missile 85, 256c, 260c, 261c, 266c, 267c

N

NAACP 26
NAFTA 42
Namibia 81
NASA 282
National Academy of Sciences 47
National Aeronautic and Space Administration (NASA) 282
National Association for the Advancement of Colored People (NAACP) 26
National Association of Evangelicals 261c
National Commission on Excellence in Education 51
National Commission on Social Security Reform 64
National Conference of Catholic Bishops 90
national debt 101
National Education Association 51
National Endowment for Democracy 78
National Endowment for the Arts 282
National Front for the Liberation of Angola (FNLA) 80
National Health Service Corps 35
National Highway Traffic Safety 62
national identity card 42, 43
National Liberation Front (FSLN) 252c
National Narcotics Border Interdiction System (NNBIS) 54
National Obscenity Enforcement Unit 50
national parks 58
National Rifle Association (NRA) 53
National Science Foundation 51
national security 22
National Security Advisor 58
National Security Agency 67

National Security Council 73–74
National Security Decision Directive 32 78
National Security Decision Directive 166 77
National Union for the Total Independence of Angola (UNITA) 80, 81
National Wildlife Federation 58
NATO. *See* North Atlantic Treaty Organization
natural gas 62, 78, 260c
naval maneuvers 67
needy 36
Neshoba County Fair, Mississippi 14, 26
New Deal 1, 13, 22, 36
New Hampshire 10–12, 16, 252c–253c
"New Jewel Movement" 68
newspaper column 8
New York primaries 13
Nicaragua 66, 71–73, 254c, 261c, 264c–268c, 270c–272c, 277c, 280c
  Address Before a Joint Session of the Congress on Central America **405–412**
  Geneva summit 94
  Grenada 68
  mining harbors in 72
  Daniel Ortega 73, 133, **202–203**, 265c
  Sandinistas 68, 71–73, 252c, 254c, 265c, 277c, 280c
  Washington, D.C. summit 97
Nicolson, Arthur D., Jr. 267c
Nitze, Paul 95
Nixon, Richard 27, 98, 99, 250c, 251c
  dispute over welfare with 36–37
  FAP proposal 36
  Gerald R. Ford, Jr. 154
  ill will between Reagan and 7
  INF Treaty 92
  national reaction to presidential campaign of 7
  resignation of 8
  Reykjavik summit 96
  support for 2
  and welfare reform 8

Nixon administration 70
NNBIS 54
Nofziger, Lyn 251c, 277c
  and assassination attempt 19
  assumption of Reagan presidential run by 8
  pro-choice position of 46
  on Reagan's gubernatorial team 6
  John Sears 12
  and second campaign for governor 7
Noonan, Peggy **196–197**
NORAD. *See* North American Aerospace Defense Command
Noriega, Manuel 56, 277c
North, Oliver 197, **197–198**, 269c, 271c, 273c, 277c
  Frank C. Carlucci III 131
  William J. Casey 134
  Thomas P. O'Neill 202
  overturning of conviction of 74
  Colin L. Powell 212
  Lawrence E. Walsh 241
"North American Accord" 41–42
North American Aerospace Defense Command (NORAD) 85, 252c
North American Free Trade Agreement (NAFTA) 42
North Atlantic Treaty Organization (NATO) 86, 89, 92, 256c, 263c, 269c, 274c
North Carolina 10, 252c
nuclear freeze movement 87, 89–90, 256c, 258c
nuclear plants 61
nuclear testing 274c
nuclear war 258c, 262c
nuclear weapons 258c, 262c, 267c, 270c. *See also* Anti-Ballistic Missile Treaty of 1972; Mutually Assured Destruction; Strategic Defense Initiative
  desire to reduce 269c
  elimination of 92, 94
  INF Treaty 89–92
  inspections of 92
  negotiations 263c–264c
  no defense against 252c
  reduction in 94

Reykjavik summit 94
"suitcase" 86
"nuclear winter" 90

O

O'Brien, David 22, 23
obscenity 49, 50
Occupational Safety and Health Administration (OSHA) 61, 62
OCDEF 54
O'Connor, Sandra Day 23, 24, **199–200**, 200, 229, 255c, 256c
"October Surprise" 15
Office of Information and Regulatory Affairs (OIRA) 60, 62
Office of Management and Budget (OMB) 29, 34
Office of Strategic Services (OSS) 66
Ogarkov, Nikolai 89
oil drilling 58
oil-price controls 62
oil tankers 79
OIRA. *See* Office of Information and Regulatory Affairs
Olympic Games in 1980 (Moscow) 17, 76, 253c
Olympic Games in 1984 (Los Angeles) 17, 265c
OMB. *See* Office of Management and Budget
O'Neill, Thomas P. "Tip" 8, 39, 64, 65, **200–202**, 201, 267c
On the Campaign Against Drug Abuse The President and Mrs. Reagan **460–464**
open borders 42
"Operation Alliance" 55
"Operation Urgent Fury" 68
Organized Crime and Drug Trafficking Initiatives 259c
Organized Crime Drug Enforcement Task Force (OCDEF) 54
original intent (doctrine of) 24
Ortega, Daniel 73, 133, **202–203**, 265c
OSHA. *See* Occupational Safety and Health Administration
OSS 66